SURVIVE
THE FATTEST 2
Now THAT'S what I call football!

An alternative review of the
'95-96 football season

Compiled and edited by

David Jenkins

&

Judi Holly

Red Card
Publishing

Survival of the Fattest 2
Now that's what I call football!
An alternative review of the '95-96 football season

Copyright © 1996 Red Card Publishing Ltd
Front cover illustration by
David Banks

First published in 1996 by
RED CARD PUBLISHING LIMITED
4 Bowater Place
Blackheath
London
SE3 8ST

British Library Cataloguing in Publication Data.
A catalogue record for this book is available from the British Library

ISBN 0 9526610 12

Reproduction by
Impressions Printing Technology, Sevenoaks

Printed and bound in Great Britain by
BPC Paperbacks Ltd

In memory of
Richard Minto

CONTENTS

Cheat's List (Reviews in order of club)

Cheat's List, cont'd.

INSTRUCTIONS ON USE

1. Buy book. Frantically search for your own club's fanzine/s

OK, so you'll probably have done this before parting with your cash. Anyway, unlike most "boring, boring yearbooks", the articles in *SOTF* are arranged in fanzine title order and not club order, so you'll have to work a bit to find your team. Unless, that is, you use the cheat's list, which is to be found on page (iv) of the contents pages.

2. Do a bit of cross-referencing

If you remember a particular game or incident last season, have a look to see if the other club's fanzine makes reference to it.

3. Place book near the bog

Continue the 'ultimate bog read' tradition. Every time you visit the 'smallest room', take a leisurely browse through the rest of the articles. In the pages of *SOTF2*, you'll find a snapshot of the emotions and key moments that made up the '95-96 football season in England and Wales. Read on...

SPECIAL THANKS

Our thanks go mainly to this book's contributors, who for the second year running, despite the many pressures of everyday life, and in some cases with last season's disasters still painfully fresh in their minds, managed to put pen to paper (or fingers to keyboard) and sent in the articles which appear in these pages.

Secondly, thanks are due to the following people, without whose help, support and advice, this book would never have got beyond the "wavy lines" of one sad Brighton fan's fantasy world:-

David Banks (Chelsea), Karen Amey (Manchester United), Maggie O'Connor (Leicester City), Nigel Fletcher (Luton Town), Richard Pedder (Chelsea).

Finally, to all the fanzine people who risk health, wealth and happiness in the pursuit of their obsession; thanks for making the sometimes frustrating and heartbreaking business of supporting our teams more enjoyable.

Dave Jenkins (Brighton & Hove Albion)
Judi Holly (Leicester City)

INTRODUCTION

Survival of the Fattest 2 is a compilation of articles from fanzines throughout England and Wales, reviewing the on and off-field goings on at their clubs in the Carling Premiership and Endsleigh League Divisions One, Two and Three.

Once again, every effort was made to get a representation from all 92 clubs, but ultimately we still finished up with a couple of gaps. However, given the voluntary nature of the contributions and the time demands on the writers, we are delighted with the 130 so articles that finally made their way into the pages of this unique football book. But if you are one of the few who are reading this book and can't find your team, then once again we're sorry; we really tried.

RANTING FROM THE EDS

Well here we are again...

To all of you who put your hand in your pockets and bought the first edition, thanks very much. Fortunately there were enough of you out there to let us continue this folly for another year at least.

It was great to receive so many positive comments about SOTF1 and to discover how many people took our advice to use the book as the ultimate toilet companion. Mind you, it is printed on bog paper to give it that authentic feel.

And what a year it was in the Red Card Publishing editorial department. The fluctuating fortunes of our own teams probably encompassed the widest possible extremes of football emotions. On the one hand, the editor in chief went ballistic as Steve Claridge shinned Leicester into the promised land of all things Carling. While on the other, chief sub and publisher endured a season where football (for the first time) was an irrelevance, as Brighton went to the brink, peeked over the edge and took a temporary step backwards.

When we got the inspiration for the book's name over the obligatory few beers, we never realised that the title would have such pertinence for both of us, for different reasons. You don't have to be a genius to understand why: having been promoted, Leicester, reasoning that survival in the Premiership will require wads of money, staged an immediate boardroom shake-up in an effort to give Martin O'Neill the funds needed to compete with the game's fattest cats. Brighton fans, reasoning that their very survival required some direct action, caused the abandonment of their final home game in a desperate bid to get someone - anyone - to listen to their cries in the dark.

And while we're beating this particular drum, we'll re hash part of last year's foreword because it is as true today as it was then. Basically, when it comes down to it, we reckon that supporters want four things: first, they want success - obvious, really; second, if they can't have success they want to feel confident that everything humanly possible is being done to change their club's fortunes; third, they want a voice so that they can 'have a go' when the necessary effort isn't forthcoming. And finally, they want to have a laugh. This is true whatever the club, whatever their division, whatever their size; it's as true for Man United as it is for Torquay. And ultimately, this is why fanzines exist.

Everyone knows that football is big business, and that's no bad thing. The main problem seems to be that the people in charge, some of whom are supposedly exceptionally talented business people, have a bewildering inability to grasp modern consumer marketing. Most companies understand the benefits that accrue from concentrating on 'loyalty schemes' that fully inform their customer about their product in an attempt to make it easier to spend with them and harder to go elsewhere. Compare that, then, to the policy of secrecy and in some cases blatant misinformation operated within some club boardrooms. Public relations? Loyalty?? AARRRRSE!!!

Anyway, that's enough of that. Enjoy this collection of personal and unexpurgated views from some of the country's most passionate supporters, and we'll leave you with a passage from one of the articles in the book, which we think sums up this whole fanzine and supporting thing rather nicely.

> **"The fanzine's influence is probably considerable, but passive. It is capable of affecting what people think, but not (currently) of getting them to do anything about it. It is, by now, part of United life, and everybody reads it: its position appears impregnable. And yet, like most fanzines, it could easily close down tomorrow if there was a row, or someone got a different job, or somebody, one day, just couldn't be bothered. No-one knows. But I think a lot of people care."**

(Thanks to *Raging Bull*, the full article from which can be found later in these pages.)

If you would like to contact any of the fanzines featured in this book, please write to the publishers who would be happy to forward the relevant details.

THE 2ND OF MAY

Bristol Rovers

Unfulfilled Expectations

When you follow a team like Bristol Rovers you learn not to get optimistic. For ten years now we've been looking for a home of our own, and every time we built our hopes up, reality had a nasty habit of kicking us in the teeth.

But expectations were high for the '95-96 season. Having murdered Huddersfield at Wembley and some-how lost, August approached with a team that was, surprisingly, intact from that game last May. The rele-gated sides, including the woeful Bris-tol City, didn't look much compared with the likes of Birmingham and Warnock's hoofers from the previous season, which gave us gullible opti-mists at Twerton something else to smile about.

The Second of May

Ashton Prepares....

GAS ATTACK '95

Our season started early, unfortunately not with a Wembley appearance in the Charity Shield, but with a 4.30 am departure up North. The hype surrounding Knighton's Carlisle duly vanished with a legendary lucky piss and a flash of Stewy magic on the opening day (when the army of travelling Gasheads were treated to steady rainfall while the rest of England blistered in a heatwave). We should have known then that getting up before the crack of dawn and missing the winning goal was an omen; yes, even at this early stage there were nagging doubts that something was amiss.

Problems with the home playing surface (something that handicapped us all season) didn't help. When a meaningless punt bounced three feet over Brian Par-kin's head and into the net to give nine man Swansea a last minute equaliser, the infamous 'Twerton bobble' had reared its ugly head again. Poor old Brian never recovered from this experience. A late winner by Wrexham at the ground formerly known as Fortress Twerton a few weeks later served merely to reinforce the view that the Swansea debacle was not a mere blip.

What followed between September and Christmas saw Fortress Twerton dubbed by one tabloid hack as the 'Twerton Takeaway'. Swindon (0-4) and Notts County (0-3) made a mockery of the hopes we had of winning the Division just two months earlier, while Bournemouth (!), Stockport and Crewe all left saying thank you very much. Even Peterborough got a point.

On our travels things swung from the sublime to the ridiculous. Wins at Bradford and Oxford (the first in 45 years) were interspersed with a dismal loss at

Brighton (why on earth didn't they have one of their legendary anti-board protests then?). In fact, Christmas came early at the Goldstone Ground, with Rovers 'keeper Andy Collett and George Parris in pantomime mood for one of the most bizarre goals ever - Parris sneaked out from behind the goal to take the ball away from Collett and score: "He's behind you" we screamed... Unfortunately it wasn't scripted but real, and at least it got us onto 'Question of Sport'.

Another trip to the seaside, Blackpool this time, and the general view was that Rovers had produced what surely would be their worst performance of the season in a 3-0 defeat... If only! That notion was firmly booted into touch when we suffered an FA Cup downfall at the hands of mighty Hitchin. Has there ever been a worse cup team in the country? Any non-league players facing Rovers should brush up on their interview technique, because they'll surely appear on Match of the Day later that night.

By Christmas, season ticket holders had been treated to a generous three home wins - seemingly a record that some of our players thought we should be truly grateful for - but hey, it wouldn't be Rovers unless they kept you in pain right until the end. No, just when we were settling back for a thoroughly mediocre season, they decided to start playing. A creditable draw on ice at in-form Shrewsbury (Robin Cousins would have been an apt substitute according to one terrace wag) set things in motion, and a string of wins culminated in the truly orgasmic evening of January 16th 1996 at Trashton, home of our beloved rivals Bristol City. Officially a crowd of 20,000 jammed in, but with all safety standards breached it was surely nearer 25,000. Lord Justice Taylor would have disapproved, but to the 8,000 Gasheads filling the aisles of the 5,500 capacity away end it was sheer poetry. Two Peter Beadle strikes sent Rovers on the way to their biggest win at Ashton Gate since 1933 and ensured that the headline writers had a field day the morning after. It also sent the vast majority of Gasheads rushing off to beat last orders.

Unfortunately, a 1-1 draw at home to Carlisle three days later encapsulated the rollercoaster nature of our season; ups and downs which we were destined to suffer right through to the last kick of the last game (and probably for the rest of our existence).

Three encounters with Shrewsbury in March only confirmed our inconsistency: a win at home in the League was followed by a draw at Gay Meadow in the first leg of the Auto Windscreens area final; then, just as we thought we'd done the hard bit, we missed a penalty in the second leg and conceded a late goal to miss out on a trip to Wembley.

That we maintained a play-off push was as much to do with other teams slipping up as anything that we did, and it was somehow fitting that the season effectively ended at Blackpool, the home of the rollercoaster, and the scene for a weekend away for the Stockport game (and even then our rivals were still trying to get us promoted, losing as they did that Saturday).

So even if the moral of the story is don't get optimistic, we know that two months down the road we'll be at it again, what with the return of the prodigal son Ian Holloway as player-manager and... wait for it... a return to a ground in Bristol (albeit at a two-sided rugby ground). We can't wait for August 17th, even though we suspect it'll all end in tears...

Fanzine Facts

The 2nd of May, 'The Fog Horn of the Twerton Masses', was formed in 1991 when Chris Scargill met Ian Marriott, who had been editing a fanzine called '9½ months' since 1989. The fanzine was re-titled, named after a never-to-be-forgotten night in 1990, when the arch enemy Bristol City had been beaten 3-0, Rovers had gone top of the table and were also promoted. Apart from Chris and Ian, there is now a regular team of writers including Hazel 'Spitfire' Potter, Rose Lowther and David King. And at this momentous time Hazel and Ian would like people to remember that "There can be little doubt that Gasheads are ecstatic at the Rovers Return to Bristol, but May 4th - our last day in Bath - was nevertheless a highly emotional day. For ten years, away supporters have descended on Twerton Park and moaned about the non-league facilities etc. etc., but one thing must be remembered - it saved Bristol Rovers FC from extinction.

Special Offer!

RENEW YOUR BRISTOL CITY SEASON TICKET BY THE END OF JUNE AND GET NEXT SEASON'S BRISTOL DERBY

FREE*

* Offer applies only if you take your seat 12 hours before kick-off

THE 69ER

Swindon Town

After relegation from the First Division in the '94-95, some Swindon supporters spent the closed season in abject misery predicting nothing good of Steve McMahon, while others boldly predicted an immediate return and a straight Championship win. As Mc-Mahon celebrated that Second Division Championship in May, he said that *he* had only doubted once: during half-time of the first game at Hull in August. At 0-0 we hadn't played well and the defence looked its usual shaky self; gloomy reminders of the season just gone. But the second half was a different story; we seemed to know what we were about, and for striker Steve Finney - a free transfer from McMahon's old club Manchester City and only playing because of a late in-

jury to first-choice striker Peter Thorne - it was the old 'dream start' as he headed home the winner. For the first time of many, there was *on-ly one Ste-eve Fin-ney*. After that, most of us were as confident as Macca himself.

In fact, part way through the season we were torn off a strip by another club's fanzine for having an inflated opinion of ourselves. That wasn't strictly true. For a side which had experienced two successive relegations, we had players who were too good for the Second Division: it wasn't arrogance; it was <u>fact</u>. But that notwithstanding, the confidence which we'd lacked in August was now there because we knew that we could have ended up on that same slippery slope encountered in the past by Wolves and Swansea - yo-yoing up and back down through the divisions with only a brief stop on the way. That we didn't do so owed much to the leadership of McMahon who, by his own admission, gave up the 'bull in a china shop' approach which had character-ised his first season in charge, to lead by example with enthusiasm and commitment during his second. At the Championship celebrations he was heard to say "I can't say how long I will be here, but *I* won't be leaving after three days." A reference to the way in which Hoddle walked out after we gained promotion to the Premiership in '93.

For the first nine games of the season then, it was bliss; we didn't care much about being knocked out of the Coca Cola in the second round by Blackburn, (two-nil up in the first leg, Alan Shearer sunk us in that *and* the second leg), because almost every away game was a party. Early season trips to Carlisle and Brentford, (two of the favourites), earned us six more points. As it happened, our superb away form contin-ued right to the end of the season, whilst at home we carried on dropping points, though only actually losing once.

Losing our unbeaten League record in the tenth game at Wrexham felt like a disaster at the time. Two goals up inside the half-hour with Peter Thorne scoring on his come back (only to suffer a bad ankle injury sidelining him for another three months), we eventually went down 4-3 in a memorable, topsy-turvy game. In our more recent history, it seems that no matter who the manager, no matter what the team, we've got this remarkable knack of throwing away seemingly unassailable leads.

The season took on a slightly different perspective starting with the visit to Bournemouth three days after an important victory at Meadow Lane. Although Steve McMahon talked about a "good, battling performance", from the terraces it looked different: we saw a tired side up against a team determined not to score themselves, and hell-bent on stopping us - and against those sort of tactics, we lacked ideas.

In terms of breaking teams down, this was the major obstacle in our home form, but thank goodness for those trips away. For the most part the opposition were open when we were on our travels. Rotherham tried to frustrate us for 45 minutes and then opened up to 'take us' in the second. It didn't work and we eventually came away 2-0 winners, both goals scored by Steve Finney, his second giving rise to a rendition of on-ly on-ly one Ste-eve Fin-ney to lift the roof off the visitors' end. In Finney, top scorer, yet invariably left out as soon as Thorne was fit, there was a replacement better than we could've ever hoped for. In fact, 'replacement' was a bit of a misnomer as he reached 15 goals comfortably by December.

Unsurprisingly, most visitors to the County Ground weren't interested in trying to win, just in trying to stop us from winning. OK, I'll give Wrexham, Walsall and Wycombe their due, they didn't lose and gave us a miserable Christmas period by each holding us to a draw, but for us, the whole thing was frustrating and highlighted our creative shortcomings: ten home draws meant that non-travelling supporters missed out on seeing the team at its best. When we won at home, it was quite often an unnecessary struggle.

After such a brilliant start, high standards were set. And so our first 'sticky patch' from the end of October to the middle of January consisted of: played 10, won 2, lost 2, drawn 6. In the midst of that, we also lost our unbeaten home record to a side bent on the most boring of spoiling tactics (Shrewsbury). And yes, that is sour grapes.

As frustrating as those ten games were, we still only conceded six goals, proving that something strange had happened to our defence: it was keeping the opposition out. This was due largely to the presence of old hand Ian Culverhouse, a masterstroke signing by McMahon (it would be difficult to quantify the number of goals he saved us), and the ever-steady Shaun Taylor, who contributed six valuable goals as well. And though it may have seemed a sticky patch to us, the teams around us at the top of the Division refused to profit. The 12 point lead held at the end of October saw us safely through until the middle of December, and then we only slipped off the top for two games when Crewe nipped in front. One of the lowest points was the abysmal showing at York where we were beaten 2-0 by one of the worst sides in the Division, and even then we still held second place comfortably.

Easy games followed against three of the sides who were to be relegated: Hull, Carlisle and Swansea, even though we still tried to make it hard for ourselves. There were more than a couple of times that Steve McMahon's post-match summary contained the phrase "we have to be more ruthless."

Oldham arrived for the fourth round of the Cup and displayed an even more negative set of tactics. Welcome relief from the League maybe, but they came to the County Ground set on earning themselves a draw and nothing else. It would be no exaggeration to say that they wasted time right from the first whistle. So you can imagine our satisfaction when Martin Ling smashed in a last-minute volley. *That* was justice. In the fifth round we drew at home to Southampton, before eventually going out in the replay. Ah stuff it, we weren't particularly bothered anyway. Only promotion and the Championship mattered.

Two away wins in early March seemed to put us back on track. Peterborough was one of the more boring victories: we were so much the better side that we really didn't have to put ourselves out. But it was worth going if only for the second, brilliant goal scored by Steve Finney. A week and a half later he was out for the rest of the season, suffering a hairline fracture of his leg in 'that' challenge at Burnley - now notorious in Swindon - after which the referee was apparently heard to say "get up, he never touched you."

Then another lowlight. A 3-0 away defeat at the hands of rivals Oxford. It wasn't so much the defeat itself which was terrible, it was the manner in which the team walked about the pitch as if they didn't care. Oxford very palpably did, and won at a canter, with Joey Beauchamp predictably scoring the third. That Oxford finally gained the second automatic promotion spot was deserved, but aside from the reasonable face of local rivalry, Swindon supporters have an additional reason for wishing they hadn't made such a good finish to the season: Division One will see two more fixtures and two more potential trouble spots off the pitch. The cause for peace promoted by *The 69er* and its Oxford counterpart *Raging Bull* this season will definitely have to be repeated next year.

During our second 'sticky patch', Blackpool jumped past us to occupy first place. Irritating, but with our four games in hand, we weren't too concerned, (well OK, maybe just a bit). The games over Easter probably clinched us the Championship: Brighton were beaten in an entertaining scrape, Notts County were seen off by a last minute overhead kick from Horlock, but arguably the best Town performance of the season came away at Crewe on Easter Monday. The train spotters had just sold three of their best players and were now fading fast from the race for second place, let alone the title. In our first meeting, it had been close, with us coming out 2-1 winners; here at 'The Alex', quite simply, we were superb. Never at any moment did we look in any danger of losing; both goals were brilliantly taken, one in each half, allowing them no reply. As we left the ground after the game, one Crewe supporter was overheard saying to another "we're just not good enough to go up." But *we* were.

From then on, it was only a matter of time before we clinched the double of promotion and Championship. Blackpool (by then the only other real contender for top spot), saw us achieve our first target and the following Tuesday we clinched the silverware with three excellent goals in a 3-1 win away at Chesterfield.

The final three games were an enjoyable and relaxing anti-climax, and we ultimately topped the pile by a clear nine points.

This year several players made the difference: Kevin Horlock, who scored 16 goals from midfield, Shaun Taylor and then Wayne Allison up front. Allison was exactly what we'd been lacking for years - a tireless, strong runner, who set up countless goals and still managed to score 20 himself. These three, and all the others who either played or contributed off the pitch, made it a fantastic campaign, for once giving us a summer break when we could sit back and reminisce with pleasure, instead of reflecting gloomily. It wasn't an ordinary season, but then we aren't used to many of those at Swindon: since '85-86 there have only been three when we haven't been either promoted, relegated or involved in the play-offs. You just can't get much more fun than that!

Fanzine Facts

The 69er was started during the '92-93 season, editors Anna Merriman and Craig Jack having met at a journalism evening class. Produced to fill the gap left by 'Bring The Noise', *The 69er* takes its name from Swindon's famous League Cup defeat of Arsenal in 1969. The coming season will be the the the 'zine's fifth, and Anna is happy to report: "It's still going strong."

JOEY SCORES !!!

Greg Ashman

A KICK UP THE R'S

Queens Park Rangers

"Not much of a game this afternoon, was it?" I ventured to Phil. "I don't know," he replied, "I couldn't see half of it." He paused, and then added. "The bloke in front of me had his programme in his top pocket."

We were talking on the phone late Saturday evening after the Wimbledon match. It's something we've done regularly for a long time now. This season, the worst in the ten years that Phil and I have been churning out our "wretched magazine ... such negative stuff" (© QPR Chairman Peter Ellis), it's been a series of inquests.

I laughed. For the only time that day, I should add. I'd not long been home from watching Rangers lose 3-0 at home to Wimbledon, our second successive defeat. The dark clouds that had accompanied me on my journey up the motorway were an ominous sign. The consensus was we were going down. And the season was just two games old.

Now, the relevance of Phil's quip may, I realise, have somewhat passed you by. If so, it's because you have obviously never seen the new-look QPR programme. Size-wise, as programmes go, it's a monster. Rolled up, it not only serves to obscure the view of anyone behind, it could probably be pressed into service as a make-shift table leg if the need ever arose. Opened up, it could quite easily shelter a small family from a sudden downpour. When it was unveiled, the cynics amongst us suggested it needed to go magazine size to fit in the names of all the players Rangers had sold over the past five years. Others ventured that it was to allow for even more rose-tinted writing in its pages. The collectors were too busy to offer an opinion; they were trying to puzzle out how they were going to fit the proverbial quart into a pint pot.

As the season wore on, and relegation became ever more likely, our Saturday night inquests began to reflect more and more on the fact that, in the face of adversity, QPR fans seem to resort to the sort of gallows humour which supporters of clubs whose expectation levels are several rungs higher can never fully understand. What other set of fans would, for example, resist stringing up from the nearest lamp-post a fanzine seller who, as the crowds trudged their weary way home after yet another home defeat, shouted out, "Never mind, Rangers will probably win the FA Cup, eh?" Or, after the third spot-kick of the season had missed its intended target by the size of a programme, loudly enquired as to whether anyone would "take a penalty next week." Or, as the 14th and most costly away defeat of the season, away at Coventry, signalled the end of 13 years in the top flight, desperately asked around to establish whether anyone had (cue impression of Baldrick) "a cunning plan."

OK, not the funniest lines in the world (and they probably lose a bit in translation), but they were greeted with relatively good humour by those within ear-shot, as evidenced by the wry smiles, before the heartache of it all came flooding back.

And don't think relegation didn't hurt. It did. But if, like rats deserting a sinking ship, the Thompson regime's legacy to Rangers fans was Division One football, they at least didn't break our spirits before they went off in search of a new toy to play with. That was never better exemplified than for the final game of the season when, even with relegation assured, Rangers took 3,000 to Nottingham Forest and had a farewell party.

Some of the humour during the season has been surreal, not least the Chinese whisper that circulated around the Ellerslie Road stand, where coincidentally Phil sits - funny, that - which had it that the reason for the unknown minute's silence before the Southampton game was "something to do with beef" - the nodding heads and unquestioned acceptance of this wisdom being the surreal part, of course. Then there was the hooligan who, in aiming a kick at a fellow type being escorted from Loftus Road during the Chelsea Cup game, managed to fall over a barrier and down the stairs, thus achieving the unique feat of ejecting himself from the ground.

But nothing was more surreal than Rangers fans celebrating each Forest goal, then turning to the home fans to mock them with the chant "You're not singing anymore." Nothing, that is, if you discount those Rangers fans wearing pineapples on their heads and the guy wearing his dressing-gown and looking more Statto-ish than the nerdy one himself.

Richard Thompson had he been there, which he wasn't, might have thought it pretty surreal, the sight of 2,000 Rangers fans refusing to leave the ground, 35 minutes after the final whistle, and singing "We'll support you ever more." And not a few crying, while doing so. But then he wouldn't have got the joke, because he never really understood the script.

And so, as we contemplate Port Vale on a Wednesday night, we're left hoping that the new owners, whoever they may be, are football people, and that Ray Wilkins has learnt by his mistakes and can lead us back at the first time of asking. It's been a long time since I last watched Rangers outside the top Division. I only hope the standard of football has improved in that time. I can't say I'm not worried about it - the fellow who sits in front of me doesn't buy a programme, you see...

Fanzine Facts

A Kick Up The R's first appeared in 1987 and was borne from the proposed merger between QPR and Fulham, which the fans of both clubs successfully fought off. Editor Dave Thomas sums up the fanzine's philosophy on "the meaning of life, liberty and the pursuit of an away win at Grimsby on a cold, wet Tuesday night in November" thus:

"An optimist sees the cup half full; A pessimist sees the cup half empty.
We're still looking for the cup... "

A LARGE SCOTCH

Shrewsbury Town

How many clubs would sell one of their best central defenders a week before the start of the season? Well Town did, and perhaps this had some bearing on the fact that we only won once in the first 15 games!

Mark Williams was the player in question, sold to Chesterfield for the pathetically low sum of £45,000. The club had refused to increase his wage by the £50 that he wanted in order to bring him in line with other players at the club. In the end we had to pay £75,000 for a replacement, in the form of Peter Whiston from Southampton. Peter was a good signing, but missed a lot of games through injury. Ironically, Mark Williams went on to win three Player of the Year awards at Chesterfield!

ISSUE 17 ONLY 50p

A LARGE SCOTCH

SHREWSBURY TOWN FANZINE

Other signings included Robbie from Take That lookalike, Austin Berkley, on a free from Swindon, Mark Dempsey, £25,000 from Leyton Orient and Steve Anthrobus, £25,000 from Wimbledon.

A poor season had been predicted by most Town fans and the team were not doing anything to change our opinion. However confidence soon improved. We had an unbelievable run of eight straight wins, including the 11-2 slaughtering of Marine in the FA Cup. After going 1-0 up after three minutes, Shrews didn't score again until quite late into the first half, but then got three in two minutes which opened the floodgates. I don't care what standard the opposition was, it was still a great achievement to score so many. We were also the only team to beat League leaders Swindon at the County Ground.

By now, the team were challenging for a place in the play-off zone and had reached the later stages of the Auto Windscreens Shield. How wrong we'd been - or had we?

We played Fulham away in the FAC, and drew 1-1 to earn a replay. However, extra excitement was added to the occasion by the fact that the winners would be playing Liverpool at home in the next round. The Meadow was packed to the rafters. In the first half disaster struck. Paul Evans was sent off for using his elbow (he never touched him, ref) and Fulham scored a goal. One nil down and only ten men. But the second half was a totally different story: Fulham were under constant pressure, Town managed to equalise and then with three minutes to go, Austin Berkley set off on a run from his own penalty box to the other end of the pitch, passed to Mark Dempsey who calmly fired the ball home. The Riverside erupted.

Singing continued long after the final whistle - "TEN MEN - WE ONLY NEEDED TEN MEN."

I know it sounds daft but drawing Liverpool in the Cup was the worst thing that could have happened to the club. League results started going against us - were the players holding back to avoid injury and missing playing against Liverpool? The club was pretty keen to switch the tie to Anfield (purely in the interests of safety, of course - the thought of all that extra money probably never even crossed their minds), but the FA refused and the mad scramble for tickets began.

The match was actually postponed twice, with more bad League performances in between. We were now sliding down the table fast. The Liverpool match was eventually played on a Sunday morning with an eleven o'clock kick-off, courtesy of the local police who were worried that thousands of Liverpool fans would turn up without tickets. The Sport newspaper didn't help by having a back page headline predicting the possibility of a Hillsborough type disaster. Thankfully their fears were unfounded.

In the end the game was a total let-down. There would have been more atmosphere if we'd gone to church instead. Fearful of the mighty red's fire-power, manager Fred Davies, always a little cautious, decided to pack the midfield and only play one forward. This resulted in Town having precisely *no* shots on target whatsoever. The Liverpool players didn't even break into a sweat and treated the match like a pre-season friendly. No wonder the crowd were so quiet; it was one of the most boring matches I have ever been to.

Unfortunately Dave Walton received all the stick from the press (and our manager) for his mistakes which led to two of the four Liverpool goals, but in reality, Davies' team selection meant that the match was lost before a ball was even kicked. Angry supporters wrote to the local paper criticising his tactics, which ultimately led to the paper and manager falling out.

Things were starting to look bad; we were getting closer and closer to the relegation zone, and the only welcome distraction to pathetic League performances were our victories in the Auto Shield. Hereford were beaten 4-1 to set up a Southern Area Final with Bristol Rovers.

This match will also be remembered for the battle of the mascots. Our mascot Lenny The Lion, dressed as a Spanish Bullfighter, taunted the pantomime cow (sorry Hereford Bull) and then stabbed it with a big sword. This went down great with the home fans but surprisingly not so with the away following. The Hereford Bull left the pitch on a stretcher. Don't worry boys and girls, it was just pretend!

The first leg was at home. Rovers with a big travelling crowd behind them took the lead. Town left it late but equalised through a long range shot from Mark Taylor. After the game the level of pessimism was unbelievable; almost everyone had written us off as no-hopers for the second leg, and the club couldn't even sell the measly 1,000 tickets we'd been allocated.

We had played Bristol away on the previous Saturday and lost 2-1, Marcus Stewart later admitting that he'd dived for the match-winning penalty. But for the area final (and for once), the manager's tactics were spot on. We were playing really well, when a Bristol player (surprisingly not Mr Stewart this time) decided to fall over in the area. Thankfully, Paul 'Eagle' Edwards made a terrific save and from then on we just *knew* we were going to win. Ian Stevens came up with the inevitable goal and we were at Wembley for the first time in the club's history.

In the seven games between the Rovers match and Wembley we only won once. Again, the League fixture list threw up our AWS opponents just a week before the final, and after drawing 2-2 at Millmoor, confidence was high. Both our strikers Stevens and Anthrobus had got on the score sheet that day, and the rest of the team virtually picked themselves for the big match at Wembley. Or so we thought...

On the day, Fred Davies had what can only be described as a total brainstorm. He decided to drop crowd hero and general cult figure Steve Anthrobus. Local lads Kevin Seabury and Paul Evans weren't even subs and instead he played two loan players with only about six games for the club between them, one a thirtysomething defender recovering from injury and the other a 19 year old lad from Wolves.

Surprise surprise, we played crap and lost 2-1. The team only started playing with ten minutes to go, and got a goal through Mark Taylor, but the final few minutes went all too quickly. What had started off as a brilliant day out full of optimism ended in embarrassment and anger towards the manager. But being at Wembley was magic - even though the place obviously needs 'doing up', it's still something very special to see your team play there. But to go there and lose is not a nice feeling. Still, at least we got there, and that's something I never thought I would live to see.

The rest of the season no longer seemed important, our hearts were broken and we just wanted it all to end there and then.

Ian Stevens won the main Player of the Season award. He was the club's top scorer with twenty goals, even though he spent a lot of time in the reserves. In fact he finished top scorer for them too! Another star was big Steve 'throb' Anthrobus. Throb is the type of player that you love if he's playing for you, but he's the dirty bugger up front if he's not. The manager was quick to point out that although we had signed him from Wimbledon, he was not part of the 'crazy gang'. Obviously keen to disprove this endorsement, in only his second game for the club he punched a Doncaster player in the head and got sent off.

The season ended as it had begun - badly, including a 6-0 drubbing at Oxford, our biggest defeat since 1964. In true Shrewsbury style, the manager was given a three year extension to his contract.

A lot of people would say a Wembley appearance and a match against Liverpool all in one season was a dream, but ask any Town fan and they will tell you it was actually a nightmare.

Fanzine Facts

A *Large Scotch* was started around seven years ago by editors Kevin and Gary Bright. Not exactly a regular publication, apparently the reaction to the fanzine is still quite mixed at the club. "The chairman Mr Bailey supports us and thinks we do a good job," says Kevin, "but there are also a lot of people at the club who think we are the scum of the earth. Especially the chap who produces the match day programme."

A *Large Scotch* got its name during the period of Iain McNeill's tenure as manager; when by all accounts he was partial to filling the Shrew's team with assorted fellow Scots.

A LOAD OF BULL

Wolverhampton Wanderers

This was a season which started early (July 10th) and finished early (July 12th). Which came as a bit of a shock, not least to the bookies who had Wolves down as 3-1 short-priced favourites for the title. Viewed from the outside, you could understand their logic: Graham Taylor was a proven club manager who had got us into the play-offs the year before. And with Dean Richards signed in the close season and the likes of Tony Daley, Steve Froggatt and Geoff Thomas due to report fit for the new campaign, surely one of the two automatic promotion places to the Premiership would finally be ours? Not, as it turned out, by a long way...

Prior to July 10th even the most sceptical of Wolves fans felt a measure of cautious optimism. But that was to be the day when the nightmare with which we had lived for years suddenly seemed about to come horribly, cruelly true: switching on Teletext and seeing the headline "Bull set to leave Wolves." And there it was; the Wolves board had accepted a bid of £1.5m from Coventry City, and the player was free to talk terms with Big Fat Ron.

Well, if Graham Taylor thought he could quietly get rid of our icon during the summer holiday season he was much mistaken. Here was a player with the small matter of 250 goals to his name in just under nine seasons with the club; now aged 30, he had been the leading League scorer in '94-95 with 17 goals in 33 games. Was it just Wolves fans who failed to see the logic in the proposed move? In the driest summer on record, violent thunderstorms erupted around Molineux that night - they were but as a whisper to the howls of outrage that arose from the town. The club was soon under siege. On July 12th Steven Bull announced his decision: he would stay at the Wolves. Why? "The fans - they've supported me for nine years." Taylor claimed to be "pleased", but few believed him. He had sown the seeds of his own downfall and they weren't long germinating.

Come August and the team kicked off the new season in front of a crowd that had suddenly and quite unnecessarily been rendered nervous, disillusioned and potentially hostile. You Know Who duly put us 1-0 up in our first game away at Tranmere, and it was *his* name and not the manager's that we were singing. Familiar defensive frailties meant that we ended up drawing 2-2 and the pattern was set. It didn't get any better.

Still determined to offload a striker, Taylor sold David Kelly to Sunderland (where he promptly got injured and won promotion) and used the money to fund the purchase of Mark Atkins from Blackburn Rovers for £1.1m. Here was the 27 year old holder of a Premiership medal who had played over 30 games for Blackburn in their title season. Why he wanted to move down a division, God knows; but if you ever wanted proof of the dangers of buying a player on the way down, here it is. He was to win the fanzine's Donkey of the Season award at an, er, gallop - something he never did in a Wolves shirt. And God knows, he had some competition for the accolade, Tony Daley to name but one.

Into November and the title favourites were by now lying 18th in this most mediocre of divisions. Taylor's net deficit on transfer dealings had now soared past £5m in a season and a half, and the performances - or rather lack of them - had turned into ones of which relegation nightmares are made. The Hayward family were big enough to admit their mistake in appointing him and quick enough to move before it was too late. Exit Taylor stage left - not pursued by a Bull, but it would have been understandable.

There then followed a quite remarkable episode and one which revealed for all to see the problems now besetting the club. Captain John De Wolf had been struggling to regain fitness since an awful knee injury the previous February, to the extent that whenever he played, he did so with a humungous brace on the bad knee, and with the turning circle and speed of an oil tanker. Caretaker manager Bobby Downes asked him to play in the reserves in an effort to improve his fitness. He not only refused point blank to do so, but went public with statements that his agent would be seeking an immediate meeting with the chairman, etc. etc. I have never seen a player move from popular cult figure to the focal point of 'should never wear the shirt again - a disgrace' accusations with quite such rapidity, but this club captain of a managerless team did so with ease. Compare and contrast this with Bully's attitude a few weeks previously when, after a three match suspension had ended, Taylor had played him in the reserves; no complaints, just a goal and then a platitude about "can't blame the boss for not changing a winning team", when he didn't make the starting line-up for the first time in his Molineux career the following Saturday at home to Stoke (we lost 4-1). One suspected that peace and goodwill was not the norm behind the scenes as Christmas approached.

On the subject of approaches, nothing much seemed to be happening, openly at least, in terms of finding a successor to Taylor. But believe it or not, the chairman of Wolves - Jonathan Hayward, son of benefactor Sir Jack - twice rang the Editor of *A Load of Bull* during the search, to discuss the attributes of potential candidates and likely supporter reaction to their appointment. How many other football club chairmen have displayed such openness? Impressive. Soon, shortly before Christmas, to no great surprise, in walked Mark McGhee and Co. from down the M69 to predictable outraged screams of 'Judas' - not that I recall Leicester fans saying the same a year previously when McGhee left Reading. Whatever else, you couldn't fault McGhee's bravery in taking over a club which had by now slipped to 20th spot in the table. But then he lacks nothing if not self-confidence, and he moved quickly to try to imbue players and fans alike with some of it. Publicly declaring his admiration of Bull at the outset was nothing if not good PR - Bull responded with a new lease of life and some crucial goals. A month later and we were unlucky to lose 1-0 at Villa Park in the Coca Cola quarter finals, also holding Spurs to a 1-1 draw at White Hart Lane in the FA

Cup. McGhee had, crucially, switched to three centre halves, and for the first time in several years we were capable of being solid at the back. It was a rich irony that he achieved this with three players signed by Taylor - Richards, Emblen and Young.

Soon the talk was of the play-offs. That though was to reckon without the one consistent feature of Wolves teams throughout our seven years of torture in this division from hell; namely, our inconsistency. And, in particular, our inability to win the big games, the ones where you have to get a result to keep a season alive. Indeed, we failed to win any of our last eight games and only became mathematically safe from relegation in our final home fixture. We finished up where McGhee had walked in - 20th. A disgraceful effort.

A disgraceful effort from the most expensively assembled, best paid and best supported squad in the mighty Endsleigh League Division One. An average gate of just under 25,000 - the 15th largest in the country - had every right to feel short-changed and were left to ponder the reasons. Purely in playing terms: inconsistent goalkeeping, average full backs, too many changes in central defence, no ball-winner in midfield (Thomas made but two appearances as sub, was sent off in the second and then had yet another major knee op) and wingers either ill and/or injured (Froggatt) or simply not interested (Daley).

That might sound terminal to the hopes of any team, but the real malaise ran much deeper. Worse, far worse, was the lack of effort from big name players, and that is inexcusable. We had far too many ex-Premiership 'stars', the wrong side of 25, who seemed to be interested only in a fat pay packet in return for not very much at all. Sometimes they would whinge about the 'problems' of playing at Molineux in front of such an 'expectant' crowd. Bloody hell! You could really see the players of say Grimsby, Reading and Barnsley (to name but three teams, assembled for a pittance, at whose grounds our All Stars team simply rolled over and gave in to abject, pitiful defeat) coming to Molineux for a game and thinking "Christ, I'm glad we don't have to put up with these facilities every week, the best stadium and pitch in the Division, and the biggest crowds and so on - it must be awful!" Couldn't you? No? Me neither.

Fact is, Wolves players are paid a fortune, and we the fans pay those wages. Ending a season nearer the drop than promotion is bad enough. But doing so in the knowledge that some players weren't giving their all leaves a very sour taste. Thirty nine teams had finished above us come May - i.e. over 400 professional footballers were in the starting line-up of higher placed teams every Saturday. So you might reasonably expect the average pro at Wolves not to be earning well into six figure sums every year, for they are hardly at the top of their profession, are they? Mid-season we witnessed the extraordinary example of Vinny Samways who came to us on loan. He very nobly stated that he was prepared to accept a cut of £3,000 in his *weekly* wages in order to join us. From £8,000 per week to a mere £5,000! The poor love.

Had he signed a three year contract, then Samways would have earned more in those 36 months at Wolves than the average person on average full-time wages in this country would earn in the course of their working *lifetime*. That's *before* signing-on fees, win bonuses, endorsements plus all previous and future earnings from football! And, of course, not every one of Wolves' 18,000 season ticket holders is lucky enough to be on average earnings. Fortunately a permanent transfer fell through - allegedly over the issue of a £400,000 loyalty bonus written into his Everton contract. *Loyalty bonus?!*

Football players are expected to earn the respect of supporters. That comes not just from individual achievement but from effort - 'fans always love a trier', don't they? Well, trying is the least that fans deserve and they have every right to vilify those players that don't. In any other industry they would be sacked. But in football we just keep on having to pay their grotesque wages. This was a sorry season in the proud history of Wolverhampton Wanderers, both in the way it began in the close season and in the way it finished. We were left once again to muse on the sorry sights of Sir Jack Hayward and Steve Bull, for each of whom time is now fast running out. The former is past 70 and with little to show but a fabulous stadium for his £30m investment; the latter has sacrificed his own career on the altar of getting Wolves into the Premiership. Both have won the enduring gratitude of town and fans for their efforts; but I finished the season wondering just how many of our ludicrously overpaid and under-performing playing staff could look these two in the eye as they sauntered out of the club in May to drive off in their expensive motors, laden down with wads of cash, to their ill-earned holidays in the sun. Hopefully, in the case of some, never to return. The Haywards and the loyal triers at the club (Bull, Thompson and Dennison to name but three, all of whom are now in their testimonial years after 10 years of loyal effort at Molineux) deserved far better in '95-96. As, I think, did the fans.

Fanzine Facts

A Load of Bull, allegedly the Endsleigh League's top selling fanzine, was started in 1989 by Dave Worton. At the beginning of the '93-94 season he handed over the editorial reins ("I've got to get a life") to long-time contributor Charles Ross. ALOB got its name following the achievements of the legendary Steve Bull over the two seasons leading up to the fanzine's launch; that it to say, Bully had scored 100 goals ('a load') during that time. Charles has a number of contributors, but singles out Tony Eagle, the ALOB cartoonist.

A LOT 2 ANSWER 4

Swansea City

Well, here we are again. I've tried to put this off for as long as possible because I didn't really know where to start. Of all the clubs included in this book, not one can come even close to the season I have just experienced - that's for sure. The misfortunes of Torquay, Brighton and even fallen aristocrats Manchester City, who between them have either had a crap team, been shit on by their board or been plain unlucky, have all befallen Swansea - and more.

Cast your minds back to last August; the Swans sat proudly on top of the Division with two wins and an away draw, but that was where the good times ended until a good six months later and the arrival of our umpteenth manager. After August 26th we only won three games out of a possible 29, and in between we suffered total humiliation in the FA Cup by losing by the odd goal or seven to lower division Fulham. Could my season sink any lower? You bet it could! We limped from bad to worse and defeat to defeat, and while the fans licked their wounds, the players were totally oblivious to the predicament and waltzed around town as if they were top of the Premiership.

Somewhere in the haze we lost our first manager Frank Burrows, who packed his bags and sodded off to West Ham to be a coach. Now don't get me wrong; it's not sour grapes or anything, but I thought he should have gone a few seasons ago. He was obviously stale and just going through the motions. Our plucky chairman was claiming he offered Burrows some money to buy players, but Burrows refused it. Now what manager turns down *any* sort of money to spend on strengthening a visibly weak team? Who was lying? Let's just say half a dozen of one and six of the other. Bobby Smith took over at the helm for his first spell, and he lasted until Christmas before a row broke out over a £200 bill for moulded boots for the players. The chairman said that the club wouldn't and couldn't pay for them. Smith left after he decided it was a matter of principle, and he wasn't going to ask the players to pay up for them either. Exit manager number two. Please, stop laughing, this is serious. It gets *worse*.

Next up in charge was Jimmy Rimmer who had been running our youth side. While the team continued its appalling run, the off the field tragedy was only just beginning. The chairman resigned and went public that a multi-million pound take-over was on the way, and the long-suffering fans should persevere a little longer. The chairman and his chief executive son had been the subject of a ferocious hate campaign for the best part of ten years, and we finally thought the nightmare was over. The knight in shining armour was supposed Shropshire millionaire, Michael Thompson, although investigations into his background yielded no proof of his wealth, his business status, or even his existence at all. I have a mate in the newspaper business who said "don't believe the hype - it's a bluff", and sure enough, only 28 days later we found out he was totally bogus. He came and went in a cloud of mystery and controversy. In the short time he was in charge he managed to plunge us even deeper into despair, by appointing our fourth manager in this torrid season - the one and only Mr Kevin Cullis.

Who, you may well ask, was he? Cullis was brought in from the hotbed of football known as Cradley Town youth team!! After speculation about Ian Rush or even Toshack being tempted back with loads of cash, this was the biggest humiliation ever. There was definitely something going on that I couldn't even begin to explain in less than a thousand words, and for legal reasons I'll just leave it at that.

I will however share with you a little tale of the horrendous week under the reign of Thompson and Cullis. The team was playing at Blackpool and on its way to a 4-0 drubbing. At half time, it was left to one of our senior players to give the team talk because Cullis couldn't summon the required kudos or respect amongst his own players. Shocking.

In the meantime, muggins here decided to take up the offer of being interviewed by BBC radio Wales about what was going on in the club. Live from Cardiff I was led a merry dance by the presenter who chuckled and guffawed through the interview about the club I love (no doubt a Cardiff City fan who had no right to laugh at us, the cheeky sod). Anyway, that same day Thompson announced that he wasn't taking over after all (losing his £40k deposit in the process), and previous chairman Mr Sharpe was taking back the club he couldn't wait to get shot of a month earlier. Cullis was now suing for wrongful dismissal (I reckon he got off lightly - he should have been flogged in the town centre by a bearded lady and then fed to the North Bank). Jimmy Rimmer was back in charge for a second time, technically our fifth manager in as many months, and the team was rooted in the relegation zone.

While all this was going on, we were being ridiculed from John O'Groats to Lands End, which is hardly surprising, but only the fans seemed to be feeling it. If the club were a dog it would have definitely been shot as a mercy killing by now. Boy, were we suffering. With 15 games to go, many had given up the ghost and were resigned to life in the basement next season. On the other hand, as they say 'every cloud has a silver lining' and this sad annus horriblus wasn't any exception. A few days before the team was due to play York away, none other than Jan Molby threw his hat in the ring and became our *sixth* manager of the campaign. Hope springs eternal and all that, but what could such a genius have been thinking of? Well, he did say he wanted a challenge!

Once again the fans of Swansea City got behind the club and Molby took us on a run of seven wins, three draws and only four defeats. With exactly the same squad we began the season with, I actually thought we were going to finish mid-table at one point. However he didn't manage to keep us up, but gave it a hell of a go and gave the club the boost it desperately needed. He even managed to prize the chairman's wallet open for five transfers, one of which was Lee Chapman who managed to get almost a goal in every game for the last quarter of the season. Anyway, the inevitable came, and after the penultimate game at Notts County we were relegated - funnily enough as one of the in-form sides in the Division.

With some summer signings and the pruning of the dead wood, as one banner at the last home game against Crewe proclaimed, we will only be "on loan to Division Three." In the immortal words of Arnie, "We'll be back!"

Fanzine Facts

Launched in March 1992, **A Lot 2 Answer 4** is edited by Dominic Daley, with the help of Dominic's brother Michael, Ralph Davis and John 'Jack London' Aspel, to whom Dominic says "Diolch yn fawr" (that's 'thank you very much' in his native tongue). As the founders were trying to think of a name for their fanzine, Swansea had experienced the farcical managerial merry-go-round of Terry Yorath leaving, Ian Evans' appointment and subsequent sacking, and the re-appointment of Yorath (seems to have set some sort of a pattern...). Following a 2-4 home defeat to Fulham, the guys decided the powers that be had a lot to answer for...

A LOVE SUPREME

Sunderland

All You Need Is Love - Supreme

From the moment Peter Reid breezed onto the Roker pitch prior to his first game in charge of Sunderland against Sheffield United on April 1st 1995, clenched fist raised in the air and his face contorted in defiant aggression, you just knew things were going to change for the better. It was not an act of egotistical bravado, but an honest football pro from the game's highest echelons saying "the crap stops here."

Little over a year later he had the Wearsiders in the Premiership, and there are still gasps of disbelief in these parts that Liverpool, the Arse, Man United and our dearly beloveds from Tyneside have replaced the Vale, Barnsley, Sarf'end and Grimsby on the fixture list for '96-97! Having changed things around so quickly (seven games from what seemed an almost certain relegation when he arrived), Reidy is becoming the biggest Wearside legend since Bob Stokoe ran on to the Wembley pitch in 1973 complete with trilby and pervy looking mac. However, something suggests that unlike Stokoe, Peter Reid will turn out to be a great manager.

This Shankly-reincarnation of the 90's exudes an air of footballing presence that promises a great deal; a top class player at club and international level, people forget that the mercurial Scouser has already taken Manchester City to fifth in the Premiership twice. How ironic then that as Sunderland went up, the Maine Road misfits went down! Not that funny-an-old-game then to the City faithful, what with United winning the League too.

Sunderland's season began none too brightly with a 2-1 home defeat at the hands of newly relegated Premiership whipping boys, Leicester City. Even at that early stage the omens were not looking good. Paul Bracewell had returned from Newcastle for his third spell. At £50,000 this was the only major pre season outlay of note and the fans were restless. But then on August 22nd, Sunderland went in at half time 0-2 down to Preston in a Coca Cola Cup second leg tie. Trailing 3-1 on aggregate, Reid allegedly read the riot act prompting a second half fight-back that secured a 4-3 overall victory. From there on the season began to pickup.

Despite the lack of chequebook activity the manager had surrounded himself with a strong backroom team in Bracewell, coach Bobby Saxton and names such as Alan Durban and 'Pop' Robson, who incidentally left Man United's hugely successful youth set-up to return to his true love as Reserve team coach. Underpinned by an excellent defence, the definitive, intelligent playing pattern that emerged in the opening months led to a 12 game unbeaten Roker run stretching from September 2nd to November 22nd. In between times they gave Liverpool a fright in the League Cup and drew warm praise for their game plan, which Roy Evans noted was similar to the mighty Reds!

Come December and Sunderland's increasingly confident team thrashed Division One leaders Millwall 6-0 (Russell got four), despite having lost the services of £900,000 David Kelly who was originally brought in to strengthen a goal-shy strike force!

Two mighty new year FA Cup struggles against Man United, in which Sunderland outplayed and out-sang United at Old Trafford, seemed to have taken their toll on the lads. Results in the League hiccuped and fans began to fear that unless money was made available to Reidy the promotion dream could easily die. Early season smiles were replaced by anguished faces as Norwich, Tranmere and Port Vale escaped unscathed from Roker. And the 0-3 thrashing at Wolves only served to reinforce the fears that 'normal service' had resumed.

As all and sundry cried out for cash to buy a striker, Peter Reid indulged in a piece of typically individualistic management. He went to Blackburn and agreed a loan deal for their third choice goalkeeper Shay Given. Up here everyone thought "if he's not ahead of Bobby Mimms in the Ewood pecking order then what are we up to?" Never fear though, within a short space of time he was hailed as "the best Roker keeper since Jim Montgomery", "one of the top ten in Britain" as he kept 12 clean sheets in 17 games. This stupendous form inspired his new team to the top of the table. He also won a couple of full Irish caps when deputising for Alan Kelly. Remember this name; at 19 he's got frighteningly massive potential and is destined to go all the way to the top.

As Sunderland's Premiership-bound bandwagon gathered momentum, a terrace chant of "Cheer up Peter Reid" (sung to the tune of the old Monkees hit 'Daydream Believer') was turned into a full length recording by a group of long standing fans who called themselves 'Simply Red and White'; and far more attractive than Mancy Mick Hucknell to boot! Despite only being sold in quantity in the North East, the song charted above Oasis for a couple of weeks! Indeed had this song (recently voted fourth best footie song of all time in the Sunday Express) been sold exclusively through chart accredited shops, it would have hit the Top 20!

To some extent the only factor spoiling the run-in was the sight of Newcastle United swanning it at the top of the Premiership. But spookily the moment they began singing their 'alternative' version of 'Cheer up' their slump began. In they rattled from Fenton, Cantona, Collymore and Woan; Sky TV's post match pan-ins captured legions of blubbering Geordies as the title slipped from their grasp. Most of these cry babies are the new breed of United glory fans; just whatever happened to those Neanderthal Gallowgate Enders? Anyway, next season's derbies will be no place for the faint-hearted, and at least the return of Wear-Tyne bunfights will end the pseudo North East showdowns involving Boro and the Mags. Middlesbrough get so riled because they hate Sunderland and Newcastle, but us Makems and Geordies just think of them as a bunch of former North Yorkshire irrelevances who should now be based in Rio de Janeiro!

For non-Roker fans reading this in particular, watch out in '96-97 for Richard Ord our brilliant ball playing centre back, midfielders Martin Smith and Mickey Gray, and Craig Russell, an ever improving striker. Reid has promised we will be prepared and we believe him after his Roker Revolution so far.

So Sunderland's season ended in a state of delirium for the Wearside faithful. The only North East championship winners and Reidy receiving the Manager of the Year Award from his peers. Kevin Keegan allegedly put his X against the Sunderland supremo's name... Wonder why Fergie never got his vote?

Sunderland's promotion culminated in a huge party at Tranmere. Modes of transport included a 20 foot hired USA Cadillac and fancy dress outfits as original as '70's Porn Stars Randy West and John Holmes, bedecked in long leather macs and 'Shaft' style fedoras! OK Premiership, lock up your daughters, the Makems are coming!

One notable thing about the new atmosphere surrounding the city was the post-promotion partying. The players and management go out and about into the bars to celebrate with the fans. Indeed after a local journalist asked Reid if he had been scared following the Tranmere game, as hundreds of supporters rushed at him and proceeded to chair him around the field, he replied "No, why should I be, they're all me mates after all."

WE ONCE THOUGHT OF YOU AS A SCOUSER DRESSED IN BLUE, NOW YOU'RE RED AND WHITE THROUGH AND THROUGH!

Fanzine Facts

A Love Supreme is one of the biggest selling fanzines in the country, its self-explanatory title taken from the John Coltrane jazz classic, a recording which was also covered successfully a few years ago by soul smoocher Will Downing.

ALS has won many admirers for its stylish design which does not gloss over a nonetheless diverse, varied internal content. Described last year by Sky Sports as "the best footie mag we've seen", it began in 1988 as a voice for supporter expression, and with sales of 8,000 plus and a readership of 20,000 it seems to have succeeded in its aim. Winner of many awards, ALS plans to go from strength to strength in the future.

A SLICE OF KILNER PIE

Huddersfield Town

The giant woke briefly for a mug of Horlicks

It seemed the sensible thing.

You know, to leave it a month or two, let the proverbial dust settle before scribbling down the outstanding memories of the '95-96 season. The League Championship, the FA Cup, the unbeaten away record and 100% home success, getting to the front of the pie queue on a matchday, only to be told that the last meat 'n' tatey had in fact been "sold to that fella over thur, luv." It would be easier to write a general overview of Town's season, I thought, rather than a week by week account. It's more reader friendly too.

"And on September 16th we travelled to... drew 0-0 in midweek at... had three pints and a pie down in..." It gets a bit boring. No, I'll wait for the best memories to stick; there's no need to mention all the tiresome away victories. Be selective, I thought.

Bollocks. You see, the trouble is, the promised rousing finish never happened. Town's surge up the table had fizzled out by Advent. The expected pastings over piss-poor opponents simply did not materialise. Where were the three, four, five goal routs of a year ago? Had we left them behind at Chester? Or Blackpool perhaps? Did Warnock take them with him? Surely not. He must have had his hands full with our reserve team (Fishy Billy, Logan, Blackwell, Clayton etc. all left with the Neilster), and it can't have been easy driving down to Plymouth with Mick Jones up your arse. No, stop it. I said I wouldn't.

I'm afraid it appears the old Division Three inconsistencies have crept back in again. A promising start, nestling nicely at Christmas, ready to pounce in the New Year, very cold February, mid-table by March. And so whilst you should be reading about our Sunday afternoon/Wednesday night triumphs in the play-offs and £5.00 programme, £3.80 hot dogs at Wembley I am left short-changed for 'outstanding memories' on which to comment. The Town 'chuckle reservoir' was, unusually for Yorkshire, a little dry last season. Memory Lane is closed for resurfacing.

I saw a few Huddersfield shirts at the cricket, though. England were playing India at Headingley so the blue army turned out in force to get pissed and throw beer bottles at each other on the Western Terrace. "You should see the Kilner Bank at 3pm on a Saturday afternoon," I told the Indian fielder at deep-backward square leg. I don't think he understood.

We've been chasing after a new club anthem all year at Town. We seemed to settle upon 'Those were the days' (or at least our version of it) at the back end of last season. It's a nice tune; I like it, although I'm a bit disappointed that no-one thought of putting words to 'Rhubarb and Custard'. Still, the great Frank Worthington always used to say that it spurred him on when he heard "We won the League three times in a row" sung from the terraces. I wish it would rub off on Simon Collins. But yes, it is a rousing anthem indeed to rival the Delilah's of this world.

Can't say much for Gina G, though. Why do we bother with Eurovision? It's not as if we ever win anything; every year we finish nowhere with bugger all points to boast of. And we never even sing at home. Maybe we should all move to Ireland...

Oh, that reminds me, Wimbledon were in town last season. We had a bit of a Cup run and the Terriers reached the last 16. Man Utd? Liverpool? Spurs? Who would we be paired with in the fifth round of the FA Cup? Which of this nation's footballing giants would be doing battle against the mighty Huddersfield on February 17th?

The Wombles. F**king Wimbledon. Cheers. What a money-spinner. Still, the blue army turned out in force once again; 18,000 filling the New Leeds Road to capacity with Sam the Man, Uncle Bulgaria, Joe Durie and Jeremy Bates keeping the stewards company in the away end. Where the hell were you guys? On the common having a picnic? Playing tennis with Tobermory? Either way, "No ground no fans, no ground no fans" proved irresistible.

Town were hotly tipped to provide an upset, hence Match of the Day gave us top billing in the evening's schedule. We were going well at the time, sitting proudly in third place when many (myself included) had tipped us to go down. We'd already disposed of Blackpool and Peterborough (what about '93, lads?) in earlier rounds, so the visit of the crazy gang posed few problems for the blue and white machine. Did it? No. Bollocks.

Seven minutes had gone when Rodney Rowe stumbled through to slot the ball home. We were one up. The Kilner Bank went mental. "Que Sera, Sera, wherever we'll be, we'll be..." echoed around the ground, if somewhat prematurely.

"It's going to be a nail-biting last 83 minutes," said the chap in the seat behind to his mate. That made us laugh, as did Mick Harford, who ambled around the pitch like a pissed Bambi on ice. In fact the whole Wimbledon side looked distinctly Third Division, and were a shocking reminder that not 15 years ago they were plying their trade in the Vauxhall Conference, regularly losing away at Altrincham and playing five at the back at home to Scarborough in the hope they could salvage a draw. But however shit and devoid of class, skill and footballing ability they may be, they are survivors, and weren't going to duck out of this one without a fight.

We went two up shortly after half time thanks to a gravity defying header from 'Top Cat' Cowan. Mount Kilner erupted once again, and a blue and white flow of lava spilled onto the pitch. The stewards caught both of them, but we still celebrated in style. "Que Sera, Sera...." No problems. This was easy. A place in the last eight was ours.

We lost the replay 3-1 after taking the lead on eight minutes through Booth. Both games seemed to sum up Town's whole season. So much promise and such expectations had threatened to be fulfilled before a big black guy called Ekoku snatched glory from under our noses in injury time. We knew we'd been cheated.

Robbed of what was rightfully ours, be it a quarter final of the Cup or a place in the Premiership.

At 4.47 on February 17th, I was convinced Town would have both. The euphoria on the Kilner Bank in the minutes leading up to that goal was unmatched all season, and was an indication of the desire shared by thousands to get this club back where it belongs. In the top flight; on Match of the Day; at Elland Road.

But by 4.48, three minutes into injury time, it had all gone pear-shaped as Ekoku drifted in unnoticed to nod home the leveller. The silence was sickening. My heart fell through my arse, I could have died. It was awful. You could say we never recovered from that goal. Like a cyclist in the French Alps, we were one minute at the top - tired but ready for the descent - and then the next on the slide back down because we realised we'd dropped our wallet at the bottom.

Sure, we thumped Palace, beat Luton, stuffed Reading, Southend and Mill-wall at home, but these were rare victories indeed. Our failure to win away since the Cup exit was to be our downfall, condemning Town to another season of long, boring away trips down the M1 to the capital and beyond.

But there's always a hop across to Valley Parade to look forward to this year; to raise the spirits and restart the motor after defeats on our travels elsewhere. We can lose at bottom of the table Port Vale, get thumped at Barnsley, surrender a 2-1 lead with five minutes left to lose 3-2 at Sunderland and even draw at bloody Luton, but we will never be beaten by the Shitty. If we can't have a go at L**ds, at least not for another season anyway, then it's fortunate Bradford have come up to take the punishment. Well done boys - you were gifted promotion; what kept you?

Like Bradford this year, our target last season was not simply to consolidate but to go all out for further honours. We knew consolidation meant relegation in the long run; there was no way we were going to sit it out in a higher division and hope to stay up. Just look at Carlisle with their ten year plan for the Premiership. I suppose you didn't account for that ever-widening gap between the Second and Third Divisions, did you guys? Is it a 15 year plan now?

The 3-0 opening day defeat at Oldham proved something of an early setback. We were outplayed, outthought, completely outclassed (basically pissed on) by rud-dy Oldham! Wandering away from Boundary Park amongst 3,000 other Town fans on that first Saturday I couldn't help but wonder what the Derby's, the Wolves, the Grimsby's of this world - the big spenders - would do to our hardy band of ex non-leaguers. In truth they all ripped us apart at some point during the season (even Grimsby put three past us at home) but up until the closing stages Town were always there or thereabouts, nestling nicely in the top five or six.

We actually played quite well for about 15 games, from Norwich City at home through the festive period and January to that Wimbledon game in February. The highlight was a 2-0 trouncing of Sheffield Utd in front of another packed away end at Bramall Lane. By the end of that period we had shrewdly risen to third place, with table-toppers Derby the only side to snatch all three points off us at home, winning 1-0 in front of a full house on Boxing Day.

Ever heard 12,000 people piss themselves laughing? Four days later we did as eighth placed Stoke City strolled into Town.

The Potters took an early lead which they held onto comfortably. Town were shite, and never looked like scoring. But whilst we knew it wasn't all over until the fat lady sang we didn't realise she was playing in goal with a Stoke City shirt on, and was to gift us an equaliser we scarcely deserved. If 'getting out of jail' is as easy as allowing a gentle back pass from your own right back to slither under your boot and scrape over the line, then I'm not surprised Cantona got away with community service. But where did Arthur Fowler go wrong? Either way the excuse from the guilty 'keeper hardly weighed up. "It hit a bobble." Prudhoe mate, this is the New Leeds Road you're talking about, not bleeding Gigg Lane after a wet January. Are you really so slow?

The second great escape during the return fixture at the Victoria Ground had a touch more OJ Simpson about it. It was March, and in recent weeks Town had begun to show signs of a faltering promotion challenge. The pressure was showing. We were crap that day, some woeful passing and a non-existent midfield were evidence enough of that. We never looked like getting away with it; everyone in the ground knew how crap we were and knew we would be sent down. Yet up stepped Rob Edwards to crash home the equaliser even later into injury time. Was he the misfit glove? He'd certainly had no problems settling in since his signing from Crewe, and the last minute reprieve adhered Edwards to the Town following as 2,000 Yorkshiremen celebrated in fine style behind the goal. The desperate pleas for Prudhoe to gift us another goal vanished in an instant as cries of Delilah rang out from the away end. Yes, I suppose that was a bit cheeky, heh-heh!

However, fortuitous moments like this were few and far between during the run-in as Town faltered, hit turbulence, began to look shaky, looked shaky, shook violently and finally nose-dived into the tarmac with only ten points picked up from the last 33 available. Yes, it was dire. And to those who would rather congratulate Town on surviving the drop than criticising them for making a complete bollocks of the final third of the season that had promised so much, I say this: our away record bettered only Oldham's; we lost 14 times on our travels and if it wasn't for a very posh fortress McAlpine and a loyal 13,500 we would have gone down.

Were we lucky? Only in that there were an abundance of other shite teams in the Division to keep us up. Next year might be a different story. Remember November 17th 1987? Town scored from the penalty spot, they scored from wherever they wanted. Ten times. Oh yes, get your tickets for Maine Road; Manchester City are back in town.

Fanzine Facts

A *Slice Of Kilner Pie* started life as a "crappy media studies project" at the back end of 1994. "It was shite", admits founding editor Phil Humphreys, "but I enjoyed it so I kept doing it." He remembered what a wise old man had once told him, "from small acorns do large oak trees grow." And *ASOKP* was that small acorn. But over the past two years it has matured nicely, and although by no means fully fledged, it is a fanzine that Phil, if not the club or the fans, can be proud of. "Parts of this mag are utterly bizarre...", said Total Football in a recent review. "I'll take that as a compliment" says Phil, and with circulation approaching the 500 mark for only the fourth issue, he'll do well to feel pleased with himself.

THE ABBEY RABBIT

Cambridge United

At Least It Was Better Than Last Year...

During our glory days under John Beck, the more cynical amongst supporters composed the following version of that old terrace favourite;

"*E I E I E I O,*
Up and down the League we go,
When we get to Rochdale,
This is what we'll sing,
We are Cambridge, We are Cambridge,
F**ked it up again..."

And, with our subsequent fall from grace being almost as rapid as the meteoric rise that preceded it, the *Rabbit* could look forward to the first return to Spotlands in years, as the Mighty U's acclimatised themselves to life in the basement.

the abbey rabbit

issn 1355-1906
feb/march
1996
issue 41

an alternative view of cambridge united f.c.

inside this issue:
psstiwanna buy united
the rabbit tels you how
boring bits
a look at the club's financial position and a report on the agm - grim indeed!
more boring bits
taking the p*ss out of p^sh
highlights and lowlights
25 years of agony and ecstasy
united rejects!
a look at the players who never quite made the grade
and much, mucch more!

looks like reggie's sprained his wrist opening his wallet again!!!

united: financial crisis situation critical?

£1

Unfortunately, as with most clubs that have suffered relegation, the season opened to the sound of players clamouring to leave. Despite a truly dodgy defensive record last term, it was the backbone of this same defensive unit that collectively felt they could perform at a higher grade, despite results conclusively proving otherwise. Centre-half Mick Heathcote took his dodgy knees to the West Country Football Academy at Plymouth, goalie Jon Sheffield decided that moving home would be far to stressful and so joined our loveable cousins at P*sh (despite still maintaining that he wanted to leave to play at a higher level) and Dean Barrick expressed a very public desire to play for anyone, thus in the eyes of most fans, going from cult to c*nt status overnight.

With no money available to strengthen the squad (isn't it nice to know that despite all the upheavals of recent times, some things remain reassuringly the same?), manager Tommy Taylor was left with no choice but to rebuild the team with a motley collection of free-transfer and non-contract cast-offs from the rest of the League.

The general consensus of opinion amongst most supporters was that mid-table respectability would be the best we could hope for. However, TT was having none of this and, in an 'exclusive' *Rabbit* interview, was remarkably bullish about our chances, stating that he aimed not only to prevent a repeat of the previous season's defensive blunders but to claim a spot in the play-offs... This was on the very day that a sad, balding git called Dave Smith was concocting a media hoax that involved Jason Donovan taking over the club! Whilst we didn't fall for that one, we were certainly taken in by TT!

Actually, things got off to a fairly bright opening, the U's recording a thoroughly merited 2-1 victory at Glanford Park, with a display as good as many fans would care to remember and one which certainly laid to rest the ghost of our totally abject opener at Wycombe the previous year. This was followed up by an equally creditable, if not totally convincing win by the same score over Swindon in the Fizzy-Pop Cup. However, with promotion perhaps our only realistic aim and due no doubt in part to our pathetically small squad, TT's avowed aim was to use as many fringe players as possible in the Coca Cola and Turtle Wax Trophy games, and so it came as no surprise when Swindon won through over the two legs.

It has to be said that for the first couple of months, with United lying third in the table, everything appeared to be going according to TT's plans. There were, of course, the occasional set-backs, including a severe 3-0 caning at Priestfield, where United, who ended up with six booked and one sent off, were lucky to get nil.

At this early stage, a number of things were becoming blindingly apparent. First, the standard of football in the Third Division was absolute cack of the highest order and any team that was able to put together a run of results would be there or thereabouts come May. Second, and more worryingly, this abject level of football was complemented by the totally abysmal standard of the match officials. Third, Cro-Magnon man look-alike Shane Westley looked over-priced, even for a free transfer! Obviously not brought in for his footballing prowess, the smart money was on his ability to curdle milk at twenty yards and frighten small children. Fourth, TT had obviously cured our defensive frailty of conceding late, soft goals. We were now likely to concede soft goals at *any* time. However, lastly and more importantly, whilst our dynamic strike force of Butler and Corazzin could keep themselves free of injury and in-form, we were always going to score more goals than we let in - so we could forget about problems three and four! Christ, to compound the feel-good factor, we even turned down a reported £300k offer for Corazzin, unloaded Westley to Lincoln and eventually swapped Dean Barrick for "Super Paulie Raynerrrrr" (© Doug Shulman) and some money. Never mind the play-offs, TT was talking automatic promotion. Pinch me! I must be dreaming...

Although we didn't take the AWS seriously, a brief mention has to be made of our home-tie against Brighton (if only because the editor of the book is a manic-depressive Seagulls fan and consequently didn't have that much to cheer about). Our tactic of fielding a second string side certainly backfired, as whilst our stiffs ran through their training ground party-tricks, the visitors remained totally unfazed and promptly coasted into a four goal lead, much to the surprise of the handful of ecstatic Albion fans!

Unfortunately, as far as our League campaign was concerned, that was about as good as it was going to get... October 14th saw the Mighty U's first visit to Sixfields and a rendezvous with the Cobblers - a local derby and a chance to pay our respects to Ian Atkins; to many fans the most reviled manager in our history (in contrast, John Ryan and Ken Shellito, the men who reigned during our 80's nose-dive are treated as the sad, pathetic figures they are). Full of confidence, a full strength United went into the match knowing that victory would consolidate our automatic promotion credentials... Whoops, 90 minutes and one total humiliation later, we scuttled away from Northampton as fast as possible.

This was the first of four defeats on the bounce, a period that saw us bow out of two Cup competitions in the space of five days. Our first choice defence at the Azteca Twerton couldn't stop Bristol Rovers romping to an embarrassingly easy 3-0 win in the AWS. Up against Swindon in the first round of the FA Cup, whatever lessons had been learnt in mid-week were quickly forgotten as we crashed 4-1. Despite the fact that we played well and defended heroically, the gap in class between the two sides was frighteningly awesome. Either Swindon have come on leaps and bounds since our first meeting or else we were going backwards... Most suspected the latter.

Our somewhat indifferent form wasn't helped by a series of debilitating injuries to key players, some truly bizarre tactical changes and a whole series of defensive gaffs that one day will surface on yet another Danny Baker video. Heard the one about the goalie who slices a clearance straight onto the opposing forward's boot? Or the defender who watches and applauds as the unopposed centre-forward's majestic header loops goal-wards? So resigned were we to these mistakes and more, that some enterprising soul could have made a fortune selling 'Golden Gaff' lottery tickets before each match!

Ah, but didn't I say earlier that providing we scored more than we conceded everything would be OK? Unfortunately, our god-like but increasingly injury-prone centre forward appeared to be another in need of a physiotherapist. In his case the problem appeared to be a rather severe and niggling groin strain. Radical treatment, including blocks of ice in the general vicinity of the testicles (my toes are curling up even as I type this), wasn't proving successful. Then, 'Bullet' surprised the medical community when he exclusively revealed that his problem was due to his twice weekly commuting from his Kent home to Cambridge. Receiving treatment at the world-famous Priestfield clinic, and despite rumours of an illegal approach, we are sure that no one connected with the Gills bothered to look up Butler's home number in the Maidstone telephone directory... Surprisingly he made a dramatic recovery...

To compound matters, 'million pound-rated' Carlo Corazzin was suffering a severe crisis of confidence, when shorn of Butler's astute touch and guidance, he looked just like the surprisingly average player he is. Indeed he was only to score twice in 17 matches before we unloaded him to Plymouth on transfer deadline day.

In came Robbie Turner, owner of the sharpest elbows in Christendom and a man that made Butler look positively mobile. He looked good whilst on loan, four goals in four games at the Abbey (OK so the one he scored whilst playing for Exeter doesn't count). Having done enough to secure another two year's regular income, his form took an unexpected(!) turn for the worse and he too eventually succumbed to striker's groin!

We travelled to Hereford knowing that a win was paramount to reinforce our (amazingly still valid) promotion credentials. At the time the Bulls were near the bottom and would surely be distracted by an impending cup-tie at Swindon, especially as we scored in only the second minute... Twenty minutes later we were 3-1 down, and the home side were cruising to an embarrassingly comfortable 5-2 win.

Never mind, things could only get better. Funnily enough we were still saying that, nine victory-less games later, a run that saw us drop from seventh to a worrying 23rd in the table. Luckily for us, Torquay were having the kind of season we used to have and Stevenage (luckily for us and Torquay) looked like winning the Conference. In the middle of this free-fall there was a brief moment of respite. We managed to keep our first clean sheet of the season, at our 32nd attempt (!), at home to then leaders Gillingham. However, any wild celebration was tempered by the fact that the Gills played the last 20 minutes with only nine players! Having regained our composure, we carried on falling towards the trap-door.

Luckily, we managed to finish with a bit of a flourish, losing only two of our last ten - although the former were fairly abysmal, being doubled by the Cobblers and a pathetic 2-0 reverse at 91st in the League Scarborough, where the home side rubbed salt into our wounds with their totally 'reasonable' admission charge of £9.50 to visiting fans.

Now, if we hadn't had that dark and dismal mid-season spell, we would have made the bloody play-offs! Bloody typical! As it was, our late spurt was enough to see us nestle into lower mid-table obscurity - just where the *Rabbit* had predicted we would finish!

So, you may ask yourselves as you read this (save for our backwards cousins up the A1, who haven't quite mastered this skill yet), why the bloody hell do you continue to support such a shower? Well, they're *my* shower, that's why! What other club can boast a player who is so keen to get a new contract that he gets himself sent home from an away match after being caught nipping into the Pub? Besides, every now and again, we'll achieve something so out of the ordinary that it makes you proud to support United (P*sh fans can allow themselves an envious glance as they compare their rather modest under-achievements against ours). Such was the case as we took on Preston at the Abbey. With most of us expecting a severe tonking as the visitors looked for the points that would guarantee them promotion, the Mighty U's turned in such a sublime display of graceful passing football (honest, I wasn't doing drugs) that we could afford to give them a goal start, miss a penalty, yet still give them a good old spanking in the second half to deservedly claim the points.

However, having survived this season, U's fans can start looking forward with just a little fear and trepidation to the forthcoming campaign. At the time of writing there is some debate as to whether our midfield dynamo Craig Middleton will ever play again following a second dislocation of his left shoulder - this after just two minutes on the field during our Preston victory. See - every cloud has a crock of shit at the end of it! Meanwhile, the full ramifications of the Bosman ruling have yet to fully impact on football in this country. However the prospect of a severe drop in transfer revenue must have serious and worrying financial implications on many clubs - not least those that have only staved off bankruptcy and manage to keep the wolves from the door, thanks to receiving over £3.5m in transfers fees in the past few years. In fact, our board is already pleading poverty (again). Despite a marked reluctance of shareholders and fans to purchase additional bundles of shares in £100 lots, they proposed issuing a preferential share scheme at only £750 a go. The sums didn't add up and unremarkably, there hasn't been a lot of interest.

Still, looking on the bright side, in Craddock, Beall, Benjamin, the two Josephs, Raynor, Edinboro' and Thompson we do have the nucleus of a good squad. But can we hang onto them? Only time will tell... By the way, what is the quickest route to the Goldstone?

Fanzine Facts

The Abbey Rabbit (named after the club's Abbey ground) is now in its eighth year. Editor Steve Jillings re-launched the 'zine last season to coincide with the club's new kit, and plans to repeat the exercise again next season... to coincide with the club's next new strip! "As well as continuing our slow and relentless purchase of shares in the club," explains Steve, "the *Rabbit*, in one of the most blatant piece of bandwagon jumping ever seen, has started sponsoring Cambridge United WFC, and being the glory-hunters that we are, latched onto their East Anglian Women's Plate exploits. Whilst revelling in their semi-final victory over Stevenage Borough, we unfortunately witnessed their tonking at the hands of the mighty... Milton Keynes in the final. Still, as goalkeeper and Rabbit contributor Michelle Kerr remarked, "At least we *got* to a final!" "

The Tea Party

THE ADAMS FAMILY

Wycombe Wanderers

I suppose there is a chance that you may have read the *Adams Family* article in last year's *Survival of the Fattest*. If you did, then there is an even slimmer chance that you may remember how our new manager was glowingly described. Perhaps the words 'one of the best talents in football today' and 'much loved, down to earth ex-Palace boss' may jog your memory. Now if this is you, and you're not one of the dwindling army of Wanderers fans who witnessed most of Mr Smith's dire drudgery masquerading as God's own game, then please listen up. The man is a charlatan. Quite how he managed to hoodwink literally all of us Wycombe fans (and we're not *all* inbred country loons, although a lot of us may look that way) into thinking him to be the second coming is beyond me.

Of course I may be as wrong now as my colleague was at this time last year, but I have to state, here and now, that I am starting to feel a well of respect filling up inside me for none other than Ron Noades - a sentiment that graphically describes the sourness I feel for Alan Smith. We at TAF attempted to start a rumour that Emlyn Hughes had been spotted sharing a cappuccino in the bus station cafe with chairman Ivor Beeks at the height of the rumour-mongering; the sad thing is he probably would have been a better bet.

You're probably thinking, and with some justification, that we Wycombe fans are a bunch of tragic whingers who should be grateful for attaining the heights we occupy now - and you'd be right. Most Wycombe supporters have never known such woe as only finishing in the top half of Division Two (just), although it's amazing how many of the new breed claim otherwise. If my memory remains sound (and it should, for I am far from pensionable age yet), Wycombe's last relegation from the Gola League to the Isthmian Premier was viewed by about 500 people. I am constantly amazed by the number of supporters who will broadcast to all and sundry about how today's team was worse now than then. Maybe there were 5,000 after all, and the official gate was merely a VAT scam.

No, believe me, most of us can handle mid-table; what we can't abide is the way Smith built up our expectations, aided and abetted by director and TV commentator Alan Parry, and set about rubbishing the work of former boss /deity Martin O'Neill. Thankfully, Parry has seen the error of his ways and has started to sling arrows in Smith's direction, but more of that later.

Anyway, in pre-season the Wanderers looked in distinctly tasty form, despite having attained the dubious services of ex-Arsenal striker Martin Hayes. The man was so arthritic he looked a second class citizen even against the 'might' of Poole Town in our first friendly. I always look forward to the first pre-season game, which is very sad in itself, for they are invariably completely shite. I mean, you have dreams of a lush pitch, cool drinks, pleasant balmy evening, and all the previously crap squad players having suddenly regained the skill that once tempted someone to sign them for money. The reality was more like this: Poole's 'specially imported from Chernobyl' turf, cool drinks taken from a scabby cold water tap in the toilets because the tea-bar only had Bovril, the balmy evening just encouraged the wasps to crawl up your shorts endangering the wedding tackle, and Jason Soloman was still a pile of racoon dung!

Still we were winning, and in a reasonably attractive manner. The main discussion centred around ex-lardman 'keeper Paul Hyde who had returned looking as slim as Wayne Sleep (although not as camp, we should add). The mystery of his missing weight was soon solved though when Terry Howard appeared with his arse protruding from his shorts in a most ungainly fashion.

But then the season started, and to be honest, it's quite difficult to recall, such was the boredom, as another witless long ball flew out of the ground. A loop of the Queen's Christmas Day speech would have proved far more entertaining. In short, the interest of Wycombe's season lay off the pitch, and so I trust you'll forgive me if I dwell there.

Despite having a much trumpeted 14 match unbeaten run, which was somewhat undermined by most of the games being entertainment-free draws, you could tell early on that we were in for a long hard slog. There was the stunning 4-0 victory at Bradford, where Miguel Desouza turned into Stan Collymore with a fantastic hat-trick, and the equally brilliant but far more satisfying 4-1 stuffing of Oxford United; the fact that it occurred at that public convenience of football grounds, the Manor ground, making it the finest day of the season.

But still the rumbles of discontent were heard around the ground; Simon Garner was constantly in and out of the side, replaced by either Steve McGavin or John Williams. McGavin's willing attitude kept him on the right side of the crowd despite his tragic scoring rate (he ended the season and possibly his Wycombe career with only one goal from open play in 37 matches), but Williams received a colossal amount of abuse. And quite rightly - our record signing appeared as an idle, skill-free loon; certainly not a patch on the sublime talents of Garner.

Then there was the shameful debacle at Walsall in the Auto Windscreens Shield, where the Wanderers capitulated to a 5-0 defeat. If this wasn't bad enough, Smith forced the players to sit out on the pitch like naughty schoolchildren. Quite frankly they didn't need further shaming, their first half performance had managed that with simplicity; all the manager's action did was to embarrass the travelling support, leaving us to endure the sarcastic taunts of the Walsall crowd.

Wycombe slumped badly after this. Already out of the Coca Cola (a 4-0 reverse at Maine Road obliterating the proud showing at Adams Park) and the Auto thingy, Wycombe turned in a disgraceful performance in the FA Cup replay against Gillingham. We should have won the first game at home where a great performance was capped by Gary Patterson's wonder goal, but failed to keep Gillingham out. Hopes were bright for the replay as we slogged our way round the orbital nightmare of the M25 at rush-hour, but Smith had once again dropped Garner for Williams, and a mix-up between Howard and Hyde sealed our fate. This was the first time in the season that the terrace mood turned ugly towards the management and some of the players, and it wouldn't be the last.

Shortly after this game Wycombe lost 4-2 to Carlisle and 'keeper Paul Hyde played his last game for the club. The true story behind this sorry tale is never likely to be revealed - both Hyde and Smith have different spins on the events that took place - and it's a question of who you believe. The bare bones of the saga were that Hyde constantly asked to have discussions about a new contract, Smith told him to wait, Hyde demanded a transfer and then asked to come off the list, and finally Alan Smith lost his rag and sacked him. Shortly after this Smith dispensed of the services of reserve 'keeper Chuck Moussadik, thus performing the managerial masterstroke of leaving us with one on-loan custodian. It's a fair point that Hyde probably made a mistake in demanding a transfer, but Smith could have earned a lot of respect by publicly making up with this popular player - however he chose the other route, perhaps to show us that he's not the lovely chap the media would have us believe. Unfortunately for Smith, Hyde was one of the crowd's favourites; he'd been with the club since non-league days, he'd played in the play-off final with a chronic dose of flu, and most importantly, he'd never played the fame game and acted the star like so many footballers. Paul Hyde was an important figure to the supporters of WWFC, a link for the fans in a time of rampant commercialism by the club itself, and above all a bloody decent bloke. Smith went too far with Hyde, and may find that this incident will colour whatever he does at Wycombe in the future.

And really, the season just died away from there. Brief excitement was tasted when the Wanderers managed to win three matches in a row, stuffing Bradford (again), Burnley, and grinding out a 1-0 victory over Walsall, with a late penalty from Player of the Season Dave Carroll. Due to the ludicrous play-off system there was a chance that the dismal season could be saved, but a 4-2 reverse by bottom club Hull, followed by a humiliating 3-0 defeat by Oxford, including a goal by that overrated pile of lanky donkey shite Paul Moody, put paid to that (fanciful) dream.

Off pitch, things were far more lively. Wycombe District Council finally did something to help the club by granting permission for a suave new stand which will replace the old terrace along the side of the ground. Despite an outrageous delay caused by a mad Tory councillor producing a Blue Peter-esque *papier mache* model of the new stand, which was so wildly out of scale it made the new stand look like a threat to the orbit of the space shuttle, the stand received permission. It has to be said how truly frightening it is that such major commercial decisions can be thwarted by people who are many, many sandwiches short of a picnic; one other councillor wanted the stand painted green so it could, "Blend in with the countryside"! If ever there is a lesson to people who consider local council elections irrelevant, then this surely is it.

Alan Smith, as all managers do, bought in a number of new players to improve the squad, including John Williams from Coventry for £150,000; David Farrell from Villa from anything between £120,000 and £60,000 (it is traditional at Wycombe for the club to brag about how much it is spending until it realises that the player is cack, in which case the fee is subtly reduced in club literature) and a host of others either on loan or on frees. Williams has turned out OK after an appalling start, and manfully resists sulking and flicking two fingered salutes at the fans who abused him so badly when scoring a goal. Farrell has proved to be a total frustration, sometimes he's literally unstoppable, at others you'll rarely see such a wet blanket of a man. Smith's finest loan signing was that of crazed custodian Euro-loon Sieb Dykstra, who has kept us amused with his wild dribbling antics; his worst loan signing is the offensive, shaven-headed cart horse known as Mark Foran. This clodhopping ape had previously played for assistant manager/football nobody David Kemp at Slough Town, and was preferred to smooth centre back Terry Howard at the start of the season. This indeed was the first sign that Smith and Kemp are often very bizarre when it comes to team selection. However nothing can beat the sheer madness of signing Brian McGorry. Managers often say that they'll only sign a player who will improve the squad. Well, McGorry wouldn't improve a cub football team. Thankfully the midfielder has been restricted to just four appearances in the first team and has now been placed on the transfer list. If your club purchases this legend, be afraid - be very afraid.

As well as Hyde, Smith had another, more subtle run-in with Terry Howard. Not that Smith ever publicised this one, but the likeable Howard certainly wasn't shy on filling in the public on the fact that Smith hated him. Indeed, Howard even came down to our fanzine stall and discussed the gaffer in far from glowing tones at the last home game. Despite coming second in the Player of the Season awards, Howard was given a free. Nice one Mr Smith!

Smith and the club received more flak by proposing to change the club's quartered shirts into a different design. The fans were given a 'choice', one being a quartered shirt with six bottles of Tipp-Ex dropped in the middle of it, the other being a mixture of plain quarters and striped ones. The latter won the day as the best of a bad bunch; I voted for it to stop the Tipp-Ex nightmare, but it doesn't mean I'll be buying it. Smith's view is that the current kit is of low quality, and he certainly has a point. What he fails to realise is that you *can* have a good quality quartered kit - could anyone imagine QPR not playing in hoops for example?

But despite all this, the most bizarre off-field development has been the 'no names mentioned but you catch my drift' row between director Parry and Smith. Parry started the row by comparing the work of Peter Reid at Sunderland to Smith's at Wycombe, causing the manager to get visibly upset at an end of season supporters forum. However Smith has been asking for it with his constant running down of O'Neill's management style - he even claimed that the existing squad was fit for relegation when he arrived, so how it finished sixth last season is beyond me. I have to give Parry credit; despite his lack of diplomacy, he is a genuine Wanderers fan and it must be difficult to maintain a balance between director and supporter. But Parry was instrumental in getting O'Neill to Wycombe and clearly got pissed off with Smith's harping, as most of the rest of us have.

In short, if Alan Smith wants to be respected at this club he must cease rubbishing O'Neill, stop kicking out players with character (such as Garner - a major mistake) and replacing them with gorillas/automatons, and take responsibility for his team. At the moment when they win they do it his way, when they lose they've not been listening. Alternatively, he could win lots of games and get us promoted - after all there's nothing as hypocritical as a football fan.

Fanzine Facts

Established in 1992, *The Adams Family* is Wycombe's sole fanzine, and according to Andy Dickinson (writer of the above) "it is still managing to survive despite the number of punters staying away from Adams Park." The editorial team is now reduced to five; in addition to the aforementioned Andy, there is Jon Dickinson, Doug Peters, Dave Chapman and Neil Peters. Life is good for the TAF team, though. According to Andy, "Despite former contributor and life president Augustus Floyd fleeing to Australia to escape the long ball nonsense, respect for TAF has grown so high that the contributors are thinking of employing a secretary to handle their constant stream of TV, radio, press and fete openings."

ALL DAY AND ALL OF THE NIGHT

Liverpool

To say that pre-season went powerful well would be like saying that Jason Lee should win the Golden Boot Award. A 5-0 trouncing by Domestos of Amsterdam (Ajax, thickos!) and a 3-0 hammering by a Norway select side gave us great hope for the new season fast approaching. As we at **ADAAOTN** are based in Northern Ireland, it was great to see the lads in Belfast, but despite a 1-0 victory, we played shite in front of a sell-out crowd. Our opening game against the Owls of Sheffield was a wee bit drab to say the least, until Stan The (Expensive) Man decided to show us wot he wuz made of with an unbelievable shot from 25 yards. His season was up and running until he bumped into donkey Pemberton from Leeds two days later, when the Yorkshire giants

(in Emmerdale anyway) kicked us all over the bloody field. OK, so Ye-boy-a scored a fluke, a good fluke mind you, but we still outplayed them for f**k all. This was to be the story throughout. A trip to London to play Spurs saw 'Digger' score twice (believe it or not) and he wasn't even wearing his f**king white boots.

November ruined us. Out of Europe by Mickey Mouse Brondby on the sad night of 31st October, the month continued to be forgettable, especially the unforgivable performance against our no-hopé neighbours at Anfield (yes, we *do* mean Everton, not Tranmere). A couple of defeats against the Geordies also didn't help our cause in the League and League Cup. In fact it was very depressing as the holders of the Coca Cola were out too (i.e. us - do we have to spell it out?!).

December, the season of goodwill to all men (especially Mancs in grey shirts), and we have to give this match a mention, cos as usual, we fucking played them off the park. This time, though, we got three points as two goals by our Robbie gave us sweet victory, not like that certain date in October when he did the same trick. (P.S. - Who the f**k are Man U). Our Robbie loves Arsenal, cause they are so easy to score against, and he duly bagged another hat-trick (again).

The New Year started well with deserved winners of both Player and Manager of the Month (our Robbie and our Evo). Day one of 1996 saw the brilliant comeback against Forest (minus our Stan); 2-0 down inside 17 minutes, we came back to win 4-2. Well done lads! Also, revenge over the boys from dingle country was sweet with a 5-0 hammering of Leeds. But the month will be best remembered in football record books when Rushie broke Dennis Law's FA Cup goals record.

February was another unhappy month, when the legendary Bob Paisley sadly passed away. Bob was our most successful boss, and will NEVER BE FORGOTTEN. The season's run-in was coming close and it wasn't looking good for the title, but the FA Cup was looking ripe and ready for the plucking. Another victory over our sheep-shagging friends from Yorkshire in the quarter finals set up a semi tie with the Villa, who within the space of seven minutes we'd demolished in the League game at Anfield. In the end, Villa were no match for the 'Pool, although they huffed and puffed, but our Robbie's two goals and one of our better players of the season Jason McAteer gave us a deserved 3-0 victory. Wembley here we come! Again!

Before we give a <u>very</u> brief comment on the final, we should mention the game of the season, if not decade, which once again involved the reds. Newcastle were the visitors; victory was needed by both sides and all hell broke loose when the ref blew the whistle to start the game. Magnificent! Roller-coaster! Game of the century! The plaudits couldn't deliver the clichés fast enough. In the end the scoreline of four goals to three went in our favour, but the scoreline should have been a lot higher. And now to round it all off, we promised you a brief word on the Cup Final, so here it is. SHITE.

So, third in the Championship, runners-up in the Cup, no victories over our blue nose neighbours, and our long time servant Ian Rush OBE joins the Dingle clan in Yorkshire. Good luck anyway, Rushie, and do us a favour; pass on a message to Pemberton - Don't dare do it again, or Stan will kick ass!!

Fanzine Facts

Cookstown, Northern Ireland based *All Day And All Of The Night* was launched in the summer of '94 and is now produced by Barry 'Bassa' Hamilton, Ali, Barney, John Boy, IBA (?), and as Bassa puts it, "all loyal red fans who do the zine for a bit of crack." He adds that "it sells well in the island and in Merseyside and also has readers in Australia, New Zealand, Italy, Hungary, France, Greece and Mauritius to name but a few. Crazy ain't it, but good fun!!"

ALL QUIET ON THE WESTERN AVENUE

Queens Park Rangers

What is it they like to call it? The Beautiful Game? The Glory Game? Ha! The '95-96 season caused me spiritual, psychological, physical and financial pain, the like of which hasn't been experienced in Shepherds Bush since 1979... the year that Queens Park Rangers last dropped out of the big time, and the year I was born to this cruel and merciless world. At least I'll be able to legally drown my sorrows next season; small compensation when I'm stood in a Merseyside pub preparing to see Rangers take on the mighty Tranmere Rovers, whilst Wimbledon fans nearby talk loudly of their forthcoming match at Anfield... Of course there are some amongst us who have seen it as a good thing for the club - a chance to rebuild, and they may have a point. But

ALL QUIET ON THE WESTERN AVENUE.
ISSUE FOUR. £1.00. AUGUST/SEPTEMBER 1995

a Championship-winning season next time around won't make up for the ridicule, the depression, and the nightmares of relegation. We saw no beauty, and felt no glory.

Actually, since QPR got sucked Endsleigh-side in May, I've often thought I'd like to have a few words with the chaps that first conceived those two over-quoted and highly inaccurate romanticised spurts of footballing philosophy. Five minutes would be all I'd need to put them right. Hunter Davies (of 'Glory Game' fame) would be no trouble at all. I'd simply explain that he shouldn't generalise. Sitting in the Tottenham changing room writing a few patronising lines and knocking off Pat Jennings' missus when the poor bloke's in North London General with a dislocated fringe does not compare to having rival fans flicking wanker signs at you, singing "you're going down with the Bolton." I'm sure he'd soon see the light, and on the next print run of his book he'd probably insist on adding a footnote along those lines. No problems with him then, though rumours that circled amongst the players' wives might suggest otherwise. (Something about leather dungarees and a Fulham rosette; still, it's not our place to comment).

Pele would be a little more tricky. I don't mean because of his little step-over-shimmie-shuffle-bamboozles (which he copied off Andy Impey anyway), but because how can you begin to explain why it's most certainly not a beautiful game to the man that has nutmegged someone in a World Cup Final? If you felt good sticking one between the legs of some herbert in a school playground game, then imagine what it would be like doing it to an Eytie in front of two billion people. I'm afraid that I'd have to lay down the facts, painful though it would be for both of us, until he understood that essentially, fundamentally, and beyond all trace of doubtful shadows, he was spouting great lumps of steaming yak cack when he made his proclamation.

Obviously I'd have to show initial caution. I wouldn't want to just spring it on him that football isn't all about being the best player ever, and having blokes who don't even know who Steve Yates is saying things like; "Ya, granted Rupert, but there'll never be another *Edson Arantes do Nascimento.*" I'll tell you something though, if that git with the sad hair and seventies retro Brazil top comes near me with his rolled up copy of the Guardian and tickets for the Euro-semi's ("Daddy knew a man"), I'll not only tell him about Steve 'Solid' Yates' defensive ability, but also where to stick his theory about football being art. Incidentally, if you are this person, then answer me this: If footy is an art then why are players like Andy Townsend allowed to be displayed publicly, bearing in mind that Damien Hurst had a dead cow banned from exhibition? Now I'm no cultural authority, but surely a sliced up moo-moo is not half as bad as letting young children sit and watch that Aston Villa monstrosity. Of course we all know that mother nature can be cruel, but stone me, the man's own family make him wear a bag on his head at the dinner table. I mean, is that a nose or what? An upturned boat-rudder?

Anyway all this ties in nicely with my chat with Pelè about his quote (ooh! Link!). Firstly I'll tell him about the false optimism instilled in QPR fans by Mr Wilkins. In an *All Quiet On The Western Avenue* interview last summer, Raymondo, as the wags at Channel Four Footbore Italia humorously called him, talked confidently about the forthcoming season. He promised that the new signings would make up for Ferdinand's departure, that we could compete with the cream, and finally that he'd stop making his eyebrows do that little dance when he talked. He promised us the earth, and speaking metaphorically, all we actually got was a tiny spot of land in the Cumbrian Marshes, where it always rains, and the television is stuck on The Shopping Channel. Just as a matter of interest, that little eyebrow jig tends to be particularly lively when he's asked questions about his share of the blame for relegation... as I say, just as a matter of interest...

Anyway, I'd let Pele know that the new signings were mostly either stuck in the reserves all year, sold on, or as in the case of record-fee Australian Ned Zelic, mysteriously wiped off the face of the planet. Actually Ned Zelic is a bit of a mystery in himself, as a mate of mine shrewdly pointed out.... It was August, and we were travelling back from a narrow opening day defeat at the hands of champions Cashburn Rovers. Confidence was high, and on the coach, and above the chants of "we're gonna win the League", I could just make out what Billy-two-seats (regular contributor to the fanzine) was mumbling about. "Pete, the general consensus is that losing Les was bad, but with Gallen, Sinclair, the other kids, and all the new faces, we're in for a good year...right?" I nodded, but his tone suggested a 'but' was lurking, so I didn't interrupt as he downed the remainder of his can of lager, emptied the crumbs from his crisp packet down his throat, burped viciously, and continued...

"But I've been thinking about this Zelic geezer." He belched again; I detected pickled onion. "How comes that we've ended up with an Antipodean midfielder in Shepherds Bush, with a Slavic name, who's been playing in the German Bundesleague? Either Butch has been using his connections or he lost a bet. It don't bode well Pete. I smell something I don't like." And so saying he belched once more. Definitely pickled onion.

By Easter, the Australian had gone, but where? There are several rumours as to what happened to Ned, who the Loft-boys christened 'Ned'. Some say he wound up Wilkins with his training ground tomfoolery, like missing out a cone deliberately on the dribbling-round-the-cone sessions, and constant jokes about 'bald crabs'. They say this caused bad feeling and led to Ned suffering a painful death involving a brick wall and a Rover with a Tango car sticker in the back window ("Let's look at this again Tony. See how transfer-market-bungler Wilkins takes out his frustration on Zelic. Smashing Stuff! You know when you've been force-fed-a-load-of-sound-bitey-cack-about-lack-of-consisitency-oed!"). Others insist that Ned (Ned) has gone to Bolivia to join a primitive tribe of naked jungle warriors. Either way I'm sure Pele would realise that Ray's handling of the millions of pounds made available was far from 'beautiful', and I haven't even mentioned Mark Hateley yet... or home defeat to Wimbledon... or going out to Chelshit in the cup...

To perfectly honest, I think Pele would have got the picture by now. However, to be conclusive, I'd insist on explaining to him the effect that this game of ours has had on a particular member of the fanzine staff; namely assistant editor Adam 'The Kebab' Wheeler, so-called because of his compulsory pre-match visit to Big Bob's Greek delicacy house on the Uxbridge Road. The Kebab was always renowned for his passiveness. At the Horn and Trumpet, Shepherds Bush, it was very rare for even the most cutting jibe to provoke a reaction. We tried jokes about his bird and his hair, and once even pretended to burn his ticket, but still he'd retain his cool and laugh along. So you can imagine our surprise, when on a sunny afternoon in early April, he became a raving lunatic and subsequently behaved in a manner which has eternally tarnished the reputation of AQOTWA as a moral guide-light in the rough fanzine sea.

There's no denying that Coventry City away was the most important game in the last two months of the season, and no-one's saying that the four thousand Rangers fans present weren't out of their minds with nerves and fear of the unmentionable. Personally I was about as tense as Salmon Rushdie passing down the Cricklewood Broadway, but even so, the Kebab's actions can't be justified. See what you think: Coventry City had just beaten us 1-0, thanks partly to their thuggish tactics, but mostly to the Welsh goon in green with the whistle who was wearing sky-blue pants. I know this because the bloke behind me kept shouting it. He also mentioned something about Rangers having to get their fucking arses in gear if they didn't want to be playing Grimsby, and this tends to confirm the notion that everyone that day was in a pant-stainingly edgy frame of mind. I mean, it's not often that the greatest team in the world is pushed ever-closer to relegation by a Midland cowboy outfit managed by a man who wears sunglasses in bed, is it? Either way, Rangers had the much-needed three points snatched away, and the blue and white sea of depression filtering out of the away enclosure wouldn't have been cheered up very much by a hefty number of Coventry pitch invaders running in front of our stand shouting nasty things about relegation and the like.

The Kebab certainly wasn't amused, and for the first time in living memory seemed to be getting genuinely angry. He began by leaping up onto a railing, and in tune with a lot of other frustrated souls, exchanged words and gesticulations with the jubilant City supporters. Now I'm prone to a bit of the verbals myself, and once threw a half-full Kia-ora carton at a particularly deserving Everton fan, but the Kebab was getting carried away. Having singled out an over-enthusiastic bloke down in front of us, he mumbled something about "letting the barstool taste some Hammersmith meat" and made a dash for the pitch.

Personally, and I'd make this clear to Pele, I think football is solely to blame for his change of character, and I'm sure it had nothing to do with that extremely dangerous-looking Chicken and Mushroom pie he'd eaten at half-time. He swore he smelt battery juice, and that something moved amongst the brown swamp of gristly gunk-slime they had the nerve to charge him £2 for, but let's not split hairs over the toxic content of his lunch. No, let's give that strange looking kid in the nice overalls (City Caterers - 'The taste of quality') the benefit of the doubt, and say for the sake of argument that it was what happened on the pitch that day, and indeed since August 19th, that made him do what he did. Bearing this in mind, I'd say there are few less glorious, less beautiful and less dignified sights than an assistant editor of a respectable fanzine leaping over rows of plastic seats, arms raised and shouting like his trousers are on fire.

Incredibly, I had a brief urge to join him. For the fleetest of fleeting moments I wanted to take nine months of heartache, of soul-destroying football torture, all out on those muppets down there. In their poxy elephant-badged shirts, and with that stupid song that Jimmy Hill wrote. I wanted to get that corner flag, find Gordon Strachan and... but then I snapped out of it as my attention fell upon the Kebab once more. Not really expecting him to actually do anything, I was dumbstruck by the sight of him hurdling the advertising hoarding and along with a few dozen other Rangers fans, charging towards the Coventry lot, most of whom had cleared off having seen a counter-attack ensuing.

The Kebab managed to escape the clutches of a rugby-tackling steward, and headed towards the character he'd spotted who'd been particularly flamboyant with v-signs and threatening postures. It's not a bad as it seems though; you see, the clash actually consisted of the other bloke pushing him in the chest before our hero did a 'foot-sweep', landing the startled Coventry guy flat on his back. Next, and as Stan Bowles is my witness I swear it's true, he ran into the goal-mouth and started doing some strange dance that Zelic's Jungle warriors would have been proud of, before flashing his arse at the unsuspecting West stand. I couldn't believe what I was seeing! Here he was, Mr Passive, running amok like a Brighton fan, and bearing his buttocks to the family enclosure. I wouldn't even like to guess at how many innocent young children were reduced to tears by the sight of the Kebab's khyber - although I'm sure I heard one boy ask his dad if he could go and get its autograph... cue an all too predictable Steve Ogrisovic joke...

Returning to the away enclosure, he managed to not only attempt a cartwheel, but picked up some change that someone had dropped. Then apparently a steward actually thanked him for returning as he stepped back over the advertising hoarding, whereas the bloke he felled had been carted off by the Midlands' constabulary. By the time he'd got back, (where I'd been stood motionless for three minutes), he was grinning like a good 'un and clutching £2.10. "Paid for the pie!" he said. What was I to say apart from; "Southampton beat Man Utd, 3-0. We're doomed." That wiped the smile off his face. The dirty dog.

So, Mr Pele, this is your beautiful game. I don't know if the Kebab will ever be the same. I certainly won't. It's not just the thought of West Brom on a wet

Tuesday night, but seeing your assistant editor's rear end on Match Of The Day is a frightening experience. I think that's enough grumbling for now though... it might just be time to pull up the hooped socks, polish the boots, pledge fond farewells to pastures Premier, and take the Endsleigh League head-on. Let's go to work.

Fanzine Facts

All Quiet On The Western Avenue, aka *the voice of Impey Fundamentalism*, was launched in the summer of 1994 by editor Peter Doherty and his assistant Adam 'Kebab' Wheeler. According to Pete, production has been a little inconsistent, mainly due to laziness, although he concedes that A-levels got in the way a little bit as well. It's been said that AQOTWA plays second fiddle to the lead violins of 'In The Loft' and 'A Kick Up The R's'. Peter counters: "AQOTWA staff opinion polls show once again that this clearly isn't true. An incredible 95% of the editorial staff and their mates have voted the mag top of the Bush-zine populars, and that's fact. With sturdy literary custodians of the contributors list such as Billy two-seats and Fanny Perrier (the view from Brittany), there's no competition... sales figures are nothing to go by really... are they?.. Oh."

BAMBER'S RIGHT FOOT

Torquay United

I was there, I saw it all. I saw every heart-breaking, tear-jerking and ball-breaking moment of it, except that bit when I slipped out for a piss, a pie and a pray. It was like the blind leading the blind, and absolutely everything that *could* have gone wrong *did*. I wouldn't dare say that we were unlucky, because as a club we deserved everything we got. The whole thing was rotten from the bottom up and the top down.

We sold players and didn't replace them, we brought in too many youngsters, we started the season without a squad and we paid the ultimate price.

Really, it was a tale of two managers, but at the end of the day it was the same old story throughout. Don O'Riordan, embarking upon his third season as Torquay manager, didn't like to bring in experienced pros who might threaten his domain, so instead he chose to fill the team with youngsters and trainees. It has been said that money was available to him, but if it was, he never used it. As for Eddie May, well, he came into the picture to haul us off the bottom with his experience of lower league management, but achieved very little. The money did flow, but it was all a bit late, and on the bottom of the basement League we remained.

Mind you, to be fair to both of them there is a certain player at Torquay who for obvious reasons cannot be named, but who has single-handedly destroyed any team spirit that was ever instilled. He's the chairman's mole, and is no more a professional footballer than I am. They say that at every club there is a player who reports back to higher echelons on what is said and what is done, and by whom, but it saddens me that such a selfish and arrogant man can be responsible for doing so much damage to a team, with only his best interests at heart. This particular person was the reason why the last manager felt that he had to leave the club. Ask almost any Torquay United supporter to draw up their retained list, and this man would be top of it. Yet, having been 'advised' to retain him against his will, Eddie May had no other option than to pack his bags. How can he be blamed for not wishing to be part of a set-up which has no ambition, and is solely run to feed the egos of a chosen few?

Everyone knows just how bad '95-96 was for the likes of Torquay United, and consequently I don't intend to bore you with the details. What I will do however, to illustrate just how inept the club has become, is give you a few examples and incidents that are so laughable you'll wonder how we've survived as long as we have.

Torquay have always been famous for picking up particularly dire accolades. If you want proof, all you have to do is pick up a copy of The Guinness Book of Records, and see for yourself.

Fastest own goal : 6 seconds - Scored by Torquay player Pat Kruse against Cambridge United in January '77.

Fastest League goal : 6 seconds - Scored by Notts County in '62. Against Torquay.

Anyway, enough of that, I was going to tell you all about our more recent debacles.

In the pre-season, QPR showed an interest in our Barbadian international wing wizard, Gregory Goodridge. Bear in mind that QPR had just sold Les Ferdinand to Newcastle for more than £6m. Well, the two clubs came to an agreement whereby QPR would cough up just £50,000 up front, and then pay an additional £100,000 a year later, and the final £200,000 after the second year. These payments were of course subject to the condition that Gregory must have his work permit renewed. Unfortunately, QPR have only played Gregory a handful of times, and therefore he's been denied a work permit! QPR were never going to lose out on that deal, were they? I mean, £350,000 was a steal to start with, but the staggered payments?! It's just incredible, but only Torquay could embark on such a stupid arrangement.

Also last season, we had a certain Matt Carmichael on loan from Doncaster Rovers. He came down and trained with the squad for a week, and we were still toying with the idea of acquiring him, when by coincidence at the end of the week the team travelled to Doncaster for the League game against the Yorkshire side. Upon arrival it seemed that Doncaster were having a bit of a squad crisis, and were unable to field a full-strength team. Half time came and the scores were level, but who was that trotting out for Doncaster to start the second-half? Why, none other than Matt Carmichael. History will bear witness to the fact that Mr Carmichael scored the goal that defeated Torquay that day, and how painful it all was.

By the way, our chairman confides in - and confers with - a ventriloquist's dummy. No, really! He even had the bad taste to go on record in a national football magazine, complete with his hand up said dummy's arse, publicly demeaning the fans of his club!

What else? Having heard certain rumours about the forthcoming game against the rather over-rated Plimuff side, the Torquay fans asked Mr Bateson at a fan's forum whether there was any truth in the story that the Popular Side (Plainmoor's own Kop!) would be handed over to the opposition supporters. He assured us there and then, in front of a hundred or so fans, the papers and the television cameras that there was absolutely no chance of that happening. He gave us his word. Around a week later that I found out that Plymouth supporters were to be allocated the Popular Side, and home supporters would have to occupy the other areas of the ground. Consequently many people boycotted the game, including this correspondent, who went to watch Stevenage hammer Woking 4-0 instead. Well, I was doing my bit for Torquay United in a roundabout sort of way!

And now, the chairman is really flying, and having forced out the manager, he has decided to go 'continental' and have a more hands-on approach with the footballing side of the club. He has appointed a director of coaching and intends to have a much greater say in what happens on the field of play. Where will it all end? Who said 'the Conference?' The man is a good example of megalomania gone to excess (if such a thing is possible). They say that all dictators eventually destroy themselves, and our chairman is fast becoming hugely unpopular, so who knows?

And just to top it all off, Stevenage decided that because they chose to ignore the rules quite clearly laid down regarding entry into the League, they would take the Football League and Torquay United to court! Now whilst I agree that the rule is harsh, it is a rule nevertheless, and Stevenage should have adhered to its criteria. I mean, what did they hope to achieve by taking us to court? The only thing that we were guilty of last season was being crap, and believe me, that's nothing new. If they were hoping to base their case on that, then we'd be facing life without parole. (They've now decided to drop their case against us, and just take on the League.)

What I want to know is what would happen to the likes of Northampton and Exeter in the event of Stevenage winning their case? Would Kidderminster and Macclesfield be allowed to join the League? By the time this book hits the shelves, we should all know the outcome, and who knows, Torquay might just be a Conference outfit.

Fanzine Facts

Bamber's Right Foot was born (and named) after a famous incident when Blackpool's big centre-forward missed his spot-kick in the penalty shoot-out of the '90-91 play-off final, giving Torquay the game. Although frequently taking the piss out of the chairman and players, editor Hayden Jones reckons that *BRF* enjoys a good relationship with the club, and is famous for its 'player on player' poll which asks the pros at the club to award marks and comment on their team-mates' performance during the season. This season, Hayden says that *BRF* is still going strong, "despite the apathy-inducing exploits of Torquay United." Hayden would like to take this opportunity to publicly like to thank all those people who make the fanzine possible. Finally, the fanzine has an established footy team, who are willing to take on just about anyone. Want a game? Get in touch!

BERT TRAUTMANN'S HELMET

Manchester City

Third Time Unlucky

It was the best of times and the worst of times for Manchester City last season. Put succinctly, the former were all too slow in coming and didn't hang around for too long, while the latter were all too frequent and lingered round Moss Side like a bad smell. Of course, the devil fools with the best laid plans so imagine what havoc he wreaked when no plans had been made at all *à la* Manchester City in '95-96...

The seeds of City's ignominious journey towards First Division anonymity were sown last summer with the laughable appointment of one Alan Ball as the club's new manager. But once the laughter had died down and the new manager's lousy managerial record had been inspected, and hastily filed under 'waste paper basket', it was time to start worrying... and worry we did.

Manchester City - in their 101st year - kicked off with their worst start in history: a miserable one (*one*) point from 27 (twenty seven). Of course there were abysmal refereeing decisions aplenty as, first, Michael Brown was sent off at Loftus Road only minutes into his debut, Arsenal were awarded a dodgy last minute free-kick which resulted in the games' only goal, followed by Richard Edghill's dismissal at St James' Park (not to mention a penalty for the home team), and then a Middlesbrough win at Maine Road when the only goal was several miles offside!

The season's first win didn't arrive until October 4th, and even then it was only against Wycombe Wanderers in the Coca Cola Cup. Liverpool managed to put ten past the hapless Blues in two games in the space of four days (League and Coca Cola Cup) and yet City's legendary fans still turned up in numbers. While there have never been any question marks over the loyalty of our supporters (unlike the glory-hunting hordes in Blackburn, Newcastle etc.) there was at least something, or someone, to warm the cockles as the nights started to draw in: Georgio Kinkladze. Virtually ignored by the Man U loving media, Gio's time was yet to come.

November brightened with the first League win against one season wonders Bolton as Manchester city centre rocked, followed by a draw at Hillsborough and two more home wins against Wimbledon and Villa. Even more astonishingly, Ball was named Manager of the Month which meant he now had as many of these awards as he had World Cup Winners' medals.

December began with an unlikely 1-0 win against West Ham at Maine Road on New Year's Day, while a goalless draw at a decrepit Filbert Street in the Cup set up a Maine Road replay. Kinkladze shone as brightly as the Leicester defender's red faces as he waltzed around them to set up four and score one in the 5-0 win... and to think that some of these cart-horses will be playing in the Premier League come August!! Gio's time was yet to come. A defeat at Spurs and draws against Coventry and Southampton sandwiched this rare victory.

After Kinkladze had been clogged up and down Maine Road by QPR in a deserved 2-0 home victory, City were robbed of Cup victory at Highfield Road by a referee who wanted to let the game flow... all night if necessary. In the very next game the familiar dodgy penalty gave Everton the lead at Goodison, before new signing Michael Frontzeck was sent off for something and nothing as ten man City went 2-0 down. Then came Coventry in the Cup replay at Maine Road when, with City fans locked out of Maine Road, Coventry's few fans congregated in the corner of the North Stand - a stand that normally holds 6-7,000! Still, at least we won to set up a meeting with the detested 'Man U' (that's what their home counties' based support call them). City took the lead of course, through Uwe Rösler, and the rest is history. At least the watching nation could see that we were truly robbed by a crap penalty decision from referee and United season ticket holder Alan Wilkie. Needless to say, 12 man United went on to cheat their way to another hollow victory. As always, the luck they enjoyed over the season was completely at odds with ours. This mismatch was followed by an equally controversial 3-3 meeting with Newcastle. Kinkladze's time finally came and the media found they could ignore him no longer, although the headlines and the FA disciplinary hearing were shared with the Messrs Asprilla and Curle - the former for elbowing and butting and the latter for *being* elbowed and butted, oddly enough!

March saw three defeats in the Capital (at Arsenal, Chelsea and West Ham respectively), and draws against Lancashire upstarts Blackburn and Bolton. But March belonged to Gio Kinkladze and *that* winning goal against Southampton. It was *the* goal of the season in all but name although (and you'll have to take my word for this) the BBC's cameras didn't do it justice.

TS Eliot wasn't far wrong when he said April is the cruellest month, and yet perversely, City's crowds increased as the drop loomed larger still. Barely one hundred more people were at the season's only true Manchester derby than were at the previous home game against Southampton, as the Mancunian club bowed to home fans' demands to limit the number of tickets made available to our visitors from Cornwall, Ireland, London and Malta. Although the score wasn't relevant, the outcome was far from satisfactory, and on the Bank Holiday Monday we set sail for London (again): Wimbledon and defeat (again), despite the backing of some 5,000 travelling fans. One-nil wins against Sheffield Wednesday and Villa kept us in with a chance but ultimately even a spirited fight-back from two goals down in the final game against Liverpool on May 5th couldn't save us.

This was my third relegation and I know I deserve better, as do the rest of City's 30,000 fans. There are some clubs in the Premier League who can only *dream* of the kind of support Manchester City get at home, while most can't touch us away. Sadly for us, a club's standing is decided on merit alone and so we'll have to endure a season or two in the First Division. But don't worry for us. Instead, start worrying about us, because we'll be back and we might be replacing YOU!

Fanzine Facts

Bert Trautmann's Helmet (formerly *Electric Blue*) is edited by Noel Bayley, who explains the change of name: "We had a scare last November when a firm of London solicitors acting for Northern & Shell (rather large publishers of another magazine called Electric Blue) despatched a three page letter to *EB* accusing me of infringing their copyright and accusing the fanzine of having caused 'damage to their good name and reputation' amongst other things. And this despite the fact that *Electric Blue* (the fanzine that is) had been going for seven years; longer than Electric Blue (the *other* magazine... nudge, nudge, wink, wink)."

So the new name was born in return for N&S dropping their damages claim. It came about because, according to Stan Boardman (unfunny scouser and alleged comic), "Bert Trautmann's helmet's the only thing in City's trophy cabinet." Noel adds "now it's business as usual for what is still the only City 'zine to come from Manchester; which means articles from a regular crew who support the Blues, and no campaigns, crusades, T-shirts or TV appearances - unlike a few other fanzines I could mention."

No. 13: Old Trafford

Age: 86.
Appearance: Steel and concrete eyesore which squats in some sort of a ditch, hemmed in on either side by a grimy canal and some old railway sidings.

THE BETTER HALF

Notts County

For Notts County Football Club, '95-96 was a case of so near yet so far, and one poor performance at Wembley ruined what had been achieved in the previous 48 League and play-off matches.

Steve Thompson and Colin Murphy received a lot of criticism (and in my opinion mostly unjustified) for the way they got the Pies playing. The truth is though that they assembled the strongest-looking defence in Notts' recent history, and we had a team that was more than capable of battling for the points away from home.

The greatest memory for me and the other fans who attended was Gary Martindale's last minute header in the play-off semi-final against Crewe, which rescued a 2-2 draw. That was the game when Notts gave

both their best and worst 45 minutes of football. In the second leg, it was Martindale again who did the necessary, superbly volleying us straight to Wembley.

Now there are a lot of people who say the play-offs are unfair because the team who finishes sixth can gain promotion over the team who finished third. Oh, stop whinging. The play-offs make the season much more interesting. Bradford City, who finished sixth, beat Notts County, who finished two places above them, because on the day Bradford were the better team, and deserve credit for their performance. For us there is always next year, and we have a squad capable of giving automatic promotion a real go, the only threats coming from Blackpool and the relegated Millwall.

Thompson and Murphy were not afraid to off-load some of our favourites, but every move they made in the transfer market was justified, especially the decision to sell Paul Devlin and Andy Legg to Birmingham and bring in Gary Jones and hero-in-waiting Gary Martindale to replace them. Also recruited for the last three months was Steve Finnan from Birmingham who gave the fans a lot of excitement and created nearly every goal we scored after his arrival. Whether or not we can talk the Brummies into selling him remains to be seen, but he could be a potential title-winner next year.

There were many highlights last season, and the way Devon White started off gave Notts the perfect platform for continued success. White of course was later sold to Watford, but will be remembered fondly by the fans of his home town club. The best game was surely the 4-3 win at Turf Moor against Burnley, where Paul

Devlin bagged two goals. We also won't forget Notts hitting four past Brentford, Bristol Rovers, Swansea and Chesterfield!

In the Cups, Notts didn't fare too well. We went out in the second round of the Coca Cola to Leeds very narrowly, drawing 0-0 at Elland Road. However Gary Speed's last minute goal at Meadow Lane gave Leeds a 3-2 victory in a game where Devon White grabbed two goals to upstage Tony Yeboah, who was superbly marshalled by Gary Strodder and Shaun Murphy. In the FA Cup we started in round one with a televised battle on Sky against the mighty York City! We scrapped to a 1-0 win at Bootham Crescent, and beat Telford United 2-0 away in the second round. In round three we came up against a Middlesbrough team sporting such international stars as Nick Barmby and the pint-sized Juninho. We gave the Teesiders a real scare, but they left with a fortunate 2-1 victory.

The season's two outstanding performers were Darren Ward and Shaun Murphy. Ward was only signed the previous summer from Mansfield, but pulled off some magnificent saves and won Notts many points, especially at Meadow Lane. Ward also forced himself into the full Welsh squad, and definitely has a bright future ahead of him. Howard Wilkinson is said to be lining up a bid to take him to Leeds as John Lukic's replacement, but at the time of writing nothing has materialised. Shaun Murphy is our laid-back centre-half whose performances often go unnoticed due to his consistency. The big Aussie is surely destined to play at a higher level and he is already worth £1m. Such was Murphy's quality this season that he won the supporters' Player of the Year award for the second time running.

I am looking forward to the new campaign with much optimism, as long as we keep together the squad we have spent a season building. With players like Ward, Murphy, Martindale, Battersby, Wilder and Agana, we are more than a match for anyone in this Division. One year on and we have grown a little wiser, and know more about the other teams. Of course the flip-side of the coin is that the other teams also know more about us, so perhaps we've lost the element of surprise we had this time last year. However, I still believe Notts will go up; how, I don't know, but others still fear coming to Meadow Lane to face the oldest League team in the world. Notts County have always been under-achievers, but for once in our lives we must strive to set the standards, and hope that the rest will not be up to the challenge. Perhaps I'm just full of mid-summer optimism, but come August I'll be up for it. I just hope that there are 11 players on the pitch who feel the same.

Fanzine Facts

Call it bad luck but Notts County's relegation to Division Two at the end of '93-94 coincided with the launch of *The Better Half*. Last season was the fanzine's second, and editor Chris Gosling got a lot of kicks reporting the goings on at Meadow Lane the way the fans like it - truthfully.

BEYOND THE BOUNDARY

Oldham Athletic

Reviewing Oldham Athletic's season without mentioning the words 'absolutely' and 'crap' in every other sentence is a challenge worthy of inclusion in the Krypton Factor. Traditionally, come the first weeks of August, supporters around the country rub their hands in anticipation of the campaign ahead. Latics fans however were faced with the prospect of a season without the services of Andy Ritchie, one of the greatest players ever to grace Boundary Park (who had been given a free transfer to Scarborough), and a squad bereft of any new faces to replace him. The simple fact was that Oldham Athletic were in no position to bring in new players because they were absolutely skint. We would have to rely on a promising crop of youngsters. What lay ahead

then was a season of survival - manager Graeme Sharp had already been quoted as saying that we wouldn't be promoted. The club that had reached a major Cup Final, two FA Cup semi-finals and won promotion to the top flight within the last four years were now back to the dark days of 6,000 crowds, free-transfer signings and relegation dog-fights against some of the First Division's also-rans. The only rubbing of hands in Oldham in August was by those who couldn't afford a pair of gloves! (Listen, it's dead cold in Oldham!)

There was a fairly bright prelude to the season when Oldham embarked on a short but successful tour of Scotland - it was the Seychelles two years ago.

The season proper started with a 3-0 win over newly promoted Huddersfield, whose only attempts on goal seemed to stem from over-priced and over-rated striker Andy Booth's attempts to cripple someone sat in the back row of the Rochdale Road end. Following a non-event of a so-called 'showpiece' game against some unmentionable red dross from down the road to 'celebrate' our Centenary, Athletic's next couple of games involved Yorkshire sides, and one win from two wasn't a bad return. A defeat at Norwich in midweek was followed by our first away victory of the season at Stoke courtesy of a spectacular own goal by Vince Overson. Athletic then went all European for the first time ever via the Anglo Italian tournament, involving a visit to Ancona where a goal two minutes from time by Lemme (a distant cousin of the lovable front man of Motorhead) ensured that the 300-odd supporters present wouldn't go home disappointed.

Around this time, the popular and influential chairman of Oldham Athletic, Mr Ian Stott, decided to double his salary to a whopping £58,000 allegedly to compensate himself for losing his place on the FA's executive committee. Public relations obviously aren't included in his various talents. On the field, Graeme Sharp had adopted a style of play which involved playing five men across the middle. Although effective in stemming the attacking ambitions of the opposition, it was hardly gripping stuff. It worked splendidly until we came up against a team equally intent on controlling midfield; West Brom, who knocked the ball around competently were obviously so astounded at their 2-1 win that they didn't pick up another point for several months. By late September a woeful inadequacy in front of goal was beginning to cause concern amongst the faithful, used to the days of 5-3 and 4-1 victories. Even a 3-1 home win over Palace failed to subdue the doubters who felt that Andy Ritchie, despite his advancing years, could still have managed to be top scorer at this level. The crop of misfits employed to fill his boots were capable of lightening bursts of speed into the penalty area - before collapsing in an ungainly heap - but when it came to bursting the old onion bag, they proved as useful as an Armani suit in Siberia, or a normal afternoon at Boundary Park, which, on reflection is probably the colder.

It soon became obvious that Oldham weren't likely to feature in any end of season push to rejoin the Premier League, but a good Cup run might bring back the absent fans. Expectations were high until the draw was made for the second round of the Coca Cola Cup and Tranmere, bogey team supreme for what seems like the last three centuries, were pulled out of the velvet bag. Bookies in Oldham immediately stopped taking money on the game after heavy betting on (1) Oldham losing and (2) Aldridge scoring. Their vision was well-founded; we lost both legs and the old man of Wirral got the only goal in the first leg. Punters would have been better advised to stake their hard earned dosh on the pools. Latics suddenly became the draw specialists of the First Division, with three single-pointers at Portsmouth, Grimsby and Port Vale and a 0-0 at Birmingham where a catalogue of missed chances added to the growing discontent with the state of the forward line.

Salvation was at hand however (we were assured) in the shape of new signing Stuart Barlow from Everton, yet another piece of the jigsaw in the Scouse take-over of Boundary Park, which started back in 1908 with the signing of Joseph Donachie for £250 and continued every other week with either the sale or purchase of yet another player willing to swap one blue shirt for another. Less than 24 hours later, Athletic managed to knock three past Wolves at Molineux without their newest recruit. A defeat against Millwall suggested that Latics' new brood of fresh-faced youngsters were a little naïve when it came to concentrating for the full 90 minutes. Added to that was the growing list of injuries and the postponement of key games. Michel Vonk, on loan from Manchester City, showed plenty of promise but we just couldn't afford him. He eventually moved on to join those masters of skill and artistry etc. Sheffield United, no doubt attracted by their positive approach to the game, sportsmanlike supporters and quiet, introverted manager. Or it could have been the money?

Despite the icy fingers of winter taking a grip on Boundary Park, Oldham managed their biggest win of the season over Birmingham, eventually knocking four past the goalkeeper Ian Bennett. Actually, they only got two by themselves, Poole helped out with a diving header in the wrong direction and Kevin Francis, obviously miffed at the lack of service from his own players, got splendidly on the end of an Oldham corner to bury the fourth in the top right hand corner of the net.

The Boxing Day game can be best summed up in three words: Tranmere, Lost and Aldridge. A reprise from the grunt and grind of the First Division was at hand via the third round of the FA Cup with a visit to Barnsley resulting in a 0-0 draw. By chance, we had to meet in the League seven days later and if it hadn't been for some dreadful misses in front of goal, Oldham instead of Barnsley might well have taken all three points. By now you'll have realised that excuses swiftly run out, whether you're an Oldham fan, manager or player. Blaming bad performances on injuries, the weather, the luck of the opposition, bad refereeing, ley lines and alien landings start to sound a little lame by the time the Christmas decorations are being packed away. Those of us who hadn't deserted Boundary Park for 'Grandstand' were looking for a scapegoat or two. The obvious target in times like these is the manager or coach and at Oldham the fans were not about to break the mould. Sharp and his sidekick Colin Harvey became the recipients of the supporters' venom. Hardly a week passed by without at least two or three letters demanding the heads (and other bodily parts) of the ex-Everton duo. However, Oldham Athletic can proudly boast its record of having had only three managerial changes in the past 28 years. Sharp and Harvey were going nowhere - both on and off the field.

The FA Cup replay was a bad-tempered affair, but thanks to a disputed penalty, Athletic ended up victors for the first time in four meetings with Barnsley. Their reward was an away tie with runaway Second Division leaders Swindon. Wembley Way suddenly seemed a lot more than 200 miles distant. And we weren't mistaken - the snow that covered Wiltshire gave Athletic a short reprise from our inevitable exit from the fourth round, again down to a late goal.

Then came a run of six games with only three points gained, including another Tranmere, Lost, Aldridge, which sent Oldham tumbling towards bottom place. Most annoying were the points dropped to our fellow strugglers.

Gerry Creaney, on loan from Manchester City, showed a few touches of class but he too caught the dreaded missed sitters disease. A 3-1 win at Port Vale on Easter Monday left us still in the bottom three but just one point away from safety. Now all eyes were on the fortunes of the relegation-haunted. If Millwall went down at Huddersfield, Reading lost at Barnsley and Portsmouth came away pointless from Stoke then we were in with a chance, providing we beat Wolves at Boundary Park. All was going well, Millwall were one down after 15 minutes, Stoke one up after ten and Barnsley and Reading remained scoreless. Nine minutes from the end of our game we got what we'd been looking for, a bit of luck: a penalty. Up stepped Creaney, right footed... save! Crawling away from the car park we learned that Reading had snatched a late goal but Portsmouth and Millwall had both lost. There was still a glimmer of hope left. Five games to go; two at home and three away including a midweek trip to Leicester whose hopes of a play-off place remained intact - we lost. Four games left. Millwall, desperate for points and three places above us. A draw would do nicely. All we needed was a bit of luck. We got it again, a penalty. This time Creaney was shown how it was done by Richardson. One-nil, a vital three points. Three minutes into the game at Southend, Creaney made up for his miss against Wolves, and despite giving away a silly penalty later on, Latics moved nearer to safety due to the misfortunes of the rest of the pack.

Two games remained, both at home. Our biggest crowd of the season, swelled by the Stoke fans hoping to claim a play-off place, saw us finally complete our survival bid. Another goal from Creaney and yet another penalty meant that we were safe from an end of season showdown with already relegated Luton. The relief was evident all around the ground.

For some unknown reason, the last games of the First Division were played on the same Sunday as the final showdown in the Premier League. Any chances of catching floating supporters were therefore lost. It was just as well. Luton, already doomed to playing Wycombe and Blackpool next season were hardly going to put in a wholehearted performance. A late goal from Barlow gave us the points, but at the end, when a lap of honour is the usual custom, many supporters had already left. No doubt they echoed the views of the majority of those forced to watch a series of abysmal performances. "I'm not hanging around to give that shower a round of applause" said one dispirited supporter "It was absolutely crap."

Fanzine Facts

Beyond the Boundary first appeared in August 1989 at a pre-season friendly. Produced, edited, printed, collated, stapled and sold by Pete Mason and Harry Crompton aka Kaptain Klueless, it slowly won the hearts of a sceptical Oldham public. Unfortunately, the former manager, Joe Royle took an instant dislike to it and they were banned from selling it on the Boundary Park premises. Sales rocketed.

Its release coincided with the most successful period in Oldham Athletic's history. A Wembley final, two FA Cup semi-finals and promotion to the Premier League. Pete says that sales have now dropped along with the attendances at Boundary Park, and Kaptain Klueless has now departed, but Pete along with Brian Green manages to knock out four or five issues a season with the help of a dependable bunch of dedicated contributors.

BLAZING SADDLERS

Walsall

The summer of '95 was a good one spent basking in the glorious sunshine of a recent promotion to the Second Division. As they do, thoughts quickly turned to the up and coming season, and while having to face the likes of Stockport, Notts County and Oxford probably meant most of us shied away from thoughts of promotion, we were nevertheless sure that we'd give a good account of ourselves. So we had a considerable degree of optimism come three o'clock on August 12th.

An hour and three-quarters later, reality slapped us in the face.

We'd been belittled by a very effective Stockport County, and in all honesty we looked more than a touch powder-puff; easily knocked out of our stride by an efficient machine. What worried us most was that the bulk of the teams we had to play in the first six weeks or so all looked just that: efficient, compact, BIG! How would we cope?

By and large, very well, actually. Apart from the Stockport opener, we were never really outclassed, despite having to tackle what we (with hindsight, wrongly) perceived to be really classy teams - like Bristol Rovers and Oxford. None of them were anything to be scared of. Maybe we paid them too much respect; maybe they were just a little more streetwise than us. Whatever, for a good two months we consistently surrendered points that were already in the bag. Examples: we murdered Bristol Rovers but only drew 1-1; we were 2-0 up against Oxford with eight minutes to go, and ended up 2-2; leading Wrexham 1-0 with three minutes left, we lost 2-1. These were just a handful of the instances that led to us being too close to the relegation zone for comfort.

It did seem apparent to us that despite playing well, we weren't taking the chances that came our way. This was borne out by a run of five 0-1 defeats away from home. It's no crime to let in a goal on someone else's patch, so defensively we weren't at fault. We were just pretty toothless where it mattered. Surely King Chris Nicholl, master tactician, could see this if we, the court jesters, could.

Oh, he strengthened the squad alright, buying in two centre-backs in three weeks (although damn fine ones at that), Adrian Viveash from Swindon and Derek Mountfield from Northampton. It seemed incredible that we'd strengthened an area in which we had a gluttony of riches, whilst our arid, featureless desert of an attack cried out for a good watering. Perversely, it seemed to do the trick though.

The first time the new centre-backs played together, we walloped Wycombe 5-0 in the AWS without breaking sweat (or, indeed, wind). Three days later we had a daunting Friday night away trip to Burnley in the FA Cup first round and demolished them 3-1. I honestly believe that night was the turning point for our whole season. We'd discovered the missing ingredient: self-belief. We'd been in awe of too many teams who didn't merit it, and this game proved to our boys that they were as good as anything this Division had to offer. November, December and January all passed by with only one defeat - at home to Brighton in the AWS (and that could be put down to complacency, having overwhelmed them 3-0 in Sussex just three days earlier). Our last League match of January was away at Stockport County, and a fine, composed 1-0 victory contrasted starkly with the opening day, and highlighted perfectly just how far we'd developed.

It wasn't all plain sailing though. An FA Cup second round replay at home to a gallant (and mystifyingly bottom of the League) Torquay United saw us enter the 93rd minute at 3-3, when suddenly a Gull with a clear sight of goal hit both posts with one shot, and supporters and players alike watched open-mouthed as the ball rolled to safety. God indeed was smiling on us, and we finished them off with three goals inside the first six minutes of extra-time. The game ended bizarrely at 8-4 - a magnificent spectacle, but tough on Torquay who were nowhere near four goals worse than us.

After just edging past Wigan in round three, a trip to Ipswich (who'd appallingly knocked out Blackburn) beckoned. It was made more tantalising as the winners were due to play Aston Villa, the big boys in our own backyard. Two postponements and the anticipation of a possible Villa tie, however, only served to upset our rhythm in the League. We had a dreadful February. From five games we took one point, and from being three points off a play-off place we once more drifted too close to the drop zone. And, to really piss us of, we limply lost to Ipswich and thus had to put on hold our assured slaying of our biggest neighbours.

March brought with it blind optimism that things simply *couldn't* be as bad as they'd been throughout February. And our rampant faith served us well too. From then until the end of the season we plundered 33 points out of 51. Championship form indeed, and we managed to finish mighty close to the play-offs. It would be tempting to look back and blame our missing out on the disastrous February. But every team has a bad run, and that was ours; our true downfall was the casual loss of points in the first three months, before we started believing in ourselves.

So, it was a good first season in the Second Division, and one in which we quite easily could have made the play-offs. With Chris Nicholl having pledged himself to the club for another year, and most of our key players doing likewise, the future's bright. The future's red.

Fanzine Facts

Blazing Saddlers was conceived on November 27th 1993 in the Early Doors pub right next to Mansfield's Field Mill ground. Peter 'Pedro' Holland, Andrew 'Pesky' Pearsall and Brian Howarth were reflecting on how sad it was that WFC had had no fanzine since the demise of 'Saddle Sore' in 1992, and thought "well, why don't we start one of our own?." And that's exactly what they did.

THE BLUE AND WIGHT

Portsmouth

It was about 4.47 pm on the final day of the season when '95-96 finally came alive for me. Pompey were clinging - no, to be fair, coasting - to a 1-0 victory at Huddersfield's space-age, but (memo to the architect) undeniably three-sided McAlpine Stadium.

But that was largely irrelevant if our fellow strugglers Millwall scored a decisive goal at Ipswich. At that moment I put my radio to my ear to hear the Five Live presenter announce '... it's all over at Portman Road; Ipswich 0, Millwall 0...'

I looked up and Huddersfield broke over the halfway line. Forget the previous week's cool reflection that, in fact, relegation might not be such a bad thing after all. And besides, the incompetence of the board (certainly) and the management of the team (possibly) had meant that they had it coming anyway. Why should I lose any sleep...

'Clear the f**king thing!', I bellowed. I proceeded to inform everyone around that Millwall had, in fact, drawn, and were not winning 1-0 as those wags on the Huddersfield 'side' (that sounds really intimidating fellas) had informed us. I might as well have saved my breath. 'Get f**kin rid', everyone else was yelling.

And so it came to pass that Pompey stayed up and Millwall (by the way did you know they were top of the table in December) went down. Couldn't happen to a nicer bunch...

My even-handed view that I'd settle for the Scummers (you don't really need me to explain do you?) staying up as long as we did went out of the window when we heard on the radio that Kit Symons had equalised for Man City with ten minutes to go. However Christmas doesn't come twice in one day to Pompey fans. Only to Man. United's...

But for all the euphoria of our last-ditch escape - and believe you me, there was enough euphoria at the McAlpine stadium that day to win the Premiership - '95-96 has to go down on record as being one of the most embarrassing and frustrating seasons in our long and generally undistinguished history. I know followers of Torquay, Rochdale and so on will think at this point I'm talking cobblers (oh yes, and Northampton fans), but success and failure in football really is relative.

In August '95 optimism was high that Pompey could mount a realistic bid for the play-offs this time. Despite the shock sale of Darryl Powell to Derby, no doubt to ward off some creditor or other, an unbeaten tour of Scotland in pre-season, coupled with a 4-2 win over Southend on the opening day did little to dampen enthusiasm.

Until, that is, four days later, when Third Division Cardiff came to Fratton in the Coca Cola Cup first round first leg and, by all accounts (I was on holiday at the time) played us off the park winning 2-0. And look how well Cardiff did last season...

A flurry of transfer activity saw manager Terry Fenwick off-load our two prime assets Kit Symons and Gerry Creaney to Manchester City, with Fitzroy Simpson, Carl Griffiths and the prodigal son Paul Walsh making the return journey. The balance of these deals probably went to see off some creditor or other! Oh, and Martin Allen (more of him later) arrived on loan. Such chopping and changing meant the team failed to gel, and between mid-September and the end of November we won just once, hitting bottom place on October 21st.

But of even more significance than this dismal run was the substance that was given to persistent rumours that a consortium with the wherewithal to restore Pompey to greatness was poised to buy out the by now universally detested Gregory family, in charge at Fratton since '88.

By early December a deal was done. The team won four on the trot. The talk was of a blind-side run for the play-offs. And we drew Southampton away in the Cup. Things were never this good again.

By the end of December the deal was off. Jim Gregory's football ambivalent son Martin - now chairman of the club - didn't think the consortium had the wherewithal to set up a whelk stall, let alone meet his £5m terms for relinquishing the family's interest in Portsmouth FC.

After the fiasco of loan signings Allen and Adrian Whitbread not being made permanent, the consortium, led by the urbane and persuasive Warren Smith, abetted by some senior members of the Pompey supporters club, tried again, this time promising a 'far-eastern billionaire' to provide enough dosh to do a Blackburn. Once again, a deal was done. Stories written and hopes raised. Only for it to collapse once more. This time for good... Apparently Gregory claimed Smith and his crew didn't have the money. Smith counter-claimed Gregory didn't have the bottle to do the deal. The fans? Who really gave a toss about them?

If you've got this far into the article you will have noticed I haven't talked much about events on the pitch. The simple reason for that is that the to-ings and fro-ings of the consortium story overwhelmed everything else. Cup match? What Cup match?

Oddly, during the uncertainty generated by the (non) take-over, the team put together an impressive run between December and February, including the scalp of ultimately promoted Leicester, while only an injury-time equaliser denied us three points against Sunderland. The loss (possibly permanently) of Paul Walsh with a knee injury didn't seem to break our stride and - despite having played three or four more games than most - Terry Fenwick at least was still talking of the play-offs.

Then, in early March, Martin Gregory announced he was taking the club off the market. Terry Brady was invited to join the board and it was his £500,000 that finally removed Martin Allen from transfer limbo - his three month loan having transpired in January.

As deadline day approached we were promised a big name signing. The local paper pictured Fenwick and Ian Rush in talks. More likely seemed the return of Mark Hateley from QPR. What did we get? Paul Wilkinson - on loan - and then he couldn't be bothered to turn up, deciding at the last minute that, er, Luton, were a better bet for him to get his career moving again. It was the defining moment of our season. Perhaps the moment when even the least cynical and sceptical of our loyal but dwindling following realised PFC were heading nowhere fast. Still, at least we were staying up...

That even such small consolation was almost beyond the set-up at Fratton Park - and I am realistic enough to concede that a team that loses five of its last six home games probably deserved to go down, whatever the circumstances - left most Pompey fans numb with disbelief.

The frustrating thing is that the First Division was - yet again - less than endowed with quality teams. Not that I fully subscribe to the view that the gap between the Premiership and Division One is now some sort of chasm. The four teams that arrived in our Division barely covered themselves in glory. Norwich bombed badly, Ipswich continued conceding goals and while Palace and Leicester made the play-off final, you know where you're money is going for 20th place in the Premiership next season. Even Southampton should finish above them...

The euphoria of staying up has very quickly dissipated. Six weeks after the bulldozers were due to move in for 'the most hectic summer Fratton has known' to finally drag our crumbling ground into the all-seated, post-Taylor age, precisely nothing has happened. £2m towards the redevelopment has apparently been pledged by the Football Trust - 50% of the cost - but Martin Gregory seems to lack either the commitment or collateral to make it happen. Six and a half thousand capacity by August? Don't bet against it...

No money, no hope, no future. Maybe. Certainly most of the smart money is on Pompey fulfilling Gregory's dream of taking us out of this Division into the terraced wilderness of Division Two this time next year. And with £500,000 of Sky's TV money to fend off some pressing debt or other. Every cloud (i.e. staying up) has a silver lining, eh Martin?

And yet, and yet. Sad, deluded fools that we are, hope springs eternal. Well-placed sources insist that an announcement on a change of ownership is imminent, indeed overdue, even as I write this during the first week of June.

Besides, with a core to the team of Alan Knight, Andy Awford, Martin Allen and Alan McLoughlin, one or two signings would make us play-off candidates. And Deon Burton and Paul Hall are young players with real potential. No, really. And if the bulldozers move in by the end of the week the Milton End could be finished by October and the Fratton End by February. It could happen. It *could*.

So while I'm in prediction mode, take a tip from me: Southampton to win the Premiership next season...

Fanzine Facts

The Blue and Wight was launched in '85 as the newsletter/fanzine of the Isle of Wight Pompey Supporters Club (hence the name). In January '93 it was redesigned and relaunched when Colin Farmery (who is also involved in another Pompey fanzine 'January 3, '88') took over as editor, assisted by Chris Hougham. Regular contributors include Alan Cousins, Tony Cook, Jess Cully and Richard Webb.

THE BLUE EAGLE

Colchester United

Colchester United finished the '94-95 season as they usually do: just missing the play-offs due to a couple of really crap results in the last few games. We have, however, been successively finishing slightly higher up the table each year, and if we continue the trend we'll actually make the play-offs next time. Of course, I'm an optimist, but then who isn't at the start of the year?

Our opening game was against Plymouth, who were the hot favourites to bounce back up to the Second, and a 2-1 win boosted my optimism so much that I thought we'd be Champions! And what's wrong with getting carried away, especially as this fine result was followed up by a 2-1 home victory over Bristol City in the League Cup (look, it *is* the League Cup, OK?). Now I know that this may not seem such a great achievement to many of you (although the Bristol Rovers fan in the office bought me several drinks the next day), but remember, not only were they in a higher division than us, but we hadn't actually won a game in this competition in over a decade - not one - and never made it to the next round either. Guess what? City beat us on penalties over two legs.

The next few League results weren't too bad, and with new signing, ex-First Division Tony Adcock (OK, so his experience was with Man City, but it still counts), we were doing very nicely, thank you. Tony had in fact played for the U's for several years in the early 80's, and was an instant hero back at Layer Road, especially when we realised he could still score. Goals as well!

We did have a bad experience at Barnet in August, when we discovered that the cost to sit or stand was £10. Well, not quite true, as the tenner got you into the seating area, and if you wanted to stand you stood on a seat! The usual away terrace was empty so Barnet were obviously out to rake in a few extra quid. Inside it got worse; I swear the 'structure' was nicked from a circus and thrown up in the morning, and unlike the covered terrace the seats were open to the elements; at least it was a sunny day, but I pity fans who travelled to this dump when the good old English winter was doing its worst!

We were well peeved to say the least, and many of us decided to stand on steps, seats or by the bit of terrace by the entrance - *anywhere* to get a decent view. Barnet's answer to Gordon Brittas got mighty flustered at this terrible behaviour, but he was overruled by the remarkably sensible police who agreed with us that there was no reason why we couldn't use the terracing. Unsurprisingly no refund was offered, but the point was made. We even scraped a draw as well, so things weren't too bad.

Wins over several teams, including the supposedly invincible Gillingham at Priestfield, meant we were on a high when we discovered that the FA Cup had given us what could be our first away game by boat. Yeah, yeah, it was only Gravesend & Northfleet, and the trip over water was the Tilbury & Gravesend ferry, but it would be a good laugh. Gravesend were in the Southern League (Beazer Homes League these days), and while no result could be guaranteed, there wouldn't be any trouble in turning this lot over, would there? On the day, all went to plan, until about 3.30 anyway. The voyage went well, and everyone found a decent pub in Kent (there are some, if you look hard enough) to have a pre-match drink. Getting in was hassle, especially as the turnstile operators weren't averse to accepting a few quid to avoid the all-ticket regulations, but we were there at the start. We soon wished we weren't, as we went a goal down. No worries though, this had happened before, and a few goals would soon put things right. When the next goal went in (and it wasn't for Colchester) things looked grim; we were just an hour from providing the giant-killing headlines for the Sunday papers. I suppose you could take heart that Colchester were considered giants, but that still didn't stop friends, relatives and, worse of all, workmates from taking the piss. The Rovers fan bought me another drink - in sympathy this time!

We soon forgot about this blip in our campaign, or at least we did when people stopped reminding us about it, and got back into League action. More strange events at the next home game with Exeter, but first, a little history. Colchester and Exeter aren't exactly bitter rivals; after all, they are on opposite sides of the country, but over the last couple of seasons there had been trouble between the fans. Mostly handbags at dawn you understand, but in these days of violence-free footy (in the Third Division anyway), the odd broken window and punch-up merits a mention. Anyway, when the game started, there were about 60 away fans on their terrace directing chants at us, and we returned the favour. A couple of the Exeter fans seemed to get really worked up for some reason and spent the entire game volleying insults at the home fans. Granted, the game was boring, but even so someone might take the bait. They did. At half-time the away terrace struck up with that all time favourite "come and join us, come and join us...", and for the first time in a while the home fans decided to take them up on their offer. All but five or so of the Exeter fans immediately decided that they'd rather the Colchester fans *didn't* join them after all and shuffled away, but a couple stayed and for what seemed like ages, but was in fact about two minutes, there was a bit of aggro. No-one seemed to get hurt fortunately, but that was more than can be said for the single Exeter flag that was liberated from the away end and brought back as a trophy, before being ceremoniously burnt as an offering. Sixteen Colchester supporters ended up in court over the incident, so I doubt it will happen again, but the trip to Exeter won't exactly be a family day out, will it!

We only drew that game, but better results elsewhere meant that going into Christmas we hadn't dropped out of the play-off zone all season. Now normally about this time, it gets cold, the team slows down, and we lose just enough games to knacker any chance of success. But weird things happen, and we didn't lose any games, well, not many anyway. In fact by the end of January we were still fifth and things were looking good. More to the point we had two games in a fortnight against Wigan, who were several places below us, and others against Scarborough and Lincoln - all walkovers. Bollocks. As always happened, this was the time to let everything slip through our fingers. Wigan beat us home and away, and Lincoln and Scarborough both managed draws. When you consider that Scarborough seemed to lose their next four or five games by about six goals, you could appreciate how poor a result this was for us. The fact that they also charged us £9 to sit (no terracing again) in an identical stand to the Boro fans who were charged £6.50 made it even worse. Some fans tried to get into the home end and save a few quid, but the Scarborough gate man noticed that they were wearing blue! They did try and insist they were ground-hoppers from Norfolk (why Norfolk?) but were told "Home fans only, no neutrals." By all accounts this practice is against League rules, and several complaints have been made by supporters of different clubs, looking to stop Scarborough getting away with this in the future. As for their new stand, they should ask for their money back, as a shot during the game hit one of the shiny new plastic seats which exploded on impact, much to the amusement of the travelling U's!

I blame the result at Lincoln on John Beck's dirty tricks, which included playing a game of five-a-side on the centre circle at half time to churn up the pitch (thus suiting the infamous Beck long ball game) and locking the radiators on full blast in the Colchester changing rooms and denying them any drinks. What a wanker.

As April approached, results meant that on the day of our penultimate game at Mansfield, we were unlikely to make the play-offs. We desperately needed to win the game and pray for everyone else to lose: how often does that happen? At a goal each we were heading for another season in Division Three, but then miracles started to happen. First, we scored in injury time to scrape a 2-1 result and send 150 Colchester fans mental on the terraces. Then, armed with the yuppie mobile phone, I frantically called home to collect the scores from the half a dozen other games in a carefully prearranged operation with the missus. And it was wonderful: three defeats and two draws amongst our rivals meant a win in the final home game and we could make the play-offs. Things got even better by the time we got to the nearest pub five minutes later, as a late goal meant that one of our rivals' draws had turned into defeat.

The following week, and things looked like this: we were two points behind Hereford and a point behind Wigan, one place shy of the play-offs, had inferior goals scored, so we basically had to win and either Hereford or Wigan had to lose. I've never seen so many mobiles on a terrace that day, everybody poised to phone someone with access to teletext as soon as we scored. Then we did score! Riotous cheering was followed by a hush as the phone calls were made. And then even louder cheers - Wigan were losing! It was great, with updates every few minutes, including one that Hereford were also losing 2-0 (which was a complete fabrication). We'd had all that sort of bogus info in the Conference so we weren't taking anything for granted. But things do go your way sometimes, and at 4.45, courtesy of a win over Doncaster, we were seventh and in the play-offs.

Kidology, that's the name of the game. Neil Warnock, manager of our play-off opponents Plymouth, used every trick in the book. He issued quotes such as "Colchester are favourites", "Play-offs are for ambitious clubs, not the likes of Colchester and Darlington", "Play-offs are a lottery and don't favour big clubs like Plymouth..." etc. etc. etc. A guaranteed sell-out crowd at Layer Road greeted the game as if it were the final. The U's comfortably won 1-0 thanks to a superb 25 yarder from (soon-to-be-International?) Irishman Mark Kinsella, and Warnock whinged that the crowd were too near the pitch! Three days and lots of alcohol later, Plymouth was the venue. Sadly, with a 2-0 deficit at half time things looked grim for the U's. A Kinsella 'away' goal in the second half, equalled the aggregate scores much to the exultation of the crowd, but a devastating last minute Plymouth goal meant our fate was sealed. Not surprisingly, the Plymouth fans invaded the pitch at the end and we were forced to watch their celebrations as we couldn't get out. But don't worry, we'll celebrate next year. Won't we?

Fanzine Facts

The Blue Eagle was started in 1993 by Jason Skinner and Robert Searle. Apparently the club didn't really push CUFC's eagle logo so the guys at the 'zine decided to do so. According to Jason, *TBE* does have a good relationship with the club, especially the commercial department, and several of the directors have been seen buying it outside the ground.

The Exeter Flag - Liberated !

BODDLE

Sheffield Wednesday

The Story of Ken Dodd, a Unicorn and a Man with no Pants.

Ken Dodd played for Wednesday last season. Did he? No, Doddy. Played for the reserves in March because 85% of the squad had got piles. He was a bit slow to be honest - kept tripping over his teeth and his tickling stick. Summed up our season really. Bloody awful it was - in fact it was our worst since 1784 when we finished bottom of all four divisions, had an average attendance of 23 and the entire squad died after contracting the bubonic plague. David Pleat's revolution? David Pleat's revolting, more like.

So when did it all go wrong? Anfield at 3.00 pm on August 9th 1995 if you ask me. Typical Wednesday. Played well but lost, and out of the title race by quarter to five on the opening day of the season. And blimey, was it just me or was it hot hot hot? It was like hotter than a really hot place, but slightly hotter. One of my mates took a thermometer along - reckoned it was 150 degrees that day - hotter than the Sahara and Liz Hurley's bumcrack put together. No wonder my Y-fronts resembled a Venetian water garden.

FRANCIS... SHOULD HE HAVE STAYED ? THE FANS HAVE THEIR SAY ..

2a Bolehill Road, Bolehill, Wirksworth, Near Darley Dale, Derbyshire, DE4 4GQ

Looking back, I blame our poor start to the season entirely on the weather. The fact of the matter is that the sun was so hot it kept expanding our players' feet, so that their boots were too tight and they couldn't run properly. All the other Premiership teams realised this and increased the size of their boots accordingly. By the time Pleaty twigged (his weight to brain size ratio is similar to that of a diplodocus) and ordered a widespread boot enlargement process, it was winter and it was cold again. The player's feet began to shrink, and before they knew it, everyone was playing in boots that were 14 sizes too big. Honest. My dad analysed videos of it. He reckons that our players looked like they'd got clown's feet. Unbelievable.

As Autumn turned to Winter, Wednesday were still struggling to put results together. New signing Marc Degryse was having trouble finding his Premiership feet, whilst the other new boy Pembridge was still trying to find his Premiership pants, forcing him to play naked in the thrashings of Leeds and Bolton. Was it mere coincidence that our best period of the season came when the ginger-haired Welsh one played without his grunties? I think not.

Around the same time, the Pleatster completed the signings of two promising Yugoslavs from Red Star Belgrade, Darko Kovacevic and Dejan Stefanovic. The deal eventually went through after a 71 year delay for work permits and an even longer hold-up for Dejan's pet goblin to get through quarantine; the jury is still out on both of them, but Darko Goalo looks promising - and so he should, he comes from a very talented family. His mother makes digital watches whilst his father works under a church carving unicorns. Honestly, I've seen pictures of him. Yugoslavs sure do love unicorns, can't get enough of them. They're unicorn crazy.

Things still weren't improving as spring arrived; in fact they were getting worse - Kovacevic was found riding a unicorn on the moors above Sheffield completely starkers, Pleato appeared on Match of the Day cunningly disguised as a garden gnome, and perhaps worst of all, Pembridge had located his pants. The pressure began to tell on everyone - the first shouts of "Pleat Out" were heard, whilst chants of "Pants Off" became commonplace whenever Pembo misdirected a pass or fluffed a shot. Which happened a lot.

Hope, though, was just around the corner, and I'm not talking about the small Derbyshire village near Castleton. It came in the shape of the dreadlocked Dutchman Regi Blinker - a brace of goals on his debut at Villa and suddenly we had someone who made watching Wednesday into something slightly more pleasurable than driving an eight inch masonry nail into your skull. What a signing Blinker was, and what a price - two pencils and a bag of balloons. Got a stationery shortage in the Low Countries haven't they - get any player you want if you know your way round a stationery cupboard. Rumour has it we're signing Overmars and Edgar Davids in the summer for a ream of A4, a protractor and a box of erasers. Daylight rubbery, I reckon.

However, although Regi brought a smile back to the club, the rest of the players still struggled to make an impression, particularly that short-arsed Welsh bloke. Like Kenny Sansom, who grew stronger the longer his hair was, Pembridge got better the less clothes he had on. The fact that he wore extra pants and socks, a cardigan, a duffle coat and a 15th century chastity belt for the game at Man City probably explains why he was so utterly abysmal. How Pleato could prefer Pembridge to the legendary Jonathan Sheridan is as mysterious as my Uncle Alan's tale about the expanding artichoke of Tideswell Moor. Not fit to lace Shezza's drinks, that ginger buffoon (Pembridge not my Uncle Alan). Haven't even got an Uncle Alan to be honest.

Saw Pembo the other day and asked him what his favourite telly advert was. He thought about it and eventually came up with that Pot Noodle one where the Welsh bloke goes "Urrrgh, not gorgeous" after taking a large bite out of a cushion. So how would you sum up Wednesday's season, Mark? "Urrrgh, not gorgeous", he said. A bit like his missing pants. Allegedly.

Fanzine Facts

Boddle first exposed the Sheffield public to its unique style in April 1992. Started by Taff Boddle, Rick Boddle and Jocelyn Angloma, the 'zine got its name in memory of Taff's cat Boddle, who had just gone to pussy heaven. Rick says that this year, they've been less regular "than a constipated ferret", and readers who would like a few more titbits about Boddle's staff may be interested to learn that Taff collects bits of lace, and Rick smells like a startled gazelle (apparently).

Footnote: *SOTF2's* eds would like to thank *Boddle* for the mysterious plastic Alan Shearer (in full Rovers kit too, not a crappy Euro '96 one), and since at the time of writing this it's only an hour since he scored England's opener against Scotland, wonder whether it was some kind of omen...

Pleaty's Top Tips

Sleeping with rabbit poo on your eyelids helps prevent river blindness

BRIAN MOORE'S HEAD
(LOOKS UNCANNILY LIKE THE LONDON PLANETARIUM)

Gillingham

If any other club enjoyed such wildly contrasting fortunes from the previous campaign as Gillingham I would be most surprised. To recap: '94-95 was an absolute nightmare for the Gills. In the bottom four of the League's basement Division, up for sale and in receivership, indeed, the club's future was only secured at the end of June '95, when Paul Scally's take-over deal assured that Gillingham would at least begin the '95-96 season.

Most supporters would have been grateful just for that, and probably would have accepted another slice of the abject mediocrity that has characterised the club's recent history, but as it turned out, '95-96 was to exceed even the most wildly optimistic fan's

GILLS SUPPORTERS IN SHOCK AS GOALS AGAINST COLUMN HITS DOUBLE FIGURES

expectations (although it has to be said that, around August 1995, wildly optimistic Gills fans were pretty thin on the ground).

For some years it had been obvious that the club needed a good shake-up from top to bottom. Right from the start Paul Scally showed that he was the man to do it, adopting a 'new broom' policy, getting rid of the dead wood (and perhaps some that wasn't quite so dead) and bringing in new faces and ideas. His first act was to appoint a new manager, ex-player Tony Pulis taking over the reigns from caretaker boss Neil Smillie (who many considered to have been somewhat unlucky not to have been given the job himself). Plenty of fans had serious misgivings about Pulis, but these were largely based on his playing record in a Gills shirt (16 singularly unimpressive late eighties' appearances, which brought to mind the words 'hill' and 'over the') and a less than successful spell in charge of Bournemouth. Hindsight, being the wonderful thing it is, proved that our doubts were all totally misplaced.

If we had misgivings about the managerial appointment, these were not assuaged by his first two signings: Mark O'Connor from Bournemouth and 'keeper Jim Stannard from Fulham. O'Connor had previously turned out for the Gills between 1989-93, and hadn't exactly set the pulses racing with his scintillating performances, while we'd witnessed Stannard letting in so many goals against us down the years that he'd become something of a figure of fun to the Gills support (although in fairness, anyone who's played behind Fulham's defence for as long as he had is bound to have let a few in!). Other signings soon followed; Leo Fortune-West (never heard of him, but it's a dead good name, we thought) from Stevenage Borough for £5,000, full back Dominic Naylor from Plymouth and Dave Martin from Bristol City.

For years it had been said that given a successful team, the Medway public would support the club in numbers. Certainly the evidence was there when we lined up to play Chelsea in a pre-season friendly. The streets around the ground were a virtual gridlock as 10,500 packed the ground, leaving many more locked outside. OK, so it was Ruud Gullit's first in a Chelsea shirt...

The opening day of the of the season proper saw Wigan pay us a visit. Their supporters seemed almost unbelievably upbeat; their optimism based on the signing of the three amigos Diaz, Seba and Martinez, coupled with some outstanding pre-season results. Initially this seemed justified, as Martinez put them a goal up, but Adrian Foster bundled home an equaliser and Wigan had a player sent off and missed a penalty, before a debut goal from Fortune-West won the points for the Gills. Perhaps the next nine months held some promise after all.

A week later we visited Sincil Bank and watched stunned as Gillingham produced a dazzling performance, utterly outplaying Lincoln, strolling to a 3-0 victory. The team had been further strengthened with the signing of QPR's Dennis Bailey for a bargain £50,000. Bailey having once scored a hat-trick at Old Trafford became the most oft-mentioned Gills related cliché since the one about us signing Tony Cascarino for a set of tracksuits. Dennis notched his first goal at Lincoln, and further goals from Fortune-West and a Brightwell oggie put the Gills top of the pile for the first time in almost a decade. "We are top of the League!" chanted the Rainham End. Little did we suspect that this early-season rendition would serve us well for the rest of the campaign.

Fifteen hundred Gills supporters descended on Underhill to watch us register our first ever goals and points at their 'quaint little stadium' (or dangerous, poky little shit-hole, depending on your point of view). The game was marred by the farcical turnstile arrangements, non-existent stewarding, and the partial collapse of the newly erected 'stand' under the weight of the expectant Gills. Can anyone explain how Underhill continues to be granted a safety certificate? Answers on a postcard...

Four wins out of four; life couldn't be better. But it could get worse, and it did, in the shape of our oh-so-charming friends from Colchester, who escaped from Priestfield with a fortuitous 1-0 win, a late defensive error gifting them the points. Amazingly, it was to be the last League goal conceded at Priestfield for another four months. Two consecutive away draws saw us slip to a disastrous second in the table, but three home wins and a 1-1 at then leaders Chester assured that we regained the summit pretty sharpish.

The second League defeat arrived on October 14th, when we went down 1-0 at Darlington in a game marred by racial abuse directed at Leo Fortune-West (something which they have attempted to either justify or deny ever since). But this was followed by our biggest win, 4-0 over Doncaster, in a game which probably marked the high point in terms of entertainment, and also contained two of the best goals of the season, courtesy of Dennis Bailey and Simian Ratcliffe. Following the events at Feethams, it was always likely that Gillingham's black players would supper further abuse at Hartlepool, and so it proved. Once again the home club attempted to deflect the blame away from themselves, but in all honesty, the insults directed at both Fortune-West and Dennis Bailey were the worst I've ever encountered. It came from all sides of the ground, including the family section, and apparently from one of their players as well. A 1-1 draw from this game followed by two goalless draws saw us slip to a season's low of third place.

The FA Cup tie at Wycombe was televised live by Sky, and we escaped with a 1-1 draw thanks to Bailey's eighth goal of the season. Remarkably it was to be another 27 games before he found the net again; a somewhat mystifying statistic for a player of his undoubted class and ability (if there was a better player in the third Division last season, I didn't see him). A 2-0 win at Scarborough saw us back up to second, and then we saw off Wycombe in the Cup replay, an immensely satisfying win over a club with huge and exceedingly annoying delusions of grandeur.

Next up was the most controversial game of the season. In an encounter that was to be dubbed 'The Battle of Priestfield', loveable old Fulham came to visit. Only they weren't that loveable anymore. They'd been transformed into an horrific mutation of a side by Ian Branfoot (ring any bells, Saints?), and had clearly come to kick us all over the park. The end result in a game which was a mess, horrible to watch and a blight on the game of football was that Mark O'Connor had his leg broken in two places by a crude challenge from Martin Thomas. Martin Gray then compounded the crime by attempting to drag the stricken O'Connor to his feet, apparently believing him to be acting (proving that Mr Gray must be exceedingly thick) which caused a 17 player mass ruck, during which the Gills' physio Wayne Jones, attempting to reach O'Connor, was whacked in the face by another Fulham player. Referee Michael Bailey showed his absolute grasp of the situation by sending off Gray for the tackle, allowing Thomas to get off scott free. Having said that, Gray certainly deserved to go, as it was his actions which sparked the whole sorry incident. He also incurred the wrath of the chief police officer on duty for inciting the crowds as he left the pitch. What a charming fellow. Fulham's Nick Cusack also went for a blatant elbow in the face of Mark Harris. The Londoner's tactics got their just reward a few minutes from time, when Fortune-West shook off the attentions of his marker to blast home the winner. Gray's red card was later rescinded by the FA and handed to Thomas instead, but in the opinion of many, Gray's should also have stood. The Battle of Priestfield was the subject of an FA inquiry come March, where both clubs were blamed equally, fined and warned. Gills' chairman Paul Scally is appealing against the decision, arguing that we shouldn't share equal blame. True perhaps, but maybe it'd be better just to bite the bullet and forget about it.

Defeat at Bury, notable only for it being £100,000 signing Steve Butler's debut, saw the club slip to third once more, but a creditable 0-0 draw at high-flying Preston was followed by a 1-0 win over Plymouth (courtesy of a Butler penalty) in front of a Boxing Day crowd of over 9,500 - "We are top of the League" sang the Rainham... New Year's Day and 2,600 supporters followed the Gills to Brisbane Road where Leo's single goal clinched the points. Even more flocked to Elm Park five days later for the Third Round Cup tie with Reading; over 3,000 watching Gillingham take the lead, before two sendings off (both atrocious decisions) let the Royals claim a 3-1 win. We enjoyed ourselves rather more three days later, Steve Butler's hat-trick sealing our own 3-1 triumph in the top of the table clash with Chester.

This had been great fun so far, but the rest of the season was to prove far more of a battle. A run of the mill 2-0 home win over Lincoln (how brilliant it is to be able to say that) was followed by defeat at fast-improving Wigan. Still, another home win soon followed, this time Mansfield the victims, before we set off on the short trip to Cambridge. Most were confident of victory, but once again the referee had different ideas. We shouldn't have been surprised because the man in the middle turned out to be Mr Barry. He'd been 'in charge' of our game at Hartlepool and somewhat mysteriously managed to send off three players. Even taking this into account, I'd like to know how a team can concede a season's low of five free kicks, yet still somehow contrive to have two players sent off! The dismissal of Simon Ratcliffe was quite the harshest I've ever encountered and was due largely to over reaction by the home bench and an Oscar winning performance from United's Paul Raynor (he'd been officially censured by the FA for over-acting a couple of years back). Down to just nine men with 65 minutes gone, the Gills did amazingly well to hang on for the 0-0. This was followed up by another 2-0 home win (against hapless Torquay, who didn't seem half as bad as their position suggested) and a rather fortunate 1-0 over Barnet.

Eight points clear at the top, and a monumental 16 clear of the fourth placed team; most of us were convinced we were going to cruse to promotion.

In truth we hadn't been playing that well and the traditional sticky patch arrived. Failure to win in four and score in three, wasn't the best preparation to face your nearest rivals, but we fought out a 1-1 draw at Preston.

Returning from Torquay with a measly 0-0, many were starting to get seriously worried as the non-winning run extended to six games. With the chasing pack whittling away our lead, a 1-0 win at Mansfield, courtesy of a debut goal from on loan striker John Gayle (describing himself as "big, black and ugly", they'd like you at a couple of clubs I can think of, John!) brought some relief, but the nerves continued to jangle. Defeat at Rochdale the following week meant we lost top spot and were only four points clear of the fourth automatic promotion place. Coincidentally, the team occupying that position were next to visit. Darlington, our friends up North, had the better of a 0-0 draw, and the Gills were booed off for the first and only time; supporters' frustrations coming to the surface after one win in ten threatened to derail the promotion bandwagon completely.

We needed a win. It arrived courtesy of an extremely physical Hartlepool side, for whom Mick Tait became their 12th, and probably most deserved, red card of the season. A couple more victories and suddenly everything was rosy again. Promotion was within our grasp after a gap of 22 years. Given the nature of the season it was perhaps fitting that promotion should finally be achieved with a 0-0 draw. At Craven Cottage on the penultimate Saturday, Bury's failure to win at Exeter meant that a point was good enough to send to 4,500 of Kent's finest into raptures. The following week another 10,000 crowd crammed into Priestfield to salute their conquering heroes. A disappointing 1-0 win over Scarborough clinched the runners-up spot, but frankly who cared because we were going on the pitch at the end.. Think again. The killjoys at Lancaster Gate directed the club to make the playing surface a no-go area. This really took a little of the shine off the day.

In hindsight it can be seen that Gillingham enjoyed a remarkable season. Records were broken, some desired, others not. We conceded just 20 goals: a record for both club, Division and 46 game season. We kept 29 clean sheets (courtesy of player of the year 'Big Fat Jimmy Stannard'), had eight players sent off while opposing teams clocked up 12 red cards in games against us (Hartlepool alone managing three). Meanwhile, gates increased by well over 100% (by far the biggest increase in the League) to a 21 year high.

After years of being a club that no-one really disliked (with the possible exceptions of Colchester and Swindon) we found that we were suddenly upsetting people with our so called physical style. Comparisons were made between us and the notorious late '80s Wimbledon outfit and even, on one memorable occasion, the early '70s Leeds side (although this was by a journalist from Plymouth who was presumably lacking a few sandwiches in the picnic department). True or not, one thing is certain: Gillingham fans have nothing to apologise for. We're proud of our team and what they've achieved. We've been on the brink of extinction, and not only survived, but come back fitter, stronger and successful. I defy anyone to say that what we've accomplished is worthy of anything but admiration. And if you don't like the way we've done it, that's your problem. Watch out second division, the big bad Gills are coming to get you!

Fanzine Facts

Brian Moore's Head (Looks Uncannily Like The London Planetarium), to give it its full name, was launched at the beginning of '88-89, a season that was to see Gillingham relegated to the bottom Division for the first time in 15 years. Named after a line in the track entitled 'Dickie Davies' eyes' by the band Half Man Half Biscuit, it pays homage to one of the Gills' most famous directors, the legendary voice of Sunday afternoon's 'The Big Match'. Only last year, editor Simon Baker pointed out that despite trying to maintain a cheery outlook, *BMH* had become increasingly cynical and pessimistic. Along with Chris Lynham and Eddie 'the bin man' Alcorn, he hoped that "one day, our turn will come." Well, what a difference a year makes, eh?

CHEAT

Sheffield Wednesday

At 5.45 pm on Sunday May 5th Jon Newsome rose to head home Guy Whittingham's centre and the awful spectre of relegation was held at bay. As it turned out, Man City, Southampton and Coventry had all drawn, so we were safe anyway, but in a season so desperate it was a consolation that we had saved ourselves.

Back in August we'd been full of confidence (mind you, don't all fans feel like that in August?), and the appointment of David Pleat was seen by most as an excellent move. The squad was still useful, only Francis' awful mismanagement had produced the previous season's debacle, and bringing in a proven boss would put it right. Pleat's only other dabble with a big club (yeah, yeah, perhaps we only think we're a big club) had seen him

take Tottenham to third in the League, an FA Cup Final and a League Cup semi. It was probably half way through the season before we worked out that it had been over a decade ago! Pre-season transfer activity saw Bart-Williams go to Forest for a tribunal-fixed £2.5m (didn't Frank Clark spend that Collymore money well - Bartman, Campbell and Silenzi!!!), while Belgian captain Marc Degryse and Derby's Mark Pembridge joined us for £1.5m and £900,000 respectively. You may notice that there had been no actual net spend at this stage. This was a theme that was to continue; every incoming was matched by an outgoing, and at the end of the season we had only spent around £500,000. The season's preparations were dominated by the much maligned InterToto Cup, in which we did fairly well; only the fact that we fielded a team of Bradford and Rotherham rejects for the first game stopped us qualifying for the knockout stages. Tottenham, you pillocks, you could have been Bordeaux. We also secured the Steel City Cup coming from behind to win 3-1 at Bramall Lane.

The season proper started off with a 1-0 defeat at Anfield with Collymore getting the goal. It's become something of a tradition that we end up on the wrong end of a headline-grabbing new signing on the opening day. This was the third time in a row it had happened, Stan joining Klinsmann and Clough in that exclusive club. The worrying thing was that the result seemed to be regarded almost as a success, and our approach to the game suggested that we were after a 0-0. The midweek visit of Blackburn brought a 2-1 win, which given our recent poor starts was something of a shock - three points already - yahoo! The win over Blackburn raised hopes but as they proceeded to get beaten by just about everyone, the value of that win soon diminished. Newcastle came for a live Sky game and departed with three points, and although much was made in the local press that they scored with their only two meaningful attempts on goal, in reality they were different class. Two decent away performances at Wimbledon (2-2) and QPR (3-0) brought more false hope, and a fairly good return of seven points from five games saw us in eighth position. Then the next four League games brought us just a solitary point, and the reality began to hit home. Frustratingly we kept throwing in the odd suggestion that we weren't that bad, the 0-0 draw with Man Utd which should have been a win and the first 20 minutes against Tottenham when we threatened to run up a cricket score. On the down side, there was the last 70 minutes against Spurs when *they* threatened a cricket score (we ended up losing 3-1), a 2-0 reverse at Leeds and a woeful home defeat at the hands of a very ordinary Middlesbrough. (Can I go on record here as predicting Boro to go down in '96-97?) We had made progress in the Coca Cola during this time, but although we were never in danger of losing, the fact that Crewe found the net four times against us over the two legs was worrying. A defeat of Millwall in the Coca Cola provided another of the false dawns. We'd totally controlled what had looked a tricky tie, but as with our early season win over Blackburn an examination of our opponents' form ever since puts the success in perspective.

Far too many mediocre sides celebrated with their fans at the Leppings Lane end at the final whistle last season for my liking, and a 1-1 home draw with basement club Man City somewhat mirrored the Tottenham game - total domination and an early goal and then complete rubbish for the last 70 minutes. In fact we were lucky to come away with anything. And even when we opened up a commanding lead, the result was always in doubt. Even three goal leads don't guarantee success down Hillsborough way; we've let 3-0 leads disappear four times in the last 12 years. Can anyone match that?

Then came the visit to Old Trafford, and we feared that the despised ManUre would notch up double figures. As it turned out, only a late Cantona goal stopped us coming away with three points. Our second goal came at the end of a 14 pass move, which had it been scored by Holland would still be being raved about now by Hansen and co. Next came by far the highlight of the season, the 6-2 thrashing of hated rivals Leeds. A brief lesson for all those readers not from South Yorkshire: everyone hated Leeds in the 70's when Revie cheated them to success, but that feeling still remains in these parts, and not just football-wise. You see, Leeds and Sheffield are almost identical in size, taking it in turns to be England's third largest city (both are bigger than Manchester if you discount Salford - which you should as it's a city in its own right), yet both the BBC and ITV local stations are based in Leeds and their bias isn't even disguised. Their basic rule of thumb is, if it didn't happen in Leeds, it didn't happen. When it comes to football they are ten times worse, indeed a resentment of this is the one thing that unites Wednesday and Unitedites. So you can well imagine how satisfying the game was. To be fair to Leeds, a four goal margin was probably a little more than we deserved, but who cares?

If that was the 'champagne moment', it was to light ale very soon. We suffered the indignity of being the only Premier side to lose over FA Cup third round weekend, and worse still, it wasn't even classed as an upset! And then came the lowest point of the season - a 3-1 home defeat at the hands of QPR. We were absolutely rubbish: out-skilled, out-fought, out-anything you can think of. Pleat saw it differently, he reckoned that we'd played well and deserved to win. There'd been the first 'Pleat Out' chants at this game, and his after-game comments turned a lot more against him. Up until this point most were concerned at Pleat's lack of success but were still giving him the benefit of the doubt; after all he hadn't had that long to put things right and Francis had cocked up on a grand scale. Now, patience ran out. We had that frighteningly familiar look of the 'surprise relegation package' - you know, the ones that come 'from nowhere' and end up plummeting into the Endsleigh chasm.

Ironically, after some fluctuating results we finally turned it on against arch bogey-side Arsenal, beating them 1-0 at Hillsborough. Everything was OK now, we were safe, more or less; a win at Man City would secure that. We lost. The villain of the piece was Pembridge who should have squared to Hirst for a certain goal but went for personal glory instead, an act for which he has yet to be forgiven by the Hillsborough faithful. Never mind, we thought, a midweek win against Chelsea who had nothing left to play for would put us safe. We drew. OK, we sighed, a point at home against Everton and we'd be safe (even if we lost it'd be alright provided Man City, Southampton and Coventry didn't all win). We lost. Got well and truly stuffed, 5-2 actually. Kanchelskis was the architect, scoring three, making one, hitting the post and having a goal disallowed. He was brilliant. Our defence was shit. Still the other three relegation battlers were all playing away and they couldn't *all* win, could they? Yes they bloody well could. And so enter that nail-biting last Sunday.

In conclusion, well it's obvious we're not very good, but where does the problem lie? Pleat has certainly incurred the wrath of the fans. Some of his misdemeanours have been covered above but others include the wasting of £4.5m on two Yugoslavs, one of whom can't play to save his life, and the other might be able to but hasn't been given the chance to prove it. Darko Kovacevic, for it is he, scored four times in nine appearances and there were glimpses that maybe he could be pretty good. The home game v Liverpool showed signs that the Hirst/Darko partnership was taking off, but for the following game Pleat played Hirst on his own up front, and for the next one he recalled Bright instead. The signing of Steve Nicol was another mistake. Such immense experience could have proven useful as a squad player coming in only now and then when needed, but he was more or less a regular, and believe me there was a good reason why he was previously plying his trade in the Second Division. Most managers seem determined to sign someone of limited ability with whom they've worked with before, and Pleat was no exception with Mark Pembridge. Don't get me wrong; he does give 100%, but so would I if someone gave me a blue and white shirt, but it still wouldn't make me good enough. Pleat's reluctance to accept that Waddle's best position is still out wide was hard to understand. He was usually given the play-maker role and then switched out wide in a desperate attempt to get something from the game for the last ten minutes. Sheridan, known as The Genius in the pages of *Cheat* was hardly ever selected and at one point packed off to Birmingham on loan for two months, whilst we were struggling big time for anyone with an ounce of skill. Oh and of course there were the bizarre substitutions and even more bizarre post-match comments. To rub salt in the wounds whilst turmoil ruled, every time we switched on the radio or TV there he was pontificating on some game or other. Managing a football team, especially when they're having such a crap season should be a full time not a part time job. On the credit side, he did sign a brilliant Dutchman, Regi Blinker for a ludicrously low £275,000, and pre-season signing Marc Degryse showed touches of real quality. But as you can see, in banking terms, he's well in the red. I tipped Boro to go down earlier in this piece, and although I hope I'm wrong I can't help thinking we will be down there scrapping it out with them too.

Fanzine Facts

Started in 1989, *Cheat* is the longest running Wednesday fanzine, but due to a total lack of organisation on the editor's part, probably the least well known (seven years down the line, they are still awaiting their first local press mention). Edited by Chris Hogg, *Cheat* is more or less a one man band, but Chris' dad Ken's help in selling the thing is much appreciated. Other contributors that Chris gives credit to are Neil Sanderson, Des and Sittingbourne Owl.

CHEEP SHOT

Norwich City

A Grim Fairytale

The summer of '95 passed happily and a bit boozily for the few that make up the *Cheep Shot* team: parties, days in the sun, even a holiday to Spain. Not that any of us were celebrating relegation to the cess-pit of English soccer (sorry, the Endsleigh League); it was the fact that we couldn't believe we'd been relegated; it just wouldn't sink in.

And who could blame us for our inability to come to terms with reality? Martin O'Neill breezed in from Wycombe Wanderers, promising great things, perhaps even the fairytale immediate return to the top Division. It must have been the sunshine or the drink (probably both) because we believed him. Everything in the Carrow Road garden seemed rosy.

Little did we know that the coming season would finally expose the financial facade that Robert Chase had everyone believing in. The most despotic chairman in soccer was in fact overseeing a sham. The actual state of Norwich City's accounts completely contradicted the official line.

As the new season approached no new players arrived, but the fixture list did. Finally the reality of relegation hit home hard: Port Vale? Luton Town? Barnsley? Surely some mistake? It wasn't!!

The first game of the season was live on Anglia's 'Kick Off' programme, laughably described as an 'entertaining' look at the region's soccer fortunes. Unfortunately there are a couple of problems with this dubious claim: firstly, the teams in East Anglia are a bit on the shit side, secondly Alan Brazil, providing the guest expertise, breaks from the regular traditions of television punditry by opting to look fat and stupid, instead of saying anything of even meagre worth. To make things even worse, those of us who couldn't make it to Luton Town for the game also had to watch George Burley partner 'Porky' Brazil in the studio. Why not just give Paul Mariner, Terry Butcher and Eric Gates a hand in the production as well? Despite this Ipswich old boys' reunion, Norwich won their first Division One game 3-1, with captain fantastic John Newsome scoring twice. Div One? A piece of piss! If only...

The rest of August illustrated how difficult things would be. Champions-in-waiting Sunderland outplayed us and hit the woodwork twice in a goalless draw.

This game also saw new signing Matthew Rush from West Ham (they must have been blowing bubbles all the way to the bank) make his first appearance of the season. It turned out be his last as well, due to a bad knee injury. In a strange way, his misfortune probably accounted for the magnificent atmosphere against Oldham. Why? Because legend Robert Fleck was once again on the Carrow Road pitch. Signed from Chelsea on a month's loan, the little genius lit up the match even though he had to go off in the 70th minute with cramp. We all love Flecky, especially the city's night-clubs owners, who watch their beer sales go up by about 200% when he's about. He eventually signed for a ridiculously low fee and the little hero has returned.

There were some erratic performances in September and the beginning of a transfer saga that would eventually bring Norwich City to its knees. But more of that in a minute. Port Vale were seen off at home, with raucous celebrations when Flecky scored. Defeat at Sheffield United brought back memories of the previous season under John Deehan with a truly calamitous performance. Ashley Ward put us one up before United equalised. Gunn was then sent off, and after scouring round for a replacement, cult hero Rob Newman pulled on the gloves. Obviously, with Rob in goal United nicked the winner. And the bad luck didn't stop there: Flecky got sent off from the bench because of alleged comments he made to the linesman. Blimey, all he said was that the referee was a cun...

Martin O'Neill continued to try and get the services of Hull player Dean Windass. Dean was willing to move, the only stumbling block being the fee. Chase was dragging his feet over paying the required million and offered the Humbersiders half. Strange this, given that he'd claimed to have seven million available at the start of the season. We began to wonder again what the bloody hell Chase was doing. As the saga ran on, the relationship between chairman and manager was becoming strained to say the least. However, none of us expected what was to happen before the end of the year.

A win over Wolves away was to prove one of the highlights of the season, with goals from Andy Johnson and Ashley Ward sealing a great 2-0 win. Draws with Millwall and Grimsby kept City in touch with the top of the Division. September also heralded the beginning of a an entertaining and often pants-filling Coca Cola Cup run. Luckily enough we were given an easy second round tie against Torquay. It ended 6-1 and there must have been a blue moon because Akinbiyi and Sheron both scored twice. We finished them off in the second leg, but then fought out a dismal 0-0 draw at home in the Coca Cola Cup third round against Bradford.

November was a good month all round. Decent results, entertaining performances and we off-loaded Mike 'wing nut' Sheron to Stoke in return for Keith Scott. At the time it seemed a good deal; now it looks like Stoke got the result. A defeat away at Huddersfield preceded the unexpectedly exciting Cup replay at Valley Parade, City winning 5-3 with Ashley Ward grabbing a hat-trick. After this it seemed a sensible precaution to wear brown trousers and bicycle clips to City Cup matches. Further good wins kept us in touch at the top. Most importantly however, we beat Ipswich 2-1 after some unbelievably dodgy decisions. The referee got a bit bored and awarded two terrible penalties, one of which John Wark converted and the other was never taken after the decision was overturned by the linesman. Nice one! Now that's entertainment! Unlucky Ipswich (ha ha).

Despite all this frivolity on the pitch, things were coming to a head between Chase and O'Neill. There were a number of show-downs. Martin asked for a board meeting to discuss team strengthening and obviously never got one. Rumours started to circulate that after an argument with Chase, O'Neill offered his resignation, only to have it rejected. It was widely acknowledged that by the time he left on December 17th, he had gone to Chase three times to quit, such was his disenchantment with the chairman's interference in playing matters. By all accounts the Windass affair was the final straw.

On the day of his departure we threw away a 2-0 lead to lose 3-2 at Leicester City, and a few days later an exit at Bolton in the CCC Fourth Round Replay looked odds on. But nothing at Norwich runs to script, and under caretaker Paul Franklin we knocked out the Premiership side on penalties with Bryan Gunn the hero, saving a couple to send us into ecstasy.

Our rapture was short-lived though, because Chase appointed Gary Megson soon afterwards, snuffing out any realistic chance of promotion. I don't know what felt worse, losing Martin O'Neill or having 'Smeggy Meggy' back in the hot seat.

Supporter anger which had simmered since the start of the season bubbled nicely as O'Neill left and now boiled over. After the Southend match on Boxing day the demos began with violent calls for Chase's head. Once again we were a club in full blown turmoil.

A move into the transfer market bargain bucket that had 'desperation' written all over it brought Jan Molby on loan from Liverpool. He played in the CCC quarter final against Brum which ended 1-1 and with City players nursing injuries after tussling with Brum's genetic aberration Kevin Francis. The replay was a an epic struggle at St Andrews. Molby scored a cracking goal, but heartbreak was once again the order of the day as Birmingham grabbed a winner in the last minute of normal time. To be honest, I haven't felt this gutted about a City result since we lost to Sunderland in the FA Cup semi-final a few years ago. Another great chance to progress toward some silverware blown. Another sorry tale of wasted opportunities.

February and March came and went in a flurry of draws and defeats (OK, and the odd win). But the real action was taking place off the pitch. Since former director Jimmy Jones had given up his duties at the club, he had taken a step back and looked at things from a fans' perspective. Obviously he was horrified with what he saw. The team was awful, the manager inept, the chairman despised and the beer tasted like piss. Immediately he stated his intentions to oust the fat controller, claiming that Chase had got things disastrously wrong. Pity it took so long. With his 19 percent share holding, Jones told the fans he proposed to call an EGM if he could win the support of both club president Geoffrey Watling and a shares trust led by a number of local figures. The support was never forthcoming and Jones failed. He had however started the ball rolling with a momentum that couldn't be stopped.

The release of the Canaries' annual report confirmed our worst fears: the club were up to their necks in it to the tune of £4m, £2m of which had accumulated in the last 12 months. It came to light that the whole squad had been circulated as 'up for sale'. As Chase had so eloquently put it: "The sale of someone like Newsome would guarantee us a six month trading period." Hardly the words to inspire the dwindling City faithful.

It was no surprise when on March 14th, club captain John Newsome was sold to Sheff .Weds for £1.6m; but it was a big shock when Ashley Ward also went to Derby for a piffling £1m. Even Megson was astounded that Chase had conducted clandestine transfer deals to put off a possible winding-up order. Where were these mythical piles of cash that O'Neill had been promised? It was now plain to see that Norwich had been in the financial shit for some time, and all the promises were pure fabrication.

Without two key players we scrabbled to avoid the drop. The farcical defeat at Portman Road only served to rub salt into our gaping wounds. I was so infuriated by Bryan Gunn's huge air shot that I nearly buried the TV set through the front door. After a number of dodgy businessmen had declared an interest in City, Geoffrey Watling and Keith Gregory finally stumped up the money to buy out Chase's 34% controlling interest.

On May 2nd the enemy finally departed. The years of wanton destruction were finally over. The real end came with a surprising 1-0 win at Palace; the travelling support going crazy. Who could blame them? Humpty Dumpty had fallen off his wall, City had won and Ipswich had blown their chance at the play-offs.

Life doesn't get much better than that... Which is a bit sad really.

Fanzine Facts

Cheep Shot first appeared in Feb '95, badly typed and clearly photocopied. Since the heady days of using an old Olivetti (still not returned to sis) **CS** has gained popularity, prestige and a better standard of production. Originally put together by Martin Betts and Jon Chapman as 'a bit of a joke' it has continued to appear bi-monthly. Next season **CS** is to merge with another stalwart Norwich 'zine *Liverpool Are On The Tele Again*. Notable contributors who have run the gauntlet of Jon and Martin's abuse have been: Dr Fust, Ian Lindsay and top cartoonist Lloyd Burr, who has a real knack of delivering a snorting joke, which only goes to prove that you can be talented *and* funny.

CHELSEA INDEPENDENT

Chelsea

Who would have thought that we would have started the season with Glenn Hoddle as manager and end it with Ruud Gullit as his replacement? Well actually I did. This is no desire on my part to appear smart but the night before we travelled up to Villa Park on October 14th 1995 to see Chelsea win at Aston Villa, a reliable source of mine told me that Hoddle would be on his way at the end of the season, and that if he went the club had a ready-made replacement in our Flying Dutchman. I filed that one away for a rainy day. So when Hoddle upped and went there was only one man who was ever going to get that job from my point of view, and it certainly wasn't going to be Stroller Graham. Still, it was fun hearing all the potential candidates being bandied about.

And if the rumours were true that Ken Bates had wanted George, and if Matthew Harding, heartbroken at the loss of Hoddle, had really fancied Ray Wilkins (not literally - with *that* hair-line?), then all Chelsea fans should then be thankful to managing director Colin Hutchinson, as he appeared to want Gullit all along. Even Alan Curbishley's name had been in the frame along with Grimsby's Brian Laws, whose only managerial claim to fame to date had been sticking one on Bonetti (Ivano, not the Cat) and in so doing put his best player in hospital.

Going back nine months, the Premier League's most optimistic fans had good reason to really believe that "this time next year Rodney" we could put a trophy in the cabinet for the first time since goals from John Dempsey and Peter Osgood saw off the Real Madrid in the heat of Athens 24 years ago. We'd had an FA Cup Final and the semi final of a European competition to look back on, and we now had Ruud Gullit and Mark Hughes. We could not wait for the season to start.

Glorious sunshine and Cup holders Everton accompanied the big kick off. We drew 0-0. You'd really think that we should have learnt by now that our early season optimism evaporates quicker than Keith Gillespie loses his wages each week. After three games we'd not scored a goal and were four places off the bottom. Then Big Fat Ron's Sky Blue Army came to the Bridge, and apart from the obligatory Chelsea ticket office cock-up leaving thousands of fans outside the ground at kick-off, we were treated to some wonderful exhibition football with Gullit, Wise, Peacock and Spencer all joining forces to play some champagne one-touch stuff that had the crowd and Glenn Hoddle positively purring. Even some of the traditional old moaning gits that occupy the East Stand could not remember the last time they had seen such exciting football played at the Bridge. We were 2-0 up at half time and coasting when it all went pear-shaped in the second half. Coventry pulled two back, nearly got a third and the final whistle was a blessed relief. If any game summarised our season this was it: early promise; cause for much optimism; inevitable disappointment.

September, and Chelsea put some points on the board while Julian Dicks put some stitches in John Spencer's head (Dicks by name, dickhead by nature).

The wheels wobbled and fell off in October. The return leg of the Coca Cola brought Stoke City to town. Danger signs were posted all over the place in the first leg at the Victoria Ground, when we were lucky to escape with a scoreless draw. Having beaten those wretched one-nillers from Highbury the previous Saturday, expectation was rising again. Stoke had Ray Wallace, we had Ruud Gullit, it was no contest. Oh no, the great God of under-achievement had bought a ticket and was surveying the proceedings. The game was heading for extra time when Mark Hughes committed the cardinal sin of trying to play football on the edge of the penalty area. Quickly dispossessed by Wallace, Rod fed Paul Pesch... sorry Mr Karen Brady, who got a lucky rebound off Frank Sinclair and slid the ball past Kharine.

The old moaning gits' club in the East Stand were in hog heaven. With the unbeaten home record in tatters they had ample opportunity to vent their spleen and were soon in full flow: "You haven't got a clue Wise"; "Get off Peacock"; "You're useless Sinclair" and wait for it; surely the final volley was just about to be delivered; something along the lines of "Off you go Dutch bloke, call yourself world class? You're not fit to lace Roy Bentley's boots." Amazingly it never came and Gullit was about the only player to escape their vitriol.

So one route to Wembley and Europe was already closed off. It would have to be shit or bust in the FA Cup. More of that later.

November, and activity off the pitch dominated the back pages. Bates fired the first salvos in the so-called 'Battle of the Bridge', and with Matthew Harding out of the country he scored the opening hits. Bates suggested that Harding was no longer necessarily going to be his successor and suggested that Harding was an embarrassment. Apparently the man whose money had paid for the new North Stand liked a drink; well several drinks; OK, so many in fact that he only stopped when he fell over, much to Bates' annoyance. The tabloids loved it and were having a field day.

With Harry Harris fighting Bates' corner and Nigel Clarke fighting Harding's, the 'war' dominated the sports desk. The Mirror and The Sun both ran phone/fax polls asking who should run the club? Harding was a runaway winner. Following a conversation with the Mirror it appeared that Greybeard's votes came almost exclusively from members of his own family. But opinion polls in national newspapers made no difference; Bates has never been a man to listen to public opinion and he wasn't about to start now.

Then he really began to lose the plot, barring Harding from all executive areas, the directors box, the car park, the players bar and removing all Matty's toys from the vicinity. He even called the *Chelsea Independent* "Harding's jackals" and seemed to suggest we were cunningly plotting behind the scenes to remove him from his throne, keen to appoint the new kid on the block as his successor. Before we got into the 'my dad's bigger than your dad' routine or 'I'll get my big bruvver on to you', Bates came down with a convenient bout of pneumonia and missed the first home game (Tottenham) for which the ban operated. If you'd believed everything that had been written over those crazy few weeks, the long-running CI plot was going to culminate in a demonstration at the Spurs game. What a load of bollocks. How paranoid could Bates get? All we've ever wanted was what was best for this club of ours. Having endured a barren, trophy-less, humiliation-strewn 20 years, would it be too much to ask for this great club to be successful , just once, and win a something that mattered. Not some Mickey Mouse competition that no one gives a stuff about, but serious silverware. Bates has had 13 years in charge, earns £160,000 a year out of our wallets, doesn't put his hand in his own pocket, never listens to the fans and on top of all that charges a quid for a cuppa. We would have forgiven him all that (maybe not the tea) if we'd had something to show for his time in charge. Harding, on the other hand, is prepared to invest heavily in the club and would make it one of the biggest in the land, if not in Europe.

Amazingly the warring factions made a truce in time to see a goal from new signing Dan Petrescu, and Match of the Day viewers were treated to the pathetic sight of the two adversaries kissing and making up in public - Yuk. Never mind that, where did Bates get that dead animal draped across his back?

The return of Gullit from injury in December heralded the Chelsea take-off. Two days before Xmas we unwrapped our first holiday present with a 1-0 win, courtesy of Gavin Peacock, and probably the best performance since Glenn Hoddle took over. A good day, a few pints on the way home and an away win with some fantasy football. Now why can't all Chelsea games be like that?

We stuttered briefly at home to the Crazy Gang on Boxing Day, but the New Year brought good fortune with our first win at the Subbuteo Stadium since December 27th 1982, when a young lad named David Speedie had scored our winning goal against the not so mighty morphin powder puff Rangers. This time round Paul Furlong, who had done nothing for 89 minutes, popped up in the last minute of the game to score the winner and send those sad Rangers off to go and contemplate Nationwide League Football next season.

Onto the FA Cup. Bert Millichip's frozen balls pulled us out of the hat/bag/machine at home to a rampant Newcastle side, and the Beeb were there to show the game live. We got the goal we wanted through Mark Hughes, but with the clock long gone past the 90 minute mark and heading towards the next millennium, Ferdinand popped up to score a cruel equaliser. As far as the nation was concerned we were out - the replay for Newcastle would be a mere formality. But remember we are Chelsea, and there is nothing like a bit of adversity and injustice to bring out the best in us. Despite falling behind twice the team kept coming back, and with a sense of poetic justice we equalised for the second time with the referee just about to blow the final whistle. The penalty shoot-out elevated Kev Hitchcock to hero status as he saved from Watson. Ugly missed for the Mags and we had a memorable victory.

Back to the Subbuteo Stadium for round four - boy how they must hate us. With Furlong scoring only his second goal of the season to put us 2-0 up they must be as sick of the sight of him as we are. Still, they won't have to play us for at least 12 months, if not longer. Shame about that. We'll really miss them.

The following week saw us reach our highest Premiership position with the 5-0 demolition of Middlesbrough. Sky TV ensured the nation witnessed the fruits of the Hoddle way, and when Venables decided to jack it in, I thought Glenn had to be in the frame. Now what did I file away for that rainy day?

However, if we could win the FA Cup then Glenn was bound to stay and sign a new contract. A jammy scoreless draw at Blundell Park saw us bring the Mariners back for a 4-1 caning and a home draw against the Crazy Gang in the sixth round.

A cracking Cup tie with four shared goals meant a return trip to the badlands of South London. We knew that Man United were waiting for us at Villa Park for the semis and we were desperate for a chance to get our own back for that 4-0 thrashing at Wembley two years ago. On a memorable wet and windy Selhurst night, goals from Petrescu, Duberry and Hughes ensured that there would be no capitulation to the Dons; we could even afford the luxury of a missed Dennis Wise penalty.

Our League form in between was little to write home about, so I won't. Settling into our perennial eleventh position meant that shit or bust time had arrived. Our season now rested on a place in the FA Cup Final, and the Scum were standing in our way. Well, you all know what happened. One thing is for certain, you can't blame Craig Burley for the result at Villa Park. Yes, in an act of temporary madness, he attempted a suicidal back pass to gift them a goal, but Burley did a fine job in his holding role and was still battling at the end when some of his more experienced team mates appeared to have given up the ghost. It was so bloody frustrating because we had the beating of them and we blew it. They didn't win that semi final, we collectively lost it. Our season was effectively over.

I suspect that the players knew he was going, long before Glenn Hoddle made his announcement, and with the exception of a 4-0 caning of a piss-poor Leeds side we didn't win another game. I can't say I was surprised or as upset at his departure as many other fans were. I'd resigned myself to it many months before. Even if we'd won the Cup, or Venables had decided to stay after Euro '96, Hoddle had had enough. No prizes for guessing why!

The rumour factory may have put regular visitor Stroller George in the frame for the Chelsea job, but Gullit was always the fans' favourite. During an emotional final game the Bridge faithful gave the boss a suitable send-off, and made sure that Bates knew exactly where he could stick Graham.

No sooner had Gullit put pen to paper than Gianluca Vialli said 'si' to Chelsea, and by the time the new season kicks off the Italian will no doubt have a new striking partner beside him. Who knows, Rodney this time next year we really could...

Fanzine Facts

The *Chelsea Independent* first appeared in May 1987. The magazine was founded to provide an opportunity for Chelsea supporters to air their opinions about every aspect of Chelsea Football Club and football in general. Edited by Mark Meehan with the help of Andrew Wrench, the '96-97 season will see its tenth birthday but the *Chelsea Independent* is not ready to claim its pension or London Transport buss pass. Yet!

Bradford City

So, what can we write for you
after Bradford City's rollercoaster season (apart from the fact that roller-
coasters tend to finish at the bottom
and we finished at the top)? Well,
putting the inability to find a proper
metaphor (or is it simile?) aside, it certainly has been a season of wildly differing emotions and experiences for
us, even by the standards of the average long-suffering Bradford City fan.

Close season saw the majority
of City fans, if not pessimistic, then
resignedly stoical, after the previous
season's early optimism that promotion was on the cards ended up with
mid-table mediocrity. Pre-season
friendlies were a mixed bag and the
tour of Scotland heard '95-96's first
concerted chants of "Lawrence out!"
as we conceded the only goal of the
game to mighty Alloa (no offence meant, Alloa fans). Early season looked good
and the League Cup win over Nottingham Forest was pure brilliance. Then came
the next round against Norwich. A good away draw brought the Canaries back to
Valley Parade where we were in the lead with minutes to go. Then, in our view, one
of the most tactically inept substitutions seen by City fans for many years allowed
Norwich to equalise and win in extra time. Many viewed this as the start of the end
for Lawrence.

But we're getting ahead of ourselves; or rather we're going off in a direction
we never intended to take in this piece. Because, if you're expecting match reports
followed by details of our glorious 2-0 Wembley victory in the play-off finals, you're
going to be disappointed. If you want a match-by-match view of our season then
City Gents 58-63 and our Wembley Special are available from our usual address
(contact publishers for details). If you need to get the impression of our fans' reaction to the various on and off field events regarding Bradford City there is no better
way to do so than read the views as they were written at the time. (You also get to
see all the photographs, regular columns, cartoons, clippings, one-off features and
other drivel we're so rightly (in)famous for.)

Anyway, we're always up for doing something a bit different, so we decided to
use this piece to make a variety of awards to a number of people, organisations and
incidents which helped to make this season a memorable one in so many ways
other than just getting promoted (just getting promoted, my God what have I written, WE GOT PROMOTED!!!!! IT'S BLOODY BRILLIANT!!!!! WELL DONE

CHRIS KAMARA, THE BRADFORD CITY PLAYERS, GEOFFREY RICH-MOND, THE BACKROOM STAFF AND ALL THE LOYAL FANS!!!

Thanks for assistance in this endeavour to 'the usual suspects' particularly those who occupy the centre rows of D Block for the reserve matches. Anyway, here goes.

Best on-pitch moaner in the City team: Ian Ormondroyd is good, very good, but he is a mere amateur compared to our winner, Paul Jewell. This man is world class. During one reserve match not two minutes went by without him moaning to the referee and linesman. We're convinced he was whinging to the ref as they came out of the tunnel before kick-off over an incident that happened years ago.

City player most likely to be caught offside: Don't get us wrong, we like the lad, but the winner has to be Neil Tolson. What makes things even worse is the fact that he always looks so surprised when it happens, as though the concept of offside hadn't been explained to him.

Heroic commitment beyond the call of duty to the cause of Bradford City: This goes to the 20 or so fans who turned up to the last home reserve match at noon on a Friday dinner time after we'd already been relegated to Pontins' Division Three and sat through to the end of a 3-1 defeat.

Most unusual managerial decision: Chris Kamara arranging for the Trinidad and Tobago national side to train with us and turn out for the reserves. Perhaps he thought we'd get Dwight Yorke off Aston Villa for nothing as a consequence. (We didn't of course, though he did turn up in the stand to watch some of his team-mates in the first match.)

Phrase most over used by fans during the year: "We need a twenty goals a season striker."

Happiest people in the area when we signed Mark Stallard: The Telegraph and Argus poster writers who must have got sick of trying to dream up headlines when we were trying to sign numerous strikers during the year and then failing.

Phrase least used by City fans: ."... the Pulse Stadium at Valley Parade...." We might appreciate the sponsorship money but we certainly aren't going to start using that mouthful; good old Valley Parade will do just fine, thank you.

Quote of the season: "I'm not going to watch City at Wembley until we get there."

City gent campaign least likely to meet with success: The 'Preserve The Old Seabrook Advertising Hoarding On The New Midland Road' campaign. (Apart from the stone wall at the bottom of Hollywell Ash Lane it's the oldest part of the ground that's visible. That is unless we really do unearth the ancient 'holy well' under the pitch before they re-seed it in the close season. We've got a water diviner and some old maps; all we need is the chairman's permission to give it a go.)

Awards for away matches are as follows:

Worst stewards at a match: We're sure most of them are OK but the winners are the ones at Peterborough who kept shouting "dirty northern bastards/f**kers" every time City went in for a tackle. This was followed by them urging their players to kick ours all over the pitch. Hardly the thing to create the impression that we could expect fair treatment from them.

Best stewards at a match: The ones at Shrewsbury who could have thrown out one of our friends but gave him a stern talking to instead. One then brought us a photograph of the streaker from the Marine match being escorted out with the chief steward's tweed hat covering his genitals. (We forgot to ask him if he'd washed his hat since.)

Best club office staff: Walsall. We wrote to many clubs for assistance during the season and whilst all helped us, only Walsall acknowledged receipt of our letter by telephone as we asked. They were also jolly nice when we went to visit them on the day of the match. Oh, and the staff in the club bars were jolly nice as well.

Most unusual City flag seen at an away match: Well done to the lads (and lasses?) who brought along the Welsh 'Bradford City' flag to the matches at Bristol City and Oxford.

Worst police: The over-officious bully-boys down at Norwich who managed 35 arrests outside the ground as a result of absolutely no trouble whatsoever. They even tried to arrest people on one of the executive travel trips.

And the 'odds and sods' awards go to:

Many a slip twixt Cup and lip award: Blackpool AFC for announcing their Wembley travel plans at half time in the second leg of the play-off. Ha, ha, ha!

Funniest incident at a football match (if it didn't happen to you): At Blackpool after the League Cup match our coach organiser was grabbed by the police and dragged off. He was then subjected to the discomfort and indignity of a full strip and body search. Nothing was found. The police had apparently thought they'd seen him selling drugs during the match. What they believed to be the packets of 'gear' they'd observed him passing out had, in fact, been the coach tickets to the following week's match at Notts County.

Anyway, we hope at least some of the above makes sense, especially if you are a City fan. If not, write to us enclosing any number of £5 notes and we will happily offer you an explanation.

Hopefully we'll see you again in next year's *Survival of the Fattest*. Bye.

Fanzine Facts

City Gent celebrated 11 years of publication in November '95, and issued a further five full 100 pages for 100p editions during the year and an 'Update' edition of 50 pages for 50p. The editorial team often produce special editions, and as assistant editor Richard Halfpenny explains, "we are hoping to issue a Wembley Special edition along with our normal (if we can use the word) 'Welcome to the Season' issue in time for the pre-season friendlies." He adds, "We have also released a tape of '12 Great Tracks of Commentaries and Songs - including the legendary - You Know We're Going To Win' called NOW That's What I Call City. (Described as 'unbelievable' by one purchaser.) This for the ridiculously low price of £2.50. Profits from sales of this tape have already raised £400 towards providing a commentary service for the blind at Valley Parade."

The fanzine got its name when Bradford City discarded their traditional logo of a chap in a bowler and briefcase, in favour of a more modern design. The guys at the fanzine snapped up the idea, and the *City Gent* was born.

CLAP YOUR HANDS, STAMP YOUR FEET!

Watford

"Ramage is clean through, with only Feuer to beat. He scores and the title is Watford's. Luton are relegated. What a season...."

Grnnbmmgh.... Oh! I was enjoying that. The dream was a million times better than reality. What a bummer of a season it was!

The previous year had finished with optimism sky high, particularly as signings were promised. Well May passed, then June, then July, and *still* nothing happened. Sure, we were linked with several players, but as the summer went on the more desperate Roeder's excuses became. He's retired, he wants £7,000 a week, he'd rather join Millwall (thanks Uwe Fuchs for that fantastic foresight), etc. August arrived and we had spent precisely £2,000, and that was on the uniform

for the Mutant Wasp that parades around the pitch before kick-off. A fat bastard of a 'keeper in Steve Cherry (a top class nutter) on a free transfer represented the sum of Watford's efforts in the summer transfer market. So, come August 5th and the pre-season friendly against Spurs, it was all rather familiar. No new players, no new system of playing, no big striker and Hessenthaler was still unable to pass the ball. There wasn't even a new kit, as the Marketing Department (starring the lovely Jeanette Cant) had decided that the game against Bristol City in April '95 was the day to launch it. In true style supporters couldn't buy it until July!!! Anyway, the game against Spurs came and went and we looked forward to the new season.

However, the headline in the *Watford Observer* did not bode well as it was announced that Ramage, without doubt our most skilful player, was not even in the squad. We wondered how the hell we would score goals. Yet come the Saturday, two goals from the most unlikely of sources sealed a 2-1 win for The Hornets. Derek 'Freddie' Payne, of all people, scored with an overhead kick and Richard 'Shooooooooot' Johnson, never the most composed in front of goal (why fanny around when a blast will do), controlled the ball and coolly curled it in from 25 yards. It clearly glossed over the cracks. An appalling performance at Huddersfield was more in keeping with what was expected. It also blew my theory that Watford were going to have a good season. In all my 20 years of following Watford, we have finished in the top four five times, and each time Watford won their first away match! Bugger! Still, Barnsley at home offered a chance to keep the home form ticking over. Errr... We lost 3-2! And then followed the *pièce de résistance* at

Charlton. And the day started so well... I got out of work early, which meant getting to the pub near Charlton in good time, and then, as our group wandered/ staggered to the away end, we were met by Freda of the Junior Hornets who had several tickets left over, which were duly taken. At £1 each we weren't going to complain. Entering the ground, in hindsight, was a mistake. We didn't deserve a goal, but we did have the cheek to go in at half-time one-up. However, the next 40 minutes were torture. We couldn't string two passes together (no, Hessenthaler wasn't playing!) and never looked like crossing the halfway line, let alone attacking. Supporters, now fed up, started chanting for the return of Ramage. It also brought a legendary quip from one of our party, "I spent more on the programme than getting in!." A cheap but very depressing evening. Still, our voices were heard and the Great Man returned at Grimsby. Full marks to everyone there, as this fixture had the lowest attendance all season. Maybe Grimsby will make a badge to say 'I was there!'. If there were any doubts about Ramage, they could be dispelled as he ripped Stoke apart the following week. This was Ramage at his piss-taking best. Stoke just didn't know what hit them. We even had the cheek to miss a penalty (Kevin Phillips finding halfway up the Vicarage Road end rather than the net). It was about this time that injuries were starting to affect the side and three draws out of the next four games started to reflect this. Still we finished September with a win at Tranmere. Victory was not tasted again until December.

October started as it meant to go on. We were, or so we thought, 30 seconds from going out of the Coca Cola when Darren Bazeley scrambled the ball home in the 120th minute to give us the lead. About two days later Bournemouth equalised and it went to penalties. Keith Millen slotted home his sudden-death penalty to win, fans charged onto the pitch, Kevin Phillips got clobbered by a police baton and suddenly we were one of the main items on the local news. Graham Taylor (Hmmm, that name might appear later on) and his Wolves side got a point and we finished October looking over our shoulders at trouble. November was no better. At least we avoided being the first team to lose at Port Vale, and Trevor Peake made his first mistake against Watford to gift us an equaliser against L***n. Another poor performance in front of the TV cameras against Norwich left us in trouble.

Watford, it seems, always have good Decembers; don't ask me why. But when I saw in the papers that Ramage had been dropped for the game against leaders Millwall (yes, that's right, LEADERS MILLWALL), I had all but given up on three points, and this despite taking Paul Wilkinson on loan. However, Watford battled away and Kasey Keller decided to test Kevin Phillips' killer instinct by spooning the ball straight onto his feet! Super Kev then ran from the halfway line to make it two, and despite Millwall pulling one back we held on. It's funny how a big striker can make a difference. Two weeks later three goals, all set up by Wilkinson, resulted in a double over Tranmere. The weather then intervened and we lost our momentum.

January was not a happy time. We went out of the FA Cup at Wimbledon, though 'Celebration of the Season' could have been claimed there and then, as Tommy Mooney's shot rifled into the top corner and was immediately followed by a 'Dead Ant' celebration. Kerry Dixon, rather than Paul Wilkinson, was signed and Super Kev had his first really bad day at the office as he missed four chances against Huddersfield. And when Sheffield United took the lead against us the following week, we were bottom. Darren Bazeley saved our blushes for a couple of weeks.

February was a momentous month. On the field we were consistent: played five, lost five. It was the middle game against Palace that was the final straw. No passion, no commitment and three days later, no manager. Roeder, his assistant Kenny Sansom and reserve manager Stuart Murdoch were shown the door. Enter Graham Taylor, who was going to be coming at the end of the season anyway to become the general manager. Also enter Mr Luther Blissett, who had been biding time working in the Marketing Department (starring the lovely Jeanette Cant), as coach alongside Kenny Jackett. Also enter Elton John, who decided that the press conference was a good time to re-affirm his involvement with the club (though not financially). Ipswich were the unfortunates, and for the first half we were all over them and 2-0 up, but we ran out of steam and lost 3-2. Suddenly it was great to be a Watford supporter again.

Taylor, Blissett and Jackett always knew it would take a miracle to avoid relegation. Looking back at Taylor's notes and comments he knew it too and was already preparing for the trials of Division Two. Still, we can all pray for miracles, and as the Terrific Trio got to grips with the squad things slowly started to improve. Pivotal in the early burst was that man Ramage. Playing up front he was a revelation as Oldham were beaten 2-1 and followed it up with two more in a bizarre game against West Brom. Watford were three-nil down after half an hour but a goal apiece from Ramage and Foster meant at half-time it was 3-2. Watford pressed but were caught 12 minutes from time when Bob Taylor completed his hat-trick. Were Watford finished? No. Two goals in a minute from Ramage and Foster again meant the game finished four-all. To say that the West Brom fans were not happy with our 'Three-nil and you F***ed it up' ditty would be the understatement of the season. Colin Wilkes of Gloucester cost us points again by giving Derby a penalty four minutes from time. If Jim Smith (never the most generous of managers to the other side) said it wasn't a penalty, then it definitely was not a penalty. And still we kept on drawing; West Brom (1-1) and Sunderland (3-3). We were proving to be hard to beat but we could not turn it into wins. Easter was a crucial period, and this is where we ultimately lost it. Portsmouth were there for the taking but it was they who did the taking as we lost 2-1 with a very poor display. On the Monday it was Southend, and Craig Ramage gave us the lead which we held until the 93rd minute when they equalised. To most people that was it; we were not mathematically down, but as good as. Maybe the players realised this as well because they suddenly went goal and win crazy.

A pre-match injury to Hessenthaler meant that David Connolly, who had been scoring goals 'for fun' (© Ron Atkinson) in the reserves, was drafted in for the game against Port Vale. Was Hessenthaler my favourite player for 90 minutes, or what? Connolly left the pitch with the match ball after bagging a hat-trick and even Devon White got in on the act by scoring his first and then second goals for Watford. The latter was a classic 'ball, goalkeeper and defender in the net' centre forward's goal. Four days later Connolly and White were up to their tricks again as Reading were beaten 4-2, and more importantly we were above L***n, who were next.

There is something about playing L***n that means all our centre halves get injured, and this fixture was no exception. Still, we didn't lose, which is as good as a victory. The lack of goal action in that game was more than made up for in the first 20 minutes against Grimsby as Ramage and Connolly helped themselves to a couple each. We let Grimsby have a whiff of getting back into the game before Connolly and Ramage each completed hat-tricks. Fifteen goals in three home games! It just wouldn't have happened earlier on in the season. Suddenly the miracle looked on. The penultimate fixture was Norwich away, never a happy hunting ground, but a Connolly penalty and a Porter screamer gave Watford a 2-1 victory. Other teams' results still needed to go our way, though, and although you can hope for one or two, all four went our way. Incredible! It was down to the last game.

As it happened it didn't matter what we did. Portsmouth won, Millwall drew, and we froze on a day when Leicester sneaked into the play-offs and beyond. To be relegated hurts, but to get so close to avoiding it hurts that much more. Oh well - at least we finished above L***n again!

With Jackett confirmed as manager, Blissett as his assistant and Graham Taylor starting his revolution by giving nine players free transfers, it's going to be a new era at the club. Expectations are high for next season, but I hope we don't fall into that trap again like we did in '95-96. There is hard work ahead for all concerned.

Fanzine Facts

Clap Your Hands Stamp Your Feet! started back in December 1989, continues to give the alternative voice at Vicarage Road and is thriving. Last season **CYHSYF** enjoyed the luxury of hiring Darren Witts to take some pictures for the fanzine at selected games. Founding member Matthew Bentote also mentions that the fanzine has its own football team. "If there's anyone out there who fancies a game, they can contact us!" The fanzine's name was meant as a rallying cry to the somewhat quiet Watford faithful.

THE CLARET FLAG

Burnley

Well, what can I say? It was the season that never was for Burnley fans, after the bookies and famous pundits (well a few small time ones anyway) had made us joint favourites to win the Second Division, along with Carlisle - and look what happened to them! We should have given up all hope of going back to the promised land of Division One. With two new all-seater stands being built as well, the town was buzzing, expecting the walk-over that never was. Firstly we only bought 'Big Bad' Peter Swan (presumably 'Bad' referred to his playing ability) from Plymouth, and in selling Steve Advise (God) to Luton Town and up and coming youngster and hometown lad John Mullin to Sunderland, things were starting to look gloomy.

"English thugs in Euro shame!"

Our fears nearly came true in the first game against a very useful looking Rotherham, when after being outplayed for long periods we ragged a 1-0 victory. After the game, we desperately tried to convince ourselves that the lads just weren't match fit yet; when they were they'd easily beat anyone in the League!

And it was the same story at Stockport, when we scraped a 0-0 after the Hatters did everything but score; they even threw things at our winger Ted Mc-Minn (and I thought all that kind of stuff had disappeared from football).

At this point I, along with many other Clarets, was concerned about our record signing Kurt Nogan who hadn't scored and didn't look like doing so; for over three hundred thousand he was looking a real pudding. How wrong could we be?

As September came and went, Jimmy Mullen (our clueless manager) tried many different tactics in the vain hope that he might save his own skin. This showed against Carlise and Chesterfield when he tried five at the back, with the players left guessing where they'd be playing week to week (hence more defeats), while against York City we once again ragged a draw with a superb Andy Cooke header giving us the lead, the Minstermen equalising after a lot of pressure.

October, and after two months of trying we finally - wait for it - WON AWAY!! Unfortunately only a thousand Clarets made the trip to Bournemouth, and it nearly killed the ones who did (it's a good job that we use Duracell in our pace-makers). King Kurt Nogan was beginning to look the part up front; shame about the rest of the team!

We beat Hull City 2-1 in the biggest non event ever Part II (the whole season being Part I), which was the last ever game in front of the famous Longside terrace. The Kop had flags, ex-players and basically a bloody good send-off. In contrast, the Longside had, well, the players kicking some balls into the crowd and, er, that was it! That's the Burnley board for you.

Having been knocked out of the Coca Cola Cup by Leicester, the approach of Christmas saw the appearance of Trelleborgs shirts (yes, that part-time team that beat Blackburn Rovers in Europe). What a perfect Christmas present for Clarets everywhere! At this moment in time we were in a play-off position, but still Mullen was unpopular, mainly due to the terrible home form. The shock sales of two crowd-pleasers Heath and Randall alienated the 'Mullen Out' campaigners even more; it seemed that he wanted rid of all the skilful ball players, and still wouldn't get the chequebook out for some quality players to get us out of the pit into which he'd dragged us.

The freezing weather around this time meant postponements and a Boxing Day derby against Blackpool at their death-trap of a ground. When we finally had a pitch that wasn't ice-bound, we played Carlisle in that Auto thing (obviously the players didn't give a toss as they were 'wiped' 5-0 by the so-called local rivals). The next game against the Burnley haters from Cheshire (Stockport) also saw five goals - fortunately this time, we got three of them. Mullen must have thought that his bacon was saved.

But defeat at the hands of Oxford sparked the nearly empty Burnley end into chants of "Mullen Out." This one was now in danger of replacing the famous Burnley chant of "No Nay Never."

February was a very important month for Burnley. This was when the well-publicised 3.33 protest took place. The idea was simple: at 3.33pm, any fans who were disgruntled with the board would turn their backs on the pitch for two minutes in silence. Amazingly, around 75% of the crowd did so at the allotted time, starting the loudest ever chants of "Teasdale Out." There was no place to hide, and Teasdale *had* to listen to what we in the stands wanted. The next major event was the departure of Jimmy Mullen, with the alleged fire attack taking up plenty of columns in national newspapers. So who was to be his replacement? Strong rumours flew around the town, with Steve Coppell, Inchy Heath, Trevor Steven, Martin Dobson, Brian Flynn and Chris Waddle all being linked with the Turf Moor hotseat. Personally, I wanted Chris Waddle or Inchy to get the place buzzing again, after it had all but gone at the end of Mullen's reign.

Inchy got the nod, and took over a team in sixteenth place. Relegation looked more likely than promotion, but at least he started with a lucky 1-0 victory at Ashton Gate, with King Kurt grabbing the goal; he was now a hero and scoring every game (or so it seemed).

The football was getting better, even though we were still getting beaten, mainly due to the back four's habit of being caught out in the last 15 minutes. To solve this problem, in came Charlie Bishop from Barnsley to stiffen up the defence, and Paul Mahorn from Tottenham to help out King Kurt up front. Safety was now the issue, not promotion.

The new stand on the Longside was opened against Bristol Rovers, and looked pretty good to boot, but as with all of these new structures, the seats are too small and it takes you ages to get out.

To wrap the season up, we got the necessary points to stay up with the goal of the season when Robbo lobbed the goalkeeper from forty yards out. A high point at last, in what was a very dismal season for the Clarets.

Fanzine Facts

The Claret Flag, originally called *The 29th,* was started two years ago by editor Matthew Pasiewicz. Trying to reflect the views of all Clarets, young and old alike, Matthew has left two co-editors by the wayside, and is currently looking for contributors. So don't be shy, Clarets, for as Matthew says, "we try to print *everything* we receive!."

COCK-A-DOODLE-DOO

Tottenham Hotspur

If I had a pound for every time Gerry Francis said: "to lose Klinsman, Popescu, Barmby and Anderton in the summer was a major blow" I'd have almost enough to renew my season ticket! But despite reservations over his tendency to moan, and the style of football he's introduced, few at White Hart Lane would criticise Francis too strongly.

Chris Armstrong and Sir Ted may vie for the player of the season plaudits, but it's Francis who has proved to be Tottenham's most vital asset. Unfortunately this may be simply because he is the best around at managing on the limited reserves Alan Sugar has allowed him. Sugar's statement halfway through the season that Spurs could never hope to compete with the big clubs was probably the

campaign's most depressing point, although the opening game against Man City at Maine Road wasn't far off.

Glorious sunshine and first day anticipation usually provide a real rush for footie addicts, but this dour draw suggested both sides would struggle. Defeat at home against Aston Villa and a total stuffing by one of the best Liverpool sides ever seen at White Hart Lane seemed to confirm our worst fears. As if this wasn't bad enough, the Spurs PA was so loud it destroyed what little atmosphere was left at The Lane, and the new announcer was embarrassingly inept. The club was becoming a laughing stock on and off the field and matters were made worst by another of Sugar's tantrums. Outraged by the fact that supporters booed off a hopelessly bad Spurs team after the Liverpool debacle, he exploded onto the back pages with the proclamation: "I'll sell up." The tabloids loved it.

Although the story was clearly nonsense, as evidenced by the asking price, Sugar's inability to take any criticism once again piled on the pressure in the dressing room. This was the pits.

Things had to improve and they did. We racked up wins against Leeds and Sheffield Wednesday and swept aside the mighty Chester in the fizzy pop cup. By the start of October we were scoring goals at a rate of three a game and only defeat by Forest, bogey team number one, upset the run. A great performance at home against pace-setters Newcastle, the Geordies lucky to escape with a point, awakened hope of better things, although a meek surrender at Highfield Road in the Coked-up Cup introduced a touch of reality.

Spurs then embarked on an astonishing run, including a satisfying defeat of Bergkamp and co, and entered the Christmas programme poised to go second, ready to set a new club record for consecutive clean sheets. Given that our opponents were Bolton, nine defeats in nine games prior to their visit, one thing was guaranteed: we'd cock it up. Sure enough the team obliged. Bolton fought hard, but never really looked capable of scoring. We were two goals up with 15 minutes to go, the crowd - now thankfully free of the overpowering PA and inept announcer - was in full voice... Then Justin Edinburgh stitched-up Walker to blow the record and Gudni Bergsson fulfilled another footie truism by snatching a vital equaliser against his old club.

That draw felt like a defeat, but New Year's Day brought a fine victory over, indeed humiliation of, Manchester United. On this glorious evening there could be no argument with the style Tottenham adopted or the completeness of the triumph (although Alex Ferguson had a good go of course). Quite simply we were superb, and Chris Armstrong showed just how much his game had improved since Francis signed him. Both he and Teddy had excellent games, Sol Campbell marked Cantona into invisibility; there wasn't a bad performance from a white shirt.

Elation gave way to confusion in the New Year. Apart from the United game Spurs had not played particularly good football. The defence was solid, Armstrong and Sir Ted were certainly a lethal partnership, but there was no creativity, and with Darren Anderton nursing a long-term injury, no prospect of any either.

The third round of the Cup threw up a trip to Hereford, a treat for those sad individuals who like to visit new grounds even if they are complete toilets. A generally friendly day out in cow country saw a nervous Spurs scrape a draw and a torrential downpour ensure a piss-poor journey home. In the replay we humourlessly banned Hereford's prize cow and roasted the team (sorry) 5-1.

Blackburn ended our unbeaten run over Christmas and Villa (bogey team number two) added another defeat to rein in our Championship pretensions. So once again the FA Cup looked like our only chance of success, especially after we cruised past Wolves at the second attempt. Then we drew *that* team again - Forest.

The fans' determination to help break the jinx was clear. Drinking in the away supporters' bar at the City ground before kick-off, I was privileged to take part in the loudest, most boisterous pre-match knees-up I've ever experienced. Fickle? No way - these supporters are the best in the world. Buoyed by the adrenaline rush of our pre-match routine we took our seats and were greeted with an astonishing snowstorm. The events of that night will remain one of the enduring images of the season, and after 14 minutes the referee bowed to the inevitable and abandoned the game.

It took us eight hours to get home through atrocious weather, all the time knowing we had to repeat the journey the following week. We did, again putting the home support to shame. Although Forest went ahead, Spurs soon went 2-1 up and finished the first half in rampant mood. Francis then made a tactical mistake by telling the team to sit on the lead throughout the second half. This muted performance allowed Forest an equaliser and a replay, at which they sneaked through on penalties after only one Spurs player could score from the spot.

Despite all the time, effort and emotion we'd invested in a game that yielded only disappointment, we resisted the temptation to indulge in public tantrums about selling what remained of our season tickets.

Our season was effectively over. Those who suspected Spurs had earlier flattered to deceive were proved right. Although we were pushing for a UEFA Cup place until the last day, needless points dropped at home against West Ham, Middlesbrough and Chelsea meant our destiny was in others' hands. One high point of our run-in was a spirited performance at Old Trafford which saw us lose to a dubious refereeing decision - something I don't think I can ever remember happening before (!).

Our last game against Chelsea was awful; an uninspired, unimaginative showing against fierce rivals who are now managed by a former Spurs hero and playing the sort of passing game we want to see at Spurs. Neither I nor many thousands of others bothered to stay for the team's obligatory lap of honour.

We crushed Leeds (but who didn't?) in our penultimate game, with Darren Anderton making a welcome return to form, then went to Newcastle on the last day needing a win and an Arsenal defeat to finish as London's top team and get that European place. Newcastle had already thrown away their chance to win the title, so any doubts we had about being instrumental in helping Man U win the League were thankfully banished. In the event a great performance only secured a draw; Spurs conceding a goal only after the substitution of the majestic Sol Campbell allowed Les Ferdinand off the leash. Wins for Arsenal, Everton and Blackburn forced us down to an undeserved eighth final place.

I missed that Newcastle game, along with a large number of other season ticket holders who'd queued for over three hours. If we'd been prepared to stump up £200 to fly to the game with the executive travel club we'd have been guaranteed a seat. So much for season ticket holder priority. Instead, I watched the game on Sky. It cost me less, was more comfortable, and I was in the midst of good company.

I still believe there is no substitute for being there, but I'm having to ask myself whether I can afford to invest the money or the energy. Football's never been so popular, but to be honest, this particular fanatic is feeling jaded. It's not just that I've been uninspired by my team, or disappointed at my chairman's mid-table ambitions. Have we gorged ourselves on so much football we're on the verge of being heartily sick? Or will the old enthusiasm return next season? I don't really know, but I've got a nasty feeling that a little of the love I had for the whole football supporting experience has gone forever.

Fanzine Facts

Now in its second year, glory came to *CaDD* near the start of the season when Total Football magazine described it as "oozing with style and confidence." "If only this would rub off on the team," laments editor Martin Cloake. This year the number of people involved with the fanzine has grown, and Martin names the in-depth profile and interview with Gerry Francis as the feature which gave him most satisfaction. Player interviews remain a strong point, which could explain why they apparently enjoy reading *CaDD*, many of them providing their home phone numbers for guaranteed access.

THE CROOKED SPIREITE

Chesterfield

In't supporting Chesterfield Brilliant!

You start off expecting a season of struggle after getting promotion to Division Two, but end up missing out on the play-offs by a point. Yep, brilliant! Or is it?

Season '95-96 has passed by with quite frightening speed. Our first in Division Two (since it was called Three) was, in the end, quite remarkable. The more positive supporters, who double as armchair fans and Wembley visitors, thought it would be a breeze. Their letters to the press and annoying phone calls to local radio hinted that last season's play-off triumph ensured that a promotion path to Division One had already been cleared.

Those of us who attended on a more regular basis just hoped we could cobble enough results together to ensure that our promotion would not be a temporary affair. For me, a season battling against relegation would have been a disaster; give me mid-table obscurity any day of the week. And to be fair, it was all I expected.

I genuinely doubted our ability to get up among the promotion candidates, fearing that the long ball game we played so frustratingly and so negatively last season would have little effect one division higher. But I was to be pleasantly surprised.

The opening exchanges were immensely enjoyable as a reformed style of play - ball on the floor passed to men in the same coloured shirts - ousted the old promotion winning thump up field and chase till the lungs collapse. It was a style of play we weren't used to, a style that only other teams seemed to adopt. Promotion favourites Carlisle came and were despatched with consummate ease 3-0. Local rivals Rotherham went back to Yorkshire on the end of a similar scoreline, and my favourites for promotion Burnley, came and played their part as we beat them 4-2. And I was enjoying it; in fact I turned to a friend during one half time and said "If we keep playing like this I don't care if we lose." And I didn't.

It was an odd kind of truth though, one I've never been faced with before, well, not under manager John Duncan at least, and it was the difference between this season and last.

So watching Chesterfield at home was a thrill again. The armchairs still talked positively about promotion to Division One while the rest of us ticked each three points gained off our mental 'points needed to stay up tally.'

SHE'S WEARING ONE!

The 'STAG' bra —
no cups · no support ·
not much chance
of keeping 'em up!

Saltergate was something of a fortress. Out of the first five games played we took 13 points, scored 12 and had yet to lose. Away from home it was a different ball game. We worked hard without really exerting the same sort of pressure. In our first five away League games we only managed four points, scored just five goals and clinched our first away win at Brentford. And the trend continued. At home between the beginning of October and the end of December we picked up 11 points, scored 10 goals and were looking almost invincible. Away from home, invincible was hardly the word to describe us; hard working definitely; shaky... maybe.

But by the year's end we had played some great stuff and were languishing menacingly in a play-off spot with games to spare. We started to see the same Division One path that the armchair mob had envisaged earlier, and as the new year opened its eyes we all started to steel ourselves for the possibility of another round of football's Russian Roulette.

Even the directors looked as if they fancied it and took the chains off the transfer wallet. It was a shock when they dipped into its murky depths and pulled out £95,000 for 'keeper Billy Mercer from Sheffield United. When they returned to the moth-eaten piece of leather and spirited out another £150,000 for Paul Holland, also from the Blades, there was collective fainting throughout Chesterfield. Ironically, we had made enquiries for Holland when he was at Mansfield, but they'd laughed in our faces. So you can imagine the broad Chesterfield grin flashed at Notts when he breezed into the club. I'm sure if we'd had a big enough load speaker we would have aimed it at the Shags, stuck out our tongues and given it the full "na-na-nee-na-na."

But all good things come to an end, and having spent £250,000 in the best part of a month, withdrawal symptoms set in and the wallet snapped shut, accompanied by the clanking of chains and the sight of a sturdy key disappearing from a substantial padlock into another bottomless pocket. Mind you, it did show a bit of ambition from a board that had previously only spent £50k on centre-half mark Williams (a signing similar to robbing a bank and leaving a tip).

One of the least exciting things to happen was the extension of manager John Duncan's contract. Mr Duncan has the classic love-hate relationship with the Chesterfield faithful - some love him, some hate him; it's that simple. Mind you, the ones who profess to love him, are also the ones who adamantly deny shouting 'Boring, Boring Duncan' just two Christmases ago. On the other hand, some of the hate brigade have refused ever to set foot in Saltergate again while he holds the reins; face, nose, spite and cut-off come to mind. However, regardless of the extremes of opinion from the terraces, the directors love, nay worship Johnny Boy, and it was they, in a quite ludicrous move, that gave him the benefit of a new five year contract. Five years... Five whole years!! You can do manslaughter and get less for that. Will the suited and booted types who 'run' football clubs ever learn?

So in the end, the board behaved exactly as we'd expected. We got two big signings as sweeteners and they snaffled up Scotch Johnny until the next century. If a host of Premiership clubs had been courting our boss, then maybe this would have been a sound move. But in reality there are now some players who will walk away from the club for absolutely nowt because they haven't got the extensions they deserved, while it will be 2001 before we can boot Duncan out without paying him a huge wedge of compensation. Believe me, that's a frightening thought.

The other main off-field wrangling involved our proposed move to some custom-built toilet. Originally the plan had been to ship us out to near the M1 (actually nearer to Mansfield than Chesterfield) and this didn't meet with universal approval, especially as the spectre of a ground share loomed with our loathed neighbours. Mind you, our chairman J Norton-Lea fiercely denied this, stating (and I paraphrase) "We will share a ground with Mansfield over my dead body." Being the eternal cynic I remembered a similar bold statement of his, "Steve Norris will leave this club over my dead body." Well, Steve has gone but JNL is still in remarkably fine fettle. It would also seem that there was more to the ground share rumour than mere supporter fright. The Shags were in the middle of their own relocation battle and a shared stadium would have certainly suited both sets of directors.

When the M1 deal fell through, the idea of redeveloping Saltergate was completely overlooked. OK, it would have needed great imagination and a bundle of the director's own money to make it viable, and there was the rub... Their expenditure is mostly calculated, designed to bring a return at every juncture, whereas mine is totally emotional week in and week out. I would see nothing vulgar in ploughing millions into the club I love, but perhaps that's why I haven't got their millions in the first place. Anyway a new site has been found, the plans paraded, and the majority of the fans bought off. Me, I still cried into my pillow every night at the thought of it.

Back on the green stuff, the play-off band-wagon rolled merrily along; we had games in hand and hard-working back to back away victories against Rotherham and Peterborough looked to have secured a place in the top six. But then the proverbial wheel fell off.

Our very own 'pocket full of Kryptonite' Kevin Davies was injured. Now while one man doesn't make a team (and his loss was a big blow for supporters) it seemed like a catastrophe to Duncan as we suddenly reverted to type: long punt down field, hoping Lormor would get on the end, and relying on the defence to cope when we inevitably gave the ball away. The fixture congestion built and when Lormor was injured at Bristol Rovers we played on without a recognised striker. Why? We had Darren Roberts champing at the bit, but Duncan wouldn't play him (oh no, don't get me started, I've got to finish this by August).

In the last two months of the campaign, fortress Saltergate was breached and our travelling army were forced into retreat: we managed to secure just 20 points out of a possible 53. If there is such a thing as footballing suicide, then we committed it - big style. By the end there was more than one wheel off our wagon.

But even then we went into our last game with that 'slim mathematical possibility' still dangling in front of us. Basically we had to beat Notts County, and hope already massively relegated Hull got something out of their game against play-off candidates Bradford. I have never seen so many radios at a match and the cheers started as soon as Hull took a shock lead. In the second half someone turned to me and said "Hull have equalised - it's 2-2." I was flabbergasted - what had happened to 1-1? And who cared, all we had to do now was score... and er, what was this?.. surge into the box... desperate lunge... trip... PENALTY!!!. Up I went, arms punching hopeful holes... YEEEEEEEEEESSSSSSSSSSS (you know how it is). My feet had no sooner hit the terrace than a hand tapped me on the back "Bradford are winning 3-2." If there is such a thing as an invisible punch in the throat then this was it; cheering our goal was almost impossible.

And that was it. The end of the craziest season I can ever remember. The armchairs were quickly into print and onto the phone blurting "Why are people moaning, they'd have settled for that at the beginning." Of course we would; I would have settled for anything as long as we stayed up, but they'd missed the whole point, just like the team. Having got so close we should have grabbed this very rare opportunity and wrapped it all up; I've been watching Chesterfield for too long not to realise that chances like this just don't come along that often.

And the cost of missing out? Less money from the football trust, more money to be found internally from an already spendthrift board, players more likely to leave and replacements harder to entice, and of course more opportunity to gloat over the hapless Shags. What started out with me proclaiming that I didn't mind losing as long as we played well, ended with clumps of hair being ripped out in frustration as we squandered the best chance of back-to-back promotions that we've ever had.

The armchairs now state with utter confidence that we're certainties for promotion next time around, but it never works like that does it. Does it?

Fanzine Facts

The Crooked Spireite started in January 1988 as a response to a board who, in editor Adam Lafarge's opinion, "seemed to be letting the club die through underfunding." Named after the town's famous bent church spire, after countless issues *TCS* still aims to be honest, up-front and outspoken, celebrating the club in good times, and acting as a pressure group in bad times. Lafarge promises to keep *TCS* going "until the readers get fed up with it."

THE CUMBERLAND SAUSAGE

Carlisle United

What a difference a year makes. In May '95 Michael Knighton was the undisputed King of Cumbria as he played keepy-uppy in front of a capacity Brunton Park crowd before the final game of a Championship season. Obviously he was taking a swipe at his critics over his aborted Man Utd takeover bid, yet the politics mattered little to Cumbrians starved of any football outside the basement Division for eight years. Happy days, but they didn't last long.

The summer started badly and got worse, laying the foundations for a disastrous season. Increases of over 30% in season ticket prices led to fierce debate amongst fans in the local media, with Knighton threatening to resign over the issue, and the top goalscorer David Reeves and Player of the

Year Dean Walling both initially turning down new contracts.

The team had won the title comfortably but towards the end of last season there were signs that the squad would struggle at a higher level, many victories being gained with backs to the wall displays. Yet new players were not recruited as funds were set aside for a new £3 million stand.

It didn't take long to see that the class gap between the Third and Second Divisions was too much for Carlisle to handle. In their Championship season United were unbeaten at home in the League until April. This time around that record lasted just 90 minutes, with an opening day defeat by Bristol Rovers.

The pattern that day was to be repeated countless times over the course of the season. Carlisle had a good share of possession with some tidy approach play, but they lacked the killer instinct. At the other end, the vital ingredient which was missing from the previous season was the stability and influence of Derek Mountfield. So many games had been won during the previous campaign with sound defensive performances held together by the ex- Evertonian. But director of coaching Mick Wadsworth was concerned about Mountfield's dodgy knees, so he was released after playing only one match.

This game at Hull in the Coca Cola Cup first round, first leg was one of just three away wins in all football last season, and things really started to look bleak when mighty Hull overturned their first leg deficit to send us crashing out of the competition.

Mountfield's absence and influence was even more apparent when his centre back partner Dean Walling floundered, hopelessly out of his depth. Walling rewarded the club for his improved contract with an inept season in which he gave away a staggering collection of soft goals.

The club's initial replacement for Mountfield was Neil Moore, a young loan signing from Everton. He started promisingly enough but after three months alongside Walling, it became clear that it was a case of the blind leading the partially sighted. Gary Bennett was eventually brought in from Sunderland in November and although he did reasonably well, the damage had already been done.

By this stage the patience of United's fans was wearing thin as fears of an immediate return to the basement surfaced. But in October, with the team third from bottom, Michael Knighton made one of his now legendary proclamations. His roll call of promises include Premiership football within ten years, membership of a British Super League and, more recently, a guarantee that he would not allow Carlisle United to be relegated from the Second Division. He added that if United were still struggling by January he would bring in new players to ensure survival. At the time many of us were gullible enough to believe him. After all, what sort of chairman would allow his club to go down while lying to the fans about his determination to stay up?

The first of many crisis points was reached in November with a home defeat by rivals Preston in the first round of the FA Cup. Not the greatest way to exit the competition, especially as their winner came in the last minute. With the threat of relegation looming large it was no consolation to see our old enemies down the M6 doing so well, but this was a season when absolutely nothing went our way.

A glimmer of hope arrived with the loan signing of striker Allan Smart, ironically from Preston. In the two games he started, United scored nine goals and moved clear of the bottom four. Just before Christmas the clubs agreed a fee for Smart and the player returned to Preston to mull over the personal terms; yet when Smart agreed to a permanent move in the New Year, he was told by Knighton that he was no longer wanted. The chairman may have decided that the club could do without the one man who looked like solving our scoring problems, but the fans didn't agree - particularly when missed chances continued to cost the club dear. The season was at a crossroads and Knighton had taken the wrong turning.

January brought the glimmer of a false dawn with a 5-0 Auto Windscreens Shield win over the old enemy, Burnley, a game notable for David Reeves' hat-trick, the first by a Carlisle player for seven years. Meanwhile, the team continued to struggle in the League, but it was still a huge shock when Mick Wadsworth resigned in the middle of January to become assistant manager at Norwich.

There was a groundswell of feeling that the director of coaching was unhappy with the lack of finance for squad strengthening, and this theory was boosted by Wadsworth's letter to the local paper in which he commented that the fans had shown an uncanny understanding of his reasons for leaving. Another factor may well have been a rumoured altercation between Wadsworth and a local radio reporter the week before his departure, which apparently stopped just short of a punch-up.

Whatever the reasons behind his move, there's no doubt that Mick Wadsworth made an incredible impact during his two and a half years at Brunton Park, winning a Championship and reaching a Wembley final. Even though he seemed to have lost his way during those fraught final months, this was blamed largely on the quality of the players at his disposal.

Bearing in mind Knighton's reluctance to use his wallet (an elusive item last seen being used by Lord Lucan to buy food for Shergar), it was hardly surprising that Wadsworth's successor came from within the club. Mervyn Day, previously first team coach, was given the Mission Impossible of keeping Carlisle United in the Second Division.

Under Day, a more pleasing style of play surfaced and players who had previous;y disappeared seemed revitalised. The performances improved but there were still short-comings in both boxes; sadly missing was the influence of Mountfield (now having a great season at Walsall), and the cutting edge of Smart.

Despite all the problems, the crowd rarely got on the player's backs. Home attendances averaged nearly 6,000 and the fans felt that the team were giving it their best, even if their best wasn't quite good enough. The level of commitment was al-ways evident, but there were exceptions: Warren Aspinall - Come on down!

This is the senior pro who had to be dragged out of the bookies for the warm-up at Peterborough; a game that unsurprisingly ended in a 6-1 defeat. During one of his suspensions he made the half-time prize draw and was abused by the opposing fans, so he responded with a "Three types of the finest coffee beans" hand gesture. Then, in the vital end of season game at Brighton, he was sent off inside the first 20 minutes for fighting. His fine example was not lost on other players, particularly a first year pro-fessional who throughout the season regularly practiced his dribbling... into a beer glass in a city centre pub every Friday night.

Some relief from the League came in the Auto Windscreens Shield when Unit-ed reached the northern final for the third year in succession. But not even the memories of Wembley from the previous campaign could create much enthusiasm. The cloud of relegation hung heavy over everything else and we lost 0-4 on aggregate to eventual winners Rotherham. But never mind, now we could concentrate on the League. Yippee!

As transfer deadline day approached, speculation reached fever pitch as to what action the club would be taking to stop the slide. Five months after his "I'll spend to stay up/We won't go down/The moon is made of green cheese" pledges, the chairman invited a couple of Barnsley players up for talks. Fine, until he sent them packing, apparently shocked by their personal demands.

Poor naïve Mr Knighton. He must have got quite a shock when he discovered that decent players don't come cheap. The expression "You've got to speculate to accumulate" was obviously lost on him. As we saw all season, if you pay peanuts you get monkeys (or is that donkeys?).

There was some transfer activity though; unfortunately it involved the club selling two of their best players while bringing in no-one to replace them. While our rivals were doing their best to avoid the drop by making new signings, Michael Knighton was taking a more unusual approach. Paul Murray, an outstanding young midfielder, was signed by QPR for £200,000, a far cry from Knighton's previous estimate of £2 m.

Then, on deadline day, left back Tony Gallimore was signed by Grimsby for around £150,000. It remains to be seen whether any of this money, along with the previous season's record profits, will go towards team building. On current evidence, if Knighton won the National Lottery on a double rollover week, he'd splash out on a packet of Rich Teas and a new light bulb for the boot room.

The depleted and dispirited squad staggered on, but their downfall was their dismal away record: one win from 23 matches, and that was at Hull. It's hard to describe the misery which the Carlisle players inflicted on their amazingly loyal away supporters. Away attendances averaged around 500, remarkable considering the distances involved and the team's League position. These fans deserved better.

A late run of home wins kept the dream alive for a while and helped to make Mervyn Day's record over the season better than that of Mick Wadsworth. Whatever the future may hold for Day, who has just signed a new two year deal, he deserves plenty of praise for improving the quality of his team's football and coming so close to achieving his aim of survival.

The end, when it finally came, could hardly have happened under more bizarre circumstances. After nine months and 46 games our destiny was out of our hands, because everything hinged on York's result in their rearranged fixture at Brighton, five days after our last game. York needed only to draw or score three goals: they won 3-1. Our future was decided for us, 400 miles away. We were down and out.

After the game Michael Knighton stepped into the media spotlight to complain that Brighton and York should have been made to play their match in the previous week, because York knew before the game what they needed to do to stay up. But the rearranged fixture was played as quickly as Football League and police regulations would allow. As an excuse for Carlisle's relegation, he'd have done better to claim that the sun was in our eyes and a dog ate our homework.

Knighton's threats to sue the League were quickly exposed as a smoke-screen intended to cloud the real reason for United's demise: Knighton himself and his refusal to invest in a squad which so obviously needed new blood.

The new East Stand, all £3m of it, is impressive. But next season, back in the basement, it's also going to be very empty. Questions must be asked about whether investing so much in the stadium at the expense of the team was a wise move.

At the moment it seems that four years after Knighton's arrival, we're right back at square one. Unless action is taken quickly to introduce new faces on the pitch and in the boardroom, last season could be just the beginning of a dramatic and painful decline.

Fanzine Facts

The Cumberland Sausage was formed in 1990 by Andy Baker and Simon Robson. It ran for three years before merging with 'North of Watford, South of Heaven' which was edited by Paul Newton and Roger Lytollis. This improved recipe supersausage has gone from strength to strength, and was recently voted one of the top ten fanzines in the country by FourFourTwo magazine.

DERANGED FERRET!

Lincoln City

Who was it that said football is a game of two halves? Nope, can't remember.

Laugh at our ignorance if you want, because it doesn't really matter to your loyal Lincoln City fan; you see for us '95-96 was a season of three thirds.

First third: August 12th '95 - September 2nd '95

Under the control of the '75-76 promotion winning captain Super Sam Ellis, the Imps treated us to a wonderful start: Preston North End 1 Lincoln City 2. It was to be the zenith and the only three points for quite some time. Come the season's end Preston had won the League and the two City goalscorers had also been promoted: Puttnam with Gillingham and West with Bury. Four successive defeats followed without a goal being scored. It was obvious to the 'untrained' eye of the fan that something was not quite right! When Gary Megson, who had been trying to play football as opposed to long ball, left after a 'disagreement' with Ellis it was clear that long ball had won. Pity the team couldn't!

A home point against Scunny, when we scored our first goals in five games saved the bosses neck (just like the buses, two came at once in the 89th and 90th minute, Scunny scoring their second in the 91st minute). But the knives were out. And when an equally poor Barnet side strolled to a 3-1 win at Underhill those same knives were well and truly stuck in his back. "What do we want? Ellis Out! When do we want it? Now!" was the chant... and the board obliged. On the same day that Ellis' departure was announced, Bury also let it be known that they had sacked their manager. With more than a hint of irony, Ellis scuttled off to Gigg Lane as assistant boss and they promptly went and got promoted!

Second third: September 9th '95 - October 4th '95

The general feeling when the new man was announced was 'huh?'. Steve Wicks, fresh from success at Scarborough (not) and Crawley (who?), was to be the man in charge as a whole new era in English football evolved. He was to have sole control over the playing side whilst the chairman controlled everything else. "We're going to play football with players who are proud to play for Lincoln City", we were told.

At first the signs were encouraging despite a defeat at Rochdale (they always beat us anyway) and a draw at Bury. The football was good and the deadwood Ellis had signed was being cut away. Allon to Hartlepool, Key and Brightwell back to their Premiership clubs and Greenall aka Judas ("I won't play for you now you've sacked Ellis") to Wigan. In came Steve Brown, Kevin Hulme, Darren Davis, Matthew Bound and Michael Appleton. Of these 'proud to play for Lincoln' players only Steve Brown remained at the season's end! Old favourites Puttnam and West were used to entice Brown and Hulme to the Bank. City fans know who came out best in one of those deals.

Disaster struck at Chester (1-5) but at least we were happy to be told we were unlucky and the victory flattered Chester. Those present would have agreed at the time, but we then got stuffed 3-1 at home to Cambridge and 3-0 at Plymouth. Still, a few of us were lucky enough to be staying in Cornwall for the weekend and were thus able to get massively drunk and obliterate the match from memory. Unfortunately, the next day's headlines proclaiming 'Easiest win in Plymouth's history' did much for our recall and zero for the hangovers. Cruel world...

A 4-3 home win in the AWS over Rochdale for the first time in bloody ages at Sincil Bank, preceded the second win of the season for... well, for Darlington actually, as they won 2-0 at Sincil Bank. A City performance acknowledged by all those 'lucky' enough to see it as the worst for over 30 years. Considering we'd been relegated out of the League in that time it was certainly an achievement!

D-Day for Wicks came ironically at Scarborough, from where he'd been sacked in strange circumstances some months earlier. Rumours were rife that he was going to get the bullet whatever the result. The fans sang their hearts out throughout the second half and the team responded, keeping their first clean sheet. Pity we couldn't have scored but perhaps we'd turned the corner. The board didn't agree and Steve Wicks was sacked after 42 days, leaving the club adrift at the bottom of the League.

Strange as it seems most supporters felt they had acted too hastily and left the board in no doubt as to what they thought of the decision. True, we hadn't won a League game since the first match, but the team were trying to play football, if a little unsuccessfully, and no one wanted to return to the hit and hope we'd been subjected to under Sam Ellis. And let's face it, 42 days was never going to be enough time for Wicks to turn things around, especially considering the mess he'd inherited. nevertheless the decision had been made and Steve Wicks replacement, as City began a new game entitled 'manager for a month', was John Beck.

Third Third: October 21st '95 - present day

The name John Beck instantly struck terror into the hearts of most of us. Having witnessed an unattractive, hopeless style of football under Ellis, we had at least seen our team try to play a passing game under Wicks. But now we had the self-confessed king of route-one football making chalk marks on the coaching blackboard - it was not a thought we relished.

However, despite all JB's negative press it soon became clear why the fans at Cambridge and Preston owed him a lot. Within weeks he had turned Lincoln City around. OK, a lot of what we saw was not pretty but when you are bottom of a very poor Division, points are all that matter. Again new players were brought in: Richardson, Holmes, Ainsworth and Fleming all came from Preston (who obviously didn't miss them!), Robertson from Wigan, Whitney from Huddersfield and Barnet from Wolves. Later came Alcide from Emley and Bos from Ysselmeervogels (some non-league outfit in Holland) as virtually all traces of the Ellis and Wicks teams were removed. Indeed by the end of the campaign 39 different players had been used, only two of whom (Minett, Onwere and Huckerby) appeared with any regularity under all three managers.

A defeat and a draw were the first results under Beck, until on November 1st City won again, 2-1 at Mansfield, aided by the fact that the Stags played with nine men for half of the game! Never mind, we'd won and celebrated in style.

Joe Allon returned to haunt us by scoring for Hartlepool at the Bank, thus cancelling out a goal by Darren Huckerby. A young lad, Huckerby had come through the ranks and the fans loved him. Inevitably a lower division talent attracts one of the big boys, but it is still felt that the eventual £500,000 that Newcastle will have to shell out for Darren will represent a real bargain. That night, whilst Huckerby carried on up the A1, City stopped a little further down and won at Darlington in the AWS.

The FA Cup came and went with a 5-0 thumping at Stockport before a mini revival took place. Between mid-November and mid-February only two League games were lost as the gap at the bottom was at first closed on Torquay and then a cushion built over them. Ainsworth became the new darling of the fans for his commitment and attitude, whilst Grant Brown, the club's longest serving player, rediscovered the form he showed when he first arrived some seven years earlier, becoming an immovable force at the back. True, the big hoof was evident, but when it was played properly it made for really exciting stuff. Problem is that sometimes it didn't work and then the games were bloody terrible!

The AWS dream died at Rotherham in January but a bigger disappointment awaited at Bury on February 17th. The Imps had only conceded 11 goals in the previous 14 games. Bury got seven in one afternoon. Sam Ellis must have laughed his socks off!! Rather than unsettle the side, they responded positively and took seven points from the next three games, including a highly enjoyable 3-2 win at Scunthorpe with a winner right at the death. Happy days for Johnny Beck's army complete with drummer! The man had got Lincoln folk talking about their football team, and in Lincoln that is no small feat.

The Scunthorpe game was the last for another of the club's young talents as Derby swooped to pay £300,000 for Matt Carbon. Within a few weeks he was playing for England U21's and starring in Derby's crunch game with Palace. What would the big clubs do without the little ones?

With relegation now just a fading memory, a run of indifferent results and performances led to some divided feelings in the stands. John Beck decided to experiment with players in different positions and some plainly didn't work. After paying good money to watch some poor games, people got frustrated. At one or two games frustration turned to anger (Hartlepool away - Allon bagged two goals in a 3-0 defeat) and calls were made for Beck to resign. There's no pleasing some folk.

In the end a 5-0 drubbing of an abysmal Torquay (they could easily have been us!) meant we went into the summer feeling more cheerful, but the question remains... Are we any nearer having a team to match the superb surroundings at Sincil Bank?

Fanzine Facts

Deranged Ferret's name came about an infamous comment about his team made by ex-City manager Colin Murphy in a Saint & Greavsie interview: "You really can do what you like with them during the week and you really can say what you like to them at a team talk. Now if that makes them run around like deranged ferrets for an hour and a half you've done the job, haven't you? Because they win!" The immortal words had been uttered, and the seed was sown.

The mag hit the terraces in August 1989, and after a brief *DF*-less gap, it was relaunched at the beginning of '94-95 by Kevin Stow and Gary Parle due to popular demand. According to Gary, John Beck is one of their 700 regulars, and thinks it's a good read.

DONCASTER ROVERS

Doncaster Rovers

Well, what a good start! The main stand was badly damaged by arsonists, the major shareholder threatened to pull the plug on the youth policy and the reserve side, and the Rovers and the council were no nearer to finding common ground over getting a new stadium. Not to mention winding up orders and players coming and going. Still, despite all the problems, wild horses couldn't stop me getting my season ticket.

Certainly the pre-season fixtures were mouth-watering: Selby Town, Harrogate, Tamworth and Hinckley with the prospect of the lucrative Yorkshire Electricity Cup against Bradford and Scarborough, the latter fixture being doubled up with the opening League fixture as the pitch wasn't ready in time. But would you credit it, we actually won the damn thing! 'Spose we'll have to buy a trophy cabinet now. The last time we won anything, Labour were in government and Wimbledon were wombling around the Southern League.

We started quite well with a good win against Scarborough. But we were soon back to our old ways, out of the Coca Cola Cup at the hands of Shrewsbury. At least we can take pride in not being slaughtered like we usually are, only going out on the away goal rule. So to our first away game, a trip down to the English Riviera, Torquay, on what was the hottest day of the year. We had to have the heaters on full blast on the bus after it overheated, got stuck in a 25 mile traffic jam, and arrived at the ground with five minutes to spare. Not even time for a drink at what must be the best social club in the League - The Boots & Laces. But it was well worth it; a good 2-1 victory even with ex-gull Duane Darby being dismissed, much to the approval of the home crowd (biased buggers!).

And soon after this trek came another example of the good old Football League's sensible fixture allocation. Away to Fulham and Plymouth within four days! I was shattered by the trips, and both times had to creep into the house at 4am without disturbing the missus (very difficult). So was it any wonder that they both ended in convincing defeats, and yet another sending off?

We were still missing a proven goalscorer, but this didn't stop Gary 'Sumo' Brabin from notching a classic goal against Northampton in the next match. This was followed by a good thumping from Rochdale 3-0, which up to February was the only failure at fortress Belle Vue.

We made the trip down to Barry Hearn's Orient, where Gob-on-a-stick Eric Hall was guest of honour, and an Orient supporter shaved his head at half time in honour of their first away win in 18 months at Northampton. I bet his hair's half-way down his back by now. It's got to be said, they've got the world's most annoying tannoy announcer, and our irritation was complete when we went three goals down.

Talk about going from one extreme to another! The following week it was Chester City, top of the League and unbeaten at home. What did we do? Win 3-0. It was also the first outing this season of the Supporters Club football team; we got walloped 9-4!!

Having put up with Robo-Gills (surely the Division's most robust and physical side), we faced Champions-elect Preston, in what many described as the best match of the season. Trust me to miss it! Weddings should be banned in the football season!

All in all, things weren't going too badly, and we were looking like promotion candidates ourselves. Then it was off to Mansfield in the FA Cup. We just knew it wasn't to be our day when our supporters team played *Follow The Yellow Brick Road* and lost 17-0, and we were lucky to get nil! I still claim to this day that the 14th goal was offside! The afternoon game finished 4-2 to Mansfield, so our FA Cup dreams had gone for another season. At least we bounced back to beat Colchester 3-2. The same can't be said about the supporters football team. We sailed into Wigan's Spanish Armada and got walloped by their fanzine *Steady Nigel* 8-1 (still, at least we were getting better).

Our dreams of the Twin Towers evaporated as we surrendered a goal lead to Notts County in the AWS. Well, at least there was still the League to aim at. Think again!

After several more promises of a new ground came to nothing, Christmas came and went, and then we signed a goalscorer from Hearts, Colin Cramb. Three wins on the trot put us up to fourth in the League, with our new player scoring some cracking goals. After Torquay on the hottest day, we went to Cardiff on what must've been the coldest, and yes, you've guessed it. The supporters coach had no heating, and as the game had to kick off at 1.00 so as not to clash with the England/Wales rugby, we couldn't even have a drink. The 3-2 defeat was the start of our demise.

More bad results seemed to kill off the players' confidence, and the management's insistence on playing people out of position and swapping the team about did nothing to help matters. After Mickey Adams' Fulham gave us a football lesson, morale seemed to be at rock bottom, and not just with the players. The fans were getting slated in the local press for lack of support, but with players coming and going and having to put up with the worst ground in the Football League, we couldn't help but agree with visiting supporters' chants of "shit ground, no fans."

At least a victory over rivals Scunthorpe seemed to paper over the cracks; we had slid from fourth to 15th in less than two months. Things didn't help when the major shareholder was arrested at the home game with Mansfield, allegedly in connection with the main stand fire. Another lacklustre performance at Hereford wasn't helped by the 'jobsworth' stewards of the season, who refused to let four of us leave the stand to join the 60 or so other fans on the terraces on a cold Tuesday night.

So it was off to Preston and a rousing 12,000+ crowd, including a good 400-strong following from Donny, but we still couldn't find the net. If only we had a ground like that - they had more fans in the souvenir shop than we get at home! In the meantime we signed our fifth player from Torquay this season (all that's left now are the palm trees and the beach, and we're still discussing terms on them). Gillingham were next at Belle Vue, and although not as physical this time, 'fortune' shone on them as Leo headed off 'west' with the points (clever, huh?).

Our end of season run-in seemed to involve all the promotion contenders, and our luck had indeed changed. Barnet were next to visit the Rovers (I didn't realise they had that many fans; they nearly outnumbered us), and a late, late winning goal by super-sub Ian Clarke wrapped up the points. A quick trip up the M18 to sunny Scunny awaited. This was a cracker of a match, both 'keepers having a nightmare, but after two belting goals by Colin Cramb and one equally as good by Scunthorpe's Clarkson, the game ended 2-2. Then the Spanish Armada sailed back into town. The day started well, when we actually drew 0-0 with *Steady Nigel*, our first scoreless draw in

13 seasons of playing against other supporters. The main match started as normal, as Rovers went a goal down very early on, but a very dubious penalty on the stroke of half time saw us equalise. Then we did something that we had not done for well over two years, since Sammy Chung was manager, we won a game after being a goal behind. Our luck had *definitely* changed, but oh, too late!

We finished the season down at Layer Road, Colchester. Fancy dress was supposed to be the order of the day, but only muggins on our bus, and a dozen lads and lasses on the travel club bus took the plunge. But it was a lovely warm day and a few beers slipped down nicely, as we hoped to dent their play-off bid. But a floater over our 'keeper on half time settled the issue and they were in the play-off spot. It was good to see the Colchester fans and players acknowledged by the Rovers supporters, and vice-versa. A stop off at Grantham for fish and chips and a few more beers gave us time to reflect on a season that had promised so much, but which had petered out with very little fight. But when you play 40 players over the season, what else do you expect?

Footnote. What a close season so far: the reserve team and the youth policy have been scrapped, so no more selling our best young players for much-needed cash. The plans for a new ground were scuppered, resurrected then scuppered again. There are more new shirts to fork out for. There is talk of scrapping the club's crest, and winding up petitions still loom large. Ever get the feeling of *déjà vu*? You Premier League supporters just don't know how lucky you are! Well, next season may be our last, and I'm just off to get my season ticket. I can't wait. Roll on August 12th!

Fanzine Facts

The above piece was put together by Paul Mayfield, a lifelong Doncaster Rovers fan, who couldn't bear the thought of another issue of *SOTF* without a Donny article. The last Doncaster fanzine, *Raise The Roof*, closed over two years ago, but there are moves afoot to get a new mag going in the near future.

DRIBBLE!

Ipswich Town

It had to be better than '95-96, or did it? Burley was still the fan's choice as manager and all the blame on last season's relegation was put at the feet of John Lyall and his ex-Hammers cronies. But how long would they give George to turn things round?

What had hurt more than the relegation itself was that people outside Ipswich had been glad to see us go down. Whereas in the past we were always looked upon as a football team who played the game the way it should be played, and were a friendly club with one of the best playing surfaces to boot, now no-one outside of Suffolk cried when we sank. Most other fans were glad to the back of us, and even the pitch was now crap!

After a very quiet pre-season, the only arrival being another in the long line of Dutchmen to make the short journey across the North Sea (a flying winger Gus Uhlenbeek), the talk was not of promotion but rather of whether we could be sure of not doing a Swindon and going straight down again.

We kicked off with a defeat at Birmingham but Gus showed some promise. We then hit a purple patch with victories over Sunderland, Stoke and Palace; little did we know then that they would all finish above us. I was out of the country for the Sunderland game but a phonecall from my dad informed me that the Mathie hat-trick had flattered us and Sunderland were the best team we'd played. Good judge, my old man. Things were looking good but the end of September saw a heavy home defeat by Charlton, aided by us only having ten on the pitch, and was followed by further home defeats by Wolves and Luton. All talk of promotion evaporated and we were one of only a handful of clubs whose crowds were dropping. We needed a new cause to brighten up our a season. The new Holy Grail was the Anglo Italian; the two trips to Italy brought back fond memories of past Euro glory, and even after the club declined to organise trips to Italy, many Town fans made the long journey and were rewarded with two fine displays: a 2-2 draw with Brescia and a 1-0 win in Brian Roy's old stamping ground Foggia. The *Dribble!* team made their way via Rome, the Italians gobsmacked that people would come this far for what they considered a meaningless game. But the fans, like the local paper, could see this comp as a big moral booster and a money spinner, especially with a trip to the twin towers on offer. The club even got into the swing of things.

They reduced the cost of admission for the home games and were rewarded by large crowds (for Anglo Italian matches anyway). But alas, when we could see that a trip to Wembley was on, the team started to improve in the League and the semi-final against Port Vale was seen as an unwanted distraction. Out we went, leaving Town followers well let down and the owners of Wembley probably considering suicide.

The home defeats in the League should've put us out of contention, but if nothing else Endsleigh One was inconsistent and unpredictable. You only had to look at Millwall who dropped faster than a Tory MP's trousers, and Sheffield United and Port Vale who strung together a few results and took off the other way. So come the New Year we were still in with a chance of the play-offs.

We then had our best result of the season in the Cup replay at Blackburn. Alan Shearer had been pretty scathing of Ipswich in '96 saying we were the only easy game in the Premier. So it was no surprise when plenty of Shearer jokes started doing the rounds of the Ipswich pubs: "There are no easy games in the FA Cup, other than Blackburn", "There are no easy International matches, unless you're marking Alan Shearer." This one is all the rage in Hong Kong as well. There were two other great things to savour about the win: firstly our support at Ewood was awesome, especially when you consider that Rovers couldn't even sell their allocation for the first game; second was the display of our 18 year old and Ipswich-born keeper, Richard Wright. A truly magnificent performance kept Uncle Jack's multi million pound strike force at bay all evening and the clean sheet was richly deserved. In fact Richard kept his place in the team over Canadian Craig Forrest and was even invited to train with Venables and the England team - it was a great honour for him to be able to train with the likes of Flowers and Seaman, something that normally only happens to Spurs players!

Despite our improving League form we were easily beaten by Villa in the fifth round of the Cup. Yet this hiccup didn't stop some other great wins and the arrival of Tony Mowbray tightened things up at the back. After a slow start he impressed everyone with his commitment, especially when he helped us beat Port Vale in the League on the anniversary of his wife's tragic death from cancer. The fighting spirit of the team was seen in most games, none more so when we came back from the brink to draw 3-3 at Barnsley. The only problem was that your name had to begin with M to score, Mathie, Marshall, Milton and Mason. Gus Uhlenbeek did manage to thump in a cracker at Watford in the turnip's return. The massed ranks of the media, slavering for a headline, were given an easy night as the Dutchman's goal helped us come back from two goals down to win 3-2 and spoil the Vicarage Road party.

At this point the play-offs looked a certainty, but home defeats to Reading and Tranmere left us having to win our last home game against Millwall. The problem was that the Lions had got themselves in such a pile of crap that they also needed a win. The resulting 0-0 did neither of us any good. So, an anti-climax and a season that finally finished on a sour note as the Millwall 'fans' ripped out the seats in the stand to hurl at the police, the second time Town has witnessed Millwall at their worst.

So we're left with the prospect of another year in the First, but at least pride was restored: we scored more goals than any other team in our Division; we stuffed Alan Shearer's words down his throat; the young lads like Wright and Scowcroft *done* well; the Argentinean Tarrico looked the part, and if Gus can learn to cross we've found yet another Dutch bargain; Claus Thomsen will play for Denmark in Euro 96 and it looks like Mathie and Marshall will still be here next year.

Oh, and what of Norwich? Well, they were crap, lost a good manager but unluckily for Ipswich they eventually got rid of Robert Chase. He will be dearly missed by all Ipswich. Also thanks must go to Bryan Gunn for his help in securing our derby win at Portman Road, it went a little way to making up for yet another ref-inspired home win at their place.

So we look forward to next year, but there will be one player missing; at 38 John Wark has eventually decided to hang up his boots. Even as he approaches 40 he still oozes class and my highlight of the season was his great free kick at home to Leicester. It just goes to show how much football has changed in the money stakes when a player like David Platt, who admittedly also has the knack of getting from midfield to score, is now a millionaire, but he is a but pale shadow of Warky at his best; thanks for the memories John.

Fanzine Facts

Dribble! was started at the start of the '88-89 season by Alasdair Ross and Dave Sheddon. Dave has since moved onto greater things (Hartlepool's *Monkey Business*). The fanzine is now run by Alasdair but with considerable help from the rest of the Ross family. They have contributions from all over the world and this year have had regular articles on Italian and Northern Ireland football. The other main contributor is Paddy Lillistone whose highlight of this particular season will always be Gunn's mishap; as Paddy said "it couldn't have happened to a nicer team."

THE EASTERN EAGLES

Crystal Palace

Outfoxed on the day

A new season dawned on August 12th 1995 and despite a few months to get over the pains of relegation, turmoil still remained. New Palace manager Ray Lewington not only had to pick up the club's spirits but he was still having to contest a dressing-room battle with some of his players, still peeved with chairman Ron Noades after his treatment of previous boss Alan Smith. Three key players had already gone: Armstrong, Southgate and Salako, together with several other fringe players. Of the 14 that faced Barnsley that opening day, eight were on (or about to go on) the transfer list at their own request. When you consider this disillusionment it makes the events of the latter part of the season all the more remarkable.

During the summer break, Lewington had set out to change Palace's direct style of play that had remained in one form or other since the Coppell days. Quite frankly, it had lost some of its attraction and effectiveness, and its demise had been partly brought about by the desire of the fans themselves. Lewington set out to have the ball played out from the back and to have players who could both hold the ball and possess good ground skills. As if to demonstrate to the supporters the type of players he demanded for this renaissance period, he purchased a rather skilful forward from the lower divisions in Barnet's Dougie Freedman, and sold the rather popular (but poor in technique) Iain Dowie. The manager recognised that in selling his centre forwards there left a lack of height and power up front, so he brought in the much-rated 'aerial king' Gareth Taylor (raved about by then Welsh boss Bobby Gould as "one of the best headers of the ball in the game") to strengthen our resolve.

New faces in the side, poor application by those on the transfer list and key injuries to Roberts and Rodger saw Palace stutter over the first third of the season, and by November, we were 20th in the Division. The chairman reacted by getting rid of the two main 'rebels' Coleman and Shaw, arguably our two best outfield players at the time, for reduced valuations. Significantly, the team started to gain more consistency but despite the efforts of Freedman and Dyer we were largely woeful up front, and by Christmas we were still hovering above the relegation zone. Particularly upsetting were some of the performances at Selhurst Park; the first 12 home games producing only 13 points, and booing became commonplace as the frustrations showed. Lewington seemed unable to lift the players and Gareth Taylor was having a nightmare in front of goal.

The Christmas period brought a brief resurgence of fortunes with three successive away wins (we always seem less inhibited on our travels). Unfortunately we immediately returned to our old ways, drawing four games on the trot and being dumped out of the Cup by Port Vale, one of the few teams we'd managed to beat during the early part of the season.

Languishing in 16th place, on February 7th Ron Noades made his move and appointed Dave Bassett as manager, Lewington being moved to first team coach. Bassett's instructions were simple: Avoid relegation.

The new boss changed little of our playing style. The passing game was retained despite initial concerns that 'Harry' was a long-ball specialist, but more urgency was brought into the build-up. One of Bassett's first tasks was the dropping and subsequent selling of 'aerial king' Taylor to Sheffield United. Taylor had managed just one goal in 20 League appearances and was fast becoming a laughing stock. The re-introduction of George Ndah's pace to the forward line (he was almost sold to Bournemouth in the early part of the season but thankfully they couldn't raise the fee!) was a significant factor, as was Harry's bubbly personality and confidence. Not only was he beginning to motivate the players, but even we began to believe that anything was possible. Palace was a team reborn.

Six consecutive home wins and only one loss in 11 games saw The Eagles storm the Division to reach third place by mid-March; a distant dream was fast becoming a reality - Palace in the play-offs?

Not satisfied, Bassett started to turn the screw on an increasingly wobbly Derby, lying above us in second place. In the run-in, we maintained our impressive away form with three successive away victories against strugglers Millwall, Reading and Wolves. Crucially however, our home form was beginning to slip once more. Two draws against Portsmouth and Port Vale (the latter after being 2-0 up) was followed by a loss (ironically against Leicester), giving Derby the daylight between us that they needed. When the crunch came at the Baseball Ground, Derby's greater will and desire saw them though and we were left with the lottery of the play-offs.

The last game, played before the largest home attendance of the season, was insignificant and Palace took the opportunity to blood some young players. Unfortunately, our regular centre half Davies got himself sent off for two rash challenges and his subsequent suspension from the play-off final was to prove costly.

Palace travelled to fellow South London rivals Charlton for the first leg of the play-off semi, were simply awful in the first half and were lucky to go in 1-0 down. A half-time rollicking by Bassett saw a more committed performance and we ended the game 2-1 victors, the winning goal coming from the unlikely Carl Veart, part of the deal that saw Taylor go to Sheffield United.

The home leg was packed out and the tie virtually decided in the first few minutes by a lovely goal from Ray Houghton, playing a more influential role under Bassett (in the first part of the season he was totally lacking in inspiration). Charlton pressed forward as we shut up shop and played a dangerous containing game. Several near misses and one shot off the line, but Palace's gamble paid off - we were at Wembley. However, the warning signs were there. Most could see that we were now only playing in fits and starts, and our 20 goal Dougie Freedman was suffering a poignant loss of form.

The final at Wembley was a sea of red and blue balloons; hope and optimism were abundant. It was a chance for both teams to wipe out the pain and misery of recent relegation. I'm sure that had Palace played to their full potential they would have seen off the in-form Leicester side. OK, we missed the suspended Davies and his fellow injured defenders Anderson and Gordon, but apart from the odd moment of brilliance we could not recapture our earlier form. Despite going ahead early in the first half through an Andy Roberts goal, we could not muster much pressure and we created too few chances. Leicester were on top for most of the game and deservedly equalised through a penalty to force extra time. Both sides tired noticeably in those final 30 minutes, and Palace had one eye on the penalties (the other on Leicester's substitution in the last minute as they brought on a specialist penalty saver) when in the dying seconds ex-Palace player Steve Claridge stole in and mis-hit a shot off his shins which ballooned into the net. Leicester were through.

Devastated, we trudged out of Wembley. Another season finally over. For six months we had been ordinary, and perhaps our past had simply caught up with us. After our dismal early showing, the trip to the Twin Towers was a bonus - but to get so close only to lose was really painful.

Post-match talk on the coach home was on the usual subjects that accompany such an ending: individual performances, players who might go, the year as a whole, but my thoughts lay with Leicester and I gave them a few private thanks. We all want to play in the Premier but there's no point in going if all you do is stay nine months, and we must build a team that can stay there. Things happened too fast and another year in Division One will perhaps give us the backbone to succeed. So, thanks Leicester, for despite the pain and sorrow you've inflicted, you've stopped us being the Bolton of next season!

Fanzine Facts

Now the oldest Palace fanzine, *The Eastern Eagles* was launched in 1991 and is about to enter its sixth season. It started life as a newsletter for Palace exiles living in East Anglia. *TEE* founder Trevor Edwards still pieces the fanzine together as well as running the group. Trevor says that the group now has over 100 members (113 to be exact) and in March released a record entitled "We all follow the Palace." Its three songs depict the ups and downs of the last 25 years and has to date sold a whopping 500 copies.

EXCEEDINGLY GOOD PIES

Rochdale

Rochdale managed to break a couple of club records during '95-96. Since joining the Football League in 1921, this was the first time that we'd managed to concede just two goals or less in every League away game. The other record we broke was the one concerning our previous 100% success rate at Anfield. This was spectacularly smashed as Liverpool beat us by seven lucky goals to our gallant nil. Oh, and there's one more record we set: we're still the longest surviving members of the basement Division. This year we extended the record to a staggering 21 consecutive seasons in football's shit-hole. We are the Arsenal of the Third Division, and just as they set a new record every year by remaining in the top flight, we extend ours at the other end of the spectrum. Mind you, we do play better football!

It all began with some pessimism, which is actually quite unusual at Rochdale. Pre-season optimism is what keeps the faithful going between September and May. The main trouble at Spotland last summer was the lack of new players. We all knew that the squad wasn't good enough to win us promotion, so we hoped the manager would unearth a few nuggets from footballing backwaters (which to Rochdale means part-timers). Manager Docherty did manage to bring in the excellent goalkeeper Ian Gray for £20,000, but Gray was already known to us due to a loan spell the previous season. He also secured the services of Dean Martin but he too had already been on loan. The squad had no new faces until Docherty signed heavyweight Ian Tompstone (quickly nicknamed Tombstone, Twentystone, Thumpstone etc. by supporters) and someone called Jason Hardy. He was so incompetent his first name should have been Fool. With two such 'notable' signings, confidence was never likely to boom, but we hadn't counted on the one real ability Docherty has as a manager.

Over the previous few seasons, hardened Dale fans were regularly frustrated at players' failure to consistently fulfil their potential. Docherty managed to develop numerous good-ish players: Kevin Formby, an erratic left back, suddenly came of age until an injury in January ended his season. Jason Peake, obviously gifted, suddenly started to run games and score goals from midfield until he had to replace Formby at left back. John Deary, who had looked rather idle after joining us from Burnley, began to keep the Rochdale engine room purring contentedly on a regular basis. He would have been ever-present but for a spate of suspensions for being a dirty git. 'Once a Claret Bastard always a...' as the saying goes! Ian Gray did the business in goal until injury in December ended his involvement, whilst Paul Butler was a rock in defence. Steve Whitehall scored a personal best of 25 goals, and younger players like Dave Bayliss and Alex Russell came into the League scene and excelled. Most of all though was the re-emergence of Mark Stuart, who responded to a threatened move to Chesterfield by scoring a rake of goals and creating many more, as he coupled his natural ability with a desire to work hard. Injury in November deprived us of his services and when he returned in mid-January his bottle seemed to have gone.

So why did we end up having such a crap season? That is a question I could provide a long and boring answer to - and tempted as I am to do so, I won't. Suffice to say that from a squad of 20 players, 10 were goodun's and the others were so bad that had they played in every game, the Football League would have allowed Stevenage Borough promotion as an act of mercy to Rochdale. It didn't help when Docherty, 'a weak man' as one player described him, changed his footballing philosophies to a long-ball game after the 7-0 defeat at Anfield. It didn't help when he proved to be 'tactfully inept', as another player called him. It didn't help when Docherty's training sessions were so weak that a player referred to them as a 'piece of piss'. Indeed, some training sessions drew an attendance of at least six or seven players. Where were the others? And of course it didn't help that three or four quality players were consistently missing from the first team from Christmas onwards. This meant the regular inclusion of duffers, although many fans suspect that some of these would have been regulars anyway. The Doc doesn't always pick his best team you know! Prankster that he is!!

Given the above, it's not surprising we were fourth in the League by November, but finished 15th in May. A 12 match mid-season run without a win scuppered any play-off hopes, and we thought it might have scuppered the manager's job too. Not so; he has done "an excellent job" according to the board. If only we were all so easily pleased...

It is better to remember the good things though, like the 5-3 home win against Rotherham in the FA Cup. It still amuses me when the local rag refers to Dale's mighty humiliation of 'high-flying' Rotherham. Since when was fourth bottom in Division Two 'high flying' over fourth top in Division Three? Still, the victory was very sweet and Jason Peake's two goals will always be remembered by every Dale fan there. Match of the Day decided to avoid Spotland on that occasion, so those two strikes were never entered onto the Goal of the Month competition... And you thought Tony Yeboah's goals were good!

There were other glorious home victories, against Exeter, Hartlepool and a 3-1 victory in a super game against Cambridge. Away victories came thick and fast with wins at Darlington, Doncaster, Lincoln and Scunthorpe. The best away experience though came at Darlington in the FA Cup second leg replay, when we knew the winners would face Liverpool. The tension travelling up to Darls was immense and the stakes during the game were so high we felt our stomachs churning every time they entered our half. Then, ten minutes from time, our right winger Dave Thompson set his own personal best by beating his man, *and* putting over a GOOD cross. Time stopped. Nearly 10,000 eyes watched the ball as Dean Martin (no, not the crooner who died) headed home. Bedlam... Pandemonium... Orgy... Our end had it all. Ten minutes later we had it again. Driving home on the cold December night was wonderful; at times we could hardly speak - we were all quietly wetting ourselves with joy!

The peak of our season had been reached, and now everything went downhill very quickly. Depressing football and depressing results. The mediocrity of the previous term came back in an all-too-familiar pattern. The spectre of '94-95 taunted us, reminding us of our pre-season pessimism and making us criticise the players, the management and the board saying, "we told you so." The good start was put there, it seems, to magnify the frustration and bitterness that the season finally brought. Some of us are thankful at least for the joyous Autumn. Others are worried that the joyous Autumn will prolong the careers of some people at Spotlands who will never be able to link that success to an equally joyous Christmas and Spring.

As April ended a good clear-out of the club's playing staff was needed. This would make room for a further six or seven players to complement the good ten that we already had. Unfortunately, not all the deadwood has been shifted, and to cap it all Docherty has offered a contract to previous crowd favourite Dave Lancaster who is now older and a lot less mobile, fit and eager. Resting some of next season's striking hopes on Lancaster is further proof (if any were needed) that Docherty, for all his good points, just hasn't the ability to build a promotion-winning outfit at a club like Rochdale. His job description, we presume, reads along the lines of 'win us promotion but there's no money in the transfer kitty'. Some managers can do this if they can spot potential in raw recruits, but Docherty doesn't have this talent. Every now and then he'll get a Deary or a Gray but he spent £45,000 on those two. There is no money available so we expect the stream of Thompsons, Hardys and Shaws to continue. Just as we ended last year's article in *SOTF*, there is plenty of doom and gloom about and pessimism will be prevalent next August unless a lottery winner comes forward.

However, I refuse to end on a sour note. Rochdale actually broke yet another record last season. We won our first ever game in London in October when we beat Barnet 4-0, and I was there. Oh bugger it, I *will* end on a sour note. In April, Barnet beat us at Spotland 4-0. And that is a true reflection of a season of two halves.

Fanzine Facts

As ever, *Exceedingly Good Pies* has chronicled the course of The Good Ship Dale during the season. The first issue of '96-97 will be forging ahead under new leadership, as editor Francis Collins retires his post as standard-bearer, and the fanzine will continue under the watchful glares of Matt Smith and Mark Wilbraham. Francis adds that "ever since *EGP* donated £300 to the players' Christmas 'do', they've been shit. We would like to point out that this £300 was not a 'bung' to make the team play badly in order to give us something to moan about, and in no way can we be held responsible for the team's loss of form. Having said that, bollocks to them next Christmas; they can go chippy like the rest of us!"

EXILED

AFC Bournemouth

After the excitement of the Great Escape, optimism was high for '95-96. The Cherries had a settled team that had shown Championship form in the second half of the previous season, and the confidence in the young team was evident with some classy pre-season performances against Crystal Palace, West Ham and Steau Bucharest. The good form continued into the new campaign and after the first Saturday in September, AFCB were joint second in the League and also had a fizzy Cup victory over Luton under their belts.

The best performance was the 3-0 defeat of Peterborough with Steve Jones scoring a hat-trick. A stylish win at Wycombe, who for some reason prefer playing with ten men, was followed by four points from home games with Rotherham and Wrexham (why does Rooster Russell always score against us?). Steve Jones didn't add to his tally against Rotherham and so failed to equal our goalscoring record of hitting the net in six successive games for the club. Still, his seven goals were good enough to make him the top scorer in all four divisions. After five games we had ten points - last year it took 23 matches to notch up that total!

But could we mount a serious challenge? Maybe not. Steve Jones continued to spread fear in defensive ranks; his opener at Blackpool was particularly Yeboah-esque - come to think about it even Tony would have envied that strike - but we still lost. Ten man Notts County, courtesy of two Devon 'Hand of God' White goals, finished us off at Meadow Lane. At least County laid on some excellent pre-match entertainment that was better than the game, and not just because the Bournemouth kids won the sprint relay. No, it was apparent even at this early stage that our blokes were being knocked off the ball too easily and the team needed a bigger physical presence to cope with such strong sides.

However, the Crewe match had little to do with the size of the players and everything to do with the man in the middle. No words can do justice to the refereeing that we witnessed. It takes a lot to turn the affable Dean Court crowd into a seething mob but rookie ref Barry Knight achieved this following an unbelievably inept display. We had seven players booked and incurred two disgraceful sendings off whilst Crewe received no cards. They were also awarded a dodgy penalty and given the first goal after keeper Ian Andrews was charged (Pathe News style) whilst holding the ball. The 4-0 League defeat was the biggest at home for 20 years. Crewe's manager Dario Gradi must have witnessed the amazing sight of Mel Machin leading the slow hand clap from the dugout; we certainly did, so it was even harder to swallow when he defended the ref. A large police presence restricted the crowd's anger to merely inflicting damage on Knight's car.

The defeat by Crewe and a penalties defeat by Watford in the Coca Cola Cup ushered in a disappointing period. Injuries to key players were an element; Steve Fletcher (last season's Player of the Year) was out for virtually the whole campaign, as was the promising play-maker Scott Mean. Tactics seemed to change as well. Machin felt a more counter-attacking style would bring success. As a result Steve Jones was often deployed as the lone striker up front, while wingers Brissett and impressive newcomer John Bailey were played very deep. Crowds dipped alarmingly to create severe cash flow problems later on. One highlight however was AFCB's first live appearance on terrestrial TV, as Meridian showed our clash with Brighton. A 3-1 win was slightly soured by Brighton's rent-a-mob element in their crowd who held up play following a pitch invasion.

As the Cherries concentrated on keeping things tight at the back, Neil Moss took over the No.1 shirt replacing the injured Ian Andrews, and proceeded to equal the club record of seven successive clean sheets. Another key player in this fine run was a youngster on loan from Chelsea, the 'unknown' Mike Duberry. He was fantastic and it was rumoured we were poised to sign him for £150,000 when Chelsea had an injury crisis, recalled him and threw him into the side to face Leeds. The rest is history... Moss' last clean sheet was at Bristol City, where apologies should be extended to the home side for their defeat that night. We could've lost 8-0 but sneaked it by the only goal! The magic of the FA Cup!

Our rock-like defensive displays saw the Cherries in tenth place by mid November, reasonably placed for the play-offs. Leaders Swindon were lucky to take a point off us as we turned in a silky performance. Then, as so often in this game, things got sticky; with Duberry departed, several injuries picked up and Jones' goals dried up the team began to look weak. So it was no surprise when in the space of five days we were dumped out of the Auto Windscreens Shield by Bristol Rovers and the FA Cup by cheesy Brentford at Dean Court. At least it provided youngsters such as Eddie Howe, Michael Dean and Ali Santos with a taste of first team football. The following week saw a dreadful 2-0 defeat at Brighton and fears of another relegation battle. However a couple of good home wins, with Steve Jones returning to his scoring ways, settled the side into a comfortable mid-table spot by Christmas. Less comfortable were the finances of the club. Brilliant goalkeeper Neil Moss was sold to Southampton for £250k to ease the cash flow.

Such is the tightness of the Division that by the end of January, AFCB, boosted by the return of Scott Mean, were in seventh place. The highlight was an amazing 5-4 win at Peterborough. We fought back from 3-1 down to level at 3-3, only to go 4-3 behind before Steve Jones scored twice in the final six minutes to secure the points. The winner was a spectacular shot on the turn from 25 yards that flew in to the net. Unhappily we only won two of our next 11 games to slide back down the table. So much of our interest focused on new goalkeeper Jimmy Glass's eccentricity and on the new stadium plans, especially the unpopular attempt by the football club to build a new stand on the site of the current supporters club. In fact things got so heated at one particular public meeting that the chairman's Jag was firebombed - an action roundly condemned by genuine fans! Away supporters will be pleased to note that the proposed ground will accommodate a pub on a corner, given the difficulty in finding pubs in the area. However, the bad news is that not many of you are likely to get in over the next season as the capacity is temporarily reduced. Of course you could always stay in the pub.

Back on the pitch the side just couldn't score away from home. Prior to the Hull match at the start of March, the Cherries had only scored in one League game out of nine away. Well, it would have been two if we hadn't suffered with the refereeing against Crewe again! Two goals were disallowed: the first for a non-existent foul on the 'keeper; the second because the ref was having a laugh. On loan Chris Casper powered the ball home only for the referee to rule his header had hit the post. The ball had in fact thumped against the stanchion and come out, a fact that the referee admitted, apologising to Mel Machin once he had seen the replay. To rub salt into the wounds, Crewe snatched two late goals to seal an undeserved win. Do we not like Crewe!

Even the home form began to slip. The crowd were beginning to show signs of unrest; unhappy at team selection, especially when top midfielder Matty Holland was deployed at the back, leaving displaced defender Mark Morris to wander around midfield! Relegation fears once again began to mount but were eased through two wonder strikes from Matty Holland at Shrewsbury to give the Cherries three valuable points. In the remaining weeks we survived a winding up order by Customs and Excise, got some of our own refereeing luck against Bristol Rovers (God, they must hate playing us!) and finally secured our place in Endsleigh Two with a point at Burnley. At last, Matty Holland and Steve Robinson started scoring goals as well as Jonesy, who achieved his target of 20 goals for the season. West Ham fans bemoaned the loss of Jones but it is Matt (who swept the board in the various Player of the Season awards) that could be the one that they will regret.

It is difficult to sum up the season. It was pretty good to see Brighton relegated but it would have been brilliant if Southampton, Portsmouth and Reading had gone as well. Alas the trio all just escaped. It is easy to criticise the side but injuries played a big part. Half the team were out with long-term injuries and the club never got the extra striker that was needed following Steve Cotterill's retirement, hence a number of on-loan players (Cureton - he of green hair fame, Ndah and Scott) who added nothing to the team. At least we did win one honour, that of the quietest fans in the League! Even this was not really merited given the superb away following the team received yet again, and plenty of other clubs seemed to have less atmosphere than Dean Court this season (the tests certainly weren't conducted at the Crewe home match).

And stop press. The news that Steve Jones has been sold to West Ham, the down payment matching the amount of the VAT debt, does not augur well for next season. OK, the reserve side won their League and the performances of the Youth side gives some hope. The club also now have planning permission for the new ground but with the debt problems it is hard to believe it will be built. At least Millwall's relegation may save some of the demolition costs!

Fanzine Facts

The Exiles Club has about 180 members all around the world and aims to keep supporters, who live away from Bournemouth, in touch with AFC Bournemouth. Adrian Smith and Gordon Buchan produce the bi-monthly 40 page magazine *Exiled*, which is one of the longest running fanzines still in existence. The magazine contains interviews with players, match reports, general features and Mike Robins' review of media coverage in 'Pick of the Cherries'. The Exiles also arrange travel to games for Cherries supporters and offer exclusive merchandise.

FERRY 'CROSS THE WENSUM

Norwich City

Well, that was the season that wasn't, as far as the actual football goes anyway. On all other fronts NCFC, '95-96 produced yet another eventful turbulent year when just about anything that could happen did, including, thank God, the one thing we thought that would never come to pass; namely the resignation of one RT Chase.

At the start most people were pretty confident. Granted, Chase was still at the helm but if all his summer talk was to be believed then he'd learnt from his mistakes and was at least going to concentrate on our team rather than his ground. Martin O'Neill was a very popular choice as manager; he apparently had millions to spend and the team started the season in an assured and quietly impressively fashion.

That was about as good as it got though. Robert Fleck and Matthew Rush may have been bought for £1m, but the main bulk of the money O'Neill had been promised never materialised. This was highlighted in 'The Dean Windass Saga', a story so long I could fill this whole article with it alone. It had it all: sex, power, corruption (well, maybe not the sex). It was a story of a chairman not talking to his manager; a chairman trying to see a club go bust in order to get a freebie player; a chairman making decisions on things he always said he knew nothing about ('the football department') and basically the story of a man hell-bent on winding absolutely everyone up without getting anywhere. And the end result? Oh yes, our manager, the man who'd taken us to second in the table and installed us as favourites for the Championship, was finally forced out.

Martin O'Neill left out of sheer frustration at one man's drainage of our club. Surely no-one else would come and work under him? Step forward Gary Megson; reserve team manager at Bradford; a man Torquay United had turned down when he applied to be their manager; a man who after declaring that we had the best squad in the Division went on to nearly relegate us for the second time.

It was at this point that the INCSA called a boycott. It had been talked about for ages, but O'Neill leaving just proved to be the final straw. There was a huge protest after the Southend game on Boxing Day, where quite a bit of damage was done to the ground and quite a bit of scrapping was done amid the general chaos of a big snowstorm (a snowstorm we had driven through that afternoon whilst coming back from Sheffield especially for the protest).

Crowds dropped considerably with the boycott. Even with the cynical ploy of thousands of kids being offered £1 tickets at each game, according to the police there were several attendances of less than 10,000, even though the official crowds were higher than this (boycott-supporting season ticket holders were counted regardless). The poisonous atmosphere that was prevalent all around Carrow Road obviously didn't do the players any good either as they were knocked out of both Cups and embarked on yet another fantastic run of League defeats - most of these being greeted by a 'told you so' wry smile rather than tears from the majority of supporters. The club was in the shit, and with Chase's position getting weaker by the day, take-over bids started rolling in. Previous Chase supporters began jumping ship or if your name was Jimmy Jones (ex vice-chairman) you jumped and bid at the same time. His attempt to force an EGM failed when the shareholding supporters trust, formed in the 50's when fans saved the club from extinction, amazingly said it would support Chase rather than Jones. Later it emerged that they were pursuing a different strategy to get Chase out. Instead we had an AGM at which two major things happened: firstly, it was revealed that NCFC was massively in debt (anywhere between £5 and £10m), totally blowing out of the water Chase's main claim for staying on, i.e. that he was a good businessman (how can you turn a £12m transfer profit into a £5-£10m debt? - very dodgy). Secondly he revealed that he had received an 'acceptable offer' for his shares; this however was immediately made void by the emergence, at last, of the club's true financial position (he had previously refused to show potential buyers the books). That night though, a 1,000 strong crowd at St Andrews Hall thought they were celebrating the beginning of the end, little knowing that Chase still had it in him to attempt a further dismantling of the club by selling both our captain Jon Newsome and our leading scorer Ashley Ward for knock-down prices.

As various take-overs emerged then disappeared, the boycott was operating in a similar fashion, on and off. While all this was going on we just about struggled to keep out of the relegation zone, Bryan Gunn's fuck-up at Ipswich not helping us feel any better. It may sound a bit pathetic but I don't think I'll ever forgive him for that. They were just the most contrasting 20 minutes of my life: Ipswich fans running about on the pitch as if they had won the League (worst); City fans ripping up their ground for them (most enjoyable).

The final home game of the season against Watford saw me abandon my personal boycott because (a) I had a gut feeling that this would be Chase's final match in charge and (b) I got a freebie ticket! (I never said I had scruples, did I?!) It was yet another terrible performance from Megson's men and more protests followed, albeit a tad more subdued seeing as half of Norwich had been arrested at one of these things (this happened after every home game).

The following Thursday there was a radio newsflash announcing that there was to be an important press conference at 3pm. Working just 10 minutes from Carrow Road I used my break to scoot off down there. Boy, if the 20 minutes at Ipswich had been the worst in my life, the next 20 minutes outside Carrow Road were the best. Firstly I had a sit in Chase's seat in his chauffeured car, followed by a row with said chauffeur. Then after finding out that he had resigned and Geoffrey Watling, the club vice president, had bought all his shares, I actually met Mr

Watling. Overcome with emotional joy I proceeded to give him a huge hug and virtually burst into tears on his shoulder (I think he understood!). Finally, after mixing with all the media lot and watching them slink off home, thinking that Chase had already made good his exit, I followed an NCFC employee and watched him pull Chase's car up outside the building. Sure enough, five minutes later out came the Fat Non-Controller himself. So I ran over to greet him, and then had great pleasure in watching the fat man struggle to get into his car while I was calling him every name under the sun. I thanked him for my criminal record, wished him luck in Spain (especially in the dodgy flight - let's hope there's a crash) and ran after his car punching the air swearing "Fuck Off ! Fuck Off! Fuck Off!."

Which was nice.

There were celebrations in the city that night and the final game of the season at Crystal Palace turned into a huge party for the 3,000 City fans with tickets. There was an amazing atmosphere, not unlike when we got into Europe at Middlesbrough a few years ago, only this time we were celebrating avoiding relegation to the Second Division. That Robert Chase did a damn fine job.

As I write, things are still very much up in the air down at Carrow Road. Geoffrey Watling is on a perpetual holiday, the rest of Chase's board are still there although there have been a couple of new additions. Gary Megson is, amazingly, still in charge and half the players have been let go on free transfers. Oh, and Mike Walker's on holiday too.

Fanzine Facts

The fanzine joined in the campaign against Robert Chase once again last season. As editor James Emerson pointed out "Original as ever we decided the best way to further the protest was to stop producing *Ferry 'Cross the Wensum*. This we did and it got a fair bit of publicity in the local press and ultimately, maybe, galvanised City fans into one final push. One final glorious push." Because of this only two issues were brought out in '95-96, but normal service should be resumed next season.

Started over Christmas '92, sixteen issues have appeared so far and by all accounts are widely read within the club and amongst the fans. According to the 'zine, Malcolm Robertson, the club's press officer and former TV reporter said "that it summed NCFC up when a fine mag like *FCTW* had to finish because of the situation at Carrow Road."

FLASHING BLADE

Sheffield United

It was a Year of Two Halves

In one way, this season was reminiscent of United's first in Division One five years ago. That year the Blades drew four and lost 12 of their first 16 games, before a miraculous run took them to a comfortable mid-table finish. But there the similarity ends.

Dave Bassett was the instigator and motivator in those days as he engendered a never-say-die spirit into his players. However, half a decade later, Bassett began the season a dispirited man carrying the oppressive burden of an apathetic chairman who had more pressing personal concerns than the running of a football club.

Despite Bassett's attempts to persuade the fans that Bramall Lane was 'buzzing', deep down everybody knew that the club would continue to stagnate, or go backwards, unless chairman Reg Brealey departed. Manchester businessman Mike McDonald's protracted buyout of Brealey's majority shareholding was becoming entangled in the sticky web of the legal wranglings of Brealey's various companies. The take-over was already almost a year old and no end was in sight. A less determined man than McDonald would have given up long ago.

It was to be another three months before McDonald finally came through, but by this time United were in desperate straits. Bassett was no longer able to fire the players up; performances were horrible and relegation was more a likelihood than a possibility. The lowest point was when two United players left the ball to each other at the second half kick-off, Marco Gabbiadini said "thanks very much", instantly setting up Ron Willems for Derby's second goal, just eight seconds into the half.

In retrospect, had Bassett resigned in May '94 when United were relegated by the last kick of the season at Chelsea, he would have remained a hero for ever more. But now the crowd was turning against him, the 'Bassett Out!' brigade becoming more numerous and vociferous by the game. At first, their chants were drowned out, but soon, even Harry's greatest admirers began to realise that maybe the time had come for him to go.

The change came soon enough. Less than two weeks after McDonald took control, Bassett was out. Which of them made the first move is not known, but McDonald had privately made it clear that Bassett would not be his choice of manager. Dave, on the other hand, was probably relieved it was all over, and could take some consolation from the fact that he had outlasted Reg Brealey, the man who had held him back for two years. Who knows - perhaps that was his only intention since that day at Stamford Bridge in May '94...

It was a sad day when Bassett left, and tears were shed around Sheffield. Even his sternest critics must have felt a tinge of regret that his eventful reign had ended. But this was no time, and indeed there was no time, for reflecting on the past - Howard Kendall was appointed the next day. This was just the beginning of an upheaval which would, initially inch by inch but eventually by great strides, lead United well clear of trouble and totally rejuvenate the whole club in the process.

As well as a new manager, McDonald recruited new board members, but it was Kendall's transfer dealings that grabbed most of the attention. After bringing in Michel Vonk from Manchester City, he dropped a bombshell by selling our leading scorer (and, to be frank, the only player who looked like scoring) Nathan Blake. Mark Patterson came in part-exchange, but most supporters were gobsmacked that Kendall had sent Blake over the M62. Tony Battersby, Paul Rogers, Jostein Flo, John Gannon, Glyn Hodges, Paul Holland, David Tuttle and Carl Veart soon followed Blake through the exit door, while Adrian Heath, David White, Chris Short, Gordon Cowans, Don Hutchison, Brett Angell (on loan), Andy Walker, Gary Ablett (on loan) and Gareth Taylor passed them in the corridor.

The team was virtually unrecognisable in more ways than one - it took a while to become accustomed to the new faces, but the biggest difference was the way Sheffield United played. The first thing was that the ball stayed on the floor except in an emergency; the second was that we stopped conceding goals. We stopped scoring them too, but that could wait until things had been stabilised. The net result: countless draws. United were slowly dragging themselves into a position that would give them a chance of staying up, but late goals conceded to Charlton, Watford and Tranmere turned three points into one each time. Defeats at the hands of Luton and West Brom balanced wins over Oldham and Barnsley, bringing a return of the feelings of doom and gloom. The FA Cup defeat of Arsenal was merely an enjoyable distraction.

When Ablett came in, United never looked back. It was still nail-biting stuff though, and it came to a head with the home game against Luton. To put it simply, the losers were in the shit. In a game riddled with tension, two nervous teams were scared stiff of falling into the brown stuff. The match, and United's season, turned on one of those ridiculous refereeing decisions that all teams dread. On this occasion, fate decreed that it would go our way for a change. Eighty three minutes gone, Roger Nilsen played the ball into the penalty area from the left. Phil Starbuck controlled it and tried to turn, but Mitchell Thomas nicked it off him, and it went back to goalkeeper Ian Feuer, who picked it up. The referee, Trevor West, was virtually the only person in the ground who saw it as a back pass. Eleven men of Luton spread themselves between the posts. Eight yards away the ball was touched and Don Hutchison lashed it through the eye of a needle into the corner of the net. In that moment the immediate futures of Sheffield United and Luton Town were decided. United won seven of the last nine, drawing a couple of others; Luton slipped silently into Division Two.

Wins breed confidence, and confidence brings wins, and as Leicester, Southend, Wolves, Portsmouth, Grimsby and Reading in quick succession were brushed aside, the Blades' only problem was that the season was just about to end.

Apart from winning promotion, I can't remember the last time a season ended on such a high. Nobody can wait for '96-97 to begin. Howard Kendall has put together a strong all-round squad, the board is (or at least appears to be) ambitious (probably for the first time in the club's history), the new John Street Stand is finally being built and season ticket sales are better than for many years. We'll soon see if the optimism is justified.

Fanzine Facts

Lanuched in 1988 by editor Matthew Bell, *Flashing Blade* continues to give the Bramall Lane faithful all the behind-the-scenes gossip. Matthew knows that the mag has always been read by the players, and was certainly on Dave Bassett's essential reading list, although no subscription has yet been received from Howard Kendall.

"*!?*☺!! REFEREE! – GIVING SAVO MILOSEVIC A PENALTY WAS BAD ENOUGH, BUT SWAPPING SHIRTS WITH HIM AFTER THE GAME WAS TAKING THE P**S!"

FLY ME TO THE MOON

Middlesbrough

Back in August '95 there was a sense of uncertainty in the air. This is Middlesbrough after all. OK, so we had been promoted, but we all knew where that road usually led: "First Division, here we come - right back from where we started." The feelings of foreboding were reinforced by our failure to land any of the illustrious crop of pre-season targets. Andre Kanchelskis let it be known that he wanted to play for Bryan Robson and then upped and signed for Everton!

Then there was the new stadium. Would it be ready? Our first home game had already been put back, but the Premier League refused point blank to sanction a second postponement. So on Saturday August 26th it would be Chelsea or bust. Strangely familiar territory...

Then suddenly things started to fall into place. Bryan Robson smashed the club record to sign Nick Barmby for £5.5m. A pre-season tour ended with us hammering Scottish runners-up Motherwell (4-1) playing exquisite, precision passing football. We went to Highbury in the sunshine and with renewed confidence. Middlesbrough threw a major spanner in the works of Rioch's Premiership all-stars as Norwegian international Jan Fjortoft combined with our terrible twins, the out of contract Craig Hignett and Nicky Barmby, for the England striker to coolly chip us into the lead. Although Arsenal eventually equalised, we had signalled our arrival back in the top flight; we weren't here to make up the numbers. Boro were big time at last.

Then it was to the Cellnet Riverside Stadium, where a safety certificate had been finally granted at the eleventh hour. That day, Saturday August 26th, will go down for many of us as one of the most unforgettable days of our lives. A giant white steel structure floated above the waters of Middlesbrough dock. Above, a mammoth red home shirt fluttered from a helicopter. We trooped in our thousands, barely able to believe that this was our new hi-tech home. Above all, it was a sight of breathtaking beauty. Inside, people were actually open-mouthed in awe. In the words of Gillandi Schmultz, we were all swan necking, gazing around the sweep of the horse shoe and over the thousands of giant Cellnet hands pointing down from the new main stand. The view of the pitch was tremendous and the atmosphere LOUD, the low roofs ensuring locked-in volumes of terrace-like proportions. All that we needed was a result. When Craig Hignett swept Fjortoft's pass into the roof of the net, we were away. Well away. A new age was born. A realm of dreams had suddenly descended on dirty, dour, underachieving Middlesbrough. And believe me, we were in no hurry to awaken.

For the first couple of months Middlesbrough was alive with excitement. Barmby was combining brilliantly up front with Super Jan and the newly re-signed Hignett. In the middle, Robbie Mustoe and Jamie Pollock were playing some Premier stalwarts off the park. And the three centre backs Vickers, Whyte and captain Nigel Pearson looked absolutely watertight. Between the sticks, new bargain signing Gary Walsh had more assurance than the always game Alan Miller. Meanwhile Neil Cox and Chrissy Morris were ever-dangerous wing halves.

We added to Manchester City's woes with a win at Maine Road and then pulled Champions Blackburn apart in front of Alan Hansen and the Match of the Day cameras. Nick Barmby was the talk of the country: 'the new Peter Beardsley'. "But they'd never call Peter Beardsley the old Nicky Barmby", pointed out *FMTTM's* Miniature G. What's more, there were still no injuries! Maybe we'd finally left our treatment table torments behind at old Ayresome.

Then came October, and while Celtic's John Collins made his mind up, Bryan Robson slipped off to Rio for the most audacious swoop of all time. Despite Arsenal's last-gasp attempt to outbid us, we finally got our man. JUNINHO. Unbelievable. I was reduced to tears in Kwik Save. Umbro couldn't produce yellow Brazil shirts quick enough. His team-mates celebrated with a victory on Sky at Sheffield Wednesday. A 50-piece samba band welcomed the boy from Brazil to the cold, murky Teesside autumn grey. The world's press came to town and tried to rip strips off us, but it wouldn't wash. Arsenal hid their shame by pretending that it had all been an elaborate dummy to allow them to sign Porto's Emerson. Oh dear! Where is Mr Emerson playing now, Brucie?!

Then there was the debut itself. The 'next Pele' versus Leeds, and an instant hit as he dissected the Yorkshire midfield with the perfect pass for big Jan to score. In the second half he even proved he could mix it by getting booked.

And then the wheels fell off. And how.

Alright, at first there were high points. A crushing victory over high-flying Liverpool showed we could compete with the big fish. A 4-1 trouncing of Man City, Kinkladze and all, gave us our first double. Then all of a sudden, everyone was either injured or suspended. Whyte, Cox, Morris, Mustoe, Pollock, Barmby and Hignett. They were dropping like flies, and so was Middlesbrough. Poised to go second on Boxing Day at Everton, we were hammered out of sight 4-0, and so the decline set in. We couldn't even scrape a single point in the next six Premiership games. Half time entertainment during an embarrassing 0-5 thrashing at Chelsea was provided by nutty, laughing boy Suggs "avin' a larf" at the Boro fans. Chelsea mocked us with "Robson for England." We even got massacred at home 1-4 by rock-bottom Bolton: "Can we play you every week?", their fans enquired. At Newcastle, Columbian superman (?!?) Asprilla got off a plane, headed off to the wrong dressing room, and then came on to turn a 1-0 defeat into a 2-1 victory for the 'Toon criers'.

The talk on Match of the Day had turned to new Premiership records... worst run ever... dropping like a stone... laughing stocks... will they go down?.. where will the next goal come from?.. Juninho's spoilt the party...

Barmby had suddenly developed the touch and finishing finesse of a three legged goat. His blinding last minute miss at Wimbledon saw us dumped out of the FA Cup. The last chance motel for silverware had gone begging with a thud of a Selhurst post.

Now we Boro fans are prone to nightmares - recurring nightmares. While Robbo and big Viv might have been as cool as cucumbers, we recalled only too vividly our past two attempts at the top League. Both times we had shone brightly, finding ourselves in the top six by November, only to suddenly and dramatically - even spectacularly - crash down and through the bottom of the League with a crazy, unbreachable momentum. So it was with incredible relief that we managed a 0-0 draw at fellow strugglers Coventry. The cheers were lengthy. When we finally won a game, it was so perfect that it should be at Leeds, Leeds, Leeds. A local derby and a bogey side of the very worst order for Middlesbrough fans. Our first victory at Elland Road in 20 years, and our first in the Premiership of 1996. Happy New Year everyone... At last!

After this we made absolutely sure of safety by slamming an appalling Sheff Weds and then dominating a 1-1 draw away at Spurs. Jan Aage Fjortoft had finally returned to the goals trail with a brace. And two new heroes were thrown into the fray. Free-scoring reserve hotshot Chris Freestone, who notched (of course) on his Premiership debut, and junior striker Andrew Campbell, 'Ginja Warrior', at 16 one of the youngest players ever to grace the Premier League (and he hadn't even completed a full game for the reserves).

The big comeback on this roller coaster ride was largely due to two factors: Firstly, the management duo kept their nerve. Secondly, the return to fitness of three vital players Curtis Fleming, Derek White and Robbie Mustoe. Maybe a word for the fans here, too. After the signing of Juninho the new stadium completely sold out of season tickets, and in spite of our terrible slump there were never any empty seats, away ticket allocations almost always fully subscribed too. The signing of our second Brazilian, World Cup-winning left back Branco led to an amazing 15,000 turning out for his debut in the RESERVES - which actually made the Radio One news.

Robson has rejected England overtures to stay on until 1999. The passion and loyalty of the Boro faithful made this an easy decision for him. Now with the signing of Brazilian whizkid Emerson, we are seeing the next steps into a bright new age for Middlesbrough FC. So a trophy-less history could be about to be rewritten. The first task was to survive in the top flight, and we've all learned a few things doing so. Now we can go places together.

As I write this review, the sun is beating down and the kids are out in the streets knocking hell out of their lumps of leather. But these days, Man U and Liverpool strips have disappeared; it's Middlesbrough shirts they proudly carry on their backs. Now THAT is an achievement.

Fanzine Facts

Fly Me To The Moon first appeared in December 1988 and has produced 157 issues, which they claim is a record for any football fanzine. Current editor Robert Nichols is assisted by Sharon and Fischer. The fanzine's title is the result of the then manager Bruce Rioch suggesting that if he ever went to the moon, he'd want to take Tony Mowbray along with him (although he didn't explain why).

FOLLOW THE YELLOW BRICK ROAD

Mansfield Town

The A to Z of '95-96

Alexander, Keith: Why did we let this man escape from Field Mill? Keith had become a firm favourite amongst the supporters; a genuine cult figure. He finished his playing career in a Stags shirt and on a stretcher carried from the pitch after everyone had buggered off at the end of the Exeter home game. Now the manager of Ilkeston Town.

Auto Windscreens Shield: A non-event this season. A chance to get to Wembley. The Stags got placed in a group along with Wrexham (home) and York City (away). Two superb games to get the crowds out and supporting the Stags (NOT!!). Why couldn't we have a nice little local group along with Notts County and Chesterfield, eh? Now that would've been fun!

Bowling, Ian: Turned up at Field Mill on a free transfer at the start of the season and played in every game apart from three (two through suspension), picking up every Player of the Season award along the way.

Bury (Home): One to forget pretty quickly. All hail the conquering hero, Phil Stant. His return to Field Mill netted him four goals to out-do the scoring feat of another Stag, Steve Wilkinson, the previous week.

Cards, Red: Not many dismissals for the Stags this season. Only seven were waved in our direction. Top of the list were manager Andy King and Mark Peters who picked up two apiece, Ian Bowling, Scott Eustace and Warren Hackett collected the others.

Cards, Yellow: It was like a ticker tape parade as far as bookings were concerned. Top recipient was John Doolan who went out of his way to collect ten. A total of 70 were flashed in our direction.

Coca Cola Cup: No giant-killing for the Stags this season, not even midget-killing come to that! A first round exit (we were lucky to make it that far!) at the hands, or should that be feet, of Burnley.

Crowds: This season it was a case of one minute they're down, the next they're down further still.

Draws: Twenty of the little buggers found their way into the Stags' final results list. They were becoming so common at one stage that Littlewoods Pools automatically marked an 'x' in the columns next to Mansfield's name on the coupons to save you the trouble of doing it yourself.

Eustace, Scott: He was dead chuffed to finally get on the scoresheet in the Stags' last home match. You could almost forgive him the one he sliced into the wrong net up at Lincoln.

FA Cup: A good cup run for the Stags is usually to make it into the hat for the first round draw. Having passed this stage, we demolished local rivals Doncaster Rovers 4-2. The glorious run came to an end with a 2-0 defeat at Crewe in round two.

Fancy Dress: The (almost) traditional end of season 'dress up like a pillock and act stupid' event took place on the crowded terraces of Chester (a dozen people would make their tiny away end look packed).

Ground, New: When the news first broke about the proposed new ground they said that we'd be playing in it by now. Not so much as a sod has been turned as yet. This is due to various companies putting forward proposals for the site. An enquiry in now taking place.

Hackett, Warren: Arrived from Doncaster Rovers (after boss Andy King said that he would never do business with them ever again - a promise that he broke twice, by the way!). Hackett's first game was the 6-0 hammering up at Preston, his second game was a 5-1 slaughtering by Bury at Field Mill. You couldn't have blamed him if he had jacked it in there and then. Would make an excellent reserve 'keeper, if the deliberate handball to turn the ball round the post against Hereford was anything to go by.

Hat-tricks: These were expected to be rare as the Stags rarely score more than two goals in a game. It was surprising, then, that Stewart Hadley weighed in with two (against Wigan and Chester); he ended the season with a grand total of eight goals. Unfortunately there were more hat-tricks scored against us, two coming against Preston North End (where we lost 6-0) and one in the same game against Chester when Hadley hit his (we managed to lose this one 4-3).

Headlines, Newspaper: Top headline of the year goes to the local paper 'The Chad': "Own Goal Hits Impressive Stags." It might not seem much, but surely this was arranged incorrectly and should read "Impressive Own Goal Halts Stags." The own goal was courtesy of Warren Hackett and was one of the best that you'll ever see.

Injuries: Almost as many people went through the doors of the treatment room than through the turnstiles. Two broken legs and umpteen knee injuries all helped to send the official end of season total to a staggering 471.

Kilcline, Brian (Killer): Arrived on the Mansfield scene from Swindon just after the Stag's FA Cup exit. He immediately started bullying the Stag's defence into shape on his debut up at Scunthorpe.

King, Andy: The manager. It seemed that hardly a match passed by without Kingy being spoken to by the referee. This ended with him twice being dismissed to the stands. His deliberate amble over the pitch at Gillingham will live long in the memory. After refusing to walk around the pitch, his 80 yard stroll included three stops to do up his shoe laces and numerous sock-pulling ups. Even more surprising is that for his dismissal he got off with a very small fine and no touchline ban.

Last minute, the: If football matches lasted 85 minutes then Mansfield would have probably conceded about 20 goals less than they did.

Legs (broken): Usually a rare occurrence amongst the Stags; this season, however, they accumulated two. Keith Alexander's appearance as sub ended on the stretcher in the last minute at home to Exeter. Mark Peters' season ended on the playing field at Hartlepool. The Stags gave as good as they got with at least three opposition players leaving pitches in the same manner.

Lincoln City (away): Under the leadership of John Beck, Lincoln have plumbed new depths. The pitch at Sincil Bank is now a grass-free zone. It looks more like a ploughed field. The ball boys are under orders to slow down the game if Lincoln are in front, by dawdling to fetch the ball when it goes out of play. It also appears to be an offence to let the ball drop within ten feet of the playing service. 'Gamesmanship' I think they call it!

Lincoln City (home): The Stags lost this game, not surprising when you consider they played most of it with ten and then nine men. For the first time as far as I can remember both managers were dismissed from the touchline, although this apparently didn't stop John Beck returning to give orders to his team.

Loan signings: The Stags used the majority of their loan spells up before Christmas. Such footballing talents as Ben Sedgemore, Nathan Peel, Phil Barber, Tony Brien and David Kerr graced the Stags team for a while. Out of these only Barber and Sedgemore made any lasting impression.

Onyora, Iffy: Bought two seasons ago, and has played in about 20 games (if that!). Always seems to be injured and an appearance in a Stags shirt is a rare occurrence.

Own goals: The Stags only scored two this season, but both were quite spectacular. None registered for us though.

Preston (away): Oh dear! A 6-0 hammering with former Stags player Steve Wilkinson netting a hat-trick and setting up two of Andy Saville's three strikes. Best forgotten. The Stags did better in the home game finishing with a creditable 0-0 draw.

Slawson, Steve: Acquired the nickname 'Don Brennan' due to his tendency to use only the one foot. Not surprisingly he was released at the end of the season.

Special offer: 'Three games for £15' was the offer but two of those three (Torquay and Rochdale) were postponed because of the weather - Rochdale was postponed 30 minutes before kick-off !

Spireites: How we laughed when we found out that they'd failed to make the play-offs!

Streaker: One brave travelling supporter bared all in the home game against Gillingham, but not before they'd had a collection to pay for any incurred fines.

Thompson, Daley: Yep, that bloke from the Olympics! Arrived in a blaze of publicity and made it on to the subs' bench, but didn't get on the field of play. Moved onto local club Ilkeston Town, now managed by Keith Alexander. Ended the season banned from playing after head-butting an opponent.

Trinder, Jason: Quit Field Mill in mid-season after being on the end of some nasty taunts by certain sections of the crowd.

X-players: (OK, I cheated!) As mentioned above, Wilkinson and Stant returned to haunt us, as did Kevin Noteman (dismissed while at Doncaster, scored against us when at Chester).

Youngsters: One of the highlights of the season was the emergence of the youngsters. Ryan Williams was regularly called up to the England U-18's and established a place in the team towards the end of the season alongside Ian Robinson and Darrell Clarke. Goalkeeper Nicky Weaver had an awesome debut at Cambridge and promises great things.

ZZzzzzz: And so to bed. Definitely a season to send you to sleep.

Fanzine Facts

Follow The Yellow Brick Road first appeared at the height of fanzine fever. It is now the oldest of two fanzines up and running, but *FTYBR* is the only survivor from those days and ended the '94-95 season on Issue 31½ (?) overseen by current editor, Keith Parnill. Founding editor Steve Hartshorn now concentrates his energies on managing the very successful *FTYBR* football team, who this year came away with the Midland Bank Five-A-Side Charity Shield which was held at Villa Park.

As well as contributing the above article, Keith suggested that the publishers of *SOTF2* also include the following piece, penned by long-time *FTYBR* contributor Marco Van Sherpa. And we thought, why not? (No prizes for guessing what the 'book' was, either!)

Book Review: The 87th Men

It was in the summer of '95 that I purchased my own personal numbered and rather expensive copy of this 'tragedy' bound in its own distinctive plastic wallet with pages enough to see me through from August until the end of April.

The cost of this volume would have proved prohibitive to many potential purchasers, but an easy monthly payment direct debit scheme was launched to help attract more subscribers and tempt those who would have found the outlay of the total cost too much of a burden on their pockets in one fell swoop.

Unfortunately, this book had lost a host of central characters from the previous year's annual and it became apparent after only a few pages that the authors had lost the plot too. The remainder was never going to be compelling reading. However I persevered in the somewhat naïve hope that there would be the occasional flicker of hope emanating from the within the text, but to no avail. If this book is ever made into a motion picture, then D'ream's 'things can only get better' would be the most apt of theme tunes, but for the remainder of this horror story things most certainly didn't get any better.

As yet another character from the previous year's potentially great volume was written out of the plot (curiously re-emerging in a rival publication from the printing house of 'Thieving Magpie Productions'), the story went from bad to worse. I became tempted to return this sorry epistle back from whence it came to demand a refund, but I'm made of sterner stuff (I'm a mug and a sucker for a sob story!); besides I'd always wondered how the tale would have finished, so once more I cautiously embraced the text.

For a while, with the introduction of a character who had excelled in different (track and) fields, the book threatened to take an unusual twist, dropping the macabre angle altogether and flying off at a tangent in slapstick comedy. This injection of bizarre mirth was short-lived, but in reality this warped humour was never really particularly funny anyway, and so this morbid tome plundered on.

Unlikely as it may seem, a hero emerged from the depths of despair; not so much a phoenix from the ashes as a supporting prop to hold the rest of the set together. He stood out head and shoulders above the rest of the cast and even turned out in a unique uniform emblazoned with a white number one on the back. However, there is only so much one man can do when carrying a nine month saga and a whole squad of bit-part actors on his back. Ultimately, his heroic quest came to nothing, because even the most noted of 'one man teams' needs a capable supporting cast standing by in the wings.

Perhaps, all along, this book had been a black humour parody; the sting in the tale being that the season actually finished after only a few pages (i.e. about October!) and the rest of the humdrum text was merely a bad joke in very poor taste to torment those of us who actually bought a copy and fell for this 'leg pull'.

We, the readers, were bored witless and were daft enough to toil on through to the very end in search of some unlikely contest. Next year's planned sequel had better be a whole lot better!

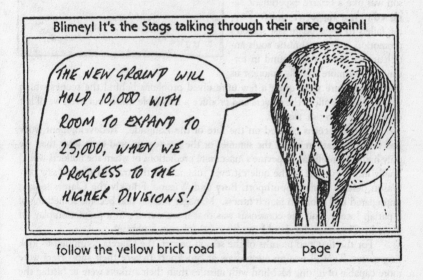

FOR EVER AND A DAY

Burnley

Look back in anger

'95-96 will go down in history as the watershed that never was. Arguably this was about the worst of the many shit seasons endured over the last two decades. After relegation, some expected a return to the promised land of Endsleigh 1, with a new ground in the same league as Highbury or Huddersfield's Kirklees. But given our board's legendary ability to do the wrong thing, should we have been surprised by the eventual outcome and the unnerving unreality of the experience? In fact the whole season was like a bizarre experiment designed to test supporter sanity. Having failed to consolidate last season's promotion, a few optimistic souls anticipated a quick turnaround in fortunes. The more worldly amongst us

knew that there were quite a few unresolved problems behind the scenes which would probably affect the players and produce a mid-table finish; but even we didn't expect it to turn out *this* bad.

Early concerns centred on the fate of the Longside. Redevelopment work had failed to start in either the summer or the pre season, and even after that, we only had the unofficial grapevine's inaccurate predictions of when the builders would finally move in. One of the quietest ever summers in the transfer market saw pre-season defeats against Southport, Bury and Wigan. Frankly the Clarets looked unprepared and short on match fitness. Manager Mullen had become something of a pariah locally, and the consensus was that if we weren't in a promotion/play off place by Christmas, he should 'get his coat' (to coin a phrase).

For the first two months of the season proper, the Clarets continued to look ring rusty. Typical was an away draw at Stockport (where their supporters were more capable of hitting McMinn with missiles than their strikers were at hitting the Burnley net). Beresford and Swan distinguished themselves in these early games, whilst up front Kurt No-guns' opportunism suggested that he wasn't the expensive flop we thought he was after all. But in general, we were reacting to relegation with poor performances, only playing for ten or twenty minutes in a game. The plan it seemed was to string five across the back and lump it long to Phyllis and Nogan up front. The midfield seemed anonymous, as creative players like Randall and Eyres were frequently bypassed or just fizzled out. Away defeats at Carlisle and Chesterfield and the away draw at lowly York saw the 'Mullen Out' movement coming into its element. Indeed some fans were supporting two teams: Burnley when we were winning and Mullenout when we were weren't. A 4-2 away defeat at Chesterfield hinted at the shape of things to come; terrace optimism after an early goal turned sour when defensive slackness resulted in two soft goals. Not even a 44th minute equaliser could prevent an indifferent midfield display and a sending off losing us the game. "We are the Burnley haters" cried yet another set of supporters, while director Basil Dearing attempted to defend the board's lack of ambition on Radio Lancs after the match.

Just to compound the on-field agony, the Longside was closed after the home game against Hull. Given only seven days' notice of the impending loss of their ancestral shrine, 10,613 turned up to witness an otherwise nondescript 2-1 victory over poor opponents, staying behind long after the final whistle. In giving such short notice, thereby preventing many fans living outside the area or working odd hours from attending this mournful occasion, the board were assured of a place in the fans' disaffections. Still, at least they were prudent enough to open the gates on Sunday for photographs and collecting chunks of terrace memorabilia.

The pairing with Leicester City in the Coca Cola Cup second round was probably as near as we ever got to a season high. In a 2-0 away defeat Adrian Heath ('Inchy') was recalled, and chants of "Inchy for manager" were the last massed renderings from the Longside fans before they were moved to the Bee Hole, where most adopted a vow of silence. Shh... Shh... Bjork must have been happy as a sandgirl at this show of devotion from such an unexpected quarter. This was when the season went really pear-shaped, the atmosphere becoming that of a dentist's waiting room. Come October and apart from Bastard Rovers' glorious European campaign (NOT!), people began saying that the season was over. Phyllis went out on loan. Hoyland, Eyres and Randall made the boo boys' acquaintances. Heath returned to Andy Jones' casualty list, Steve Thompson had a second operation, McMinn drifted back into the Pontins League, whilst the optimists wondered if the campaign would ever get started. Hovering between obscurity and the play-offs, Clarets fans found a third team to support: Teasdaleout. Nevertheless, away wins were at last registered at Peterborough and Bournemouth. But a pitiful attendance of 4,605 for Leicester's return visit confirmed that faith was wearing thin in the ranks. However, such is the fickle nature of football that it seemed Jimmy Mullen only needed a couple of wins to re-establish his managerial credentials.

A see-saw affair at home to Notts County brought the first League home defeat (3-4) with a late offside goal putting the game beyond our reach. Then an early goalmouth handball and subsequent red card for Harrison (three appearances at full back - three failures to complete 90 minutes) sent us crashing to a 0-3 defeat at Shrewsbury - whose supporters weighed in with the 957th claim to be the "Burnley haters" of this Division. We were the first club eliminated from the FA Cup (a Friday night reverse at home to Walsall), and the faltering AWS Trophy progress against Chester and Crewe merely confirmed Clarets in their support of Mullenout and Teasdaleout. The board decided to 'act' by going live on a Radio Lancs phone-in. Teasdale didn't bother to appear, and Holt, Blakeborough and Dearing were singularly unimpressive. Surprisingly, JM was adjudged the only man to have any passion and ambition for the club. But this wasn't enough to stop the rumours doing the rounds in the Burnley pubs and clubs: he was washed up; the bottle was his only remaining friend; he was unable to motivate his squad and implement tactical decisions; he was directing abuse at well-meaning supporters.

Some did feel sympathy for JM. Certainly his was a no-win situation. The loss of the Longside had decimated the atmosphere, and this seemed to be getting to the players. When they played badly or made individual errors Mullen was held directly responsible, but when things went right the players got the credit and he was forgotten. Much was made of his alleged drinking and inability to handle training sessions. He was also under threat of replacement by Inchy (who made no secret of his wish to move into management, preferably at Turf Moor, later moving to Sheff U as Howard Kendall's number two).

At the same time, another interesting sideshow was developing in the board-room. According to - ahem - 'sources', JM cleared the 'vote of confidence' hurdle on more than one occasion, only the chairman's casting vote saving his bacon. News of a split emerged, and a power struggle looked a certainty as various anony-mous figures were making bids for shares, according to the local press. Eventually Basil Dearing resigned on a matter of principle, leaving the balance of power in the hands of the 'Young Turks'. Were drastic changes afoot? Against this backdrop of turmoil the Clarets remained undefeated in December, and the Bastards provided a bit of comic relief with Le Saux and Batty's attempts to show that they could regis-ter 'a bit of clout' in Europe. Still, it was good to see the McEwans Lager Louts licked by Urengoigazprom Kulaks. Trelleborgs remained our unofficial second team and their shirt was the most popular Xmas present.

When competitive action resumed in the New Year it was the AWS trophy at 'Burnley haters' # 19,507 (Carlisle). They were fired up and eager for action, while we played like it was our first attempt to shed some holiday flab. The result was never in doubt - 0-3 down after 30 minutes, we finally capitulated 0-5. The critics had a field day. Ex financial director, Derek Gill, publicly criticised Teasdale's leadership, leaving no doubt that if Teasdale resigned and allowed Gill to form another reconstituted board, his business consortium would willingly invest. The die was cast.

Then came the straw that broke the camel's back. No, not the next away defeat, but an unpardonable oversight by the board. As any supporter knows, there will always be individuals who personify a football club, such as Bill Shankly and Ian Rush at Liverpool, or Matt Busby and Bobby Charlton at Man United. To Joe Public, Burnley FC means Bob Lord and Harry Potts. Unfortunately the Burnley board was so far removed from Mr Public that when Potts passed away, they showed insensitivity on a monumental scale by deciding that the commemoration of his death could wait until the next home fixture. It was left to the Burnley faithful away at Rotherham to find their own way of marking Harry's death. The poignant chant of "Harry Potts' Claret And Blue Army" highlighted the board's gaffe. The local media was deluged by supporters as they erupted with volcanic fury. A deaf-ening silence from Teasdale prompted the '3.33 turning of the backs' protest, organ-ised for the next Saturday home game, a visit from Crewe Alex (a creditable per-formance but 0-1 defeat). At the allotted time, 70% of the crowd turned their backs and although media coverage was mixed, subsequent events tarnished the image of Burnley FC. JM's dismissal/resignation was a direct result of his wife being at-tacked by 13 year olds with a cigarette lighter. This was reported nationally as an orchestrated hate campaign, the facts massaged to make good copy; the juveniles becoming fully grown thugs, and the attack taking place inside a restaurant rather than outside a takeaway. It's not the first time that the national press has been woefully inaccurate because of a penchant for sensationalising soccer violence.

The 3.33 protest re-dubbed itself Target 10,000, an ambition for future attendances, and there was a notable increase in crowd backing for the home draw against York City (in which old favourite Adie Randall starred for the Minstermen). But with the uncharismatic Clive Middlemass in temporary charge, disservice as normal was soon resumed with spineless defeats at home to Blackpool and Hull away. Strong rumours abounded that Steve Coppell had met up with Frank Teasdale on that day to throw his hat into the ring. In all there were nearly 30 candidates for the job, including ex-Clarets Trevor Steven, Martin Dobson and Mick Buxton; ex Bastard Don Mackay and luminaries of the lower League such as Dario Grady. A good number of candidates were written off as being unaffordable by the 'Inchy at all costs' brigade. Given a choice between an ambitious set-up or perpetuating the pattern of penniless romantics most fans opted for the latter. The board took a month's pontification before appointing Adrian Heath as new manager. The intelligentsia on the supporters' internet only rated Inchy as joint 5th. It must be said that Inchy's popularity was like something out of the X Files, he'd certainly put in some Fox-like performances in a Burnley shirt - unfortunately they were more Mulder than Ruel. Maybe all the other Clarets fans had been beamed aboard a UFO to watch a different Inchy in action. It's the most rational explanation I can offer.

By now Burnley had plummeted from sixth to 16th. Although the dead men seemed a number of points adrift, the spectre of relegation was creeping up. Totally out-footballed at Ashton Gate for Heath's first game in charge we nevertheless snatched a 1-0 win with Nogan finding the net. During the next couple of games, the seeds of kamikaze defending in the dying minutes were sown. We travelled to Oxford and seemed to be making a good fist of fighting back from a first half 0-1 deficit. Fifteen minutes from the end they brought on their sub who scored a hat trick as Clarets crashed 0-5. It was similar at Wycombe were we went from 1-1 to 1-4 in 12 minutes. Where was the fire and the faith that made Burnley FC?

As the season drew to a close, the most noteworthy observation was that air sickness pills, parachutes and field glasses were needed in various parts of the new stand. The final game also saw next season's kits given a public airing: a couple of Adidas cast-offs, one the quartered job Liverpool use as away kit done up in Claret and Blue, the other a fading stripes design similar to the Eire World Cup number. Rumours also circulated that admission prices were set to rise to £15. Those blokes in the boardroom are determined to make following Burnley a long and bitter struggle.

Fanzine Facts

For Ever And A Day is the successor to Marlon's Gloves. After five years the author is taking an indefinite rest from fanzine activities as circulation has peaked. Supporters still have three other fanzine titles to choose from, various supporters group newsletters and a couple of internet groups. Also there is an Independent Clarets Association being formed in the close season.

FOREST FOREVER

Nottingham Forest

According to the record books, '95-96 season saw Forest reach the quarter finals of both the FA and UEFA Cups and finish a respectable ninth in the Premiership. Trainspotters will also point out that an unbeaten run from the end of '94-95, which continued over the first 12 games of '95-96, established a new Premiership record of 25 games undefeated.

Looking at these bare facts, it would be easy for one to get the impression that it was a pretty good season. However, most of our supporters would probably disagree. And not because the team fared particularly badly; it's just that the quality of their play was so uninspiring. Basically, Forest struggled throughout the season to score goals. This wasn't such a problem in home games, because most of the time Forest could get away with scraping narrow victories or low scoring draws. But away from home it more or less got to the stage where supporters travelled knowing that we were unlikely to get anything from the game unless Mark Crossley kept a clean sheet. Over the course of the campaign they won away four times in the League, a statistic which couldn't be blamed entirely on the club's putrid new yellow away strip.

FOREST FOREVER ISSUE 31 £1

PAUL MCGREGOR ON HIS FEAR OF SPIDERS

Exclusive interview inside!

No, the cause of Forest's goalscoring problems was basically a failure to replace star striker Stan Collymore, who was sold to Liverpool in the close season for a British record £8.5m fee. Frank Clark did spend most of the money on new players, but neither of the two strikers he purchased were able to fill Collymore's boots. Due to injuries Italian import Andrea Silenzi never really had a chance to impress, although the same can hardly be said for Kevin Campbell. Somehow he kept his place for most of the season, even though he scored only three League goals. Apparently Campbell puts in more effort on the dancefloors of Nottingham's night-clubs than he does on the pitch, although that's another story...

At one stage it looked as though the unlikely figure of Jason Lee may be able to replace Collymore single handedly. Lee found himself in the team, and began weighing in with an impressive quota of goals. This inspired a classic terrace song:

My eyes have seen the glory of the coming of the Lord
Number 12 on his back, many goals he has scored,
His name is Jason Lee, he's got a pineapple on his head,
And the Reds go marching on,on,on!

Unfortunately, David Baddiel and Frank Skinner of TV's *Fantasy Football* soon latched onto his bizarre 'pineapple' hairstyle as well, and week after week of piss-takes on said programme saw him become a standing joke with opposition supporters. Unsurprisingly Lee's confidence soon dried up as a result of this, and consequently so did his supply of goals. Once again Forest were left to struggle without a prolific goalscorer.

To make matters worse, shortly after the start of the season skilful midfielder Lars Bohinen was allowed to exercise a clause in his contract and move to Blackburn for a measly £700,000 and there was no way Clark could ever replace him for that sort of money. OK, we still had a lot of good players. To name just a few, Colin Cooper and inspirational captain Stuart Pearce ensured that the back four remained solid, while Steve Stone and Ian Woan are arguably the best wing pairing in the country - the former being a rightful England international, and the latter a renowned scorer of spectacular goals.

But the gaps left by Collymore and Bohinen proved critical. Without Bohinen the midfield struggled to carve out goalscoring opportunities. When chances were created, inept finishing from the likes of Campbell meant that they often went to waste. There was still Bryan Roy, but without Collymore beside him he struggled to maintain his form of the previous season. In some games Forest failed to register a single shot on target. It was very uninspiring, to the extent that Alan Hansen went as far as suggesting that Forest were becoming ' the new Arsenal'. Unsurprisingly this caused outrage amongst the City Ground faithful, although in all honesty his comments probably weren't all that far off the mark.

To be fair, we did have our moments in the League and FA Cup. There was a 1-0 victory over Liverpool, although the game will be best remembered as Collymore's return to the City Ground. Having angered Forest supporters with some of his outrageous comments when he left the club, he was booed whenever he touched the ball and eventually substituted to wild cheers, after contributing practically nothing to a futile Liverpool performance. There was also a glorious, if nerve-wracking, 3-1 victory on penalties in an FA Cup replay at White Hart Lane, largely due to the heroics of Mark Crossley. He saved three out of four Tottenham penalties, and ironically it was his save from former Forest striker Teddy Sheringham which confirmed Tottenham's fate. Crossley celebrated in style, sprinting the length of the pitch and diving headfirst in the mud in front of the travelling Forest supporters. For a player not exactly renowned for his sleek figure, this was quite a spectacular feat!

But in general the domestic season was at best mediocre and at worst embarrassing. More than once the whole team fell to pieces and succumbed to a heavy defeat. The first of these thrashings at Blackburn was actually quite a novelty, and the sight of several thousand Forest supporters singing "Nil-seven, to the Nottingham" and generally laughing in the face of adversity really was hilarious. But by the time Forest had suffered further heavy defeats, against Everton, Manchester United and Blackburn once again, the joke had begun to wear rather thin. Worse still was going out of the Coca Cola Cup to Bradford, made all the more embarrassing by the fact that we conceded two goals by the not exactly legendary Ian Ormandroyd.

This leaves the season undoubtedly best remembered for Forest's UEFA Cup run. Again, the quality of the football from Forest often left a lot to be desired; each aggregate victory was by the narrowest of margins, and to be honest it was sheer determination and team spirit rather than skill which saw them conquer some good sides and reach the quarter finals of the competition. But with all the other British teams going out in early rounds, Forest soon became the nation's sole survivors in Europe. This was obviously a great source of pride for everybody connected with the club, and made all the more satisfying by the fact that none of the so-called experts had given Forest a cat in hell's chance in the first place. Needless to say, 'there's only one team in Europe' became the signature tune of the City Ground faithful.

Going abroad to watch the games was also brilliant. The camaraderie amongst the supporters who travelled was always fantastic, and none of the trips were ever short of a laugh. Getting to Sweden for the first round tie against Malmo involved travelling through half a dozen different countries and three ferry crossings. In all, the journey took a gruelling 28 hours. What's more, on arrival it transpired that the going rate for beer in Sweden is a cool £4 a pint! But those Swedish girls were something else, and the sight of hundreds of Forest supporters staging an impromptu conga around the terracing after Ian Woan scored the opening goal was most amusing. Malmo fought back to win 2-1, although a stunning goal from Bryan Roy in the second leg secured a 1-0 victory and Forest went through to the second round on away goals.

Auxerre in the next round was a mixed bag. The trip gave the travelling supporters their first real opportunity to stop at Calais for some dirt-cheap beer, although the French public toilets were the cause of nightmares for weeks after. The game itself epitomised the way Forest played throughout the UEFA Cup run - basically, maintain a nine man defence and counter-attack whenever possible. Steve Stone got an early goal which Forest proceeded to hang onto for the remainder of the game. Somehow they prevented Auxerre from scoring, largely thanks to some brilliant saves from Crossley and four goal-line clearances. The second leg was pretty much the same - Frank Clark just about summed up the game by describing it as "like the Alamo all over again." Again, Forest somehow prevented Auxerre from scoring with some brilliant defending, which meant Stone's goal in the first leg was enough to send us through.

The third round saw Forest pitted against another French club, Lyon. This time the first leg was at the City Ground, and it got quite dramatic late on. With the game still scoreless and time running out, Forest won a penalty. Stuart Pearce stepped up to take it, and one could hear the collective curse of 20,000 or so people as his shot was saved. However, the agony became ecstasy within a couple of seconds as young substitute Paul McGregor fired in the rebound to provide Forest with a priceless lead. They finished off the job in the second leg, holding Lyon to a goalless draw thanks to more magnificent defending. This put Forest through to the last eight, something which naturally saw mass celebrations amongst supporters and players alike. Indeed, Steve Stone was allegedly observed swigging from a bottle of champagne with his trousers round his ankles during the Forest party's flight back to England, although that's another story entirely...

Germany in the quarter final was quite a nostalgia trip for many supporters, Bayern Munich's Olympic Stadium having been the venue at which we won the European Cup back in '79. On the day of the game the city's streets, or its bierkellers to be more precise, were awash with Forest supporters (one of whom was even decked out in full German army uniform!). When Jurgen Klinsmann gave Bayern an early lead it looked rather ominous, but Forest hit back within a minute, Steve

Chettle heading home at the far post. Although Bayern scored again, Forest put up a spirited performance which gave the travelling supporters every confidence for the second leg. After all, they only needed a 1-0 win to go through. And if they could get as far as the semi-finals, what was to stop them from going all the way?

The second leg had the makings of a truly memorable night, with the fans really doing the occasion justice by creating a crescendo of noise and colour. On the pitch things appeared to be going according to plan as well, with Forest piling pressure on the Bayern defence. Unfortunately, it all turned out to be a huge anti-climax. The Germans scored two flukey goals before half time, and suddenly the UEFA Cup dream was in tatters. OK, we could still go through by scoring four, but with Campbell in the side it was just never going to happen. But to their credit, the players never let their heads drop and threw everything at the Bayern defence, although in doing so they left themselves wide open at the back and the Germans went on the score three more. To rub salt into the wound, Forest would have had Barcelona in the semi-finals!

In the aftermath of their UEFA Cup exit the press treated Forest like some sort of laughing stock, although getting things into perspective Clark and his players could still hold their heads high. After all, they did far better in Europe than any other British team. But even so, the end of March left Forest out of all the Cup competitions and with little chance of finishing high enough in the Premiership to qualify for Europe again. In other words, there wasn't a lot for them to play for, and consequently the remainder of the season seemed rather meaningless.

To be fair it did get quite interesting in the final week though, with Forest facing both Manchester United and Newcastle in the last few games. The pressure of the title race was taking its toll, and using the fact that there are a number of Geordies at the City Ground as his incriminating evidence, Alex Ferguson made outrageous claims that Forest would be doing all they could to help Newcastle's cause. As things turned out, Forest did anything but the sort. We were humiliated in front of a Sky TV audience in a 5-0 defeat at Old Trafford, while restoring some pride by holding Newcastle to a 1-1 draw at the City Ground four days later. We then finished off the season in style with a 3-0 win over QPR.

So in the end Forest became quite heavily involved in the title race. Although in this case it was never really likely that we would win the Championship, I would love to end on a high note by saying that the trophy may well end up at the City Ground in the not too distant future. However, with Clark having been told by his unambitious board that he will have to sell to buy, the future doesn't look all that promising. Still, with sheep-shagging rivals Derby County having just gained promotion to the Premiership, at least we are guaranteed a six point head start in the new season...

Fanzine Facts

The first edition of *Forest Forever* appeared in December 1991. Edited by Richard Fisher with invaluable assistance from a wide range of contributors, it's "rather bland title" (in Richard's words) belies the fact that it is a highly rated publication, and was last year voted eighth best fanzine in Britain by readers of 'fanzine collector'. Now over 30 editions old, *Forest Forever* is probably not so popular with certain members of the Forest board, although that's another story...

GRORTY DICK

West Bromwich Albion

"Some report a sea maid spawned him; some that he was begot between two stock-fishes. But it is certain that when he makes water his urine is congealed ice."

Grimsby Town fanzine editor and Shakespeare lover Steve Plowes talking about Alan Buckley.

"You know nothing about playwrighting!"

Albion manager Alan Buckley, talking about Shakespeare.

And so we at *GD* Towers say farewell to season '95-96, quite honestly the most bizarre I've ever witnessed. During the course of the campaign just gone I've had the twin dubious pleasures of seeing my lovely Baggies spectacularly ascend Cape Canaveral-style to that ionospheric region of the Endsleigh where Premiership hopes are earnestly coveted and secretly nurtured by the faithful; conversely I've also witnessed our precipitous descent into that Slough Of Despond, the penultimate position in the First, and all in the space of three months, dear reader. Then came our fight for survival, which we achieved on the last day of the season, finishing 11th, as Midlands Endsleigh top dogs. Wolves, to the unabashed delight of many Albionites, only missed relegation by a couple of points... Shame!

Such was the roller-coaster nature of Albion's season, the club should have displayed at the turnstiles several of those gaudily-written notices one sees at amusement parks debarring pregnant women, children and people with heart conditions from the 'white-knuckle rides', those fiendish contraptions calculated to impose G-forces, disorientation and severe motion-sickness on the unsuspecting punter. Had they done so, no Albion supporter could have sued under the Trades' Descriptions Act!

The season started unremarkably enough with an undistinguished home win by the odd goal over Charlton Athletic. This was followed by a 1-1 draw with Wolves, on their own odious dung-heap. This result, on a scorching day with temperatures in the nineties <u>did</u> make our faithful sit up and notice, not least because Wolves were at that time hotly tipped by pundits and bookies alike to achieve escape velocity from Planet Endsleigh; in fact, we should have done far better than draw; only a classic own goal from Welsh international defender 'Captain' Mardon prevented us grabbing all three points. Supporter consensus at the game's end was "If that's the best in this Division, what have we got to worry about?" What indeed...

And as the gloriously hot summer melted into Autumn, this in fact seemed to be the case, as we notched up victories over Northampton Town (Coca Cola), Sheffield United and Oldham; drawing, creditably, with early pace-setters Ipswich and Tranmere. A televised 1-0 victory over the Bluenoses (aka Birmingham) put us firmly into the promotion places. Two weeks after this event, the writing was on the wall, though we didn't realise at the time - another televised match, this time our noses being rubbed into the dirt. No great surprise to report that it was the old enemy Stoke that did the rubbing... a note to my Fairy Godmother; will we <u>ever</u> beat these people? Come late October, several victories more, and like James Cagney, we were "Top Of The World, Ma!!" And just like Cagney's mobster, it was to end explosively and in tears. We now examine the tricky Christmas/New Year period, our fall from grace, and our recovery from the mire; events which inextricably revolve around three principal factors; the manager, the supporters, and what I've come to call the "Holy Trinity." The last of these I'll refer to later. But first, our manager...

I think it's fair to say Alan Buckley came to The Shrine some 18 months ago toting in his suitcase a pretty fair reputation for acerbity and taciturnity in his former dealings with Grimsby Town supporters. The aforementioned Steve Plowes ("Mr Angry") gave us plenty of warning of what to expect from Buckley, reporting that our manager was not at all well-regarded in those parts. Not totally because he defected to us; simply because his idea of public relations broadly approximated to those espoused by the late and unlamented punk rock group The Sex Pistols. One example Steve cited was of a Grimsby aficionado who had the temerity to ask a perfectly innocent question about then Grimsby favourite Paul Reece. The response, was apparently just two words, the second one 'off'! Not an isolated incident, apparently, according to Steve. "You wait 'n see!" said that fishy luminary to us all that time ago; so we did...

When we at **GD** Towers heard of Buckley's reputation, and then discovered for ourselves his abruptness and abrasiveness in supporter relations, we automatically assumed that he'd been given a hard time by Grimsby fans and had presumed Albion supporters to be of similar ilk, and therefore not to be trusted. Besides, as I mentioned earlier, the bloke was getting results; just one victory, or series of victories, tinges everything with a rosy hue. Consequently, during that winning run we weren't overly concerned when a few supporters told us of our manager's hostile attitude to perfectly reasonable questions. At a supporters club meeting in those early season days when the leaves were falling from the trees and our favourite footie club was experiencing the heady heights of the Endsleigh summit, Buckley stated amongst widespread Baggie puzzlement that he felt Albion supporters "weren't warming" to him... Pardon?

Then came our 'Runnus Horriblus'. Following our top of the table clash and 2-1 defeat against Millwall at the New Den came 12 agonising and humiliating League and FA Cup games with absolute zilch to show for the effort. During this time, West Bromwich Albion became a national joke, our pointless sequence frequently alluded to in risible vein on national TV, radio, and - on one memorably humiliating occasion - in the leader editorial of The Guardian. The smelly stuff flew in every direction; during this time I heard vituperation verbally hurled in great dollops in the direction of our board, our chairman Hales, and certain of our players. Even normally bomb-proof performers like Andy Hunt and SuperBob Taylor weren't totally exempt from the Brummie Road's version of Orwell's Two Minute Hate. And yet, despite the verbal dissent (which reached its rather unpleasant nadir at both Crewe and Charlton), there was hardly a scathing word uttered in criticism of our hirsutically-challenged leader. Unusual that, for an Albion manager; in fact, I'd go so far as to say it's practically unique, given our dissent-ridden recent history.

Which brings me neatly to the next point; that of <u>loyalty</u>. Given our all-too-recent record of adversity, how many supporters of other League clubs would have backed their manager so wholeheartedly in the same circumstances? Not many, I suspect; I can think of several First Division outfits where it would have been death-threat/anonymous telephone call/vandalism to car time by now, reprehensible though that may be. You didn't know how lucky you were, Buckley - so why mar for supporters a radio forum at the fag-end of the season with offensive answers to questions asked in a perfectly reasonable and polite manner? To tell one questioner "I'm not being personal, but you know nothing about football" - and that to a guy who'd been a Baggies season-ticket holder some 35 years - or to bluntly tell an equally polite enquirer to "mind your own business" bordered on the totally unacceptable, and furthermore was not a good example to set to younger and more impressionable players who might see their manager as a role-model.

At the moment Buckley's public performances remind me very much of those of Margaret Thatcher. Intransigence, arrogance, obstinacy - "There Is No Alternative!" - the patronising putting-down of dissenters and the belittling of questioners. A certain 'way with words' is all well enough at the right time and moment, as the Tories quickly discovered with Thatcher. And just as quickly discarded once the Leaderene's verbal blitzkriegs outlived their electoral usefulness. It's a pity Buckley can't grasp the fundamental fact that we're all on our manager's side, really; something he would quickly find out if he only loosened up a little. God, I feel better now I've got *that* lot off my ample chest! Enough of all this catharsis, though; back to the Endsleigh, and the second part of the triumvirate - our supporters...

With the patient showing terminal signs of relegation come the New Year, Albionites found ourselves confronted with a dilemma. Having run the gamut of the usual reactions to customary ignominious defeat (sarcasm and abuse against Crewe; irony and gallows humour against Charlton), following the first goal against at Portman Road, Ipswich, the thousand and a half away following (honestly!) decided to go for broke and take a different tack...

Although the Baggie faithful had been relatively mute during the first half and even during the breach of our cataleptic defence in its dying minute, it soon became evident that Baggie-people had decided to meet their fate in a similar manner to the band on the Titanic. Like all such things, come the second half, it started in a small way. First, as if from an unseen signal, there was an almost unanimous lusty - even defiant - rendering of the Twenty Third Psalm, better known as 'The Lord's My Shepherd'. Then first one Baggie, then another, took up the strains of 'Alan Buckley's Blue and White Army'. Pretty soon, nearly everyone in the Portman Stand, from juvenile to geriatric, almost every man-jack of them, were roaring the refrain. The volume shook the very foundations, a Baggie-Gestalt almost; the whole greater than the sum of all its parts, the vocal ferocity of which undoubtedly caused a massive surge in laryngitis remedy sales around the West Bromwich area the next day.

Our 'Alan Buckley's Blue And White Army' marathon started with 39 minutes remaining on the clock, becoming surreal, hypnotic; a mantra. Just those words over and over again, merging into one long syllable, on and on... ALANBUCKLEYSBLUEANDWHITEARMY, one word, spiritually uplifting... A single unit, us against the world, almost Orwellian in nature. There was a joyful limb-flailing interval for equaliser celebrations with 24 minutes showing on the clock. And then again, seemingly louder than before, swollen with rare triumph and pride, ALANBUCKLEYSBLUEANDWHITEARMY!, slamming those reddened palms again... and again... and again... until there were just ten minutes of the game remaining. In case you're wondering, my co-editor timed it. Did we, metaphorically at least, blow the equaliser in? I wonder...

Physical proof of our efforts was provided by the small boy behind us who, mid-chant, proudly showed his Dad his somewhat lobster-red hands. His Dad merely urged him on to greater efforts. Then there was the reaction of the Ipswich Town supporters; confronted with what was in effect a 'no contest' situation: what feeble vocal support they had been able to muster during the first half and the beginning of the second was stunned into complete silence, only to be resurrected disguised as somewhat embarrassed relief when their winner finally went in. In 33 years of Albion supporting I can honestly say it was without precedent.

To me, it seemed our beleaguered faithful were sending the players, management and board a number of urgent messages. First, whoever was to blame for our current crisis, it *wasn't* the supporters, who'd honestly tried their best to lift the team, and second, it was an affirmation of support and encouragement for our crisis-ridden manager, despite his disdain for supporter opinion, positive or otherwise. An almost Churchillian mood prevailed, "in defeat, defiance"; a gut feeling that we were singing not so much for the club as for ourselves, and all conducted with a dignity and self-respect that was anything but quiet...

We didn't realise at the time, but that match was to be the turning point in our fortunes. Having two weeks previously stopped the rot with a bloodless encounter versus the Steptoes Of Wolverhampton and their customary supporting cast of numerous insectiles, we then tackled the 21 game run into the fag-end of the campaign, losing only three along the way, truly promotion form had we not made such a pig's ear of the middle. So how *did* we extricate ourselves from the smelly stuff, then?

During the worst parts of the abysmal run, in the dark days of winter, supporters quickly fathomed that our precipitous plunge to the nether regions of the Division was largely due to injuries, plus the fact that both of our strikers were way, way off form. Lack of service, exacerbated by an imbroglio of a midfield didn't exactly help either. That, plus a defence somewhat diaphanous in nature; we had a square peg central defender shoved into the round hole of right back. The left back suffered a 12 month injury in September. Buckley feverishly (desperately?) cast round for people to do a hasty shoring-up job.

Enter from stage left our midfield general Peter Butler, who came to us on loan from Notts County, and added some definitely-needed 'oomph' to the engine-room. Hopefully Notts can be persuaded to give us his services on a permanent basis before the start of next term. Enter also a certain Mr Holmes; no, Watson, not the violin playing, cocaine-ingesting gumshoe of literary fame, more the quick, accurate-crossing round peg defensive-stiffener sorely needed by the beleaguered

Baggies. In fact, forget about Watson - this Holmes' was quickly ably partnered by recent import Shane Nicholson. Elementary...!

Which, as Conan Doyle would say, brings me to The Singular Case Of The Dutchman Sneekes. Bought for four hundred grand from Bolton Wanderers (what on earth were Bolton thinking of when they sold him?) our Rapunzel-haired goal-machine and Michael Bolton lookalike was to instantly electrify the Hawthorns faithful. For far too long the Brummie Road had dwelt without a hero; now they had one, make no mistake. Making his debut versus Watford at the Shrine he scored; nothing remarkable about that - what *was* remarkable was the fact he repeated the performance the following game, and the game after that, and the one after that... And not just yer run-of-the-mill tap-in either; all of his strikes were quality ones; more often than not from the edge of the box, with the 'keeper usually left thrashing and floundering like a netted cod in its death throes. His inevitable apotheosis in the eyes of the Baggies faithful came during the away fixture with subsequently-promoted Leicester City where he launched a strike of exocet proportions from some 30 yards, the velocity of which caused the ball to lodge firmly in the right-hand stanchion of the net. Most goals are greeted by aficionados with a roar; this one caused a great cry of "BLOODY 'ELL!" to gush forth from the lips of the travelling Black Countrymen - and what's more, some Leicesterites joined in too...

Slipping into the 'hole' behind established strikers Andy Hunt and Bob Taylor, the 'Flying Dutchman' has become a Hawthorns cult. His late appearance at the Player of the Year night caused absolute chaos (it's awfully difficult for a presenter to proceed while the audience below is madly genuflecting and chanting "SNEEKES, SNEEKES!" ad infinitum). Since his Hawthorns arrival, pre-match crowds around the Players' Entrance have swelled to Royal Visit proportions, totally blocking the street on occasions. Then there's all these burly Black Country blokes who insist on buying long blonde wigs and wearing them in honour of You Know Who; what capped the lot, however, were the scenes outside the ground the day prior to our away fixture with Norwich - no less than SIXTY Baggies turned up merely to get a glimpse of The Holy One stepping onto the team coach! The lad deserves the adulation; his final tally of ten goals in 13 games proved to be our First Division salvation. That and the industriousness of Andy Hunt plus the latterly-rediscovered goalscoring form of 'SuperBob'. No surprise then that we at GD Towers have since christened the three of them the "Holy Trinity."

Talking of Sneekes, the lad provided GD with the season's best laugh at the last home fixture of '95-96, versus already promoted Derby. At the game's conclusion (Albion were the winners by the odd goal in five), several score Baggies ran onto the pitch. Not so unusual, given it was the season's end. What made it unusual was that the 'invaders' made a beeline for our Flying Dutchman; in a trice the lad found himself sans shirt, socks, boots, and finally, shorts, a masculine version of Lady Godiva, long blonde tresses and all. I must admit, I was spellbound as our hero, clad only in his all-too skimpy underpants, flew for the nearby players tunnel, hotly pursued by his 'admirers'; 'will they, or won't they?' I wondered... Thankfully our No. 4 had blistering pace sufficient to reach the tunnel's sanctuary before his pursuers, thereby avoiding a charge of indecent exposure by a short head... or something!

So what can we expect from the Baggies next season? I'm pretty hopeful of better things come '96-97; our recent share issue, underwritten for £2.5m, looks to be quite a success. We've already been able to acquire the services of classy midfielder Paul Groves from - you've guessed it - Grimsby! Unless I'm sorely mistaken his team-mate Clive Mendonca will be Hawthorns-bound as well; looks as though we'll have yet another torrid time from the Grimsby faithful come the next campaign! As things stand, I reckon we're not too far off a promotion side, and a classy one at that; after the penultimate away fixture of last season, venue Roker Park, I watched the Sunderland side collect the Championship trophy and their medals, and wistfully observed their supporters' joyful celebrations - after all, it was their day. As they partied, the thought ran through my head "I could do with a basin full of that!" It's high time Albion had their own personal moment in the sun, therefore the message I wish to give to the readership of this publication is simple; next year, baby, just watch us go!

Fanzine Facts

Grorty Dick has been in existence as a fanzine since 1989. The name derives from an ancient Black Country cheap belly-filler, consisting of shin beef, leeks, onions, rolled oats ('groats'), and water. Editor Glynis Wright describes the 'guilty party' as consisting of herself, husband and closet Hereford supporter Simon Wright, book-keeper extraordinaire Steve Carr (whose parsimony is apparently legendary), plus his partner Dawn Clennett and bouncing sprog David. She also mentions co-editor Andy Beaglehole and 'typesetting whizzkid' Scott Wills.

Glynis promises that their first issue of next season will include a pirated copy of Issue 7 of *Steak And Chips*, the Albion players' fanzine - surely the only players' 'zine in the Endsleigh League? She also claims that a *GD* publication 'With Hope Kaye and Clark' was also the inspiration behind the success of the Lightning Seeds/Skinner/Baddiel record brought out for Euro '96. The book is prominently displayed on a coffee table on the accompanying video, which Glynis reckons prompted thousands to dash to their record shops to buy the record, and quickly the single rose to become Number One! "How about some royalties, eh Frank?!"

GULL'S EYE

Brighton and Hove Albion

I'll get straight to the point. It was an absolute season from Hell. The only highlight came in April, right at the death, when the club's directorate - or should that be dictatorate? - announced the club would be playing next season at its home for the past 94 years - the Goldstone Ground - rather than Fratton Park, Portsmouth. Admittedly, we would only be tenants in our former home, but at least we would be staying for a little while longer, and the Fratton Park experience is something to look forward to the season after next.. The 'beautiful game' in general, though, when viewed through the Sussex seaside air, had turned into nothing short of an ugly grouse, disfigured totally by boardroom shenanigans. Be warned, the season's account that follows could happen to a football club near you. The clues are there, as Gross Lloydman might say.

Football, the game, had a brief walk-on part, and fluffed its lines spectacularly. Talk during the pre-season had been of a play-off place. Liam Brady, on a local television sports bulletin, forecast the same. He qualified it by saying 'famous last words' through a wry, Irish grin, which proved all too prophetic. What he knew at the time of the interview the supporters didn't. He could do nothing but be bullish with the bullshit, rather than bearish with the truth. More about that later.

For those to whom a dressing gown and slippers are *de rigueur*, here are some of the vital statistics. The Albion won a total of 13 games in all competitions - that includes two wins in the Auto Windscreens Shield alone - and yes we were talking about playing at Wembley when on the crest of that particular wave. Headline writers were frenetic, throwing tabloid alliteration aside in favour of 'Auto Windscreens Fever Grips Sussex'. Bah, humbug - mighty Shrewsbury Town put paid to that little excursion in the Southern area quarter finals. Fulham (from Division Three) squeezed past us in the Coca Cola Cup/Bottle/Tin - by five goals to nil over two legs, and through 22 legs belonging to an inept collection of blue and white stripes. The co-incidence of knowing a football League linesman meant I didn't have to pay to see the second part of this pantomime. "It's behind you", the back four cried out in unison at our keeper Nick Rust at alarmingly regular intervals. In the FA Cup, Canvey Island of ICIS League Division Two - or non-euphemistically 'a pub side' - held us to a first round, 2-2 draw in their *bijou* stadium that encloses several square yards of reclaimed Thames mud flat. Liam Brady, answering probing 'ifs and buts' type questions from a radio reporter after the game replied with; "Yeah and if my Grandmother had balls, she'd have been my Grandfather." And would have been slammed up in Reading gaol with Oscar Wilde, presumably? Things were beginning to look a good bit downbeat on the managerial front.

The Saturday before the replay with Canvey, Liam had had enough. The Albion were at home to the pride of the West Midlands - Walsall, and losing by the slender margin of 3-0. Normally, in this position, at least one substitute would have been thrown on. Today, though, nothing. Liam had banged his head against the boardroom wall, and the wall had scored a resounding victory. The next day he phoned Bill Archer, the chairman, and on Monday a press conference was convened at the Goldstone where he stood and read out his resignation statement in competition with the groundsman, who was cutting the grass aboard a turbo charged XR3i lawnmower. At least, I think it was the groundsman. It might have been Bill Archer. Nothing at the Albion was ever made easy for Liam.

The official reason for his departure was down to the good old cover-all-and-give-nothing-away 'mutual agreement'. Pull the other one, it's got Pompey chimes on it. It was mainly due to broken promises made by the club's owners, specifically over the availability of funds for new players; and the uncertainty as to the future of the club caused by the sale of the Goldstone Ground during the close season, and the devastating effect this had on all those who cared - players and staff alike. Liam's commitment to the club was total, and never in doubt to the supporters. He, his assistant Gerry Ryan, and coach Jimmy Case, instigated a cut in their own pay in order to strengthen the playing squad. This proved to be futile, and deep down Liam always knew it would be. In fact he was going to resign the previous April, knowing the side would struggle without the funds that had always been promised for August, but were not now going to be forthcoming. He stayed on against his own better judgement - not even Alex Ferguson would have kept the Albion clear of relegation with our board of dictators (sic).

Back to the story. Jimmy Case took over as manager for the Canvey Island replay, which we won 4-1. A new era was upon us - not. It got worse. Fulham (again!) were our opponents in the next round, and after an insipid goal-less draw at Craven Cottage, defeat followed in the replay at the Goldstone. The replay was a glimpse of how the future might look. BSkyB came along to broadcast the match live to an expectant nation, or at least to those with more disposable income than they know what to do with. They were suitably rewarded with an even more insipid 0-0, on this occasion taking in extra time, and thereby rendering most of the 6,209 crowd comatose. The Albion lost on penalties, Fulham's last being converted by their goalkeeper. Albion fans that night were left more than a little dehydrated: Fulham had extracted the urine totally. Our future was indeed staring us in the face. We had played Fulham four times in under five months, not won, and failed to score in open play. Sights were being set on a local Division Three derby against Woking the following season.

Woking blew it, but we didn't. The football, though, paled into insignificance against what continued to go on behind the scenes, and the sheer frustration it induced in most of the supporters. And for our last home game of the season, against York City, all hell broke loose; metaphorically, the fans hit the shit. Anyone who travelled down to the Sussex coast this summer might have noticed how well the allotments were equipped with blue and whited netting, supported by particularly robust runner bean frames. These gardening sundries came into existence at 3.16 pm on Saturday 27th April, when as goal posts, they ceased to be. The whole sorry scene that afternoon, during what most believed to be our last game at the Goldstone, was a fitting celebration of the Albion's nadir.

Discontent amongst the supporters had been festering since the previous summer. Bill Archer seemed determined to drive the club down the Portsmouth Road for a temporary period in exile while a new stadium was built in Sussex. However, his directional sense prompted most people to believe he was driving us in completely the opposite direction: down the Maidstone Road and into oblivion. But what evidence was there in support of this doom-laden view of the future? Here is a brief scenario: the Goldstone Ground had been sold before a new site had been secured; no agreement had been obtained from the Football League for the proposed ground sharing arrangement at Portsmouth; a planning application had been submitted to Hove Borough Council for a stadium on a site which the club didn't yet own and never looked likely to, let alone be permitted to build on; the no-profit clause preventing the owners from collecting a return greater than their original investments should the club be wound up had been 'accidentally' removed from its constitution (but was hastily reinstated once the scam had been rumbled); and lastly, and to the fore at the time of the York City game, the purchasers of the Goldstone had offered a one year stay of execution at a cost of £480,000 'rent', which the club needed to agree to by midday on Tuesday 30th April. Suffice to say, on Saturday 27th April, they had not agreed, and remained adamant that they wouldn't.

Such a stance was typical of the club's public relations, which had been an unqualified failure throughout the season. As a result, the target for the verbal frustration of the fans was the club's chief executive and deputy chairman, David Bellotti. Bellotti wrote (or lent his name to) articles that appeared sporadically in the match day programmes attempting to appease supporters concerns. Such articles only served to fan the flames of discontent further, and demonstrate his total ignorance of what a football club means to its community. Bellotti's press and media statements faired little better, and often contradicted other statements issued by the club and himself. Bellotti, though, is nothing but Bill Archer's monkey, being a paid employee of the club with no personal financial investment in it. But it was Bellotti who turned up to home games - God knows why - and even the match day stewards resented his attendance. Bill Archer, on the other hand, lives and works in North West England and couldn't be arsed.

Stranger, and more perversely still, Archer, the organ grinder, bought a controlling interest in the club for just £56.25 (yes the decimal point is in the right place - five thousand, six hundred and twenty-five PENCE). Beware of holding companies - they are Trojan Horses looking for a club's Achilles heel. The Albion's went on full view when the club was being dangled in the High Court, subject of a collective noun of winding up petitions in 1993. In sailed Foray 585 Limited, with Archer at the helm, and bought out the previous directors' interests. The co-owner of Foray 585 (and therefore Albion) is Greg Stanley, worth a cool £40 million (£5 million more than Martin Edwards!). Words to describe Greg Stanley fail me, or rather, if written, would embroil me in litigation. The fact that he stood back and allowed everything I have described earlier to happen probably speaks for itself. Oh yes, I almost forgot, he is also a Chelsea season ticket holder.

Cries of "Sack the board" had become trite by the time we played York City, and so it was no surprise that events took the turn they did. Claims that true supporters of the Albion were not involved in the media-speak 'riot' are ridiculous; most of those protesting on the pitch were true Albion supporters, and proud of it. There were, undoubtedly, a small number of the ubiquitous 'rent-a-mob' involved, one of which assaulted a (female) supporter for no reason whatsoever. (A club in our position does not need big brave soldiers such as that scumbag, whatever the cause.) But what the 'rent-a-mob' did that afternoon was to lift the lid of the pressure cooker, and allow every single Albion supporter's cry for help to be heard on a national stage. They also, unintentionally, made the referee's decision to abandon the game an easy one by destroying the goal posts and, in consequence, the police were able to bring the afternoon to a peaceful conclusion without the undue pressure of getting the game restarted. Last, but by no means least, a big thank you to the York City supporters who made the round trip for 16 minutes of football: your support for us that afternoon was second to none.

Can such so-called direct action be justified? In the cold light of day probably not. However, the ferocity with which it happened could, oh so easily, have been reduced if the club had attempted to empathise with its supporters. The previous Saturday's game against Carlisle had seen a dress rehearsal of what was to come. A pitch invasion after the game, followed by a re-enactment of the storming of the Bastille, for which, owing to the absence of a French prison, the director's box was deemed an acceptable substitute. Plush blue vinyl cushions plumed upwards and outwards like sparks from a Roman candle. It was clear to everyone, except the board of dictators, that enough was enough - WE DID NOT (AND DO NOT) WANT TO MOVE TO PORTSMOUTH. Consequently, further action was inevitable. Surely no surprises there? Certainly not to the Sussex Police, who asked the directors to stay away from the ground on match days from then on for their own safety; they also implied that the board had no-one but themselves to blame for what was now happening, and it was down to them, and not the Police, to sort the problem out.

At 11.50 am on Tuesday 30th April, ten minutes before the deadline, the club paid over what it would cost to allow it to stay at the Goldstone for another year: no real surprise there either, if the truth be known. The deal was subject to a confidentiality agreement, binding on both parties, so no one outside it knows what the agreed price actually was. The eleventh hour striking of the deal did, though, explain why a lorry load of chemical fertiliser had been delivered to the ground the previous week. Someone at the club knew BEFORE we played York it was going to be hover-mowers, and not bulldozers, that swept majestically across the Goldstone turf during the summer. I wonder if directors can be charged with bringing the game into disrepute?

So that was the season that was. The sound of leather on willow's arrived, and not before time. It has become a custom in this 'trophy-challenged' part of old Blighty for *Gull's Eye* to hold an end of season dinner/wake. The top table guests this year, amongst others, were Steve Foster, club captain and centre back of considerable years, and Ian Chapman, who regularly occupied the left back position, was born in Brighton, and who has been with the club since 1986. Both got to their feet and proposed a toast to us, the supporters. Perhaps there is some beauty left in the game after all. Sadly, neither will be wearing an Albion shirt next season. People more cynical than myself can draw their own conclusions as to why.

The search goes on for an oasis in Albion's desert of under-achievement and crass stupidity. Some might say that sunshine follows thunder. Some might say you get what you've been given. I look forward to the day when all Albion supporters can say, unambiguously, there's no 'f' in Bellotti, and there's no 'f' in Archer either. As for Greg Stanley, well, any leopard would change its spots when the cheque book comes out - wouldn't it?

Fanzine Facts

Gull's Eye, Britain's most prolific fanzine, was launched in 1988 by a dedicated but largely anonymous team. *GE* has campaigned tirelessly for the administrative mess that is the Albion boardroom, to be sorted out once and for all. However the strain started to show, and towards the back end of last season Billy and Lenny announced that it was time for the mag to close for good. However, with the venue for next year's *Gull's Eye* dinner already booked, the rumours of a comeback seem to have some substance. Thanks once again to Eldrich, who relived the ghastliness of the last nine months to pen this article.

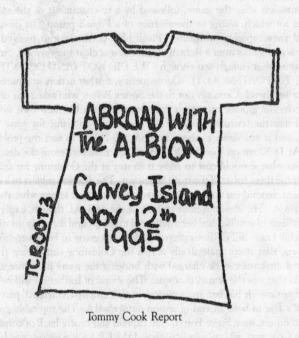

Tommy Cook Report

GWLADYS SINGS THE BLUES

Everton

Gloating over another team's defeat is always something which I have looked upon with a certain amount of disdain. I frowned with cringing embarrassment as my fellow fans have screamed "Nay-eeeeem" whenever anybody so much as entered the Arsenal half when we played them in August, and at the gesticulations which Andy Cole received week-in week-out whenever he let another gaping chance go amiss for United. Going back a few months further, who could forget the nation's crowing at Man United's ability to win absolutely nothing during the '94-95 season? What perverse satisfaction do these morons get from watching the suffering of a fellow football supporter? Childish, puerile and immature all spring to mind when looking to describe those who delight in the disappointment of others.

However, in the case of Liverpool Football Club I make an exception. For years they have revelled in the failings of Everton, basked in their own glory and that of others (when it meant an Everton defeat) and waxed lyrical about how they are the greatest club in the history of the entire universe (which they're not). The '95-96 season provided ample opportunity for revenge. The first derby game at Anfield, a ground in which we had failed to record a League victory for a decade, provided the setting for Andrei Kanchelskis to plunder his first two goals since signing for £5.5m, a deal which had been protracted by Man Utd's refusal to pay a contractual fee to the Ukrainian's first club. When that matter was finally settled, Kanchelskis was then injured just 194 minutes into his Everton career, ironically against the Mancs. When the winger eventually forced his way into the Everton side he proved to be a revelation, scoring 16 times in 32 games, including a hat-trick in the rout of Sheffield Wednesday, in what was described by David Pleat as a "world class performance." Without his pace on the right, Everton looked a little lost, but with it they were a force to be reckoned with.

The second glorious defeat of Liverpool should have been the third. You see, had it not been for Robbie Fowler's 87th minute equaliser, Everton would have recorded the double over their Mersey rivals. However it was not to be, and Everton had to rely upon United beating the Anfield side in the FA Cup Final before having the chance to once again crack open the Champagne. For years the red half of Merseyside has fuelled a hatred for all things connected with Manchester, yet the passion for this hate remains a complete mystery to most people. One thing is certain, the majority of Evertonians do not share this animosity, and by Cup Final Day we were all decked out in those atrocious grey away shirts, bought on the cheap after Alex Ferguson refused to let his young stars wear them. Watching my neighbours crying into their pint glasses was made all the more enjoyable by the fact that defeat was inflicted by a team which they hated more than us. The manner in which they accepted the defeat was almost as bad as their performance; one gracious loser spitting on Cantona and another belting Ferguson. The papers needed no further excuse, and launched into vengeful attacks upon the city and its apparent jealousy of Manchester. Oh yeah? Don't forget that this so-called 'bad feeling' between the two cities resulted in no arrests at the '95 final between Everton and United.

Despite all the moaning by kopites, it was Evertonians who spent the early part of the season in a subdued mood. Aside from a Charity Shield win, after which Ray Harford cited Everton as Blackburn's chief title rivals (a prediction about as accurate as his own side's finishing - Alan Shearer excepted), we stuttered through August and September with just two League wins and two scrappy victories against a bunch of Icelandic part-timers in the Cup Winners Cup. The only bright spark was Anders Limpar who livened up proceedings at Goodison, putting in a few magnificent performances and fulfilling the maxim of one of his predecessors on the Everton wing, Duncan McKenzie, who once commented that "Entertainment is what it's all about."

By now, the patience of the Everton support was being stretched, and wary of a repeat of the previous season in which Mike Walker had led us to just one victory by the time of his sacking, one or two individuals started to call for the head of Joe Royle. How anybody could suggest that Joe should be sacked after he'd saved Everton when they were virtually unsavable and as a bonus led us to Cup Final victory the year before remains a complete mystery. But when we lost 2-4 at home to Millwall in the League Cup, the letters flowed in to the fanzines and the local papers alike. Although it could be argued that Royle had borstalised the so-called school of science since his returned to Goodison, in his favour it ought to be remembered that he had the same nucleus of players who'd scraped past relegation in the previous two seasons. As if things couldn't get any worse, on Wednesday 11th October 1995 Duncan Ferguson was sent to prison for head-butting Raith's John McStay. It seemed ludicrous that in the year in which Eric Cantona had attacked a supporter, Julian Dicks had stamped on John Spencer's head and Paul Merson had admitted cocaine addiction, Ferguson was the only one who received a custodial sentence. It was whilst the big man was confined to Barlinnie gaol that there was an upturn in the blue's fortunes, and by the time of his release at the end of November we'd risen to 12th from 18th after a run of wins, including the scalps of Champions Blackburn and of course Liverpool.

Ferguson was in the headlines twice more before he'd even had the opportunity to get his No. 9 shirt off its hanger. First, because one or two newspapers thought it 'inappropriate' that Goodison should applaud their hero when he stood at the mouth of the players' tunnel the day after his release, and again the following week when his 11 match ban was overturned. This enabled him to play in a 5-0 reserve victory over Newcastle in which he scored twice to delight the crowd of 11,000 who'd braved arctic conditions to see his return. By the start of January he was back to his best with a brace against Wimbledon. In spite of a further six goals, the rest of his season was marred by a niggling groin injury, which resulted in him pulling out of Scotland's Euro '96 squad and being told to rest. Hopefully the best is yet to come from the fiery Scot.

The Blue revival was stunted by defeats against Newcastle and Coventry, but some Christmas cheer was brought in with a convincing 4-0 trouncing of Middlesbrough who at the time boasted the best defensive record in the League. There followed a 2-0 win over Leeds when we had to do without captain Dave Watson for most of the game after an early sending off. Joe Parkinson and Graham Stuart played a quintessential part in this game, both fulfilling roles alien to them but nevertheless excelling. Stuart, a right winger by trade, played most of his games at centre forward, and only injuries at the start and end of the season prevented him from being top scorer.

January was an indifferent month with an early victory against Wimbledon apparently setting us up nicely, but draws against Chelsea and Stockport saw one or two disgruntled fans question Royle's tactics. Stockport were seen off in the replay by a late John Ebbrell winner. It was nice to see the midfielder back to form as he'd received some horrific abuse from the crowd the previous season. There are few things better than seeing a player respond in such a fashion... unless of course it involves a Liverpool defeat!!! An away win at Arsenal kept the steady rise up the table going, but this was followed by the blues losing their grip on the FA Cup when we crashed to a 2-1 defeat at Port Vale. The performance was so bad that it marked the end of both Gary Ablett and Matt Jackson's Everton careers; two players who'd been stalwarts in the previous year's Cup victory.

Being out of the Cup might have seemed like the end of the world, but it provided Everton with less fixture congestion and a more realistic chance of qualifying for Europe. By the end of March, a place in the top five looked distinctly possible, especially following a Kanchelskis-inspired 3-0 drubbing of Blackburn, and this on the back of a run of just two League defeats since Christmas. However a surprise reverse at QPR appeared to have stifled our continental plans, as Everton slipped back to seventh, not helped by *that* late equaliser in the Goodison Derby.

A UEFA Cup place still wasn't out of the reckoning, and defeats for Arsenal, Spurs and the hapless Sheffield Wednesday meant that the calculators were out for the last game of the season against Aston Villa. A full Goodison Park saw a game without much incident until the pocket genius, Anders Limpar, was brought on to a standing ovation. Just as he had inspired Everton to victory on the last day of the season two years previously, when Everton needed a win to ensure survival, he provided the inspiration for a late Joe Parkinson winner, drilled home from outside the box. For that moment, Everton were in Europe, as Spurs were drawing at Newcastle and Bolton were beating Arsenal. However, two late goals at Highbury meant that Europe wasn't to be; at least not in '96-97.

But like the Murphy's, us Evertonians weren't bitter. We knew that a Manchester Victory in the Cup Final would alleviate the blues, and the following Saturday a certain Mr Eric Cantona duly obliged.

Fanzine Facts

Gwladys Sings The Blues, now the second largest Everton fanzine, was started in August '94 by editor James Corbett and artist David Pearson, who gained the help of Rory O'Keeffe, Steve Masterton and Claire Redhead along the way. Unfortunately, '96-97 will be **GSTB**'s last full season as James and some of the others head off to various 'seats of learning' around the country. As James laments, "That probably means I'll be stuck in Leeds or some other shit-hole, miles away from my beloved Goodison."

When Skies Are Grey

HANGING ON THE TELEPHONE

Huddersfield Town

Sex and Drugs and Rock and Roll

Huddersfield Town achieved promotion to the Endsleigh First Division by winning an enthralling play-off final beneath the Twin Towers of Wembley at the end of May 1995.

Seven days later the club had no manager and no chairman.

Manager Neil Warnock scurried out of West Yorkshire amidst rumours of sordid goings on that involved other people's wives and girlfriends together with copious amounts of whipped cream and chocolate sauce (a complete fabrication of course).

Hot on the heels of Warnock went Terry 'The Fish' Fisher, the only Huddersfield Town chairman in recent history to be popular with the supporters, ousted only hours later in a boardroom coup. "Difficult to contact and a bit of a loose cannon" came the official explanation, "pissed up and ego out of control" whispered the gossips (more fabrication).

Hardly the pre-season preparation the supporters were hoping for as we faced the bright new dawn. Still, with the new chairman proclaiming ambitions about the Premiership things could only get better...

The wheels appeared to have fallen of the wagon immediately however, when aforementioned new chairman Geoff Headey announced that Terry Dolan was one of the favoured candidates for the vacant manager's chair. Now the words 'ambition' and 'Terry Dolan' do not belong in the same sentence as far as Town fans are concerned. Indeed a worse choice to lead the team (other than perhaps Malcolm MacDonald) Town fans could not imagine. Here was a man who, having failed as a Town player, had sought to denounce the club's supporters on every subsequent visit to Huddersfield in his capacity as a manager. Thankfully, tremendous supporter pressure forced a re-think and Dolan was gently dropped from consideration by the board and allowed to successfully guide Hull City into the Football League's basement.

The appointment of supporter's choice Brian Horton (who the board now pretended had been their first choice all along, honest) as new manager three weeks later, heralded a rush for season tickets that saw sales top 8,000 for the first time in the club's history.

Horton unfortunately had little time to assess the capabilities of his playing staff, and amid expert pundit opinion that dismissed the side as "simply not good enough at this level", a very familiar Town side showing little change from the one which completed the previous campaign began their season at sunny Boundary Park. With supporters revelling in the club's new found lofty status, it should have come as no surprise when the players entered into the spirit of things by looking on in awe of their opponents and losing 3-0.

Then they lost at home to mighty Port Vale the following Tuesday, to make us wonder if a know nothing journalist fool might actually have a point.

But things were slowly beginning to change, and having had a good look at his squad Brian Horton decided who was and wasn't good enough and began to do something about it. Welsh international defender Steve Jenkins was stolen from Swansea for a mere £250,000, together with the emerging Kevin Gray and the cool, calm and collected Tom Cowan, in order to stabilise a suspect defence. Lee Makel, the only ball-playing midfielder on Blackburn's books was the next arrival, brought in to add a little finesse to our play (and he looks an exciting prospect despite resembling, and being slower than, Brian the snail from The Magic Roundabout). Finally, 'the best winger outside the Premiership' Paul Dalton (who?) joined us from deserter Warnock and striker Rob Edwards was prised from Crewe. All this for a mere £1m.

With the squad complete and growing in confidence, the ball began to spend more time on the floor (something we weren't expecting) and Town established themselves in the top six (something we *definitely* weren't expecting).

Town were serving up some top class football and demolishing supposed superior opponents along the way. For example, during November we were unbeaten and accounted for Norwich, Leicester and Wolves at home, whilst earning draws away at Portsmouth and Millwall (who were then top) to move into a vertigo-inducing second place.

The FA Cup also saw Town make some significant progress for the first time in almost a quarter of a century. The fifth round tie with Wimbledon at the McAlpine Stadium and Town were cruising at 2-0, only for Wimbledon to claw their way back into things and then sickeningly equalise four minutes into injury time. More sickening was the inevitable "Naive defending" post match analysis from Alan Hansen on Match of The Day. Even more sickening still was the fact that he was right.

Despite this relative success I wasn't really that convinced because any number of early season games, where we scraped home, could so easily have gone the other way. Inevitably, as the season went, on a greater number of games did in fact go against us, prompting critical eyes to focus on a playing 'surface' which, beginning to suffer under the weight of 60+ football matches and 25+ rugby matches, was used as a convenient excuse for our declining fortunes.

An over-utilised and badly managed pitch, we asked? "Not at all" came the reply; all the problems were caused by covering the pitch for two days back in July so that REM could bore everyone to death for two hours with their MOR American pap. So *that's* why it's worn out down the middle and in the goal mouth then huh?

By mid-April, Town's play-off chances were slowly waning and an away record of only three wins (the worst in the Division) told its own story, and has most of us quivering about the forthcoming campaign. "I can't understand our poor away form" claimed Brian, "it's not as if we approach the games differently or try to alter our tactics." Brian, I think perhaps now might be the time...

The season didn't just fade away however; we were still treated to a bout of fiststicuffs at Wolves between Town players Tom Cowan and Mark Ward that Sky Sports would have been proud to present as 'Big Time Boxing'. Even more entertaining was Man Utd loan signing Ben Thornley getting booked six times and early-bath'ed twice in 12 appearances (the best of which came at Sunderland when Ben threw the ball at the referee after the half time whistle had gone, apparently for talking to him in a stern manner. Poor temperament or typical club upbringing?)

To top it all, 'Huddersfield Superstar' Craig Whittington propelled himself into the headlines for the one and only time in his footballing career by failing a drugs test for cannabis for the second time. "Explains why the dope missed from only one yard in his only game for Town" declared one fanzine contributor in a fitting epitaph.

Our slide in form meant that our last game had little meaning for Town fans, but was rounded off in the now usual McAlpine Stadium fashion by a pitch invasion of travelling supporters who'd just witnessed their club achieve the impossible (Portsmouth avoiding relegation this time, Barry Fry's Birmingham winning the Championship the last).

So have a quick look at the fixture list. If your team are visiting Huddersfield for the final game of this season, now's the time to order your party costume.

Oh, and yes, we *do* know we've only got three stands.

Fanzine Facts

HOTT is concocted five times a season by Mick, Mini and Wights. Foundered one drunken evening after an especially inept Huddersfield performance, *Hanging On The Telephone* is now into its seventh season, has many regular contributors (to whom *HOTT* are very grateful) and still remains largely ignored by the club.

THE HANGING SHEEP

Leeds United

Out of the smouldering wreckage that was the '94-95 season we had the good news that Leeds hadn't bought some waste of space from Sheffield Wednesday (e.g. Nigel Worthington). The bad news was that Supremo Wilkinson had managed to surpass this miserable and thoroughly unpopular signing by delving into the footballing wasteland that is Sheffield *United*, bringing Paul Beesley to Leeds. "I can't believe a club like Leeds has come in for me," he exclaimed. "You're not the f**king only one pal", was the collective groan of the fans.

Three victories at the start of the season had us sitting aloft the Division like some demented fairy on the Christmas tree. Could this squad of players actually live up to Wilkinson's boast that they were "the best squad I've had at the club" (manager's handbook cliché No. 43).

THE HANGING SHEEP
the independent leeds fanzine
£1   issue 40

All Clapped Out!

Brolin: Kicked into touch?

The 'close your eyes it might get better' Special

Our surge towards the end of the previous season had gained us a UEFA Cup place. The draw gave us a sexy sounding trip to the South of France to play Monaco, with its yachts, big cars, helicopters and poodles. Our plane was delayed and the 500 Leeds fans on board consoled themselves by drinking enough beer to send Tetley's shares shooting through the bloody roof.

Upon arrival it was clear that the local police were, erm, crapping themselves. Baggage and passport control was at the bottom of the steps, with the coaches as close as they could get without breaking aviation rules. Once again we were given a police escort of royal proportions into the centre of Nice. For being good boys and girls we were allowed to wander into the bars for a few hours, which we naturally did. Before departing Nice, the local police commander waddled across the road to inform us that, "Monaco, zey are to win four nussing'. Yerssss, Pierre.

As we wound our way into the bowels of the Principality, the scale of the wealth was clearly evident. Yachts the size of which P&O would have been proud bobbed about in the marinas. On closer inspection, most of these huge vessels were bedecked with bimbos of one description or another. Who says size isn't important?

More drinks were on the menu and our little group chose the yachting club at the Hotel Ramada for our quaffing venue. Orange waistcoat clad waiters served the rich, famous and downright pompous. They were a bit disturbed by the drunken antics of one group of Englishmen, but enough of the press. The alcohol took its toll and as I claimed my place in the toilet amongst the 24 carat gold taps and marble urinals (I kid you not), I could sense that some of the Versace-clad locals were less than impressed with my attire. I don't suppose they were used to seeing Adidas Sambas topped off with a cheeky little Nike tennis T-shirt number.

The match itself was a fairytale story of orgasmic proportions. I could hardly contain the euphoria as Yeboah smashed his second from 25 yards. Two-nil up in Monaco and bloody cruising. A third ensured that we'd hit the headlines for all the right reasons, for once. The bars of Nice were bristling with happy United fans that evening, I can tell you. Outside the ground our ever-popular MD Bill Fotherby appeared to wave the fans off. He was greeted with umpteen thousand 'V' signs for his trouble. Well liked bloke our Bill...

The only down side to the Monaco trip was the fiasco over tickets. The simple rule (apparently) was that you either travelled via one of the official travel clubs or you didn't travel at all. As it turned out, the official fans (some of whom had spent 30 hours on their coaches) had to fork out £15 per ticket. Those who had travelled independently paid £6 at a booth outside the ground. This was the starting point of a severe season long rumpus over ticket prices.

Nothing is ever predictable watching Leeds United, and just four days after the glory of that 3-0 victory in Monaco we were ripped apart by QPR in a 3-1 defeat which flattered us somewhat. The annual Coca Cola Cup upset hadn't materialised, although it took two titanic struggles to dispose of Notts County. Next to fall to a late Speed header were Derby County.

Our European tour would take us to Holland next, Eindhoven to be precise. In typical Leeds fashion we'd finished Monaco off in the second leg of the previous round by losing 1-0 at home and scaring the shit out of ourselves. Oh, how we laughed at the time... A storming start saw us lead 1-0 against Eindhoven inside ten minutes. Dutch masters my left buttock! Half time arrived with us firmly 3-1 down. Oh shit. The stands erupted for the second 45 in a backs-to-the-wall cavalry charge type of thingy. The players responded and with 20 minutes left we'd clawed the tie back to 3-3. With the hordes baying for blood and the 1,000 travelling Dutchmen looking distinctly uneasy in their segregated area, the Leeds players did this; sat back, admired what a good job they'd done and conceded two more goals in the last eight minutes. Three-five; goodnight Vienna.

The second leg saw large scale pilfering across Belgium. As one fan observed, "Well - we did bail them out in the war." Yes, quite. Upon reaching Eindhoven we were ushered down a fog-bound lovers lane by the police, who were decidedly nervous of our presence. That would obviously explain why 123 Leeds supporters were deported for the heinous crime of not carrying their passports. Great this European Community lark innit?

Our collection of youngsters and wasters didn't stand a cat's chance as the Dutch queued up to take pot-shots at our goal. Three-nil on the night and 8-3 on aggregate was United's worst ever defeat in European competition. The only consolation was the magnificent support from the 1,500 who were allowed to attend. A full 30 minutes' continual chanting of "We are the champions, champions of Europe" more than confused the 25,000 locals and police. They could only stand in silence until it was all over, and then a rapturous round of applause greeted our ears. They appreciated loyal fans and weren't scared to show it.

Things from here on in started to go pear-shaped. Tomas Brolin, that impish Abba-esque Swede was bought for a club record fee of £4.5m and was promptly installed as the most expensive substitute in Leeds' history. When we break records at Elland Road we don't do it by halves. Having outplayed (and outsung) the magnificent (sic) Toon Army in their own backyard, we came away with a 2-1 defeat. This was followed by a gut wrenching 1-0 home reverse against Man City.

The slide which in truth had started in September, now resembled a sledge with a 21 stone wrestler going down the side of Ben Nevis (I think you get the picture), with a 6-2 mauling at Sheffield Wednesday. Next the players ripped the Reds apart to record a morale boosting 3-1 win (which could easily have been six). A 2-0 loss at Everton brought us crashing back to earth once more.

The FA Cup saw us paired against Derby. The Rams had a man sent off for looking at Brian Deane and Leeds pressed home the advantage by going 2-0... down. Miracles do occasionally happen and two goals in the last minute somehow helped us to a 4-2 win. I was even spotted on Sky by a mate whilst joining a chant of "we're shit and we've beat you twice" being directed at the pissed-off locals.

The League form was all over the place and with Nigel Worthington suffering horrendous abuse and ridicule, the rest of the players seemed reticent to try anything (including passing, tackling, heading, running, shooting, how long is this book by the way?) for fear of the same.

Things were grim as Tony Yeboah was back in Africa for their Nations Cup. Noel Whelan had been sold, much to the fans' collective dismay, and we had Liverpool and Villa away looming. What should we do? Bring in Jamie Forrester from the reserves? Na, he'd already been sold to Grimsby earlier in the season. I know, we'll get Lee Chapman back on loan from Ipswich reserves some two and a half years after we'd sold him. Brilliant! As it turned out Chappy contributed to goal number one after 24 minutes against West Ham. A minute later he was turning the showers on after harshly being accused by the blind bastard in the green of using his elbows. Looking across at the Leeds bench I'm sure I could spy Wilko trying to rig up a noose.

Leeds battled like madmen and with Tomas Brolin off the bench and on the pitch for once we could sit back and marvel at his obvious ability. With the Whites and Tomas two goals up and cruising for the third, Wilkinson decided that he'd had enough of this popular little Swedish shit and subbed him. Howls of derision and chorus upon chorus of verbal abuse was the fans' response. A truly disgraceful decision.

The farcical idea to sell Whelan to Coventry was further made to look like the mother of all cock-ups with a 5-0 rout at Anfield and a 3-0 drubbing at Villa Park to console the travelling fans. The defence was now playing a blinder (or like blind 'uns to be more accurate).

If the League form disappointed (!), our Cup exploits offered some comfort. A 2-1 scrap against Reading had us paired with Birmingham in the Coca Cola Cup semis (having avoided Arsenal and Villa). A 5-1 aggregate win meant that despite all the crap performances, crazy transfer dealings and overall apathy emanating from the gates of Elland Road, we could look forward to our first major Cup Final appearance for 23 years.

Before that we had to settle our FA Cup sixth round tie against Liverpool. Having held the Reds 0-0 with the most defensive, boring and ultimately pointless display I can ever recall seeing at Leeds, we set ourselves mission impossible by travelling to Anfield just days before the Coca Cola Cup Final. We curled up and died, 3-0.

The two Cup ties highlighted an undercurrent of alienation felt by the fans against the club as a whole. Leeds had been charging over the top prices for all the Cup ties, and against Liverpool they tried to screw top prices out of the fans just once too often. With the 'cheap' seats costing a mere £19 (£1 dearer than the cheapest seats at Wembley v Villa), fans staged a boycott which resulted in only 24,000 (including 5,500 visitors) turning up. The replay saw Leeds' once proud travelling army reduced to 1,100 hardy souls. The fans were making a very clear point to those in charge. This time, enough really was enough.

Our great day out at Wembley ended in total humiliation for both the fans and the manager. When have supporters ever called for a manager's head at a Cup Final? Villa hardly had to break sweat to canter to a 3-0 win. The supporters who had been asked to witness largely second rate performances for two years or more had seen more than they could take. Wembley exploded in a vitriolic attack on the manager and his lacklustre players. This abuse clearly shocked Wilkinson, and I personally feel that he was close to quitting. I wouldn't have shed a tear.

The season was now well and truly over, except that the gutless bunch of players that Wilkinson presides over contrived to break a few more records before the season was out. A losing streak which was the club's worst for nearly 50 years confirmed that what had been witnessed by all at Leeds was nothing short of dire. Only a 0-0 bore draw at Coventry saved face. We couldn't even have the consolation of sending Big Fat Ron's team down. The oh so predictable pitch invasion by both sets of fans gained our supporters yet more notoriety. But it wasn't much more than people venting their anger and sheer frustration. It doesn't make it right, but it does help to explain why it happened.

One supporter was perhaps spot on, when, on witnessing the Leeds hordes surge towards the home fans on the pitch after the match, observed "It's about the only time Leeds have attacked so positively all season..."

As I write, Wilkinson has promised to rebuild his team, and I hope for his sake he does just that. The fans don't want second rate players giving second rate performances. If the public humiliation that Wilkinson suffered at Wembley stings him into action, then everybody at the club will hopefully benefit as a result. Roll on August...

Fanzine Facts

The Hanging Sheep first saw the light of day on a train going to a pre-season friendly at Carlisle in 1988. Along the way, as editor Chris Stringer says, "we've had some bizarre correspondence from fans across the world and it's perhaps this, above all else that makes it all worthwhile."

THE HATCHET

Bury

For Bury FC the '95-96 season got off to a distinctly muted start. Following the huge disappointment of losing in the play-off final at the end of '94-95 (our first ever trip to Wembley incidentally), many Bury supporters were not exactly in high spirits for the start of the new season.

The position of manager Mike Walsh was not exactly rock solid either. During the summer a number of letters from disgruntled supporters appeared in the local press, calling for Walsh's head on a plate. A few of them reminded the directors of their promise earlier in the year - that failure to secure promotion would mean Walsh would be sacked. As the new campaign got under way, however, Walsh was still in the hot seat - even if he was considering investing in a pair of asbestos trousers.

The Shakers' Wembley hangover didn't only affect the supporters. The team embarked on a less than inspiring run of just one win in their opening six league fixtures. It was the sixth match, in fact, that proved to be the final straw for Mike Walsh - Bury collapsed to a humiliating 5-0 defeat at home against Plymouth. Within a day or two, Walsh was out by 'mutual agreement' as they say in football circles. Whatever.

The fans now waited with baited breath to see who the board would choose to lead us into the promised land of Division Two - although at this stage, some pessimists thought avoiding the drop into the Conference would be an achievement. Many Shakers supporters clamoured for the appointment of Sammy McIlroy. Famed as the last of the 'Busby Babes', Sammy had been a big favourite with the Bury crowd when he had played out the latter part of his career at Gigg Lane. Not only that, but he had recently shown the right stuff as a manager by leading Macclesfield to the Championship of the Conference. McIlroy's supporters felt that appointing such a popular successor would, at a stroke, help to rally support and provide an instant boost in morale to everyone at the club. In these circumstances the board had little choice - they offered the job to Walsh's assistant, Stan Ternent.

Still, things seemed to pick up as Bury bounced back to win the next two games. The first of these was a 2-1 victory against Chesterfield in the Dandelion and Burdock Cup - only the tiniest crumb of revenge for the Wembley let-down a few weeks earlier - and the second was also a 2-1 win, away against the Pie Eaters at Springfield Park. It proved to be a false dawn, however, as we failed to win any of the next five matches. Brief respite was gained with a stirring 4-2 success in the home leg of the Pop Cup against Sheffield United, followed by the rare treat of a League win at home, Leyton Orient being the victims (well, no surprise there then). The next three were lost, however, and by the time struggling Scarborough turned us over at Gigg Lane we were in 22nd place in the Division - our lowest position since ads first appeared on kit tops.

Ternent's reign desperately needed something to turn it around - and on Saturday October 28th, veteran striker Phil Stant duly pulled the rabbit out of the hat, with four superb goals in a 5-1 victory at Field Mill (ironically, Mansfield are one of Stant's former clubs). Bury won the next game too, and we then went on to be unbeaten through November and December. Oh yeah - apart from being knocked out of the FA Cup at home, by... Blyth Spartans. "Never mind", we muttered through gritted teeth, "at least we can now concentrate on the League..."

Apart from a 3-0 hiccup on New Year's Day when Hartlepool beat us, things really started to look up in the New Year. Out of the last 24 games, the revitalised Shakers lost just five, drew five and won the other 14. Particularly enjoyable results included a 7-1 annihilation of Lincoln City at Gigg, and a brilliant 4-2 away win at Cambridge - all the sweeter since we'd had to claw back a two goal deficit.

As the season drew towards its end, it was undeniable that promotion was a distinct possibility, although everyone was absolutely desperate to avoid the play-offs this time. Preston and Gillingham were home and dry in first and second place respectively. With only three games left we were lying in automatic promotion third place, a position which was also jealously eyed by Plymouth, Wigan and - most dangerous of all - Darlington, who'd been in superb form in recent weeks.

On April 20th, almost 1,500 Bury lads and lasses charged up to Feethams for a match which had been billed as the 'promotion decider'. Spurred on by a big following with everything to play for, a real carnival atmosphere and brilliant sun-shine, Bury responded in classic fashion by losing 4-0. As a few of us sat dejectedly in the railway station afterwards, a large advertising poster caught my eye. I hoped to God it wasn't an omen. The slogan proclaimed 'Hartlepool - The Future'.

Still, we reasoned, we might yet do it, as long as we beat Exeter at St James next week (trying hard not to dwell on the fact we'd looked incapable of beating an egg when we played Darlo). We drew. Still, we reasoned, becoming more desper-ate, we might yet do it. All we had to do was beat Cardiff at home in our final game... and pray that Darlington didn't win at Scunthorpe.

For the Cardiff game Gigg Lane was packed. Well, the two main stands were, anyway. The Manchester Road stand was still off-limits, and, despite all the hype in the press about an invasion from South Wales, I reckon there were less than 200 Bluebirds fans in the Cemy End. The game itself was mostly one-way traffic, the cheers for Bury's goals being matched by more cheers as news filtered through of Scunthorpe's strikes against Darlington. Early in the second half, though, an eerie silence descended over the ground, as reports came through that Darlington had scored twice and Scunny were just holding onto a 2-2 draw. With 20 minutes to go, Bury were 3-0 up, but we were in torment. The Cardiff fans were having a great laugh at our expense, yelling in unison every now and again to make us think Darlington had scored again. Things got very confused. Some people said that

Darlo were winning 3-2, others that it was 3-3, "but hang on - Darlington have just hit the crossbar!." I couldn't take it - remembering from painful personal experience how we had all been misled by fake reports during a similar 'crunch' match at the end of '82-83, I chose to ignore the rumours.

As the final whistle blew at Gigg Lane, hundreds of us ran onto the pitch - but it was a very strange feeling just standing there, waiting for the final score from Scunthorpe. Four whole minutes ticked by before it was announced that Scunthorpe and Darlington had finished 3-3 and we were up! The place went absolutely crazy as Bury celebrated promotion for the first time since 1985. The intervening period had seen us fail in no less than four sets of play-offs and suffer relegation once, so this success seemed even sweeter. Stan Ternent had somehow managed to pull the season around and lead us to promotion - an achievement which had seemed extremely unlikely before Christmas.

Now, all we have to do is get promoted again next season, and we'll be where we should have gone, back in '89...

Fanzine Facts

The Hatchet editor Chris Bainbridge was born on Tyneside, but moved to North Manchester with his family in the late 60's when he was still a bairn. He began watching Bury, and became seriously hooked after watching the Shakers beat Aston Villa 3-1. "This team will go far" he confidently predicted. And indeed, within a few years they had tasted both Premiership and European glory. Villa, that is. Bury on the other hand, have spent the last 28 years alternating between the bottom two Divisions.

His confidence boosted by having letters printed in 'When Saturday Comes' and 'Talk of The Tyne', in 1995 Chris decided to launch The Hatchet. "There comes a time," he says, "when writing to the local paper is no longer enough."

Chris says The Hatchet is aiming for quality rather than quantity, and he has been encouraged by the standard of writing sent in by guest contributors. He was also delighted that the magazine seemed to act like a lucky charm for the club, promotion being clinched in its first season of publication. "If we go up again next year, we shall definitely expect an invitation to the civic reception." In case you hadn't guessed, the 'zine's name is based on the old saying 'bury the hatchet'.

THE HEATHEN

Birmingham City

Frying Tonight!

Just when we thought it was all over this summer, Blues managed to hit us with the bombshell of the season! After 156 games in charge, 61 signings and 349 players used, Barry Fry was asked to make his final trip through the (much used) revolving door. It came as no surprise that he left in such circumstances - Birmingham City have rarely failed to hit the headlines since David Sullivan, Karren Brady and David and Ralph Gold arrived. So here follows the story of Barry's last season at St Andrews.

Quote from an early season issue of *The Heathen*: "The Gold Brothers feel that our club has all of the elements of being a Premiership club. They identify the following: a stadium that will be completed in the next two years, Barry Fry - a Premier manager, Karren Brady - a terrific administrator and negotiator, outstanding supporters that are Premiership fans, and a team that will do better in the First Division than in the Second."

ELECTRIC BLUE. There was an abundance of optimism after last season's Wembley and Championship double. Barry's balance book had been boosted by the big crowds (beat that, Sun sub-editors!), and the boys were brimming with bravado (oh God, I can't stop now). Within the first month we had already seen 21 players and a glimpse of how far we were behind the top teams. Relegated Ipswich and Norwich were beaten at St Andrews, but Charlton and Huddersfield saw us off away from home.

BARNS-STORMER I. A 5-0 win away from home at Oakwell would put the most pessimistic fan in a brighter frame of mind. It was an all-out Fry team performance, and as Barry's scouring of the lower leagues (as we like to patronisingly call them) has been his strength, it was good to see the new signing from Kidderminster, Richard Forsyth, play his part. He would probably be most Blues fans' choice for find of the season, especially when he had to deputise at right back for a while.

FROM GENOA TO GRIMSBY. For the next month Blues had to live on that glory. There was only a home win against Grimsby in the League Cup in the plus column. But 20,000 against Genoa in the Anglo-Italian Cup showed that we know a good thing when we see it. The 'good thing' in this case was the club's pricing policy - £5 anywhere in the ground, and kids for a quid (don't tell Barry, he'll want a few hundred thousand!). It's almost perverse that in their eagerness to attract new supporters, the club mistreated its most loyal fans. For instance, charging £15 to join the travel club which was supposed to be the only way to get a ticket to an away game.

DEN OF INIQUITY. In November, St Andrews saw its worst crowd trouble for a few years with the visit of Millwall. The incident was caused by the coming together of the uglier minority of both sets of supporters, but it was made worse by mismanagement beforehand and ill-advised comments afterwards. As Blues fans "cast the first stone" they were considered to have sinned.

CHAMPIONSHIP FORM. Blues started to play like they knew each other for a while. Away Cup wins at Tranmere (after extra time earned by the Hand of Aldo) and in Italy, courtesy of Ancona (relatively trouble-free, apart from the much-publicised alleged punch-up between three of our players and the histrionic Ancona coach) hinted at Premiership form. But the real thing came from Derby County, who tore us apart 4-1 and remain the best team seen at St Andrews this season.

OUR CUP RUNNETH OVER. Of course, you know you've arrived back in the big time when you can go to a team at the top end of the Premier League and hope for more than a huge embarrassment. The credibility of Barry Fry's 'minnows' was raised tenfold by the performance at Middlesbrough. Juninho didn't get a look-in, (and isn't it funny how other teams' nippy little skilful foreigners are always 'diving cheats'?). Incidentally trivia fans, this was a rarity because Barry ONLY MADE ONE SUBSTITUTION! (and that was due to injury.)

WINTER SQUARELY BITES US. December will undoubtedly go down as the month that broke Birmingham City's season. A superb goal by Kevin Francis as we beat Middlesbrough could not disguise the fact that Southend and Oldham outplayed and humiliated us. The form we showed in the Coca Cola Cup was absent in the League, and Barry was in the unusual position of substituting Oldham's two scorers after Poole and Francis gave them the lead. (Think about it...) We were left freezing cold, utterly humiliated, tired and weary with a long journey back to the capital ahead of these London-based Blues. Still, keep right on!

NEW YEAR'S DAZE. Blues did not win a League game in January or February, a fact only made more bearable by West Brom's failure to even draw a game over the same period. Unfortunately, the run ended with a 2-2 draw and 3-1 penalties win at St Andrews in the Anglo Italian Cup. Were Liam Daish's efforts in Italy wasted? The FA Cup draw against Wolves also signalled the loss of Ian Bennett for the rest of the season after he broke his arm failing to save from Bull. (STATS: Bennett 41 goals in 37 games, Griemink 40 goals in 24 games.) In between the Wolves draw and their victory in the replay, we saw a brief glimpse of what Barry Fry's philosophy had promised when he took over. "I don't care how many we let in as long as we score more at the other end." Unfortunately, in-form Charlton were more efficient up front, especially speedy Kim Grant. They won 4-3.

THE CUP THAT CHEERS. Well, it took us two attempts, but we did win something in January. In spite of a goalkeeping crisis - with all Barry's transfer dealings he had forgotten to get a spare goalie - and another missed penalty, we still beat Norwich in the League Cup thanks to a storming Liam Daish headed goal from a set-piece. We knew that the victors would face either Leeds, Arsenal or The V***A, which was incentive enough to win. And as it turned out we may have been better off if we had drawn the local rivals.

Quote from February's *The Heathen*: "Barry talked about leaving Southend to come to Blues, "After a short time, I thought, 'kinell! But whether I lasted three months or three years, I never regretted coming to Birmin'ham." "

SHOULD AULD ACQUAINTANCE BE FORGOT? Leeds United in the semi-final of the League Cup, and the chance of a crack at The V***A in the final. The pre-season promise of David Sullivan that we would be challenging for promotion had gone stale, but we were within two games of Wembley (although perhaps the more realistic chance had been lost in the Anglo-Italian Cup.) Blues' biggest crowd of the season was sure to bring out a few idiots, and the match reports were overshadowed by news that a pool ball had been thrown at Gary McAllister as he prepared to take a corner near our fans. But for Chris Whyte's old pals' act, we might have given them something more to report. Kevin Francis showed a large TV audience that he is not useless on the ground by running onto a through ball and firing a rocket past John Lukic. Blues were on top, but not for long. That was where our season ended. By backing off against Tony Yeboah and then deflecting a shot into his own net, Chris Whyte brought back some fond memories to the Leeds fans. It was going to be an uphill task at Elland Road.

MID-SEASON SALE OF THE CENTURY. What's the best way to prepare for a big match? Well, I can tell you what isn't. With the transfer deadline still a month away, Barry sold Liam Daish, the captain and main inspiration of last season. He almost sold Steve Claridge too, and as he missed a penalty, perhaps he should have done. Blues never really impressed in the return leg, relying on the heart and passion of non-league signings Forsyth and Richardson.

CLARIDGE'S AUCTION. The missed penalty wasn't the last straw for Cladger, but arriving late at Selhurst Park was (he was allegedly talking terms with Leicester City). He had not scored for 14 games, so a million quid didn't seem such a bad deal. As we now know, Leicester got a bargain...

FUNERAL MARCH. Away from home, Blues were becoming rather unlucky. Palace bundled their way to the points, Tranmere scored a freak equaliser against special guest goalie Fred 'the mask' Barber and then Wolves staged comeback of the season. But it was at home that the fans were getting fed up. The early season hammering of Barnsley was wiped out by their more skilful attacking tactics, and Sheffield United came to bury football, not to play it. Results actually picked up at St Andrews until Sunderland emphasised the gulf between us and the Premiership. There was still a chance of the play-offs when Mark McGhee called us an average team, but we lost to his less than average team after twice taking the lead. Realism set in.

KARREN GETS HER MAN. Barry had sold Paul Peschisolido to Stoke because he thought that having the managing director's husband in the squad undermined his authority. But on transfer deadline day, with the first pangs of withdrawal symptoms setting in, Barry said that signing Pesky back was just what the club needed.

BARRY GETS HIS MAN. More significant was the arrival of Paul Barnes a month earlier, at last giving us a goal scorer who scored goals. Barry had been trying to sign him almost since he arrived at Blues.

DEN OF INEQUITY. After the nastiness in the Millwall game at St Andrews, perhaps the BCFC plc administration should have been a bit more sensitive. They deemed that the return match should be all-ticket, and only 250 fans fulfilled the criteria to join the convoy of official coaches that visited S. Bermondsey. The scenes were very similar to those at St Andrews in November, but the media interest was for Barry Fry's comments that he was unwilling to put his son at risk by taking him on the bench as he usually did. They ignored the crowd of locals throwing bricks at our supporters coaches. Amid all the fuss, we almost accidentally kept Millwall up by providing them with a 2-0 win.

BARNES-STORMER II. If you looked at our home results in April, you would think that the new boys had clicked to give Blues a chance to go up. Don't be fooled; the 4-0 win against Luton was universally recognised as the WORST 4-0 win ever seen at St Andrews. It only happened as a result of Kim Grant hobbling off when Luton had used all their subs. For a forward, his defence missed him an awful lot.

FADE AWAY. Apart from a spirited draw at Derby, which not many Blues fans could have seen, the team did little for '96-97 season ticket sales in the last few games. Defeats in the League and an embarrassing 6-0 defeat by The V***A in John Frain's testimonial game gave you the feeling that the players had already given up.

VOTE OF CONFIDENCE. David Sullivan certainly likes to keep Blues in the public eye, and when he intimated that if Barry Fry were to leave (even though funds had been promised to the profligate one), they would consider Trevor Francis the ideal candidate to replace him, eyebrows were raised.

IT'S NOT OVER UNTIL THE FAT BARRY SINGS. Barry Fry's last game in charge of Blues was the defeat of V***A in the Birmingham Senior Cup Final. So it was a cruel twist of the old 'vote of confidence' that saw him attend the League managers' end of season function with a Cup under one arm and a P45 under the other.

TREVOR FRANCIS IS THE KING OF BRUM. Twenty years ago, if anyone mentioned Birmingham City, you would immediately think of Trevor Francis. He is still held in high esteem by Blues fans, and even those who never saw him play will know he is the best player the club ever had. Since his milestone £1m transfer, he has been linked with a return on numerous occasions, and now the dream is real. With classic Brummie pessimism, we still manage to think the worse: "What if he is a failure and we lose those happy memories of him?" But it is another chance for optimism as we start to sign Premiership cast-offs instead of lower league hopefuls. Barry set the ball rolling with the double winning season, mid-table consolidation and a Cup semi-final. But now we have the thrill of the return of the Wonderkid to get us 'looking forward', as the club's motto says.

Fanzine Facts

The Heathen started as a newsletter circulated amongst London supporters of Birmingham City but by August 1989 it had developed into a more recognised fanzine. Originally named 'BAD', the 'zine was renamed in 1991 following rumours of a ground relocation away from Small Heath, the current home of St Andrews. Adrian Brown, founder and editor, has decided to stop publishing The Heathen, although he's not retiring from fanzines altogether. According to Adrian, "it's the editing and all that cutting and pasting that I won't miss!" Next season, his scribblings will appear within the pages of other Blues fanzines such as Wake Up Blue and Blues News.

HEAVEN 11

Reading

Jim'll Mix It!

Last season's review in *SOTF* concluded with the following quote: "One season wonders? They said that last year!"

Well, as much as it pains us to say it, the doubters got it right, and any achievements from a hugely disappointing season will be remembered for their rarity value.

Out went Shaka Hislop, Scotty Taylor and Simon Osborn. In came Michael Meaker, Martyn Williams, Steve Swales and Trevor Morley. Within a month Meaker had become a victim of terrace booing, Williams had been subbed (having already come on as a substitute) against his old club, Morley had nearly been killed in a game with a skull injury and Steve Swales had disappeared into oblivion!

"Sing your Hearts Out For The Lads"

The fixture computer provided Stoke's Victoria Ground for our first game, and a late equaliser up there was followed by three points against Derby at home. This got expectations around the club buzzing, just like they had been three months previously. However, that buzz soon turned into a collective groan as the Lions of Millwall roared into Elm Park nicking a win in a ferocious manner. Our season ended there - we had performed so abysmally that even the most optimistic fan amongst us must have foreseen what was to lie ahead.

'Keeper Borislav Michaelov, or as he prefers Bobby Mihaylov (or as teletext would have it, Mick Haylov!) joined us from some unpronounceable team in the Eastern Block. Rumour has it, he thought Wembley was our home ground, having seen us on the box, and that we were in the Premiership. Nevertheless he signed, but the saying 'hair today, gone tomorrow' most definitely applied to him as he never played more than five games in a row, and was vulnerable to injury (supposedly) to say the least! One felt that if the Bulgarian farted forcefully he'd be in danger of slipping a disc; thus our great international star just didn't shine. Therefore, it was left to loan 'keepers Chris Woods, Steve Sutton, Eric Nixon, Nicky Hammond, the nervy Simon Shepperd and our player/manager/centre-forward/coach/media man Jimmy Quinn to keep goal. In fact, only Quinny managed to keep a clean sheet!

In the Cup, bogey team Bury trotted down to Elm Park, grabbed two early goals, much to the disapproval of the incensed Reading fans. And then the gods smiled on us. The referee sent everyone off for an early bath as the pitch looked like becoming one! A couple of well-rehearsed puddle shots from Reading players had swayed the ref's decision - and we thank the gods (of cats and dogs) for it! When the game was replayed at Elm Park it was heading for 90 minutes when Jimmy Quinn decided he wanted to enter the affray. Warming up and preparing for his entrance, he was told by the linesman that there were only seconds left and he was probably wasting his time. Nah! Our player/manager thought nothing of this, got onto the field, legged it into the penalty area and immediately knocked in the winner. Bury must hate us, and Quinn even more. Bogey team? This time, the finger was up the other nostril!

Later on in the Cup, spoon-bender and number one psychic fan Uri had predicted a 2-1 win against Man Utd, so a curse was on the game before a ball had even been kicked. I wish he'd kept his spooky premonitions to himself. Come February and we were out both Cups and caught up in the dreaded relegation dog-fight.

The belated arrival of play-maker Darren Caskey did little to inspire the Royals ranks, and inconsistency continued to play its unwanted role. The penultimate game saw us playing host to Wolves, Mark McGhee making his hugely publicised return. As expected everyone labelled it our 'Cup Final' and although there were no medals handed out, we were satisfied with our own equivalent of gold (definite Division One footy next season) as we spanked Wanderers. With nothing to play for the Royals dished out more Brummy misery, as we took three more points (and probably Barry Fry's job) at St Andrews on the last Sunday.

So where did it all go horribly wrong? The management must hold their hands up for the majority of the season's calamities, although it was the performances of the two joint managers on the field that kept us in it, to be fair to them. At too many times discontent was etched on the players' faces, but unfortunately changes at the management level just don't look like happening.

Have they learnt anything from this campaign? We'll have to wait and see. If not, it'll be *au revoir messieurs* before winter sets in. Under the right guidance, the squad has the strength in depth to be quite a force. Basically, any team can win this Division; all it takes is consistency in all aspects of the game - something Reading Football Club seems to have forgotten.

In a nutshell, the team used a grand total of 33 players (including seven 'keepers), had no ever-presents, let the fans wait until May 5th to record two wins in a row and basically disappointed far too frequently. However, there is light at the end of the tunnel - and it will soon shine onto the pitch in a new 25,000 all-seater stadium. Elm Park will be no more come December '97. Gone will be the historic terraces, the piss-stained shoes, inaudible tannoy, tepid burgers, Victorian facilities and totally inadequate parking. Its replacement will be, quite frankly, the complete opposite and the dog's dangly bits, but the all-important question surely is - can we fill it? I'm not going to answer that one; especially given last season's far-fetched hopes.

Rome wasn't built in a day, and 125 years on, neither is Reading Football Club. But we're getting there.

Fanzine Facts

Heaven 11 has maintained a steady readership since it launched, and remains at 50p an issue, although its editor (who wishes to remain anonymous) looks forward to the day that the price can go up to £1 when Reading get into the Premiership. "I've always fancied being the editor of a fanzine with a four figure issue number", he quips.

When one Reading player was asked whether he read the fanzine, he replied "Yeah; it makes great bog roll 'n all!" "Which probably explains some of the crap I put in it" says the ed.

HEROES AND VILLAINS

Aston Villa

2.55 pm on August 19th 1995, and not many Villa supporters viewed the forthcoming opening game with much optimism. We'd only escaped relegation because there were four teams worse than us, and the summer had seen a long run of players turning down the chance of joining the Villa - Collymore, Ferdinand, Gascoigne, to name but a few. The only additions to the team which had performed so badly the previous season were the unknown Serbian Savo Milosevic, Gareth 'who?' Southgate and Mark Draper, famous for being relegated in the past two seasons. With all these factors combined, we confidently expected to be comfortably adrift at the bottom of the table by October.

Savo's message to defenders

3.45 pm, and the ground rose to acclaim a three goal lead, some Manchester United supporters having already left. The scene was set for what was one of the greatest, most delightfully unexpected seasons in decades. Villa spent the next few months not only playing great football, but showing a passion for the club and sheer will to win that was totally removed from the collection of deadbeats Brian Little had inherited.

Dwight Yorke was a revelation, the most attractive striker in the country. Andy Townsend finally showed his true form, Southgate was converted into an international central defender; everything in the garden was rosy.

Even the odd setback in the League was shrugged off and Christmas arrived with Villa looking good in three competitions. The FA Cup third round saw all the clichés brought out and dusted off, as Gravesend and Northfleet from the Beazer Homes League brought 15 times their average home gate with them and played well above themselves, losing just 3-0. In the League Cup quarter final, Villa faced Wolves and despite not playing at top form, a Tommy Johnson goal was good enough to put us into the semi-final yet again.

Things were now really hotting up, although there was no realistic chance of winning the League, and with the fatalism of supporters who are used to seeing regular false dawns and hopes destroyed, we waited for things to start going wrong. Dwight kept scoring, Savo didn't do very much but when he did it was always worth watching, the midfield was magnificent and defence the best in the country. Alex Ferguson called Villa dour and uncompromising; we laughed at him and things just got better and better.

Anyone who knows anything about the Villa know that they never, ever do things the easy way; and so it proved in the League Cup semi-final. Away to Arsenal in the first leg, the team started off well but were caught by a classic sucker punch, courtesy of two goals from Dennis Bergkamp. In days gone by the team would have given up, but roared on by a set of supporters who simply refused to accept defeat, they stormed back with a rampant finish to claim a share of the spoils thanks to a brace from Dwight Yorke (cliché overload there). The second leg will, I feel, prove to be a milestone in the club's history. The players battled for two hours, out-Arsenaled the masters of grinding out results and the jubilation that greeted the final whistle was awesome. In fact, we found it difficult to get worked up for anything else for the rest of the season. It was as though there was a pre-ordained plan, the Villa were headed for glory and nothing could get in their way.

Then came the usual ritual of an away sixth round tie in the FA Cup. This was the seventh quarter final we'd been involved in since 1959; we'd been drawn away in all of them and lost the lot. Against Nottingham Forest, Franz Carr made his debut 12 months after signing, and naturally scored the only goal of the match. As if we expected anything else.

Sunday March 24th, and off we went to Wembley for the formality of winning the League Cup. Compared to the events of our victory there two years previous, when we treated the day as a one-off, the build-up to this occasion was so laid back as to be almost routine. The day passed by almost without incident; we knew we were going to win, and Leeds were equally aware that you can't interfere with the laws of certainty. Having suffered a lot of criticism Savo naturally scored one of the greatest goals the National Toilet had ever witnessed, Ian 'Villa Fan All His Life' Taylor (who'd been a spectator in 1994) got one, and Dwight made it 3-0 in the last minute.

And so to the FA Cup semi-final at Old Trafford. Stupid ticket prices coupled with the sheer expense of two big games in a week meant that there were 10,000 empty seats against Liverpool, and the whole event was an anti-climax after the previous Sunday. With Southgate going off injured early on, the defence was unbalanced and conceded a goal straight after, and despite Villa dominating long spells of the match Liverpool did what they're good at by wrapping things up with two late goals. But if we were ever going to lose an FA Cup semi-final, this season was the least painful one in which to do it.

Things didn't exactly fizzle out after that, but then again we hardly battled to the last. An horrific injury to Garry Charles showed that although he comes in for a lot of criticism the team missed him, and with only one point from the last four games they eventually struggled to finish in fourth place. The poor run-in gave the last few remaining supporters of our ex-manager Mr Fat Ron an excuse to find fault with Little, but no-one with any sense could disagree that the whole season from start to finish was anything but exhilarating, great to watch, unforgettable and, best of all, a marvellous surprise. We've got England internationals, players who should or will soon be in their national team and a crop of youngsters as good as any in the country. If only we'd had another regular goalscorer we could have made a real challenge for the title. For a team that even its own supporters thought would finish at best in the middle of the table, and who many tipped for relegation, it was a tremendous achievement. Looking at the average age of the squad and the spirit and enthusiasm running throughout Villa Park from the boardroom down, the best is yet to come.

As an encore, Villa Park had easily the best atmosphere of any Euro 96 ground and Gareth Southgate established himself as an England regular.

Those of us who rejoiced when Brian Little was appointed manager of Aston Villa have double reason to celebrate. The most talented Villa player in recent years is on his way to becoming the club's greatest ever manager.

Fanzine Facts

Heroes and Villains was started in 1989 by editor Dave Woodhall and is now firmly established as Villa's biggest fanzine. It is still very much a one-man-band and Dave is often asked by the media to comment on the latest issue facing the club. This has brought him to the attention of the infamous Mr Ellis who apparently hates the 'zine. However, *Heroes and Villains* continues on its way and is now, according to Dave, generally ignored by the club.

HEY BIG SPENDER

Derby County

Was it a bird, was it a plane? No it was the Bald Eagle, come to take us on a whirlwind ride over the dross of Endsleigh League Division One. In truth, after the departure of Roy McFarland, we were expecting the appointment of one of those young and trendy (not to mention overpaid and inexperienced) 'tracksuit player-manager' types. Steve Bruce was the favourite, but we got this old baldy fella and, to be honest, we were all a bit pissed off with it. Then we played 11 of Tottenham's finest superstars in a pre-season friendly and a couple of our new lads, including £300,000 Ron Willems (who'd only lost his place to Bergkamp and Van Basten at Ajax through injury - and then been turned down whilst on trial at Nottingham Forest because Cloughie couldn't be

bothered to turn up), ran the show - and we won. Perhaps things weren't going to be too bad after all.

The opening games were a disappointment, both in terms of results and attendances. Drawing with Port Vale and Grimsby (or was it Barcelona in the blue and red stripes) and losing at Reading hardly set the pulses racing. However, some of the individual performances were promising, especially as Jim Smith was restricted to 'wheeling and dealing' to get new blood. Players like Sean Flynn (in from Coventry with Paul Williams going in the opposite direction) and Gary Rowett (same thing, from Everton, passing Craig Short en route) who were supposedly only 'make-weights', turned out to be quite evidently better than the 'big names' we sold.

By mid-November we'd made our customary early exit from the League Cup and were sitting in an uncomfortable 17th position with only 18 points bagged from a possible 45. The day before Bonfire Night had seen our regulation disaster at Prenton Park (1-5 to John Aldridge's team this time), but it also saw something else that was to change the course of the season and ultimately the history of the club. Lionel Pickering, club chairman and all round local hero, did something he'd promised not to do since Arthur Cox had wasted millions of his hard-earned a few seasons earlier - he spent a fortune on a player. Igor Stimac was the guy's name, and 'a sensational coup' was how his arrival was greeted by the local press and club officials alike. Nobody knew a thing about him except that he was expensive (£1.57m), big and tall, played sweeper (whatever that was) and came from somewhere called Croatia (wherever that is). News that he had crashed his car (some technicality he hadn't got to grips with on his journey from the airport about driving on the left), and his claims to be the bee's knees only added to the confusion in supporters' minds... was he really the answer to all our prayers? He scored at Tranmere and although we were hammered, the thousand or so that made the trip from Derbyshire soon made their minds up about this mountain of a man: hero and saviour, no question about it. That's when we started to take the piss out of the rest of this Division.

Jim and brilliant young coach and ex-Ram Steve McClaren instigated a system based around a five man defence - or more accurately around the abundantly talented and massively confident Igor. In the next match we beat West Brom 3-0, at a canter. As the Baggies began their desperate slide to the bottom, we went in the opposite direction, only twice as rapidly. From then on, despite being 'Premiershiped' (i.e. cheated) out of the FA Cup by Leeds in January, the Rams didn't lose another game until we visited Roker in mid-May. Seven points clear of the chasing pack was the summit, I believe, and the football observed in that 20 (yes, 20!) match unbeaten run was some of the finest witnessed at the Baseball Ground since the days of Hector, Hinton, O'Hare and company. Quality sides that had either beaten us earlier in the season or would finish in promotion contention come May were swept aside like so many Sunday morning pub teams; Birmingham's latest first eleven were totally humiliated at St Andrews, and Charlton, Barnsley, Reading, Stoke, Sheffield United and plenty more besides were played off the park. Home or away, it mattered not a jot. It was total football, the Bald Eagle way. Robbie Van Der Laan, Jim's admitted vision of himself as a player, was the central force in the success; the Rams 'ticked' when he wore the captain's armband, such was his leadership and commitment - it was that simple. Along with Darryl Powell and either long-serving Paul Simpson, fiery Sean Flynn, or young Paul Trollope; Derby had the best midfield in the Division for the majority of the season. The back line wasn't unbeatable, but generally very reliable and as effective a weapon in attack as defence. Dean Yates' solid performances made him Player of the Season, Chris Powell fitted in nicely at left back after he replaced the workmanlike Shane Nicholson, Lee Carsley had his best season at right back and 21 year old Gary Rowett's magnificent contribution cannot be accurately described in words; he looked like he'd been playing top-flight football for a decade, rather than taking part in his first full season. Igor is simply the best player to play for the club, ever. "Watch out Premiership centre-forwards" is surely the message that Aggrieved of Wolverhampton, Southend and Huddersfield would convey. Messrs Bull, Regis and Booth - Igor just cruelly toyed with them. We also scored one or two goals during '95-96; this was due in the main to two players, already at the club before Jim's arrival, hurtling out of the blocks, keen as mustard in August, and putting in the best season's work of their respective careers. Marco Gabbiadini and Dean Sturridge (who we were willing to unload to Torquay last season for £100k - but they wouldn't take him), along with the aforementioned Dutchman Willems, who flourished when moved to play in the 'hole', were each averaging a goal every third game. During the unbeaten run they seemed to be engaging in their own private battle to top the Division's scoring tables. This race reached epidemic proportions around November/December when they contrived to score in four games out of six; that's all three of them, scoring in each game!

There have been some memorable moments on the pitch, but also, for the first time in years at Derby, the club's attitude to their supporters, and therefore relationship with them, has improved beyond all recognition. Not only had we previously been asked to choose which song the team ran out to and which kit design we preferred, possibly seen as early token gestures from a newly organised board, but as the season progressed the fans have started returning in their droves to watch the improved performances, to find that they are no longer treated like sheep (!) but as small but essential parts in the one big happy family that is Derby County. A lot of the credit for this has to go down to the clean sweep in the administrative department. Fans' complaints and suggestions for improvements have been accepted and acted upon honestly and positively; the work of chief executive Keith Loring and his team has been as impressive as that of Robbie Van der Laan's. Jim Smith's honesty and acceptance of criticism has also compared favourably to the 'us and them' attitude of his predecessors. Strange tactical and selection decisions have been plenty, but they have always been explained openly and more often than not reaped positive and immediate rewards in the form of points. Writing a fanzine has been nigh on impossible - there's sod all to complain about! Instead we've found ourselves welcomed into the club with open arms, when before we've been shunned and ultimately banned.

But it's the football that matters the most, and it's not been all plain sailing, despite the fact that there has not been one club in this Division capable of stopping us taking points off them. Jim has used just 28 first team players (if that sounds a lot, look at Barry Fry's record) and we didn't see a red card in 46 League games. Amongst the downers have been: throwing the lead away at Fratton Park with a lax clearance in the dying minutes; being totally out-played at Oakwell by that fat old bastard Molby; playing doomed Watford twice in 11 days in March and getting just two points from them; losing at home to a frigging ten-man Leicester when John Harkes missed a penalty (I mean, losing a home game - that's a bloody disgrace - thank Lionel Pickering it was only once); and all those wasted points at places like Grimsby and Ipswich after Christmas when we actually had something to lose - fingernails have never had it so bad in the East Midlands.

But the poor and the mediocre, and the fact that the season's been such a bloody serious business are greatly over-shadowed by the highlights: Ron Willems' goal about four seconds into the second half at Bramall Lane; Robbie's pile driver free-kick at Pompey; the almost embarrassing mauling of the Brummies; the four goals against the Blades at the Baseball Ground when the place seemed to spontaneously combust every five minutes, such was the atmosphere and fervour generated by a crowd that realised that at last we may just be on to something; expert (!) pundits Jimmy Greaves and Tony Francis trying to deny they said we were relegation material earlier in the term (we'll really miss them!), the last-minute winner against Norwich on New Year's Day; the 6-2 destruction of Tranmere Rovers; coming from a goal behind (something we did a lot of this season - about 13 times) to overtake Sunderland and go top two days before Christmas; even recent £1m signing Ashley Ward, who struggled with form, injury and illness after his arrival from Norwich managed to break his goal-scoring duck during the final day party at The Hawthorns; and ultimately the victory over form team Crystal Palace which booked our Premiership place on that magical date - Sunday 28th April 1996, fifty years and a day after another glorious day in the club's history, their only ever FA Cup win.

The emotions encountered on that day alone are fulsome enough to deserve a book of their own: "20 minutes and we're in the Premiership", "Shit, they've got a corner, I can't watch", "Just eight minutes Derby, just eight more bloody minutes", "Sod going for goal Deano, get the bleeding ball down near that corner flag and hold on to it", "Just blow the fucking whistle ref" - you get the picture. There are some truly wonderful memories from an incredible campaign, which have meant that ultimately we have achieved the goal that has eluded us, the club and about £15m for the past four seasons. But all this has meant we could sing that sweetest of football songs, "And now you better believe us... the Rams are going up." Watch out Forest - we're coming to getcha!

Fanzine Facts

Hey Big Spender, edited by Mark Aldridge with the help of Simon Evans, first appeared in September 1992 and is named after the club owner and chairman and his legendary spending spree a few years back. This season Mark points out that they have "gotten a little bit serious and arse-licky as '95-96 all went very 'swimmingly' for Derby fans. No doubt we'll get back some of that much needed attitude that is expected of fanzines when we start to be treated like crap by Sky TV and the Premier League hierarchy in the coming season. Then again, we might be taking ourselves just as seriously as we worry about whether Manchester United, Liverpool and Newcastle are capable of closing that seven point gap we've got at the top of the table!"

HIGHBURY HIGH

Arsenal

Rioch's Big Challenge

When the Highbury crowd stood and applauded at the final game of the season, there was a reassuring familiarity to the proceedings. It wasn't just the manner of our qualification for Europe with almost the last kick of the League campaign, or the fact that Arsenal had once again proved their superiority in the North London stakes with Tottenham. Above all, it was the traditional, victorious ovation to the man who had presided over the resurgence in the club's fortunes - the one and only Georgie Graham.

But this year something was strangely amiss. For a start, George was not the manager of the Arsenal, but disgraced party in an unsavoury 'bung' scandal. And wasn't that rotund figure starring in the Arsenal midfield none other than the fat Geordie bastard we'd swore never to forgive for his part in the 'Black Sunday' semi-final against Spurs in '91?

INTERVIEWS WITH CLIVE ANDERSON AND TOM WATT

EUROPE EUROPE HERE WE COME?

Of course this was no ordinary match, but Paul Merson's testimonial. And indeed Gascoigne, being Gascoigne, had played his heart out to finally win the affections of the initially hostile crowd. But, although testimonials do not have much bearing on the real world, Bruce Rioch cannot not have failed to notice the warmth of the reception received by George Graham as he strode onto the pitch with the rest of the '71 Double squad during the half-time break. After a year in charge, it still felt as though Rioch was living in the shadow of his predecessor. After all, when had the Arsenal crowd ever turned up the volume in such a way for him?

In fact, Rioch can justifiably count his first season as a success. The standard of football had undeniably improved, especially when the graceful Bergkamp was pulling the strings. With the decline of the previous few seasons, European qualification was the only realistic target for the club, and this had been achieved despite extensive injury problems which sidelined not one but two current England captains. And the interest in Arsenal had ensured sell-outs for virtually every game. But Rioch was made painfully aware at the Merson testimonial that Arsenal fans have become accustomed to winning things. Welcome to the world of high expectations!

When the huge Arsenal contingent trooped out of the Parc de Princes stadium last May, we were all certain of two inevitabilities: first, the Graham era had finally run out of steam. The decline in the team could no longer be disguised by Cup successes, and there was no doubting that there was a need for a radical overhaul. Second, we knew that a lot of rival fans would take real pleasure in Nayim's long distance winner. A year on we were still hearing "Nayim from the halfway line" at every club from Hartlepool to Southampton. Of course, these poor fans have to sing about our European Finals because no other English club ever gets close to one!

The start of the summer was no better, as we missed out on long-term targets Ferdinand and Barton, largely because we had no boss. Our manager-less state continued with the farcical approach for Bobby Robson, whose habit of forgetting players' names extended to forgetting that he was still under contract. So in the end, the lower-profile, second choice was appointed, although it shouldn't be forgotten that Graham was also chosen only after a failed attempt to land Terry Venables.

With Rioch in charge, it seemed likely that he would soon acquire the talents of Stubbs and MacAteer, but in the end we had to 'settle' for Dennis Bergkamp, David Platt and the promise of more to follow. Suddenly Paris was no more than a distant memory and the rush for season tickets and replica shirts began in earnest.

The expectation, fuelled by the press hype, was so intense that the opening day draw against Middlesbrough was immediately reported as a big money flop by the tabloids. Bergkamp in particular was targeted by the hacks, desperate to knock him off the newly-assembled pedestal they had built for him. After only a couple of appearances without getting off the mark, the tabloids launched a campaign to discredit him. The witch-hunt quickly reached ridiculous proportions, culminating in the Cup tie against Hartlepool when the back page of one of the rags had a banner headline 'Hartlefool'. Arsenal had won the game 3-0!

If it was taking a while for Bergkamp's first goal in the Premiership, none of his team-mates were complaining about his contribution to the side. Ian Wright was particularly enjoying the Bergkamp influence. Even so, when Dennis finally broke his duck against Southampton, the release of the pent-up anxiety almost took the roof off the stands. With the weight lifted off his shoulders Dennis began to demonstrate his full range of skills, including a long distance wonder goal in the second half. Of course, Wrighty wasn't going to give up the spotlight that easily, and he duly stuck in Arsenal's fourth of the afternoon after turning the defenders so many times they must have felt sicker than a Vogue model at a medieval banquet.

It was all starting to look so perfect. The team was getting better and better, including a fine 3-0 victory at Elland Road and an exciting victory against Man Utd. Even the hospitalisation of David Platt after only four games (in which time he became our most prolific midfielder for years) couldn't dampen the optimism of the faithful. Ray Parlour was playing out of his skin, and Martin Keown was well on his way to achieving cult status. At *Highbury High* we confidently declared on the front cover, 'Rioch: So far, So good' - with which it all came crashing down!

And of all places it had to be at White Hart Lane. For the first 20 minutes, we took them apart. Spurs couldn't get near the ball and it was only a matter of time before we would add to Bergkamp's first derby goal. But then from an Arsenal corner, Sheringham scored on the break, and the confidence drained out of the team. Spurs scored again and could have had more. A dismal run of results ensued, the only respite being two victories at home against Sheffield Wednesday (but then again we always beat them at Highbury). By Christmas any early season Championship hopes were well and truly buried. And New Year had hardly started before the FA Cup dreams burst after a spineless third round replay at Sheffield United.

We were in bad need of a tonic from the dire League form, but unlike last year there were no glorious Highbury European nights to lift the spirits. Luckily, Newcastle stepped in to boost our flagging morale. Their first visit in January for the quarter-finals of the Coca Cola Cup saw a resumption of the Dixon/Ginola battle (which had began two years previously when Ginola was at Paris Saint Germain). Lee Dixon is clearly Ginola's worst nightmare. For all his gallic guile and flair, whenever he comes to Arsenal he never manages to find a route out of Lee's pocket. His inability to make his mark on the game, combined with his frustration at the refereeing, was enough for the red mist to descend in the form of an elbow to Dixon's face. Tempers were no better on the bench with Rioch squaring up to Keegan and McDermott. It was one of those dream nights, and I haven't yet mentioned Wright's winning brace of goals.

Of course, the tabloids were indignant, and the two-faced toilet-paper merchants had another opportunity to combine the words 'soccer' and 'shame', as well as providing more ammunition in the demonising of Dixon (what has he ever done to upset these people?). But no amount of media moralising will change the fact that these are the games that us fans love, and it certainly didn't do Rioch any harm in the eyes of supporters.

When Newcastle returned a few months later with Batty and Asprilla in tow, the result was the same, but this time the outcome was never in any doubt. The cracks in their defence had become chasms and there was little doubt amongst the crowd that their title dreams were in tatters. The chants of "Keegan, get your cheque book out" were cruel but funny. To be honest none of us wanted to see Man Utd win the League, but those games against Newcastle were absolutely vital for Arsenal's confidence.

By this time, European qualification was the only way we were going to salvage anything out of the season, and worryingly our main rivals in the quest were Tottenham. We had crashed out of the Coca Cola Cup despite never losing a game, in the process scoring 17 goals and only conceding three. The semi-final against Villa looked in the bag, after Bergkamp, relishing the big occasion, put us two up in the first half of the first leg. His team-mates then conspired to surrender the lead in the second half, crucially providing Villa with two precious away goals.

Arsenal put up a spirited performance at the return leg at Villa Park, but never looked likely to score the vital goal. So this game signalled the end of any silverware ambitions for the season, but it may also have sounded the death knell of Arsenal's famous back four. The rock on which our success has been built over the last eight years had been the formidable defence of Dixon, Winterburn, Adams and Bould (with cover by Linighan). Despite the long-term absences of Bould and Adams this season through injury, and worries about the advancing years of the fullbacks, it was still a shock to see Rioch turn out a three man defence of Keown, Morrow and Linighan. Yet the system had no apparent effect on the 'goals against' column - Arsenal still conceded the fewest goals · and it released the wing-backs to maraud up the flanks, a role in which Dixon in particular flourished.

In the pursuit of the last UEFA Cup place, Arsenal didn't exactly blaze any trails across the Premiership, but the record of only two defeats in the last 14 games sufficed. To be honest, most of the action was happening off the pitch. Arsenal were linked with virtually every European international, but not a single player was actually purchased during the season. This was interpreted widely in the press as being caused by a rift between Rioch and vice-chairman, David Dein, who controlled the coffers. Of course this was largely a media-fuelled and perpetuated story: the more the press speculated (i.e. guessed) about who Arsenal would buy, the more they could report a crisis when the chequebook remained closed. The stories of behind-the-scenes battles intensified when Ian Wright declared his intentions to leave the club because of rows with the boss. This saga was endemic of the problems at the club, with Wrighty publicly praising Dein, and rumours circulating that Wright had floored Rioch's assistant, Stewart Houston, after the Cup tie against Sheffield United.

On top of all this, the manager had yet to sign a contract with the club.

In this context, it was clear that Rioch had to get us into Europe, or else his future would have appeared very shaky to say the least. And so it came down to the last game - victory over his old club, the already relegated Bolton, would ensure qualification. Anything else would be a disaster with three other teams still in contention. Surely Bolton wouldn't create any problems, would they? The game was as tense as any we've endured over the last few years. With a plethora of missed chances, and news of a Spurs lead at Newcastle, it seemed it couldn't get any worse, until that is, Bolton took a late lead. But the game and the season was dramatically salvaged by Rioch's only signings, Bergkamp and Platt.

Only minutes away from feeling the wrath of the crowd, Rioch could now at last bask in the glory. European qualification had saved his skin and dissolved all of those back-room tensions. After all, would Ian Wright want to leave if there was a European foray to enjoy? Surely Rioch can now confidently step out of Graham's shadow. Or can he? George's most notable quality was his ability to pit his wits against the top Italian and French clubs. Now he's made it into Europe, Rioch's next challenge is to emulate Graham's success there. Good luck, Bruce.

Fanzine Facts

With the fanzine world's penchant for sarcasm and the love of the darker side of the game, *Highbury High* could hardly have been conceived in such a perfect environment. The club was embroiled in every conceivable scandal or embarrassment: Georgie's bung, Merson's charlie, Ray's pizza parlour exploits and the captain's drinking binges. But as editor Ian Trevitt points out, "we did not arrive on the scene to join in the piss-taking, there was already far too much Arsenal abuse going on from every quarter. We decided it was time to stand up for the club, and give the abuse back to the capital's non-achievers." Now ten issues old, the team at *Highbury High* doesn't shy away from criticising the club when necessary, but never forgets who they support.

THE HOLY TRINITY

Aston Villa

After a forgettable '94-95 campaign (well, it would be forgettable if I didn't have to keep mentioning it in articles), Villa fans were right to expect changes in personnel. These changes were a long time in coming. After a very public rejection by Les Ferdinand - we weren't a big enough club apparently - Villa were linked with a number of big name players such as Collymore, Gascoigne and Bergkamp. However, the official line was that Ferdinand had been the only serious target.

Nevertheless, Villa fans were becoming more and more impatient as several other top players were linked with a move, only to be transferred elsewhere. The cheque book eventually appeared at the end of June, when Brian signed two players from relegated clubs and an unknown Serb striker for a combined fee of nearly £10m. Hardly something to inspire even the most optimistic of Villa fans, but a closer look into the pedigree of these new acquisitions revealed a blood-line that would please the faithful.

Gareth Southgate was widely recognised as the only good thing to come out of Selhurst Park in recent years. After playing in over 100 consecutive games for Palace, and becoming their youngest ever captain, Gareth had earned a reputation as an extremely competent midfield player. So Brian played him at the back.

Despite paying £3.2m to relegated Leicester for his services, Villa fans were not worried by the acquisition of Mark Draper. We'd already seen him in action at Villa Park as he had pissed all over our entire team to bring Leicester back from a 1-4 deficit in February '95. Draper was also on the fringe of the England squad, having been called up to attend one of Venables' get-togethers. Finally, the unknown Savo Milosevic, although only 21 years of age, had scored 79 goals in three seasons in Yugoslavia, and seemed to be a great prospect.

By the time three o'clock on the opening day of the season had arrived, a fair degree of optimism had built up around Villa Park. Pre-season performances had been good, and the team trotted out in bright sunshine to a capacity crowd, many of whom were wearing the new, excellent (for once) replica home shirt. That day there was only going to be one winner. What followed was 45 minutes of near perfect football as Villa rattled up a 3-0 lead against the side that eventually went on to become Champions.

This set the pace for the rest of the season. Villa lost only once during their first ten games, and by the end of September we were in second place. For the first time in ages, Villa fans were able to sing, 'we're going to win the League', and it gave us great pleasure performing it at Highfield Road, having competed a 3-0 win over Fat Ron's latest excuse for a football team.

By October, the initial momentum had faded. Two defeats in a row were followed by unconvincing wins over Stockport (in the League Cup) and Everton. One of the most disappointing aspects about Villa is the fact that we seem to have more than our fair share of fickle supporters. Not missing an opportunity, as soon as we reached the gloomy depths of seventh place (our lowest position all season), and the high standards had started to drop, the knives immediately came out. The target was Savo Milosevic.

Savo had struggled to settle into the English game. By the end of October he had only scored three goals (two of them in one match against Coventry) and had missed many other chances. But the majority of the crowd realised that he was only young, that the surroundings were new to him and that we would be wrong to expect miracles from him. Furthermore, many recognised his contribution to the whole team. In the aforementioned game against Manchester United, he supplied the final pass for Draper's goal and also won the penalty. Unfortunately, the minority of non-believers were far from silent, and at times, Savo was subjected to some disgraceful abuse from certain sections of the crowd. It was the kind of treatment that had previously only been reserved for 'favourites' such as Tony Cascarino, Nigel Callaghan and Dalian Atkinson. Incensed by this behaviour, *The Holy Trinity* printed a 'get off his back' message on one of its front covers, a move that won favour with many supporters. Savo, though, was to have the last laugh.

November brought one of the most significant moments of the season - an injury to Andy Townsend. At Upton Park, with the match finely poised, Townsend's injury meant a chance for Tommy Johnson (who, before this game, matched Savo in the popularity stakes of some supporters) and a change in formation with three now playing up front. The result was outstanding: Villa dominated the second half with a superb display of attacking football and came away with a 4-1 win. The new-look side was maintained for the next two games. Against Newcastle, Villa gained just one point for outplaying the League leaders, whilst two days later at Southampton, Villa registered 30 attempts on goal to entertain the Sky viewers - and to move back up to third place.

As the end of the year approached, the team's form took a bit of a nose-dive with defeats away to two of the worst teams in the division: Manchester City and QPR. Steve Stone's late equaliser also ensured that the youngest Villa side for years only came away from the City Ground with one point, even though they deserved all three. Nevertheless, December did include a 4-1 win over Coventry. Home wins over Coventry are now as certain as summer following spring, but this particular victory was especially pleasing because of who their manager is, and also because Savo's hat-trick marked his first goals at Villa Park.

By now though, the media - for once - were beginning to sit up and take notice. Three of Villa's games during January were shown live on television - and we won all of them. Dwight Yorke's chipped penalty in the FA Cup win over Sheffield United will stick in the memory, whilst the two League games shown on Sky against Middlesbrough and Tottenham only helped to enhance our growing reputation. However, the best team performance during the month came at Old Trafford with a real 'backs to the wall' job similar to Scotland's performance against Holland in Euro 96. Villa left Manchester with a well-earned point but Ferguson was not happy, lambasting us for our negative approach and having the cheek to label us a "boring" team. Maybe Alex had his eyes closed during the 3-1 thrashing that we dealt out on the opening day of the season - or perhaps it was just a severe case of sour grapes.

The first game of February resulted in a 3-0 win over Leeds. After this result, Villa occupied fourth place in the table - and this was to be our position for the rest of the season, although just one point from our last four games meant that we finished nearer the chasing pack than the top three.

The culmination of all the hard work over the season was rewarded on March 24th with victory over Leeds United in the Coca Cola Cup Final. The emphatic nature of the result, and the confidence with which the team played, was consistent with what many Villa fans had seen week in, week out. The most satisfying aspect was undoubtedly Savo's goal. By now, even the national press were beginning to make jokes at his expense. But the majority of Villa fans and, more importantly, Villa's management team had stuck by him, and his goal at Wembley was a massive repayment of the faith shown in him.

Joy turned to disappointment the following week as we were unceremoniously dumped out of the FA Cup by Liverpool at the semi-final stage. However, the fact that we were there in the first place was a remarkable achievement, as it had strictly been a no-go area for the team since 1960.

So, all in all, it was a great season; League Cup winners, FA Cup semi-finalists and fourth place in the Premiership. There is a real buzz around the club nowadays. We have a good blend of youth and experience, and a wealth of talent in the squad. Behind the scenes we are developing our own vision of the Liverpool boot room with ex-players Evans, Gregory, Withe and Shaw (amongst others) all involved in some capacity.

Although it is obviously a team effort, one man can take more credit than most. Writing in last season's *SOTF*, the Birmingham City fanzine *The Heathen* commented, "Smiling Ron left Villa Park... but the best laugh came with the appointment of Mr Charisma as his replacement." Brian Little may not be one of the most outgoing people around - but he's turning out to be one hell of a manager.

Fanzine Facts

'96-97 will be *The Holy Trinity*'s fifth season, making it Villa's second longest-running fanzine. *THT* usually takes a light-hearted stance, and readers seem to like the fact that it is not overly critical. Editor Stephen Whitehouse comments, "Football had become so expensive nowadays, so what's the point of going along to the match and moaning for the entire 90 minutes? You might as well enjoy it as much as you can."

Bearing this in mind, the European trips during the forthcoming campaign are strongly anticipated, given that past excursions to Bratislava, LaCoruna and Milan have provided the fanzine with some of its best material to date.

THE HORN

Watford

Watford were relegated, but there were no fan rampages or seats ripped up; not even a chorus of "Petchey out." That's not to say that relegation was acceptable; rather, the lack of outrage was a reaction to Watford's form in April - you see, they'd really made a fight of it, unlike the other two relegated sides. At the final whistle the players had that haunted look; and yes there were tears, but no boos. Instead, defiant choruses of "We'll be back as Champions" reverberated around the ground, and Taylor had to rouse his players to accept the applause from the Vicarage Road Stand.

Watford went into the final game having to beat Leicester and relying on Millwall and Pompey losing. Let's face it, it was never going to be a satisfactory arrangement. Within eight minutes, some herbert with a tranny spread the doom and gloom: "Pompey are winning at Huddersfield." The pre-match buoyancy was punctured as easily as the thousands of balloons handed out before the game.

A tad over 20,000 turned up for that last fixture, 6,500 of them from Leicester. It was our biggest gate so far this decade, but I wonder how many of them will be back watching in the Second Division? Seventeen years ago, Taylor took over the seventh place club in Division Four and left us as one of the top ten sides in the country. Now we're back amongst football's low-life: time to do your stuff again Graham.

Yet one unbelievable month almost put the whole thing right. When Taylor returned in February the team were 24th and without a win in '96. Ironically, Glenn Roeder was given a one year contract just a week before he was sacked, when a spineless defeat at Palace left him with more time to spend with his greyhounds, or fishing with Gazza. At Palace there had been no "Roeder out" chants. Instead, we targeted the board. The club has been run by the media-shy Jack Petchey since 1990, a man whose profile is lower than Lord Lucan's. Fans collect "I Spy" points for spotting his metallic blue Roller at games (apparently he finds watching the team a chore). The club does actually have a 'chairman' in Timperley, but his impotency can be summed up by the fact that even before he'd handed Roeder a renewed contract, the other directors were already plotting Taylor's return without him even knowing about it.

Roeder had two full seasons. In his first, Watford stayed up (just), but in his next (the one before last), they had their best campaign of the 90's: finishing seventh, they kept 19 clean sheets, including a record nine in a row. No-one found us easy to get past, but the downside was a lack of fire power. Kevin Phillips scored nine in 15 and was brilliant, but he couldn't carry our attack on his own. A slightly-built 5'9, he needed at least one partner with physical presence. All we had was Peter Beadle, a 6'1 striker from the Trevor Senior 'Hall of Donkeys' and a skinny Jamie Moralee (who Daniella Westbrook reckons is the Guvnor in bed). Shame he can't score more often on the pitch!

All summer we scanned teletext and the papers, and some desperate die-hards even phoned the Hornet Hotline, but there was nothing substantial to report. We were linked with un-named, out-of-favour Premiership reserves, but Watford's budget couldn't match even those players' expectations. We were close to signing Uwe Fuchs (phew) and the reserves manager flew to Norway to try and badger Rushveldt to 'come on down', but he didn't. We did however sign Steve 'Fatbloke' Cherry, an eccentric goalie (although not quite in the Schmiechel mould). Roeder wasn't going to be hurried into signing a short-term solution, and the board had no intention of funding any ambitious spending, despite that encouraging seventh place.

This was definitely a factor in our relegation. In December, ex-Hornet Paul Wilkinson came back on loan from Middlesbrough. After not winning a game in October and November, we began December at leaders Millwall. Wilko added a new dimension to our team; he won the ball in the air and gave Phillips a new lease of life. Our win seemed to spark Millwall's catastrophic decline - a real bonus! Watford fans reckon the £500,000 they spent on our full back Gerard Lavin helped send them down! Wilko didn't score in his four games on loan, but the team won twice, drew once and lost narrowly at Birmingham. The deal to bring him back permanently was called off when 'Boro demanded a quarter of a mill', and the player's wage demands were also beyond the club's budget. We were furious... well, there were some stern letters in the local press anyway! Wilko was a realistic sort of target; he had a tendency to stray offside but had top scored in his previous three seasons with the Hornets. We had signed Penrice from QPR but he is as injury-prone as Frank Spencer and lasted four games; at £200,000 he'd also cut a deep hole into Roeder's transfer fund.

Kerry Dixon did arrive, prompting the board to send out newsletters explaining why they'd signed the cheaper, older and short-term option. Dixon was booed when he made his debut, guilty by association with Luton. He did as good a job as Wilkinson, but some still viewed him as a sort of Mo Johnston figure. There was even a fight at Southend between those fans who sang his name and those who denied his existence. Personally I liked him; he could look after himself, often sending so-called 'hard men' squealing to the ref, he won most of the aerial battles and laid off intelligent balls.

So the burning striker issue was never properly resolved in Roeder's time. Injuries also affected team selections; a graph in the local paper demonstrating that we had more long term walking wounded than any other club in the Division. To make matters worse, long-serving physio Billy Hails had been sacked even before the manager was, amidst rumours that he had only a rudimentary knowledge of sports medicine. Whatever the truth of this, poor old Billy deserved a testimonial given his long service, not a P45. What was becoming glaringly obvious though was that we needed a bigger squad to compensate for the casualties. It got so bad that the reserves were fielding our 'football in the community officer' Jimmy Gilligan and Stuart Murdoch, an irritating old geyser who'd somehow managed to get the job of assistant manager despite his blank footballing CV.

Taylor took on a team with a losing mentality, who were bottom and without a win in eight games. He did however inherit some good players. Ramage had fallen out with Roeder, been fined and dropped for reporting back for training a few pounds over his fighting weight. This developing rift meant that his ability to pass and strut about in midfield was missed by the fans, and on the pitch too. So he didn't 'play' for Roeder and it was a surprise he was still there at all in February. Phillips limped off in Taylor's third game, it was for him an injury-hit season including an incident at Bournemouth when during a pitch 'invasion' (yes, a dozen or so Watford fans spilled onto Dean Court), he was mistaken for a an interloping supporter and truncheoned. Taylor had lost our key attacker, yet without any new signings of his own he transformed the team into an attack-minded one.

He bought in Kenny Jackett and Luther Blissett as coaches. Elton John spoke of the club needing an "enema", and although he didn't promise to invest any of his £140m fortune, he vowed to spend more time helping the club. There was no instant cure; Taylor fumed about peeling paint in the dressing rooms and "the deterioration in standards on and off the pitch." Fighting (provoked by our goading fans) interrupted the Portsmouth game, then there was the civil war incident at Southend. Watford looked doomed, despite a 4-4 draw at West Brom, during which the chants of "There's only one Graham Taylor" took me back to the mid 80's. But when we left the ground at a quarter to five after defeat by Portsmouth on April 6th, we were convinced there was no chance of us delaying relegation for much longer. A late equaliser by Southend on Bank Holiday Monday added to the fatalism. We did draw 3-3 with Champions Sunderland and had two draws with Derby. Oh, and we failed - yet again - to beat Luton. But they're not important enough to be mentioned too much in this article; suffice to say that I wish they'd fold and re-emerge in the ICIS League Division Three and stay there.

Watford then started to score goals in a manner in which they'd failed to do for years. In-form Port Vale were beaten 5-2, Reading 4-2, a blip at (where else) Luton 0-0, and then Grimsby 6-3. We weren't bottom anymore and had started to show promotion form. At Norwich, my hands were numb and my throat was hoarse, after countless choruses of "Elton John's Taylor made army" (he was on the bench), while the Norwich hordes were preoccupied with their "Chase out" chants.

When 18 year old Connolly, who'd scored two hat-tricks in recent weeks, put us 1-0 up with a penalty, I've never been on such a high. Watford were still probably doomed but on that afternoon the team and fans were determined to alter their fate. Then Norwich equalised. That fat, square-jawed jock Fleck managed to aggravate us yet again. Porter then hit a 30 yarder into the top corner; cue frenzied leaping around in the away end. At the final whistle both sets of supporters applauded each other, a sort of 'love-in' as someone said. All the other relevant results went our way: Luton lost (cheerio!), Reading lost, Oldham drew, Millwall lost and Pompey lost. It now went down to the last day. Reading and Oldham winning in mid-week narrowed the field down to us, Millwall and Pompey. Of course, history shows that Portsmouth got out of jail that day, but had we stayed up it would have been the ultimate 'great escape'. The board would have then felt vindicated, but their budgeting for mere survival has been exposed for what it is: a sure fire recipe for relegation. Watford struggled for six seasons out of seven in the years before they finally went down, and not once did Petchey spend to try and improve the situation. He isn't a Watford fan; he doesn't give a toss about us. To him, the club is purely a business; well at least he won't make anything out of relegation. I know that fans always blame the board, but what's the point of selling players for millions, having a smart ground and a second Division team. "PETCHEY OUT!"

Watford have gone down with players who don't belong in the Second Division: goalkeeper Miller, Phillips when he gets fit, Player of the Season Mooney, local lad (and Eire international) Connolly, Hessenthaler, Holdsworth and Page. Injuries were a factor, loss of form as well, but most of all lack of ambition. One final mention must go to Devon White. If there's ever someone you'd want to help you out if you were cornered by a gang of Luton fans, he's your man. He shows the odd good touch but his game is based largely on his 14st frame. He looks more like Frank Bruno than a footballer but he's our current hero anyway!

Fanzine Facts

The Horn first appeared in January '90 and got its name from the Vicarage Road chant 'Come on you 'Orns.' Editor Mark Evans says "I was once confronted by a Claire Short lookalike who spotted The Horn's title, and grilled about the mag's possible sexist connotations. But FourFourTwo probably got closer to the truth when they described it as "refreshingly polite and well mannered." He adds "We're like the Beano really, good wholesome reading... well, usually!"

I CAN DRIVE A TRACTOR

Norwich City

Over the years, Norwich FC has become synonymous with the villainous name of the archetypal, dictatorial chairman himself, Robert Chase. Whenever, during conversation with a football fan anywhere, you revealed that City held a place in your heart, you could guarantee that part of their reply would mention Norwich's former heartbreaker and how he was destroying the club. The fact that the titles Norwich City Football Club and Robert Chase were virtually interchangeable really does show just how much power he held. And didn't he know it as well!

It was this power, plus his refusal to accept defeat, along with a complete lack of ambition, which turned last season into farce. Indeed, if it wasn't for the fact that Chase's

actions hurt City supporters so much, his misdemeanours could be classed as perfect comedy material, transgressing the boundaries of the laughable and heading straight into the absurd. Although it would be a hackneyed description of Chase to say he was unambitious, conceited, pretentious, two-faced and self-centred, this really did sum him up perfectly. That doesn't mean to say he wasn't adequately described through the use of much more hard-hitting, derogatory remarks. Needless to say, it wasn't uncommon for him to be colloquially likened to an area of the female genitalia or a participant in self relief methods (need I say more?).

This all came after a summer when he'd played the part of heroic leader, leading us into war, reeling off battle-calls to prepare fans for a no-holds-barred campaign aimed at thrusting us straight back into the Premier League. He masterfully managed to convince many supporters that he'd changed his unpopular ways, and caused a degree of optimism to be carried into the season. Chase himself said on numerous occasions whilst attempting to gain forgiveness and provide justification for his misdoings that "hindsight is an exact science." Well, with the benefit of hindsight, I would guarantee there are literally thousands of supporters who wish they'd never bought a season ticket last year. Like me, they'd been conned by Chase into believing he really was going to make an effort to get us straight back up. He'd talked of "putting everything on a back burner", "freeing up funds" and told supporters how "our first chance is our best chance", as well as guaranteeing that something in the region of £4-5m would be made available to the manager for new players. To accompany this bellicose repertoire, he'd appointed Martin O'Neill, signed Robert Fleck, and unlike previous seasons, every player had signed a new contract and seemed ready to don the yellow and green come the start of the new campaign.

All these factors earned Chase a temporary reprieve from the demonstrations.

Soon enough, everything started to go horrifically wrong. The catalyst for this turnaround? Yes, you've guessed it, Mr Chase. It seemed that once again with the benefit of hindsight, he'd thought to himself, "well, maybe we haven't got quite as much money in the kitty as I thought." It was soon made blatantly obvious that Chase thought we could make do with what we'd got, and that no funds were going to be made available for new faces. It was mainly the promise of this money which had lured Martin O'Neill to Norfolk in the first place. And like Mike Walker before him, O'Neill's wasn't just going to let Chase walk all over him. Trouble began brewing at Carrow Road almost immediately, and very soon, publicised verbal battles were being aired by the local TV channels.

The boardroom friction reached its climax on December 17th, the morning of the Leicester away game, when Martin O'Neill handed in his resignation. From a supporter's point of view, to be told upon walking towards the ground that your highly regarded manager had just resigned was absolutely soul destroying. This to many of us spelt the beginning of the end, and O'Neill was subsequently replaced by Megson, who, needless to say, was hardly the fans' choice. Admittedly we weren't playing spectacular football under O'Neill, but he was starting to get things together (we were second by December), and I feel sure that had he been allowed the courtesy of getting on with his job unhindered, then he would have been lifting the play-off trophy at Wembley as the manager of Norwich, rather than Leicester. I would even go as far as to say that one of the automatic promotion spots wouldn't have been totally out of the question.

When speaking to a Leicester supporter prior to the match, upon hearing the news that Martin had jacked it in, he confidently predicted "he'll be here on Monday." He was nearly right (only four days out) and it was revealed soon afterwards that the morning O'Neill had quit, Chase had been on the blower to Martin George to wrangle out a compensation package for the Ulsterman's services.

From then on, the season took a kamikaze nose-dive. If there was one saving grace following O'Neill's departure, it was that Chase was put under more forceful than usual pressure, if only for a brief period. Norwich supporters aren't really renowned for adopting a revolutionary attitude. Indeed, sometimes it seems as though many fans are so laid back that they're on the verge of falling over, which was why it is surprising to say the least when following the Southend home game on December 26th, after the obligatory post-match demonstrations, groups of fans made genuine attempts to storm Carrow Road in an effort to hang, draw and most likely quarter the rotund figure of Norfolk's most hated man. This hostility subsequently led to members of the local constabulary warning him that his safety couldn't be guaranteed, and Chase resorted to hiring a personal security firm. Police vans were also positioned outside the entrance to the City Stand for the remainder of the season.

During this period, it seemed that Chase's stranglehold was beginning to weaken. He was being squeezed between a vice of supporter pressure from the two hundred or so committed revolutionaries stationed outside the City Stand after every home game, and financial pressure from those boycotting Carrow Road. But, as was proved, Chase is not an easy man to crush. Having boycotted Carrow Road myself for a time, I can tell you it's not an easy thing listening to your club on the radio, when, but for one man, you would be attending. Conscience is an amazing thing. You want to go to the game. Yet you know that by not going, you will hit the enemy where it hurts - in his pocket. And if by not going you eventually remove that enemy from his stronghold, then your guilt at causing short-term damage to the club you love is far outweighed by the long-term good of helping to start a new regime. But it hurts nonetheless.

In the aftermath of O'Neill's resignation, at one stage, three consortiums were attempting to prise Chase out of the chairman's seat. One was even reported to accommodate the serious financial clout of the 20th richest person in Britain, worth a cool £200m. As per usual, Chase remained adamant that not one of them had the required credentials of "having the club's best interests at heart." Incidentally, this had become a much-coined phrase, which, due to the constancy of its use, is becoming increasingly irritating to hear. It seems everybody knows what's in the 'best interests of the club'... except the supporters. Needless to say, nothing happened.

The boycott began to take its toll on the attendance figures at Carrow Road, although that's not to say Chase didn't try to hide the fact, like a follically challenged man combing his remaining hairs over his ever-expanding bald patch. Thousands of schoolkids were given free tickets in an attempt to halt the erosion of the City support, and this cover-up came hand in hand with a blatantly obvious 'fiddle' of the attendance figures (allegedly!).

February 28th brought with it the shock revelation that from now on the phrase 'cash rich Norwich' was to be replaced with 'debt ridden Norwich', as news was disclosed that Chase had blown all the club's money. Every penny which had literally poured in from the UEFA Cup run, and from the sales of star players such as Sutton and Fox, had gone. What's more, he'd managed to put us £4.5m in debt, and the banks were getting restless. Chase the business supremo? Don't make me laugh. He tried to fob us off with excuses that it had all been necessary expenditure. What surely *would* have been necessary was more investment in the playing side of things, then the on-field success would have more than covered his off-field financial requirements.

The next day he released a letter to the other 91 League clubs putting every player up for sale, in an attempt to clear some of his self-inflicted debts. And now, Chase's legendary transfer wranglings which usually dragged on for months were replaced by the rather more desperate approach of 'well, we'd better take what we can get'. Ashley Ward was sold for £1m to Derby, and Newsome was offloaded to Sheffield Wednesday for £1.6m, prices which can only be described as bargains.

Very surprisingly, Megson, in total contradiction to his 'Chase's puppet' image, blasted the chairman the next day in a verbal attack which came totally out of the blue. That's not to say the supporters changed their attitude towards him as a result. The consensus was that he'd known what he was letting himself in for before he decided to take up the manager's vacancy, so he was afforded little sympathy.

On March 21st, an AGM was held whereby Chase informed shareholders that he'd found a buyer for his shares. Oh yeah? We'd believe it when we saw it.

And sure enough, nothing happened... until, that is, May 2nd, six weeks after Chase had made the initial announcement, when it was finally revealed he'd shut the door and turned out the lights, so to speak.

By all accounts, the boycotts and mounting personal debts had been the instrumental factors in Chase's departure. When my aunt phoned with the news that Chase had sold his shares (at greatly reduced value) to club president and former City chairman Geoffrey Watling, the sheer relief of Norwich finally being a Chase-free zone brought the most unbelievably childish grin to my face. It was like being a kid at Christmas unwrapping your presents and finding the one you'd put at the top of your list. To be honest, I don't think it will really sink in until the start of next season that we're finally going to be free to progress without being held back like a dog on a lead. At last, the melodious club anthem 'on the ball City' will once again ring out around Carrow Road, and when we sing it, we'll really mean it. I know the notion of a supporter wanting their team to lose may sound unthinkable (and even blasphemous), but last season, many fans had reached such a low that losing could be seen as a good thing in that it put more pressure on Chase. Hopefully, with a bit of ambition shown by the new regime, much-needed communication with supporters and the installation of Mike Walker in his anointed place as City manager, maybe the club can begin going forwards again, after such a long period of retrogression under Chase.

Although I don't profess to being a visionary, the future could be bright, but it ultimately depends on both club and supporters healing the damaging fissure between them and working together. Nobody is so naïve to think that recovery will be an overnight process. All we want is for whoever is in control of the club to at least try and match the ambitions of the supporters, because, as some eminent philosopher once said; 'you can't ask for any more than that'.

Oh, and as for the football. The season peaked on the first weekend with a 3-1 win over Luton in front of 2,000 vociferous Norwich fans who were under the sad impression the rest of the season would continue in the same vein.

Fanzine Facts

I Can Drive A Tractor was launched by Darren Alcock in April '94 at an away game against Manchester, and in Darren's words, "in all honesty, it could adequately have been described as bollocks. Not the dog's bollocks, just bollocks! Quite what the Man City fans thought after reading **ICDAT** and then their own fanzine *The King of the Kippax*, I wouldn't like to even try and imagine." However, he'd like to think it's steadily come of age over the last season or so, in both content and layout. Darren acknowledges the huge input given by assistant editor Phil Keenan, and also praises regular contributors James Francis, Suffolk Yellow and Peter Gates. The fanzine's name derives from the age-old Norwich song: *"I can't read, I can't write, but that don't really matter, cause I'm a Norwich City fan and I can drive a tractor!"*

INTO THE O'S ZONE

Leyton Orient

Our worst season ever!!

We thought things couldn't possibly get any worse. The '94-95 season had seen us: finish bottom of Division Two; have a player sacked at half-time; sack our two managers; go a whole season without an away win, and threaten to sink out of football altogether.

But despite all of this, most O's fans were pretty optimistic. Barry Hearn had arrived at Bristol Road full of ideas and promises. We had a new management team in charge and new players were arriving with alarming regularity.

Well, congratulations to the '95-96 squad! This season we managed to: finish fourth bottom of the Third Division; have a player sacked for co-caine abuse; go a whole season with just one away win.

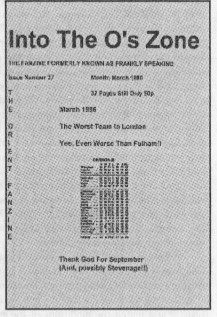

Yet it all seemed so different back in August. Eight thousand plus arrived at Brisbane Road to see us open the season with a 1-0 win over Torquay - the new Orient had arrived! And despite our normal Coca Cola Cup first round exit, August and September were promising months. We lost just one game, and in September we managed to remain unbeaten.

Fulham were defeated at Brisbane Road and we managed a 1-1 draw at Plymouth. Then came the magical night. September 12th 1995. We won 2-1 at (yes, _at_) Northampton Town - the highlight of our season. Doesn't sound too good, does it, the highlight of your season being a 2-1 win at Northampton. Remember, though, this was our first win on our travels since October 30th 1993. Yes, the O's had gone a month under two years without an away win until goals from Ian Hendon and a last minute winner from Alex Inglethorpe gave us a 2-1 win. YESSSS!!! After this historic victory, we beat Hartlepool and Doncaster (at Brisbane Road, of course) and drew at Exeter to end the month in third place.

Sadly, this is where we peaked, and things then started to go wrong. We lost the next nine games including Cup defeats against Shrewsbury (in the Auto whatever it is called now) and Torquay in the FA Cup. But _no-one_ lost to Torquay!! In their four games prior to our FA Cup tie, the Gulls had conceded 18 goals and had been stuffed 1-8 at home to Scunthorpe. Yet we lost to them!

Soon after this came Barnet away. We lost 0-3 and were truly awful. After the match, several O's players were selected for drugs tests. Sort it out, we'd just lost 0-3 to Barnet and our players were being tested for *performance-enhancing* drugs!

In January, it was announced that our left back, Roger Stanislaus, had tested positive for cocaine. Stanislaus came up with the story that he'd smoked the stuff on the Thursday prior to the Barnet game. The medical experts reckoned that if that were so, he must've taken a lethal dosage for it still to appear in the test on the Saturday. Whilst that might explain some of his performances, the FA sided with the medical experts. Stanislaus was banned for a year by the FA and sacked by Leyton Orient.

On the pitch, the team was making a successful bid to become the worst O's side ever! We dropped into the bottom six, but the Conference was never a real prospect; Torquay were rooted to the bottom. They did beat us in January, though. It was their first victory since November when they'd beaten... us!! Also in our favour was the fact that Stevenage were top of the Conference.

It has to be said that pretty soon after Christmas, most O's fans were praying for May 4th to arrive. But there were still some highlights left: Westy's hat-trick against Cardiff; Andy Arnott's late equaliser at Gillingham to give us a 1-1 draw; a massive Degan James Beer/Football/Horse Racing Special (Hereford for the football and Wolverhampton for the floodlit horse racing); coming back from 1-3 down to Barnet to draw 3-3 and effectively end their play-off hopes.

Finally the prayed-for day arrived, and our season ended with a 0-2 defeat at Cambridge, with two players sent off. It sort of summed up our season. We were fourth bottom of the Third Division - 89th place overall - our worst finish ever!

Our away record is legendary - we have now won just one away game since October 30th 1993 - a pretty sad statistic. But our bids for 15 minutes of fame include the Channel Four documentary which showed one of our ex-managers giving an exhibition of bad language to put Graham Taylor in the shade, and or course the Stanislaus cocaine incident.

What a joyful game football is!! Still, since then we've managed to sign two ex-Premiership players whose combined age is nearly 80, and we've also beaten a near full -strength Wales side 2-1 with our winner coming from a player who must have been all of 15 stone!

In a strange sort of way, that summed up what being an O's fan is all about!

Fanzine Facts

Originally known as *Frankly Speaking*, the fanzine was born back in '91 "for no obvious reason at all" according to editor Andy Campbell, and was retitled **Into the O's Zone** in August '95. Andy acknowledge Fiona Campbell, Degan James, Steve Snell, Jason Starr, Grant Conway, Paul Simmons, Becontree Bill, Richard Lawton and others, without whom **Into The O's Zone** would not be around today.

IRON FILINGS

Scunthorpe United

EIGHT-ONE! Eight-Bloody-One!

We were in a 'phone box next to Torquay Harbour at 2.30 in the morning. Our mate Andy wasn't. He was in bed back in Scunny, asleep. Or rather he *had* been until he got a load of drunks on the 'phone for the third time that night to confirm the result of the afternoon's shenanigans at Plainmoor.

It's not often you win 8-1 (once every 31 years is Scunthorpe's current average) and so you have to make the most of it. And there's nothing quite like the sadistic pleasure of being able to ring the Man Who Hardly Misses a Match in the early hours of the morning to gleefully inform him that the first game he'd missed in ages just happened to be a club record 8-1 away win.

Of course, at that stage (end of October), no-one realised quite how bad Torquay were going to be and, with hindsight, the result did nothing but raise our hopes falsely. In effect, it was to be the high spot of the season. Three days later, we ground out a 1-0 win at Cardiff, our third consecutive victory, which lifted us to ninth in the table.

After a bad start things were beginning to look up, and the biggest crowd of the campaign so far turned out at Glanford Park for the visit of Rochdale on November 4th. Inevitably, the Iron rose to the occasion in fine style, losing 3-1. Those stay-away fans who'd been tempted back by the Torquay and Cardiff results went home muttering "same old rubbish."

The Rochdale defeat saw us drop three places to 12th and we would never be as high as ninth again all season. Yes, indeed, it was to be the 'same old rubbish' for much of the year.

Back in August, the feeling had been very much different. Much to everyone's astonishment, striker John Eyre - eight goals in just nine loan appearances the previous season - had been prised away from Oldham for £40,000; lanky forward Andy McFarlane came in from Swansea; Lee Turnbull's loan move from Wycombe was made permanent for £15,000 and full-back Paul Wilson was signed on the eve of the season from York.

The general consensus was that we had a decent team. We hadn't been that far away the previous year, finishing only one place below the play-off positions, and, in Dave Moore, had a young and ambitious manager who could only have learned from his first full year in the hot seat during '94-95.

It didn't take long for our illusions to be shattered; the opening day in fact. All was going well at home against Cambridge as we led 1-0 with little more than ten minutes to go. Result - lost 2-1.

The topsy-turvy nature of the season to come was perhaps best summed up within the first ten days by the two matches against Rotherham in the first round of the Coca Cola Cup. In the home leg United were magnificent, romping home to a 4-1 win with a superb performance, which effectively booked our place in round two. Even the manager thought we were through; "It would take a horror night for us at Millmoor to let them back in it," Dave Moore told the local paper.

Scunthorpe fans, however, have suffered more than their fair share of 'horror nights' over the years and Rotherham is not a ground which holds happy memories. Our 'relegation party' was held there in '84 and we became the first ever team to go out of the FA Cup on penalties in '91.

Still, we were 4-1 up, we all thought on arrival at Millmoor. Surely we weren't going to mess this one up? Ahem. One 'horror night' and a 5-0 gubbing later, and that was the end of our League Cup hopes for another season. When the final whistle went, someone suggested Moore should keep the players on the pitch for another half an hour to practice passing to each other as they hadn't managed it all evening. Another wag interrupted: "No, they've got to master the real basics first, they should be practising tying their bootlaces."

Quite how we managed to be so good and so bad within the space of eight days and two matches was inexplicable, and though it was only early days, they were two results which shaped the remainder of the season: very good and very bad in alternating spells.

The first couple of months were largely bad. The Rotherham away leg may have been the worst performance, but the results weren't coming in the League either.

A first win was recorded at home over Barnet but that was followed by a collapse at Lincoln (1-0 up with three minutes to go; 2-1 down with a minute to go; then a last kick equaliser from Eyre) and defeat at Exeter. The air of despondency was becoming tangible, and after Chester turned us over 2-0 on a miserable Tuesday night at Glanford Park (the scoreline in no way reflecting their superiority), we were third from bottom.

The rest of September showed signs of improvement; a fortuitous penalty helping us to a lucky draw at Preston and Big Andy Mac's knee coming to the rescue at Mansfield in the 90th minute after they'd taken the lead in the 89th! But after defeat at Hartlepool in mid-October - thankfully on the day of the Scunthorpe Beer Festival so the weekend wasn't a complete waste of time - we were down to third from bottom once again.

Manager Moore came under fire for the first time at Hartlepool as disgruntled travelling supporters vented their anger, but then the team embarked on their first sustained spell of decent results. A surprise 4-0 win over Bury in the Auto Windscreen Wipers was followed by victory over Leyton Orient at home, the 'Torquay Farce', and the win at Cardiff.

If Scunthorpe are consistent at anything, however, it's being inconsistent. No sooner had we started winning than we started losing again. November and December were disastrous, the only consolation being that we avoided the humiliation of an FA Cup exit in round one at Northwich Victoria.

A 3-0 lead at home to Scarborough was squandered in a 3-3 draw; a 1-1 draw at home to Shrewsbury in the FA Cup inevitably meant we missed out on Liverpool in the third round (we've never won an away replay in the Cup since entering the Football League in 1950); and a dismal display on a wet Tuesday night at Hereford confirmed the worst suspicions of even the handful of die-hards at Edgar Street - we weren't actually any good.

The Christmas and New Year holiday period was surprisingly quite enjoyable for United fans: the bad weather wrecked our entire programme and we didn't play again for almost a month! And what a transformation followed. No-one would have put money on Dave Moore becoming Manager of the Month for January but after a home win over Wigan and three successive away victories at Cambridge, Plymouth and Fulham we were suddenly right back in the play-off race. But as so often happens, his award virtually killed our season. Twelve points out of 12 in January turned into two out of 15 in February, which in itself was a glut compared to the start of March, which yielded four straight defeats.

The alarm bells were clanging off the wall as we plunged to third from bottom, casting anxious glances in the direction of Torquay as we fell. The thought sent shivers down my spine - being overhauled by the Gulls on the final day of the season to be condemned to a Halifax-like existence alongside the wannabes of the Conference. The horrendous prospect of Tuesday night trips to Gateshead just didn't bear thinking about.

Urgent action by the board was called for and the inevitable happened. Moore was sacked - only a fortnight after receiving his Manager of the Month award. Although a good number of supporters had some sympathy for Moore, an amiable and honest man who had tried his best with limited resources, there was a general feeling that a change was essential as the slide down the table into relegation trouble went unchecked. The big surprise, though, came with the announcement of Moore's replacement our former manager Mick Buxton, who'd been sacked by the club in January '91.

Buxton had twice taken Scunthorpe to the brink of promotion in his previous stint but lost his job after an indifferent start to the '91-92 campaign. His arrival hardly fired the imagination of supporters who were desperate for a big name boss (a big name boss at Scunthorpe? Last time we had one of those, Allan Clarke got us relegated). But now he was back; initially only until the end of the season with the task of getting us out of trouble.

Buxton may not be the most charismatic man in the world, but he is a good manager at our level. And after a derby defeat at Doncaster in his first match (having only met the players a couple of days beforehand), he promptly inspired a run of five successive victories which, somewhat ludicrously, even revived the notion of a play-off place.

Admittedly, it was one of those 'if we win all our remaining games and they lose all of theirs' affairs, but that's the beauty of the play-offs. Third from bottom in mid-March, and on course for promotion in mid-April... Well, almost.

In the end, we came home 12th, being pipped for a play-off place by a meagre 12 points (I did say it was a ludicrous notion) but at least finishing in the top half.

The season ended on a high with a 4-1 win at Scarborough (always nice to beat our former bogy team) and a 3-3 draw with Darlington, which put the tin lid on their promotion hopes.

And so yet another Scunthorpe season was consigned to the file marked 'mediocre'. Despite a couple of near misses under Buxton, and the Wembley play-off defeat on penalties by Blackpool in '92, the fact remains that we have been in the basement Division for every season bar two since 1973, and after Rochdale and Hereford, are the longest serving members of the Fourth/Third Division.

That's a pretty dismal and depressing record, but one that Mick Buxton will hopefully be able to put right. As we say every February (or March if we happen to be having a good year), "there's always next season..."

Fanzine Facts

Iron Filings was conceived at the launch of the Scunthorpe United London & South East Supporters' Club in August, 1987, when five United fans living in the capital got together at The Chandos pub in Trafalgar Square to form the Iron's southern branch. Messrs Vaughan, Dunn, Pearson, Kemp and Skeels intended to have a plaque erected in the pub to commemorate such an auspicious occasion but never got round to it. Andy Skeels was nominated as *Iron Filings'* editor and has been (in his words) "lumbered ever since."

IT'S AN EASY ONE FOR NORMAN

Sunderland

"Cheer Up Peter Reid! Oh what can it mean, to a... Sunderland supporter to be top of the League!"

So went the most original terrace anthem for years, soon to be a chart-topping hit, and later copied and adopted by fans all around the country, including Newcastle's very own abusive ditty! Far more important was what inspired it: a Sunderland side which had only just beaten the drop the previous year racing to the Division One Championship. It was something that no Sunderland fan had even dreamed about at the start of the season. Yet against all expectations, straight-talking Peter Reid guided us to top spot with virtually the same squad as the relegation-haunted one he'd inherited from Mick Buxton. In the process, he guaran-

teed himself Messiah status amongst the Sunderland faithful who'd long been waiting for someone to restore our pride in a football club that for too long had been a complete joke in the North East.

When it all began, only the most insane optimist would have predicted the outcome. Most fans were hoping for a summer clear-out after the traumatic '94-95 season, and a transfusion of new blood in the squad. How else could a team that finished one place above a relegation spot possibly challenge for promotion? When it became clear that there was to be no money for new signings, the groans of Sunderland fans could be heard from Land's End to John O'Groats. "Here we go again" was the universal cry of red and whites, as we looked on enviously at big-spending Newcastle and Middlesbrough enjoying life in the Premier League and throwing wads of cash about. Sunderland, on the other hand, didn't seem to have the proverbial pot to piss in.

However, canny manager that he is, Reid used the few farthings the board gave him to good effect. The capture of Paul Bracewell from the black and white enemy as assistant player/manager for fifty grand was a masterstroke. Ironically, Bracewell had been signed from Sunderland by eagle-eyed Keegan in '92, immediately after Bracewell's appearance in our FA Cup Final against Liverpool, and after our short-sighted board had not offered him acceptable terms. The fans were delighted to have him back, but didn't think that he alone would make us realistic promotion challengers.

An opening day defeat by Leicester at Roker seemed to confirm our worst fears. However, one bright spot was the masterly performance of Bracewell, who controlled the midfield with contemptuous ease. The void that had existed there since his acrimonious departure three years earlier, and which had been unsuccessfully filled by nonentities like Shaun Cunnington and Derek Ferguson at a combined cost of £1.4m, had at last been filled.

Despite this, Sunderland's start to the campaign was not spectacular. We won only one of our opening five games, and were hovering near the bottom of the table. Even worse, Third Division Preston North End had almost embarrassed us in the Coca Cola Cup, going two up in the first half of the second leg at Roker, before a suitably bollocked Sunderland side scored three in the second half to win the tie. The prize was a second round clash with Liverpool!

Sunderland's season gradually began to gain momentum after a slow start. Peter Reid, with the influence of Bracewell on the pitch, had moulded this team into his own. Players like Michael Gray, largely ignored by the previous boss, had a new lease of life. Restored to his favourite position on the left wing, Gray was a revelation. Those who witnessed the Old Trafford Cup tie will have seen him at his brilliant best as he tormented the Man Utd rearguard. Another player rescued from obscurity was Richard Ord. Restored to his natural centre-half position by Reid, Ord had an outstanding campaign, culminating in the Player of the Season award. Craig Russell, a strong aggressive forward with an eye for goal, was another young player who was transformed, and was leading goalscorer for '95-96. Later in the season Reid also introduced the extremely precocious goalscoring talent of Michael Bridges. Just 17 years old, the lanky forward made his debut at home to Port Vale in February and showed great promise in the short time he was on the pitch. He would later make his mark by scoring two goals in five minutes at home to Huddersfield Town, after coming on as a substitute late in the second half when Sunderland were 2-1 down and chasing the game. All four will make a big impact in the Premier League.

But I digress. At this stage of the season (autumn), although Sunderland were a much improved outfit, promotion still seemed far off. However, although we unluckily lost 3-0 over both legs, the Liverpool games did show what we were capable of. But were we good enough for promotion? Most fans were still doubtful.

However, by the time leaders Millwall arrived in December we'd climbed to second place. It was a top of the table showdown. A closely fought game was anticipated, but Sunderland turned on the style for their best League performance of the season, massacring the Lions 6-0, Craig Russell bagging four. We were top of the League! But not for long, swapping top spot with Derby County just before Christmas after a 3-1 defeat, and we'd suddenly lost our League momentum.

The third round of the FA Cup saw Sunderland give their all in two memorable games against Manchester United. No-one gave the lads a chance of leaving Old Trafford with a victory, but they nearly pulled it off. Backed by 8,000 passionate frenzied supporters that even Alex Ferguson praised after the game, United were given the fright of their lives by a Sunderland side that took the game to them. Despite going a goal down against the run of play, we hit back in the second half, scoring twice in a five minute burst. A famous Cup victory looked on the cards. However, United showed the fortitude that would bring them the League and Cup Double, and with ten minutes remaining Eric Cantona (who else) brought them level with a close-range header. An epic encounter nevertheless, and a performance that every single Sunderland fan was proud of. Roll on the replay!

Once again, we gave our illustrious opponents a scare, dominating the first half and going in a goal to the good, when it should really have been two. The Roker Roar was at its loudest, but in the second half a reorganised and revitalised United slowly turned the screw on the tired Sunderland players. The equaliser inevitably came, but worse was to come in the very last minute with extra time beckoning when Andy Cole scored one of his not-so-frequent goals to put the Red Devils into the next round. While the United fans went mad, Sunderland's could only reflect on what might have been, but a bigger prize than Cup glory was still very much up for grabs - promotion.

Was it a New Year hangover that loosened our grasp on the prize? We won just one game in seven, and suffered a 3-0 mauling at Wolves, which seemed to many to signify the end of any dreams of automatic promotion. We'd slipped to fifth, but more worryingly were having trouble hitting the net. So it was a massive surprise when rather than a striker, Reidy decided that a fresh custodian of the green jersey was needed. It was another masterstroke that was to inspire a nine (yes, nine) game winning run - a sequence which had not been achieved since the days of handlebar moustaches and penny farthings. On January 21st in came 19-year-old Donegal-born Shay Given. We'd never heard of him! But it didn't take long for the young lad to capture the hearts of the Sunderland faithful with a series of magnificent performances. By the time he played (possibly) his last game for Sunderland at Barnsley on April 6th, Shay was a full Republic of Ireland International. His record of 12 clean sheets in 17 games had helped steer us well within sight of the winning post. Sunderland fans would love to see Shay signed permanently, but that depends on moneybags Blackburn (from whom we had him on loan) releasing him.

The Roker juggernaut was unstoppable! A crucial game saw top of the table Derby County visit Roker Park on March 9th. Straight victory number five! Roker Park echoed to the chorus of 'Cheer Up Peter Reid' as the ecstatic Sunderland faithful lapped up the occasion. We went top again after the 2-0 defeat of Birmingham at St Andrews on March 17th, and stayed there. In a near-perfect away game, Sunderland comprehensively outplayed their hapless opponents with a swagger that had Champions written all over it. Their fans did not appreciate the footballing lesson that we handed out, judging by the many reported attacks on our lot after the game (why is it that Midlands supporters, the Baggies apart, have a taste for violence?).

On a lighter note, the 'Cheer Up Peter Reid' anthem had been recorded in the studio by a group of fans under the name 'Simply Red and White'. It proved an immediate hit on Wearside, outselling Oasis' 'Don't Look Back In Anger' and reaching number 41 in the national charts! (Sales on Tyneside were not reported to be good, though!) A higher position would have been reached but for the fact that some outlets stocking the cassette were not registered record shops. A cancer charity was the beneficiary, to the tune of several thousand pounds.

The Championship was clinched by the point won at home to West Bromwich Albion amidst raucous Roker Park celebrations. At last, the fans had a team to be proud of and a manager who shared our same burning passion for success. Had it really been just a year since Sunderland were tumbling towards the Second

Division and possible extinction? It is impossible to over-estimate the impact Peter Reid has had on Sunderland AFC. His Manager's Manager of the Year award is well and truly deserved. True enough, Alex Ferguson won the Double for Man Utd, but Reid's achievement in turning a club round from being down and out to Champions in a year with virtually the same squad is something that is frankly unbelievable.

And what about the future? Well, it's never been brighter. The Premiership will of course be a challenge, but this time we're confident. After 99 years, season '96-97 will be the last one ever at Roker Park before the club moves to the biggest (and best) new all-seater stadium in the country. Currently under construction at Monkwearmouth on the banks of the River Wear, on the site of an old colliery, it is fittingly just half a mile from Roker Park. The new stadium and its money earning potential means Sunderland should be able to compete in the top echelons of the Premier League, hopefully leaving the years of mediocrity behind us forever.

What an emotional year it's going to be, and how fitting for a world famous old ground like Roker Park to be playing host to top-flight football and the likes of Liverpool, Arsenal and Everton. All that is needed to really put the top hat on the occasion will be some silverware, which, incidentally, Newcastle have conspicuously failed to collect despite spending £45m in the last few years and leading the Premiership by 12 points in February! Well, you didn't think I would forget to mention *that*, did you?!

Fanzine Facts

It's An Easy One For Norman got its name following a much publicised and televised mistake by the then Sunderland 'keeper Tony Norman. An innocuous looking goal-bound ball drew the words "it's an easy one for Norman" from the commentator. Where did the ball go? You guessed it! As Tony Norman has not been resident at Roker for more than a year now, main protagonists Robert Stein and Mark Jennings plan to give the 'zine a new name for next season.

JANUARY 3RD, '88

Portsmouth

As final days go, our trip to Huddersfield was the greatest many of us had experienced. It was a really big occasion. We were as wound up for this one as we had been for those epic semi's against Liverpool in '92, the near automatic promotion miss and subsequent play-offs in '93 and our Cup heroics at Ewood Park and Old Trafford in '94. This time though, there was an important difference... A happy ending. Miraculously, we secured a win which our recent form had suggested was unattainable; Millwall's dire run had extended itself just enough, and we were staying up.

At the final whistle, delirious fans invaded the Kirklees pitch, hugging each other and the players, and lifting the once much-maligned Jason Rees on to their shoulders to join in with the songs of triumph. Suddenly, the thought of a trip to Barnsley was like dreaming of a holiday in the Caribbean; a match at Roots Hall was a game in the San Siro, and the prospect of Neil Aspin in the opposing line-up was as exciting as facing Eric Cantona. We were as euphoric as the Frenchman's fans, jubilant over their latest title win which was clinched the same day at Middlesbrough. Pompey were staying up and that's all that mattered. Finishing 21st has never been celebrated so wildly.

Like that last day, Fratton Park was never a dull place in '95-96. If the team weren't either dangerously near the play-off zone or chalking up their longest ever winless run, there was plenty to keep us occupied off the park.

Manager Terry Fenwick was surely only thinking of our entertainment as he produced quip after quip. At least we assume he was joking when he said, for example, that Alan Knight's fifth minute error against Port Vale was to blame for the defeat in not only that match (we did equalise before losing), but also in the subsequent game against West Brom. He also had us rolling in the aisles when he pledged to "Get a fresh face or two" in the side for the game against (insert name of our next opponents). His targets - which included Mark Hateley, Ian Rush and, when he was particularly desperate, Paul Wilkinson - were never likely to arrive.

Another form of off-field entertainment (and don't worry Pompey fans, I'm not about to wax lyrical about the efforts of the Pompey Belles and their pom-poms) was the 'On-Off' game. A consortium of northern businessmen headed by Des Lynam lookalike Warren Smith seemed to spend most of the season saying they were on the verge of buying out the Gregory family, only for MD Martin Gregory to deny any such take-over.

Most fans would have loved a new owner, although not all were convinced that Smith & Co had the spending power they claimed to possess. However, things got so desperate - never more so than in the aftermath of the 3-0 FA Cup defeat at Southampton (God, it hurts just to say it) - that the clamour for the take-over grew. But all to no avail, although as summer arrives Warren Smith is still sniffing around, no doubt encouraged by signs that Martin Gregory has apparently had more than enough.

Gregory's disinterest and/or desire to sell is the only possible explanation for the lack of progress on the plans to carry out the now essential terrace replacement which is now needed on all four sides of the ground. And just to complicate the directors' box line-up, Terry Brady (Karren's old man) arrived in the spring with a posh car, personalised plates, a breath of fresh air and a bulging chequebook that secured the popular signing of West Ham battler Martin Allen. More cash was promised for other players - a truly strange phenomenon in our recent times.

So even without 46 League games and three Cup matches (yes, yes, just three - but then Cardiff are bloody good on their day) it would have been an eventful season.

Out where it mattered though, our form was to put it mildly up and down. Or maybe up, down and down a bit more was nearer to the truth.

At 4.45pm on Saturday August 12th, we sat proudly at the top of the pile following a sun-baked 4-2 win over Southend. It couldn't last, could it? Well, er, no. The downward spiral started quickly with the Cup exit against Cardiff, the sale of our best player, Kit Symons, and a dire League run which saw us hit the bottom after a late goal sunk us at West Brom - which incidentally was their last win for absolutely months. During that desperate period, which also included the sale of Gerry Creaney, only the return of our old hero Paul Walsh saved us from despair. He wasn't quite as sharp as before, but was still in a class of his own, before his season was ended by a serious knee injury sustained against Leicester - more on that game later.

If November was drab, December was remarkable by comparison. We reeled off straight victories over Oldham, Tranmere, Luton and Norwich (the latter our best of the campaign) and the inevitable play-off talk began. One win from our next six soon put an end to that and by January's end we were too near the bottom for comfort, the take-over seemed dead and we were still suffering from the jibes that followed defeat at the Dell.

February started well with a win over Reading on their rubbish heap, and reached ecstasy levels a week later when Leicester came a-visitin'. Football lore decrees that you will hate, nay despise any team that secures a flukey win over you, but few teams can have inflicted such pain on another as Leicester have on us in recent seasons, the worst being their off-side goal which knocked us out of the '93 play-offs after we'd finished about 20 points ahead of them (I said 'about' didn't I?).

So when Paul Hall got his shin in the way of a fierce cross to divert the ball past Leicester's helpless and probably hopeless 'keeper in the last minute, it meant more to us than I can possibly describe. Let's just say it was the first of the two high points this season... Yeeeeaaaasssss, 2-1, you beauties!

Walsh's injury coincided with another bad run of results, broken only by a 2-1 victory over Charlton clinched with a spectacular overhead kick from Deon Burton.

March was a bleak month and an extremely rare point at Crystal Palace was the only one in a five match run. Transfer deadline day came and went with our arrivals lounge not required. If Terry Fenwick had spent more time in concrete negotiations to secure potential signings rather than just telling us who they were, he might have had some joy. Instead, the only change to the squad was the departure of Carl Griffiths, who had come to Fratton in September to escape from the shadow of Paul Walsh at Man City, only to find two weeks later... you can work out the rest. The failure to sign anyone was almost fatal - it meant that spare strikers were thin on the ground at a time when Burton and Hall's form had taken a turn for the worse.

The good done by winning at Watford on Easter Saturday was more than undone by a measly haul of one point from the following four games. Suddenly, with Oldham and Reading's improved form, the maths was simple. Having played the 'On-Off' game until it wasn't funny anymore, it was now time to play the 'ifs and buts' game. If we could win at Huddersfield, and if Millwall failed to win at Ipswich, we'd be OK. But anything less and Bury, Walsall and Shrewsbury beckoned.

Few it seemed had much in the way of hope. Some lied and said it would be nice to visit some new grounds. Despite widespread pessimism we trekked to Yorkshire with our blue and white wigs, red and black faces and bags of tickertape - if not bags of confidence. We feared we were there to be condemned, but as it turned out, our last wish was to be granted. And isn't that what makes this such a wonderful game? See you at Oakwell.

Fanzine Facts

January 3rd, '88 was named to commemorate Pompey's last win over bitter rivals Southampton in Division One. Launched in 1995, ten issues spilled forth from the pen of editor Steve Bone and his merry band of contributors. Steve reckons that this coming season will only see about five issues, but all will be jam-packed with "witty comment, humour, nostalgia and anything else we can lay our grubby mitts on."

KING OF THE KIPPAX

Manchester City

Brian Horton was sacked as manager of Manchester City within a few days of the end of the '94-95 season. After failing to entice about three or four 'second choice' replacements, the board appointed their original 'first choice' (ho, ho, ho, do they think we are daft?). With a spectacular playing career behind him and a World Cup winners medal under his flat cap, more recently he is better known as the holder of a spectacularly bad managerial record with a unique talent as a relegation specialist. His name? Alan Ball.

On the opening day of the season Uwe Rösler headed an equaliser against Spurs at Maine Road. The game ended 1-1 and that point was to be the only one which came our way in the opening nine League games.

We could have scraped a couple of other points I suppose, but Arsenal snatched a last minute winner from an iffy free kick, and Boro went home with all three points thanks to a goal that was scored by a player who was a mere three yards offside.

During this abysmal run we did manage to beat the 'mighty' Wycombe 4-0 in the second leg of the League Cup after a pathetic 0-0 at Adams Park, but Liverpool beat us by the same margin in the following round. To add insult to injury they put six past us in the League three days later. During this none too auspicious start to the campaign Franny kept telling us that "Alan Ball is a football genius." Yes folks, the pressure was already getting to Mr Chairman!

It wasn't all bad news, though. Kit Symons was looking good at the back, Eike Immel was playing well in goals (great shot-stopper, crap with crosses), and Georgiou Kinkladze was absolutely brilliant in midfield. Up-front we had nothing, but that was hardly surprising when you consider that Niall and Uwe both preferred to play with wingers, and Ball didn't have one available. Beagrie, who had played so well last year was injured, and Ball wasn't interested in youngster Scott Thomas who had made his debut towards the end of the previous season.

We had to wait until November for our first win, 1-0 against Bolton, and the following game brought our first away point at Hillsborough. We kept the ball rolling with home wins against Wimbledon and Villa. These heroics earned Ball the Manager of the Month award, and we celebrated with a win at Leeds in our next game.

But we were soon back in trouble. After three defeats on the trot, our final beating of the year came at Ewood Park on Boxing Day night. Eight degrees below zero was the forecast and I think they were being optimistic. Nevertheless, several thousand masochists made the short journey north and gave the locals a 90 minute singing lesson. This travelling support was one of the few highlights of the season, and if the players had matched the fans' effort then survival would have been a mere formality. New Year's Day saw another record bite the dust as we scored twice in a League game for the first time that term. Not bad against a 17 year old goalie eh?

We also found the net a few times in the FA Cup, as Leicester were hit for five without reply in a replay after a dull 0-0 at Filbert Street. That was the night that Kinkladze really announced his arrival. (He had scored a beauty at Boro in December but the morons at the BBC were more interested in a Juninho tap-in). This time there was no ignoring his genius as he provided Uwe with the first, walked past a few defenders before burying the second in the bottom corner, and then had a hand in the other three.

The fourth round was played at Highfield Road where the visiting fans spent an hour and a half raising the roof and snowballing the nearside linesman. The team were playing silly buggers as well and allowed Dublin a simple opportunity to make it 2-2 deep into injury time. We won the replay 2-1 which set us up for a visit to the swamp for the fifth round. The nation watched as Uwe put us in front, but the ref knew the score and awarded the rags the most ludicrous penalty in the history of the game.

Once again, we were left with Premiership safety to concentrate on and we started with a cracker against the Geordie bottle-losers. Not only did we have a six goal thriller, but we also saw Asprilla use both his elbow and his forehead against Keith Curle; needless to say the ref missed both incidents.

Blackburn were the next visitors to Maine Road and Ball was happy with the draw, even though they had a truly awful away record. This was to provide the script for the rest of the season. Draws against anybody were seen as points won, and defeats were seen as very close games where we could have got a draw. Let's face it; if you don't acknowledge a problem then you have no chance of resolving it.

Southampton and Kinkladze. Put them together and you have the on-pitch highlight of the season. Geo picked up the ball outside the box, danced round half the visiting side and chipped the ball over the advancing goalie and into the net for his second of the game. It was a moment of pure and unadulterated magic. It was a goal which encapsulated the beauty of football. Basically it was bloody brilliant!

Another Georgian, striker Mikhail Kavelashvili, had been signed to give Geo someone to talk to, but he was hardly ever used. This could be because he wasn't ready, or because Uwe and Niall were scoring so frequently. Or perhaps it was just that Ball didn't have a clue...

The Easter weekend had been good to us in the relegation battles of '94 and '95. Both times, six points had given us a platform for safety. Look, Premiership clubs may be dumb, but even they aren't dumb enough to fall for the same trick three years running - we were the only relegation candidate to fail to pick up a point over Easter, while all the others collected at least three.

Three games left and a miracle was needed. Sheffield Wednesday came to Maine Road as the ref-bribers went in search of three easy points at Southampton.

It hurt to support the festering rags but my prime concern was for our survival. We won 1-0 but the useless, blind incompetents lost 3-1 because their grey shirts 'made them invisible'! Funny, they wore red against York City and Rotor Volgograd... Maybe the ref's cheque got lost in the post.

By this time it was clear that Bolton and QPR were on their way down. The third place was between Coventry, Southampton, ourselves and possibly Wednesday, and our goal difference was much worse than any of theirs.

Our final away game was at Villa. The home side didn't want us to go down and we managed to scrape a win. Unfortunately Coventry and Southampton did the same, and so the third relegation place would be decided on the final day of the season. It was not a simple equation: if we lost we were down, if we drew we were safe if Coventry or Southampton lost, if we won we were safe if Coventry or Southampton failed to win, or if Sheffield Wednesday lost. With me so far?

Liverpool were our final opponents and were totally disinterested (apart from David James), however despite their lack of commitment they went 2-0 up by half time. A penalty from Uwe and a volley from Kit Symons pulled it back to 2-2 but would it be enough? 'Yes' said a selection of dickheads because Southampton were losing. 'No' said the tranny men because it was still 0-0 at the Dell.

It wasn't enough.

Alan Ball confirmed his talent for taking clubs down, and the papers began their game of 'guess who will be leaving the sinking ship'. In this race Ballie is a non-starter - Franny won't sack him and no other club would be daft enough to poach him.

Fanzine Facts

As editor (and ex-'fan on the board') Dave Wallace explains, "*King Of The Kippax* derives its name from City's equivalent of the Kop, the Kippax Street Stand, which ran the full length of the pitch opposite the main stand. The heaving mass is now sadly defunct, having been replaced by an all-seater job, but has kept its name - so far! The 'King' was, of course, Colin Bell, but to us, all Blues are Kings."

KK is now in its eighth year, having first staggered into life in September 1988. Dave goes points out that "the 'zine finds itself flat on its arse and back where it started, down in the Second Division/Nationwide League." Fifty issues on, Dave says that *KK*'s half century celebrations were delayed until the end of the season, "on the night which completed arguably the worst week in the history of the club, KK held its 'Bollocks to the Cup Final' party. Downhearted? No chance....!"

LATIC FANATIC

Wigan Athletic

Latics' '95-96 season was like a game of snakes and ladders: we almost got to the final winning square, we thought we were home and dry, and then up loomed a bloody big snake which sent us all the way back down to the middle, while those around us conquered the pitfalls and made it to the end.

Of course there's a whole series of pitiful excuses that could be offered to explain why things fell apart so badly in the closing weeks of the season. It's a phenomenon not totally alien to other clubs in our area (just look at Blackpool or Crewe), but perhaps we can offer more excuses than most, because the whole season was filled with frustrations and 'could have beens'... The only predictable aspect of the campaign was its unpredictability.

Let's face it, for a team that started as promotion favourites, we hardly lit the Division up. Inspired by the 'three amigos', we still could only muster three victories in the opening ten games, and then following an embarrassing 6-2 home defeat against Mansfield, millionaire chairman Dave Whelan finally lost patience with his team's inconsistencies. Exit Graham Barrow, one of the few managers to be sacked without being denounced on the terraces, and to this day one that still remains a popular figure with the Springfield Park faithful. However, in those opening matches it was easy to see where precious points had been thrown away: goalkeeping errors by Barrow's worst signing David Felgate and penalty trouble (spot kicks either missed or not awarded).

Ex-Norwich boss John Deehan arrived with John Benson as his assistant. His first month or so in charge was pretty unspectacular - five draws and one defeat in six games; however the turning point came in an FA Cup first round replay against Runcorn. Thankfully, we'd already helped erase nightmarish memories of an FA Cup defeat at Altrincham the previous season by drawing 1-1 in a rain-soaked, mundane first tie at Runcorn, once again in front of the Match of the Day cameras, no doubt praying for another giant-killing act. Sorry to let you down Aunty Beeb! The replay saw the non-leaguers take a 2-1 lead before professional superiority prevailed and we won 4-2.

The second round took us to Barrow who were promptly dispatched 4-0, and we all waited intently for the big third round draw that smaller clubs always dream about. "Walsall or Torquay versus Wigan Athletic." Brilliant. God once again chose to vomit in our face. Torquay would provide a nice weekend by the seaside and not exactly stiff opposition, but Walsall? Hardly giants of the Midlands are they, and a club not in a totally dissimilar bracket to ourselves, but they had a team capable of beating us with the aid of home advantage. As it transpired, Walsall beat Torquay in a high-scoring second round tie, so we put the flip-flops back in the wardrobe and our FA Cup dreams back on the shelf for another season, going down 1-0 on a pitch more suited to a crop rotation system than a football match.

In the meantime, League form took a shape that would stay with us for the rest of the season - great, attacking football at home producing good results, while away, dull negative performances brought little by the way of either points or admirers. At the club's AGM, one supporter stood up to ask the chairman if we could keep John Deehan for the home games but bring back Graham Barrow on our travels. The question made everyone chuckle (except Deehan).

A rare victory at Colchester in February raised hopes that we'd turned the corner and away form was at last looking up. Ahem, a 5-0 defeat at Barnet seven days later brought us back down to earth. Two comfortable home victories against Scarborough and Torquay again put us back on the promotion track, three of the five goals scored in these games coming from the Spaniards Diaz and Martinez. This made it all the more bizarre when Diaz was dropped for next game, a proverbial six-pointer at Bury.

Despite brave words that he was going all-out for a win, Deehan dropped his leading goalscorer and brought Chris Lightfoot back as an extra defender. The result was a 2-1 defeat that left the supporters so irate that they bombarded a local radio station's phone-in show. "Why change a winning team?" they howled.

Yet again, though, the home form deflected some of the criticism, as we walloped a depleted looking Cambridge side, before travelling to Cardiff for a midweek match. Guess what? Yep, you should know the script by now, we got stuffed 3-0, and to cap it all, Diaz was sent off for racing 80-odd yards to protest to the ref about a blatant penalty he'd just turned down.

If we thought our luck had deserted us in South Wales, then worse was to follow. The forward line had looked lightweight all season; in fact, we haven't had an out-and-out striker for many, many years. The manager finally took the plunge and signed Graham Lancashire from Preston just in time for the Lincoln game, after an impressive loan period in which he scored three goals in four games. The result? We won 4-2, but the game was badly marred by the fact that the aforementioned Lancashire was stretchered off with a leg injury thought to be just as bad as a break. Thanks to a lumbering donkey, his season had finished two months early.

Three out of the next four games emphasised just how up and down the season was becoming. A goalless draw at Chester should have been a win, but for Martinez making a rare mistake and missing a last minute penalty. If that boob could be considered to have lost us two points, then the comedy of errors that took place four days later was of such epic proportions that it'd make JFK resemble a ten minute documentary. Indeed, "Carry On Rochdale" as it's now become known was unique in that the game contained not one, not two, but three moments of farce. The first was when the Dale 'keeper, intent on hoofing a harmless back pass out of the ground, only succeeded in kicking thin air, and watched helplessly as the ball bobbled embarrassingly over the line. This was followed by two Rochdale penalty misses, the first almost snapping the cross-bar in half, the second flying straight over the stand. To rub salt into the wounds, Wigan wrapped up the game with a well taken Biggins penalty.

Once again, Lady Luck brought us down with a sliding tackle from behind, when seven days later one of our fastest players Tony Black finished the match in the local hospital's casualty unit with a badly dislocated right ankle. To add to the misery we lost 1-0.

Recognising that the injury list was building up at a crucial point in the season, Deehan was given more money to spend, and former Latics favourite David Lowe returned to the club in a £100,000 deal from Leicester City. It was Lowe's arrival that helped with two crucial victories in as many weeks over Orient and Hartlepool, before an impressive and well-organised Darlington side brought the run to an end by taking a point back to the North East in the Division's top game of the day. Little were we to know that this was the last point we'd pick up.

If you collect *null points* in the last three weeks of the season, you really don't deserve much unless your form before that has been outstanding - and ours hadn't. The fact that two of the last three games were away from home spelled trouble. At Fulham the supporters' fury once again turned on the manager at the end of the game. He later criticised the fans for jeering the players, but it wasn't the players who were in the firing line; they were simply obeying the indifferent tactics of the manager.

The game at Doncaster resulted in the same 1-2 scoreline as Fulham. But this time, you couldn't blame the manager; the result was down to yet another dodgy referee, who turned down one blatant penalty appeal for Latics, awarded the home side a penalty after their man had tripped over one of his own players and then sent Deehan off for protesting when the Doncaster captain kicked Neill Rimmer in the head whilst he was lying on the floor. Unsurprisingly, the official was later reported to Football League.

The last game saw us entertain Northampton, and we needed nothing less than a victory to guarantee a place in the play-offs. After we'd hit the post and Northampton had slotted in an equaliser to our first half goal, it was always on the cards that there was no way back. Our players' heads dropped and the Cobblers finished 2-1 victors. But no complaints - it was in our own hands, and we blew it.

So just like in Bullseye, we made it right through to the end but just when we most needed a good performance, we did the equivalent of scoring fifty-odd with six darts.

"OK lads - come and have a look what you could have won..."

Fanzine Facts

Latic Fanatic first appeared in February '93 to replace the defunct 'Cockney Latic'. Andrew Werrill leads a team of many contributors that includes Bernard Lang, Steve Halliwell, Jeff Rourke, Deborah Callaghan, Ken Werrill (Dad and head of sales/PR) and the mysterious 'S.I.C' (you know who you are, even though the *LF* doesn't). *The Latic Fanatic* has built up an enthusiastic following, although probably not amongst the supporters of Wigan Rugby League, who are affectionately known as the Muppets (so called because according to Andrew, they're "thick and ugly").

LEYTON ORIENTEAR

Leyton Orient

The tortuous, pointless waste of time that was the '95-96 season

In front of me lies a copy of my local paper. It contains an advert boasting of Leyton Orient's never-ending quest to bring the biggest names to Brisbane Road. It is the kind of thing you would never have expected to see two, or 20 years ago. The ad is upbeat, triumphant, even cocky... but it is for a 'Football Legends v Sports Superstars' end-of-season charity game, featuring such luminaries as Jeremy Beadle, Caesar the Geezer, Nigel Benn and George Best, none of whom I can safely predict will be turning out for Leyton Orient next season. This is what the new-look 'fun-oriented' Barry Hearn-inspired O's set-up has so far amounted to.

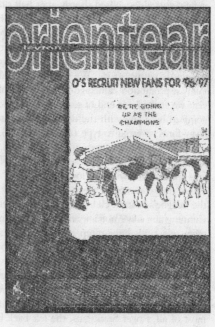

Another example: Our last home programme contained a glossy leaflet advertising season ticket prices for 'London's family club' next season. Its cover is illustrated by ten small pictures of various features of Leyton Orient Football Club - only one contains a direct action picture from a game, in which the ball is being ballooned in the air, naturally. Other shots include Steve Davis, Bestie (again) and a couple of page three girls (all of whom starred as celebrity walk-ons at various games), as well as shots of chairman Hearn and manager Pat Holland. These images say more about the kind of Saturdays we have had to endure than 1,000 words detailing the soul-destroying awfulness of the games ever could.

Yep, we've got a new theme tune, Queen's dire *We Will Rock You* replacing Herp Albert's distinctive and charming *Tijuana Taxi*, we've got a cheeky chirpy DJ who bellows "gooooaaaaalllllll", Brazilian style, on each of the rare occasions we score, and finally, we've got the fourth worst team in the entire country. Orient came 89th out of 92 teams in '95-96, which was by some distance the lowest League position in the club's history.

After last season's emphatic relegation and brush with bankruptcy, we at least thought that under Barry Hearn's bright and breezy stewardship it couldn't get any worse. We were wrong. On the pitch at least, it did.

But it all started so well, and for the first two months of the season we believed the hype. This was less down to our gullibility than to the witnessing of a truly astonishing event, an Orient away win, the first for nearly two years. Around 900 O's fans packed out the away end at Northampton Town's Sixfields Stadium

on a balmy September evening and saw possibly the ideal away triumph. We dominated the game, played some great passing football, went 1-0 down to a flukey
deflected goal, equalised shortly after half time, and won it in the last minute with
a tap-in from Alex Inglethorpe. The travelling faithful piled onto the pitch, misty-
eyed and euphoric, and the world was a lovely place once again. Emphatic home
wins over Hartlepool and Doncaster and an entertaining 2-2 draw at Exeter followed, and by the end of September we were in third place. And then it all went
hopelessly wrong again. We are used to end of season collapses at Brisbane Road,
many a promotion campaign having come off the rails in March or April, but this
year we started our end of season slide in October. Can anyone top that? I'm not
going to bore you with the details of the rest of the season; suffice to say that our
away form reverted to type (and then some), and our home games, including most
of those that we won, were unspeakably dull. Football's great appeal is that it is an
activity in which you can lose yourself completely. But never have so many Orient
fans spent so many games longing to be lost - somewhere else. Arguably the lowest
ebb of the season came when we were knocked out of the Cup in the first round by
the League's bottom club Torquay. Manager Pat Holland and his assistant Tommy
Cunningham have not impressed in their first season in charge. Their tactics and
team selections have often appeared clueless and confused and, while Orient are
not one of the more crude teams in Division Three, they have lacked any sort of
creativity. New signings have appeared, but few have proved to be of any use.
Defender Alan McCarthy, forward Alex Inglethorpe and the lively but raw winger
Joe Baker might just be worth persevering with, but Holland has bought a whole
load of duds - Tony Kelly, Danny Chapman, wobbly 'keeper Peter Caldwell and,
most of all, Roger Stanislaus, the left back bought from Bury last summer.

As was widely reported, Stanislaus was banned from football for a year and
sacked by the club in February after tests revealed that he had taken a 'performance
enhancing' amount of cocaine prior to Orient's abysmal 3-0 surrender at Barnet at
the end of November. Quite how the FA decided that cocaine boosts performance
(if that were the case, surely Noel and Liam Gallagher would be turning out for
Man City) is something of a mystery, but Stanislaus' flat denial of the charge did
him little credit. Whatever the rights and wrongs of the affair, for Roger to take
such a large amount of the drug before an important game was totally unprofession-
al and cast serious doubts over his commitment to the team.

The Stanislaus affair was the last time O's had cause to make the national
papers, as the rest of the season just slowly deteriorated. By May most fans had
decided that this *was* even worse than last season.

Talk to Bazza Hearn himself and he will doubtless tell you that, yes, he's
disappointed with the team's results, but off the pitch it's all changed for the better.
And, to an extent, he's right. The £10 season tickets for kids and all sorts of other
offers have helped push the O's average attendance up to almost 5,000 (although
they tailed away towards the end). The club shop has had a revamp, Hearn grants
interviews to any scruffy fanzine editor that wants one, he meets the fans at public
meetings, and he has raised the club's profile considerably. In many ways, this is
exactly what lower division clubs need to do in these desperate times for the League's
little fish. Which is why it's so maddening that despite being one of the best supported clubs in the Division, Orient were unable to compete with nearly every team
in it. Holland wants more money for the squad (urgently needed), Hearn's pre-

pared to make *some* funds available but would rather concentrate on redeveloping the stadium (no work has been started yet, mind). He also wants to buy the ground from Waltham Forest council, a pointless waste of money given that the club has a harmonious relationship with its local authority.

So the manager is right to demand more money and less bluster and bullshit from his chairman. The trouble is, however, that not many fans have much confidence in Holland's ability to spend wisely. We glance enviously at Gillingham, a club who, like us, were threatened with bankruptcy and subsequently saved last year. They got their heads down, appointed an experienced manager, and went on to win promotion; although it should be pointed out that their success says as much about the new lows to which standards of football in the basement have sunk as it does about the Gills' own credentials. Still, us O's fans would just like to be convinced that the club is serious about promotion first and foremost. The doubts remain and optimism for next season at the time of writing is hard to muster.

Fanzine Facts

Leyton Orientear was founded in September 1986 by Dave Knight and friends who were worried about the financial uncertainty surrounding the club and angry at the secrecy which surrounded goings on at Brisbane Road. The mag touched a chord amongst the numerous miserable gits on the terraces and a solid editorial team developed. The editor's post was passed on to Stephen Harris in 1991 and then to Tom Davies in 1993, and from the summer of 1996 the new man at the helm is Jamie Stripe. The fanzine has been produced monthly throughout every season since 1986 and issue 100 is due later on in the '96-97 term.

THE LION ROARS

Millwall

Season '94-95 had finished disappointingly, with mid-table mediocrity replacing early forecasts of promotion glory.

So many thought '95-96 would be completely different. If the annual mid-season player sale could be avoided, the existing squad would be good enough to improve, and for the first time in years the manager was actually given money to strengthen key areas. We didn't even take much notice of the latest big money sale; Andy Roberts leaving for Crystal Palace for £1.5m. Little did we know how influential he would turn out to be in their play-off quest.

The key problem area was undoubtedly in attack. Chris Malkin was brought in from Tranmere for £400,000, and Uwe Fuchs from Kaiserslautern for £750,000. Fuchs' tally of nine goals in 15 games for Middlesbrough at the tail-end of the previous season had helped Bryan Robson's stuttering side to promotion, but Robson declined to make the move permanent. With hindsight, Robson obviously knew something McCarthy didn't. Club chairman Peter Mead predicted that "the Malkin and Fuchs partnership will terrorise First Division defences." Ahem.

Bobby Bowry and Ricky Newman were both bought from Palace and Maurice Doyle from QPR to strengthen the midfield. Mickey Bennet from Charlton and Anton Rogan from Oxford completed Mick McCarthy's transfer activity. In all, over £2m had been spent. Only Wolves spent more.

Twelve games into the season and Uwe Fuchs still hadn't scored. However, it didn't really seem that important, as we were second on goal difference to leaders Leicester. There weren't any stunning victories, and home defeats to Barnsley and Sunderland were even overlooked as the Lions were in the middle of a ten match unbeaten away run, including yet another glorious Cup night at Goodison Park. Millwall once again made nonsense of Premiership status as they trounced Everton 4-2 in the Coke Cup. There were less than 800 Millwall fans there. You see, it wasn't a Cup shock to us, we *expected* to win! That attitude was also shared by the players. Unfortunately. Good when playing top class opposition, but bad when playing average First Division sides.

The club's first win for 20-odd years at bitter rivals Palace, seen live on TV, took us to the top of the table outright. The good form continued until the begin-

MILLWALL WERE A SPINELESS, GUTLESS RABBLE OF A SIDE WHO HAVE GONE FROM INVINCIBLES TO INCOMPETENCE IN WEEKS

ning of December when our lead was reduced by three consecutive defeats. It wasn't until the fourth though, 6-0 at Sunderland, that Millwall plunged from the top to seventh.

It was now clear that whilst our defence was solid, our new look attack hadn't gelled properly, and the service they were receiving didn't help either. Kingsley Black had come, done well, and gone again, much to the supporters' surprise. Instead, the half a million remaining transfer fund was spent on Gerard Lavin from Watford, who was to replace Ricky Newman at right back.

By Christmas we had much to reflect on. The press had made an example of a one-man pitch invasion against Sheffield Wednesday, making it look like a full scale riot, (as opposed to the real one that took place at Hull at the season's end, which was barely reported on), and they even tried to pin disgraceful scenes at St Andrews on the Millwall faithful. This time Millwall fans were the innocent party, as a Tooting and Mitchum fan had actually supplied the press with their first exaggerated story and then Birmingham fans with the second.

Then a new problem occurred. Eire lost to the Netherlands at Anfield, thus precipitating Jack Charlton's departure. Not only was McCarthy the favourite, but he was the only manager that made it openly known that he wanted the job.

The supporters came to three conclusions: First, we're used to the bad press; it's the price you pay for being the nearest high-profile unsuccessful club to Wapping. Second, we had all come to terms with the fact that we probably weren't as good as we'd first thought, but knew it didn't really matter because all the teams were as good (or bad) as each other. And finally, Millwall supporters to a man thought McCarthy should have resigned or been gently pushed out of the door. It was obvious the speculation would affect the team. Unfortunately it was this latter conclusion with which the club disagreed. Not only did they want McCarthy to stay, but gave him a couple of Russian internationals to keep his spirits up.

As expected, McCarthy was finally offered the Ireland post at the end of January. The Irish FA and the Millwall board had unforgivably allowed the situation to drag on, during which time the team's form went into sudden free-fall.

And what of the 'transfer coup of the season' (© Capital Radio)? Vasili Kulkov and Sergei Yuran were brought in on loan from Spartak Moscow until the end of the season, on £5,000 a week each. Kulkov (the play-maker of the Russian national team) didn't seem too enamoured with the delights of South Bermondsey, playing barely four times before getting injured and returning to Moscow. Yuran was undoubtedly class, but showed the frustration of his technical superiority to his team mates by frequently posturing with hands on hips when a defence-splitting pass wasn't capitalised on. This didn't endear him to the Den faithful either.

To give the club (and in particular Peter Mead) some credit, the replacement for the outgoing McCarthy was sorted out with the minimum of fuss. He spoke to the players and even the supporters before Jimmy Nicholl, who had worked wonders at Raith, was appointed. *TLR*'s first choice then swapped the middle of the Scottish Premier for the middle of Division One. I'm sure Peter Mead, one of the country's leading advertising men, managed to paint a far rosier picture of Den life than truth would have it, but the fact was, when Nicholl arrived, Millwall could still have challenged for the play-offs.

Home form immediately picked up, with the side showing a passion rarely seen in McCarthy's last few weeks, but Nicholl was in for a sharp shock. After being kicked around by the Wolves defence for 90 minutes, Sergei Yuran finally lost his cool and shoved Eric Young over right in front of the referee. He had spent the entire match whinging to the match official for more protection, and the inevitable red card was shown. This was one of seven red cards shown to Millwall players during the season, easily the worst disciplinary record in the Endsleigh League, and a direct legacy of McCarthy's relaxed regime. It prompted Nicholl to give us the quote of the season: "There is a lack of discipline at this club the likes of which I have never come across anywhere. It must have something to do with the old Millwall character and it is frightening." Unfortunately for the Lions, the side suffered the consequences of this ill discipline - frequent suspensions - at just that time in the season when every game was crucial.

Another unlucky defeat, at home to Palace, along with a poor sequence of away results, meant that by the end of the Easter period, Millwall were left anxiously looking over their shoulders at the likes of Portsmouth, Oldham and Reading. However, after an easy win at home to Birmingham, in a match predictably hyped up by the press, it appeared that Millwall were safe, but fate still had another cruel and vicious card to play.

A poor Oldham side turned up at The Den for a relegation six-pointer, wholly intent on gaining a point. Despite the absence of the entire Millwall back four it was a credible performance and one which certainly deserved three points. However, as we all know, football doesn't work like that. Ninety minutes, one attack and one penalty later, Oldham escaped from town with an inconceivable three points. Suddenly both Oldham and Reading were above Millwall. Watford were thrashing everyone out of sight, and all of a sudden it was two from them, Portsmouth and us.

The penultimate Saturday of the season saw Stoke leave The Den with a fortunate 3-2 win, but with Portsmouth losing 0-1 at home to Ipswich and Watford winning at Norwich, it would go down to the wire, with only Luton definitely assured of one of the dreaded three places.

In the end, Jimmy Nicholl's draw tactics at Ipswich back-fired, as Portsmouth grabbed their decisive win at Huddersfield to condemn us to relegation on goals scored. One small consolation: the Lions easily blunted the Division's most potent attack, thus denying them a play-off place. It was one last glimpse of what the players were really capable of. A glimpse that came far, far too late.

As you can see, it is a very difficult season to summarise. It's easy to find excuses: Russian wasters, disappointing signings, or even part-reasons: a new manager and the incredibly even Division. But the damage was done much earlier.

Both Bolton and Sunderland have gained promotion whilst residing at ropy old stadiums during a time when many of their rivals are financing new stadiums, stands and futures. Millwall were the first club to relocate, and Lord Justice Taylor had cost us this team: Keith Branagan, Phil Babb, Colin Hurlock, Alex Rae, Mark Kennedy, Jimmy Carter, Teddy Sheringham, Chris Armstrong. And these are just a few of them; surely we're the only club to have sold what would be an entire Premiership eleven.

Not only has the sale of players like these prevented us from gaining a Premiership place, but by having so many good players in such a short period of time, everyone connected with the club has come to think of Millwall FC as something far bigger than the team we all grew up with. This has had its natural conclusion both in the general attitude and in the team's standard.

We have no doubt that Millwall were as good on the last day of the season as they were on the first, and indeed they were as good as any team in the Division. Therefore, in theory at least, if the players display the right attitude as opposed to the disgraceful collective attitude that was at the heart of Millwall's problems, and if Jimmy Nicholl spends more wisely than his predecessor, it could be the start of a brand new era for the club. Alternatively, Millwall could just return to the backwaters from whence they came. They have just one season to find out.

Fanzine Facts

The Lion Roars started life at Christmas '87, as a number of fans decided that the press attacks on Millwall had gone too far, and it was time for a voice to speak up and attempt to rectify the perceived image of Millwall FC. There were less than a dozen fanzines in existence at that time, and the editors Paul Casella and Carl Prosser never imagined that *TLR* would develop, with the help of several trusty contributors, from an A5 cut and stick fanzine, to a monthly 32 page A4 desktop published magazine.

GOOD EVENING LADIES
& GENTLEMEN, AND
WELCOME TO TALK
BOLLOCKS - THE
TOPICAL CHAT SHOW.
AND WOULD YOU
WELCOME, FROM THE
WORLD OF FOOTBALL....
....ERIC CANTONA AND
KARREN BRADY

LIVERPOOL ARE ON THE TELE AGAIN!

Norwich City

Some ginger haired people have got the gift of the gab, e.g. Chris Evans. He may be an irritating, loud mouthed, self opinionated Man United fan, but almost single handedly he's dragged Radio One out of the gutter and gets his fair share of decent looking women too. He may be no oil painting but he's obviously got something!

At the other end of the scale, you've got Gary Megson. His record as Norwich manager reads: played 32, won 5, drawn 10, lost 17. Megson in his defence claims that his appalling record is misleading because he's only been in office in times of crisis. Bollocks!

If Gary Megson is still manager of Norwich City next season, I can see us getting relegated again. We were lucky this time because we started so well. After the 2-0 victory at Watford on November 27th the Canaries, under the leadership of Martin O'Neill, strolled up to second place in the Endsleigh League Division One. In O'Neill Norwich had a manager who looked capable of achieving promotion back to the Premiership. He eventually did of course, but with Leicester City!

O'Neill walked out on Norwich after a disagreement with infamous chairman Robert Chase. It's claimed that the announcement of O'Neill's resignation was greeted with a loud cheer by the Norwich players the night before the 3-2 defeat at Leicester on December 17th. I couldn't give a toss about that. All I was concerned about was the fact that we had lost the only manager (apart from Mike Walker) who was capable of getting Norwich back up with the big boys.

Although the reason for his resignation was unclear at the time, it's obvious that he'd become impatient with Chase's unwillingness to stump up transfer cash, even though the fat git had claimed in the summer that all off-pitch plans were to be "put on the back burner" and £5m would be made available to spend on new players. However, O'Neill was only allowed to fork out just under £1m on West Ham winger Matthew Rush and former Canary folk hero Robert Fleck. The relationship between the two reached boiling point when Chase pulled the plug on the proposed £650,000 transfer of Hull City striker Dean Windass. Negotiations between the two clubs went on for three months, and when Chase finally backed out of the deal Hull's chairman labelled him "a disgrace."

This coincided with Gary Megson's infamous remark on Anglia TV that Norwich had "*the* squad in the Endsleigh League." This comment was enough to convince Chase that he should bring Megson (now assistant manager at Bradford) back to Carrow Road as O'Neill's replacement, since it implied that he wouldn't want to spend any money. As John Deehan's right hand man, Megson had coached Norwich to relegation from the Premiership in '94-95, and now he was back as manager. Whatever was Chase playing at?

Typical of Gary Megson's astute leadership was his defence of our 'keeper Bryan Gunn after his boob had cost us the derby game at Portman Road. (This was a regular thing with Gunn in '95-96. It's time Andy Marshall is given a chance). Megson's Norwich eventually finished the season in 16th place, our worst since 1964.

On Wednesday May 2nd 1996, after weeks of speculation, Robert Chase resigned as chairman. Dubbed by his biggest supporters as an astute businessman, Chase left the club up shit creek with debts over £4m, despite receiving millions upon millions from selling all the club's best players. After such a dismal season we had something to celebrate at long last. The "Chase out!" chant was now a thing of the past. Suddenly there was hope. But now as I write, things don't seem any different. Chase may be gone but his board of directors still remain and so does our hopeless manager. Thanks to Chase, players like Darren Eadie (*LAOTTA!*'s Player of the Season) and Keith O'Neill will have to be sold to pay off our debts. The writing is on the wall for next season, unless there are drastic changes and fast. Getting Mike Walker back would be a good start.

Fanzine Facts

LAOTTA!, the brainchild of editor Ian 'Duke' Lindsay, first came out in March 1990 (since when nine other Norwich fanzines have fallen by the wayside). Now in his sixth year, Ian's regular contributors are Gary Parkins (former editor of the Watford fanzine 'Mud, Sweat and Beers'), Kit Circuitt, Stephen Copeman and Simon Whittaker. Next season *LAOTTA!* will be merging with fellow City fanzine *Cheep Shot* and will continue to shock, entertain and abuse Alan Brazil.

LOADSAMONEY

Blackburn Rovers

We're Shit But We're Champions

Before a ball had been kicked, Rovers supporters, still celebrating last season's Championship victory, suffered what can be best described as a killer blow. Kenny Dalglish resigned. But if any cloud had a silver lining, then it was this one: 'God' Alan Shearer signed a new four year contract. At least Dalglish wasn't leaving Ewood; just moving to the position of 'Director of Football'.

Ray Harford was offered the manager's job and he accepted. Transfer speculation was rife, but only two players came in: Adam Reed from Darlington and Matt Holmes from West Ham. Departing Ewood were Tony Gale and Robbie Slater. Rovers were unbeaten in the close season friendlies on tour in Scandinavia, and in the invitation games to open Kilmarnock's new stand and the McAlpine stadium.

Next up was a return trip to Wembley for the Charity Shield, where we lost 1-0 to Everton. The lowest ever Wembley Charity Shield attendance of 40,149 endured pitch-side temperatures of 107°F, and those supporters who stayed at home washing their cars were the fortunates.

The season proper kicked off with a flurry of red cards. In the home win against QPR (thanks to Alan Shearer), Tim Flowers became one of the first casualties of the tightening of the professional foul rule. Mark Atkins was next to go at Hillsborough. Against Manchester United, the referee again held centre-stage, dispatching Roy Keane for diving, which still didn't prevent them beating us 2-1. The match at Bolton was like going back in time. Did the powers that be forget to send a copy of the Taylor Report to Burnden Park? It was like watching Match of the Day on UK Gold. The only good thing to come from this game was that Rovers finished with 11 players on the pitch.

Domestic fixtures sandwiched our home game against Spartak Moscow in the Champions League. The nation held its breath. How would the Champions of England fare this year? Mmmm; a crap game where Tim Flowers' mistake gave the Russians the points. Say no more...

A 3-0 hammering at Anfield followed, but the scoreline flattered us and Henning Berg was the latest Rovers player to be red-carded. The pressure was building, and a trip to Second Division leaders Swindon in the Coca Cola Cup only turned up the heat further. After only 25 minutes Rovers were 2-0 down, but a huge fight-back left us a goal in front with five minutes to go. Incredibly, the action didn't stop there: with the last kick of the game Swindon's Paul Bodin missed a penalty. Phew!

A brief good run continued with a 5-1 thrashing of Coventry, Shearer net-ting three. Sadly it wasn't to last, and another pitiful performance in the European Cup gave the Tabloids plenty of ammunition to slag off 'the English game' as we lost 2-1 to Rosenborg.

September closed with a trip to the Riverside Stadium. Another defeat; another poor performance. Some of the natives were becoming restless (well at least six of them) and were chanting for Harford's head. It was going to be a long season...

After Alan Shearer's goals had seen off Swindon in the second leg of the CCC, Harford signed Forest's Lars Bohinen and Dundee United's Billy McKinlay. Bohinen's influence was immediate. His debut strike in our win against Southamp-ton was only part of the story; he helped create so many goalscoring opportunities that even David Batty had two attempts at goal.

More misery followed in the Champions League with a 1-0 defeat in Poland against Legia Warsaw. Is it any wonder though, since back in Blighty, we had to wait until the end of October for our first away point of the season; a 1-1 draw at Upton Park. The reception given to Miklosko by the Rovers fans was amazing, after his heroics against Man Utd last season had denied the Urinals the win they required to secure the title. We finished October in 11th place with 14 points, the ubiquitous Shearer having scored 10 of our 16 League goals. If United shelled out £7m for Andy Cole, what price Shearer?

Still, the international hex that hangs over our number nine came to bear again in our return game against Legia. In injury time he was six yards out with only the 'keeper to beat; you would have put your life savings on him scoring. Unfortunately the 'keeper saved it and we had to settle for a goalless draw - still, it *was* our first point in the competition.

After a totally abysmal performance at Goodison Park and another reverse at Newcastle, we faced Nottingham Forest, unbeaten in their last 24 Premier League games, with some trepidation. No need, as Rovers and Lars Bohinen were superb. Bohinen shut the Forest supporters up, scoring two of our seven goals. Shearer got another three, and Newell and Le Saux also found the net. It was difficult to believe: seven shots and seven goals.

In typical 'roller coaster' fashion, disaster followed in Moscow. It wasn't so much the 3-0 scoreline or the Hendry sending off. No, this time Rovers gave the media some serious meat to get their teeth into. A ball went out of play and Graham Le Saux and David Batty both went to take the throw-in. Innocuous enough, you might think. A couple of words were exchanged, and a gentle shove turned into a solid hook from Le Saux which landed square on Batty's chin. If *his* jaw didn't drop, then the rest of the watching millions' certainly did. The grapevine says the incident was a response to a dressing room campaign of resentment of Le Saux's alleged aloofness, intellectuality and general Guardian-reading arty-farty-ness. Rumour has it that Ray Harford contacted the UN for the services of a peace envoy. As usual the club wouldn't comment.

The following Sunday both Batty and Le Saux (complete with middleweight-type bandaging) played against Arsenal. Another away point; no fighting, no goals, and an uneventful game. Even Andy Gray found it difficult to say anything positive about the match.

By the end of November we were out of Europe, out of the fizzy drink cup (having lost to Leeds) and we had no chance of winning the Premiership. Come on you blues.

Thank God for Alan Shearer - another hat-trick in a 4-2 win over West Ham. Again the Hammers' keeper was given a tremendous ovation by the entire Ewood Park crowd, and Robbie Slater celebrated the return to his old ground with a brilliant goal from the edge of the area.

At last, and with the pressure off, we finally nailed one of our European opponents in the final game in the Champions League. Rosenborg still had an outside chance of qualifying for the knockout stages, but Rovers thumped them 4-1. Mike Newell scored a memorable hat-trick, the best being his second. The move was made up of 27 passes - football at its best. But the red card voodoo struck again as Paul Warhurst was sent off early in the second half.

Personally, I reckon the following Saturday was the lowest point of the season. We lost 5-0 to Coventry with a shite performance; Bohinen being substituted at half time because he was having problems seeing the orange ball. Colour blindness!!! So what were the other ten's excuses? Next, Bryan Robson's boring, boring Boro came to Ewood and went away with what they deserved: nothing. The only thing that I can remember about the game was the horrific injury to Graeme Le Saux, when an awkward landing (or was that a piece of sushi he slipped on?) badly broke his leg. We were all treated to repeated slow-mo's of the flapping limb - why do they insist on doing that?

Christmas came and went, and on Boxing Day, Batty (perhaps inspired by the appropriateness of the day's name) suprised us by scoring his first goal for Rovers in a 2-0 win over Manchester City on a bitterly cold night. Shearer finished '95 in indomitable style by notching his 100th Premier League goal in a 1-1 against Spurs. We were ninth in the Premiership with 31 points.

January 13th was a day etched in the minds of the 800 travelling Rovers fans. An away win at last, and who else but Shearer to get the only goal? The last time Rovers got three points in an away game was also at Loftus Road.

Cup replay time, so bring on the Ipswich. Filled with doubts about the team progressing, we watched Rovers as they continued the trend of losing replays at home. It has to be said though that Ipswich's third choice 'keeper, 18 year old Richard Wright, was superb. We wouldn't have beaten him if we'd played all night; no doubt about it, Ipswich deserved their victory.

Having finished January with nine wins out of the last nine at home in the Premiership, a local derby victory against Bolton gave Shearer his fourth hat-trick of the season. Next on the agenda was the 'Theatre of Dreams'. The best thing in a toilet of a game (which they scraped 1-0) was the torrent of abuse directed at the United fans. A thousand Rovers supporters taunted them with "Did you cry at Upton Park", "Who're the Champions now scum" and the one that really pisses them off: "Do you come from Man-ches-ter." We couldn't work out why hoards of the red bastards started to leave the ground at 4.10, until someone explained that the last train to Plymouth departs Manchester Piccadilly at 4.30. Oh, Right.

Next up, Liverpool. Our record of ten successive victories came to an end with a 3-2 defeat. The talking point was Collymore's first goal. Thirty yards out, he looked up and hit what can be best described as a tame shot that trickled towards Tim Flowers. As all world-class keepers do, he went down on one knee with his body behind the ball. The next thing you knew the ball was in the back of the net. On Match of the Day later that night it was plain to see what had happened: the ball had hit a cunningly-placed scouse divot and flew past Tim's right shoulder. What scallies, eh?

Injury problems and suspensions hit Rovers for the Leeds game; the midfield of Gallacher, McKinlay, Marker and Holmes had played only 25 Premier League games between them so far this season. Warhurst partnered Shearer in the first half, but due to a rib injury didn't re-appear for the second. Graham Fenton replaced him and got the only goal. Flowers made one superb save from a McAllister free kick. Before the match a minute's silence was observed for the victims of Dunblane. Credit is due to all 24,000 supporters who marked the senseless loss of life in total silence on a bitterly cold night. It brought home to many how insignificant football really is.

Shearer's fifth hat-trick of the season at Tottenham gave us our second away victory. It also marked the return of the SAS with Chris Sutton's re-appearance as substitute after missing 15 games through injury. It was his defence-splitting pass which led to Shearer's third. Then it was time to parade our big new signing, Gary Flitcroft, for the Everton game. He certainly succeeded in making an early impression by getting sent off after just three minutes. Kanchelskis then tore us apart, giving Kenna in particular a torrid time.

Monday night football and the Champions-elect Newcastle came to Ewood, hell-bent on closing the six point gap Man Utd had opened. After a goalless first half, things changed when Gillespie replaced Asprilla. New Magpie Batty left-footed from 20 yards out, putting Newcastle in front. Then, in what many would see as the defining moment in the '95-96 title race, Ray Harford made an inspired substitution. Super-sub Fenton came on and scored his first. That was not the end of the entertainment though, as Wilcox's massive clearance found Shearer, who in turn found Fenton. Again, he made no mistake. The Newcastle supporters had their heads in their hands. What a wonderful sight!

The home game against Wimbledon would be Shearer's last; the following day he was to have a groin operation to get him fit for the European Championships. He didn't disappoint, scoring two in a 3-2 victory and becoming the first player to score 30 League goals in three consecutive seasons.

Rovers' Championship reign formally ended at a sunny Stamford Bridge. Glenn Hoddle was saying his good-byes to the Chelsea supporters before he took over from Terry Venables as England coach. Rovers spoilt the party, winning 3-2 and ended up seventh in the Premiership, and despite poor early season form, we still had a sniff of Europe during that last mad Sunday afternoon. I could go on about injuries, blah, blah, but every team gets them. No, we've had our hangover after the title bash; now it's time to look forward to next season with renewed anticipation.

Fanzine Facts

Loadsamoney was launched in February 1993. From humble beginnings, a stencil set and works photocopier, it is now on glossy paper and sales are steadily increasing. Editor Paul Loftus is the first to admit that he relies heavily on contributions from Kevin Nolan (who wants to have Colin Hendry's children), Andy Carruthers and John Cook. Apparently **Loadsamoney** is read by the players. By all accounts this can be proved following an incident involving warm seats, hotpies, poems and Mark Atkins' (Rovers mid-fielder at time of writing) wife! If you want to know more, contact Paul! **Loadsamoney** got its title because... Oh, you know, Jack Walker and all that!

let's kick racism out of football!

MAD AS A HATTER!

Luton Town

The summer of '95 had seen myriad changes at Kenilworth Road, with David Pleat involved in an acrimonious departure to Sheffield Wednesday (apparently widely regarded as a good manager, but his best in his second spell at the club had been 16th place in the First Division), and eventually the appointment of a virtual unknown, Terry Westley, as the new manager. Westley made his mark immediately by raiding the transfer market and eventually spending an incredible £2.5m on new players. When Luton Town spend that sort of money, optimism soon follows, and so it was as the season commenced.

The opener was a televised game at home to Norwich City, which saw the visitors win 3-1. We all thought that Norwich were a good side and a sound bet for promotion! Still, a win at Southend was more like it, but then we suffered our customary exit from the CCC against lower Division opponents (Bournemouth obliging after a draw at Kennilworth Road). It was during the next six matches, when we scored only three times and picked up just two points, that the doubts began to surface. During this time we had sold 'keeper Juergen Sommer to QPR for an almost unbelievable £600,000 and replaced him with another American, Ian Feuer, initially on loan, and later bought for £580,000.

A 3-1 demolition of Portsmouth raised some hopes but was followed by a couple of defeats (including West Brom's last win before their long dry spell). Westley's head was already being measured for the noose, when we got an unexpected victory at Ipswich in mid October, a result which Westley called "hermendous" (?!), celebrating like a man who'd been granted a last-minute reprieve. The only goal had been scored by David Oldfield, one of Westley's relegation-victim signings (the list also included Steve Davis (Burnley), Darren Patterson (Palace), Bontcho Guentchev and Gavin Johnson (Ipswich) - recognise the pattern?). Guentchev had been hailed as a World Cup striker, but had singularly failed to score from anything other than the penalty spot.

Securely in 23rd spot, we went into the local derby at Watford expecting defeat, which would probably be the end of Westley, but praying we could have victory and *still* lose the manager. As it turned out, it was a 1-1 draw with Town's oldest ever player Trevor Peake gifting the equaliser with a back pass so feeble that if Watford hadn't intervened, it would still be on the way back to the 'keeper now.

December opened with a rare victory, as we beat Tranmere 3-2 at home. The following week however, showed this to have been a fluke as we lost by the same scoreline to struggling Wolves. In between all this misery, we had been participating in the Anglo Italian Cup, and over three matches had acquired a goal difference of 2-10 (which is why I didn't use the word 'competing'). On December 13th Ancona arrived at Kenilworth Road and charitably allowed us a 5-0 win, presumably by way of thanks for the opportunity to get a Christmas shopping trip in London (their substitutes, knocking the ball about at half time were wearing those ridiculous 'Santa' hats). And so to Portsmouth on December 16th. Three-nil down at half time, Pompey spent the next 45 minutes compiling present lists, and only bothered to register a fourth when all the Aunts and Uncles had been taken care of.

That really was the final straw, and within two hours Westley, along with his talismanic sidekick Mick McGiven, had been sentenced to walk the plank. When asked if he would've done things differently if he'd had the chance to start again, Westley responded that he would have asked for a longer contract - a comment which, like most things done by Westley, baffled everyone. The board acted quickly, and within the week Lennie 'Houdini' Lawrence was appointed as replacement. With no choice but to manage with squad of players bequeathed to him, he had 'weakness in depth', and a real battle on his hands. But the next match seemed to show an improvement as we fought out a 2-2 draw with an impressive Huddersfield. Christmas was postponed to the extent that our next match was away to Grimsby in the FA Cup on January 6th (we really get the glamour ties!), but the players were determined that their generosity should not go unnoticed. It didn't, and we finished on the end of a very sound 7-1 thrashing (for the record, this was one goal short of our record defeat and meant we had conceded 13 goals in our last two FA Cup games - is this another record?).

Then out of the blue, we were the victims of some unexplained phenomena: we started winning games (bizarre), and Bontcho Guentchev started scoring goals (spooky!). We won five of the next six, with Guentchev scoring in four of them, and escaped from the relegation places. Houdini Lawrence was working his magic - we even beat Grimsby - and the beast called optimism reared its ugly head again. Lawrence even won a Manager of the Month award. But every statistic tells a story, and in that spell we had scored a quarter of the entire season's goals. And, just as hopes were raised, they were dashed again when leading scorer Dwight Marshall suffered a broken leg at Sunderland, in a match we lost 1-0 due to an outstanding own goal by Julian James. The Rokerites never looked back, and by contrast we turned and faced relegation head-on, rather than just glancing over our shoulders.

It would be five weeks and six matches before we scored a goal from open play again, with a solitary Guentchev penalty in the interim. Yet during this period only one of the subsequent defeats was by more than one goal, which backed up the view that the defence was OK, we just needed someone to stick 'em in at the other end. Enter deadline day signing Kim Grant from Charlton, who set about redressing our lop-sided goal difference. He scored three in the next four games, and might have been the answer to our prayers. (Too little, too late?). One of these matches deserves special mention. The victory at The Hawthorns was our first midweek away League win since 1989 (previous to that it had been 1983) - a rare result indeed. But suicidal tendencies resurfaced, and 1-0 up at home to Stoke with just five minutes remaining, we contrived to lose 1-2, and then four days later, conceded four goals against Birmingham (their first arriving in just 17 seconds with the remainder being bagged in a five minute spell). A tame goalless local derby was the penultimate nail in the coffin, before Port Vale and Barnsley drove the final one home. The only small consolation was that in the final home game, before the season's smallest crowd, a bunch of youngsters played with some flair to secure a rare victory. The campaign ended with a whimper, the final game being true to type as Town had loads of possession, not one shot on goal, and, of course, we lost. Another bonus - at least Watford's late revival shot its bolt at the last!

It is a fair reflection that the Player of the Year awards all went to the goalkeeper, Feuer, except for the Junior Supporters' award, which was received by Dwight Marshall, in spite of being on crutches for the last ten weeks. As for the future? It is generally accepted that we must go straight back up, but with no money to strengthen the squad that may prove difficult. Unless, that is, the existing bunch turn out to be a damn sight more capable than anything seen to date has suggested.

Fanzine Facts

Mad as a Hatter! enters its seventh season still going strong, with sales holding steady in the face of falling attendances. Editor Keith Hayward, 'star of radio and television', says that "the public respond to our cries of 'Mad as a Hatter! Only 50p', with the comment 'We must be to come here'. And probably think that they are being funny."

Keith claims to do all the hard work, with sales managers Phil and Mark Argueson offering considerable help. The other founder was Andy P - whatever happened to him...?

THE MEMOIRS OF SETH BOTTOMLEY

Port Vale

Seasons To Be Cheerful

'Living with Schizophrenia' is a pamphlet issued by the NHS for patients and families coping with the psychological disorder that is characterised by wild mood swings, unpredictable behaviour, split personality and phobias, paranoias and delusions.

'Living with Port Vale' is a pamphlet issued to Port Vale fans. Its content is identical.

I was asked to try and summarise the season to date and had to sit and think of a scenario that could possibly generate the vast array of emotions encountered over a season at Vale Park. I could have brought you this report from a padded cell on a top security ward at a mental hospital, under sedation, and wearing the Vale's new kit, a very tight little

number in white with sleeves that tie round the back (presumably in an attempt to suppress hand-clapping). However, in the spirit of 'Care in the Community', I will attempt to describe the events since last August in the style of a Vale fan... on the edge of a nervous breakdown!

The start of the season provided a well documented example of the potential naïvety that lingers in the nooks and crannies of Vale Park. After a goalless draw at Derby and a one goal first leg Coca Cola lead at Huddersfield, the manager and the local media leaned their heads back and bellowed up to the heavens to invite the gods to send Fate down and teach us a lesson. Within an instant our two most important players Aspo and Foyley were out for half of the season, and the trouble began. Out of the Coca Cola (a tradition upheld anyway) and it was off to Stoke for our usual drubbing. A drubbing was indeed dished out, except it was Stoke who completely fell apart. We prepared for an extended feeling of well-being and satisfaction as we basked in the glory of stuffing City, but then went on to take just ten points from the next 16 games.

Mixed emotions so far, then, by early December. The final frontier for us at that time appeared to be Division Two, though the Klingons from Bootham had been neutralised. Manic depression was taking hold, and I was mixing in bad company. I was spending more time than is healthy in places like the Albion in Hanley, and Shipleys Amusements in Hanley's East Precinct. On more than one occasion I was seen staggering into Roseby's Curtain and Linen shop, bleary-eyed and rather drunk, MacDonalds in hand, complaining to the bemused lady behind the counter that, "if this is supposed to be 'student alternative night', the music's crap", only to find that it was four o'clock on a Tuesday afternoon and that Chico's was next door. This is what being in the bottom three does to a fan!

A visit to the doctor and a prescription of valium. It did the trick, and the visit of Huddersfield got me out of the house, gave me my appetite back (I'd lost 4lbs) and got me talking to people again. We then did Reading 3-2, and then came a hat-trick for Lee Mills in Perugia (that's in Italy folks, where they're good at footy). I left half of the course of valium on the bathroom shelf and began to take more care in my appearance (scraping a two week old encrusted cornflake from the collar of my Vale shirt (also clear evidence of an improving diet). It stopped raining, I went out for a walk and in an optimistic mood, decided to go to Wolves on Saturday. And what a refreshing change it proved to be. Like the toddler pageboy stealing the show on the wedding reception video with some cheeky dancing and 'grown-up' antics, Andy Porter sent us all home from a very grown up contest bragging like kids that, "Our team's better than YOUR team... nerrrrrr!." I was enjoying my work again, the gas bill wasn't as high as expected and I was seen window shopping at a pricey boutique in the Potteries Shopping centre. West Brom 3-1 at home at Christmas, and I decided to have a shave for New Year's Eve as part of my recovery to self-esteem.

New Years Day dawned, I had little in the way of a five o'clock shadow but soon got a three o'clock hangover with the 5-1 mauling by Ipswich. Several Phensic were taken over the following 48 hours. My headache cleared, we got a Cup replay win against Palace thanks to a Raymondo blinder in a fog so thick it looked like a volcanic eruption of Andy Berry's pea and ham soup from his stove in Dresden had descended on Burslem. Ray's lob in the lobby gave us a fourth round tie away at Everton. That'll do nicely, thank you! We were still in relegation territory, so the trip was considered to be just one for the scrap book; a mere pick-me-up as 'the drop' was still a real possibility.

The depression that hung over this odd season then began to evaporate like Andy Berry's minestrone on the Lorne Street on a January night when, from absolutely nowhere, a run of just two defeats from 22 games heralded the return of four things: Aspo, Foyley, team spirit and happy fans.

It came out of the blue, like a vision in the night and when the burning bush told Moses "Get down the Vale, youth, it's gonna be a stunning next three months." The stylish performance at Millwall got the press talking about us and totally ignoring the debuts of their Russian Internationals. Off it went like a runaway train! A draw with League leaders Derby and a 4-2 thraping away at Ipswich in the Anglo-Bubbly was a warm-up for the trip to Everton. But this is the part it all went a bit weird - downright outrageous performances started to flow with impudent abandon. A 2-2 draw at Goodison?! Doctor, I'm fine, really, just feeling a little high at the moment. But not as high as I was after we'd beaten them in the replay. What a performance - surely the best match of the season. Bogie's opener on 17 minutes was so good, even the referee joined in the mosh. Back at the psychiatrists for my check-up, he advised me that the depression was all but passed and that no more Sanatogen tonic would be needed.

Leeds United away in the fifth round was a good opportunity to give them what their crap support (at both home leg and replay) deserved. We should've won and they knew it. Beam me up Scotty.

My mental state was now quite healthy, and with an Anglican-Bishop Cup Final first leg draw at West Brom followed by another away draw in the League, it was very nice indeed to know that the Baggies ought to be suffering from chronic inferiority complexes, after three games in ten days confirmed that it was they who'd finish well below the Vale in all competitions this season. The golden glow continued and life was sweet.

Just *how* sweet we found out a week or so later. They say the most traumatic events in life are usually births, deaths and moving house. Conversely the most euphoric events must be local derby wins, convincing local derby wins and convincing local derby doubles. I was pissed for a fortnight after our despatch of City after 12 seconds, on nothing more alcoholic than a half time cup of Bovril and the memory of Super-Bogie's outswinger. What a buzz. And to cap it all we then got to take our fine form to Wem-ber-ley to play mighty Genoa in the Angling Times Cup Final. It was an event that reminded us of our own mortality, but which at least gave us a Martin Foyle diving header in front of the 'home' fans to prevent a possible entry in the Wembley record books under the 'heaviest defeat' section.

Where did we go from there? Well, another four straight wins in the League for a start and we were now talking about the play-offs. At this point, with us flying up the table, the thought of competing for Premier League status got the jitters going again, this time in dread fear of somehow stumbling into the Prem like a couple of clean-cut mormon lads knocking on the door of a big old dodgy house occupied by a coven of devil-worshipping Hells Angels. Our fears of promotion to the top shelf of English soccer faded just as rapidly, with fatigued defeats to such class acts as Birmingham, Oldham and Watford, but more disturbingly letting in 11 goals in three games. We were almost mathematically safe, yet only three places above the drop zone. Then grubby wins over Grimsby and Luton and a dodgy draw with Tranmere propelled us up seven places, back into area of the table reserved for those with a 'mathematical chance of a place in the play-offs'. At this point in proceedings I preferred to call it a day on the football front for fear of a return to a state of mental turmoil that only this proximity to Paradise and Valhalla combined could bring.

It's been a great season. It's been serious, worrying, exciting, fun, boring, and spectacular, but above all it has not been short of action and incident. All this from a team who still want to pass the ball about. As with the early Hang-Glider Trophy games against Ancona and Genoa, those matches with least at stake were rare moments of angst-free football entertainment, so get yourself down to Andy Porter's testimonial and give thanks for a great season once again. See yer next season at the outpatients folks!

Fanzine Facts

The Memoirs of Seth Bottomley is named after a fictitious ex-Vale winger from 'the Good Old Days', and was started in January '89. It is now considered one of the 'originals' and according to the editors anyway, is easily the best 'zine in Burslem. Edited by four Vale fans from the now famous Seth Mansions, set in the rolling countryside around Alton, it basically comes out when they can be bothered, but usually sees the light of day four or five times a season. Quality not quantity, as with Vale supporters, is their motto.

MISSION IMPOSSIBLE

Darlington

If someone had said to Darlington fans at the beginning of the season that their team would finish in a play-off spot and just miss out on automatic promotion in May, then I'm sure they would have been carted off to the nearest psychiatric department!

Darlo were even the bookies' favourites to drop into the dreaded Vauxhall Conference. But they reckoned without two signings from Portugal: Pedro Paulo and Rui Neves. Thanks to David Hodgson's connections as an agent, instead of free transfer signings from over here we could sign them from abroad. Well, at least it added a little bit of momentum to the early proceedings. Pedro, a winger, was fast, tricky and prone to diving. Rui on the other hand had all the mobility of an arthritic snail. Neither were to last more than three months.

The appointment of a new management team in former Middlesbrough teammates David Hodgson and Jim Platt had done nothing to whet the appetite. Little did we know that within six weeks of the season commencing Darlo would be in the national limelight after Hodgson's post-match outburst (threatening to put the whole team up for sale following a particularly depressing 2-1 home defeat against Scarborough) had the national media beating a path to his door. It had all started so brightly in the August sun at Exeter's St James Park, when a first half goal by the rejuvenated Paul Olsson was enough to pick up the first three points of the season. Reality was to hit Darlo fans the following week when yet again after the Lord Mayor's show the Quakers underachieved, allowing Rochdale a late winner to sneak the points. Two successive draws gave no indication of the storm that was to brew in September.

A 1-0 home defeat at the hands of a dreadful Cardiff City side wasn't helped by goalkeeper Mike Pollit's tenth minute sending off; it really was a strange sight to see a team with an extra man desperately trying to defend a one goal advantage for 70-odd minutes. Crewe Alexandra accounted for our Coca Cola hopes but at least we went out with some conviction; our neighbours Hartlepool may as well not have bothered turning up at Gresty Road, as they left Cheshire with an 8-0 thrashing into the bargain. So it was reasonable to hope that we might give the Bash Street Kids a thumping in the local derby at the Victoria Funeral Park, but in the end, honours were even.

October was the vital month. The fans were starting to get restless at the team's poor performances at home and something had to give. At Lincoln's Sincil Bank we introduced a sweeper system, which proved effective and was the key to a lot of success thereon in, particularly away from home. Table-topping Gillingham were accounted for at Feethams thanks to a single goal from the influential Gary Bannister, but the Quakers were the victims of an unwarranted after-match slur by the Gillingham chairman Paul Scally that stank of sour grapes, as the former Millwall fan accused us of shouting sustained racist abuse at Gills striker Leo Fortune-West. According to Scally, in this part of the world, racism is prevalent because there are no proportional sections of the population of ethnic origin. All this coming from a person who was making his first ever appearance in the North East, and who formerly supported a club with an infamous reputation for bigotry and racism. The words 'cockney' and 'banker' somehow seem appropriate. It was true to some extent that Fortune-West's style of play did not endear himself to the home fans; apparently he'd had similar problems at Hartlefool and Mansfield, but the Gills striker was certainly no angel when it came to dishing out stick.

A third consecutive League victory at Cambridge was then followed by a superb 2-0 performance against promotion favourites Plymouth Gargoyle in front of the home crowd; a fully deserved victory in which Darlo's mixture of free transfer cast-offs ran the Pilgrims ragged. Finally the month ended with a 2-1 last-gasp victory at home to Wigan. Director of coaching Dave Hodgson picked up the Manager of the Month award, but perhaps more importantly, the team's good performances throughout October had convinced the faithful that better days lay ahead.

November brought with it the FA Cup tie at neighbours Hartlefool. Anything less than victory against the old enemy would have killed a lot of the renewed optimism. In glorious style, we administered another season-crippling victory (4-2). Willing as ever to take the shine off a brilliant victory, Darlo sold our first team 'keeper to Notts County reserves for £75,000. Our general manager Steve Morgon reckoned Politt was the best goalie in the Third Division, it was just a pity he forgot to tell County that when negotiating the size of the fee, and what's more we didn't even have a replacement lined up; instead we got the 'evergreen' John Burridge on a match to match contract that was eventually to cost us a place in the next round of the FA Cup... at Anfield of all places!

Following our only away defeat in the League against high-flying Chester, December ushered in an FA Cup tie at Rochdale, where Burridge did his best to ensure that Rochdale were given another chance at Feethams. In true Darlo style the players huffed and puffed but couldn't find a way through, and ten minutes from the end Rochdale scored the all-important goal. Ha! It was just reward that the Anfield goal machine stuck seven past them!

But the Rochdale Cup match had brought with it a shock of another kind... Dave Hodgson had resigned!! It seemed he was unhappy with a certain general manager, and had been told that the two most saleable assets, Matty Appleby and Sean Gregan would be sold if an offer came in for them. Hodgson, trying to build a winning team, delivered an ultimatum: it was either him or Steve Morgon. The club tried to whitewash the saga by printing contradictory information in the Rochdale Cup programme, but Darlo fans of long standing braced themselves for the inevitable collapse.

It goes without saying that initially the new management team of Jim Platt and Gary Bannister steadied the ship and kept the Quakers on course for a play-off spot. Away from home the lads were picking up points galore, but problems persisted at Feethams. Following official bickering about the lack of home support, and certain remarks made in the local media, the club was told in no uncertain circumstances by readers of *MI* that if they wanted people through the turnstiles then they should start winning at home.

And to prove our point, both eventual Champions Preston and 92nd'ers Torquay both gained away wins at Feethams. Funnily enough, Torquay played better than Preston for their three points (in their only away victory all season). Luckily, home form picked up in the final run-in with wins in glorious fashion against promotion rivals Bury and Chester. Away, we ran Preston ragged in front of 12,000, forcing Tom Finney to concede it was the best performance he'd seen by an away team for many years; even Preston's *Pie Muncher* fanzine admitted that despite the 1-1 scoreline, they should've been beaten 4-1.

Finally, assured of a play-off place, our destiny was in our own hands for the third automatic promotion spot. We just needed to beat Scunthorpe at Glanford Park, never a happy hunting ground as far as the Quakers were concerned. Sadly, a 3-3 draw, after an immense fight-back from a two goal deficit, wasn't good enough.

Hereford were easily overcome in the play-offs; then it was off to Wembley for Plymouth in the final. The club sold 15,000 tickets, and although Darlington supporters were outnumbered almost three to one, that wasn't of much importance on the day. Matty Appleby probably had the best chance in the first half when he went on a mazy run which caused havoc in the Argyle penalty box; his subsequent shot was inches wide. Despite having most of the possession we just couldn't convert our territorial advantage, and in an act of sheer frustration one Darlington fan took all his clothes off and streaked across the pitch (some people thought the identity of this mysterious person to be none other than our main benefactor - let's face it, it was the most we'd seen of him all season!), but it was to be Plymouth's day, when a short corner caught the Quakers' defence momentarily off-guard and the cross was headed in by Mauge.

Looking at it from a realistic perspective, Plymouth will be far better equipped to cope at a higher level than Darlo. The club had made it obvious to all and sundry in the local media that no money would be spent new players, although despite these comments the directors of Darlington FC claim they still remain ambitious (funny, the meaning of the word must have changed since I last looked it up in the dictionary). It's just as well they do because unless they invest in bringing some quality into the team, they will never attract more than the 2,000 hard-core to Feethams.

The season has been eventful and positive on the pitch, with some fantastic away performances regularly undermined by erratic home form (one reason why the public of Darlington only responded towards the end of the season perhaps).

But at Feethams, events off the pitch always tend to overshadow achievements on it. It speaks volumes for Jim Platt's man-management skills, together with player/coach Gary Bannister, that working on a budget that only gives scope for signing free transfers, he has been able to keep the players' minds focused on the job at hand.

The identity of the club's main backer is thought to be former Sheffield United chairman Reg Brealey, who set up a trust (in Gibraltar!) in the name of a shareholding company called St Philip Ltd, the patron saint of small clubs. It is rumoured that he has a similar involvement with Chesterfield too, yet he still denies that he has had any direct influence on Darlington FC. Whoever owns the club cannot alter the fact that Reg has acquired a 78% shareholding (according to the club's accounts).

As the season ended the club announced the news that a new shirt sponsorship deal had been arranged with unheard of leisure firm Soccerdome for three years, worth £150,000. The identity of the people behind Soccerdome was revealed in a newspaper article as St Philip Ltd! They also announced to the local press that building work is to begin on converting the main East Stand into a 3,400 all-seater "within two to three months." It is intended to have a total capacity of 10,048 seats, of which 100 will be for the disabled.

Fanzine Facts

Mission Impossible began life in March 1989. Contributors Steve Harland (who wrote the above article), Steve Raine, Dave Sowerby and Keith Wallace were heavily influenced and encouraged by various people, in particular Frank Ormston of York City's now defunct Terrace Talk. "If it wasn't for his advice and help" says Steve, "we would probably never have got started."

MI's relationship with the club has been less than harmonious. This year, letters from the club's solicitor threatening legal action were not uncommon, and general manager Steve Morgon wrote to the local media on more than one occasion with various accusations and demands that the *MI* team refrain from attending any future home matches. The club also introduced their own fanzine, about which Steve Harland is pretty disparaging, although he thinks that a new Darlo mag *Where's The Money Gone* is in the best of fanzine traditions: loyal and witty (despite being produced by an 11-year-old schoolboy).

MI remains wholeheartedly dedicated to the cause of Darlington FC. It has been active on many fronts, including matchball sponsorship, money-off vouchers promoting future home games (of which 725 people took advantage), and a free of charge Wembley special along with 500 'Darlo FC - Wembley '96' badges.

MONKEY BUSINESS

Hartlepool United

At the end of the last campaign, our chairman said that '95-96 would be a season of "consolidation and improvement"; ever-cynical me wondered whether it could possibly be any worse than the previous two. In many ways we were both correct. From the club's point of view they achieved their main targets, i.e. we didn't finish bottom of the League, they got rid of the inherited debt and the lingering spectre of a winding up order, and improved the ground beyond recognition. From the fans' viewpoint, the season was effectively over in mid-November when we crashed out of the FA Cup to local rivals Darlington, and were once more looking at the League from the wrong end. Poor discipline on the pitch, appalling standards of refereeing and the lack

of any semblance of flair from most visiting teams made for yet another season of depressing mediocrity, thinly disguised as football. Off-pitch events usually proved more interesting. Indeed, the kids' half-time penalty shoot-out was usually more entertaining than the actual game.

The completion of the highly impressive Cyril Knowles Stand, and new covered terracing for home fans behind the Town End goal made Victoria Park look like a real football ground, and one with a lot more character than some of the new pale grey kit-built grounds which seem to have been designed by an architect using Lego bricks (just a thought - is Deva the Latin for breeze-block?). New Chairman Harold Hornsey has invested large amounts of his own money in putting the infrastructure in place - now all we needed was a team to encourage the fans to come and fill the new stadium.

The latest away shirts hadn't arrived for the first game of the season at Chester, so we played in a stop-gap yellow and black outfit. Good job we lost or the team would have wanted to play in them all season, and the club shop would have been left with hundreds of the proper Sunday League Cricket-style version when they eventually arrived.

Notable games were few and far between, but some stayed in the memory for differing reasons. Drawing 1-1 with Scarborough over two legs in the League Cup heralded the first penalty shoot-out that I had personally witnessed. Over the space of 18 kicks, Pools eventually won 7-6 in one of the most tense, nail-biting occasions I have ever endured at a football ground. It was after 10.15 when the tie was finally decided. This victory won us a chance to play a Premiership club, but we were slightly disappointed to draw 'Boring, Boring' Arsenal for the second year running. In the first leg at home we had the satisfaction of extending Dennis Bergkamp's score-less run, even after 'keeper Brian Horne had been sent off for handling outside the area. The Daily Star went to town, featuring a minute by minute account from our veteran centre-half Peter Billing on how he handled the Dutchman. Little did Shane Reddish know when he took over in goal that he would be one of seven to wear our No. 1 shirt in the season. For the away leg, Arsenal did us the dubious honour of playing a full strength team this time. The 27,194 crowd was a bonus; the 5-0 defeat wasn't.

At the end of September, our first away win of the season at Cambridge was memorable to most *Monkey Business* contributors more for the free crisps and Doritos (courtesy of match sponsors Walkers) than for the football. Our visit to Crewe in the Mickey Mouse Cup was also hard to forget because of the size of the hammering we took. However, the competition's dumb rules meant that we only had to win our home tie by two clear goals to still qualify for the next stage. The 3-2 home win over 2nd Division high fliers Blackpool didn't quite achieve this, but produced the best home game of the season, albeit witnessed by a mere 895 fans.

Poor away and indifferent home form had left us in the bottom quarter of the table. We seemed to be plagued by the most incompetent bunch of referees I have seen in my 35 years of watching Pools (I know, you get less than that for murder these days!); we picked up bookings and sendings off galore, and I can barely remember one being for a bad foul. Things came to a head with the visit of leaders Gillingham in late October. Their previous game at Darlington had led their chairman to complain of racial abuse of some of his team, although the press cuttings and eye witness reports told of provocation from various Gills' players. They came predicting more of the same from the Neanderthal north-east, and promptly played in a manner certain to bring about a self-fulfilling prophesy. The allegedly skilful Leo Fortune-West ignored the ball for most of the first half and berated, pushed and pulled his markers before falling like a sack of potatoes to win a penalty. In an ill tempered game the referee managed to book eight players and send three off in a cracking display of lack of control and gross ineptitude. Fortune-West spent most of the game gesturing to the crowd, as did Bailey after converting the penalty, and both were widely abused from all sides. Gillingham complained vehemently that they had once again been the victims of racial abuse. Our view was that both players had provoked the crowd and would have been treated identically whatever the colour of their skin. Not surprisingly this view wasn't shared by their chairman, who went on to accuse us of having colluded with Darlington. The abuse of his players was unpleasant, but he was clearly displaying his lack of experience in lower league football with his latter accusation.

Our poor League position meant that the visit of Darlington in the first round of the FA Cup in mid-November was our last hope of maintaining fans' interest for the remainder of the season. Lacking the experience of player-manager Keith Houchen and recently re-signed Joe Allon (suspensions for their sendings off against Gillingham!), we were yet again forced to rely on the products of the youth team. Sadly they weren't up to it and we went down 4-2 to a pretty slick Dar-low side.

Goalkeeper Brian Horne, now in his second season, had built a decent rapport with the fans, but as the season developed it became more and more apparent that he did not have the same relationship with manager Keith Houchen and some of the senior players. Houchen proceeded to use up three of our five allowed loan signings to bring in 'keepers, two of whom (to add insult to injury) were recalled by their clubs after one appearance. This did little to endear Houchen to the faithful, and combined with poor results put pressure on his position. The local paper then ran a phone-in poll on whether or not he should go (which incidentally gave him overwhelming backing, despite a fairly low response). Houchen took real umbrage to this and ran up a large 'phone bill... allegedly... and refused to speak to the press for months. Indeed, he is still apparently not speaking to the local sports reporter!!

Horne won his place back at regular intervals, but the friction was obvious. Veteran defender Peter Billing squared up to him in one home match and Houchen did likewise away to Gillingham, replacing him at half time with reserve 'keeper Steve Jones. This led to further public slanging matches in the press. Horne was eventually sacked after two home matches where the crowd took his side, booing Houchen's every touch and displaying banners supporting the 'keeper. He was later voted the Supporter's Club Player of the Year, by a large majority, much to the embarrassment of the management who declined an invitation to attend the presentation night.

The chairman's investment in paying off inherited debts and completing the development of the ground meant that little cash was available for the playing staff. The exceptions were the signing of former golden boy Joe Allon from Lincoln for £50,000 and Kenny Lowe on loan from Birmingham. The former came back to a hero's welcome, which soon turned sour as he piled on weight and seemed to lack interest. Thankfully he worked hard later in the season to return slimmed down and somewhere near to his former fitness. Lowe was the mainstay of our midfield for three months and exuded class, but financial restrictions meant we were unable to sign him permanently (so he went to play for Gateshead !!!).

On a more positive note several of the younger players developed well during the season, and Stephen Halliday in particular is unlikely to be with us much longer. He often showed mesmerising ball skills only to fail with the final pass or shot, but his finishing improved as the season drew on. Denny Ingram and Ian McGuckin developed into mature defenders, occasionally abetted by Graham Lee fresh from the youth team. Late in the season a combination of suspensions, injuries and lack of form in the more established forwards, prompted us to blood 17 and 16 year old Paul Conlon and Paul Walton. Conlon scored an excellent individual goal after 90 seconds of his full debut, and continued to give his more experienced colleagues lessons in finishing with both goals in the away win at Scarborough plus the winner at home to Fulham. His father found himself seriously out of pocket after promising £100 for every goal he scored when he went on to score four in six games. Both players seem excellent prospects with skill and pace, but suffer from the traditional Hartlepool problem - lack of height. As the end of season clear out started, other youngsters were brought in and given experience as the season wound down,

The final twist to the goalkeeping fiasco came when Horne's departure left reserve 'keeper Jones to cover the last five games. Ironically, Jones pulled a muscle in the warm up for the first, and then fell off the club's mountain bike when exercising said muscle later in the week requiring 15 stitches. The transfer deadline having passed we had to ask the League for a concession to play a non-contract goalkeeper, Paul O'Connor from Blyth Spartans, in a meaningless game against Lincoln, but had to return the injured Jones stitches 'n' all for the last two games against Preston and Gillingham. Jones ended the season conceding 32 goals in nine games.

Ten red cards and a staggering 64 bookings would seem to indicate a dirty side, but that certainly wasn't the case. The vast majority were for technical offences or dissent. In this area manager Houchen certainly led by example with 45 points! The quality of refereeing was almost universally abysmal, yet we never seemed to learn that telling referees how crap they were was a fail-safe way to naff them off. The hierarchy will always support referees, no matter how inept they are, and the refs simply say that they were carrying out FIFA directives. I don't know what the rule makers are trying to turn football into, but it certainly isn't the game most of us want to see. The black clad ones (yes this is Endsleigh football) seemed superb at spotting the minor offences, whilst remaining oblivious to the real incidents and villains.

What of next season? Well, the obligatory clear out has begun with a vengeance. Houchen and assistant manager Mick Tait have stated their intentions not to be regulars in the side. This leaves us with a basis of six professionals, some of whom have ambitions to move on to better things, plus a similar quantity of young first team fledglings. According to the club, next season should see us pushing for at least a play-off place. Hmmm... As usual, we await the summer signings with baited breath; getting hold of a decent keeper to replace the one we've wasted would be a good start. You never know, we might actually sign someone that we've actually heard of. Now *there's* a novel way to restore the fans' faith.

Fanzine Facts

Monkey Business started on December 16th 1989, which also marked Cyrill Knowles' first game as manager. The current team of Dave 'Wallace & Gromit' Shedden and Paul 'PM' Mullen are the only listed helpers that editor Mervyn the Monkey has. All the profits from the fanzine are returned to the club.

MOULIN ROUGE

Rotherham United

At the beginning of every season I want Rotherham United to go unbeaten throughout and win every trophy in sight. I have reluctantly come to recognise that maybe my dreams will never come true, so I look for a suitable second best. Last August I had a bronze, slightly slimmer body than now, refreshed from a week swimming in Ullswater and drinking in Lake District pubs, and I was full of anticipation for the new season. A quarter of a million spent on players and lots of predictions from club and press that we were going places; this was backed up by friends and some not-so-friends. Come August 12th we had played Bradford Park Avenue and won 4-2, lost 3-0 at Preston Nob End, drawn with Leeds 1-1 and had a kick-about with Washday in a testimonial

MOULIN ROUGE
THE ROTHERHAM UNITED
FANZINE
AUTO WINDSCREENS SHIELD FINAL SPECIAL

The Bird has landed

ISSUE 12   £1

for Nigel Johnson, so we should be prepared for Burnley anyway.

Had Shaun Goater been wearing his boots on the correct feet we may well have wrapped this one up in the second half. As it was, he - and others - wasted numerous chances, and being only 18 miles from Burnley I was in for some stick that night in the boozer. Never mind; there was the Fizzy Pop Cup at Scunny on Tuesday, and we should piss that and make the second leg a formality. I didn't make it to Glanford and I'm not too disappointed either as we went down 4-1. It looked bad enough on Teletext but those present said it was awful. The only win in August was the return leg when we stuffed the Iron 5-0 to set up a two-legger with Middlesbrough, the first in their brand new ground in smogland. A battling performance (in other words outclassed) gave us hope at only 2-1 down, but Paul 'Ted' Danson put in his usual shite refereeing display and the ten-man Millers went down 3-1 on aggregate. Never mind; there's always the League and FA Cup and that Mickey Mouse effort, isn't there?

Some inconsistent results up to Christmas saw us in the bottom half and sinking; some were calling for the managers to be replaced, but by whom? Matt Clarke had been injured at Stockport at the end of October and boy did we miss him. With Steve Farrelly also crocked we had no experienced 'keeper, so Carl Muggleton came in on loan although he wasn't eligible for the FA Cup tie at Rochdale. Youngster Craig Davis made his first team debut at Spotland and couldn't really be blamed for us going 5-1 down before pulling a couple back to give the score some respectability. You'd think that things couldn't get any worse. Oh, but they did, a week later at Wrexham when the 'experienced' Muggleton let SEVEN in and we had our worst League defeat in 20 years since letting seven in at... Wrexham. Funny how things work out like that. There was only the Auto Windscreens Shield to concentrate on now, apart from avoiding relegation - AGAIN! Muggleton was actually our Man of the Match against Wigan in the first round proper and ensured that our season stretched past December.

The new year began with a 2-2 draw at home to York, having been 2-0 up, ensuring that the critics were still on the backs of Gemmill and McGovern. We were promised that when everyone was fit we'd start winning, but with Mike Jeffry sold to a Dutch side and captain Chris Wilder packed off to Notts County, things didn't look too promising, especially when it looked as though they wouldn't be replaced. As it turned out, replacements weren't needed as we then went eight games unbeaten, including a couple of wins in the AWS. Shortly afterwards, though, the old 'sod's law' reared its ugly head as we went eight League games without a win to slump back down the table.

Sandwiched in between were the two legs of the Auto Windshield Northern Area final against Carlisle United, who I had seen in the final at Wembley last year. The first leg was a tense affair, and it wasn't until late in the game when a piece of brilliant skill by Shaun Goater sent us wild with delight. Ten minutes later Neil Richardson calmly slammed away a penalty after Jemson was fouled. So a 2-0 lead to take to Cumbria the week after; would it be enough? A lot of people seemed to think so. I heard my eight year old son Jonathon assuring a Rotherham pub landlord we were going to Wembley. But over my pint, I couldn't help being cautious: "Oh shit, what if we don't do it?." On the day of the second leg it snowed like mad, and we all thought it was certain to be off. At 4pm when the MR crew met up in Skipton town centre, the tension reached a climax as we realised it was ON, and tonight would decide whether we were going to make it to Wembley for the first time ever.

Carlisle's manager had said in an interview the week before that judging by the reaction of some of our players, they thought they were at Wembley already. "Well, they're in for a rude awakening next Tuesday - I can assure you of that." Those words had been ringing in my head for seven days and nights, and I'd been praying that he was wrong. As it was, I had no need to get so worked up, and the Millers put in probably the most professional performance I've seen from a Rotherham side in the 30 years I've been watching them. Nigel Jemson took the glory with two first half goals, but it was really a good all-round display, with even Andy Roscoe shining. I haven't seen celebrations like that for 15 years since we clinched promotion from the old Third Division with victory at... Carlisle! Funny how things work out like that...

Meanwhile, life in the relegation dogfight was getting tense, and it wasn't until we played promotion-chasing Notts County at home that we got our act together. Previously injured players surprisingly re-appeared to give us a 2-0 win, and followed it up with another eight match unbeaten run including wins over other high-flyers Blackpool, Crewe and Stockport.

The Blackpool game was our last before Wembley, and our better League form put us in a position to enjoy ourselves at the twin towers, which we did. We took the train down to London on Saturday morning, checked into our hotels and had a quick look around. That night we met up in 'The Angel in the Field' pub on

Marylebone High Street. A roaring time was had by all, and it was up early for breakfast, Millers fans everywhere, singing at the breakfast table and in the lifts. Nearly an hour was spent applying the war-paint to my son's face, followed by some ill-advised sight-seeing (only *we* could ask French tourists where Trafalgar Square was!). We then returned to the scene of the previous night's festivities, our numbers swelled by a couple of Canaries (now adopted Rotherhamites who - rightly - thought that a day out at Wembley was a better bet than the East Anglia derby). Several beers later, and with the itchy face paint now ineptly removed in the bogs, it was time to make our way to the tube station, by this time full of noisy Millers and a terrific atmosphere. Not that many Shrewsbury fans about, though.

The walk up Wembley Way was absolutely fantastic, an experience to which nothing else in football compares. The support for Rotherham that day was magnificent. Twenty thousand had made their way from all over the world, and Rotherham too. It was a real red & white party atmosphere. All that was left now was to win the game. All of my pretensions of "just going down to enjoy ourselves" flew out of the window as the tension began to mount. I was desperate for us to win.

About 20 minutes in, some superb work by Goater gave Jemson the opener (**MR**'s Hugh missing the historic strike, having just nipped off to the toilet, the pre-match beers proving too much to hold on to). When he returned to his seat, he ranted "I saw all of Wrexham's seven, and I bloody missed that! We'll just have to score another." The team obliged in the second half, and despite a nail-biting last nine minutes after the Shrews pulled one back (I won't begrudge them their moment), it was our day.

The celebrations carried on for hours, well actually weeks. Walking up the stairway at Baker Street Station I described it as the greatest day of my life, duly receiving a slap from my wife (quite right too; promotion was far more important), and I was made to watch the video when we arrived home at midnight (that's the video of our wedding of course). So many memories of a terrific day, but spare a thought for the utterly dejected Shrewsbury players as they left the pitch to the strains of "We are the Champions." "No time for losers"; how true. I honestly felt really sorry for them.

So we come to the end of another season, and what a season. A few pounds heavier (too much celebrating), a few less hairs, a few more grey ones... God, I hope we're not this successful next year! I'm looking forward to a rest this summer, but as I write, the club is up for sale and we are uncertain about what is happening. Some things never change!

Fanzine Facts

It's over two years now since Matt Norcliffe launched *Moulin Rouge*. Matt says that they are getting on better with the club now; they're even allowed to sponsor a player's kit and to present a Player of the Season trophy (which went to Shaun Goodwin this year). Matt's main helpers are Hugh Vaughan, Steve Brookes and Phil Hawes, and he also thanks contributors Rob Hindle, Martin Gibbins, Mick the Miller, Betty Swollocks, Russ of the Muns, Sickly Child, AN S60, Life Long Miller, Des Pejko, Symbol (formerly known as the Lucky Cigar) and Jonathan Norcliffe (aged 8 and a bit).

MOVING SWIFTLY ON

Walsall

For the realists amongst the Walsall FC faithful, the '95-96 season was always going to be one of consolidation. Our main objective was to hold on to our Second Division status, after having worked so hard and gone through so much to finally escape the claws of the Football League's basement Division.

It was widely believed that with the step up we would meet more teams who shared our philosophy of playing the ball around on the deck, and as a result life would be a whole lot easier than the 'route-one', 'smash-and-grab' days of Division Three. Not so, and to be perfectly frank, I felt a little let down by the overall standard. Only a couple of teams had any real quality about them and most would struggle if they ever reached Endsleigh One.

But, at 4.45pm on the opening day I was left in a quivering mess. What did this Division have in store for us? The day had started well enough, as do all opening days. The sun was shining, and decked out in a new replica top I'awaited the visit of Stockport County with great anticipation and excitement. A new era had at last arrived at the Bescot Stadium!

What a rude awakening! The Stockport players appeared to be a stone heavier and a couple of feet taller than our lot, and gave us a rather frightening welcome to the Division. All that pre-season confidence and anticipation drained away within the space of just 90 minutes. What on earth was to become of us??!

Things got back on track in our next League game as we went to Shrewsbury and were given our usual three points by our kind Shropshire 'neighbours'. But hey, let's keep our feet on the ground here; after all, it's no great achievement to beat the Shrews, but at least we left safe in the knowledge that there was someone worse off than us.

September and October ushered in an extremely worrying and damn frustrating trend of losing late goals and vital points. It all began on September 6th at Burnley when our 'keeper Jimmy Walker let a 96th minute free-kick slip through his body and we had to go home with just a point, when a confidence-boosting three had been on the cards. We managed to gift Swansea a late goal in the next game; still, this is Swansea we're talking about, and we'd already bagged four goals for ourselves! However, in the next match (v Oxford), things became a little more serious as we managed to go from coasting along 2-0 up with just ten minutes left on the watch to grimly hanging on for a single point in injury time. The malaise continued when against Peterborough we snatched a draw from the claws of victory due to yet another defensive cock-up, but the worst was still to come... We were 1-0 up with just four minutes to go at home to Wrexham; surely now we would be OK for a point? If only... The Welshmen proceeded not only to equalise, but to win! To use a common football phrase, I was absolutely gutted! You'd have thought that lessons had been learnt by now. Hmmm... October ended in a rather apt fashion on Halloween night up in Bradford, as former Saddler Neil Tolson grabbed their winner four minutes from time after we had defended stoutly and frustrated the home side for much of the game.

The fans were completely at a loss to explain why this was happening, and to a certain extent so too was the boss, Chris Nicholl. Action was taken, and in came centre backs Adrian Viveash and Derek Mountfield, both on free transfers from Swindon and Carlisle respectively. They joined summer signings Darren Bradley (from West Brom) and Ray Daniel (from Portsmouth) in a side that contained no fewer than SEVEN centre backs! Three guesses what position our gaffer used to play??? Ultimately, someone had to go, and the obvious choice was the likeable Stuart Watkiss, who had a decidedly rocky relationship with Nicholl after the boss made some rather misguided comments about injured players on a radio show, when it just so happened 'big Stu' was injured himself and quite rightly took offence. Watkiss was one of just two players to exit Bescot over the course of the season as he eventually joined Hereford on a free. You may remember that in last year's *SOTF* I took great delight in the fact that Hereford had shelled out £75,000 to take our former player Dean Smith to Edgar Street; well, in Stuart Watkiss they've picked up one hell of a bargain, and it certainly makes up for paying over the odds for Smith. Oh, before I forget, the other player to leave was Colin Gibson whose days were numbered the moment that 'Razor' Daniel arrived. It was a great pleasure to know 'Gibo' as he was a true professional and a good bloke too.

Back onto matters on the field, and we continued to lurk around the middle of the table, occasionally dipping our toes into the 'lower reaches'. We enjoyed some good victories, but absolutely nothing can compare to the 8-4 triumph over Torquay in the FA Cup second round. In a truly bizarre match, we kept falling behind before dragging ourselves back from the dead, and in the very last minute of normal time, with the scores level, Torquay had a great chance to win it, but somehow the ball hit both posts without crossing the line. In extra time, there followed the craziest 30 minutes of football I have ever seen. The goals fairly rattled in as Walsall started to take the upper hand, but I could swear that there were two balls on the field - one for the Walsall forwards to play with, and another for Torquay at the other end! It sure appeared that way. The Torquay fans were absolutely brilliant, and I can't for the life of me understand how their team has struggled so much... Still, as a certain Central TV football 'expert' once said, "It's a funny old game", and this particular game was as funny as it gets!

In the next round we were drawn at home to Wigan Athletic. On the one hand there was disappointment that it wasn't exactly a glamorous, money-spinning tie, but at least we had a very good chance of making the next round, which we duly did, but in far less gripping fashion than against Torquay. Still, our reward this time was much greater as we looked all set to make the trip to reigning Premier

Champions Blackburn, until Ipswich had other ideas and forced us to head East instead. As expected, we made a very quiet and unspectacular exit from the competition, going down 1-0 and missing out on a home match with Aston Vile in the process... Oh well, that's football for you I suppose!

Back to the 'bread and butter' of the League, and we were now starting to look like a decent outfit. We hit the dizzy heights of 13th in the table and managed to win at Stockport in the process, proving how much we'd come on since the opening day. Our biggest enemy now was the weather which was doing its very best to interrupt our flow, and sure enough the month of February was a total disaster with only one point picked up from the 15 on offer. So who was to blame? Suzanne Charlton? or perhaps Michael Fish!

In March, the forecast looked brighter, but there were storm clouds on the horizon. A sweeping low accompanied the news that our inspirational captain, Martin 'God' O'Connor was set to leave us prior to transfer deadline day. Although the money would have been very welcome, we needed O'Connor to 'pull our strings', especially with a play-off place very much in our sights. As it turned out, 'God' decided not to become yet another Birmingham City player and remained at Walsall for the rest of the season; however, a summer move is widely anticipated, so watch this space.

They say that things even themselves out over the course of a season; well, in March and April it was our turn to benefit from a series of late goals. First, we scored a 95th minute equaliser to take a very good point home with us from eventual Champions Swindon. Next, we pulled back from an early 2-0 deficit to win 3-2 against Crewe with a last minute goal. We recorded another 3-2 success a few weeks later, as we won at Peterborough with another last gasp winner, and finally beat a decent-looking Bristol City side 2-1 with another late 'un.

With the news that we had O'Connor until the end of the season, we embarked on the final month determined to give it our best shot and maybe nick a play-off place. However, as the month progressed, our sights were lowered somewhat and the objective now was a top ten finish, but at the end of the day even that was out of our reach as we ended up 11th - some nine points clear of 12th place, though (Statto fact!).

Missing out on the play-offs was a big disappointment, but still being in with a sniff right up until a couple of weeks before the end of the season is testimony to the team's efforts. We would have grabbed an 11th place finish with both hands after our opening day disaster, and looking back, there have been some very encouraging moments over the course of the season, none more so than the flourishing defensive partnership of Messrs Viveash and Mountfield, and the goalscoring exploits of Kyle Lightbourne despite carrying a niggling injury for much of the campaign.

It is widely anticipated that this pre-season is going to be one of the most interesting in the club's history. Manager Chris Nicholl is going on about needing "a new challenge" and skipper Martin O'Connor is looking to display his talents at a higher level. It will be a very sad day if the pair leave us. Nicholl is a good manager and got us to mid-table in a higher Division without spending a penny on new players. Just imagine what he could do with £500,000+ from the sale of

O'Connor. Still, if he is not 100% committed to the club, then perhaps he should go off and look for his 'new challenge'. Having said that, as I write, Barry Fry is seeking employment... Oh God, no!!

Fanzine Facts

Andrew Poole first had the idea for *Moving Swiftly On* back in December 1989, but a combination of youth, hostility from the 'official' programme editor and discouragement from the club thwarted two previous launch attempts. Now, the 'zine goes from strength to strength, and the relationship with the club has got stronger. They even allow the editor to present an award on the pitch at the end of the season. Andrew claims that even the programme editor has come around to the *MSO*, and it is now available at the Bescot programme shop. As Andrew says, "What more could you ask for?"

Blazing Saddlers

NEW FRONTIERS

York City

This season ended with York City scrambling to safety with a 3-1 win at Brighton. The team that had done what the whole of the Premiership couldn't do, i.e. prevent Manchester United from doing the treble, had to suffer the ignominy of needing to go to Brighton after the season had supposedly finished, and get a result to avoid relegation back to the basement Division.

The low point of the season was the original game at Brighton. As soon as I arrived on the South Coast, I sensed a mood that the game wouldn't be completed. The prospect that this could be the last ever game at The Goldstone more than hinted at trouble, and I was very surprised the game was not all-ticket. The police seemed to have a minimal presence around the home fans, although the were very evident in front of the City supporters and around the director's box. No one seemed to make any attempt to get the game restarted after the pitch invasion (although I'm reliably informed that Brighton didn't have the money to replace the goalposts anyway!). Then to cap it all, The Football League took their usual stance and hoped that it would all go away. No decision was made on a possible replay despite the protests from Carlisle (who were disputing the last relegation place with us), until results forced them to act. While Michael Knighton rightly complained that the rescheduled game gave us an unfair advantage in knowing precisely what we needed to do, it also worked against us. We knew we needed a result to avoid relegation. Pressure - who needs it?

While everyone said that it was a good humoured pitch invasion and they could understand the reasons why, I'm not so sure. You must have to be a funny kind of person to want to wreck your own ground and bring shame onto the club you support. A week later a more sinister element surfaced. In a similar situation, Hull supporters demonstrating at their last home game of the season turned their grievances on the visiting supporters who they apparently attacked. Once again, football violence hit the front pages. What would have happened at the Goldstone Ground if Brighton had been playing someone other than York? Perhaps a more local club with a support of a couple of thousand instead of York's 500. Say, a Millwall or a Portsmouth? Perhaps if the 9,000 plus who were at the York game had been regulars, there would have been no need to contemplate leaving The Goldstone Ground. Just a thought...

Obviously York City's '95-96 highlight was the 3-0 Coca Cola Cup win at Old Trafford. We may have got a few lucky breaks on the night (poor 'keeping and a 'dodgy' penalty included), but really, there's nothing lucky about a 3-0 win. United were outplayed by a very young (even younger than United's) City side missing several key players through injury and unavailability. As two-goal hero Paul Barnes said when United bleated about their (out of choice) understrength side, "we might have won 5-0 if we'd had a full squad available."

As usual, our youngsters looked good in parts, but lack of consistency saw us struggle all season. Two of our stars that night at Old Trafford, Scott Jordan and Darren Williams, soon lost their form and spent much of the remainder of the campaign in the stiffs. Who knows whether they will recapture their form, or whether they will be starring for the likes of Harrogate and North Ferriby in a couple of year's time.

Another success of sorts was to see Paul Barnes and Jon McCarthy sold to higher division clubs where they both made their marks. You probably saw McCarthy's trickery for Port Vale against Everton in the Cup, and international recognition was soon to follow. Barnes' feat was even more notable. He joined Birmingham in early March *and retained his place* in Barry Fry's strike force for the rest of the season!

As ever, their departures were followed by cries of "where's the money gone?." The sale of three players and our Coca Cola Cup run probably netted over £1m, around our total income for the previous financial year. We twice broke our transfer record, yet neither of the two signings have made their mark. Indeed, we sold Rob Matthews on for a £10,000 profit to Bury within four months. The other, Adrian Randall (£140,000) flatters to deceive.

Over the last year, we've been, overactive in the transfer market, well, for City anyway, so far without really improving the squad. We started with a large playing staff, to cope with any potential injury problems that might be encountered during an expected push towards Division One. By the end of the season, we'd shed some of the fringe players and ended up with about three full midfields and an acute shortage of defenders.

If you're looking for stars in our team then the aforementioned Jordan and Williams are ones to keep an eye on. You can add Graham Murty, Steve Bushell and Richard Cresswell to the list too. Cresswell, a young central striker, started to establish himself in the team after Christmas. He's very skilful, but for my money he's going to have to be more prolific than he's so far proved to be. However, he's only 18, so he's got time. Over the years, we've had a succession of promising youngsters so don't hold your breath in expectation of these five being seen in Premiership action every weekend. If I had to nominate one, though, I'd go for Murty. He's versatile enough to play wide or more centrally either side of the field. Our beloved chairman is forever telling us that he's better than Jon McCarthy was at a similar age.

Personally, Gary Bull is my favourite; it was immediately obvious why he scored a lot of goals at Barnet but then failed elsewhere. He's class. You could see him moving into positions, waiting, waiting, waiting for a colleague to play the defence-splitting through ball that he wanted. When the ball was eventually played, Bull had strayed offside. He got booed, but once his colleagues realised what he was doing, the goals went in and his confidence came back. Those goals probably saved us from relegation. Let's hope that Cresswell learns from the master.

With most of the squad under contract, we don't expect to see a much changed side from last season. Indeed, only three of the lesser squad members were released.

One change may be in goal where Dean Kiely is out of contract and isn't too keen to sign again. He suddenly discovered an Irish grandmother during our pre-season trip to Dublin two years ago and came back wanting to play for The Republic in the '98 World Cup Finals. I suspect that with Blackburn's unknown 19 year old keeper, Shay Given, coming from nowhere to win full international recognition, Dean feels a bigger club is the place to be if he wants to play international football. Well, Deano, learn to kick straight and you'll be in with a chance!

I'm afraid expectations are not very high for the new season. The talk is that we were too good to go down last season and that we can mount a promotion challenge this time around. A lot depends on the youngsters, who will have to graduate to star players if we're going to have a chance.

If changes need to be made, might I suggest a new manager? Alan Little has been at the club for years, as assistant to the two previous managers and now into his fourth year as top man. He took John Ward's side up into Division Two within three months of taking charge. However, his record of signings isn't good; more steady than spectacular. Admittedly, he's generally recouped his purchase prices, but there again, you've got to question whether a player sold for a profit within 15 months of signing has been a success or a failure.

We remain a good side to watch as Alan Little tends to retain the neat footballing style that John Ward introduced. Our problems seem to stem from a defence which went to pieces last season. Our attacking options at set pieces are restricted to two dead ball specialists who sometimes beat the wall, and I can't remember the last time we scored a goal from a corner kick!

I'm afraid that the general downbeat mood has reached New Frontiers. At the moment we're not publishing. As crowds struggled to top 2,000, motivation dropped and sales fell. However, the plan is to be back next term. Who knows, maybe even at our Coca Cola Cup round two game. I wonder what the odds are on us doing the double over Manchester United?!

Fanzine Facts

The first issue of *New Frontiers* hit the streets in November 1992. Nearly four years later, editor Chris Forth would like to say it's still going strong. But all he can say is that it's still going! Like its author, and unlike fellow York fanzine Terrace Talk (one of the pioneers of the fanzine boom of the 1980's and 90's, now demised), *New Frontiers* isn't too controversial. Chris likens its progress to York City: "it chugs along."

NO MORE PIE IN THE SKY

Notts County

What's The Story? (Magpie Glory... Well, nearly)

If the previous season's fiasco had been an exercise in *Don't Look Back In Anger*, then this season's promotion-chasing campaign was to become more of a *Definitely Maybe* scenario. The close season saw two new passengers board the Mayhem Lane rollercoaster ride. Colin Murphy and Steve Thompson, both infamous for various escapades and misdemeanours at such glamour clubs as Lincoln City and Southend Utd, took their seats and strapped themselves tightly in.

A year of *Cigarettes and Alcohol* had left the club in a right old mess, and Murphy set about "Changing them before they change us." Two early signings were landed from the transfer ocean. Overboard went two

'keepers and various other bits of deadwood, as they reeled in the young and highly-rated Stags goalie Darren Ward and Gary 'no nonsense' Strodder from the Baggies.

An impressive pre-season saw Notts unbeaten as we *Rolled With It* towards The Racecourse Ground for the opening game of our season on loan to Division Two. A 1-1 draw was followed by wins over The Adams Family and The Posh, and four Goals from Devon 'Bruno' White sank Lincoln in the Fizzy Pop Cup. Only a defeat against a well-organised Bradford (we scored early) City spoilt the holiday mood as August drew to a close.

September began with Notts in generous heart. A trip to Brighton rewarded the home side with their first three points, but a half-time demonstration, free from trouble, brought to light the unrest that lay ahead for the misery-stricken Seagulls. We returned to our winning ways as fellow 'bucket and spaders' Bournemouth were sent packing with two second half goals from big Devon. In the Cup, we returned from the intimidating Elland Road with a good 0-0, and for the return, Notts unveiled a new third kit of all-yellow, hoping to give Leeds a sense of *déjà vu* ('keeper Wardy and Mansfield Town returned home last season at the same stage of the competition 1-0 up). Finally, a *Supersonic* evening was capped by neighbours F***st losing 3-2 away at Bradford City.

In October Oasis released their second LP, an important step for any band, and the next evening we also faced a difficult follow-up. Our success was not quite as marked, however, as Leeds returned home from the second leg of the Coca Cola

Cup much relieved, after a last minute goal (which was maybe a blessing in disguise for the Pies). Twice Devon 'who's this Yeboah chap anyway' White equalised for Notts, making him the nation's leading hot-shot, but with extra-time looming, and County down to ten men, we'd given our all. So we exited the competition with pride and honour still intact. But at least the infamous Bradford curse struck Nottingham again the next evening, as the Bantams knocked F***st out of the Cup too!!

League form fluctuated from one extreme to another: boring at Brunton, re-kindled against Rotherham, ballistic against Bristol Rovers and a swizz against Swindon. Not to forget the 2-1 defeat in the Auto Windswept Shield at Saltergate, home of unfanzine-friendly Stewards and things that resemble stray asteroids rather than what we supporters know as Meat Pies!!

November was *Wonderwall*. We thrashed Brentford, we thrilled at Burnley in the game (and pies) of the season and we wreaked revenge over the Spireites. And all this together with Euro-flops Blackburn Rovers annihilating F***st 7-0! Cans of '7-Up' all round - now *that's* entertainment! The two remaining Cup competitions brought more success, with a win over Stockport (AWS) and a Sky-televised victory over York (FAC), while a late, late, late 3-1 come-back at Belle Vue left only a 0-0 at the moon-like Vetch Field (no goals and no atmosphere) to finish a rewarding month.

December arrived, but there was to be no FA Cup glory for the infamous giant-killing non-league Telford Utd. Bruno returned after 'being rested' to nod home the second in the 2-0 win at Ashton Gate, but we dropped points against promotion rivals Crewe and Blackpool, and a hat-trick of postponed games brought a slightly chilly end to the year.

January saw us *Slide Away* to Robson's Middlesbrough in the Cup, and to revenge-seeking York in the League, and February wasn't too bright either. The Devon-shire cream was spilt and lapped up for £100,000 by Watford, while our luck finally ran out in the third 'clash of the Counties' as Stockport snatched victory with two late goals. Then the March sales got underway as Barry Fry took advantage of the Meadow Lane 'buy one, get one free' sale. He paid £½m for TWO players (Devlin and Leggy were both worth *at the very least* that amount each), which leaves a bitter taste in the mouth even now. The hectic pile-up of games continued with still no sight of consistency. Performances ranged from a boombastic 3-1 at Bootham Crescent to a braindraining nightmare 0-0 at bottom-of-the-pile Hull City (home of the famous Boothferry Boff Burgers). Added to that were a well dodgy off-side decision against Blackpool and yet another defeat against Bradford, and the alarm bells started to ring. In response the strike force was augmented by the recruitment of the 'G-force factor', as the two Garys (Jones and Martindale) were signed from Southend and the Posh.

The only thing worth noting about April's trips to Rotherham and League leaders Swindle Town was the massive void between the stewards at each club: Millmoor's trouble-seeking posse tried (unsuccessfully) to evict me for selling the 'zine at half-time, while the County Ground crew couldn't do enough to help, and even bought a few copies! On the pitch, a trio of draws saw any hopes of automatic promotion begin to *Fade Away*.

We faced the final Saturday of the season with many issues still undecided. To gain automatic promotion Notts needed to win, while Blackpool and Oxford both had to lose. But there was no five o'clock hero at Saltergate that afternoon, Chesterfield looking for a last-chance route out of the Division themselves, and we had to settle for the play-offs.

After a 2-2 draw at Crewe in the play-off semi, a superb second half volley from Martindale in the second leg was just enough to take the Pies through to our fifth Wembley trip in the space of seven years.

Sunday May 26th, and a huge convoy of City supporters were en route to the football Oasis. A 1:3 difference in support was no doubt due to the novelty value of a first visit to the Twin Towers. Many Notts fans now know that Wembley isn't all that it's cracked up to be and decided to stay at home in the rockin' chair... The game itself was by no means a classic. In a day of taking chances, Bradford converted theirs while we left our shooting boots back at home. A final result of 2-0 took Bratfud up. The trip home is a long one when you've lost, made just that bit longer by jubilant Bantams keen to remind the down-hearted Magpies of the score using 'hand signals' all the way back up the M1.

Some Might Say finishing fourth and a trip to Wembley after the previous season of misery would be glory. But there's a wider picture to view. The football this season has been at many times *Up In The Sky*, devoid of any cohesion, method or skill. What the fans want is to return from matches entertained - win, lose or draw. Maybe we *are* asking too much too soon. On Bank Holiday Monday, Colin Murphy commented in the local paper "We were as close as a whisper - now we want to change the way we play next season." It finally seems that the management may have taken note of a factor that we the fans worked out months ago. All the pieces are now in place for what should be a successful '96-97 promotion push. A world-class international 'keeper and a well-balanced squad, plus of course a stadium capable of gracing any Division.

But I'll leave that story until next year...

Fanzine Facts

Founded in January 1994, *No More Pie In The Sky* is primarily a Notts County Fanzine but also has allegiances to Stockport County and The Almighty Chris Waddle. Edited by Oasis/Weller fan (never!) Ivan 'Bart' Bainbridge, this year *NMPITS* has also launched a successful 'Hitchhikers Guide To Division II'. Apart from himself "on lead guitar and vocals", 'Bart' names his a regular line-up as:

Andy 'Statto' Gordon - keyboards
Moulinuex - Drums
Levi - Bass Guitar
Mad Mik Wyer - Rhythm Guitar

NO-ONE LIKES US

Millwall

When most supporters look back at their club's season they usually come out with something like "It was a roller coaster of a season, full of ups and downs." In the case of Millwall '95-96 was like a free fall parachute jump when the 'chute doesn't open. Could someone explain how a club could go from top of the League in December to relegation in May, winning only four games in the process? 'Cos we're buggered if we know!

The close-season gave us hope that this would be nine months to remember (little did we know!), and although Andy Roberts was sold to Palace, the money, for once, was invested in rebuilding the team. In came Newman and Bowry from Palace, Doyle from QPR, Bennett from Charlton and a million quid was invested

in the strike partnership of Chris Malkin and Uwe Fuchs. Scoring goals had been the problem for Millwall since the sale of the god Sheringham, and these two were hailed by new chairman Peter Mead as "the pair who will at last bring us 30 or 40 goals." Malkin ended up scoring 12 and Fuchs five! That was the first of our problems. Although *No-one Likes Us* owes a debt of gratitude to Uwe for keeping us provided with jokes and cartoons for most of the season, as a goalscorer he followed a long line of striking flops (Paul Goddard, John Byrne, Clive Allen... the list is too painful to go on). Spending huge amounts of time on his back, Uwe earned himself the nickname 'Duvet', but despite all this, thanks to a rock solid defence, we ground-out some impressive away wins, topping the season for six weeks without ever really hitting top form. A fine battling performance at Goodison (widely highlighted on the box) saw us come back from two down to beat Everton 4-2 in the Coca Cola Cup.

But the wheels came off big time at Sunderland with a 6-0 defeat, and although we didn't realise it at the time the parachute was already failing. Gerrard Lavin was bought from Watford for five hundred grand and it was 16 games before he played on the winning side, earning him the nickname 'Lucky' and a fine from the FA for gobbing into the crowd at Luton. Then came the second problem: Ireland lost to Holland, Jack Charlton stood down, and Mick McCarthy was set to take over as his replacement. What should have taken two days, thanks to a group of old farts on the IFA, took two months. Big Mick was seen as Charlton's nominee and they jumped at the chance to exact some revenge for the way they had been treated by Big Jack; their fucking-about effectively flushed our season down the toilet. During two months of deliberations we didn't win a game. The crowd turned on the team, the manager and performances went from poor, through dismal, to shambolic. In an attempt to halt the slide Peter Mead pulled off what outsiders called 'the coup of the season' signing Vassili Kulkov and Serguei Yuran form Moskow Spartak. A near sell-out crowd greeted their arrival and stood open-mouthed when the two overweight Russians attempted to make some sort of sense of the Endsleigh League. Major problem number three had arrived.

To say their signing was a disaster would be putting it mildly, even by Millwall standards. Paid five grand a week EACH, Yuran couldn't even be bothered to turn up for training. Kulkov played half a dozen games, picked up a knee injury and spent the rest of the season in his Hotel counting his money. Yuran produced one of the most spectacular failures in living memory. He ended up 'playing' 13 games, hurling himself to the ground every time he was challenged, only to spring to his feet making yellow card gestures; I can't remember him getting a single foul! The high point came against Wolves; winding himself up to a fever pitch of fury he ended up chinning Eric Young and getting sent off. In the meantime he was also charged with drunk driving, providing that old adage: "you can bring a Russian to Millwall but you can't stop him having a drink." Jimmy Nicholl from Raith Rovers was appointed as Mick's replacement with the promise that he would get us out of the First Division (well, at least he kept his promise!). We were in 12th place at the time and still hopeful of the play-offs. On arrival Nicholl took one look at the huge squad and said they were overpaid and all playing for their places. The players responded to this keen psychology ploy by racking up five red cards in seven games... Say hello to our fourth big problem.

By the time the penny dropped that there really was an outside chance of relegation, our entire defence was suspended for the vital game against Oldham. We lost to a highly dodgy penalty (Oldham's only shot on target in the entire game), had several penalty appeals turned down, a goal disallowed and Alex Rae sent off. The writing was on the wall. A loss at home to Stoke and a battling point at Ipswich saw us relegated on goal difference along with Luton and Watford. No comfort can be taken from the fact that all three teams hardly deserved their fate when awful sides like Sheffield United, Oldham, Reading, Portsmouth and Grimsby survived. Not even Barry Fry getting the boot could lift our gloom. It's a funny old game... NOT FOR US IT BLOODY WELL ISN'T!

Fanzine Facts

No-One Likes Us is in its sixth year and got its name from Millwall's famous terrace song. Famous for ploughing its profits back into the club, the fat bastards (otherwise known as 'the Albatross' and 'the Jocko') point out that "they still have to take our money through gritted teeth." NOLU says that its policy "has always been influenced by the fact that life at Millwall has never been easy, so why make it more depressing by being serious?"

NOT THE 8502

AFC Bournemouth

I could have probably chronicled the events of this season in June 1995. After the mind-blowing excitement of '94-95, when relegation was somehow avoided, the side reclaimed their perennial mid-table position, occasionally looking like play-off candidates, sometimes flirting with the relegation places. It was very much business as usual.

The lack of a 'big' draw in the Cup also saw the many thousands of Bournemouth's glory fans miss out on their annual visit to Dean Court. Did you know that the latent support at Dean Court is the most dormant in the country? It's true: for the size of the town, we are the worst supported team in Britain. Still, with planning permission for the new stadium finally being passed, perhaps the missing thousands will flock back... you never know.

STEVE JONES DENIES 'JEALOUSY' CLAIMS IF OTHER PLAYERS SCORE

Anyway, so what actually happened?. Well, the majority of it was pretty mundane with a few notable exceptions, most of them involving Crewe, a homely club liked by most people but now loathed at Bournemouth. The season was ticking along nicely, the side playing good confident football, and Steve Jones, who it transpired was merely on loan from West Ham (AFC Bournemouth reserves), was banging the goals in left right and centre. Then, the watershed. September 16th... Crewe were in town... And the referee was Barry Knight, a name that now strikes fear in every Bournemouth heart. In 30 years of watching the beautiful game, I can honestly say that I have never, ever seen a more incompetent refereeing display. What should have been a good game of footie ended up a riot. Two Bournemouth players were sent off and seven booked, in a game where there honestly wasn't a bad foul. Possibly the worst challenge was when Bournemouth keeper Ian Andrews was blatantly bundled over, giving Crewe the softest of goals. Needless to say, Knight(mare) said "no foul" and the goal stood. Our players were kicked all over the park, whilst Crewe's were given protection beyond belief. The trainspotters finally ran out 4-0 winners, and Knight needed a police escort off the pitch. But this didn't deter hundreds of Bournemouth fans laying siege outside the official's entrance. After an hour he emerged, mob-handed with stewards and police, and the look on his face as he attempted to drive away with Bournemouth fans hanging off his car was a picture. Of course, the obligatory FA charged followed, but at least we never saw him again.

The next home game saw the visit of Brighton for the first ever live televised game at Dean Court. The Seaweeds, not too popular with us anyway, decided to 'protest' by invading the pitch and attacking Bournemouth fans. What hurt most, about these two incidents was that while the Brighton supporters were described in the press as 'protesters', our lot having a go at a ref were described as a 'mob'.

And to round off the trilogy, the next home game against Watford in the Coca Cola Cup saw the visitors go through after a penalty shoot-out, after which the police decided to 'have a go' at the visiting fans for celebrating on the pitch. Someone should have told them that if people are wearing football kit and boots, you shouldn't really attack them with truncheons!

The season then reverted to type: a few home wins and a few away draws. Neil Moss kept seven clean sheets in a row, including one at Bristol City in an FA Cup replay where he single-handedly kept the Robins at bay - we were awful, City outplayed us, and we won 1-0! Ha!

Following a team like Bournemouth every week home and away is made all worthwhile by the occasional incredible game, and we had a real belter on January 13th. Peterborough v Bournemouth doesn't sound very exciting, but it is a game I'll never forget. One-nil up, Boro' equalised, and by half time it was 1-1; all fairly run-of-the-mill. Second half, Boro' went 3-1 up but we produced a hell of a fight back to square it at 3-3, before the home side made it 4-3 with a superb goal. With six minutes left, I was thinking, "we've blown this; still, we fought brilliantly." One minute later, it was 4-5 and 150 Bournemouth fans were going absolutely mental in the away end. Both goals came from Jones; the second an absolute peach.

The next dose of 'excitement' came, once again, against Crewe. Now everyone's heard the theory that lightening doesn't strike twice. But don't believe it. Chris Casper was on loan from Man United and it was a game that I know bothered him deeply. Crewe were abysmal and it seemed only a matter of time before we would take the lead. On the half hour we did, only for the ref to rule it out due to a push that no-one saw. In the second half we really stepped up the pressure, and from a corner, Steve Robinson flicked the ball to Casper who knocked the ball home to spark off glorious celebrations - oh, revenge was going to be so sweet. Then, a Crewe player booted the ball in disgust, and incredibly, the referee gave a corner!! That hurt, and it still does to this day. We scored.. "WE BLOODY WELL SCORED" I screamed at the ref. Even the police that we thought were rushing over to tell us to sit down (as usual) agreed: "It was a goal!." Then injustice piled on injustice when Crewe scored two late goals to give them the undeserved win of the year. And you wonder why we hate Crewe!

Despite a poor spell, enough points were gathered to finish in a comfortable position, and the last weekend of the season still held the promise of being one hell of a knees-up. It wasn't to be. First, a last day out at Brentford ended up as flat as a pancake as Bournemouth went down tamely 2-0. Second, Poor Old Pompey only had to draw at Huddersfield and they were down. They went and won. Last, and worst of all, S*********n drew with Wimbledon, and once again stayed up by the skin of their teeth. God, football can be a cruel mistress.

Yet with a young side, we are looking to the '96-97 season with some optimism. Players being sold every two minutes doesn't help, but when you're as skint as we are, it's a fact of life. Machin is doing a good job, and with the new stadium on the horizon, things could be looking up as the club may finally start to realise their potential. Then again, it could be just another false dawn.

Fanzine Facts

As the fanzine is now in its tenth season, Editor Mick Cunningham can look back at '95-96 with a lot of pride. Fed up with the poor quality of the official match day programme, he complained the club, and ended up editing it. His efforts won him the Second Division Programme of the Year award. *Not the 8502* continues as well and was banned twice last season, just to prove that some things never change. Mick has proved to be a 'bridge' between the supporters and the board, something which (so far) has worked very well. The fanzine takes its title from the difference in size between the first and last crowds of AFC Bournemouth's successful '86-87 promotion season, and as such it is dedicated to the 'real fans'.

THE NO.9

Newcastle United

Football is a passion. It's not about money, or individuals; it's about supporting your team through thick and thin, through the good times and the bad. And as a Newcastle fan I have seen a *lot* of bad. The season that was '94-95 had promised so much, yet delivered nothing; even a place in Europe was stolen away from us by Leeds.

As usual, no sooner had it all finished then the season ticket renewal forms were on my doormat. I filled them in with haste and worried about the money later. The summer dragged on as Geordies everywhere waited for the fixture list to be released by the FA. And when it was published, opinions were mixed. An easy start but a hard run-in, depending on how far up the League we would be. The papers were rife with speculation about who Keegan would be signing. In came Les Ferdinand, Warren Barton, David Ginola and Shaka Hislop, taking Newcastle's spending up to the forty million mark since King Kevins arrival. Needless to say the papers were very wide of the mark with their predictions.

The opening day saw Coventry visit St James, Big Fat Ron and all. The Toon sent them packing 3-0. Les (or Sir Les as he was to be known) scored a memorable 25 yard goal in the famous number nine shirt. Bolton away next: 3-1 win. Sheffield Wednesday away: 2-0 win. And so it went on. After a slip-up at Southampton, Newcastle's next League defeat was not until we played Chelsea away; a three month spell. This was the stuff dreams were made of and I like many others could not believe it. There was however that niggling thought in the back of my mind that we may throw it all away again... No, we had a bigger squad, we would learn from last season... God, was I trying to convince myself! I waited for the men in the white coats but they never came. Unbelievably we were still in the Coca Cola Cup after easily disposing of Bristol (8-1 on aggregate) and Stoke (4-0 away), and then beating favourites Liverpool at Anfield 1-0 - oh, how the scousers howled. As '95 drew to a close my beloved Newcastle were on course for glory on all three fronts, and we'd welcomed local neighbours Middlesbrough back into the Premiership with a 1-0 defeat. Life could not have been sweeter.

January arrived, and I wish it hadn't. The old year had gone out with a whimper; again the scum that is Manchester United had beaten us 2-0 at Old Trafford. We then fell at the first hurdle in the FA Cup after a replay against

Chelsea, going out on penalties, something I've never really agreed with (mainly because we can never score from them). Three days later it was the quarter final of the Coca Cola Cup against Arsenal at Highbury. Having beaten them rather convincingly eight days earlier, confidence was high, and many Geordies were once again relishing a trip to the Twin Towers. But the only relish we got was in the dodgy North London burgers, as two Ian Wright goals dumped us out. Suddenly we were out of both Cups with just the League to play for. This was a little bit too much to take for some fans who began to vent their anger in the local press, a lot of it total crap, some even suggesting Keegan should leave. What short memories some people have.

By the end of February rumours of Alan Shearer's imminent arrival spread through Tyneside like wild fire. Various sightings of the genial Geordie striker in bars and bus stops were reported, however once again these rumours proved to be somewhat misleading. The 'genial Geordie' turned out to be Colombian, and was called Faustino, not Alan. Asprilla's on-off, on-off transfer had the whole of the country in awe of Newcastle's prowess in the transfer market... until they read his criminal record. It appeared that Keegan had lost it. There was uproar in the national press. This bloke had used firearms, damaged buses and slept with loads of women! "So have we!" cried the Toon army! Asprilla made his mark within two games. He turned an almost certain defeat against Middlesbrough into a win with some scintillating ball control and the cross for a Steve Watson winner, and he elbowed and head-butted his way into disciplinary trouble with the FA. Genius or Jerk? The jury was out (on both Keegan and Asprilla). To accommodate the Colombian, Keith Gillespie - a major supplier along with Ginola for Ferdinand's early season form - was, much to the annoyance of the fans, left on the bench when he returned from injury. It was not until Keith's betting exploits were revealed by the bookies that we all realised there was more to this than met the eye. Keegan, ever the disciplinarian, was once again showing he was the gaffer. By the start of March we had opened a 12 point gap on our nearest rivals Manchester United. And so - D Day. The Mancs entered the fortress that is St James' Park, and were treated to an explosive Toon Army welcome. The game kicked off and the first 45 minutes was all Newcastle; wave after wave of attack, but to no avail. Then up popped the Frenchman - no, not ours, theirs! The man who should have been banned from English football, Eric Cantona. Look, last word on this, but what would have happened to Vinny Jones had he done the same as the temperamental Frenchman, I wonder?

Anyway, 12 points was soon whittled away to six and suddenly Liverpool were back in the equation; the title was now a three horse race. After a lacklustre performance again at Arsenal, another 2-0 defeat, we visited Anfield for what turned out to be one of the greatest televised matches of all time. It was a night that saw David Ginola at his mercurial best. The Frenchman's absence through suspension after being sent off in the Cup quarter final at Arsenal had made him sit up and realise that playing football and not play-acting is what the English game is all about. 'Tino Asprilla was also in mouth-watering form for this clash of the titans. Tied at three goals apiece, Collymore scored in injury time. The TV cameras fixed themselves on the travelling fans, and captured the devastation on many of the Toon Army's faces, something many of the pundits perversely revelled in. As I walked away from Anfield I felt like a relative had died. Such was the affect that in my heart of hearts I knew it was all over, but still hoped for the impossible. The signing of David Batty could have been a godsend, if only he'd arrived five games earlier. He gave us that bit of bite in midfield that we'd sorely missed and also had experience in winning the title. So unfortunately did Manchester United, and apart from their 'grey day' at Southampton, never really looked like slipping up again.

In contrast, those two Graham Fenton goals at Blackburn in eight minutes which turned a certain win into defeat summed up our run-in. We dropped too many points, and although we took it to the last day, not even the most optimistic Geordie thought we could still do it. As we played out an entertaining draw at home to Tottenham, the Mancs were slaughtering Boro, and as the final whistle blew on another massively exciting but fruitless season, we were left to reflect on what might have been. 'There's always next year' is an old cliché with Newcastle fans, but this time I think we're in with a shout. The treble and Europe, but first the Charity Shield and an old score to settle. Look out Manchester, we're behind you...

Fanzine Facts

The No.9 was founded in August '89 by Steve and Rob Wraith. Formerly known as The Mighty Quinn (during which time Micky Quinn-style curly black wigs and 'tashes were obligatory for many at away games), it was re-named *The No.9* when their inspirational centre forward left the club. Steve and Rob explain that "*The No.9* is all set for the leap into the big time. It's increasing in size to A4, 20 pages and full colour glossy! Interviews already lined up include Lee Clark, Les Ferdinand, David Batty, and Robert Lee." The mag's first team includes Steve and Rob, plus John Wraith and "new signing" cartoonist Joe Mckeough.

THE OATCAKE

Stoke City

Surprise, Surprise!

Without question, the '95-96 season was a remarkable one for Stoke City. By finishing fourth in the table and reaching the play-offs, Stoke (for the first time in living memory) actually managed to exceed the expectations of the supporters.

We usually go into each season fully expecting the team to be right up at the top pushing for promotion, but that wasn't the case at the start of last season. An ongoing feud between supporters and the board had done much to create an air of resentment and apathy, with many City fans vowing not to return to the Victoria Ground as long as the present board remained in control of the club; something borne out in the plummeting season ticket sales.

If that wasn't bad enough, Stoke then decided to introduce a new 'signing-on' policy for players at the club whose contracts were due for renewal. Rather than pay them their signing-on fee in instalments over a period of time, the club decided that players would only receive the money after the completion of a set number of appearances. You don't have to be a genius to work out that the players didn't express their entire satisfaction with this new policy. Other clubs got in touch to commend Stoke on their course of action, but the hard truth is that rather than being a brave stance against the spiralling wage demands of greedy players, as they would have you believe, it was actually a desperate measure from cash-strapped club, trying frantically to save money however they could. Other clubs may have been quick to pat Stoke on the back but I'd be interested to know exactly how many of them introduced the policy themselves?

With supporters in open revolt against the club, not even one new player coming in to strengthen a team which had nearly been relegated the season before and persistent rumours of a severely demoralised dressing room, it seemed that the prospects for success in the coming season were somewhere between slim and non-existent. We settled down and waited for nine long hard months of battle to beat the drop. Sure enough, after six games, everything was going to plan. We were second bottom of the First Division and looking in big trouble. An appalling performance in an early televised match against hated local rivals Port Vale confirmed our very worst fears about what lay ahead, and the general feeling was, as Fraser from Dad's Army would put it, "We're doomed!."

The situation at the club had become a joke; supporters were totally disillusioned, the dressing room morale was rock-bottom and even Lou Macari seemed to chuck the towel in by announcing that he was moving 'upstairs' and leaving team affairs to his two coaches. If ever there was a time for people to stand up and be counted then this was it. Cometh the hour, cometh the man; club captain Vince Overson challenged everybody to get their act together and start pulling in the same direction. The chairman ordered Lou to re-take control of the first team (which turned out to be the only good thing he did all season) and suddenly things started to happen.

The dramatic turnaround in Stoke City's fortunes was as steady as it was spectacular. One rousing rallying call from Overson and Lou's decision to remove the two main dressing room protagonists (Keith Scott and Toddy Orlygsson) transformed the club from relegation certainties to promotion contenders. It was as if the players had something to prove to everybody, as they played with an intensity and self-belief which caught a good few opposing sides off-guard - none more so than our traditional South Staffordshire rivals Wolves, who succumbed to a thrilling 4-1 home defeat at the hands of The Potters. It should have been 5-1 but Paul Peschisolido missed a last minute chance which he really should have buried. OK, so 4-1 is a sound thrashing, but 5-1 would have been a complete dicking! The sight of dejected Wolves fans streaming out of Molineux, having witnessed their overpriced and over-rated heroes get a thumping from Stoke's two-bob outfit was one of those rare moments that makes up for all the pain and misery you have to suffer at other times.

Good results were flying in from all over the place now, and Stoke's remarkable turnaround in form and fortunes was no better highlighted than in the Coca Cola Cup victory over Chelsea at Stamford Bridge, when Pesch's late goal sent the huge travelling Stoke support into a bout of serious celebrations - not even Ruud Gullit could stand in our way! Apart from the winning goal, the two-legged tie was also memorable for the non-stop 180 minute battle between our Vince and Chelsea's Mark Hughes, which would have graced any episode of International Gladiators!

Stoke brought in the only new arrival of the season in November when Lou Macari finally managed to off-load the useless Keith Scott. It seemed as though we would be stuck with trouble-maker Scott until his contract ran out, but amazingly Lou managed to strike up a cash plus appearances deal with Norwich manager Martin O'Neill whereby Scott was swapped for out-of-favour Carrow Road striker, Mike Sheron. Sheron had arrived at Norwich just a year and a half before in an £850,000 move from Manchester City, but had failed to impress. That said, I still can't believe that he had played so badly that Martin O'Neill thought that Keith Scott (who'd played for him in his Wycombe days) was a better deal. Significantly, this turned out to be just about the last piece of business conducted by O'Neill before he walked out on Norwich to join Leicester City!

To the considerable surprise of everybody connected with Stoke, we were now blessed with an embarrassment of riches in the forwards department. Pesch was banging in the goals, Simon Sturridge (who had spent most of the previous two years in the reserves) grabbed his chance of a regular first team place with a vengeance and Mike Sheron, once he settled in, showed just what a quality player he is. Unfortunately, it was exactly this strength in the Stoke side that enabled our board of directors to once again show just why the vast majority of supporters hate them with such a passion. On transfer deadline day they used the excuse of having three front-line strikers to sell Paul Peschisolido back to Birmingham City for a bargain basement £400,000; considerably less than the £580,000 we'd paid for him just 18 months earlier!

This visible display of such a total lack of ambition highlights perfectly why so many supporters dream of the day when the directors are gone from the club. It also gives another indication of just how well the players and staff had done to get involved in the promotion race at all. Supporters had been screaming out for the club to buy that extra player who could push the club towards promotion, but instead the board sold off one of our best players!

Despite the best efforts of our directors the team continued to confound their critics and though we could scarcely believe it, we went into the last third of the season with promotion still very much on the cards. From time to time we would stutter, stumble and look set to drop out of the race, only to bounce back with a string of results to push us right back into the thick of things. The run-in was littered with unforgettable games as our chances of success seemed to swing wildly with each passing game.

We suffered the ignominy of Vale completing a League double over us when we lost the return match at Vale Park. We had gone into the game keen to avenge that early season defeat, and part of our masterplan was to avoid conceding an early goal as we had done in the corresponding fixture the year before, when Tony Naylor had scored inside two minutes. Somewhere along the way, the masterplan went awry. We managed to find ourselves a goal down; this time after just 12 (yes, TWELVE) seconds! Suffice to say it was the only goal of the game.

Disasters like that one and losing 2-1 at Charlton, having led with just five minutes to play, were painful, but amends were made in games such as the 2-0 home win against Mark McGhee's resurgent Wolves team in a pulsating local derby, and thrilling away victories at both Luton and Millwall - both of which contributed greatly to their eventual respective relegations. Luton fans saw their side batter Stoke for 75 minutes only to watch in horror as we stole the game with 87th and 90th minute goals from the flourishing 'SAS' partnership of Sturridge and Sheron. That prolific pair also scored the goals that brought about a 3-2 victory for The Potters in Millwall's last home game of the season. Stoke fans mercilessly baited the home supporters throughout that match, only to be reprimanded for doing so by the Radio Five reporter afterwards. OK then, in future when we're near the top and winning a game which could help relegate our opponents we'll be sure to keep our mouths shut so as not to offend!

A quick word here for Mike Sheron whose incredible goalscoring exploits towards the end of the season saw him write himself into Stoke City's record books. He scored 15 times in 22 appearances, including a run of scoring in seven consecutive games, a feat never before accomplished by a Stoke player. One of our favourite post-match pub pastimes was to wonder what the Norwich fans would make of seeing Sheron's name on the scoresheet again and again while his replacement, Keith Scott, was on loan at Bournemouth!?

After more ups, downs, pressure and heart-stopping moments than it seemed fair for one club to have to suffer, we finally made it into the play-offs by beating Southend in the final game of the season. Fate paired us against Leicester City, who, despite having a pretty mediocre season had fluked their way into the play-offs courtesy of victories in their final four games. We knew that we were a better team and had two League wins to prove it. However, this counts for nothing in the play-offs and even though we easily held them to a 0-0 draw in the first leg at their ground, we bottled the second leg and lost to what turned out to be their only decent chance of the entire tie. No complaints about that second leg score though. Leicester may have only managed to carve out one clear goalscoring chance, but it was one more than we managed! On the night they wanted to win the game more, and they did. For us it was a case of one game too many. When you play all season with a patched-up outfit that flies by the seat of its pants, then inevitably you're going to have games like this. It's a pity that we had to choose a game of such importance though to have such an off day.

What the games against Leicester did show is the basically unfair nature of the play-off system. Endsleigh victories counted for nothing and the law of averages were stacking up to work against us. Let's face it, if we kept meeting Leicester they'd be bound to win one sooner or later, and that's exactly what happened. It's not sour grapes either. They no more deserved another crack at us than we deserved another crack at third placed Crystal Palace. The sooner the play-offs are buried and we return to automatic promotion for the top three teams the better!

Stoke supporters were thrilled at the team's achievement of finishing fourth in the table. In the face of adversity they did us proud; the only thing demanded of their team by Stoke supporters is effort - and we got that by the bucket-load. The players gave their all throughout the season and they were clearly as choked as we were to fail in such a fashion.

Our joy at the efforts though can't disguise the fact that we missed out on the Premiership by just six points; half a dozen measly points. Look back in anger? Hell, why not: losing League doubles to such average teams as Vile, Grimsby and Oldham, and four points surrendered to quite probably the jammiest team in the entire four Divisions, Huddersfield Town certainly screwed us up. Huddersfield's manager Brian Horton witnessed City give Town an unbelievable late own goal in our first encounter, and then watched as we hit the woodwork three times before they claimed a last gasp leveller in the second, a goal which went in off, go on, have a guess, the underside of the crossbar. On both occasions he reckoned that his side were worth a draw, thus earning him the prestigious Endsleigh Award for the biggest dose of verbal diarrhoea delivered last season.

While these dropped points were factors, the biggest single reason for our 'near-miss' was our own board of directors, who gave the manager not one penny to spend. Macari was a known admirer of Bolton's Richard Sneekers, but when he became available for transfer Lou could only watch as West Brom moved in with a £400,000 bid. Then while our midfield pulled up during the final furlongs, Sneekers was banging in the goals at the rate of one a game for the Baggies!

Yes, in many ways, it was a truly memorable season that ended in ultimate disappointment. And what really sticks in the throat is that our ultimate failure was down to those in charge of the club. No doubt, they are at this moment bemoaning the millions lost by Stoke for not making it into the Premiership, yet they still refuse to acknowledge that it was they who were most responsible for bringing this about! With such people in control, it makes you wonder if we'll ever make it out of this Division... in an upwards direction, that is!

Fanzine Facts

The Oatcake was born in September 1988 when editor Martin Smith and a group of friends decided to do something about giving supporters a greater say about the way their club was being run. It would also give them the chance to lay into anybody they didn't like! Inspired by Glasgow Celtic's campaigning fanzine *Not The View*, there was much debate as to what to call the new fanzine. After toying with several ideas based around the word 'Victoria' (after the stadium), they settled for *The Oatcake,* after a rough-looking pancake made from oats (surprise, surprise!!) which is a local delicacy, unique to the Potteries and North Staffordshire. *The Oatcake* is a compact fanzine that appears every weekend home match, and aims to give supporters a bang up-to-date offering on a regular basis. It is a full-time commitment for Martin, who claims that Stoke has a very fanzine-friendly following.

ON THE TERRACES

West Ham United

When, in years to come, West Ham supporters look back upon season '95-96, it will probably be remembered as a watershed in the club's history. After so long spent yo-yoing between the top two Divisions thanks to the spendthrift nature of the board of directors, there was a dramatic awakening to the realities of football in today's (rather than yesterday's, or last year's, or last decade's) world; and, with so many outsiders (i.e. non-locals) now playing for the Hammers, we mean 'world' in its very widest sense.

You might have been hard pressed to think such a thing as the season got underway though; bookmakers William Hill took a total of one bet on West Ham to win the Premiership ("a rather embarrassing £2

bet each way" according to spokesman Graham Sharp), and as had been the case for the two previous seasons, we were - along with the Premiership's whipping boys Bolton Wanderers - favourites for the plunge. Performances during pre-season seemed to indicated that the old 'favourites for the drop' tag was one the team would find it eminently easy to live up to: Bournemouth (with our then ex and newly re-signed Steve 'Steptoe' Jones leading the way) beat us on penalties; Oxford thumped a full strength (bar Julian Dicks) team, and there were uninspiring draws at both Charlton and mighty Peterborough.

With manager Harry Redknapp having already used most of his summer finances bringing in Marc Rieper and finishing off the payments for Don Hutchison, there was very little left in the kitty. However, there was just enough to secure the signature of Dutch striker Marco Boogers, of whom managing director Peter Storrie famously said "We have signed a top quality striker, and maybe this will answer the critics who have been having a go at us."

For the second season running our opening fixture saw Leeds United visit Upton Park. Danny Williamson opened the scoring on five minutes but it never looked enough, and the first of Tony Yeboah's spectaculars saw them take the points. A similar scoreline was repeated at football's equivalent to Disneyland. Redevelopments at Old Trafford meant no tickets for West Ham fans and a red card for substitute Marco Boogers just two minutes after coming on as a substitute. No points from six became one from nine as a Martin Allen header meant we shared the spoils away at Forest, a total we doubled after a similar result at home to Spurs.

Things went from bad to worse, especially for Julian Dicks who saw a tackle on John Spencer in a 3-1 defeat by Chelsea (not deemed worthy of so much as a booking at the time) highlighted again and again by Sky, until the FA chose to haul him in for a disciplinary hearing. Five days later Julian tangled with Ian Wright and received yet another red card. The Arsenal game also saw the return of Iain Dowie (a move criticised by 99% of us at the time) and Les Sealey, making his Hammers' debut as a striker! Having to use our 'keeper as a makeshift outfield player was probably the straw that broke the camel's back; I mean, when the board saw Les foraging for openings against the gunners' back four the penny finally dropped: some drastic action was needed. As we left North London in 19th place and with just two points from 15, the mood was generally that things could *surely* never get any worse than that...

When barely 800 of the 1100 tickets for the midweek Coca Cola trip to Bristol Rovers were sold, this only highlighted the frustration being felt. Mind you, those who did go were rewarded with a John Moncur stonker and our first win of the season. This very timely morale booster sparked a run of three wins and two draws in five League matches: two Julian Dicks penalties beat Everton; Ludo's first clean sheet got us a point at Southampton, and a Cottee goal saw all three gathered at Wimbledon. Finally there seemed to be a bit of light at the end of the tunnel.

Michael Hughes had by now been lured back from Strasbourg to add a bit of balance down the left and, despite not scoring, Iain Dowie was providing some necessary muscle up front. The one time boo-boy target got off the mark in a 1-1 draw against Blackburn, and a week later went one better with the only goal of the game dominated by Sheffield Wednesday at Hillsborough (don't you just love it when that happens). A string of fine performances soon forced many Hammers' fans to concede that perhaps Dowie was doing OK. The longer the season went on the more and more Dowie's fortunes seemed to mirror that of the team as a whole. So much so that Redknapp picked him as his Hammer of the Year (he was runner-up to Julian as it turned out). He's actually turned out to be wiser investment than Railtrack, and I reckon that you'd be hard pressed to find a better pound for pound buy anywhere during the last year.

A Wembley appearance in the Coca Cola Cup Final had disappeared after a sloppy defeat at the Dell, and the unbeaten League run came to an inglorious end when Milosevic finally came good for Aston Villa with a hat-trick in their 4-1 win at Upton Park. Still, next up were Bolton, and a 3-0 win was capped by Danny Williamson running the length of the pitch in the last minute to score one of the finest individual goals I've ever seen. If that was one of our best away wins for a few years, it was followed by a handful of our worst. We went three down inside the first half hour at Blackburn (Shearer amassed seven against us in '95), saw Dicks go in goal after Miklosko was sent off at Everton, and then had Juhnino rip the defence to shreds at Middlesbrough.

However, our improved home form kept us out of the bottom three and there was further good news when it was announced Santa Claus was bringing us a couple of new players, both of whom would have to be kept wrapped up until - as it turned out - well into the New Year. Unfortunately the 'traditional' big freeze brought the inevitable postponements. But can someone explain why clubs and referees collude in such an irresponsible fashion when the thermometer drops below zero? The calling off of our Boxing Day game at noon was nothing short of scandalous.

We kicked off '96 with the sort of farce that we'd hoped was a thing of the past. Remember Les' appearance up front at Highbury! Well, Miklosko's sending off at Everton resulted in a one match ban that couldn't be served because of the weather. Ludo, now set to miss our New Year bash at Maine Road, was due to be replaced by Les, who somehow crocked himself. Ian Feuer meanwhile (our only other senior 'keeper) had been sold just before Christmas, which left the boss with somewhat of a crisis between the sticks. Redknapp tried to sign someone as cover but League spokesman Mike Foster was too busy playing golf to be interested in West Ham's problems, so youth team keeper Neil Finn became the Premiership's youngest ever player. Two Niall Quinn goals against one by Ian Dowie ensured Finn didn't become the youngest player ever to earn a win bonus though... Redknapp's eventual response to was to go to the other extreme and sign Peter Shilton (who is almost old enough to be Finn's GRANDAD) on loan.

January began as a frustrating month. Three consecutive defeats in the League saw us slide down the table, and we were prevented from signing Romanian Ilie Dumitrescu thanks to petty interference by the PFA and Department of Employment. Despite the Dumitrescu situation (which was to drag on for days, weeks, months... until changes were made in the rules themselves), good news was just around the corner. Three points from a crucial win at home to fellow League strugglers Coventry, Croation Slaven Bilic finally getting his papers cleared and the news that Harry had blagged Portugese wonderboy Dani on loan from Sporting Lisbon meant January ended on a happier note. Dani's film star looks might have caused Iain Dowie a few sleepless nights had the pair of them been in competition for most handsome footballer of the year, but since it was a place in West Ham's first team at stake, Dowie was not going to be intimidated. Even though Dani bagged the winner and headlines away at Tottenham in the fans' favourite match of the season, the more significant contribution was from new centre back Slaven Bilic, who in his first proper match for three months gave perhaps the finest debut I have witnessed in more than 20 years of watching football.

Typical of West Ham was that just two days after the excellent win at Spurs, they threw away the other route to Wembley with a performance at Grimsby Town as bad as the Spurs one had been good; still, since many fans are painfully aware of the fluctuations of West Ham's fortunes, most of us travelled up to Grimsby with a sense of foreboding anyway. However, three more points from another derby victory (away to Chelsea) helped ease the embarrassment and rounded off a strange five days.

As Bilic settled in and steadied things at the back, confidence spread throughout the team, and a string of impressive performances put daylight between us and one of the relegation places, culminating in a 4-2 win against one of the teams who'd finally fall, Manchester City. Unlike previous Easters (usually a time for us to hope for resurrection), if survival was not literally certain this time, it did appear that way to most of the players. However much they might deny it, if the players are honest with themselves - and us - they would admit that they were not giving it their all in the last few games. And that could've proved fatal.

Redknapp knows he needs to strengthen his squad and seems to have been given the necessary finances to do so, the signing (s) of strikers (s) Florian Radiciou (and Paulo Futre) show he is in no mood to mess about. He's also determined to push West Ham towards the next Millennium as a recognised Premiership club capable of challenging for Europe. He doesn't want the club constantly looking over their shoulders, selling their top youngsters and making do with rejects, cast-offs and old has-beens. And as well as bringing in the best, Redknapp also has an eye on home-grown talent. The title winning youth team - with the likes of Rio Ferdinand, Frank Lampard junior, Lee Hodges and Lee Boylan - show that the club can produce its own as well as casting the net as far and wide as Australia, America, Croatia, Portugal, Denmark, Romania etc....

West Ham enter season '96-97 more optimistic than at any time in many years. I don't see us pushing Manchester United, Newcastle or Liverpool for the title but one of the cups and a top eight finish are well within grasp.

Fanzine Facts

OTT was started by editor Marc Williams in the summer of 1988, with the help of an Enterprise Allowance Scheme. It has remained a one man op since, but Marc is the first to admit that *OTT* couldn't have survived without the help of Chas the suit, Jonno, Johnny Ingram, Dr H Ball, Peter, James and Darren Webb.

ON THE UP

Brighton and Hove Albion

Down But Not Out

Depressed? Downhearted? Me? No, of course not - why should I be? But as I start to look back over the past nine months: the sale of our ground, the threat of the bulldozers, no club to support next season, pitch invasions, the fact we were relegated being the least of our problems; my heart begins to beat a little faster and my palms grow moist... "Nurse, quick, my pills!"

I missed the first few games (family holiday you understand), but I was still optimistic enough. We enjoyed a very pleasant fortnight in Devon, except the drinking water got contaminated and... sorry, where was I? Like many other Albion fans I seem to be in a very confused frame of mind these days; hopefully I can hold myself together while I complete this review.

Things could be worse!

We lost a couple of games, drew a couple, and then, ah, yes, it was the old Coca Cola. Unfortunately, I missed that particular 'Cup run' (still in Devon!).

News then broke that our ground had been sold, and mild panic ensued. But our kindly chief executive calmed us down, telling us not to worry, he'd arrange for us to play our home games at Pompey next season. Phew! That's alright then!

Our first home win came on September 2nd against Notts County. There was a half time demonstration and some of our supporters had a sit-in on the centre circle. I would have joined them, except I was preoccupied with my Mars Bar, which had melted in my pocket; it was a warm afternoon. Liam Brady came out and chatted with the protesters, and they ambled back to the terrace (another vicious riot quelled at the Goldstone). Sometime around then, the chief executive got all phobic about newspapers with *Evening* and *Argus* in the title.

Bournemouth, one Sunday in September, made lousy TV viewing. We lost 3-1, and on top of that had to watch 'our' fans (?) invade the pitch and wreck the afternoon.

Further defeats and we slipped into 23rd place. I thought, if we try hard enough I'm sure we could make this place our own, somewhere to settle down and feel at home. October continued in a rather miserable vein, losing again and again. "Nurse, bring me my STRONGER medication."

Our home game against Bristol Rovers was strange, as we'd obviously decided that if we couldn't win by fair play and sheer excellent skill, then we'd have to cheat a bit. George Parris started a game of hide and seek with their goalie. George found a really good hiding place behind the goalpost, just off the field of play as it happens, but that doesn't matter does it? Then, just as the goalie rolled the ball out for a little kick, George tiptoed up behind him, nicked the ball and trundled it into the net! Ooh, he cried and cried. Then Denny Mundee had his shorts pulled down, but fortunately he'd remembered to wear a clean pair of pants.

November was a bad month; first Jimmy Case (our player/coach, ex Liverpool and Southampton hard man) retired from playing, and second we only managed a draw at Canvey Island in the FA Cup. Then of course came the big event of the year, my son's sixth birthday party. It went very well, and... sorry, where was I? Oh, the big event, yes, losing 3-0 to Walsall at home, proved to be the final straw for our manager Liam Brady, and we parted company by mutual consent. A sad day for all of us here, eased only by the fact that Jimmy Case took over more or less right away. Having to lose a brilliant manager doesn't hurt so much when another of your old favourites steps in.

Jimmy's first game in charge was a real test: our FA Cup replay against Canvey Island. Hmmm, they're five divisions below us on paper, we should win easily. Unfortunately we don't play on paper (mind you if there is such a pitch in Sussex/Hampshire/Dublin our board's probably looking for a ground share). Fortunately, things went according to plan for once, and we won 4-1, now facing Fulham away in round two.

A fascinating (!) no score draw set up the replay, which to our great excitement was televised live on Sky! Oh, wow. I enthused my daughter into coming, mentioning the thrilling atmosphere and excitement involved in a Cup tie! And sure, we trembled and quivered, but from cold - not excitement. Call me a soft southern girlie, but it was absolutely freezing. The game was awful, no score, boring and very long. As it got to the end of 90 minutes everyone was hoping someone - anyone - would score, saving us the torture of extra time. Unfortunately no goals came, so extra time it was. Of course, being the thoughtful and wonderful mother that I am, and realising my daughter might become ill if she stood in the cold for much longer, I dragged her out of the ground, and we watched the rest of the match at home on Teletext (we don't have Sky). With both cups out of the way (pens = lost), we could concentrate on our League position.

So, with Jimmy Case in charge, had we noticed any changes? Well, one of our players, Peter Smith, had certainly let his hair down. He used to wear his dreads up in a little pony tail, but now it flapped in the breeze. Jimmy himself got quieter, and we didn't see so much of him shouting at referees and linesmen. On the odd occasion he did venture out of his dugout, he'd be clutching a green towel. He reminded me of a small child who wouldn't go anywhere without his security blanket. I expect Jimmy will grow out of it soon.

A few days later we lost away at Shrewsbury, and Jimmy was reported as saying that we were not getting much luck at a time when we needed it. So, after much soul searching and hard thinking, I decided the only thing to do was send him my lucky four leaf clover. (No, I did - really!) That should do it - we'd be alright now.

The Albion unveiled plans for a super-duper new 30,000 all-seater stadium at a local Hove beauty spot called 'Toads Hole Valley'. I had grave doubts as to the viability of packing 30,000 football supporters into a toad's hole. I started to feel as though I was living in a surreal fantasy, and walked around expecting to bump into Ratty and Mole. I decided to go late night Christmas shopping instead of watching us lose 0-2 at home to Chesterfield.

My surreal world continued as I read several of the Albion players had come out in a rash. It turned out to be the fault of the kit man, who having run out of washing powder, used 'Happy Shopper' shampoo to launder the kit. Bet Man United never had that problem...

After Christmas, we won at Brentford (hey, maybe the lucky clover was working?) and we moved into 23rd place in the table. You know where you were there. But wait a minute, somehow or other we won 3-1 at Bradford, and rose majestically to 21st. I felt quite dizzy and required more medication at once. Hopefully we'd soon return to 23rd, where I felt at home.

Ah, it's OK, we're back there again, after we lost at home to Peterborough - nice away shirts lads! Has anyone mentioned 'curtains' to you?

February, and we were on TV again. This time a local documentary type thing. It was very depressing viewing, and didn't give one much hope that there would be a club to support next season. About this time there was also news that the FA wouldn't let us go to Portsmouth unless there were definite plans for a new stadium in Sussex. What would happen? Once again I wrote to our friendly and approachable chief exec. The reassuring reply came back that I wasn't to worry, the club would survive and be successful. Oh good.

Halfway through February, and something very unusual happened - we paid money for a player! Wow, how exciting, it'll be that striker that we've need then, one with some height and weight on him that we've lacked all season. Paul McDonald from Southampton arrived, weighing 10 stone dripping wet, and measuring up at 5'6" (did anyone see that Vic Reeves' 'Boost' ad featuring 'The Whelk'?). Maybe all of him hadn't got here yet, and would be sent under separate cover? *On The Up* went for broke and sponsored him for the rest of the season.

March kicked off with another new signing - good grief, where was all this money coming from, and why wasn't it there earlier? Craig Maskell arrived, also from Southampton. A couple of games later Paul McDonald's season ended as he was stretchered off in our win at Wycombe. We then beat Hull at home 4-0! I must admit, I'd forgotten that great buzz you get after a really good win, and rushed off home to tell the family, even though I knew they wouldn't be interested. In my hurry to park the car I scraped alongside a lamppost and took the paint off my passenger door; never mind, I was still a happy bunny. My husband was delighted to see me so happy, and suggested I support a team that wins more often. I won't tell you my reply to that suggestion!

'Total Football' ran a survey of which fans give their club the best vocal support, and we came... next to bottom. Thank goodness for that, 'our place'. In another poll our attendances were shown to have dropped by 29.3% on last season. That also put us next to bottom in the attendance league. When you find a place to stay, stick there. Next to bottom suited us fine, thanks.

At the end of March, much to our amazement, three new players arrived; this was strangely unsettling when you'd seen the same faces all season. Derek Allen came from Southampton (would you believe it), we borrowed Zeke Rowe from Chelsea, and rather strangely we shelled out for Gary Hobson, a defender from Hull.

At the beginning of April we were away at Swindon, and I thought I'd follow this game on text pages. It didn't prove to be a good evening for me, as I watched it with the 'hold' button down, thereby suppressing the score. I spent ages watching what I thought to be a no score draw, only to release the 'hold' near the end. Blink and it was 2-2, blink again and we'd lost 3-2. It was probably more exciting if you were actually there.

As time marched on, and there was still no definite news about the ground for next season, I could often be found hunched over my telephone, furtively dialling an 0891 number. I began to get addicted to the sultry and sensuous tones of... "Hello, you've called the Seagull line."

Into April, and it was time to vote for the Player of the Season. In my opinion (and subsequently everyone else's too), Ian Chapman was far and away the best. I happily mailed my entry, only to read in the evening paper that he'd been given a free transfer. What?!

Towards the end of April, and with no saviour in sight, I splashed out on tickets for us all to sit in the stand! Why do they call it the stand, when you sit? Anyway, I'd always wanted to 'try it sitting down', and this could be my last chance. It was also the first time I'd brought my son, as I wanted him to remember the Albion. We played Carlisle, and won 1-0. It was very exciting, and also very nice to see Mervyn Day, their manager. I used to have a soft spot for him, many years ago. Hmmm, he'd got a bit plumper, and his hair'd gone grey! I looked down at myself. Hmmm...

The company that now owned the ground offered to let us stay another season for a price. The board for some reason wouldn't agree. We lost away 2-1 to Notts County, and that was it, we were down. Were we down and out, though? However as Jimmy said: "Things could be worse, at least we're playing attractive football." Great! I'll look forward to relegation again next year then!

The offer to let us rent the ground would run out on a Tuesday, and after that the demolition men would be in. I was sure some announcement would be made before the game against York, which for all we knew could be our last game at the Goldstone, and possibly our last game ever. So it came as no surprise when there was a pitch invasion, and people we had never seen before rushed onto the pitch and broke both crossbars. Fearing the bulldozers had arrived a few days early, we were unsure whether to dig up a turf to take home or leave quickly. It was a bit scary and not just for us; apparently the referee was a bit apprehensive when Jimmy Case locked him in his dressing room.

Tuesday morning I listened to the local radio, and an hour before the deadline expired came the great news - the Albion could stay at the Goldstone for one more year! The euphoria soon turned to despair as we realised we'd have to go through the whole thing again next season.

The York game was replayed at 11.00 am on a Thursday morning. We lost of course, sending Carlisle down with us. Sorry Mervyn.

But what's this? Stop Press. Brighton prices announced for '96-97 and terrace tickets start at £8. We're top of the prices league. Top of a league. What?! Oh my word. "Nurse, my pills!"

Fanzine Facts

OTU had a very successful first year at the Goldstone, and with the sad departure of *Gull's Eye* has arguably established itself as the no. 1 fanzine. Editor Paul Libel says "with a name like *On The Up*, the season your club gets relegated, it was bound to come in for stick and that's why it may soon be changing its name." He adds "We've earned our 'cheap and cheerful' tag because we try to always look on the 'Brighton' side of life." Thanks go out to Marc Twibill, Jackie Mooney (review writers), Richard Darlington, Roy Scarborough, James Forbes, Helen Mackenzie, Sarah Glaskin, Louisa Hill, James Waite, Marc Edgar, Graham Sturges, Daniel Roberts, Michael Spillman, Chris Heath, James Camp, D Spair, Tony Bowie, James Fry, Chris Twibill, Paul Sampson, Paul Atkins and many, many others. They are the fanzine.

ONE MORE POINT

Crystal Palace

Following a season of drudgery, conceding few goals but scoring even fewer, to start the campaign with a 4-3 win was something of a shocker. Mind you, we'd almost let a 4-1 lead slip, and something of a trend was set.

The following week, it became apparent that we wouldn't romp this Division as we went down 1-0 at Ipswich, despite the backing of a very noisy Palace turnout. August 26th '95 saw the opening of the impressive new Holmesdale Road stand for the visit of Charlton. Reasonable prices ensured that the stand was packed. Trouble was, the other three sides of the ground were virtually empty! Still, up the road at the New Den, all four sides are empty, so I shouldn't complain! Fittingly, the first goal in front of the new end was a classic. Unfor-

tunately, it was scored by Charlton's Lee Bowyer. Thankfully, normality was restored, and a second half equaliser ensured our long unbeaten run against our former tenants remained intact.

A run of mediocre performances, mainly draws, confirmed my belief that the Division was very even, but pretty poor in quality. Games at Selhurst were becoming a drag to attend, as fans started directing abuse at Noades and the management team, as we meekly surrendered yet another three points. While not on the same scale as the Chase or Swales Out campaigns, there was increasing discontent, and at some stage, fans started to divide into pro- and anti-Noades factions. Meanwhile, the playing squad had been bolstered by the signing of Gareth Taylor from Bristol Rovers, and the skilful high-scoring Dougie Freeman from Barnet. We were at least trying to play classy football, but ultimately, results weren't coming, and frustration grew. The shotgun sale of crowd favourite Iain Dowie to West Ham didn't help, and was a big blow, and the cryptic remarks in the programme suggested there was more to this deal than met the eye.

The televised win at Port Vale suggested we'd turned the corner, but a defeat at home to Millwall the following week nipped any optimism in the bud. This game was particularly galling as I'd failed miserably in my attempts to pull at The Zone nightclub in Gillingham the night before, and I needed cheering up. Seeing ex-Palace boys Bowry and Newman do so well while our new-season signing Andy Roberts had yet another poor 90 minutes was terrible. This really was the low point of the season for me.

Another appearance on the box at Southend turned out to be something of a watershed. An abysmal first half display led to saddening scenes of Palace fans from opposing sides of the Noades In and Out debate come to blows.

While results were at times disappointing, the performances were encouraging, and at least some cohesion was becoming evident. Annoyingly, Palace threw away a 2-0 lead at home to Oldham, in what was to be the last game in the Palace career of Welsh International Chris Coleman. It was an unfitting end for this popular player; however, on reflection, it was noticeable that his heart wasn't in it, and a move was probably in everyone's interest. A 2-1 win at Stoke saw Freedman score again, and Gareth Taylor finally break his duck, much to the surprise of the loyal following who'd braved a freezing day. Typically, having had so many beers before the game, I was having trouble focusing on the pitch, and actually missed the goal, even though I was standing on the terrace! Equally typically, we were forced to suffer unnecessary stress, as Stoke scored neared the end to leave us praying for the whistle.

It wasn't to be the last time that we wished a game would finish either, as we were making a habit of seeing two and three goal leads chipped away, but then a string of draws stretched our unbeaten run, although we seemed to be forever stuck in 15th place.

Following another draw, this time 0-0 at Charlton in February, there came what was to be the most significant move of the season. Dave 'Harry' Bassett was appointed first team boss. Fans were initially sceptical, despite Harry's claims that the long ball game would not be introduced. Another 0-0, this time against his former club Sheffield United, did little to appease the doubters. However, the Bassett magic started to work the following week, with a 4-0 win over Watford, and three days later with a stunning 3-2 victory at Tranmere, having been 2-0 down at one stage of the game. A run of wins soon followed, including a 5-0 over Grimsby which featured an 11-minute hat-trick from Freedman to set a club record. Players like Houghton, Ndah and Dyer noticeably improved during this period, as Palace shot up from 17th to third in little over a month. Blimey - all of a sudden it looked like we could make automatic promotion!

The highlight of this spell was undoubtedly our 'doing' of Millwall, in which Nigel Martyn elevated himself to god status with a first half penalty save. From being up against it for the whole of the first 45 minutes, we came storming back, and when George Ndah scored with an audacious overhead kick to make the score 4-1, it was symbolic of both clubs' seasons: Palace starting poorly then coming good in the end, while for Millwall it was the exact opposite. That afternoon it was great to be a Palace fan, that is, until we had to walk back to South Bermondsey station. Lesson One in visiting the New Den: If your team wins 4-1, then you'd better have a get-away helicopter parked right outside the away end!

The televised penultimate game of the season at second placed Derby was basically a promotion shoot-out. Whoever won would be favourites to automatically join Sunderland in the Premiership. Derby got off to a stormer, scoring almost immediately, but on-loan Kenny Brown popped up to equalise just three minutes later to set up a potential classic. Inevitably, the game settled down, and although we played well, Derby secured the win mid-way through the second half to go up. Oh well - at least the walk back to the station would be less hazardous!

The final game against Norwich was truly memorable; not for the football, but for the scenes which followed the announcement of Millwall's relegation. Brilliant!!

So, it was down to SE7 to face Charlton in the play-off semi's. After a week of arguments about ticket allocations, the tie finally got underway. Within 55 seconds, Norwegian defender Leif Andersen attempted Own Goal of the Season with a spectacular diving header. Despite Martyn's parry, Charlton's Newton was on hand to poke it home. Not quite the start we wanted! Thankfully, the second half saw a drastic transformation, and we got two back to take a goal lead into the second leg. This time round, the tie was killed off with a great strike from Houghton, and Palace were off to Wembley.

We were favourites for the final against Leicester, but they'd won at Palace only a few weeks previously, and we knew that this one would be close. Much was made of Bassett's great record as a promotion specialist, and I for one hoped it would continue. Our Player of the Year Andy Roberts opened the scoring early, and although Leicester made the running, as the first half went on it looked like it might just be enough. It wasn't. Leicester continued to pour forward, and on 77 minutes won a penalty, which Parker slotted home. Thirteen minutes from promotion and now we had to score again. I was drained. In extra time Leicester were the better team, and as time ran out I just knew we'd lose if it went to penalties. I prayed for the game to be settled in open play. It was, but unfortunately it was Claridge and Leicester who responded to my prayers.

I was so depressed that I couldn't even be bothered to stick around to drown my sorrows. Still, at least I got back in time to watch the Dr Who film on the telly!

Fanzine Facts

One More Point started in September '93, after Palace had failed to avoid relegation by that margin. Editor Cris Lehmann says that after the season just gone, he's considering renaming it *Two More Seconds*.

ONE-NIL DOWN TWO-ONE UP

Arsenal

It started with a miss. After all the hype surrounding the arrival of Bruce Rioch, David Platt and Dennis Bergkamp, Sunday August 20th 1995 couldn't come quickly enough for Gooners still traumatised by the events of '94-95. Could the new men galvanise an ageing team? Would Bruce lead the Arsenal to the Promised Land? And was Eddie Mc-Goldrick still around and, if so, why?

On the evidence of the opening match with born-again Boro, the answer to the first two questions was a resounding "well, perhaps. Or, then again, perhaps not." A dour encounter saw Wright open his account and Nick Barmby return to plague us, but as the faithful filed out into the warm streets it was 'ho hum, here we go again' rather than 'hi-ho, silver lining.' Things had to improve.

The 2-0 win at Goodison a few days later looked like the start of something big, with Wright and Platt doing the damage. Expectations for the Coventry match were never greater and legions descended on Highfield Road to witness a Championship campaign in its lusty infancy. We were on the march with Brucie's army...

Oh, dear. This was probably the worst football match ever played anywhere by anyone. A few disquieting aspects about the team had already become apparent. Dennis Bergkamp was the obvious one. He'd flutter onto the pitch like a Cabbage White butterfly and thereafter flit innocuously from one mildly diverting situation to the next with a kind of languid grace. "Was he a lot of money well spent?" we asked ourselves. Was the future really orange? Not on the evidence of his showing at Coventry, for sure.

Nigel Winterburn was (and still is) a problem too. He's been a marvellous club servant for the Arsenal, but time seems to be tugging his shirt more insistently these days and it gets embarrassing when a desperate ball-boy, heading for the bogs, flashes past our No. 3 as he's making a 'run' down the left. We left Coventry with a fab 0-0, of course.

Then there is the moot question of Platt's radar. Legend has it that Dave's outstanding ability in life is to surge (great verb) late into the box and score priceless goals. Well, he did do that a few times over the season, most notably against Forest, but a more typical characteristic is his inability to pass accurately to a team-mate. He finds opponents with unerring precision; thumps advertising hoardings with monotonous regularity; bombards the fans in Row Z of the West Stand as if his life depends on it. Arsenal scientists are working hard to solve the problem but it was still very much in evidence during Euro 96, when his cameo in the Switzerland game included a 'pass' which exactly bisected four team mates and thumped an advertising hoarding. Houston (Stewart), we have a problem, although a lengthy absence through injury spared us many blushes.

The season flared briefly with the visit of Southampton, traditional British beef to the Highbury incinerators. The pessimists were by now despairing of Bergkamp ever bulging the net, but the Dutchman found his range on this occasion with a lolly-sweet volley and a 25-yard shot on the run into the top right hand corner. Oh joy that day it was to be alive and in the East Stand! Seven matches unbeaten and next up were the floppy-eared quadrupeds at Stamford Bridge.

We should have known. Rioch tinkered with the formation that had annihilated the Saints and decided John Jenson was the man to do what John Jenson does so well - although no one currently existing on the planet had a clue what this is. Cue a predictable defeat, and as we don't want ever to mention the dismal Dane again in connection with our lovely club, suffice to say he left us early in '96, having contributed one goal in the best part of three seasons.

October saw a couple of excellent victories over Leeds (3-0) and Villa (2-0) and ended with a trip to Burnden Park which Sky, in its wisdom, decided to screen on a Monday night. Sometimes you just know that fate has it in for you. Bolton would have had problems beating a primary school XI but they nevertheless notched a first half strike and spent the rest of the game denying furious Arsenal attacks and, come the end, a deserved three points for the Gunners. Suffice to say, Manchester United were beaten 1-0 in the very next game, evidence of the inconsistency which was to plague us all season.

Rioch was getting a few good results, no doubt about it, but his efforts to make Arsenal play a passing game were not bearing such rich fruit as we'd hoped for. Rumours circulated saying that a number of senior players were unimpressed with the new gaffer's approach and that there were 'tantrums' in the dressing room. Ordinary fans take these things with a pinch of salt, although ordinary Arsenal fans do not take 2-1 defeats by the auld enemy with anything like equanimity. Despite playing their best 20 minutes of football of the season, and with Bergkamp plundering a brilliant goal, Arsenal capitulated and Spurs ran out 2-1 winners.

This kind of infuriating result dogged the Gunners throughout the remainder of '95, 'climaxing' with a 3-1 home defeat by Wimbledon on December 30th which showed clearly how Joe Kinnear had tactically outwitted Rioch. Adams had also been lost to injury and was not to play again during the season, a severe blow which the loss of Bould a few days later at Newcastle only exacerbated.

Still, there was always the Cups, and the Gunners had made good progress in the Coca Cola trophy, beating Newcastle 2-0 on January 10th to set up a semi-final with Villa. The 1-1 draw with Sheffield United at Highbury in the FA Cup on January 6th had just been one of those embarrassing blips that sometimes happen to the best of us, and the replay at Bramall Lane would see natural superiority triumph and harmony prevail in London N5. And the rest! Sheffield, under the revivifying influence of Howard Kendall, won 1-0 (shades of Bolton) and we were out, all the more galling for having fallen at the same stage to Millwall the previous season. The League was similarly anti-climatic, with a 1-2 home defeat by Everton on January 20th and an atrocious 1-1 with Coventry on February 3rd (God we hate Coventry!).

The first leg of the Coca Cola semi-final at Highbury began well enough, with Bergkamp putting the Gunners 2-0 up, and all the signs pointing to a handsome victory which would see us marching up Wembley Way in pursuit of another trophy. Naturally, then, Villa were allowed to pull back the deficit and a fortnight later we spent two hours trying to score with the likes of Morrow, Linighan and Hillier in the team. The 0-0 result sent the Villa fans into pitch-invading raptures and much unpleasantness ensued. Most unpleasant of all, however, was the fact that we'd been dumped from a final without losing a game. It's enough to make you want to call Esther Rantzen.

After this major disappointment, the season trundled down an increasingly forlorn road with only qualification for the UEFA Cup at stake. Newcastle's title ambitions were dealt a major blow in their 2-0 Highbury defeat on March 23rd and it's a fair bet that we're not the most popular club on Tyneside. Ah, well, we're not popular anywhere, not even at Highbury sometimes, especially when we take three points from a possible 12 in the UEFA countdown, including a defeat at Hillsborough (God, we hate Sheffield!) to a team that has re-defined the word 'appalling'.

So it all came down to a clash with Bolton, already relegated, to determine whether or not we'd be meeting our European brethren next season. Arsenal being Arsenal, they went 0-1 down, the situation rescued by Platt (who'd been told to aim for an advertising board) and Bergkamp, who blasted a stunner from 20 yards. Symbolic really. The two new boys had saved the day and, according to some, Bruce's bacon. It wasn't convincing but it'd worked.

After eight years of George Graham it was odd to go through a season in which he wasn't at the helm. The considered opinion of *One-Nil Down, Two-One Up* is that Bruce Rioch is out of his depth at this level and blood-curdling stories from the dressing room in the season's latter stages support this view - if they're true, of course. Arsenal needs a true leader if the club is to prosper and '96-97 will test Rioch's mettle - let's hope he's up to it.

Fanzine Facts

One-Nil Down, Two-One Up was launched in December 1987, the brainchild of Tony Willis and Ally Wolfendale. Its name is derived from the events surrounding the 1987 Littlewoods Cup campaign, when the Gunners came back from 1-0 down in both the semi-final and the final to win 2-1. *ONDTOU*'s first issue contained an interview with Charlie Nicholas and a seminal piece by Jeff King on 'The Cult of the Manager'. "The smart-arse, pseudo-intellectual tone was set right from the beginning", according to Mike Collins, co-editor and writer of the above piece, who joined at issue three. Never using one word where a paragraph will do, it now sells 4,500 copies per issue to Arsenal supporters sceptical of the anodyne dross in the programme. New writing stars Chas Newkey-Burden and Sarah Doyle are continuing the rich vein of destructive sarcasm copyrighted by the magazine, and the contributors hope to continue taking the piss for the foreseeable future.

ONE TEAM IN BRISTOL

Bristol City

We Beat The Gas 4-2

As the new season started in August, we could still somehow hear the now infamous words of our year-old board, promising us "Premiership football within 2-5 years and European football within 10 years." But it was difficult to accept, as we seemed to be taking the scenic route to the top. We were still trying to come to terms with the fact that we'd been relegated only a few months earlier, and realising we would be trudging off in all weathers to Chesterfield, Carlisle and Crewe instead of assembling gantries for Sky TV.

During the close season however we had acquired a new board member, a youthful (in comparison to the others) Scott Davidson, former backing musician for bands including Bros

and The Pet Shop Boys. He now owned a local newspaper and rumours spread that he had a £1m to buy players with. The main problem was the lack of a goal scorer, made worse by the fact that nearby Swindon had purloined our previous season's top scorer for a tribunal-agreed figure of £475,000. Earlier, manager Joe Jordan had turned down £800,000 from Millwall saying it was not enough. So as the new season arrived we wondered who would be firing the shots. Our two strikers came from Australia (that footballing hot-bed); we weren't filled with optimism.

As many fanzine editors will tell you, we usually miss the first couple of minutes of each game in favour of the chance of a much-needed sale to any latecomers, however nobody could have imagined the welcome we would get to life in Endsleigh Two. After only 15 seconds Blackpool's Jimmy Quinn smashed any illusions that this was going to be a stroll in the park. The game ended 1-1.

After struggling to beat Colchester in a penalty shoot-out in the Coca Cola, we won our first League game at home to Stockport. We'd started with back-to-back home fixtures due to Crewe's inability to get their eight row stand ready in time for August - the game was eventually played in a blizzard. We travelled to Shrewsbury mid-table, but in sight of the leaders with a game in hand. The first half performance had us drooling; we ran the proverbial rings around them and came off at half time 1-0 up (should've been at least three). Things looked rosy for us; our Aussie duo had already scored six times and the local press delighted in their new-found puns such as Wizards of Oz. Original, eh?

The Championship looked ours, but what happened in that dressing room at half time is still a mystery. In a case that would surely fascinate 'Spooky Mulder', our silky footballing machine was abducted and replaced by an outfit that capitulated totally. In the space of 15 minutes, bottom spot Shrewsbury had put four past us. The slump had started.

The next Saturday we travelled to Peterborough and watched our new £200,000 ex Gas Head defender Richard Dryden (seemingly still playing for our hated rivals) make one of many costly mistakes throughout the season to gift Boro a goal. Goalkeeper Welch was carried off with two broken bones in his back and another summer signing, the ageing Alan McLeary, was also a stretcher victim and subsequently ruled out for three months. Another super strike by Seal gained us a 1-1 draw.

Chairman Russe stepped down due to business commitments and Mike Fricker took over the reins. The board showed just how out of touch they were when they announced that they'd budgeted for a break-even attendance figure of 9,500. We were now losing £10,000 a week and Brighton - even more strapped than us - plundered a 1-0 win from the Gate. Crowds were going down, our Aussie sharpshooters had long since ran out of ammo, we were now in the bottom three and sinking fast.

At least a plum tie in the Coke Cup brought a little respite from our depressing League form. Kevin Keegan gave us the courtesy of fielding a full strength side and the Geordies proceeded to administer a football lesson. Never out of second gear, Newcastle coasted through a game that saw Ginola save our 'keeper from a red card after he'd handled outside the box; he was obviously happy to let him stay on as the Magpies compiled their five goals to our nil.

It was now over four games since we'd troubled the scorers and despite have loanee Dykstra from QPR between the sticks, we still went 2-0 behind to Notts County at their place, before the Aussie boys rediscovered their aim and inspired us to a draw.

Before our next game there was time for a bit of swapsies in the transfer market as the unpopular Ian Baird was sent packing to Plymouth in return for Kevin Nugent. Baird had been dropped ever since his two fingered salute to City fans during a pre-season game against Chelsea; by all accounts he was pissed off at the stick he got for being crap in front of goal and his attempt to decapitate Gullit. Then, as only football managers can, Jordan dropped eight goals in 12 games Seal for lack of work-rate. What?! Still, this keen tactical nous that the average fan can only dream about worked wonders as we walloped exactly ZERO goals past Wycombe.

Thank God for Hull City! The reward for the losers of our encounter was the honour of being bottom of the pile and even we managed to stuff four past them - more than we'd managed in the previous 810 minutes.

Now when the local media described our away win against York as "impressive", it really made us appreciate how far the club had sunk; an outfit of our size should murder them every time, especially with our financial clout... If only! By now, redundancies in the admin. department were being made in a bid to save money, but sadly, the hatchet men didn't look as far as the dressing-room when they were making their cut-backs.

The season sort of meandered aimlessly towards the end of the year when the scent of a local derby started to focus everyone's attention. December 30th, 1995 was to be Judgement Day. When it arrived the weather had decided to throw a spanner in the works and decimate the whole football programme. So you can imagine our surprise when at 11.30am the Ashton Gate pitch was passed fit. Ninety minutes later as most of Bristol descended upon our ground, the game was called off due to ice in the stands. Oh Bollocks! Even worse, at 4.45pm the pools panel gave it as an away win - that *couldn't* be right, could it?

With our New Year's Day game also called off, we could at least stretch a mini unbeaten run up until the rearranged derby on Tuesday January 16th. This turned out to be one of the darkest nights for City, as rumours were rife that the stuck for cash board had sold tickets twice and were allowing money to be taken at the turnstiles. And they looked to have had some substance too. An hour before kick-off the ground was already over-full, with fuming season and match ticket holders stranded outside and demanding to get in. Well, the pushing turned into a crush as the gates were forced open, leaving a lady steward with a broken leg as thousands more tried every conceivable way to get in. Most surprising was the reaction of the police who seemed disinterested, but at least chairman Scott came out of the shambles with some credit as he tried to sort things out throughout the game. It was estimated that the 20,000 capacity was breached by at least 4,000 and a further 6,000 were locked outside. The only small consolation was that in this total chaos, the 2-0 defeat by the enemy went by almost unnoticed!

However, the team were affected and we lost a further couple of games on the bounce before Jordan turned to David Seal to sort out the lack of goals. And what d'ya know, after ten minutes of his return he scored against Bournemouth to instil the boys with renewed confidence that culminated in a 3-0 pasting of Brighton at the Goldstone Ground. We were now in 11th place and the talk was not of debt, but an overlapping run to the play-offs.

Now, is it just us being paranoid or do clubs who appoint a new manager always choose to do so just before they play Bristol City, getting so fired up in the process that they're odds on to piss on our bonfire? Jan Molby breezed into Swansea just as City turned off the M4... we should have just kept going round the roundabout and headed straight back to England. And then Burnley wandered down to Bristol complete with Adrian Heath as new boss, and sure as eggs are eggs they left with all the points.

Consequently the build-up for the return derby wasn't great, and the laughable 1,200 tickets they allocated us were snapped up within hours. Saturday March 16th 1996 was a day to remember for years to come. It was one for the grandchildren, as our hastily made T shirts testified, proudly announcing "We Beat The Gas 4-2." In fact we not only beat them, we out-sang them, outplayed them and ensured that their play-off dreams were shattered. It was hilarious to see John Ward on TV, seemingly swallowing something sharp and jagged as he desperately tried to grasp anything from the game, finally proclaiming "Well, over the two games it was 4-4." If we are being petty, Johnny boy, WE WON ON AWAY GOALS!

Our outside chance of a play-off never really gathered the required momentum and we are left to reflect on a season that will be remembered for the appointment of a new chairman who has given us fresh hope, and for our famous victory at Trumpton Park. Now that the rent boys have been evicted from their latest squat, they will never be able to avenge the fearful mauling they received that afternoon.

Fanzine Facts

One Team In Bristol has now been going for four years and is still the only City fanzine. It has a small staff of dedicated workers and additional contributors including Robbo the Editor, Andrew Jefferson, Smiffy, Clevedon Codger, Dave, Jim, The Robin, Wiggy, Elliot, Martin, Julia and Johnny K. Robbo says "As the established fanzine we are frequently invited to discuss local football matters on radio and television, and we have a good relationship with the club itself."

Sorry mate can't help, we have a contract to supply Mr Ward and Mr Ward only!

THE ONION BAG

Chester City

"The Football League season is a half-marathon, not a sprint." Hmmm. Maybe not precisely what some wiseacre once said but, based on Chester City's '95-96 season, it bloody well should have been. Top of Division Three in December, scoring a ruck load of goals and playing some damn fine togger to boot it seemed the side were inexorably heading for promotion to maintain their reputation for being a yo-yo club. Sad to say, no sooner had the midnight chimes rung in the New Year than Chester capitulated "Devon Lock" style to slump so horrifically they couldn't even make a play-off berth. Shrugging off the disappointment of missing out on a chance to secure that elusive first Wembley appearance, supporters wondered how Chester could undergo such a topsy-turvy season? Let's have a look through the arched window shall we...?

As fans idled away the hot summer months in the park, trampling over prostrate loving couples in pursuit of errant Frisbees, Kevin Ratcliffe prepared unobtrusively for his first full season in management. In truth his hands were tied. Bound by a tight budget and contractual agreements that meant he had to retain the majority of a team relegated so abysmally the previous campaign, Kev invested modestly in his squad. The new faces included Touché-Turtle lookalike Dave Rogers (Tranmere), Neil Fisher (a cast-off from Bolton), rather surprisingly the veteran ex-England and former "Three Degrees" hearthrob Cyrille Regis (Wycombe) and lastly goalie Billy Stewart (Northampton). Mind you, Billy could scarcely fall into this category. Having already amassed in excess of 270 appearances for Chester during a lengthy first spell at the club, he would only have qualified as a 'new face' had he endured extensive treatment under the scalpel of Michael Jackson's cosmetic surgeon.

So, it was with relatively low expectations that Hartlepool arrived at the Deva in August for the big kick-off. It was hardly the most auspicious of starts. In spite of a 2-0 victory (an ecclesiastical double from Messrs Priest and Bishop no less) Chester struggled against a side denied a clear penalty and later reduced to ten men. Worst still, Roger Preece, all smiles before kick-off when he picked up his '94-95 Player of the Year award, sustained a knee injury that was to rule him out for the season - that perennial old thug Mick Tait responsible, you won't be surprised to learn.

Matters quickly perked up though. Wigan, who effectively fielded a Chester Reject XI, were dispatched emphatically in a Coca Cola grudge match before City embarked on an unexpectedly joyous autumn goal-scoring romp which saw Plymouth, Lincoln, Torquay, Scunthorpe, Darlington, Rochdale and Mansfield all suffer in the goals against column. Obviously not everything was sweetness and light. There was inevitably the odd hiccough and, hell, the home defeat by Doncaster descended into the sort of unremitting tedium reserved only for a Chris De Burgh album, but generally speaking no-one was complaining. Most people were too busy pinching themselves as Chester enjoyed the privilege of basking in the limelight with fellow promotion rivals Preston and Gillingham.

If the lofty position was surprising, the manner of victory was often quite staggering. Crikey. Crisp inter-passing! Slick counter-attacking! Calmness and maturity on the ball! Was this *really* Chester? Although September had seen the arrival of rock-star wannabee Nick Richardson (Bury) and winger Kevin Noteman (Doncaster), much of the credit lay with Eddie Bishop and "Big Cyrille." Eddie was an unlikely hero. Suggesting that even he thought he was past his best, he had relinquished full-time status to concentrate on a career in welding. Sensationally he started the season like a house on fire. Lashing in six goals in his first five games he intriguingly attributed his early success to finding a new girlfriend. Even when he missed the Hereford game with a groin strain (no doubt attributable to that self-same girlfriend rather than all the thunderous tackles he'd been putting in), he still couldn't be kept out of the action and burst into the PA's office to shout out across the tannoy system "Come on ref! Open your eyes man!" when the match official chose inexplicably not to award a blatant spot-kick. He missed punishment because the ref claimed to have heard nothing for the boos from the City fans! Tremendous. And what can we say of Cyrille Regis? Destined surely to be the only City player to hail from Mariapousoula, French Guyana, here at last, albeit at 37, was that colossus of a centre-forward that fans had prayed for - that someone who could hold the ball up. With his power, strength and aerial ability he brought the best out of strike partner Andy Milner and was a dream of a target man for playmakers Chris Priest, Neil Fisher, Kevin Noteman and the barely recognisable, so much had he improved, David Flitcroft. When Cyrille crashed home an awesome header against Plymouth (to commence re-payment of the five he netted for Coventry against the lads back in 1985) the cheer virtually took the roof off. An instant cult-hero, Cyrille won so many Man-of-the-Match awards we assumed he was tempted to enter the champagne retailing business.

By the start of January however, just like the best of dreams, things were poised to turn horribly sour. The signs were already there. City's solitary hard-tackling midfielders, Bishop and Flitcroft, had by now joined Preece in spending the remainder of the season on crutches drawing the half-time Cash Bonanza ticket; their silky skill and fancy-flick-merchant colleagues, having seen the lush swards replaced by cloying mud, had decided they didn't want to get their shorts dirty; and Iain Jenkins, facing a lengthy lay-off after a car crash, was proving impossible to replace at right-back. Worst still, Big Cyrille was finding the winter chill was taking its toll, which would herald the return of Stuart Rimmer. Stu maybe the clubs' record scorer - over 120 goals, you know - but nowadays, with his pace long gone, was as likely to be shoulder-barged off the ball by Lena Zavaroni as by a burly centre-half. Then, to cap it all, the weather and the fixture card combined to ensure Chester had an unremitting diet of demoralising trips down south in foul weather as the waterlogged Deva Stadium was only capable of hosting one game in 50 days.

Sure enough, one win in nine games set the ball rolling. Nagging doubt set in as Stuey, bless his heart, proved a predictably hopeless replacement in the No. 9 shirt despite putting in the proverbial 110% and scuffing in a few flukey goals. With the confidence visibly draining away, City nose-dived down the table. The dispiriting run continued unabated through Easter to much wailing and gnashing of teeth. Thumping wins over woeful Cardiff and Scarborough sides, coupled with the signing of full-back Ross Davidson (Sheff Utd), couldn't stop the rot and Chester finally gave up the ghost when they failed to win any of their three precious rearranged home games. Eighth place it was ultimately to be. And thus, lying just two points off the play-offs and aware of City's vastly superior goal difference, fans could only ruefully reflect on occasions such as the needless corner leading to Exeter's 95th minute equaliser or Fisher's missed penalty on a glue-pot pitch at Lincoln where those priceless points were lost. Pah!

Enough self-pitying and what of the cups? Reward for the aforementioned immensely enjoyable slaying of Wigan was a two-legged tie pitted against the mighty Spurs. Chester predictably got stuffed (7-1) but, in spite of inadvertently kickstarting Chris Armstrong's career by goading him into scoring two goals thanks to cries of "Wrexham Reject", the trip to London was well worth the effort if only to chalk up a new ground and listen to the sexy, sultry voice of the women on the PA (even if it got a bit wearing by the time the fourth went in). Just a shame that 1,500 fans couldn't make the similar journey to Gillingham three months later for a game that *really* mattered. On to the Auto-Shield thingamajig which was even more lowkey than usual and consisted of an exit at the preliminary stage courtesy of a home defeat to eventual winners Rotherham (they seemed bloody awful at the time) and a creditable draw with Burnley. The FA Cup draw provided further disappointment considering that the unfamiliar names of Blyth and Spennymoor were still in the velvet bag by the time Blackpool's ball came out to enforce a familiar visit to the sadly now decrepit Bloomfield Road. At least Andy Milner's late header sparked off the most exuberant goal celebrations of the season - a rather frenzied imitation of the entire 633 squadron. It was just a shame about the Seasiders scoring two pigsickeners in the last minute. Twats!

Briefly a mention for the key Chester personnel. Kevin Ratcliffe, even at the club's zenith, never really won himself over with the fans who still recall the petty exchange of gestures and harsh words during the previous year's lamentable campaign. There may have been the odd "Kevin Ratcliffe's Blue'n'White Army" from what seldom constituted more than a blue'n'white platoon at away games, but that was about it. On one occasion though he leaped up enormously in fans estimation. With three crucial home points against Rochdale about to slip away skipper Peter Jackson become embroiled in a fracas with the visitors' dug-out. Jacko duly departed for an early bath but Kev joined in the ongoing mêlée to, depending on your eyewitness, push, kick, punch or garrotte the 'Dale boss John Docherty. He still awaits the FA rap for his ill-discipline but laughed off the incident by expressing his wish that the players had shown as much commitment as the two dug-outs. Quite right. Player of the Year eventually went to Peter Jackson for his stalwart efforts at centrehalf though he must have jeopardised his chances late on with an abysmal showing in goal versus Orient. Replacing Billy Stewart, dismissed for a professional foul that warranted purple not red, he put up the most unconvincing display of kicking and handling ever witnessed between the sticks and let in a Colin West shot that frankly your brittle-boned great grandmother would have held comfortably. Pushing Jacko close for star man was Chris Priest - a tireless performer and joint top scorer with Stuart Rimmer. Undoubtedly Chris is the club's greatest asset and won't be staying around long if he shows a bit more consistency in front of the posse of scouts that are perpetually watching. And finally, another mention for the veteran Cyrille Regis. Admired by both sets of fans (except at Cambridge, strangely enough, where he was repeatedly referred to as a part of the female anatomy and, hey, we're not talking fallopian tubes here) he was simply a revelation - when his body allowed him to play that is. As a Born-Again Christian we only hope God's decreed he's got one more season in him before he becomes a full-time bible basher.

To summarise - an enjoyable season (two facts for Statto: City, somewhat flatteringly, were the only team to beat Darlington on their travels and it was also the first time no-one achieved the double over Chester since '74-75! Cor!) and certainly a year which justified the theory that if club's like Chester haven't got the cash then they're better off in the Third. Just a pity it was such an anticlimax. Next season maybe it won't be so arse-about-tit.

Fanzine Facts

The Onion Bag (whose name was exploited later by a national satirical football mag) first started out in the autumn of 1988, when it was primarily preoccupied with a Chester and District Sunday League Section 'C' side called Dee Rangers with proceeds going to buying the lads a well-earned new kit. By the start of the '90-91 season however, realising the scope for mickey-taking a handful of footballing nonentities was rather restrictive (let alone esoteric in the extreme), editor Jon Wainwright began to harbour ambitions of selling the Bag to a wider audience. As a lifelong fan, Chester City were the obvious target. Fortunately the club's only fanzine at the time, 'Hello Albert', was edited by a vicar (seriously) and was thus somewhat toned-down by nature. Seeing the niche for a raucous, controversial, and politically-incorrect alternative *OB* hit the terraces away at Wigan. John says "He is desperate for new contributors" so come on you Chester faithful - take up thy pen.

OVER LAND AND SEA

West Ham United

The seven days between February 12th to 18th can readily sum up the season for Harry's Hammers. Why? Well, who else could reach such heights yet sink so low in the same week?

Monday was White Hart Lane, with another of our famous Monday night live matches. We put on a show for the cameras, completely out-classed Totts and came away with three points. On the Saturday the team went to Stamford Bridge and took the piss there as well. Again three points; again some very stupid looking London rival fans.

But, here's the catch: on the Wednesday night between the two, the Hammers showed their true colours. You've got to support them to understand what I mean. Grimsby Town - Cleethorpes: cold, wet and fishy (and that's in the middle of August). You can imagine what a February night was like. West Ham, on the back of that outstanding victory at White Shite Lane looked hot favourites to go through to the fifth round of the FA Cup, with the prospect of facing Chelsea at Upton Park. Well, you don't have to be Einstein to work out what happened next; even Andy Gray could've probably got it right. Yes, the Happy Hammers soaked up every possible pressure, before their class told and they steamed their way through poor bedraggled Grimsby... and lost 3-0!

It might be funny to some, but to the few hundred of us up there, it was a complete waste of a night out. And you'd have thought that we could at least take comfort in the local delicacy, but even the fish and chips were crap! If I have to follow the lads there again in fifty years' time, it'll be too soon.

So, there you go; a typical week as a Hammer. But what about the rest of the season? West Ham finished in a very respectable tenth place so it couldn't have been *all* bad. Or was it?

On the first day, Leeds United took the points away with them - nothing unusual there. West Ham have this unrivalled habit of blowing any hopes on the first day of every season, so it was quite comforting to see them lose! Actually, Leeds eventually took the full six points, but still finished lower than we did. So they weren't *that* good a side after all, were they?!

It took West Ham seven matches to get a win - and that came against Bristol Rovers in the League Cup. The week before, Julian Dicks had given Andy Gray his finest moment on Sky when Chelsea's John Spencer had nutted Julian after a tackle. Typical of Andy Gray, he managed to turn the whole thing around and put the blame on poor Dicksy. I mean, how on earth did Spencer think that just because he was lying on the floor he would get away with head-butting the bottom of Julian Dicks' boot? It was a reckless thing to do! It was great for Gray and Sky, as they made a weekly series of the incident, showing it from every possible angle at least a million times. OK, I might be exaggerating, it was probably only 999,999 times. What puzzled me though, and made me think that Julian had been set up, was one particular camera angle. It could only have been taken from a camera up Spencers' arse!

But I will say "fair play" to Spencer over the incident. When he apologised to Dicks for what he did, he shook hands and said he'd never do it again and they both had a lemonade together after the match. Which was nice.

Julian was back in the news a few days later, as he was unjustly sent off at Highbury. Two mis-timed tackles, they said. Apparently one was in the tunnel coming out onto the pitch and the other was in the bar afterwards. Oh well, it can't be helped.

But seriously, those two incidents were Julian's only wrong-doings and he went on to play the best football of his career for the rest of the season. How he didn't make the England squad for Euro 96, only Venables knows.

One particular highlight was a run of five successive wins in the Premier League starting at the end of January: Coventry, Nottingham Forest, Totts, Chelsea and Newcastle all came a close second. With a run of League wins like that, Harry Redknapp was a banker for Manager of the Month. Obviously, Alex Ferguson got it instead! Had it not been for that little run, though, things might well have ended a tad differently for us, as we won only three more times in the final 11.

One of the most unusual things to happen last year to the Hammers was the fact that we signed (or at least seemed to sign) about 500 new players. And they were all foreign! It was ever so funny to keep reading about "West Ham United Nations." My, what a hoot. Those journalists really know how to capture the imagination, with those funny headlines, don't they? Tossers.

We had players from France, Croatia, Denmark, Czechoslovakia, Portugal, Russia, Holland, Australia and the United States of America to name but a few, and of course, two lads from Middlesex. But the best one was the player we signed before the start of the season from Holland for a million quid. He was going to be our star striker - everyone knew his name (in his own family): Marco Boogers.

Uncannily, just like last year with Joey Beauchamp, we bought a complete and utter social misfit. It went completely pear-shaped almost immediately. It even got to the stage where Boogers fled the country and was apparently living on a Dutch goat farm in a caravan! Harry Redknapp was less than impressed. When interviewed in *Over Land and Sea* about Boogers' apparent pre-season apathy, Harry told me: "I wanted to pick a team for the first game of the season. I pulled him aside and he said 'when the games start proper, I start playing proper'. I wasn't prepared to have that. I said 'you're here now, and if we're running, you run up the front like everyone else, not a hundred yards behind. This is England, you fucking do it like we do it in England, this ain't Holland.' "

Talking about Harry, I spent hours upon hours with the guy last season, and I have to say that as a football manager in the top Division, he comes across with a biting honesty. On one occasion, I asked him about players at clubs he'd been at and what it's like to pick a side. He replied: "When you pick your team, you don't pick footballers because you like them, because you don't like them all, do you? Some I fucking hate the sight of. I wouldn't want to spend a minute of my life with some of them if I had my way really. I pick the best players because I need results. I have had players before when I was at Bournemouth and I hated them, their wives were fucking aggro but I still picked them every week because they were the best players." Let me ask any of you: can you imagine your team's manager saying that sort of thing to you? If you think this is a ball-crunching statement from Redknapp, he is also a very funny guy with a wicked sense of humour.

I'm lucky, as I can normally get into the after-match press conference and hear first hand what both managers say about the game that has just been played. Redknapp, at times, says the most unbelievable things. Last season at Villa Park when we had Portuguese wonder-boy Dani at the club, and the press were going on about the kid's good looks and calling him by the wrong name, Redknapp quipped: "Dani, not DARNI. He sounds like a tart when you call him that. *Darni?* I keep thinking he's going to fucking start singing in the Eurovision Song contest or something. No, that was Dana wasn't it, oh yeah, fucking hell. But don't call him Darni!"

Another hack with brains like dog shit called out: "He's a good looking boy, Harry!" Harry murdered the poor guy with a classic one-liner: "Sure. When he comes on, they don't know whether to mark him or fuck him, know what I mean?" They threw away the mould when they made Harry Redknapp.

But he wasn't always our favourite person last season. Early on he signed Iain Dowie back from Crystal Palace and we couldn't believe it. He was always selected in the worst West Ham teams. But, by the end of the season, Dowie had proved us all wrong and had proved Harry right. He was a great performer for the side last year and justly deserved his runner-up slot in the Hammer of the Year awards.

Of the foreign imports? One player in particular really stood out head and shoulders above the rest: Croatia's Slaven Bilic. I never saw Bobby Moore play in the flesh, only on video and on the box, but I'm not alone in making the comparison between the two. Bilic is one hell of a player. His reading of the game and the timing of his tackles are impeccable. His work-rate and distribution are equally impressive and his temperament is just right (he just doesn't like Germans). If West Ham keep him, he will no doubt go on to be one of the greatest ever Hammers.

And we also had the on-off saga with Ilie Dumitrescu to keep us amused through the winter. The 'will he-won't he' work permit situation was getting well out of hand and Ilie finally found out what he paid his PFA subs for, when they turned around and argued against him getting a work permit. Nice guy, that Gordon Taylor.

The real highlight of last season for me though came with the emergence of home-grown Hammers-supporting Danny Williamson into a fine Premier League player. He fulfilled his promise and proved right everything *OLAS* had been saying about him for two or three years. Also the ability and sheer guts and determination our youth team showed as they lifted the South East Counties League title and were runners-up in the FA Youth Cup Final. There are four or five players in that side who really could make it in the game. That's what it's really all about.

Last season, the League table showed we finished tenth, above teams that spent fortunes. Harry Redknapp spent shillings, swapped a few players and achieved a very good result with the side. I can honestly say that for the coming season, there is a real feeling of optimism around the place, and if we don't make Europe we'll feel that we've failed. But every Hammer will also tell you in the same breath that we also wouldn't be surprised if we went down.

That's West Ham, and that's us!

Fanzine Facts

Last season *Over Land and Sea* published their 114th issue. Gary Firmager started the fanzine solo eight years ago and retains ownership and full editorial control, although he quite readily acknowledges that he couldn't keep it going without the hundreds of regular contributions that come in through the season.

Published every single home match, *OLAS* now incorporates the independent matchday programme 'Home Alone'. As Gary says, "The gamble to combine the two and put the price up paid off, and after eight years, the fanzine has finally begun to look the way I always intended." *OLAS*' honours include being named as Sunday Times Fanzine of the Year and Sky Sports Fanzine of the Year three years ago, and making the Top Ten in the 1996 FourFourTwo magazine Fanzine of the Year awards.

THE PETERBOROUGH EFFECT

Peterborough United

From Baldy to Barry

As all football fans know, the start of a new season is a wondrous thing. Hope springs eternal and every side in the League look beatable. The new additions to the squad have all been plucked from under the noses of big Premiership sides and... this is going to be *our* year.

Well, that's how it's been for most clubs most of the time, but since the start of Premiership football the gulf has not just widened between the Premier League and the Endsleigh League; it grows ever wider between the First, Second and Third Divisions too. The spending power of most First Division sides can only leave the average Posh fan shaking their head in bewilderment. Yet Peterborough United by the end of '95-96 season took their spending to £1m in under three years; the sort of sum that the majority of our fellow brethren in Endsleigh Two and Three could only dream about. Not only that, the demolition of the old uncovered Glebe Road terrace had made way for a smart new 5,700 seater with season tickets at just £115 a go! Surely this season more than any other, Posh fans would be brimming with interest and optimism.

Not so. John Still (The Bald One), our manager, had hardly inspired confidence in his first year and whilst he had unearthed a gem in Gary Breen he had imported some obnoxious characters who just weren't up to it on the pitch. What Peterborough fans needed was a sign that things were going to happen, and soon.

Pre-season friendlies against Hitchin, Chelmsford, Cheshunt, Maidenhead and Chatteris certainly weren't arranged to fill the new stand and with the exception of Bruce Rioch's son Gregor and ex-C**bridge goalkeeper Jon Sheffield, all of the new signings were household names... in the ICIS League. Slightly unfair perhaps because Still also brought in Gary Martindale from Bolton reserves, Lee Power from the NHS and Danny Carter from Orient.

The season proper started predictably enough with a win, Posh only having lost on the opening day five times in their 35 League seasons, 3-1 against an appalling Brighton side. Gary Martindale was an instant hit with the fans, scoring on his debut; his err... robust style winning over a lot of Poshies. Then it started 'properly': six League games without a win and a 4-1 drubbing against Swansea in the first leg of the Coca Cola cup. Miraculously the inept Welshmen managed to surrender that advantage and Posh went through on away goals with a 3-0 home win. That gave us the dubious honour of a home and away tie with form team Aston Villa. We warmed up nicely with a 1-0 win over Wrexham but then Mr Still abandoned his 4-2-4 attacking formation for a bizarre 4-5-1 set-up which seemed to please Villa and their ball-playing wing backs, as much as it baffled the Posh faithful. Villa duly won 6-0 and obligingly let us draw 1-1 in the second leg to avoid further embarrassment. A 3-1 win over Bradford came between the two Villa matches, our last League victory until October 28th. Posh did manage to beat Plymouth 3-0 in the Auto Windscreens thingy and registered home draw against the hapless Cobblers (who haven't beaten the mighty Posh for seven years or scored against us for five!) to progress to the knock-out stages of said competition.

The last defeat in October was away at Brentford 3-0; it was a day when the increasingly loud barracking of several players (Dave Morrison and previous season's hero Billy Manuel, specifically) and John Still in particular, reached fever pitch. Son of God and chief executive Chris Turner condemned the fans' reaction and said the club would not sack him. John Still predictably added that the boo boys would not drive him out. It was therefore no surprise when Still resigned after lengthy meetings with chairman Alf Hand and Turner. What was a surprise was the appointment of Mick Halsall as boss, given that Mike Walker was being tipped for the hot seat by all and sundry.

Halsall started his second stint as Posh manager with York at home, promising a more attacking style and better discipline at the club. It has to be said that the local bookies didn't have too many punters to pay out when Peterborough blitzed them 6-0 on the Saturday! The biggest difference to the side was Paul Shaw, on loan from Arsenal, who at last gave us a midfield. Suitably stiffened, we embarked on a run of just three defeats in the next 13 games which saw us climb away from the relegation mire, progress to the third round of the FA Cup and the area semi-finals of the Auto Washwipe. In the process Peterborough notched a first for the club by beating Swansea 1-0 in sudden-death extra time, a goal celebrated by nine of the 11 players sprinting straight from the pitch as soon as the ball hit the net. Laughed? Swansea didn't!

Things then went decidedly strange. A 5-4 home defeat to Bournemouth after leading 3-1 and 4-3 was irritating but entertaining; a 2-0 defeat at Huddersfield in the FA Cup was expected; a 1-0 home defeat to Bristol Rovers in the AWS wasn't, and a 6-1 thumping of a truly chronic Carlisle side was hilarious. By the way, why did Michael Knighton blame the FA for Carlisle's relegation, the rest of the Division knew it was because they were shite. Also the sale of Gary Breen, an undoubtedly talented footballer but totally devoid of personality and unloved by the fans, took place, with one Kenneth Leroy Charlery, ex-Wembley hero of this Parish, coming in the opposite direction. Ken, sold several times for more than he was worth and bought once again for his true value, was about to commence his third stint for Posh.

The results were all over the place: away wins at Stockport and Bristol City, home defeats to Walsall and Brentford; you just couldn't predict what was going to happen next. All the time the side hovered precariously above the relegation zone; Paul Shaw had long since returned to Arsenal and the midfield was limp once again. That didn't stop us buying centre backs, full backs, centre forwards and wingers, but midfielders? Nope. Things looked to be reaching a crisis point when Posh splashed out a record £225,000 for Carl Griffiths (a forward) on deadline day, to add to a strike force already containing 18-goal Gary Martindale, 12-goal Sean Farrell, Ken Charlery with six goals in 11 games and several young pretenders such as McGleish and Furnell waiting in the wings - bizarre. This signing spelled the end of the road for Gary Martindale. Adored by the fans but rubbished by Halsall and Turner (players who 'allegedly' wanted to leave shouldn't play for the first team), this 20-odd year old starlet with golden boots was sold for £175,000 and replaced by a 31 year old who cost £50,000 more. Oh, by the way, Marcus Ebdon handed in a transfer request in February and played almost every game until the end of the season. It's the sort of consistency Posh fans have come to expect

Five games into April the side had not won a game, but fortunately Hull, Brighton, York, Carlisle and Swansea were equally dreadful. Posh secured safety with a victory over Hull at London road and then went on to lose gloriously at Crewe and Oxford. Another boy wonder striker Guliano Grazioli, who'd scored 28 goals in 27 reserve and non-league games, made his full debut against Crewe... and scored. If only we could find midfield players as easily.

The season stuttered to a halt and, if anything, interest for next year was even lower than it had been for this. Then BOOM. Enter Barry Fry with his legendary appetite for the contents of the chairman's money clip. Before the European Championships have even started he's bidding for players that we've only associated with proper clubs, he's re-named the new stand the Chris Turner stand, season tickets are selling like hot cakes and Posh are in the news every day as Baz makes a bid for everybody from Pele to Collymore. He's talking of an all-seater stadium filled with 20,000 every week, winning the League, the Cup, the World Cup and God knows what else. Do we believe it? Hell no, but it's the most fun Posh fans have had since relegating our hapless county cousins from the swampy south and seeing them slide into obscurity.

Hang on to your hats and wallets 'cos Fry's in town. Whatever happens next season it ain't gonna be boring or predictable.

Fanzine Facts

The Peterborough Effect was born in the Highbury Vaults, a pub not far from the centre of Bristol, on April 9th 1988. Founders Andy Groom, Russ Morris, Mark Papworth and Paul Rush had seen the last ever League hat-trick scored at Somerton Park, Newport, that day, and realised with sadness that what they had witnessed was a football club dying. Although Posh at the time were pushing for the play-offs, they were also in administration, and for these fans it appeared that no-one really cared if clubs like theirs or Newport died.

A few pints of Smiles Exhibition, and starting a fanzine seemed the most logical thing in the world to do. The name came from the Peterborough Development Corporation's advertising slogan of the 70s and 80s that enticed businesses to move to Peterborough ("Why do people move their business... it must be The Peterborough Effect"), although as editor Andy Groom points out "It probably means more to folk in London who were the subjects of the campaign than it does to Peterborough people."

PRESTON PIE MUNCHER

Preston North End

Winning promotion from the Third Division was the cake. Doing it as Champions gave us a bit of icing to go on it. But if Preston North End are as big a club as we 'glory-hunters who can't help but live on our history' (© every other Third Division fanzine) like to think, just how big an achievement was this? You're about to find out: this is the story of what '95-96 meant to the people of Preston.

The apprehension that preceeded the season was fuelled by the events of the one that had passed. Maverick manager John Beck had been sacked and his assistant Gary Peters appointed in what at first glance had seemed an ambitious move. In retrospect, it was a master stroke; Peters took us from 16th to fifth in the second half

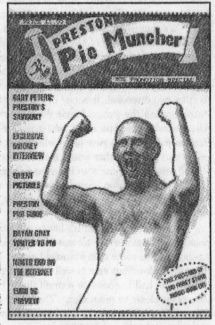

of that season, and the almost inevitable defeat in the play-offs seemed acceptable considering Peters' record of just three defeats in his first 25 matches as a football manager. The squad that helped him clock up such a record was also skillfully pruned by Peters in the summer of '95. Out went a very long line of those pointless members of the squad who you know will eventually leave to be quickly forgotten (every team has them). In came Steve Wilkinson who had just scored 26 goals for Mansfield (£90,000), Andy Saville, who was to become the Division's leading scorerer (£100,000), and the Doncaster Rovers Player of the Year Russ Wilcox (£60,000). Oh, and we also signed the former Newscastle and Everton midfielder Neil McDonald (£30,000). And the Finnish under-21 goalkeeper Teuvo Moilanen (£75,000). And the lower divisions' most prolific striker of recent years Gary Bennett (£200,000). And... well there were two or three more, but what I'm basically saying is that we bought a few much needed quality players.

Despite this, our season started slowly. Our first nine games yielded just two victories, and the pleasant presence of some attractive attacking football on the immaculate Deepdale turf was no consolation. We didn't want to watch nice football. We wanted football in a nice Division. We needed the team to click home and away - to start picking up three points on a regular basis, and in October that's what we got. A run of six wins and a draw in seven games, with a stunning 23 goals scored in the proccess, hoisted us from eighth to first, and we at last enjoyed that great feeling in life. Returning to the world the morning after a night of celebratory beering, currying and hoplessly fumbling with birds in the grim alleys of Preston town centre, to find a copy of the News of the World with the words 'Preston' 'North' and 'End' above those that make up the names of the other 23 teams in the Division. Bloody brilliant! Now all we had to do was stay there for six months and we'd be up. Which proved surprisingly easy.

We fluctuated between first and third until January, when we settled in second spot until the end of March, and then decided to go back to the top until the end of the season. But more on the run later. It's time for a cake update.

The Tom Finney stand opened on March 16th. It is (and every person who visited Deepdale in the spring of '96 said this) without doubt the best stand in the bottom two divisions. It is one of the most distinctive structures in British sport - incorporating the pyramid-style flood-lighting of the Luigi Ferraris stadium that Genoa and Sampdoria share, and a unique mosaic of the face of Preston's most famous player of the past (after which it is named), into a £4.5m 8,000 all-seater stand with facilities that would make all but the biggest Premiership clubs jealous. Three other matching stands are to follow, starting with a new 6,000 all-seater Spion Kop this season to make Deepdale a cross between the stadiums of Wolves and Huddersfield... with knobs on. If *that* isn't icing on the cake, I don't know what is.

Anyway, this is what it's like to get promoted. On Easter Monday we needed four points from our last six matches to clinch promotion, and ten for the Championship. Escape route one: Mansfield away. The team turned up at Field Mill for a morning kick-off but may as well not have; the match was so dour that at the final whistle you had to convince yourself that it had actually taken place. Still, 0-0 and one point closer to promotion. Three now required.

Escape route two: Northampton at home. Surely we could get the required win against this lot - the 12,000 fans that turned out to watch certainly thought so. Wrong! An unbelievable yet almost predictable 0-3 defeat left the party well and truly gate-crashed, its guest casting aspersions about possible match-rigging, foul play, and North End being shit. Four matches left to get the three points that would take us up. Escape route three: Cambridge away. The U's had absolutely knob-all to play for and posessed one of the worst home records in the country. Their victory over us on this hot summer night left our promotion push in an official state of crisis. Surely after all we'd been through we weren't going to be subjected to another season of the Third? Popular opinion that it was looking a strong possibility. Arse.

Escape route four: Leyton Orient away. A return to the venue of our '86-87 Fourth Division promotion clincher, for what could be a bizarre replay of what was for younger fans one of the greatest days in our history. And it bloody was. Two superb Saville strikes took a relieved North End back into the Second Division and sparked a mad dash up the M6 to join the celebrations that had taken over the town centre. Fans sang in the streets; players were carried shoulder high; DJ's dedicated records like "*Movin on up*" to the Whites; young Mexican women danced naked in the streets; the Mayor gave everyone free kebabs. It was rather fab. Ahem, cake update...

The Third Division Championship would have provided a little more icing for this here cake. Two games to go and six points were required - or three and a Gillingham slip-up. Hartlepool away was our first chance to do it, and 3,088 fans (more than most teams in the Division can muster for home matches) made the trip. Two spectacular goals from Davey and Saville (obviously) gave us an impressive 2-0 victory, a result that meant we would almost certainly clinch the Championship at home the following week. Enter the Hartlepool tannoy man: "Fulham nil, Gillingham..." At half-five we left the ground for another night of free kebabs and Mexican babes, etc... Now, do you remember at the beginning of this story when I asked if Preston North End were really a big club? Well, our final match was at home to Exeter. We won it 2-0, but that's beside the point. We were presented with the Championship trophy and were entertained by a brass band, a schoolboy match, skydivers landing on the centre spot, an after-match party on the pitch and an aeroplane circling the stadium carrying a message of congratulations. But none of that makes us a big club. What makes us a big club is that at a quarter past two, supporters would've had to scale the fences to get in. The ground, with the spectacular new stand fully operational, was filled to its 18,700 capacity, only 200 of whom were away fans. There were 3,000 supporters outside the ground at kick-off, who had to make do with watching the highlights on Granada Goals Extra. Now let's put this in perspective: this is Exeter City at home. This is the Endersleigh League Third Division. The Championship had been clinched, the match effectively meant nothing other than a chance to thank the players for a marvellous season. Twenty one and a half thousand people turned up. That's more than many Premiership games. And it wasn't a one-off - we had a five-figure average attendance last season when the Divisional average was 3,000. If *that* isn't proof that Preston are a big club then I was lying about those free kebabs. Let's just hope that we can pick up where we left off and finally fulfil our potential by getting into the First Division. Who knows what the crowds will be then.

N.B. If the above account sounds like the perfect season for any football supporter, get this: our rivals Blackpool were virtually assured of automatic promotion from the Second until a disastrous run saw them drop into a play-off spot on the final day of the season. They won their first leg match away from home 2-0 before somehow losing the return tie 3-0! The following week, their chairman was sentenced to six years in prison for rape, and the manager (a former Preston player and downright traitor) was sacked by the accused's wife. I was going to have a slice of cake to celebrate, but sadly I couldn't find a sledgehammer big enough to smash the icing on it. Oh, what a season!!

Fanzine Facts

Launched in November 1992, *Pie Muncher's* success is entirely down to the qualities of the people involved in its production, according to editor Steve Brennan. Describing himself as "a genuinely nice guy", and co-writer Ken Robinson as "a scheming devil-worshipping door-to-door dishcloth salesman with a penchant for fine wines", Steve explains that the other contributors Joe Gudgeon, Karen Pearson, Howard Irving, Sharon Gifford, Pete Dimmock, Jean Davies and John Billington became part of the editorial team as a result of "a freak soapy pogo stick incident in which a young kitten became mysteriously separated from its fur. And that's weird, because that's how fanzines start."

RAGING BULL

Oxford United

So what's the point of all this anyway? Why would *you* care how our season went? Are we trying to share something with each other here, something we have in common? Now there's a thing. Being football fans, we're supposed to have little capacity to take an interest in anything, let alone each other, while in English football nowadays, the word 'share' relates to something you hold in Tottenham or Manchester United. As for the idea that anything is 'in common' in football - well, that is very quaint. Football today is about money, the pursuit of money, and the disposal of anything that is not dedicated to that pursuit. We have nothing in common, except our status as consumers.

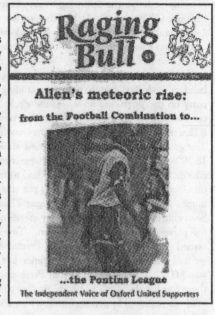

Allen's meteoric rise:

from the Football Combination to...

...the Pontins League

The Independent Voice of Oxford United Supporters

But that's not why I follow my team with passion and dedication, nor why anyone else does. We have that in common. They have made a grotesque circus of our game, a machine for the production of profit and the promotion of everything synthetic. Sooner or later, they will rearrange the League again, and lock out the Oxfords, the Southamptons, the Barnsleys and the Darlingtons; those who are not revenue producers. They have turned the major clubs into huge, expensive, antiseptic parodies of themselves, halfway between NFL and a hypermarket. So celebrate while we may. It was a celebration season - Oxford were promoted. But whatever happened, it would have been worth celebrating in times like these, simply for the fact that it took place.

Reminiscences? For most of the season, there was little worth recalling. There was a Cup run, memorable because we set our record score, beating Dorchester 9-1. But the League was rubbish. United didn't win away until the end of January. We were still 13th in February, when leaden performances gave way to alchemy. United started winning, and then just kept on winning, except for the glitch at Stockport. Matt Elliott, our imperious centre-back, was suspended. His father apparently commented that "they'll have to play for a draw, then"; the rest of the squad were not amused, and in the end four goals were conceded. Daddy knew best! Elliott played in each one of the other 14 games from the end of February and we only conceded four in all of them put together.

This was supposed to be a nothing season. I'd practically stopped going to away games altogether by the middle of October. Even by the end of March, when we were fifth, they still hadn't won me over enough to lure me to *that* Stockport game. (OK, so I was moving house, but the point is that I *chose* a Saturday to move.) Still, nine days later, I cycled 30 miles to Wycombe, and cycled and pushed the 30 miles back, which was almost as much fun as the game itself, 3-0 and easy with it.

Even so, after Stockport, we had had eight games left, and were 14 points behind Blackpool, the sort of lead you'd expect them to hold even if they never won another game. Blackpool obviously agreed, and tried to prove it. When we went to Crewe on the penultimate Saturday, the gap was down to two.

Crewe was a real game, memorable for its atmosphere. TV commentators, power-worshippers who would have done well under Big Brother, marvelled at 'this magnificent stadium' (it's big), and 'this passionate crowd' (it's big) and 'this parti-san atmosphere' (the home fans are supporting the home team). But at Crewe, there was a truly original atmosphere. What was special about it was all the usual end of season clichés: the radios in the crowd, the nerves and passion. But what was bizarre and unique about it was that the away crowd turned up before 12 o'clock, got in by one and at half past had filled their end, while the rest of Gresty Road couldn't have been more deserted than if Alex were playing away. Ninety minutes before kick-off we could have been forgiven for wondering if we'd come to the wrong place. Now for internationals and Cup Finals, grounds fill up early, and when they are stupidly not made all-ticket, those games fill up at both ends. The first Crewe fans turned up, those sad cases who rather than have a drink will lose 75 minutes from their day in order to reserve their traditional spot. Expecting to see the back of all four stands, they nearly fell over when a packed away end picked them out for waving and singing.

So we were there for hours, and it never abated, it never wore off, it was an atmosphere of momentum. (I'm trying here, really I am, but I'm sure you either get it or you don't.) It was all momentum and melodrama. Blackpool behind, every-body celebrating, United one up, then, being the melodrama that it was, it almost fell apart, as Stuart Massey was sent off and Crewe got one back, and then played ping-pong in front of our goal. Which, mercifully, was at the far end, while we covered our eyes, ate our fingers and grasped chairs, posts and pillars for emotional reassurance.

But we won. We also won the last one, home against Peterborough, 4-0 after a nervous, nervous game was mercifully turned by a Peterborough own goal. After that it was easy (too easy, for the bloke next to me had, I believe, £20 on a 3-0 result. But money's not the point, is it?). The whistle went, the pitch was briefly invaded, there was a lap of honour.

This was not as fine as the Saturday before; there was something not quite satisfactory about it, something incomplete. The church bells should have been rung, and if they weren't, I wanted at least to celebrate all night. But people and the evening drifted away. It wasn't meant to be a private thing, this triumph; it was supposed to enthuse a whole community.

However, Oxford are back, or may at least be edging back, however slowly. Four years previously, we stayed up on the last day, got back to Oxford - and found nobody who understood why this mattered until the fourth pub we visited. This time, every so often on the street there was a familiar face, or a little knot of carous-ing fans. It is beginning to matter again.

United were relegated from the old First Division in '88, and since then football had been changed to ensure that as far as possible, clubs like United should have no chance whatsoever of challenging for honours again. (How archaic, how anomalous that word sounds now. 'Honours'. I mean financial opportunities.) When we have, in effect, only a few clubs left, because the others are financially dwarfed by the rest, we shall be told two lies: first, that the clubs who 'failed' did so because they were not wanted, and second, that those who succeeded did so because they proved their worth in a tough market. This will happen because in a market economy success is its own justification, and there are plenty of journalists eager to tell it how the powerful want to hear it. We, however, know the truth. We can see the difference between a level playing field and what's happened in football. The difference is growing bigger all the time, and that was never the way we wanted it.

Two days after Peterborough, many of the fans met up again at Fun In The Parks, a sort of annual carnival in Oxford. This is real Oxford, nothing whatsoever to do with academia and far more representative even than the Manor - more multiracial and a greater balance of the sexes. It's the best thing Oxford has. It's about an Oxford aware of itself, proud of itself while hostile to nobody. The best carnivals are like that; they have personality, community, involvement for everybody and plenty of time for you. They are a pleasure, not a task, not a means of making money. If we had that, would we give it up for a bright red shirt and a satellite dish? I sat in the Bank Holiday sunshine, surrounded by friends and fellow citizens, and thought of how much I would like football to be like this. Which of course will never happen. But isn't that dream a million times more preferable than the drawn-out nightmare that we're having at the moment?

Fanzine Facts

Raging Bull was founded in '88 following an advert in When Saturday Comes, and by the end of '95-96 had produced 40 issues. There have been around a dozen different editors, and well over a hundred different contributors. Last season's editors could have been summarised without injustice as one Trotskyite, two ravers and one bloke who thinks we should leave the planet and make a new life for ourselves on Mars. The editors have, at different times, been thrown off the ground, and invited to run the club administration (Ian Davies, the current club manager, was an editor for seven years). They have been threatened by Nazis, assaulted by their own supporters, criticised in the programme and asked to contribute to it, invited to meet the board and refused permission to buy shares. They have distributed leaflets against various Maxwells, against ID cards, and have appeared on a number of television programmes. They enjoy an appalling relationship with the local press.

According to Ed Horton, who produced this review, "*Raging Bull* has occasional lapses into humour but has tended to move away from the hackneyed, cliché-friendly 'just a bit of fun', or 'just putting our point of view' sort of thing, and become deadly serious and very concerned with events off the pitch and financial affairs. This is a reflection of the club's enormous debts, its frequently opaque and occasionally shady financial dealing, the current state of football generally, and my own political preoccupations." Ed Horton writes agitational articles whenever he can get them past the editors of When Saturday Comes, and is taking a year off from editing Raging Bull to write a book about the commercialisation of football. "Hopefully while I'm away it'll lighten up a bit" he muses.

Ed continues: "**RB**'s influence is probably considerable, but passive. It is capable of affecting what people think, but not (currently) of getting them to do anything about it. It is, by now, part of United life, and everybody reads it: its position appears impregnable. And yet, like most fanzines, it could easily close down tomorrow if there was a row, or someone got a different job, or somebody, one day, just couldn't be bothered. No-one knows. But I think a lot of people care."

RANDY ROBIN

Swindon Town

Writing this article proved to be a great deal harder than I expected, after all Swindon were Champions in '95-96 and you can't get much better than that, but for some reason my piece last year on our disastrous second successive relegation flowed a great deal more easily. Whether the fact that I find it harder to write about positive things is a sad reflection on human nature, the British way of life or how much I had to drink last night is a question that remains unanswered. So, on with the show...

"Steve McMahon, we're proud to sing your name, Swindon Town are going up again!!" Had you sung that one around Swindon in May '95 then you would have probably been locked up in an institution. Twelve months on, it seemed to be a civil offence *not* to be singing it.

This change in attitude can be explained by one word: CHAMPIONS!

The season started optimistically; a 2-0 win at Hull brought some happiness back into hearts weary after two years of unbridled crapness. Best of all, one of the goals came from a bloke called Steve Finney. Finney was the unexpected success story of season; the omens though when he first signed were not good. At the time he had declared that this was his "last chance", and if it went wrong then he would "go back to bricklaying." At the time the fans were not impressed, one commenting that "Macca's turning us into a bloody pub team." One year and 14 League goals on, Town fans now think that Finney was either joking or being unnecessarily modest. His success and that of Macca's other great free transfer acquisition, a certain Paul Allen, gave confidence to fans who, after McMahon sold leading goal scorer Jan Aage Fjortoft for a meagre £1.3m the previous year, thought that when it came to wheeling and dealing McMahon was football's equivalent to Nick Leeson.

The first few months flew by. We remained unbeaten for ten League games, equalling our all-time record. And as if being top of the League with a quarter of the season played wasn't enough to whet even the most pessimistic Town fan's appetite, there was also the visit of Premiership Champions Blackburn Rovers in the Hokey-Kokey Cup to look forward to. With 30 minutes gone we were two up and all over them. There were pigs flying over the Wiltshire downs; this was going to be the greatest League Cup giant-killing since the Swindon class of '69 did Arsenal at Wembley in the final. If only. We were eventually soundly beaten 5-2 on aggregate, but Alan Shearer was the only real difference between the sides. This proved that Swindon now had a side capable of rising to the big occasion; Macca's name was being chanted at every opportunity, and they were already whispering that word down Wiltshire way, "Champions."...

However, all in the Swindon Garden was not rosy; Chesterfield's visit to the County Ground in September showing an uglier side of football. Chesterfield's Darren Carr, sent off for a second bookable offence, went with a team mate to remonstrate with the linesman who had spotted the foul. An angry Swindon fan jumped onto the pitch, Carr pushed him and - WHAM - it all went off, with over 30 Swindon fans on the pitch. Cantona in reverse - or so the tabloids the next day would have you believe. It was in fact over as quickly as it began with no real damage done, but the incident and Carr's behaviour left a sour taste in the mouth. The media slavering over this and other flare-ups (such as before and after the Oxford and Cardiff home matches) threatened to spoil what was overall a highly successful season for Swindon. Thankfully at the end of the day '95-96 will be remembered for the football.

October continued in much the same vein with three wins and one draw, and despite a slight slip in November when we failed to win a single League game, reasonable results over the Christmas and New Year period left us well in the running for the top spot. We were chanting it by now: "Champions!.."

Into February, and attention was diverted from the League, with a sell-out crowd at the County Ground for a fourth round FA Cup tie with Southampton. Once again it was a case of 'so near but yet so far' as Swindon squandered a lead to draw 1-1 and take the game into a replay at the Dell, in which despite another sterling Swindon performance, we lost 2-0. However, round about the middle of March it all started to go wonky; we drew three easy-looking games on the trot and Finney broke his leg. There was even worse to follow.

Tuesday March 19th is a night most Swindon fans would prefer to forget. We lost 3-0 to our hated local rivals Oxford United. To make the temples throb even more, the third goal was scored by Joey Beauchamp (or Beauscum as he's known round these parts), who'd been transferred back to Oxford from Swindon earlier in the campaign. Beauchamp, not for the first time in his career, demonstrated his lack of maturity and common sense by giving the Swindon fans a V-sign to celebrate his goal. Ironically, he'd played for Swindon against Oxford at the County Ground earlier that season. The Oxford fans celebrated by printing T-shirts depicting a Mad Ox and the initials BSE, which on this occasion stood for 'Beat Swindon Easily'. We started to get a nasty feeling that we were going to throw it all away. Over the next few games the chants became muted and unsure: "Champions?"

Thankfully these jitters were not shared by the Town players, who with wins over high-flying Notts County and Crewe went to Blackpool, at that time our nearest rivals, and managed a 1-1 draw which secured us automatic promotion. Swindon fans had a beach party to celebrate, although the real festivities didn't take place until three days later, when a win at Chesterfield gave us an unassailable lead at the top of table with two games remaining. Champagne corks were popping, we were shouting it from the rooftops by now: "CHAMPIONS!"

It was Sunday May 4th, and Swindon fans were making their way through the town centre to the civic offices for a reception in honour of the Second Division victors. A man with a Bible was preaching at the 'sinners' about turning away from

God. For those at the civic offices, there was no doubt who was God that day "*Steve McMahon, We're proud to sing your name...*"

Fanzine Facts

When Swindon schoolboy Matthew Arnold founded the **Randy Robin** in January 1994, he hoped it would bring him fame, fortune and a place in Swindon footballing folklore. Since then, the fame has turned to infamy with numerous appearances on local TV, radio and in the local press for various crimes ranging from being banned from selling the fanzine around the ground to participating in demonstrations against the board of directors. And as for the fortune and the place in folklore, let's just say he's still waiting. Fanzine Motto: "Well, it seemed like a good idea at the time..."

RED ALL OVER THE LAND

Liverpool

Two Tribes Go To War!

I thought long and hard about how to review Liverpool's season, but I kept coming back to that magical night in April. A football match of such quality that it stirred the nation, and stood head and shoulders above anything else the season had to offer. It epitomised everything that a football supporter hopes to experience at least once in his or her lifetime. So I thought - hell, why not? I'll just tell the story of a magnificent game. Here it is:

**RED
ALL
OVER
THE
LAND**

A LIVERPOOL FANZINE FREE ONE MARCH NO. 11
A TRIBUTE TO THE LATE GREAT BOB PAISLEY

Wednesday April 3rd will long live on in the memory of 40,700 football fans who turned up at Anfield to watch Liverpool play Newcastle United. This was almost certain to be a night of passion, regardless of what happened on the pitch, simply because of the two sets of supporters. The fact that Liverpool fans had also decreed the match to be a Flag Day would add to the atmosphere. Flag Days were first introduced by the kop when Liverpool met Spurs in the final League game of the '92-93 season. Such was its success that others followed, the most famous one being the event billed as 'The kop's Last Stand' which heralded the final day that standing was allowed on the world's greatest and most famous terrace. The match with Newcastle was to be the kop's eighth flag day, so the scene was set. Flags did not just appear on the kop, they were also in the Centenary Stand and the Anfield Road Stand, and there were also unconfirmed rumours that one did actually appear in the Main Stand, and, yes, Lord Lucan was waving it! The Geordie Boys were also up for it, and in support of their French 'Diving Ace' Ginola, there were a few Tricolours to be seen in the away end. The event couldn't fail really. Liverpool had just beaten Aston Villa to reach the FA Cup Final (sponsored by Littlewoods Pools!), while Newcastle were hoping to regain their form (away from home) in a desperate bid to take the title.

Before the teams took the pitch, the whole of Anfield sang 'You'll Never Walk Alone' with huge passion. The kop was a magnificent sight; a sea of different flags, including some of overseas sides such as Juventus. It gave you that eerie feeling of anticipation. Something special was going to happen, but nobody knew just what.

Anfield was a cauldron of noise as the tribes made their feelings for their respective sides known, and inside 90 seconds the volume of noise reached a crescendo that was almost 'fever pitch', and not for the last time that night. And why? Robbie Fowler had given Liverpool the lead. How the kop reacted! First with the chant of 'Fowler!' and then to the strains of 'Scouser Tommy', the famous kop anthem. It was mayhem. We stood, and we sang, and we shouted.

But the Geordies came back at us; Keegan would not let his side meekly surrender, despite the volume of noise and the emotion that was almost tangible. Within ten minutes not only had they levelled, but they had gone ahead. First of all Les Ferdinand had suckered our defence and put the ball into the net straight through the hands of David James. Then Ginola scored, staying on his feet long enough to run about 50 yards before clipping home a beaut. Whether or not he fell over then I do not know, I was staring at the ground hoping that he had missed. I hoped against hope! Now the noise emanated from the other end of Anfield. The kop, as if its pride had been wounded, responded with sound. The noise was already deafening and both teams responded with an all-out attacking display that at times bordered on reckless. Defence? Forget it! This was what the fans wanted, regardless of what the coaches and 'experts' thought, and later said. This was raw attacking English football at its very best. Surprisingly the interval came with scoreline still reading Liverpool 1 Newcastle 2. It could have read any combination up to four each and nobody would have been surprised.

If the first half had been pulsating, then it was to be over shadowed by events after the 15 minutes respite. The second half got underway with both teams having just one thought. WIN!! It was mind-blowing stuff, and 40-odd thousand throats were being put to the test as they roared out support for their team. Suddenly it was two-all, and more mayhem on the kop. McManaman had found Fowler and the genius scored again. Pandemonium reigned, but no sooner was it level than Newcastle were back in the lead through Asprilla.

For a moment or two the kop was suddenly silenced. But not for long. Liverpool were soon back on the attack, and the fact that they were attacking the flag-waving 12,500 must have acted as an inspiration to them. The thought occurred to most of those hoardes that perhaps Liverpool were tired following the exertions of the previous Sunday in the semi-final. But any doubts were suddenly removed when Macca again set up a goal. This time it was for Stan Collymore, who had been relatively quiet up until that moment. Again, the kop was alive with songs, the flags waved madly and the battle for the winner was on.

At 3-3, most teams would have probably settled for what they had. But not these two! And not on this night! These were two heavyweights throwing heavyweight punches. Two Tysons, and not a Bruno in sight. It was a case of kill or be killed, let's see who hits the hardest and who can survive. Emotions were at an almighty high. I swear that during the second half I'd hardly sat down, and neither had anyone around me. The kop, and all of Anfield, was on fire as the tidal wave of passion, emotion and will to win flowed down from the stands onto the pitch and carried the players of both sides forward. In return, the commitment and desire from the players similarly inspired the legions of support to even greater noise and passion. I don't know how the legs of the players felt, but mine had turned to jelly, as nervous exhaustion took over my aching body.

Ian Rush came on. Liverpool came forward; Newcastle responded. The noise, amazingly, grew louder. The referee started to play what has now become known as 'Manchester United Time' (previously known as injury time). Liverpool came forward once more, Barnes swapped passes with Rush until they almost got in each other's way. But Barnes was in control of his brain; he'd spotted Stan Collymore unmarked on the left, and threaded the ball through the gap. And then it happened. Colly netted and wheeled away in uncontrolled delirious delight. I saw him running down alongside the Centenary Stand while everyone in the kop and in the home areas of Anfield went absolutely barmy, crazy and stupid. Who cared? Yes, in time-honoured tradition, strangers hugged one another. I'm sure there were tears in the eyes of some. Anfield was electric - you could have lit up the night sky of the North West on the power and emotion that was being generated.

The final whistle blew. The noise got even louder, and I doubt if 'You'll never walk alone' had ever been sung better! The red shirted players walked towards the kop, and how they must have felt, God only knows. It was a mass of flags being waved with pride, and anthems belted out into the night air. Outside Anfield the streets were alive with the sound of Liverpool songs. It was said that the noise that greeted the winner carried for miles; well, if any of the residents around Anfield had hoped for an early night, they could forget it! It took an age to get out of the ground, and even when we reached our car a mile away, fans were still singing.

Yet we spared a thought for Newcastle. We now even had to live with the thought that we had just made Manchester United a good bet for the title, and we felt for the black and white Toon Army. How must they have felt; their team had given their all, and so had they. But we had outfought them, outlasted them, beaten them. No doubt that on the Thursday morning some forty thousand people had woken up with sore throats, and many others (the armchair brigade) would have woken with the game still spinning through their minds. Those in Anfield had been privileged to watch what was being described as the game of the season, the decade - the century! Which one depended upon who you listened to or which paper you read. For once though, the media couldn't exaggerate, they could only understate what had happened. Both on and off the field, football had triumphed. *TWO TRIBES HAD GONE TO WAR!*

Fanzine Facts

Red All Over The Land was launched in November 1995, ironically on the day that Liverpool lost in the Merseyside derby. Edited by John Pearman, the mag comes out monthly during the football season, and has so far produced seven issues.

RED ATTITUDE

Manchester United

It's difficult to put into words the emotions I felt as I watched Eric Cantona lift the FA Cup at the climax of the '95-96 season, although come to think of it, 'undiluted ecstasy' would just about sum it up nicely! After all, what could be better than winning the League and Cup double, while watching local rivals City drop through the relegation trap-door into the Endsleigh League, a sentence I find difficult to write without indulging in a celebratory jig around the living room. United's success tasted even sweeter this year, not least because everyone had written us off at the start, especially a certain ex-Liverpool defender and smoothie TV pundit who just couldn't resist kicking a man when he was down.

Red Attitude

20 Trophyless Years...
City fans take It Badly

50p

INDEPENDENT UNITED FANZINE ISSUE 0

The week before Wembley had seen United winning the League Championship at Middlesbrough. United fans celebrated with jubilant chants of "you'll never win the League with kids", a sarcastic reference to Alan Hansen's arrogant assertion that a squad filled with youngsters had no chance of winning the Premiership. I didn't join in with that song because although I resented the conceited and almost gleeful manner in which he rubbished United's title hopes, I had grudgingly agreed with his analysis at the time. After all, we'd lost Hughes, Ince and Kanchelskis in the summer, Eric was banned until October, Cole was misfiring badly, and the squad was filled with gawky-looking inexperienced youngsters. The phrase 'transitional season' was being bandied about a fair bit by those in the know, and even Old Trafford itself reflected the sense of a club that was prepared to tread water for a year, with the North Stand only partially rebuilt after its demolition in the summer. For the first half of the campaign I suspect most United fans would have been happy with a UEFA place and a decent cup run. Alex Ferguson knew better, which I suppose explains why he gets paid more in a week than I do in a year. The big difference between us reds and Hansen however was that we were more than happy for Fergie to prove us wrong.

After an opening day defeat at Villa, the vultures hovering over Old Trafford were sharpening their carving knives and ironing their dinner suits, but a ten match unbeaten run saw the boys grow into men in a process that did much to reassure the doubters, although early exits in the Fizzy Pop and UEFA Cups against York and Rotor Volgograd underlined our inexperience in certain areas. Of the two knockouts, it might surprise you to learn that the European exit hurt most; after all there is nothing like a good Euro away trip (and Volgograd away was nothing like it at all!), although on the plus side, at least the bars and hotels of numerous European cities were spared the attentions of hordes of Mancunian beer monsters for another year.

In between times of course, there was the small matter of King Eric returning from an eight month exile for assaulting a South London fascist sympathiser (I can never understand why anyone should have a problem with that!). One of Old Trafford's favourite sons returned to a hero's welcome, and he responded within minutes by supplying the pass for United's first goal, and then coolly slotting home a penalty for the second. If there was one significant event upon which the whole season turned, the return of Eric Cantona in a red shirt was surely it. On that day, even our lucky escape with a draw against our bitterest rivals paled into insignificance.

Christmas saw United defeat Newcastle 2-0, and also registered possibly the first sighting that season of the strange affliction known as Blubbering Geordie Syndrome (first reported at Italia '90). No-one knew it at the time, but this highly infectious ailment would sweep through the massed ranks of the Toon Army as the Championship race drew to a close (so if you've got any spare hankies you know where to send them). However, that victory was the only bright spot in a festive period that saw three consecutive away defeats against Liverpool, Leeds and Spurs. These were results which prompted at least one *Red Attitude* contributor to conclude in a doom-laden article that "we're going to win fuck all this season." Typically, the release of the issue containing this article coincided with the beginning of a 17 match unbeaten run that culminated in United overhauling Newcastle, while at the same time progressing to the Cup Final. Boy, did *we* have egg on our faces.

February was the month where it all came right. It included three easy wins over Blackburn, Everton and Wimbledon in the League, as well as an FA Cup victory over City in the most keenly anticipated derby in years (the Bitters were unhappy about that penalty, but then they always need something to whinge about to camouflage their own inadequacies). The month concluded with a six goal defeat of the village idiots from Bolton, a result that finally destroyed their ridiculous conviction that United are somehow their local rivals, far more suitable candidates of course being Wigan and Bury. As we waved them goodbye we sang "you're going down with the City" and "you'll never see us again." And given the strictly small-time attitude of the clog wearers from hell, it'll be a long time before they ever get another chance to disgrace the Premiership. Driving back from Bolton the pessimists amongst us noted that it was all beginning to look remarkably similar to this time last year. Then, it had all gone horribly wrong at the final hurdle, but now there was one major difference...

Eric was back! Not only that, but he was on a one-man crusade to restore the League and FA Cups to their rightful place in the Old Trafford trophy room. His renaissance matched the rebuilding of the North Stand almost step-by-step. Every time another tier was added, Eric would step up another gear. We always suspected that he felt he owed us one for our undying support during his troubles, and the determination which he showed during the last dozen games confirmed this belief beyond doubt. Priceless goals and performances in victories over City, Newcastle, Arsenal, Spurs, West Ham and Coventry, plus a late equaliser against QPR had all the hallmarks of a man on a mission to repay a debt of honour. Football supporters know that loyalty has its own reward, and just for once it's nice to confirm that a player knows it as well.

In the final weeks, Eric's contribution to United's cause was recognised when he won the Sports Journalist's Player of the Year Award, although the cynics amongst United's support suspect this was more an act of contrition rather than an acknowledgement of Eric's genius. They had gone completely over the top and tried to hound him out of the game following the incident at Palace, and now he was back to prove them wrong. The award was a guilt-ridden act of penance for their past sins against one of the greatest footballers of his generation.

As an aside, it is interesting to note that a cameo court-room appearance by Matthew Simmons degenerated into farce after he leapt from the dock and attempted to strangle the prosecutor. A tempting proposition admittedly, but one hardly likely to help your defence as a nice young man who was picked on for no reason by the nasty Frenchman. A moment of light relief for the United faithful in a season heading towards an increasingly tense climax.

Being naturally pessimistic, we all expected some horrendous end of season sting in the tale which would deprive us once again of both trophies, but in the end it was all fairly easy. We needed a win against 'Boro, but a draw would probably be enough to put the title beyond the reach of the Toonies. The Teessiders offered no real resistance as we put three past them with consummate ease. Meanwhile the travelling red army celebrated United's third Championship in four years with the obligatory conga and drunken festivities 'Down by the Riverside'.

Having won the title, the pressure was off for the Cup Final, although the Scousers were very confident, having had the better of our two League encounters. Perhaps they were over-confident. Who knows? Who cares? All I know is that they deserved to lose for wearing those awful cream coloured Armani suits. John Barnes on the other hand deserves to be drowned slowly in a vat of warm treacle for wearing those hideous white boots, a fashion crime which even Alan Ball, the original perpetrator, eventually disowned. The final itself was certainly no classic, but I don't suppose anyone present at Wembley actually stopped to consider whether we'd be watching it on Match of the Nineties 20 years from now. Eric confirmed his omnipotent status by slotting home a late winning goal, afterwards revealing that it had always been in his mind to settle the final in exactly that manner. Some of us began to suspect that he had sold his soul to supernatural forces in exchange for the gift of genius. Nevertheless, we all went mental, the Scousers left early, and United went down in history as the first ever double Double winners.

In many ways, the future at Old Trafford has never looked brighter. The United board are said to be considering supporters' proposals for singing areas and a freeze on ticket prices. The stadium now has a 55,000 capacity, money is available to sign the world's best players, and with the lifting of the three foreigner rule it looks like we can at last mount a serious challenge in Europe. United's youth policy still has plenty more to offer, with the names Ben Thornley, Terry Cooke and Jovan Kirowski being prominent amongst the crop of exciting youngsters waiting in the wings.

On the debit side, United supporters will face another season of renewed pressure from the PLC to squeeze them out of Old Trafford in favour of middle class day-trippers from the far-off corners of the globe. Despite the enlarged capacity, there will still be overwhelming demand for tickets, especially for the big games. It makes financial sense for a board concerned solely with profit to ensure that tickets go directly to Mr and Mrs Well-Heeled from the Home Counties who spend a fortune in the Megastore before the game, rather than a local lad who spends his money in the pub and gets to the ground 10 minutes before kick-off. The problem is nowhere near as bad as many would have you believe, but it is a growing trend that has to be reversed.

Hostilities will be renewed in August... In more ways than one!

Fanzine Facts

Red Attitude was originally launched at the start of the '94-95 season by members of Man Utd Anti-Fascists. Since those heady far-off days, the fanzine has gone from strength to strength, slowly increasing in terms of both size and circulation. Main contributors are Dave (who has managed to convince everyone that he's the editor), Griff (the old one), Steve (the tall one), and Glen (the other one). However, "all our efforts would be wasted without the help of numerous contributors, sellers and the occasional support of our security advisors" as Dave maintains, adding, "It goes without saying that the fanzine has absolutely no relationship with the club management."

RED CARD

Chelsea

For more than a generation Chelsea's name has not been seen amongst football's role of honour, and silver polish has not been in their list of overheads.

Glenn Hoddle's appointment three years ago was meant to change all that. In his first year he led us in a playing role to the Cup Final. The pain of our 0-4 defeat at the hands of Double-winners Manchester United was eased with a place in the Cup Winners Cup. Against all the odds we advanced to the semi final, losing to eventual winners Real Zaragoza, and as the dejected throng filed out of Stamford Bridge, few if any would have guessed that just over a month later those same fans would be rejoicing over Hoddle's two sensational signings.

The first sent shock-waves throughout the football world, as Ruud Gullit joined on a free transfer. At 33, the cynics claimed that his knees had gone and he'd be spending more time browsing the Kings Road's antique shops than doing what he was being paid for. Shortly after, Mark Hughes, sensing his assured place in the United line-up would only last until Cantona's ban was completed, decided to come to London and play for his childhood heroes. The effect that these two had on the club was awesome; season ticket applications and shirt sales rocketed as the fans clamoured to be part of the revolution.

Their first public appearance was in a non-playing role at Kingstonian, where Chelsea played their first pre-season friendly. Even though the non-league ground only holds 4,500, Gullit and Hughes' appearance broke the ground's previous attendance record and ensured the first lock-out of many to come.

A few days later, they made their playing debuts at Gillingham, a club which three months earlier had been just 24 hours from oblivion. An 11,000 capacity crowd (with a further 3,000 locked out) helped swell the Gill's recovering coffers. A comfortable win including a Mark Hughes goal sent Chelsea's fans home happy, and as the pre-season tour moved to the West Country, Torquay, Exeter and Bristol City all experienced Gullit fever.

Traditionally, Chelsea's pre-season games are played away, but this year we staged a benefit match for Paul Elliott against the Portuguese Champions Porto.

Sixteen thousand turned up for a glimpse of our two new stars, beating all previous testimonial gates since Peter Osgood's over 20 years ago.

The Premiership campaign began against Cup holders Everton. Thousands were turned away as Gullit played a starring sweeper's role, and despite the game ending in a goalless draw, the fans wanted more. We travelled in our thousands to Nottingham, and then played the first game at Middlesbrough's new Riverside Stadium.

Three games gone but still no goals. Then, at home to Coventry, Hughes opened his account, although the game ended in a 2-2 draw. At West Ham in front of the cameras a John Spencer double helped Chelsea gain their first victory, and we followed that up with a 3-0 win at home to Southampton. Hughes contributed one, but the best goal, a sharp volley from Gullit, just about took the roof off.

Bouncing back from a disappointing League Cup defeat at the hands of Stoke, we shone briefly with a win at second placed Villa, but losses followed, and during the home game with Sheffield Wednesday, Gullit added his name to a growing injury list which already included most of our recognised defence.

Enter find of the season Michael Duberry. Saved by our injury crisis from anonymity at Bournemouth (where he was on loan), he was hastily recalled and became a star overnight, remaining a linchpin in the side for the rest of the season. Lining up beside him was David Lee, who had spent most of the previous three seasons in the reserves or out on loan. Perhaps of more significance was Lee's performance in Gullit's role as sweeper; he had always been comfortable on the ball, and with Duberry and Myers became the mainstay in Chelsea's new-look defence.

Off the pitch, mega-rich Matthew Harding had incurred the wrath of his chairman Ken Bates, who although absent from the Leeds game through illness, had banned Harding from enjoying directors' privileges. He denied him access to the boardroom, the directors box and withdrew his car park pass. Harding was unpeturbed and enjoyed the hospitality of the Leeds directors, even watching the match in a Leeds United coat, a gift from the club.

The festering power battle at The Bridge didn't appear to affect the players' form, and Harding began watching home matches from the North Stand, which had been built with £5m of his own money. Even more incredible was the fact that Harding also owns the freehold to Stamford Bridge and is in fact Bates' landlord. By now Chelsea fans had long since become accustomed to Bates' antics, and concentrated on watching the football.

As the Christmas programme approached, Chelsea's back line was completed when Dan Petrescu, the world-class Romanian right-back, joined from Sheffield Wednesday and Terry Phelan returned to London from Man City. Slowly but surely, our form, with Gullit inspirational in the middle of the park, was improving. Hopefully just in time for the tie of the round against Newcastle in the FA Cup. Chelsea looked to be heading for a sensational victory, until Kharine's mis-kicked clearance in the fourth minute of injury time went straight to Albert, who headed into Ferdinand's path. Cue one very controversial equaliser, almost as the final whistle blew. The Chelsea fans and players were distraught, whilst their Newcastle counterparts were ecstatic.

Ten days later and 'mission impossible' was accepted. Newcastle had won all of their previous games at St James' Park and were odds-on favourites to progress. Hitchcock had replaced Kharine, and although the club was quick to point out that he was injured, many believed that this was just an excuse. What transpired that evening may have been the catalyst for their subsequent surrender of what appeared to be an insurmountable Championship lead. We had the audacity to equalise twice, the second coming from Ruud with just two minutes left, giving the Geordies a taste of their own medicine. A goalless extra time, and it was penalties. Chelsea scored four times, Newcastle missed one and two were saved, giving us a sensational victory.

In the fourth round at QPR, Wise and Hughes were both missing, but Paul Furlong (too often the villain of the piece) scored a superb goal with Peacock grabbing the other. QPR pulled one back, missed a penalty a minute later, but it wasn't enough. We now had Wembley in our sights, and even though our League position gave us a chance of Europe, all eyes were on a return to the Twin Towers.

In round five, a nervous draw was gained at a freezing cold Grimsby, and during a sensational period in the replay, Chelsea smashed three goals in as many minutes into Grimsby's net to move into the quarter finals against Wimbledon.

After a thumping draw at the Bridge, the home side enjoyed a rare full house for the replay, despite half of Selhurst's new stand not being used (apparently due to a row over rent with Palace). Just as the Chelsea fans dominated the ground (taking over 80% of the 17,000 seats), the team swarmed all over The Dons, and cruised to a silky 3-1 win.

Cup fever was back in earnest with fans relishing the prospect of revenge against Man United in the semi final at Villa Park. Determined not to miss out, Chelsea fans queued all night for tickets. Despite the pitch resembling Camber Sands, Chelsea played the better football and Gullit headed home Hughes' cross to give us a first half lead. But in the second half, our worst fears were realised. First, Andy Cole finally hit the proverbial barn door, then Burley hooked an attempted back-pass into the path of Beckham who raced into the box to put United ahead. After that, Cantona of all people headed off the line and Wise was twice denied by Schmiechel.

Chelsea's and Gullit's Cup dream was over for another year, and as we played out our remaining fixtures the rumours regarding Hoddle's future began in earnest. Out of contract in the summer, he always denied being approached by the FA for the England job, but refused to sign a new deal at Chelsea claiming that he was unable to commit himself until the boardroom battle had been resolved.

But every cloud has a silver lining, and following Glen's unsurprising departure the fans got their wish granted when Gullit was installed as the new player/manager. His influence has already been felt, with the signing of Italian superstar Gianluca Vialli.

So as we look forward to the new season, the fans are more concerned about what happens on the pitch rather than the ongoing boardroom battle and ground redevelopment. And who knows, someone yet may be sent out to buy some silver polish!

Fanzine Facts

Red Card was first published at the beginning of Chelsea's Second Division Championship season of '88-89, and 71 issues later it's still going strong. All this despite several costly legal battles including a High Court appearance after Ken Bates sued editor Alan Collis for libel. In a attempt to resolve the matter Alan asked the chairman for advice, to which Bates replied "Try getting on your knees and grovelling!." Eventually an apology in front of the judge was accepted but by then the legal bill totalled over £3,000. Luckily, *Red Card*'s readers rallied round and this was paid off within a year. Recently, a truce between the two was celebrated when Alan had lunch with the chairman (paid for of course by Alan). But at least a costly lesson had been learnt: if you take on Bates there's only one place you'll come - second!

Chelsea Flower Show Special

for sale

summer mayflowers

only

£164,614 per crate

Legal note: They mayflower, they may not.

Chelse Independent

THE ROOTS HALL ROAR

Southend United

It was during a turgid, mean-ingless end of season home match against Tranmere Rovers that I heard it. My brother Tony had acquired two tickets for the director's box from work and asked me along to get another angle for the *Roar*. The prawn parcels at half-time were certainly different, as was the eerie feeling of sitting back down on a comfortable cushion after offering some passionate advice to our lacklustre heroes. That is where we stood out like sore dicks; the rest in the hangers-on box (there was not one director in sight) remained impassive and motionless. That is when *he* spewed out these immortal words... "You don't actually support Southend do you?." I think Tony was too stunned to utter a reply, let alone chin him, before our neighbour continued... "I mean with all the excellent communication links you have down here and everything." Those few words summed up not only our season, but the apathy towards our club in general. Despite a huge catchment area, Grimsby Town and ourselves were the worst supported clubs in the Division. We are now officially a London overspill rather than a seaside resort, and many of the local populace therefore have allegiances to the Capital's 'finest', and even when the club introduced cut-price tickets, Southend townsfolk failed to respond. The national press either ignore or ridicule us and I can no longer bring myself to respond to away supporters' boorish chants of "shit ground - no fans!"

If you didn't know any better I may have given you the impression that we had just experienced a dismal season. Far from it. It was Southend United's most successful campaign ever. *We are the 34th best club in the country.*

After the first two games I was convinced that I had seen three certain relegation candidates: Portsmouth, Luton Town - and, well, Southend, frankly. Surely I would not bear witness to such ineptness elsewhere, but I was wrong; the standard of Endsleigh League Division One was even worse than the previous season (Sky TV, what have you done?!?). At least our manager Ronnie Whelan recognised our shortcomings and managed to persuade our loveable chairman to part with some of his Collymore fund. Mike Lapper (American international), Mark McNally and Paul Byrne (both ex-Celtic) and Mike Marsh were added to the squad. They could actually keep the ball on the deck and soon made favourable impressions with the Roots Hall faithful. Ronnie could certainly spot a defender and a midfield player, but when it came to strikers he seemed to have a mental block. Throughout we played minus a forward line (to label the two people that filled those positions thus would have violated the Trade Descriptions Act). Whelan tried his luck abroad and signed a Norwegian - Peter 'The Viking' Belsvik - on loan. Hmmm, 'The Smurf' was nearer the mark. I would go as far to say (and please don't laugh) that if we'd had a decent pair of strikers this season we would now be rubbing shoulders with the likes of Manchester United and Newcastle. And wouldn't they have just welcomed us with open arms?!!

We didn't enjoy too many run-ins with the board this year. Chairman Vic was ill for quite some time so I decided to interview his sidekick John Adams instead. Alas, John objected to our usual questionnaire type format, claiming that it could be slanted; I protested that we were a vehicle for his supporters and would only ask the type of questions that they never got the chance to put to him personally. In the end, I refused to be dictated to and our brief meeting ended with John accusing me of being "entrenched", (and long may *RHR* continue to be). I also managed to gain entry to the shareholders' AGM and found it most illuminating. Our chairman informed us that we had a better stadium than 70% our First Division rivals and that our two superstores (sic) (actually two tatty club shops) took in approximately £200 a week - between them! My abiding memory was the way the floor were discouraged from asking questions: "My question is can di..." "That's not a question, it's a speech and is not acceptable..."; you get my drift. Transfer deals apart, we suffered a record loss in the last financial year, but this didn't stop Vic awarding himself a 35% pay rise. Nice work if you can get it.

The mistake of the season was not made on the field of play, it was committed by yours truly. Five off us bombed down to Italy in a Lexus (it took us ten hours to get to Milan) to see the Blues play in the Anglo-Italian Cup. One local couple drove down in a Reliant Robin! We pulled up outside the San Siro at nine in the morning and, after some pidgin Italian at the gate, we persuaded someone to give us a tour of the ground. I took numerous snaps of the boys inside the vast stadium in their Southend shirts ('a piccolo club' we informed the affable groundsman), had a picture taken of me climbing out of the bath in the Meeeelan dressing room (which was surprisingly Spartan) and took one of Charlie doing a splendid Keef Richards impression outside the drug testing room. The next night I had to confess to the lads that I didn't have any film in my camera.

A couple of them do still talk to me.

We grabbed a 1-1 draw against Reggiana's reserves, roared on by 100 loyal/crazy fans. There was only one unsavoury incident to report during the trip, but naturally it did not involve our traditionally well-behaved fans. A female member of the club sponsor's party got shit-faced, trashed her room, punched several people and consequently spent a night in the cells. When we arrived at the hotel to team up with our mates who had travelled by plane, the sheepish rep who had just got her released was handing out Southend United pens to appease the hotel staff and the ever-present Polizia. Needless to say the biro's didn't work. On the way home we bought one of those huge pink publications that James Richardson brandishes on a Saturday morning. The headline read "Not Even Southend Can Make Reggiana Happy."

Hypocrite of the season was my mate Andy. En route to Filbert Street to take on high-flying Leicester City, we heard that the diminutive Julian Hails was in our starting XI. Andy was instrumental in the 'turn the car around we've got no chance' movement. We did get into the ground, albeit ten minutes late, only to discover that Hails had put us one up. He went on to score the perfect hat-trick in one of those rare games that everything seemed to go right for us; we eventually triumphed 3-1. And who did we meet on the way home? None other than Mr Hails himself, who'd travelled alone to Leicester after missing the team bus. Andy went straight over to him and patted him heartily on the shoulder, "Well done mate... you deserve it!." Aaarggh, this prompted mass derision all the way home.

The flashpoint of the season was Dave Regis' last act in a Southend shirt. He decked Derby County's Croatian defender who'd subjected him to a torrent of racist abuse throughout the game. Jim Smith leapt to the defence of his new signing, claiming that the lad couldn't speak a word of English. Unfortunately for Jim, Igor had just conducted an impromptu press conference in perfect Queen's. He soon picked up a quaint new Essex expression when one of our passing players called him a f*****g foreign c**t, in the tunnel.

Our best player in '95-96 was without question our young custodian Simon Royce. I will be very surprised, and delighted, if he is still with us next term as so many Premier League clubs have reportedly been monitoring his performances. A supreme shot-stopper with handling to match, the lad can now also drop-kick the ball over the half-way line; definitely one for the future. I estimate that he alone was responsible for the fact that we did not have to endure the usual chore of relegation avoidance. Our less blessed squad members were Phil Gridelet and Keith Dublin. Phil started modelling this year and admits to being last out onto the pitch as he is busy studying himself in the mirror. "If you've got it flaunt it", professes our midfield 'dynamo'. We have yet to see him flaunt 'it' out on the pitch. Gridelet's speciality is the lofted pass - from within the opposition's penalty area. As vain as he is I bet he is still bewildered that Venables left him out of his Euro 96 squad. At least Dublin is a battler; despite his shortcomings he never gives less than his all, and that is why he has less hecklers than our resident beefcake. I recently read that in America, sports stars can patent their own individual mannerisms and celebrations. If this had been introduced many years ago the likes of Dick Fosbury would be coining it in. My advice to Keith is go out and put a copyright on that unique step-over-then-trip-over-the-ball routine now.

Finally, the highlight of the season. I was sitting at my desk when one of our messengers tapped me on the shoulder and begged the question "Apart from winning the lottery, what would make you the happiest man alive? Birmingham have sacked him haven't they?." It was the moment I had been waiting for so long. Bazza was apparently "stunned and disappointed." Now he knew how *we* felt. All of a sudden the 'sleeping giants' he'd ditched us for were not all that after all, they were a long way from being a top outfit, claimed the bitter Mr Fry. Strangely enough he does not appear to have been deluged with job offers since. My Sunday side were briefly interested, but our secretary flatly refused to take on all the extra administrative work that comes with a flood of new signings. We toasted his ill-fortune; we even heard of Birmingham fans raising the odd glass at the news of his demise. From now on, May 7th will be forever commemorated in south-east Essex, it will always be a *fryday* and my muckers will be seen proudly wearing an emblem consisting of thirty pieces of silver on their lapels.

As for next season, I can't wait. Considering the average opposition we are going to encounter (especially if Alan Ball remains at Maine Road), and the fact that we may manage to sign somebody who can put the ball into the net (Tony Cottee I hear has just moved to Thorpe Bay), then there is no reason why we cannot extend our five-year run in the Division that our knockers never thought we would or should become a part of.

Fanzine Facts

RHR has been going since 1991 and is mainly written by Bob Sills and edited by Mark Withers, with a hard core of five regular contributors that help to keep them going. Like many fanzine writers, they often used aliases; indeed when one former employee of the Blues (upset by a particular article) demanded to know who wrote the *Roar*, the club (as clued up as usual) pointed them in the direction of an Andy Fairweather-Low; needless to say he couldn't be traced in the Southend directory!

RUB OF THE GREENS

Plymouth Argyle

Division Wot?

If there was a hangover from the Shilton era at Home Park, it soon cleared up once Neil Warnock arrived. I was never a fan of Shilton the manager, and he got his come-uppance. However, he effectively wrecked Plymouth Argyle along the way.

Warnock wasted no time in getting rid of Shilton's signings, most of whom had expressed their wish to leave before his arrival anyway.

These exits more than financed all the incoming journeymen - Mauge, Heathcote, Clayton, Leadbitter, Logan, Baird, Billy - that Warnock signed, although we were touted as big buyers. By the time we had a settled team, only Patterson, Evans and Barlow remained of the pre-Warnock players. The rest all seem to have played for Huddersfield and/or Cambridge before...

We still don't have a goalkeeper to call our own. Hammond was signed from Swindon and sold on to Reading in double quick time following our disastrous start of six straight defeats. Kevin Blackwell the youth team coach took over for half a season before a succession of loanees grappled for the green jersey. Steve 'Sumo' Cherry has been there for the last three months but the play-off final was his last match for us.

Despite the fact that I am writing this the day after Plymouth Argyle won on our first ever visit to 'Wemberlee', I am totally against the play-off system for deciding promotion issues. As far as I am concerned, we have competed in a LEAGUE for the last nine months, so why make it a cup competition at the end?

OK, it was wonderful when we scored, and at the final whistle, but I had no fingernails left and I'll swear my hair is greyer! Only the 'part timers' and 'hangers on' could really enjoy the day to the full. The loyal 6,000 only really celebrated once the game finished.

It was unreal to be at the 'Mecca' of English football, watching my team doing a lap of honour with a play-off trophy having finished fourth! I wonder how the fans of Preston, Gillingham and Bury felt about it?

At least justice was done this time. Two years ago we finished third in Division Two - 12 points ahead of Burnley, who then knocked us out of the play-offs at the semi final stage. I'm not the only Argyle fan who has enjoyed seeing two seasons of struggle for the Turf Moor mob! One division lower, we again finished in what would have been a promotion position pre-play-offs, so it is only right that we should go up. I had to laugh at Argyle 'player' Chris Billy's comment of "Thank God for the play-offs - if we didn't have them we wouldn't have this chance to go up." Fool! If it wasn't for the play-offs, we'd have been up anyway!

Having played well for most of the season, I began to feel sorry for Darlington as they looked so dejected after the final whistle at Wembley. However, I have since seen a recent copy of their fanzine *Mission Impossible* and I don't feel sorry for them at all. Their fans deserve to stay down.

That's true of Colchester too. Alex Ferguson was heavily criticised for his comments in the press towards the end of the season. It was nothing compared to the diatribe of the Colchester manager prior to our clashes in the play-offs. The Essex press did their best to drum up bad feeling too. To his credit, Neil Warnock did not rise to the bait and let the team do the talking.

Argyle's first ever season in the basement has had a few highs, but on the whole it has been awful. A Division of shit teams playing shit football in shit stadi... grounds. To call some of them 'stadia' would be a total falsehood. Anyone who has visited the delights of Barnet, Doncaster, Rochdale and Cambridge, to name just four, will know what I mean.

Some of the grounds have been a welcome surprise, though. Hartlepool, Bury and Scarborough were a revelation compared to previous visits and the new stand at Preston is magnificent. Fulham is still one of my favourite away grounds - despite our 0-4 defeat there. On the whole, though, it's like being in the Conference, except that most Conference grounds are more modern. The 'gates' that some of these teams survive on is unbelievable. How they get by is completely beyond me.

The football was something else again, and we were as bad as anybody else in this respect. We always looked more effective when we passed the ball, rather than hoofing it the length of the pitch. However, our best footballers, i.e. pre-Warnock signings, hardly got a look-in. Not surprising really, because he often accused them of playing too much football! Mind you, ironic cheers greeted every move with more than three passes - he must have got the message!

Our season really turned when Martin Barlow was selected regularly. One of the best passers at the club and rightful winner of the PASTA Player of the Year. Sadly, all the other supporters groups gave their awards to Mick Heathcote - a centre back in the classic Fourth Division mould, i.e. a good 'stopper' but no distribution skills. Every team in this League has got a centre back like Heathcote and some have two or three. No prizes for guessing the 'style' of football played by most teams! Here Gillingham deserve a special mention as they have eleven 'players' in the Heathcote mould. Their success this season is due to the way they have intimidated teams into submission. Hopefully they will be found out next year.

There *have* been exceptions of course. Preston deserved to win the Championship as they were the best footballing team, and with their support they could go far. Darlington's football warranted a better fate, but as I said earlier, their 'supporters' got exactly what they deserve. Bury played some neat stuff at times, but it's hard to believe that a team we thrashed 5-0 away finished above us!

Another major difference in this Division is the lack of organisation. Barnet didn't seem to appreciate the size of Argyle's travelling contingent and had to keep opening extra bits of the ground. Colchester didn't realise they had a chance of getting in the play-offs so didn't sort out tickets for their home game until five days before the event.

Exeter City are a sad club - in the hands of the receiver, pride was more important to them than money. When we played at St James Park, instead of allocating a larger area of terrace to us, we had a condemned area, capacity 1,000. What happens? 500 Argyle fans go to Exeter and buy tickets for the 'home' area. The gate that day was 6,500 which could have been a capacity if the club had been sensible or realistic. Torquay did just that and benefited with 2,500 Argyle fans in the crowd.

On the whole, the season has been one long hard slog and I'm not sorry to be waving Division Three goodbye. We finished on a high with the Wembley appearance but that can't mask the nine months of dross we suffered before. The only other highs were Bury away (5-0) when our season really started, Lincoln and Fulham at home (both 3-0) - yes we can win well at home - and the two games with Torquay - the Gulls played some great football!

Other positives from '95-96? The supporters matches meant some very early starts on Saturday mornings, but we made loads of new friends, particularly those at Bury, Darlington, Preston, Fulham, Rochdale and Mansfield. We also re-visited a great bunch of Wycombe fans when Argyle played Slough in the Cup.

Several at the club deserve the promotion. Neil Warnock, who didn't promise anything this season, but delivered despite much criticism and Dan McCauley, who has piled loads of his own money into the club with nothing to show until now. But most of all the loyal fans - the ones who have supported the club through thin and thin in recent years.

I shan't miss Division Three - roll on '96-97!

Fanzine Facts

Rub of the Greens was launched by Tony Scowcroft (aka ROTGUT) in March 1990, and is aided by the editorial team of the Plymouth Argyle Supporters' Club, including chairman Steve Nicholson who wrote the article above.

THE SEADOG BITES BACK!

Scarborough

The same again please, barman!!

When people say 'things can only get better' they are either a) singing D:Ream's hit song from a couple of years back, or b) a Scarborough fan. After the descent to 91st place in the League during '94-95 a vast majority of Seadogs, including some of the most loyal, were feeling sceptical of what was to come during '95-96.

The scepticism soon turned to optimism after the pre-season, as a string of fine wins and a draw against Leeds United (Yeboah and all), coupled with what seemed at the time as excellent signings, combined to turn the heads of the ever doubtful supporters. In fact it was so good that some believed the coming campaign would be our most successful since '88-89,

which culminated in the play-offs. Undoubtedly the biggest and baldest (!) signing was Andy Ritchie, who'd been released by Oldham Athletic. His free signing was hailed by chairman John Russell as "the biggest Scarborough Football Club could ever make." Manager Ray McHale said he was looking for between 20-25 goals from Ritchie, and most agreed this would not be too hard, given his top-flight experience and the influx of new talent around him.

Among the newcomers, all on frees, were: Don Page, the former Rotherham and Chester striker; Richard Lucas, a central midfielder or left back from Preston; Lee Thew, a midfielder from Donny Rovers; Ronnie Robinson, another left back from Exeter; Mark Todd, a midfielder from Rotherham and Oliver Heald, a Canadian international striker from Port Vale.

With a virtually rebuilt team, a new kit and a feeling of contentment, we rolled into Doncaster on the opening day looking to take three points back to the coast. Our plans were scuppered before we even kicked off. New signings Lee Thew and Ronnie Robinson were involved in a car accident on the Friday night and had to be replaced at the last minute. All the chopping and changing didn't help as we fell to earth with a bang after a 1-0 defeat. But we soon cheered up when reminded of the 45 games still to go! Great!

The Coca Cola Cup was guzzled down at Hartlepool after a 7-6 loss on penalties. This rates as one of my most emotional nights as a Boro fan, not that I cried or anything! It just hit me really hard, harder than Vinnie Jones, Julian Dicks and Stuart Pearce put together! The fact we had two chances to win it during the shoot-out made it worse. In the end we fluffed it, or at least Lee Thew did, and Hartlepool went through to play Arsenal in the second round.

One of our best finds came and went within a month. Jimmy Gardner, a Scottish winger, joined the club initially on trial, and then signed a three month contract (or so we thought). His displays on the left flank and his eye for a cross helped Boro to a couple of decent wins, but as soon as he received a better offer from Cardiff City, he hopped on the first train to South Wales. It was a kick in the teeth for Boro, who had helped revive a career which was going nowhere in St Mirren's reserves. Yet like most of today's young stars, Gardner opted to raise his bank balance rather than Boro's League position.

In the meantime, we'd been knocked out of the FA Cup, and the Auto Windscreens Shield. Sixteen year old YTS lad Mark Lee became the youngest ever Boro first team player against Preston, but youthful exuberance couldn't help us, as three defeats saw us slip to 18th in Division Three, any early promise slowly fading away. Even the North Riding Senior Cup had been abandoned until the summer! Andy Ritchie was then interviewed for the vacant manager's job at Wigan Athletic, but nothing came of that.

December, and new signings and departures took centre stage. David D'Auria left to join Scunthorpe for £50,000. Oliver Heald (who'd scored the goal of the season against Fulham in August) and Ronnie Robinson were released after five months at the club. Don O'Riordan, the former Torquay manager, joined as coach, and the signings were finished off with wingers Kevin Magee (a free from Plymouth) and Craig Midgley (three month loan from Bradford). Yet all this to-ing and fro-ing in the transfer market had no immediate impact as we slumped even further in the League. The 2-0 defeat to Donny and the 1-0 reverse against Fulham were voted worst home and away games respectively in our end of season poll.

We were now in 23rd place. Obviously something had to be done to halt the slide. Midfielder Chris Myers was brought in after the release of Mark Todd. Also arriving at the McStad was Andy Curtis, as back-up for Craig Midgley. Andy Ritchie, who'd been on the transfer list since November, was linked with a loan move to Shrewsbury, which he turned down. A Sheffield United quartet of Carl Veart, Charlie Hartfield, Phil Starbuck and former Boro loan star John Reed were all linked with moves to North Yorkshire's greatest team, but unsurprisingly the moves fell through.

And shock, horror, the latest changes to the side actually seemed to help, as we ventured with trepidation into the unknown: an unbeaten run of five games. These included a marvellous 2-0 away win at Rochdale and a 1-0 win at home to Cardiff. The former saw Craig Midgley score one of the goals of the season, and the latter saw Steve Charles make his 600th League appearance, and the return of Jimmy Gardner who was given a suitably hard time throughout the game. Many Seadogs thought the run would help us towards mid-table security. Wrong! We were brought back down to earth in Challenger Space Shuttle style by Wigan's Roberto Martinez (Martinez 2, Boro 0), as we started a further 13 match stretch without a win.

The redevelopment of The McCain Stadium came under the spotlight in March. The new West Stand was opened for away fans against Hartlepool, and John Russell collected an award at the Wembley Fizzy pop final for stadium redevelopment. The Hartlepool game itself finished as a 2-1 loss, Stuart Hicks gaining our consolation with a net-busting 35 yard free kick. He didn't stop talking about it for weeks!

By now, it was becoming apparent that we'd be bottom if Torquay hadn't been so crap, and after a 1-0 defeat at Barnet, manager Ray McHale was 'asked to step down', or in other words he was sacked but kept on as assistant. Don O'Riordan wasn't so lucky, his tour of seaside clubs was to continue elsewhere.

The new manager needed to be a name, someone who could demand and gain the respect of the chairman and the fans: Glenn Roeder, Jimmy Mullen and Mike Walker were all in the frame, but instead Russell opted to appoint Mitch Cook, a former player, as 'director of coaching' (or manager). Relations between supporters and players improved immediately when Cook ordered the team to go into the supporters bar after the games to face the fans. However on the pitch things were, to be blunt, crap! Unfortunately, Cook's management skills didn't live up to his talent for PR. We lost the first five games under his guidance, conceding 17 goals along the way and only scoring three.

A trip to Plymouth was fraught with controversy. As a morale booster, the night before the game Cook decided to take a few players out for half a Guinness. The original story which hit the tabloids was that the whole team had gone out on a bender. If only it were true; at least it would explain the 5-1 defeat that followed. Truth be told, we were just a pile of pooh, that's all there is to it.

Speculation was rife that Cook was about to be ousted. At one game, Gordon Cowans was spotted in the stand, pen and paper in hand. But nothing happened - not then, anyway. The season petered out with a couple more losses, and Andy Ritchie a mile short of the 20-25 goals we were looking for, only getting seven (but was still top scorer). Winger Andy Curtis also broke his leg for the third time in his career in training, but the blow was softened when he was given £300 from the players' pool.

Possibly the biggest achievement for Scarborough was when full-back Darren Knowles was voted second in the North East Player of the Year contest, only losing out to Les Ferdinand.

The season over, all attention was focused on the managers job. Unsurprisingly the axe fell on Cook. Youth and reserve team coach Phil Chambers, who had been at the club since '89, and had a spell as manager in '93, also felt the cold steel. This turned out to be a weird few weeks, as a total of 60-odd applicants applied for the job. The main front runner was still Gordon Cowans, and indeed the job looked as though it was his until late May, when he pulled out, preferring to stay at Sheffield United and see out his playing career. The job again looked settled with David Hodgson ready to take charge, until he took his bucket and spade elsewhere due to contractual differences. At the moment it is hard to see who else there is to take the job - at this rate, I'll be on the bench in August. But I know one thing: whoever accepts the challenge will have a mighty hard task. Hardly any money, only eight players and an average attendance of under 1,600; let's see what Fergie would do with that raw material.

Hell, no-one wants to finish 91st in the Football League for a third time. But there's one consolation: at least I don't support York City!

Fanzine Facts

In a recent article about Scarborough Football Club in FourFourTwo *TSBB* was described as a 'friendly polite' fanzine. This is quite true. Given the plight of the club, editor James Hunter tries to look on the bright side. "I am an optimist in every sense of the word" says Hunter, "You have to be here, if not you'll end up ringing the Samaritans every five minutes."

The 69er

THE SHEEPING GIANT

Wrexham

Imagine my excitement when I, humble Dai Shovett, Welsh Sports Writer of the Year (according to my mum), was asked to pen this fine piece of work! From my modest beginnings as an apprentice journalist, polishing the boots of the professionals, to this! My break in national publishing! From John O'Groats to his brother Billy, everyone will be able to enjoy my thrilling prose style, so purple I am known throughout North Wales as simply 'The Journalist Formerly Known As Prince'. Or was that 'The Simple Journalist With A Dog Called Prince'?

Previously, being Wrexham FC correspondent for a local paper has, surprisingly, limited my profile in the rest of the country. I do occasionally get to cover other teams, but it always tends to be an anti-climax. I went on that stupid Far East tour with the England team, but it was so dull! Nothing newsworthy happened! I was so bored I slept all the way back, despite what sounded like the noisiest in-flight movie ever! I never thought I'd sleep through "The Lion King", although I do have a vague recollection of a previously unbroadcast scene where Simba trashes his hotel room.

Mind you, it's not all roses; writing about football is a job for a man willing to pour the very fibre of his being onto the page, to re-invent himself and bend the boundaries of conventional prose in order to challenge, clarify and purify the consciousness of his audience. Pays well too. Writing is a very painful process, tearing something from your soul every time you put pen to paper. Ernest Hemingway killed himself, and he didn't have to watch Wrexham every week.

Anyway, on to Wrexham's season. It began in exciting style, when I made up a story about the Reds buying Gianluca Vialli from Juventus ("**WOP THIS WAY - FANS TELL FLYNN 'JUVE GOT A BARGAIN' "**). After that we actually did go to Europe, playing crack Romanian outfit Petrolul Ploesti (32 points in Scrabble, not counting double word scores). The commies were hardly a cheerful bunch - no doubt still hung over after celebrating the tenth anniversary of Chernobyl - hence my thrilling headline summing up Wrexham's chances - **FISSION IMPOSSIBLE**. Still, considering we had a half strength team we did pretty well to limit them to a 1-0 win described in the local papers as "Acestor bilete se pedrepseste." Euro runs are always lucrative for local journalists, as Johnny Foreigner often asks for background on our region. I wrote an article on Wrexham for the Ploesti paper, with the headline "RIVER SHEEP MOUNTAIN MINE", which apparently lost something in the translation.

On the home front, Wrexham's form was disappointing. Indeed, I was so distracted that I often forgot to tape 'Countdown' (I like to freeze-frame that luscious local lovely Carol Vorderman and gaze at her fabulous thin hair). The Rockin' Robins were missing 100-Goal Gary Bennett, who had been forced to leave the country after my "BENNETT IN SEX QUIZ" exclusive, and sign for Tranmere. Some malicious scoundrels had the nerve to accuse me of making the story up, but it was totally true - I'd stopped him in the club car park and asked him to name three differences between a man and a woman, and if that isn't a sex quiz then I don't know what is!

Little Brian Flynn's replacements failed at first to fill the gap left by centurion Bennett, but by God, he could handle a spade. Experienced Peter Ward came from something called Stockport and did well (which was a shame as I was keen to run the headline "WARD, HUH! WHAT IS HE GOOD FOR? ABSOLUTELY NOTHING!"), but Elusive Craig Skinner looked as comfortable as a claustrophobic man in an open space, while Kojak of the Kop Kevin Russell suffered from unfavourable comparisons with an identical-looking super-striker who had played for us in the Eighties. Funnily enough, he was called Kevin Russell too.

Fortunately, both Russell and Skinner enjoyed remarkable turn-arounds in their form, resulting in their becoming firm favourites with the fans. I tried all season to find out how the coaching staff had managed such a swing in their fortunes, but without success. My informer, Pete Throat, told me that they pump them up so full of drugs before each game that they sometimes pass the ball to big green monsters with check jackets on, and the club lay on massive bowls of corn flakes for them to eat at half time. When oh when will he ever find me a story worth looking into?

In August we had our annual defeat at Blackpool, although some good did come of the game as I wrote a brilliant report. Blackpool is a venue that offers plenty of scope for those clichés that can make a writer's career. Take this paragraph from my account, which I sent to the judges for the Nobel Prize for Literature:

"Humes towered over the Blackpool donkeys, but in the second half Wrexham's defence dissolved like candy floss in a strong sea breeze as the Tangerine Dream Team blew in like a breath of fresh Ayre."

Ironically, I forgot to enclose an S.A.E., and therefore never received a reply from that Nobel lot. Could I have won the prize and not heard about it?

The turning point in the season came after a disappointing draw with Mansfield, which is only a shoe shop. Next we played runaway leaders Swindon at home. Apparently Little Brian Flynn had introduced a revolutionary new shape to his team, but I couldn't tell the difference. Mind you, after Swindon went 2-0 up after 15 minutes I decided to go home and watch 'Brief Encounter' on Channel Four - I could make the report up on Monday morning. Frustratingly, it turned out that Wrexham won 4-3, and, despite the title, the film didn't have any underpants in it. There ought to be a law against such misleading titles - I haven't been so disappointed since I forked out £2.30 to see 'Free Willy'. And that Pepsi Max tastes nothing like the old bloke who used to be in 'Hart to Hart'.

Anyway, The Reds, or "Little Brian Flynn, Ably Assisted By Nice Kevin Reeves, Committed Joey Jones and Sensible Mel Pejic,'s Red and White With a

Yellow Advert and Black Boots Army" as the fans affectionately know them, went from strength to strength. Victories at home were augmented by a string of fine away performances at a succession of grounds which I either couldn't find or couldn't be bothered to go to. I did manage to turn up at some away matches, more out of curiosity than anything else, but I often found these journeys to be anticlimactic and even suspicious. I arrived early at Eastville and Fellows Park only to find myself completely alone. And yet, despite no trace of a match taking place, Wrexham were credited with 2-1 victories in each and scaled the table! Furthermore, we were supposed to have drawn at Wycombe, and everybody knows there's no such team! When it came to playing them at home my suspicions were aroused. They were wearing ludicrous rugby outfits (as if old-fashioned shirts will ever come back into fashion!) and were freaky 6' 11" Neanderthals to a man! When they actually started playing they were ridiculous, just thumping the ball as far as they could! We beat them easily, but eased up to leave it at 1-0 to make it look realistic. They clearly weren't a real football team so, sensing a cover-up, I contacted Woodward and Bernstein. Unfortunately they turned out to be a firm of solicitors in Llandudno, and when I tried to phone Oliver Stone, Frank Clark told me to get lost. Never mind.

Controversy was to continue to dog Wrexham's season. In January the following headline appeared in "The Sun":

"ULRIKA AND HUNTER MADE LOVE IN MY BED."

Obviously I couldn't just ignore this shocker so I penned the following front page exclusive:

"WREXHAM CENTRE BACK IN LOVE TRIANGLE PROBE"

"Wrexham star Barry Hunter has been named as the shadowy third man in Finnish blonde bombshell Ulrika Johnson's messy divorce."

The libel case comes up in August, but I'm confident I'll be alright as no-one ever reads what I write. That's how I got away with the **"HODDLE KILLS 12 IN BROTHEL CARNAGE"** story.

As the season progressed the Reds maintained a top ten place. In February Little Brian Flynn delved into the transfer market, looking to make a double swoop to strengthen our play-off hopes: to boost our attack he brought Leapy Lee Jones back on loan from Liverpool; and to tighten up our defence he attempted to sign that goalie with the massive wings from the Nike advert with Eric Cantona in. He came for a trial and played for the reserves in a friendly against a Brymbo Steelworks Golden Select Eleven featuring Mike Duxbury and one of the blond blokes out of Bucks Fizz (both of them would have been just too much). He was a confident lad and certainly filled the goal, but Flynnie's expert eye had spotted a flaw - he had an irritating habit of exploding when the ball was hit straight at him. Bearing this in mind we only offered him a one year contract, and he politely declined, claiming that he had decided to give up football and work in the strangulation-related industries. The club shop were particularly sick about this, as they were already planning to up the cost of the letters they put on the back of their replica shirts in anticipation of a rash of requests for 'Beelzebub' (24 points in Scrabble, bonus ball back in October).

The Boys from the Racecourse were beginning to look like thoroughbreds in a sea of donkeys as they flew on the express train towards the chequered flag of promotion. They developed the irritating habit of not losing very often, which seriously limited my scope for stories - nothing sells papers like bad news (or a diahorrea epidemic). Even though the defence was still leakier than a Yorkshire Water pipeline, the attack made up for this by scoring lots of goals. Last season I'd had plenty to moan about, but now nothing! We'd suffered our own mad cow scare in the boardroom last year, but the promotion of Birmingham City meant that I couldn't even write about that this time round. Still, there was some consolation, as the play-off bid fizzled out like a candle in the wind, never knowing who to cling to when the rain set in. Defeat at home to Burnley effectively ended our chances, and protesting fans burnt effigies of the Wrexham manager. Desperate not to be outdone, Burnley's fans set fire to the real thing, and a fun time was had by all. Actually, that's all a lie. It's the journalist in me, which reminds me of something Pamella Bordes said to me once.

Of course, all seasons lead to the farewell of old friends. I was particularly sorry to see Hull go down as they are a veritable gold mine of headline material. Every time we play them I compile a list of possible ones. You know the sort of thing: "BLOODY HULL"; "A LOAD OF HULL"; "WINDASS GIVES FOOD FOR FART." In the end I plumped for "HULL ME, THRILL ME, KISS ME, NIL-NIL ME." This is the longest headline I have ever written, and therefore the best. It is also ironic as we beat them 5-0.

The future's bright for Little Brian Flynn's men. They were Welsh dragons who breathed fire into the hearts of the Kop faithful, the Division's outstanding footballing team whose attacking style poured cold water on the opposition, except for after they lost, when they were a mediocre bunch of underachievers whose failure in the bread and butter matches left no crumbs of comfort to the long-suffering red army. The milk of their human kindness was one hundred per cent proof, but sadly not Bradford-proof as we missed out on the play-offs and failed to make the Bantams wait.

The future's bright for me as well. My dashing style has been recognised by the scouts (the Italian girl guides having decided not to take up their option), and I've been asked to contribute to "SMELLS LIKE KHARINE SPIRIT", an "exciting new mag all about footy and lads." It can't fail now!

Fanzine Facts

Like most "bastard offspring", according to co-editor Gavin Evans (aka The Green Anorak), *The Sheeping Giant* was conceived in the back of a transit van on the way home from the '89-90 Welsh Cup Final. Originally set up to raise cash for the 'Wrexham Revival Fund' which was formed to raise money to buy players to help the club maintain its League status, today, Gavin and his co-editor Darren Morris turn most of their profits over to the club as sponsorship or use it to produce *TSG* merchandise. *TSG* has a team of regular contributors, which include Bryn Law, Herbert Phlegm, Damon Williams, Richard Sympson, Andrea & Jayne Davies (Ewe's Eye), Sumo, Peter Ellis and Gareth M Davies.

SING WHEN WE'RE FISHING

Grimsby Town

Season '95-96 was to be the first one under the exclusive guidance of Brian Laws, who, we were given to understand, would be happy with nothing less than the Premier League. We'd finished tenth the previous year, and despite mixed feelings about Bri's sincerity, sound-bytes and continued residence in Nottingham, Town fans were prepared to give it a go.

His first two matches saw him:

- involved in a fight with Millwall's Alex Rae, by all accounts (i.e. Brian's testimony) a remarkably easy thing to do, and
- scoring the most sensational goal seen at Blundell Park for many a year; an absolute screamer against Pompey in the first home game of the season. No one witnessing his two-fist-

SING WHEN WE'RE FISHING
The nauseous voice of Grimsby Town supporters

41

IVANO ENDORSES LATEST PRODUCT

CRISPS WITH THAT 'KNUCKLE-FRESH' TASTE

ed salute to the Pontoon and the concentrated belligerence of his facial expression could have doubted the manager's enthusiasm for the task. However, the nature of the victory against Portsmouth boded ill for the season, if we had but paused to consider it; the two goals were the result of tremendous individual effort and inspirational skill in a patternless performance, lifting the fans from frustration into a state of euphoria with their very glamour.

The same could be said of the Norwich match a month later, which would set another trend that matured and developed as the season progressed: 2-1 up with no time left at all, you just KNEW that we were going to concede a goal to a powerful bustling centre-forward - in this case it was Ade Akinbaye (it was to be Southend's Dave Regis later). We spotted what looked to be another trend: Laws in a confrontation with a member of the opposition who was furious at one of his challenges (Eadie?). A coincidence surely? Or perhaps the incident at Millwall had not been entirely Alex Rae's fault...

The give-away goal syndrome was becoming a constant as time went on, and the most worrying factor was the management's apparent inability to do anything about it. In fact, one startling feature of the season was the manager's propensity for blaming someone else; this was encapsulated in his remark to me during a phone-in: "Once they're across that white line, they're on their own..." Another smart sound-byte on the surface - but what's a manager for, for heaven's sake?

Laws' penchant for mayhem was applauded in the case of the game v archrivals West Brom, for which the Mariners, including 'Bri', as we have continued to call him, were well fired up. Woe betide any former Town player (i.e. Dave Gilbert) who stood in their way, and indeed the manager proceeded to give him a real clattering. The winner in that one was scored by Town's most worshipped player for many a year, Ivano Bonetti.

Bonetti, a former Serie A player who had decided to come to Grimsby to further his career (?), was signed in a moment of inspiration under a deal which brought him to Blundell Park till the end of the season. The arrangement also involved the fans stumping up fifty thou to "purchase his image" from his American management company. For some reason, the club were not allowed to contribute to this; the whole thing would have sounded very fishy (!) indeed to anyone listening - but nobody was. The fans' money was held in trust by local businessman and club sponsor, Brian Huxford.

Bonetti's brief appeared to be to raise awareness of the club both on the field and locally; he accomplished the former with a brand of attacking skill which had the crowd wetting themselves with appreciation and excitement, and the latter by appearing at every social occasion they could get him to, and some he wasn't supposed to be at. The result was a wave of enthusiasm and confidence that shot Town to second in the First Division at the end of November, with the fans discussing how we would spend the Premiership loot that was clearly headed our way.

But it wouldn't be Grimsby if everything went according to plan, would it?

Involved as we were in a sensational Cup run, no one seemed to notice that League results were suffering badly, and there were disturbing reports of indiscipline amongst the players, who by all accounts enjoyed 'a good Christmas'. We were giving late goals away with alarming regularity, and playing with a lack of conviction that saw us sliding down the table as winter began to play havoc with the fixture list.

The Leicester match at Blundell Park proved that if no one else cared, Bri cared enough for everyone. Former team mate Gary Parker ruffled his hair after a 93rd minute equaliser and he set about him on the spot. No one knew better than Parker the sensational effect that this action would have upon Laws - look what happened when Aldridge did it in the League Cup Final after Bri's own goal - and it worked a treat as our gaffer throttled him and had to be torn off his ex-pal in the tunnel.

But few were willing to bend their minds to that as the West Ham match approached, and there was a nasty feeling about that the players were unable to 'get themselves up' for such mundane fixtures as the fatal Luton away game...

After turning a 2-1 deficit into a 3-2 victory thanks to some more clueless play by Town, Luton gratefully sent in the refreshments and the lads tucked in. Enter one furious manager, who told them to stop eating; Ivano, halfway through a chicken leg, carried on - and the rest is history. Well, three onfield confrontations with the opposition might be considered a lapse, or even a good thing by the socially maladjusted, but lamping one's best player? Surely he had to go!

Well, no! Ivano retired to Brescia with a shattered cheek-bone, and Town thrashed West Ham against all the odds. Cup fever had in effect postponed the manager's Waterloo, which did not come until a Ruud Gullit-inspired Chelsea beat us 4-0 and ended the Cup dream, after a heroic 0-0 draw at the Park.

Now in the relegation zone, we were exposed in all our disorganised fallibility, and our feeble attempts to escape looked doomed. There were some shocking performances; the players looked as if they didn't know what they were supposed to be doing, and Laws, in a gruesome echo of the dread days of Mike Lyons, tried to play both midfield and up front (and against Palace, all over the terrace too). We scraped a couple of victories against teams that were having even worse days than us (Stoke, Birmingham) and eventually finished 17th, with little conviction about the '96-97 campaign - basically, we fully expect to be relegated.

What has made it worse is that there is now unrest behind the scenes:

the aforementioned principal sponsor, Brian Huxford, has pulled the plug over the Bonetti affair, saying he will not deal with such people. Huxford, of Imperial Motors, claimed the board had reneged on a deal to make up any shortfall in the collection, and that the fund he looked after had also had to pay for 100 raffled season tickets. So, no cars, no money - back to the Skoda for chairman Bill Carr!; the ex-chairman has gone to press saying he'll come back and help if required, as the club are obviously clueless; Bonetti is suing Laws, who, incredibly is still there, although this does NOT extend to living in Grimsby; we've just sold our best player and captain Paul Groves to arch-rivals West Brom, managed by the reviled Buckley, who left us in the lurch so sensationally; the manager is now reputed to have punched the assistant manager on the training ground.

Oh, and there's more: One Town player abandoned his car on a traffic island, another challenged a mate of mine to a fight whilst pissed, and the manager has been caught speeding again.

Well, that's a brief rundown of the season, but it could scarcely give a flavour of the desperate disappointment and nasty taste it all left. And that's not all. Ivano Bonetti, who spent his time here in a luxurious log-cabin in Lincolnshire, is reputed to have got a hotel chambermaid pregnant and to be on the run from her furious father. So good is *la dolce vita* in Lincolnshire that Vialli and Ravanelli are rumoured be playing for Town next year, and Ivano is going to stay around to start a chambermaid escort business.

"I hope the truth will out," says Bri earnestly, "he acted as if he was lord of the manor." Town fans didn't give a shit about that; one little man came along and brought the magic back to Grimsby Town for the first time in years, until the hooligan in the manager's seat punched his lights out. Go for it, Ivano - sue the arse off him!

Fanzine Facts

Steve Plowes, editor of **Sing When We're Fishing**, explains the history of the fanzine: "SWWF began as a cartoon strip, 'The Magnificent 7', the brainchild of cartoonist Jim Connor, and continued with 'Leave it to Nobby', satirical stabs at the powers that be at the Park, which thrilled us all immensely but which provided little feedback from a population seemingly steeped in the marinade of years of disappointment.

"The magazine's title is typical of the defiant attitude of the supporters; "You Only Sing When You're Fishing" was a regular taunt by opposing supporters, which apparently first happened during a Cup thrashing by Liverpool. The taunt became a sort of battle-cry, and it is still chanted to the tune of 'Guantanamera' when things are going well. The delicious irony is that we are no longer fishing, so we don't sing much any more... "

SKY BLUE ARMY

Coventry City

In 1967 Coventry City won promotion to the First Division. In 1968 we drew on the last day of the season, finishing third from bottom and sending Sheffield United down. In 1969 we again finished third from bottom, one point ahead of Leicester City who only needed a point from their last game to send us down. Needless to say, the sad bastards lost and went down instead. In 1970... shall I continue? The fact is, we've had more last-minute escapes than Harry Houdini. Many managers have tried to get us relegated and many have failed; the truth of the matter is if they'd have painted the Titanic sky blue it would never have gone down. Every year we're the bookies' (no, everyone's) odds-on certainties for the drop, and every year come August we're still there like a bad case of herpes. By now you would have thought the pressure wouldn't get to us, but each year these last day shit or bust situations don't get any easier. I know the season just wouldn't be the same without the annual relegation dog fight, but the thought of Grimsby away on a cold November night just doesn't bear thinking about.

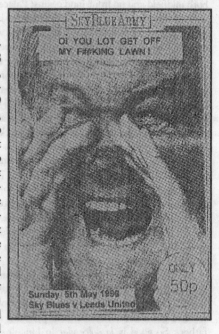

So, '95-96 has gone and we're still here, albeit by goal difference, so where did it all go pear-shaped? It certainly wasn't lack of ambition. With our chairman prepared to put his hand in his pocket, we've spent more money this year than in the last 29 put together. You can't blame the support either; we're sad gits really, despite being in the bottom three all season, we've just had our best average gate since Wallace and Ferguson were scaring defences shitless back in the late Seventies (mind you, they were ugly f**kers!), and have supported the team throughout. I wouldn't even blame the management, Big Fat Ron and 'Bianca Jackson' have spent well on some quality players and have tried to play decent football despite our predicament. So, what about the players? Well, the new signings have all looked the part and the old farts have held together well. Admittedly we've leaked the odd goal or 69, but that's down to the fact that we could never play the same defence twice. It seemed that players only had to sneeze and they would pull something (certainly the case with Peter Nndddluvv if you believe everything you read in the Sunday Papers), or fart and they would get a red card. It got so bad that against Wimbledon we had Dion Dublin playing centre-half and Richard Shaw looking like something out of the phantom of the Opera (nothing new there then!). So at the end of the day I wouldn't even blame the players. No, it all boils down to... Aston Shitty Villa! "Why?" I hear you ask. Well, whilst the smug bastards stuffed us home and away, with Donkey Bollocks Savo Mouldysausage getting an inconceivable five goals, the tossers were the only team in the entire universe who failed to take a single point off Man Shitty. If they had've done so, then the Mancs would have been dead and buried by Easter, whilst we could've had a party on the last day, smugly looking forward to '97. Instead, we had to rush out for new batteries for our trannies and live through yet another brown trouser day. OK, we can't completely blame the Chim Chimmenies, but you have to come from Coventry to appreciate our intense resentment towards them. If there is one thing that has Coventry fans reaching for the strait-jackets, it's our inability to win at Villa Park. In our 113 year history we have failed to gain *one measly victory*. There has been many a Coventry fan who's gone to the grave never fulfilling that one simple ambition 'to see the Sky Blues win at Villa before I go'. If we ever do go down, and let's face it we try our hardest every year, it would almost be tolerable if we beat the Brummie bastards on the way. Besides the embarrassment of being turned over by the Villa, was the season as bad as our position suggests? Here's the abbreviated run-down.

August: Away at Newcastle for the first game is hardly the start most would ask for; still it's nice to get the easy ones out of the way! We played better than the 3-0 scoreline suggested (which was somewhat the case all season). Back at home on the Wednesday, and a victory against Man Shitty. Little were we to know that this would be our only League win till nearly Christmas or Telfer's only League goal till... well, till now!! Credible draws against Arsenal and Chelsea gave little indication of how we were to struggle.

September: A point at home to Forest was all we could muster. Defeat at Middlesbrough after going a goal up was followed by annihilation at Blackburn (5-1) and embarrassment at home to the Scum (0-3). It was never going to be our day with them scoring after around 0.7 seconds (approx), but how did we let that donkey Saveloy Mildewsausage get two?! The only consolation was a home win in the Pepsi Cola against Hull.

October: Our Virgin Cola form continued with us finishing off Hull, and then the comeback of the season against Spurs. Nil-two down at half-time we looked dead and buried, but goals by Nuddy, Busst (there it is) and Salako gave us one of our few highs of the season.

November: Spurs took revenge for their Sainsbury Classic Cola defeat, whilst Man Utd stuffed us 0-4 and another fight-back saw us snatch a dramatic 3-3 draw against Wimbledon. But defeat at Wolves in the Barcardi and Coke Cup finished off a forgetful month.

December: Despite Dublin getting a hat-trick, thanks to some kamikaze defending we managed to lose 4-3 at Sheffield Wednesday (the first of five doubles over us this season). But wait - get the flags out! At last, a win! And what a win. Five-nil against the defending Champions finally lifted the doom and gloom from Highfield Road, but didn't we just come crashing down to earth again, losing 4-1 at the Scum, with that twat Milosovic getting another two against us! Enter the saviour! Whelan arrived from Leeds and scored on his home debut as we beat Everton. Another Whelan goal and a Salako penalty (after a foul on Whelan) give us a late and vital victory at a freezing Bolton, which would have given us a somewhat more cheerful end to the year except for the fact that I wrote off my car. Not that it's got anything to do with the City but I thought I'd mention it anyway!

January: A wonder goal from Whelan got the New Year under way, but it was only enough to get us a dire 1-1 draw against Southampton. Despite going a goal down and losing Busst to a red card, we came back well to beat Plymouth in the FA Cup. The rest of the month saw us lose at home to Newcastle, draw away at Man City and despite coming back from two goals down (Dublin and Whelan) we still managed to blow it in the final minutes away at West Ham.

February: We got a credible draw at Arsenal (Whelan again), but then had to wait for the snow to clear before Whelan and a last minute Dublin goal gave us a replay at Maine Road in the FA Cup. A goal from Whelan (who else?) gave us an impressive 1-0 win over an in-form Chelsea. But with a trip to Old Trafford the prize, we failed to beat Man City in the Cup replay. This was the start of a run of games we should've won but didn't. Despite the signing of Jess from Aberdeen and Daish from Brum we could still only manage a dreadful 0-0 draw with Middlesbrough.

March: draws against West Ham and Everton were the best we could scrape out of March. Pitiful defeats at home to Bolton and away to Southampton and Spurs, looked to have given us a mountain to climb. Tempers were wearing a little thin with big Ron threatening to stick his headphones up Andy Gray's arse on Sky Sports. Dublin also came in for some stick for legging it off the pitch without so much as a glance over his shoulder at the travelling support.

April: having dropped ourselves deep into the shit by our March results, our Easter program looked horrendous. But Whelan (thank you Leeds!) gave us a desperately needed win against Liverpool, and despite losing Busst and the match at Man United, we showed that we weren't about to lay down and die. The Busst injury was horrific; I've never heard anything like the huge "Urrrghhh" that echoed around Old Trafford as the groundsman threw a bucket of water over where Busst had been laying and it immediately turn bright red with his blood. Needless to say, we wish him a speedy recovery. Next came a momentous game at home to QPR. If we lost it, we would have been down; instead Jess's first goal for the club doomed Rangers to the dreaded drop. A hugely important point at Forest meant that our fate was in our own hands. The win at Wimbledon should have made it party time for the 8,000+ City fans that had headed South, but thanks to Aston Shitty Villa's failure to take a point off the Mancs, it meant we had to sweat it out on the last day against Leeds. It was a hugely disappointing game, and with Man City staging a comeback against Liverpool, it was all very bloody tense. Thankfully some dozey bastard spread the news at Maine Road that we were losing, so they went into smug mode and played out the last five minutes thinking they were safe (sad eh?!). The fact was that our 0-0 draw was enough to keep us up by goal difference and have the Mancs crying into their Bovril. The brain-dead Leeds fans decided to ruin our celebrations by invading the pitch and kicking anyone that wasn't wearing flares, tank tops and hob-nail boots, but they couldn't diminish our joy and relief at avoiding the drop once again.

In respect of my original question I suppose the answer has to be yes, it was as bad as our position suggested, but at least we lived to tell the tale!

So what about '96-97? Bookies favourites? Well to be honest, I don't think so. In fact, now the new players have had time to settle, we have the making of an excellent team. Oggy at 58 remains one of the most consistent 'keepers in the country, Liam Daish looks like becoming a cult figure and the backbone of our defence, Eoin Jess looks class in midfield alongside Player of the Year Paul 'if it moves whack it' Williams, whilst Whelan is a god up front. With Dublin signing a new contract and if Peter Nddlluuvve can take a break from his mission to shag every tart in Coventry, then we should have a potent strikeforce. So for once I can't see us being involved in the relegation dog fight. But then again...

One thing's for sure: as much as we've been relegation-proof over the last 30 years, the Sad Bastards from up the M69 have been up and down more time than Fergy's drawers (and I don't mean Alex. Or do I?). So it's a sure-fire bet that come May they will be filling one of the relegation spots, and with their country bumpkin neighbours Derby also guaranteed an immediate return, at least it means the rest of us are only fighting over the one spot. As for winning at the Villa? If we do, I'll hire the open top bus for the team's victorious tour of Coventry myself!

Fanzine Facts

The *Sky Blue Army* was first published in 1989 when Dave Rose convinced his cousin Mick Rose to join him, and since then they have produced over 50 issues. Dave admits it's hard work for just two people, but at least it cuts down on the arguments! "A centre page article in one mag depicting the Villa players as an assortment of penises did create quite a stir.", says Dave. He admits it was probably a bit near the knuckle, but still believes it was the funniest thing they've ever done. The humour side is important to *Sky Blue Army*. "We're not into slagging everyone off, although naturally, the Villa and Leicester both come in for a fair amount of stick, but generally we just aim to give the fans something to read on the bog, and hopefully put a smile on their faces at the same time."

SO JACK ASHURST, WHERE'S MY SHIRT?

Carlisle United

Last season broke a fair few Cumbrian hearts, but more significantly for the wider footballing public, it shattered the myth of the Eddie Stobart wagon.

Away day supporters and fanzine writers up and down the land have long believed that Eddie's trucks possess a mystical power, and all that's required to unleash the force on their team is to spot one en route to a game, thus guaranteeing a win.

For Carlisle's Blue Army however, there was no need to lorry spot last season, for our boys' away strip was in Eddie's red, green and yellow colours (or as one of our writers put it, 'blood, turd and custard'). What's more, as a money-saving measure the shirts seemed to have been cut directly from one of his wagon's canvas covers.

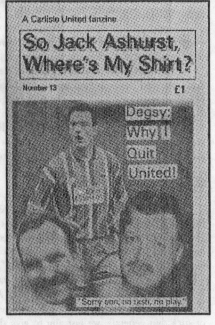

A Carlisle United fanzine

So Jack Ashurst, Where's My Shirt?

Number 13   £1

Degsy: Why I Quit United!

'Sorry son, no tash, no play.'

Gone was the legendary deckchair strip which had taken United to the Division Three title and Wembley the season before. Instead, United wore Eddie Stobart seconds.

So attired, we believed Lady Luck wouldn't merely be smiling on us, but beckoning us to her bed every matchday afternoon and Tuesday night. As Hilda Ogden once said, the world (or at least the Division Two bits of it) was our lobster.

Only it didn't work out that way. Far from instilling fear into the opposition, the Eddies inspired at best a moment's shock at the sheer awfulness of the design, and usually mild derision, followed by a hefty defeat. And when United did win away, they only did so three times (and twice at Hull, which hardly counts), and on each occasion they wore the blue home shirts. I can't remember any Eddie Stobart wagons parked behind exposed away ends either, so United couldn't even use the excuse that they weren't able to pick each other out against the crowd...

Although Carlisle started the season as promotion favourites (no, don't laugh!) we thought this more than a little silly. After the excitement of the previous year, we were prepared to settle for mid-table mediocrity, an Autowotsit Wembley win, and reaching the fourth round of the FA Cup for the first time since the Big Bang.

After all, Michael Knighton's Ten Year Plan permitted a three season sojourn in Division Two, so this would be a snug consolidation of our ever-improving fortunes. We'd flirt with a play-off place whilst continuing, in the words of that much loved championship anthem, to 'shit on the bastards below' (especially Burnley) and keep our noses well clear of the relegation stench.

The season began with the visit of Bristol Rovers, play-off finalists the season before and a good test of our Division Two mettle. It was a difficult fixture on paper and even harder on grass. United did their best, played reasonably well in parts, but weren't as good as Bristol and lost. Which is a pretty accurate summary of the way things went over the next nine months.

There were some very bad days (Chesterfield and Peterborough leap to mid like a Roy Keane tackle) and watching United fail to win away so often did get a bit monotonous, but even now I can't quite believe United are back in the basement, which next season seems more gloomy and grotty than ever.

"The Premier League in seven years, Division Three in one!" gloated Darlington's *Mission Impossible* fanzine, with reference to Michael Knighton's famous (now infamous) boast.

Ah yes, Michael Knighton. Many of your will be tutting "I told you so" and rejoicing in the humiliation of a man whose ego, it seems, is only marginally smaller than his mouth. Most Blues too blame him for last season's relegation. Having a go at him however is rather like publicly criticising your father. Knighton, after all, saved our club four years ago, buying it for the price of a Paul Gascoigne shin pad, and not only have we the memories of that Championship success and Wembley appearance to savour for ever, we also have a spanking new 6,000 seater stand. It's just a pity it's over twice the size of an average home gate for our Third Division opposition next season.

And it's an even greater pity that it cost United their Second Division place, for despite Knighton's promise to spend, spend, spend should United still be in trouble in January, his wallet stayed tighter than a Baresi-led defence. As the stand went up, United went down.

In thinking big, Knighton had overlooked the small problem of the team not being good enough to stay in Division Two. And yet, as I've said, every Blue I knew felt just as confident (or complacent) as Knighton. Had he later admitted, "Sorry lads and lasses, I've boobed", or explained his promise to bargain buy at the January sales as a bluff to get the team to play better, we'd have understood and forgiven him. (Well, maybe.) Instead, Knighton spoilt matters by bleating on about the lack of financial support from loyal Blues in taking up his debenture plans and share offer.

We weren't the only ones cheesed off. So too was manager, sorry, director of coaching Mick Wadsworth. He left in January, for a reason which was never made public, and we wondered whether it was simply a case of Mick's heavily foliaged upper lip being one tash too many for a club Carlisle's size.

The real reason however, seems to have been a wrangle over a little known Preston reserve named Alan Smart. United had been the dumping ground for several loanees and trialists, the worst being Spurs has-been Clive Allen, the only United player in recent seasons who'd refused to come over and sign my son Sam's programme during the warm-up. It wasn't as if the extra seconds he spent posing and pouting did him any good either. After three games and no goals off he went.

Smart however, looked the part. "At last!" we cried like desperate parents watching our beautiful daughter slowly turning into a thirtysomething spinster, "here's a partner for Reevsey." In the two full games Reeves and Smart played together, United scored nine goals. Smartie was the answer. But whilst the clubs agreed a fee, Smart couldn't fix his price with Knighton, so he stayed at Preston, Wadsworth went to Norwich (another club with a philanthropic chairman) and United stayed in trouble. No one did well out of it, least of all us supporters.

Micky Tash was replaced by the clean-shaven but ever-greying Mervyn Day, widely regarded as 'too nice' a manager to save United, but a touch-line dust up with a Bradford City jobsworth who came between Merv's rage and a rotten referee put paid to that notion. Anyway, United's relegation was no fault of Merv, who did the best he could.

Meanwhile, Knighton was suggesting that a successful season back in the third mightn't be too bad (that went down a treat), and the relegation writing spilled off the wall and all over the 6,000 seats of the new stand on transfer deadline day.

Left back Tony Gallimore went to glamorous Grimsby for anything up to £200,000 and midfielder Paul Murray left for the bright lights of QPR. Murray's departure had long been expected, not least by Murray himself, an arrogant young man by all accounts, whose ego and first touch need careful control, but when he did turn the talent on he destroyed more than one team single-handed (just ask Burnley, ho, ho!).

Neither player however, was a vital part of the spluttering United machine, and with the cash from their sale Knighton would surely now buy a striker: maybe even Smart. But what's this, read the smallprint. The words 'on loan to QPR' put these dreams, like the teletex page, on hold. United's most saleable asset had been given away; we didn't even borrow a QPR player in exchange.

United's last survival hopes sat square on the shoulders of our deadline day signing, the mighty Wayne Dowell, a loan transfer from bitterest rivals Burnley - talk about rubbing it in. To be fair to Wayne he didn't do badly, and in reply to an autograph request from Sam, Wayne wrote him a letter (Clive Allen take note), but a left back loanee wasn't the answer to our survival prayers.

United lurched on. For a while we dreamt the beautiful dream of United staying up at Burnley's expense and of reaching the Autowotsit final, but with Reevesy, who'd had more partners than a Royal Princess now starting to play like the old slag he must've felt, the end was nigh. What's more, when Rotherham's Nigel Jemson crawled into our box before collapsing to con a penalty out of a ref so far behind, he was still refereeing the previous week's game, United were washed out in the Windscreen semi-finals too.

Relegation, though inevitable, was delayed because of the Brighton riot. That resulted in York playing their last game five days after the season had finished, which in turn gave Knighton the excuse to blame the FA for United's demise. But we'd stopped believing him long before.

So now it's back to the basement, albeit for just a season. United will win promotion because there's no club to match our set-up, size and, above all, support. (And if you want one to watch, note the name Rory Delap - a player of huge potential and even bigger ears.)

But I can't get too excited about another Championship season. God willing I've got maybe another 20 years of active home and away support for United, and I didn't want to waste one in the Third. Mind you, the club recently announced they're keeping the Eddie Stobart strip next season! Perhaps I'd better wait a while before counting the chickens. Or lorries.

Fanzine Facts

So Jack Ashurst, Where's My Shirt? appeared for the first time at Brunton Park the day Michael Knighton made his debut in the director's box. Whilst Knighton's made the greater impact in the four seasons since, it's hoped the fanzine has at least lightened the load on the long haul back to Carlisle after another away day defeat. Publisher Tim Pocock, exiled 113.4 miles from Brunton Park in deepest, darkest North Yorkshire, explains that the fanzine is dedicated to "the Blue who was so fed up at one home game, that he decided to leave at half time. The gates however were locked, and with no-one about to open them he was forced to climb <u>over</u> the walls to get out before waiting in his mate's car with only four cans of Special Brew and half a pound of cheese for sustenance."

Spitting Feathers

SOUR GRAPES

Wimbledon

Death of a football club?

It's difficult to know whether to laugh or cry when talking about Wimbledon last season. On the pitch there was the short-term relief in avoiding relegation after flirting with it for most of the campaign, yet in the long-term it may have proved beneficial if we had been relegated, as the proposed Irish take-over may not have materialised had we been displaying our talents in the Nationwide.

The club's future appears to hinge around what owner Sam Hammam wants to do with it. Reports in the Irish press suggest that he has sold his majority shareholding in the club to an Irish consortium headed by U2's manager, Paul McGuiness, who are prepared to inject £10m into the club to keep it in the Premiership in prep-

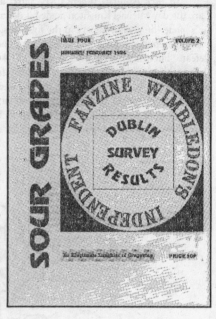

aration for the wholesale removal of the club to Dublin, and 'up yours' to 107 years of Wimbledon FC's history. This disgraceful example of greed gone mad would confirm to all Dons supporters that the club has sold its soul to the devil and spat in the face of its loyal supporters.

Season ticket application forms which worryingly were not included in the last couple of programmes have now been sent out, and it seems the club will be staying at Selhurst for one more season at least. Pitch invasions which were proposed at the inaugural meeting of Wimbledon Independent Supporters Association (WISA) were, in true Wimbledon tradition, rejected as detrimental to security in the light of Euro 96, and therein lies the fundamental problem: too tiny a percentage of an already small hard-core of fans is prepared to rock the boat, when Brighton-style match abandonments are what is called for to get national attention focused on the death of a football club. An article last year in one of the national papers highlighted the fact that Dons fans are on average amongst the highest earners in the country (or the 'Toff's club' as the tabloids put it), and too many of these are too smug and complacent to get involved in demonstrations and such like, preferring to observe rather than participate, and doubtless they will disappear should an Aldershot-style resurrection of the club be required.

Returning to on-field activities and the main reason for our struggle. Two late-conceded goals by Bolton on the last day only just pipped us for the 'honour' of most goals against. Only Chris Perry, can hold his head up and say he defended consistently well, whereas in goal the initially promising Paul Heald was only slightly better than the antics of Neil 'not up to it - when can we sell him to Fulham' Sullivan. Leonhardsen won Player of the Year which he didn't really deserve as Perry was clearly better, although 'Leo' did benefit from the mid-season absence of Vinnie Jones who was rightly dropped after being too much of an automatic choice to be healthy, but after transfer talks broke down he returned to inspire the side to safety.

An 8-7 aggregate defeat against Charlton in the Coca Cola Cup highlighted the defensive shortcomings of the side, but the FA Cup run compensated for it, even if it did prevent the team realising their full potential in the League. My personal favourite moment of the season was when our laziest player Efan Ekoku equalised in the third minute of injury time in the FA Cup fifth round tie at Huddersfield, followed by yours truly going completely ape-shit. The day was completed by local five year olds handing out verbal abuse and mooning at us in the station afterwards, reminding us of the quaint joys of the Endsleigh. Another high was Holdsworth's late equaliser at Chelsea, a minute after Gullit had put them ahead with possibly the flukiest goal of his career - the tannoy screaming "The Man is a Legend", which wiped the smiles off the faces of the Chelsea fans who were behaving like Man United supporters (i.e. arrogant scum).

Christmas was not a happy time. The Dons had not won in any competition for three and a half months, since beating Liverpool at Selhurst on September 9th, including throwing away a 3-1 lead at Coventry and successive home defeats against Premiership 'giants' West Ham and Southampton. On Boxing Day morning I was hoping the game at Stamford Bridge would be called off as we had not beaten Chelsea for over five years, and to be honest I fancied watching England in the test in South Africa. In the end, the game was not cancelled, I did go, and the long drought was broken with a 2-1 win; we could even afford a missed penalty! This was followed up three days later with a 3-1 win at Arsenal. Hans Segars played in both these games but missed the majority of the season through injury, yet the club saw fit to give him a free transfer. It seems to me that at a time when he most needed support, the rug was tugged from beneath his feet and he was treated quite shabbily. He is innocent until proven guilty, after all.

Changing tack slightly, what a joy it was to be in Europe at last - seven years after we should have been - albeit in the Inter Toto Cup. When we moved from Plough Lane to Selhurst, Hammam promised to buy Batistuta and Rodriguez from South America for £5m to compensate for our upheaval. We had also been promised Paul Davis and Alan Smith from Arsenal. All we got were a load of Man Utd third teamers. Arriving at (rather ironically) Brighton's Goldstone ground for our first 'home' match, the sound of 500 crazed Turkish supporters filled the air, and their 4-0 victory over our youth team was greeted with wild celebrations. If that was surreal, crossing the Hungarian/Slovakian border a week later to be greeted by the sight of thousands of pilgrims heading away from Kosice in ramshackle old buses having heard the Pope speaking on an airfield near the town was equally as bizarre. That our youth/reserve side got a 1-1 draw against the team who finished runners-up to Slovan Bratislava was equally incredible. To be later banned from Europe for fielding a weakened side was frankly ridiculous, and in the end, common sense (a quality that seems to desert some people where football is concerned) prevailed and the ban was quashed.

As I write, our landlords Crystal Palace have contrived to lose the play-off final in the last minute of extra time at Wembley and tears of joy are rolling down my face. They may have the last laugh if we bugger off to Ireland, but as that famous twat Emlyn Hughes once said "I'm enjoying it because it's happening now"; never mind that our first game the season after next will be against East Thurrock rather than West Ham. We've had ten consecutive years in the top Division, and I've enjoyed every bloody minute of it.

Fanzine Facts

Sour Grapes has continued to have a loyal readership and has now over a dozen contributors, this article being written by one of them, Richard Crabtree, who took it like a man last year when he wasn't credited for his contribution to SOTF1 as editor Jane Hart forgot to mention it!

Incidentally, in the process of selling *Sour Grapes* Jane was interviewed by Julie Welch for the Sunday Telegraph; an experience akin to meeting God for any woman who can remember the pre-Julie period when girls were shunned from the terraces and ladies' loos were non-existent at most northern football grounds. Needless to say, Jane has not been the same since!

This season *Sour Grapes* ran a survey to find out what Dons fans thought of the proposed move to Dublin, "not that we needed to ask" as Jane points out, but this led indirectly to the formation of *WISA*, the Wimbledon Independent Supporters' Association which with 600+ members is already showing far more clout than the official supporters' club which only has about half that number. As Jane says, "the fight for not just a new ground in Merton but *survival* goes on."

Finally, *Sour Grapes* sends its greetings to all Seagulls fans. In Jane's words, "It's a disgrace that fans should be treated like that, and if fanzines serve any purpose at all it is to keep the views and hopes of all fans alive."

SOUTH RIDING

Barnsley

When we started this fanzine in 1990, one of the names we considered was 'Second Division Barnsley' but this was rejected on the grounds that we would look incredibly silly should BFC get promoted, or more likely, relegated. When you consider however that out of Barnsley Football Club's 110 years of existence no fewer than 70 of those years have been spent in the old Second (now First) Division, then the proposed faznine title perhaps wouldn't have been too outlandish.

It was no surprise then that season '94-95 ended with BFC in the oh-so-familiar position of 'shit, just missed out on the play-offs again'. It is now 15 years since we won promotion from the Division formerly known as Three, and despite a couple of scares

at either end of the table, we have never seriously looked like disturbing the status quo. Mind you, we did have a fright a couple of seasons ago when we needed to win our last game and Brighton *not* to win theirs, in order to make the play-offs. At the end of the game, after we'd duly beaten Middlesbrough 1-0, the PA announcer informed us that Brighton had drawn and we were in the promotion play-offs. He then went on to announce the date and venue of the first play-off game, before sheepishly informing the delirious Oakwell crowd that Brighton had in fact won and that... er.. we weren't in the play-offs after all, sorry, but - phew - lucky escape, eh?!. Barnsley had once again managed to stave off promotion and the dickhead announcer went on to become Mayor of Barnsley (honest).

And so season '95-96 was greeted with all the foolish optimism that only the true football fan can muster, as we travelled to Selhurst Park to take on freshly-relegated Crystal Palace, and proceeded to take an early lead courtesy of defender Steve Davis. Could we start with a win? Not on your bollocks. Bruce Dyer the Palace striker ran through the middle and was caught yards off-side. Realising his predicament, he turned and ran back towards the half-way line and the referee waved 'play on', presumably because he felt that Dyer wasn't interfering with play. Unfortunately for us, however, as Dyer was trotting back, the gorgeous Iain Dowie passed him going in the opposite direction, took a pass from Ray Houghton and slotted the ball home. That crap decision turned the game and as was to happen all too often during the season, we gave away a lead and ended up losing 4-3.

Another quiet close season at Oakwell had seen only the departure of big Gerry Taggart to temporarily promoted Bolton for £1.5m and a replacement drafted in, in the shape of 72-year-old Peter Shirtliff, local lad but big Wednesdayite for most of his career, for a fee of £100,000. A few years ago journeymen like him would've come for free!

Shirtliff was in the side however for the 3-2 win at Watford following on from the home defeat at Oldham, although quite why he was preferred to the very unfortunate Gary Fleming is a mystery to most Barnsley fans. Still, everything looked fine and dandy as we handed out a footballing masterclass to Tranmere (OK, we won 2-1) to go second in the table. We only needed to beat-up on Birmingham at home on the Saturday and we'd go top. Sod the play-offs; automatic promotion as Champions should be a piece of piss at this rate.

Barnsley nil, Birmingham City five. Sack the players! Sack the manager! Sack the board! Kill the groundsman's dog! Vote Tory! Watch Man-O-Man! Christ!! Why are we football fans? It's a crap game. OK, so I took it all back a week later when we beat top of the table Millwall at their house. But *really*!!

A few years ago, we had hardly any Yorkshire derbies. Now we had three in eight days, and another in a fortnight. Someone suggested the days of the week had been renamed Sunday, Monday, Huddersfield, Wednesday... First to 'Udders, where the up and down nature of our season continued with a sever drubbing. How many things can go wrong in one game? Let's start with the abysmal attitude of the players, summed up by their third goal as no-one could be arsed even to pretend to put a tackle in. Again, Fleming didn't start the game. Wilson criticised him for putting in a transfer request, but as he'd been dropped for not being tall enough, and as he'd reached the age where he was unlikely to start growing again, all his excellent performances over the last few years seemed to count for nowt. And to be dropped for Bishop. Well - wouldn't *you* wand to leave?

Further bad results followed. The Blunts were gifted a point, but in truth we stopped playing at half time. Most tragic was Fleming's injury; it must have been enough to make him stop believing in God.

Two days later, we were back at 'Udders. This time, in the League. And we added a 2-0 defeat to the 3-0 that we suffered in the League Cup. This all smacked of a rapid decline, and something had to be done to salvage it. To everybody's amazement, Danny Wilson pulled off a major coup by signing Jan Molby on loan from Liverpool. Now I know our midfield was lacking solidity and width, but I was reckoning on at least three players being needed to fill the gap! Still, he inspired us to beat Derby. And so it went on. Old friends 'Udders came to Oakwell for the League Cup second leg. Given our first leg stuffing, there was little chance of pulling this one out of the fire. Eh? Wrong! The performance of the season so far saw us thrash 'em 4-0 to set up a home tie against Arsenal. Dennis Bergkamp at Oakwell. Ooh 'eck!

We missed a penalty, Bergkamp was brilliant, they won 3-0. On top of that, the evening was marred by an outbreak of racist shit which was dished out to Ian Wright. An enquiry was announced by the club, as one of the stewards was spotted joining in with the monkey noises. The steward was sacked and signs were erected asking people not to be racist. That'll stop 'em!

Meanwhile, back in the League, we gave Wolves a good pasting. They were truly awful and deserved to be splattered. What is it about big clubs? They spend squillions and still end up with a team that plays like football's equivalent of Spinal Tap. The Midlands seem to specialise in them.

The signing of centre-half (Dr) Arjan de Zeeuw from Telstar in Holland for £250,000 seemed to have made a difference as we didn't concede a goal during November. This guy looked class. And as yet, no weak points have shown up in his game. Watch him turn out to be a Jehovah's Witness or something! The cracks were beginning to show, and our only win in December came courtesy of our favourite benefactors Stoke City. The draw for the third round of the FA Cup gave us a chance to gain revenge for a defeat suffered at the same stage two seasons ago, when a dodgy penalty cost us the tie. And since we'd done them twice in the League already, one more win and we got to keep them!

Step forward one George Cain of Bootle. When Gunnar Haller fell over in the box, Mr Cain, the referee, was the nearest person to him, so when he blew up everyone in the ground thought he was going to award Barnsley a free kick and book Haller for being a cheating bastard (er, well alright - ungentlemanly conduct). The entire crowd plus all the players were stunned when he pointed to the spot. Now everybody who watches football will have seen bad refereeing decisions. But this redefined the word 'bad'. If this had happened a few years earlier, Whacko Jacko would've called that album 'George Cain's Penalty Decision At Boundary Park Against Barnsley'. There can never have been a worse call in the history of professional football. Ever! I can't wait for George's next visit to Oakwell.

A string of good results including further trouncings of Huddersfield and Tranny in the early part of the year kept us in contention. Only Stoke upset the apple-cart by blatantly flaunting tradition and beating us.

March 9th 1996 will live forever in the memory of everyone who visited Oakwell that afternoon. Barnsley were comfortably thrashing Ipswich 3-0 when at 4.38 pm the Barnsley team collectively decided to reserve a place for themselves in the record books. Those remaining seven minutes saw an utterly beaten Ipswich team drag themselves back to steal a point, to which they had no right. The most dramatic come-back ever, bettering Hull City's in eight minutes against Wednesday in '82. If shells had fallen on Oakwell that afternoon, we couldn't have been more shocked. It was totally inexplicable. "A freak result", Danny Wilson called it, and he was probably right. I just wish it hadn't been us. It doesn't bear thinking about how he would've felt if we had missed the play-offs by a point. It didn't come to that though, as we failed to win any of our last six home games, and thus achieved mid-table mediocrity once again.

It certainly had been an incident-packed season in one way or another. But even allowing for all the drama, and the, at times, brilliant football, and the equally bad football, you still get the feeling that all we're doing is treading water. Hmmm. Rochdale in the League Cup, eh? Can't wait! Roll on next season!

Fanzine Facts

South Riding first appeared in 1990. Started by John Wray, Keith Norman and Gavin Talbot, it got its name from the one Yorkshire Riding that never existed. The 'zine has a fairly decent relationship with club; as Keith puts it: "from surprising encouragement at the start, now it is just a case of you get on with your job and we'll get on with ours."

SPEKE FROM THE HARBOUR

Everton

Joe Royle's programme notes for the first home game of the season declared that a good cup run and a top six finish would constitute progress. Twenty two thousand season ticket holders seemed to agree as they signed up to watch European football and the world-class skills of Andrei Kanchelskis.

The previous two seasons had both ended with the possibility of relegation. So the first priority was to shore up the defence, the second to find somebody to guarantee some goals. Craig Short, the towering Derby centre back who had kept Duncan Ferguson quiet in the previous year's FA Cup tie, was the first piece of the jigsaw. The second was Stan Collymore, or so we thought. Collymore elected to end the season at the trophyless Anfield. So, to plan B: Chris Armstrong. No luck there either as he opted to join the mediocre Tottenham. With some £8.5m burning a hole in his pocket Joe noticed that a certain Ukrainian at Old Trafford was having trouble warming to his beloved managers' charming personality. And so began the first convoluted transfer saga of the season. Peter Johnson the Everton chairman contacted his counterpart Martin Edwards and agreed a deal (what some people might call a 'gentleman's agreement'). Andrei Kanchelskis met Joe Royle and agreed personal terms, having turned down the bright lights of Middlesbrough. United then decided that they didn't want to pay any cut of Andrei's transfer fee to his previous club, Shakytor Donetsk and decided that Everton should pay instead. The deal was therefore 'Kancelled' (© Daily Mirror) and we found ourselves embroiled in yet another transfer farrago. Everton threatened to report United to the FA, United failed to respond, saying that no deal had been entered into. After much wailing and gnashing of teeth United finally capitulated and allowed Andrei to leave, blaming everybody except themselves for the whole sorry mess.

The season started brightly at Wembley with a 1-0 Charity Shield victory over the Champions Blackburn Rovers. Vinny Samways got the goal in what was to be the highlight of his season (despite getting a good kicking by David Batty). League form was patchy with our first win coming against a fairly poor Southampton side. The first big game was against those loveable Manchester United rogues. Once again the tabloids decided to try to make the game into some sort of a grudge match with stories about Kanchelskis, trying to whip up as much hatred as possible

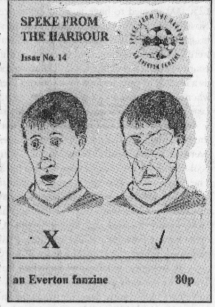

SPEKE FROM
THE HARBOUR

Issue No. 14

.X   ✓

an Everton fanzine   30p

between the two sets of fans. As it happened the only thug to whom the idea of violence appealed was Lee Sharpe who put Kanchelskis out of the game for the next five weeks without managing to earn himself a card. (I was some 200 miles away at the time being a best man - Thanks Joll - but I have it on good authority from my brother-in-law!).

The next highlight, and I use the word advisedly, was our first European fixture since winning the Cup Winners Cup in '85. The mighty Reykjavik of Iceland provided the opposition and we managed to dispose of them over the two legs with what was to be our customary clinical disposal of inferior opponents in the cup competitions. (Millwall, Stockport, Port Vale, ahem!) Sandwiched in between the two legs was a rather shaky debut for Craig Short, and images of Glenn Keeley sprang to Evertonian minds as he trod on the ball with his first touch.

The Blues' brief sojourn into Europe ended at the hands of Feyenoord; an honourable display in Holland not being enough to avoid a 1-0 loss on aggregate.

A home victory against Blackburn and the now ritual humiliation of our dearest neighbours were to set us on a mini revival. "Blues Kan-Kan" was the witty headline in the Football Echo as Andrei opened his account. The first was a 'change of roles' goal as Paul Rideout provided the cross for him to head home, and the second resulted from a piece of Anders Limpar magic as he waltzed past three Liverpool players before setting up Andrei who blasted the ball past the helpless (or should that be hopeless) James. Victory at Anfield was certainly very enjoyable, especially after seeing Rush, Harkness and McAteer celebrating their 'goal' in the first half, which was unluckily disallowed.

The new Everton megastore threw open its doors in November, enticing Evertonians to purchase all manner of things that they never knew they wanted. Some criticism has been levelled at the new regime and their money-making exploits, but the general feeling seems to be that it was fulfilling a genuine need.

Back on the pitch and Anders produced the pass of the season (from just inside the QPR half out by the touchline onto Graham Stuart's boot on the penalty spot) to help ease us into a 1-0 lead. Then, Jurgen Sommer made the worst goalkeeping mistake at Goodison since Hans Segers, allowing a tame Paul Rideout trickler past him, and Everton cruised to a 2-0 victory. Things were already starting to look grim for Rangers, who could only afford cheap numbers and letters on the back of their shirts. Was Kevin Gallen's 'G' falling off in the middle of the game a ploy to con the Everton defence into thinking he was in fact a reincarnation of ex-QPR great Clive Allen?

December brought the long awaited return of a certain Mr D Ferguson. A judicial review in Scotland had decided to quash the remainder of his 12 match ban and the big man was free to play. Almost 11,000 turned out for the hastily rearranged reserve team game at Goodison to welcome back their hero. Duncan got two goals in a 5-0 win to send the crowd home happy. His next appearance was as a substitute against West Ham live on Sky a week later. The game itself was ruined by a rash challenge from Miklosko on Amokachi which saw him sent off. Stand-in goalkeeper Julian Dicks didn't really have an awful lot to do as the expected cricket score failed to materialise. The loudest cheer of the night was reserved for the introduction of the big Scot.

With the return of one striker, another was allowed to leave. Stuart Barlow, the nearly man, decided that it was time to move on when ex-Evertonian Graeme

Sharp came in for him. Stuart was a nice guy, but it has to be said he was one of the worst finishers I have ever seen in a blue shirt, (well, since Brett Angell anyway!).

A bumper 40,019 crowd turned out to see the Blues' Boxing Day fixture against high flying Middlesbrough, complete with Brazilian Juninho in their ranks. The day was special for three reasons. First, Everton played with the trendy three centre backs formation. Second, Craig Short got his first goal for the club, and third, Joe Parkinson introduced Juninho to Goodison with one of his trademark 'hard but fair' tackles, which ensured that the Brazilian was about as effective as Stan Collymore in a Cup Final.

The second of the festive games got off to a good start as David Weatherall placed a perfect chip past his own 'keeper. However, things took a turn for the worse when Dave Watson was unluckily sent off for a second bookable offence only 17 minutes into the game. Step forward that man Andrei Kanchelskis, with one of his best goals of the season as he cut in from the right, beat two men and planted a perfectly placed shot in the corner of the net to guarantee the three points.

A New Year's day trip to Wimbledon was the archetypal game of two halves. Everton raced into a 1-0 lead after less than a minute, courtesy of John Ebbrell. Duncan scored a brilliant twisting volley to earn my vote for best goal of the season, and celebrated by kissing the badge on his shirt (always a good way to curry favour with the supporters) in what he described as a 'thank you' for the support he had received. Wimbledon poured the pressure on in the second half but could only pull the score back to 3-2.

The Everton publicity machine was now in full effect with the launch of the now legendary Radio Everton marshalled by DJ Alan Jackson, whose strange pronunciation of our Ukranian winger's first name (Anderay) was one of his many unusual broadcasts over the Goodison airwaves.

It was the end of January, and enter convoluted transfer saga No. 2. Marc Hottiger, the Swiss international full back was signed from Newcastle United and a work permit was applied for. A formality, we were assured by the wise men of Fleet Street. Except that it wasn't. The application was turned down because he had not played enough League games for Newcastle last season. This despite the fact that he was first choice right back for his country. And so Everton appealed, and we waited... and waited... for five weeks in fact.

Having unconvincingly disposed of Stockport in the first round, our defence of the FA Cup stuttered on as we meandered to Port Vale for yet another replay. February 14th was the rearranged date, and to be quite honest I should have stuck to my original plans of a romantic meal for two with my girlfriend. Where do I begin? Matt Jackson 'played' his last game of the season, and quite possibly his career, in an Everton shirt. But he wasn't the only one who had an absolute howler. It would have been easier to name the two or three players who did themselves justice on that sorry night. Everton had ignored all the warning signs from the first game and played right into the hands of their lowly opponents. They got what they deserved from the game: nothing.

Unable to get tickets for the away tie at Manchester United, I had a night out at Goodison watching the Jumbotron screen erected on the pitch. The lack of a recognised right back prompted Joe to give young reserve team regular Jon O'Connor a dream debut. Just imagine the questions to Jon in years to come : "How old were you when you made your League debut, Jon?" - "Nineteen." "Where was it?" - "Old

Trafford." "Who were you marking?" - "Ryan Giggs." Joe also introduced Michael Branch as a second half substitute making him the second youngest player at 17 to play in the League for Everton (the youngest being Joe himself). Andrei was predictably booed and Everton were predictably beaten.

Being woken up at 8.30 on the Saturday morning of the Nottingham Forest home game to do an interview on Radio Nottingham did have its consolations. I was able to tell all their listeners that Everton would beat Forest by at least three goals and that *they* wouldn't score any because they didn't have any goalscorers in their team. I was right. (Smug grin).

Now a 'media personality', I was checking out Radio Rovers on the way to Ewood Park, and heard their new signing Gary Flitcroft who was at pains to point out that he would not be changing his all-action (dirty bastard) style. Sure enough, six minutes into his home debut he was breaking the seal on the Lux. Kanchelskis was irresistible once again, scoring two.

Another gutless performance at Goodison by Liverpool resulted in a trademark last minute goal by the Red filth to fluke a 1-1 draw, Andrei scoring his third goal in only two derby appearances. Meanwhile Liverpool were shooting up the record charts with their Cup Final single, 'Pass and Lose'. (PS Note to Roy Evans: If you want to see how to beat United in a Cup Final, the 1995 Cup Final video is available in the Everton megastore, priced at only £12.99.)

A trip to Hillsborough saw the final ever appearance of the garish white away strip (christened our 'Real Madrid' kit). The score was 3-1 after 23 minutes and my mate turned to me and said "It's like watching the highlights on the telly." Kanchelskis ripped them apart with a fine hat-trick and he was unlucky not to get five, having one disallowed and hitting a post in the 5-2 demolition of Wednesday.

Going into the last match of the season against Villa, it was exciting to still be in with a chance of the last UEFA Cup place. Joe Parkinson did his bit by getting a goal 12 minutes from time, but sadly it was not enough.

On the whole it was a satisfying season. We may not have actually won anything, but we have made progress and should be there or thereabouts when they're handing out the prizes next year.

Fanzine Facts

Speke from the Harbour was launched in 1990 by John McAllister and friends, who would look forward to a trip from Northern Ireland's Harbour Airport to Liverpool's Speke Airport on match days, hence the name of the 'zine. In '94, John handed his blue editor's pencil to Mark Staniford, and other contributors include Blue Peter, PJ and Spikey. Mark and also gives credit to cartoonists Shaun McCoy and Joll Benn and regular sellers Danny Jones, Chris Keenan, Colin McMullan, Sara and Mark's mum Adrienne, who as he quite rightly points out "are all absolutely invaluable braving the elements when they could be in the pub."

SPITTING FEATHERS

Sheffield Wednesday

Look *pessimism* up in any thesaurus and you'll find the noun *Wednesdayite* near the end of the myriad definitions offered. Well, it's the cross that all Owls followers have to bear. So, it was no surprise to find that the coach I boarded on the final League day of the season was about as lively as Filey in a fog. We were heading for the Boleyn Ground and hopefully we weren't going to lose *our* heads. A mere point was required to secure our place in the Premiership; the fact that we had needed this point for what seemed like absolutely ages didn't help. Our misery had been compounded the previous week when we were reliably informed that for Wednesday to be relegated, all three teams below us had to win both of their final games, whilst we had to lose both of ours. We had smiled uneasily when the odds of such a happening had been put forward. And then the impossible happened - Man City did the Villa, Southampton nicked it at Bolton and Coventry easily beat Wimbledon... all of them away from home. And us? Well, we got stuffed by Everton. They'd all done the hard bit, now they each had a home game to win, whilst we had to strike The Irons who (for the first time in years) were actually hot. (That must go down as the worst pun in football history - surely now I will be offered that job on the Sunday Mirror's sport's desk?)

I stared out of the coach window as we headed down the M1. It had been a long season. Yet when it began in the middle of the hottest summer this century, things looked pretty bright. Wednesday were even in Europe. Better still, we hadn't had to win anything to get there - they just asked us; in fact the League had offered to pay us to enter. The Intertoto (which apparently *isn't* a sexual offence that Tarzan once committed) Cup was looked upon as a joke (yet Bordeaux have made full use of it as a route to the UEFA Cup Final). Wednesday, unlike Tottenham and Wimbledon, actually made a credible attempt at qualifying, but, as ever, we didn't quite make it.

The new season had beckoned with the supporters' choice, David Pleat, installed to steer us away from the doldrums into which Trevor Francis had guided us. New signings Mark Pembridge (a fiery Welsh dragon), and Mark Degryse (a skilful Belgian, er....) that I'd actually heard of, both looked sharp and ready for the fray. It's weird, but Wednesday fans' normal pessimism seems to evaporate in the summer months - perhaps it's a form of that S.A.D. disease (you know, the one where people get depressed in direct proportion to the lack of sunlight). Anyway, I, like many other Wednesdayites, am prevalent to bouts of optimism at the start of the football season. It's not until around October that I look at the points difference between Wednesday and the League leaders, and have to concede that we aren't going to win the Championship this year (again), and that the best we can hope for is a cup.

The opening skirmishes would certainly test our mettle: Liverpool away, then Champions Blackburn followed by Newcastle (everybody's favourites) at Hillsborough. With our usual good grace we allowed Collymore to steal the show on his debut with his only chance (Wednesday are notorious for succumbing to debutantes, Klinsmann and Clough amongst others). Blackburn arrived and were duly dispatched, reinforcing the prevailing feel-good factor: if we can sort Blackburn out, what have we to fear? Consequently everybody sorted Blackburn out (away from Ewood anyway), and our non-performance against Newcastle (live on Sky) in which we allowed Ginola the freedom of Hillsborough further compounded our fears and slapped the optimistic smiles off our faces.

Creditable away performances at QPR, Wimbledon and Coventry were counterbalanced by home defeats, David Pleat hinting (as had Trevor Francis before him), that the players were scared of playing at home. Apparently they don't like it when we go *Boo!*

Having reached the stage when the title was beyond us, we looked forward to a good run in the cups. Crewe and Millwall bit the dust, and then those dreaded words *"Arsenal will play Sheffield Wednesday."* I felt a bout of terminal pessimism coming on...

The Premiership match at Highbury happened to pre-empt the Cup game, and Wednesday played their best 45 minutes of the season to take a 2-1 lead, before reality tapped us politely on the shoulder and we lost 4-2. A feeling of déjà-vu in the Cup match followed, as a 1-0 lead was given away and, well, there's always the FA Cup isn't there?

Sky TV viewers were treated to a feeble display of defending as Wednesday conceded the lead three times before coming back to win 4-3, against perhaps the only team whose defence can out-inept us - Coventry. Things started to look up as we drew at Old Trafford and outplayed United; buoyed by that performance we reached the highlight of the season - a 6-2 thrashing of neighbours Leeds United. Waddle and Degryse gelled for the first time and gave Wilko's mob a footballing education. New signing Steve Nicol looked the part as midfield destroyer, and the visitors' latest acquisition Thomas Brolin managed to score with his face, whilst falling over. For four and a half million you expect that kind of ability, though.

Christmas came and Pleaty unwrapped his presents. A pair of Serbs; he'd have preferred cuff-links, but what the heck. Darko Kovacevic (according to World Soccer, "the best young striker in Europe") and defender Dejan Stefanovic were bought from Red Star Belgrade for £4.5m. Not bad value, considering both are internationals and still in their early twenties. Kovacevic made his debut on Boxing Day in the 2-2 draw with Southampton, but it was in the New Year's Day game against Bolton that he scored a brace, as did co-striker David Hirst. Thinks were definitely looking up - bring on the Cup run!

Oh shit! A miserable performance against Charlton inspired a barrage of headlines about 'into the Valley of death' as Wednesday became the Premiership's only third round casualty. Let's face it, the way we played we could have been knocked out by *Susanne* Charlton. Well that's it for another season, I thought, I might as well send my article to *Survival of the Fattest* now. But wait - was that a light at the end of the tunnel?

At that time, Wednesday as a team were playing with all the passion and power of the concert party in *It Ain't Half Hot, Mum*. Winter came to an end and The Times was inundated with readers claiming to have heard the first "Pleat Out!" of spring. Villa away looked a daunting prospect, but dreadlocked Dutchman Regi Blinker bought from Feyenoord for less than £300,000 seemed a bargain as he be-witched the Villa defence to score Wednesday's goal of the season (he started with the ball at the corner flag... beat Ehiogu, Charles and McGrath before netting... I guess you just had to be there!). His second goal was a consolation as the Owls conceded three, but at least we had a new hero to sing about: "Super, super Reg" etc. Another pre-deadline signing was Jon Newsome from Norwich. Big Jon is Sheffield born and bred, and was returning to the club that let him go and win a Championship medal with Leeds. The prodigal's return helped us beat Villa at home and then nick a win at Southampton with a first minute goal that your correspondent missed 'cos he was outside selling fanzines blissfully unaware that it was a 7.30 kick-off and not the usual 7.45. Degryse's strike was not met by the incessant chanting of his name, due to the fact that Wednesday fans don't know quite how to pronounce the little Belgian's moniker. Is it Degreese... Degrice... Degreezer... Degrizer... let's call the whole thing off!

Hey, we're on a roll. That was two wins on the trot! And then the Trotters put an end to it. A victory over Arsenal was but a blip as Wednesday failed to get the necessary points from our remaining games to pull us clear of the relegation dogfight. Everton arrived and Kanchelskis discovered Wednesday's weak spot - the team.

David Pleat further endeared himself to the Hillsborough faithful by declar-ing that it was far more exciting to be involved in the relegation battle than to be playing meaningless matches in the sanctuary of mid-table. He is obviously the love child of John Motson and Anne Widdecombe (Special Minister for Sheffield... she talks bollocks too!). Church attendances across the city rose (after all, United fans were praying for us too - praying that we'd get relegated, that is!).

It is at this point that I realised just what that light at the end of the tunnel was... It was the Endsleigh Express thundering towards Hillsborough, and I was woken out of my reverie by its screaming whistle. Blinking, I looked out of the coach window to see other Blinkers walking down the Barking Road, all proudly wearing their Regi wigs (which are in fact the remains of a job lot of Ruud Gullit wigs that Ken Bates offloaded on us - that guy will get on, you mark my words). Wednesdayites (despite the pessimism) are innately a proud lot, and the noise gen-erated by the two and a half thousand was undoubtedly greater than that made by equally desperate fans in Coventry, Manchester and Southampton.

During the game, one in twenty had an ear superglued to their Sony Walk-man and mutterings of *"Liverpool are winning 1-0... 2-0..."* brought a smile to our faces. *"The other matches remain at 0-0... it's 2-1, City have pulled one back... they've got a penalty... 2-2."* Two and a half thousand Zantac tablets were ingested... "Bar-my Army! Barmy Army!." Then the expected happened (I told you we were pessimists): Dicks headed (I had to be careful how I wrote that - or perhaps I shouldn't have worried) West Ham into the lead. "You're not singing anymore." Yes we were - "Barmy Army! Barmy Army!." ."..*still 2-2 at City... Pressman keeps Wednesday in the Premiership for another minute...*" in the dying seconds... ."..*it's 0-0 at Coventry*", we're safe!! "Barmy Army! Barmy Army!." Sheffield's number one son Big Jon Newsome directed an equaliser into the Hammers' net... Delirium... Orgasm... oops, sorry about that!

Isn't it bloody typical of our lot; they spent 89 minutes (and a few weeks) trying to get a point to be safe and only managed it when we didn't need it any more. A sea of happy faces was warmly applauded by West Ham fans who had delighted in an afternoon of "Going Down" chants, but were nothing but gracious in their acceptance that Wednesday didn't deserve the Endsleigh, if only for the sake of their fans. Still, that will be little consolation to Manchester City, about whose followers the same could be said.

That coach ride home was not the wild party that I'd expected. Tension, fear and the resulting elation takes it out of you. I drew on a cigarette (not easy that you know, the pen goes through the paper usually, ha ha), and turning to the person at my side, said "How was it for you?"

Fanzine Facts

Spitting Feathers (formerly known as *A View From The East Bank*) was started in September 1992 by Peter Holmes and has produced 36 issues to date. New editor Graham Lightfoot decided to give the mag a new name as he felt that the previous one was "a bit straight for a fanzine." Still, he promises that *SF* will continue to have the same mix of articles, letters and cartoons, but will also feature a tongue-in-cheek look at visiting sides. Wednesdayites can expect an issued every home game, if Graham gets his act together!

SUPER DARIO LAND

Crewe Alexandra

Shattered dreams

A bunch of anoraks scribble madly as the cliché-laden gravy train pulls out of Crewe station heading for the rich trappings of the First Division. Crewe Alexandra aren't on it, but their fans are on the platform, waving a fond farewell to several of their former players who jumped ship and are! Instead, the Alex are currently working on a place in the Guinness Book of Records as the team who lost out the most times in everybody's favourite May hobby, the play-offs. Don't get me wrong, I think that the end-of-season decider is the business. If you're good enough to go up, you'll do so automatically, won't you? Let's shut up whinging about how unfair it all is... for us it was a safety valve which kept our season alive when we

had, at one stage, looked dead-certs for top-flight football. But then we sold three key players at a time when all around us were boosting their squads, our form slumped and suddenly we were wishing ill fortune on others just to retain a spot in the top six. That's what I call desperate, and so were we during the last three months of a now familiar topsy-turvy formula.

Nothing surprises me about football anymore, especially at Crewe. You become increasingly cynical, only betting £20 on promotion (yes, it used to be more!), and even consider booking holidays in May. I think I've learnt my lesson and try not to expect the earth. Fairy tales only materialise on dusty bookshelves once frequented as an expectant child. Older, but only very slightly wiser, you still hope that dreams come true. But if you allow yourself to surf the euphoria that surrounds the League's longest-serving manager, his associated talented midfield dwarves, a chairman who thinks big and reckons we need a 14,000 all-seater stadium (our current average attendance as a reasonably successful Second Division team is about 3,900), then you shouldn't be too surprised when you find yourself drowning. You can't tread water indefinitely without additional support, and unless the minnow develops, it's not long before you're out of your depth, swept away, spiralling down the plug hole. Doom and gloom. Christ, I'm sounding like that daft Frenchman!

Reading this drivel you'd be forgiven for thinking that we'd just endured the worst of seasons. That's not true. Come the halfway point, we were up there head-to-head with Swindon looking like potential Champions. We had entertained Southampton (FAC4) and Sheffield Wednesday both home and away (that other Cup), with Waddle and Le Tissier both oozing class after all these years and all that criticism. Watching them, our players learnt a lot, and the fans certainly took plenty of enjoyment, even in defeat. We scored seven times against our supposedly superior Premiership rivals, but out we went, to concentrate on the League and all that. The scheduled fixture at the Dell in late January was postponed due to frozen toilets. Really. You could say they were shit-scared of losing to Second Division opponents. Then again, neither team's season was flushed with success, Southampton's nearly going down the pan, ours rising then disappearing out of sight... no, stop it.

I could start to ramble on about numerous triumphs against any one of our 20 League opponents. But you expect these victories, especially when you've been put on a pedestal - Dario's conveyor belt of talent, blah blah. This season was no different, and we had a flyer; who could stop us? Blackpool and Swindon could, that's for sure, with not a single point stemming from either League or AWS fixture. Blackpool is our new bogey team, and we've had a few! In fact, all we've got on Blackpool is a marginally better nickname - can you imagine having to chant "Come on, you Tangerines..."? No, neither can I - and if it came to the crunch, our lion (Gresty the mascot, a bloke in a furry suit who gives sweets to the kids, but doesn't get arrested) would have no problem biting that ridiculous inflatable piece of fruit which bounces around pre-match Bloomfield Road. And who didn't have a little chuckle at Owen Oyston's demise?

Apart from the result, Blackpool was just one of several eagerly anticipated jaunts to the always sunny English seaside - Brighton, Bournemouth, Hull and Hartlepool... OK, so Bournemouth was a bit of a shithole. But these away-days really make the season: inflatables, singing and dancing, discarded burgers, sticky fingers - and that's just the gents' toilets in Brighton. But your spirits are lifted (especially in Hartlepool, unless you nail them down), it's a mini holiday with football incorporated where you enjoy a distant town without being herded onto coaches and trains immediately after the final whistle. Why, I don't know, but they all have the edge on an excursion to Scunthorpe. It's a different atmosphere. It will be a tough decision this coming season as we hop off the train at Gillingham instead of spending a dull and tedious day in run-of-the-mill Paris, courtesy of that Euro-bullet thing.

Talking of the Gills, we saw a couple of revamped stadiums on our travels. Ours isn't too much of a disgrace these days, either! The new-look red plastic buckets (ergonomically designed for added comfort) are a partisan sight to behold, with C.A.F.C. spelt correctly in dashing white so nobody's in any doubt as to who's stadium it is - as if anyone else would try and nick it! New ticketing facilities ensure you'll get your matchday ticket within, er, about an hour, and the home fans' toilet facilities wouldn't look out of place at the Ideal Boat Exhibition. When the final piece of the jigsaw is put in place next summer (the reconstruction of our irresistibly quaint wooden main stand), we'll probably be one of the host stadiums for World Cup '98. OK, so it's being held in France, but we've got one of those swanky EuroStar connections and Crewe-Paris can't take much longer than Bordeaux-Paris. I bet you're already dreaming of sipping a good red as the evening sun goes down on the Royal's terrace bar, waking up to croissant and freshly ground coffee before nudging your new-found sleeping partner you met over a romantic meal... then you remember how pissed you got, losing your keys and having to crash at some drunken yobbo's flat; yes you've woken up next to a hairy Stockport fan. We never could score in Europe!

I suppose I'd better speak briefly about the football, and we continued to play some cracking stuff. Neat passing, beautiful triangles... everyone seemed to compliment us. All this can start to get you down, though, when your front-men (the ones that aren't sold, that is) continue to fluff chances or pussyfoot around refusing to shoot. Apart from Rob Edwards (striker come good, treated badly, who not surprising didn't sign a contract before defecting to Huddersfield for a bag of peanuts), most of the goals came from midfield. We're good at producing them. Small ones. I challenge any visiting supporter to deny that they've had a smirk at the average height of our team. Of course, size isn't everything (we've all used that line, haven't we?) but we continue to get battered on and off the ball each and every game. Being perennial winners of the Bobby Moore Fair Play Award is scant consolation for losing games through physical inferiority. I'm not saying that your entire squad should tip 6'2" but Dopey, Sneezy and Sleepy would probably force a place in our midfield. We need a little balance, a couple of players to counteract the donkeys that endeavour to destroy our total football.

All that I do ask is for 100% commitment from the players. There's nothing worse when you believe someone wearing your colours is slacking. So it's a positive note on which I'd like to end, describing the attitude of the Alex players who fought tirelessly for a place at Wembley in the play-off final. We'd started well, at home against Notts County, going 2-0 up with some electrifying football; a return to our best, football we had always been capable of. But it went horribly wrong towards the latter part of the first leg, with County fighting back and Crewe snatching a draw from the jaws of victory. No complaints, they deserved it. Meadow Lane was a different matter, though. An evening match at their impressively remodelled stadium. Floodlights setting the scene, casting light on the theatre below where one team would be victorious. The Alex were magnificent, and we sang until hoarse, until the ref had blown and our efforts could lift the team no more. The players really wanted it, and how the ball stayed out of County's net is a mystery. We lost, but it didn't hurt. Any doubts about the players' ambition were quashed that night. Perhaps the club's management have different priorities, but the players earned respect from all those present.

Football. It's the most potent of drugs. A dependency where substitutes exist but you know you could never reap the same irresistible highs and lows. A non-evil lure for which you'd sacrifice much. So I'll be there come August, cynical as ever, a fresh bet in place, with dreams intact for at least a few months, hoping that the Alex will succeed where others fail. As for that holiday in May, well, maybe not... we'll be in the play-offs again. Probably.

Fanzine Facts

Editor Jules Hornbrook explains that *Super Dario Land*, which started at the opening of the '93-94 season, became *SDL* during '95-96. "No reason, except a bit less ink I suppose." Still boasting an issue each month, it's now more popular than ever. Jules reckons that about a quarter of the home support read each issue and the contributors' list hasn't stopped growing. Response to the fans' survey was excellent with most wanting plenty more anti-Stoke material, who remain Crewe's favourite rivals, although they've been apart for some years now.

TALK OF THE TYNE

Newcastle United

In all of my years following Newcastle United I can honestly say, like the majority of the tens of th.., well the tens, that call themselves the *Toon Army*, that I have never seen my team win anything.

OK, perhaps I tell a white lie. There was the prestigious Anglo-Italian Cup and the never-to-be-forgotten... er, what was it called again? Oh yes, the Texaco Cup, back in the days when Supermac was God, beer was 20p a pint, fags 30p, and the country was run by the Labour Party. Yes, *that* long ago.

The League title was always something that only the 'big boys' could scrap over, while we were like some snotty nosed kid with our face pressed up against the sweet shop window. Look, but don't touch! Quite simply because we didn't have two pennies to scratch together.

1927 is the most famous year in Geordie history. It's the year our famous landmark - the Tyne bridge - was built; Newcastle Brown Ale was invented; and the last time our run-down and barren trophy room housed the League title. Yes, and we certainly had those facts perpetually rammed down our throats during '95-96.

And this season was going to be *so* different: Keegan had been spending money like it was going out of fashion - £24m to build the squad, and the arrival of England stars Warren Barton and Les Ferdinand meant we could boast a team of 11 full internationals. Incredible though it may seem, to emphasise how much United had been in the backwaters, Barton was the first current England player Newcastle had bought since Ivor Broadis in 1953! And this point alone showed that we could at long last call ourselves a 'buying' club and rid ourselves of the tag that we produced the stars (Beardsley, Waddle, Gazza) only to sell them on to the big cats.

During Keegan's reign, Newcastle have had an amazing tendency to start a season like an express train but finish it like a blind man pulling a rickshaw. His first season in charge ('92-93) saw us win the first 11 League games and dominate the First Division for almost the entire campaign, at one point putting us 16 points clear at the top. Then we faded badly and with three games to go ended up in second spot, with West Ham and Portsmouth looking the likeliest to win the automatic promotion places, before three wins in the last three games gave us the Championship.

Next came our introduction to the Premier League, and after a poor first week the team went ten games unbeaten in League and Cup.

The following year started with an unbelievable run of 17 games undefeated before falling away and losing top spot in mid-November, never to regain it.

And so to '95-96:-

The express train left Newcastle Central on August 19th with a convincing 3-0 win over Coventry City, followed by equally strong performances at Burnden Park (3-1) and Hillsborough (2-0). All in all, only one single defeat in the first 16 League games.

French star David Ginola was quite simply the best footballer I had ever seen in a black and white shirt. He defied logic. The first rule I was taught in football was how to trap a ball, yet Ginola has probably never killed a ball dead in his life. It was a tool of expression and had no place lying motionless on the grass. People still rave about Glen Hoddle's sweeping 50 yard passes, and rightly so, but Ginola made them five or six times a match!

Early in the season the balance felt right, and even though there were times when the two full-backs Barton and Beresford played more like wingers than defenders, we always looked capable of scoring twice as many goals as we were likely to concede. But somewhere along the line, something went sadly wrong.

Keegan dabbled with the three centre-back system which was the initial cause of our downfall the previous season, and three players who I interviewed for *Talk of the Tyne* openly declared that they hated playing five across the back. One, a midfielder, told us that the system would never work because using overlapping full-backs with two wingers meant that the midfield only consisted of two players who were up against an opposition brick wall of four or five. Another said "At the start of the season we let other teams worry about us. We had no fear and we went out and tried to express ourselves and it worked brilliantly. Now [March], we seem too concerned about how other teams play rather than let them worry about us."

Suddenly that 12 point gap at the top of the table became minus 6 and my world started to cave in. Sky TV showed the anguish of the fans as we watched the torment at Liverpool and Blackburn, but all I can say is "Don't look back in Anger..."

We finished second when we should have had it in the bag by March, but this is our highest League placing for 70 years, and '95-96 was truly a memorable season.

OK, we can all ponder on that 12 point lead that was chipped away and say it could all have been so different. If only we'd done this, done that, played so-and-so and played a more defensive formation. We've all got our theories, and who's to say they wouldn't have worked either? The plain facts are: we have a manager who wants success just as desperately as we do; we have the greatest Newcastle team any of us under the age of 45 has ever seen; and unquestionably the greatest supporters 'the world has ever seen'!

Newcastle is the place to be. This is not the disaster everyone is making it out to be. Sure, we are all devastated, but no more so than the team and the manager, and we must all remember that this is just the beginning... Not the end.

The couple of days leading up to the last finale against Tottenham were the most nerve-wracking I have ever experienced. We had a mountain to climb and despite the odds we just had to convince ourselves that we were in with a chance, even though that chance depended on the Smogmonsters of Middlesbrough winning a match - a tall order in itself; monumental when you consider they were playing Man Utd. They did us no favours, but perhaps we can return the compliment one day.

It has been a major disappointment, there's no disguising that, even more so knowing it was the Cockneys (Man Utd) who took it from our grasp, but we have seen some classic matches this season and some equally classic performances. David Ginola has captivated us with his silky skills, Les Ferdinand has worn the famous number nine shirt with pride, Peter Beardsley has run until he dropped... But the new kid on the block David Batty has been an inspired signing. This man is going to have a major say where the Championship goes next season. And it won't be Manchester!

We lost out this time but Keegan and the players are now even more determined. Sunday May 5th was a day of mixed emotion for us all and I'm sure there was a river of tears. We were so close, yet so far. Still, the future of this club is in safe hands and there is that ever increasing optimism that the best is yet to come.

Fanzine Facts

Talk of the Tyne is now one of the biggest selling fanzines in the country despite only being in circulation since 1994. Editor Kev Fletcher was involved in the Newcastle fanzine explosion at the outset in 1988 when he was co-editor of *Black and White*. He says: "Back in the late 1980's I thought the fanzine movement was nothing more than a fashion craze that would have as much longevity as John Travolta's white suit, but happily I was wrong. The standard life-span of a publication is probably only two or three years due to work involved, and it does take a man with a big heart to keep the enthusiasm going after standing out in the rain, hail and snow continually saying "No, it's *not* the programme."

"But as one fanzine editor calls it a day, there invariably is someone else who believes they can do better, so the craze is as healthy as it's ever been. Down-to-earth humour is still the most important ingredient and the reason for the success of fanzines."

TALKING BULL

Hereford United

In last year's *Survival of the Fattest*, our prediction for the coming season was that we couldn't see "the motley crew of expensive failures, promising youngsters and typical lower division journeymen bringing the long-awaited success to Hereford in '95-96." So while what actually happened might not seem like success to some of you, to us it certainly was.

I should have guessed that something good would happen because it was my first season living away from Hereford since I first started following United in 1983. My relocation to Leicester and a change in priorities (i.e. marriage) suggested that a good year for United might be on the cards. The squad was virtually the same as last year's, the only difference in personnel being the appointment of Graham Turner as manager to replace John Layton. The latter was in dispute with the club over a new contract, and with only a couple of weeks to go before the first game kicked off, no-one knew who was going to be the boss. Once it became known that Graham Turner was interested, there weren't really any other candidates (even though *Talking Bull* first suggested his appointment over a year before!).

The first positive proof that the season might actually deliver something special came in the first match when Barnet ("who could still make the play-offs" as Gabriel Clarke and Ray Clemence never tired of telling us all season) were stuffed 4-1. Our man between the sticks, Chris MacKenzie, became one of a select band of 'keepers who have scored from open play since the war, guaranteeing United's place in history as a team who have been both on the giving and receiving ends of this feat, as the 846 (total attendance!) who were at our match at Maidstone on Rugby World Cup Final day in 1991 will testify. A quick exit from the Coca Cola Cup followed when we lost 5-2 on aggregate to Oxford in the 'big local derby', as Central South would surely have described it (seeing as Oxford, Swindon and ourselves are the only League teams in their region). A worrying trend soon became apparent as we won away at Plymouth - the sort of place where we would never normally be expected to get a result.

October 1st marked a very sad event, when our excellent and beloved Supporters' Club was destroyed by fire (later found to be arson). The end of October saw a double-header away at Fulham and Leyton Orient. The first of these was notable for United having two players sent off in the first half but still holding out comfortably for a 0-0 draw, and also for some stewarding reminiscent of 1930's Germany, while Barry Hearn's boys were on the receiving end of another of those 'unlikely' away wins.

November is of course FA Cup time, and our fame is inextricably linked with the competition. After three successive defeats against non-league opposition, we weren't exactly overjoyed with a home draw against Stevenage, who were beginning to show signs of what they should rightly have achieved. Matters didn't improve when we went 1-0 down, but the supporters lifted our game and carried our hard-working players to a 2-1 win. Two weeks later we were visited by the worst Cardiff City team witnessed in recent years, but the swines still beat us to extend their unbeaten run in proper matches at Edgar Street to 20 years. That was followed by another 'big local derby' as we won 1-0 at Swindon in the Tesco Trolley Trophy (Auto Windscreens Shield to the uninitiated), where Steve White was applauded by the entire crowd after his winner. We survived yet another encounter against non-league opposition (yes, two in a row!) with a 2-0 win against Sutton.

December, and the first appearance of something which would play a prominent part in the rest of our season - postponements. Northampton on Boxing Day should have been called off too, but the Cobblers probably realised that they would never get 5,222 people on a Tuesday in February, so we all had to freeze and watch a lottery on a skating rink (the pitch-side thermometer registered -5°C).

Our reward for those non-league victories against Stevenage and Sutton was one of the biggest - Tottenham at home. Much to our delight the club resisted the chance of making quick money by switching the match to White Hart Lane. Instead the media had to consult their maps and descend on Edgar Street in hopeful search of an upset/patronise the locals (delete as appropriate). Our confidence in believing that we could beat Spurs did not look misplaced as we tore them apart, but finally had to be content with a 1-1 draw and a chance to make some REAL money. The replay was one of those nights when having a good time was paramount, and although we lost 5-1, 4,500 United supporters out-sang 27,000 'all-seater stadia' customers, *and* we scored the best goal of the night. The raucous rendition of "Graham Turner's Barmy Army" that was still going on 15 minutes after the final whistle is something that will remain in my memory for a very long time.

Before we'd taken our wellies on a day out to London we'd already qualified for the area semi-final of the Tesco Trolley with a win against our friends from Sixfields. The game was away at Gay Meadow, home of our near-neighbours the Sloppies. Unfortunately our players still couldn't get the hang of playing on ice, and a desperately disappointing 4-1 defeat resulted.

Shortly after this a copy of Lincoln City's 'The Deranged Ferret' arrived with a prediction that we were their tip to come from nowhere to qualify for the play-offs. Oh, how I laughed! Hereford? Play-offs? My cynicism largely rested on the fact that we still had to play Lincoln twice and they invariably beat us. Another desperately cold night at Sincil Bank lived up to my prediction, our only consolation for the 2-1 defeat being that we could take the piss out of John Beck's teams' 'style' of football.

At the start of March there were ten League Saturdays left, but we still had 17 matches to play. While some of us realised that winning our games in hand could take us to the verge of the play-offs, others looked at our small squad and saw how easy it would be to get sucked into the relegation dogfight if we had more than a couple of injuries and suspensions. The first of the 17 was Northampton at home, and Tony James' return to the first team after more than a year out injured. In the 89th minute he went upfield for a corner and scored the only goal of the match - if you'd written the script it would have been rejected as too far-fetched! A win in our next match at Hartlepool saw us going to Scunthorpe chasing our Holy Grail - three successive wins, which hadn't happened for several years. Well, it did on 9th March 1996, and I doubt whether anyone was prepared for what was to follow. In April, we won our next six matches to take us above that mystical dotted-line that we'd only ever seen from a distance. Highlights included another Chalkie White hat-trick as Plymouth were beaten 3-0, and revenge for last season's club record 7-1 defeat at Mansfield. The equation was now simple - two wins in our last four matches would see us in the play-offs for the first time. Defeats by Darlington and Cardiff put the pressure on; we now needed two from two. Hartlepool and Rochdale were dispatched with relative ease and the unthinkable had happened. Unfortunately the ultimate happy ending didn't materialise, as Darlington completed their third and fourth victories over us within the space of six weeks to reach Wembley, leaving us to miss out at the last hurdle for the third time in our history.

In spite of that, it was a successful season for United and one which has restored some of our belief in our club. It also means that expectations will be higher than they have been in recent years. With appetites whetted, a return to anywhere near our traditional 17th place just won't be tolerated!

Fanzine Facts

Talking Bull, the fanzine at the heart of all things HUFC, began back in 1989. One of the original editors, Keith Benjamin, is now the supporters' representative on the board of directors, and the fanzine is represented on a club committee, taking decisions on pricing structures, ground development, etc. Without *Talking Bull,* editor Chris Jones feels that the fans' views would not be heard, especially with the lack of local media in Herefordshire.

THE TEA PARTY

Stockport County

The place was Millmoor, Rotherham, on a sunny Tuesday in April. "We only need to win our last four games to make the play-offs..." Stockport County fans had been saying this since before the previous Saturday's 3-0 defeat of York City; a statement which, ignoring as it did the fact that we hadn't won four successive games all season, encapsulated the false optimism of '95-96.

That optimism had been founded on good early performances. A 2-0 win at newly-promoted Walsall on the opening day was quickly followed by the return of manufactured rivals, Burnley. The Purples (Clarets is so twee, don't you think?) were making their first visit to Edgeley Park since the infamous play-off final of '94 ("Daddy, where

were you during the great Play-off of '94?" "Block 148, Row 26, seat 182, my son. God, it was hell"), and the County crowd were hell-bent on verbal revenge. Gratifyingly, the recipient of the majority of the abuse was Ted McMinn, a man confirmed, in the words of his team-mates as "a bit of a wind-up merchant" following the Wembley débâcle, in which County had become the first team to have two players sent off on the hallowed turf. The other main culprit on that dreaded day had been referee David Elleray, who this time was thankfully detained elsewhere (in a Bangkok hell-hole, with any luck). The non-stop chants of "Ted McMinn is a wanker"; for variety, "Ted McMinn is a bastard"; and, to demonstrate the full extent of the County fans' verbal dexterity, "Fuck Off McMinn", led to him being substituted early in the second half, eyes brimming, and bottom lip a-tremble. Unable to admit to being intimidated, McMinn resorted to stories of being hit by missiles, the size of which ranged from boiled sweets, to bricks, to some of the largest of the works from Henry Moore's "big" period, depending which newspaper report you read (needless to say, County's concerned monitoring of the surveillance film showed that in fact nothing more dangerous than a tantrum had been thrown).

The game? Well, Burnley were hammered out of sight, 0-0. And thus that first memorable home game represented County's season in microcosm. For the first few months, we were playing teams off the park, and not getting the results. Burnley, Crewe, Wycombe, Swindon... all came and pinched a point, and yet none of them deserved it. Away from home, the side was performing well enough - indeed, the final tally of 11 away wins was the best in the club's history. A mere eight victories at Edgeley Park, however, only three of which were achieved before FA Cup third round day, tell their own story.

Ah yes, but FA Cup third round day... Easy victories at home over Lincoln City and Blyth Spartans made sure we were participants in the FA's attempt - with the help of the least amusing double act in the country, Law and Venables - at spicing up an event which, most people would agree, requires spicing up in much the same way as Man United need to pull their bloody finger out and start winning trophies. Everton was the name drawn out prior to ours from the Heath Robinson contraption that seems to have replaced the velvet bag. Dave Watson's smug "we'll settle for anything at home *(thinks: Stockport! Yes! That's round four for us, then!)*" comments during the post-draw TV interview with the Cup holders' representative gave no hint of the classic to come.

Following Liverpool's 7-0 thrashing of Rochdale on the Saturday (the Reds having won the toss for choice of day), Everton fans were apparently heard to make noises of the "we'll score as many as Liverpool" variety, which made it all the more enjoyable when County outplayed the Scousers, and were desperately unlucky to have to settle for a mere *(mere!)* 2-2 draw, twice coming from behind, and having at least three clear-cut chances to clinch it. Walking back through Stanley Park afterwards - or, to be precise, six inches or so above Stanley Park - amongst the small knots of Evertonians, I experienced the euphoria that is denied to supporters of Premier League clubs: the pride that can only be experienced when you play one of your supposed betters off the park. *"I'm* a County fan" I wanted to say to each group of Everton supporters in turn, the members of which would then have queued up to congratulate me personally for the way County had played. In reality, of course, they would probably have kicked my head in, so I pulled my coat about my County shirt, kept quiet, and floated back to my car.

The replay was a classic, marred only before kick off by a massive price hike by the ever so fan-friendly County board. We took a first half lead through Matthew Bound, fluffed a couple of great chances early in the second half, but were still ahead after an hour, before Everton - in fairness on top by then, and playing much better than they had at Goodison - scored twice in quick succession, and, with substitute Amokachi running riot, threatened to overwhelm us. But we rallied, and in the 89th minute got the equaliser our late pressure had warranted when star striker Alun Armstrong took three defenders out of the game with a single flick from the outside of his right foot and equalised right in front of 5,000 delirious County fans sitting in the new Cheadle End Stand. Cue ape-shit celebrations both on and off the pitch, which were probably a major contributory factor to the ease with which John Ebbrell ran unchallenged and scored Everton's winner 30 seconds after the restart. Armstrong in tears, disbelief in the stands, yet, slowly, that pride once again swelling in the chest. The only sour note was struck with our ex-Evertonian manager Dave Jones' post match comments of the "if we had to lose to anybody, it was nice we lost to them" variety. At that precise moment, County fans could not have cared if we'd lost to Accrington Stanley, the Faroe Islands, or Real fucking Madrid.

But memorable Cup performances (we also put First Division Ipswich out of the Coca Cola Cup over two legs) do not a successful season make, especially with the new Sky TV deal promising up to a million quid a season for Division One clubs. The curate's egg which was County's League form saw points dropped at home to nonentities such as Wrexham - and even sound wins over promotion rivals Notts County, Oxford and Crewe merely prolonged the agony, until, sure enough, on that April Tuesday, the Millers, buoyed up by their pre-match parading of the Auto Windscreens Shield, psyched up by pre-match "entertainment" from the Chuckle Brothers (the most inappropriately named duo in the history of misnomers, although marginally funnier than Law and Venables), and creased up by Jim Gannon, returning from long-term injury to fill in at full back for County, and treating the match as an audition for the position of third Chuckle Brother, duly won 2-0. And that was that. Crewe won their game in hand, Bradford eased above us into sixth place, and, despite our battling 0-0 draw at Champions Swindon on the last Saturday, the Bantams, doing what we had earlier failed to do, won at Hull to earn sixth spot, and, ultimately, a crack at Division One next year.

Off the field, the unfair dismissal case of ex-manager Danny Bergara grabbed most of the local headlines. He eventually won his case (with 75% liability awarded against the club), leaving County with a large compensation bill to pay. The hearing provided lurid local headlines for a few weeks mid-season, with details of Bergara's alleged heavy drinking, and a reported brawl between chairman and manager during a sponsors' function at a local hotel. What was most depressing, however, were the allegations, revealed in testimony given by an ex-employee who herself is due to launch an unfair dismissal claim against the club, of sexual harassment against "everyone from the chief executive to the safety officer", and including several players. The fatuous "Friendly Football Club" slogan, dreamed up a few years ago, was thus shown up as nothing more than a marketing gimmick, and a fairly inappropriate one at that.

It was rather sad, then, that, Cup heroics apart, off-the-field activities seemed to provide the season's most noteworthy events. The stark reality is that, for Stockport County, '95-96 was barely an improvement on the previous season. Of course the Mr and Ms Reasonables, the "My club right or wrong" merchants, the pains-in-the-bloody-arse, quite frankly, have been out in force, claiming that fans should offer nothing but unqualified support, and - perish the thought! - never criticism, constructive or otherwise. Following a disappointing season on the pitch, and one in which fans were shafted by club policy on more than one occasion off it, it is gratifying, however, that there are still enough supporters with more than a few hundred brain cells to enable the fanzine to remain viable.

In summary, and whatever their viewpoint, no County fan can deny that last season, was, by any criteria, not a successful one. At best, we stood still. And what's worse, the club seem to have got their priorities, not for the first time, completely arse-about-face, with most of the ambition at the moment seeming to lie off the pitch. A shiny new 5,000 seat stand has indeed been built, but with price rises of almost 30%, and our 13th new kit in seven seasons, it's easy to see who's going to be exploited to pay for it. The commercial department's turnover is one of the largest in our Division, but there's the rub - we've remained in that same Division for another year. We can be the most successful "trading organisation" in the lower leagues, but, frankly, if we don't get promoted fairly soon, who gives a toss?

I'm probably just depressed; you've caught me at a bad time. In fairness, the squad Jones has assembled looks a good one, with Armstrong due an exceptional season any year now, and players such as Chris Marsden, John Jeffers and the ever-reliable Mike Flynn looking a class above most of their opponents. However, I distinctly remember harbouring similar thoughts last close-season, and the events described above soon gave the lie to that optimism, leaving me with the dread thought that '96-97 might prove another false dawn.

I hope to God I'm proved wrong, however, no matter how much word-eating will ensue. Indeed, I hope to God that, come next May, I look a complete and utter fool (more so, that is, than I do normally). In fact, I hope to God that, come next May, people will be actively seeking me out, in order to nudge their friends, point, and say "you're the one who wrote the County bit in that review of the season thing, aren't you? HA!."

Fanzine Facts

The Tea Party, edited by Dave Espley, was started on August 1st 1991, and derives its name from Stockport County's nickname - the Hatters. Dave relies on a host of contributors and sellers, all of whom helped to make *The Tea Party* Four-FourTwo's Fanzine of the Year 1995.

THERE'S A GOOD TIME COMING
(BE IT EVER SO FAR AWAY)

Exeter City

Saved from closure, a return to 70's style hooliganism, 200 City fans locked out at an away match and the usual failure to win a single Cup game - another season in the life of Exeter City.

But while finishing 14th in the Third Division may not seem much to some, it has been a triumph for Devon's finest. The only thing that went wrong was when Neil Smallcock (sorry - spellcheck doesn't recognise Warnock's) Plymouth Argyle fluked promotion via the play-offs.

None of us City fans even expected to start the season. The club were skint and in the hands of the administrators. We'd sold our ground for a paltry £600,000 and quite frankly only about two and a half thousand people were even bothered.

THERE'S A GOOD TIME COMING

Issue 1
Jan 96
50p

(BE IT EVER SO FAR AWAY)

After finishing bottom the season before, only Macclesfield's crap ground saved us from going into the Conference; the bookies made us favourites for the drop this time. And who could blame them? Even the most optimistic City fans were saying that if we finished second from bottom it would be time to crack open the champagne.

But we did have a new player/manager in goalie and Player of the Year Peter Fox, and he made the inspired decision of bringing in Noel 'hardman' Blake as his assistant and centre-half. After an opening day home defeat against Darlington, City then embarked on a ten match unbeaten run. There was even a touch of early season play-off fever as 5,500 came to the Park to see our 2-2 draw with Leyton Orient. And what made it all the more enjoyable was that all this time, Plymouth 'we'll have won this Division by Christmas' Argyle were rooted, along with Torquay, to the bottom.

But while the local paper banged on continually about play-offs, we the fans knew differently. For the first time in ages we were tight at the back thanks to Blakey, but we still couldn't score goals, and the best striker we found all season wasn't even ours. Lee Bradbury came on loan from Portsmouth and showed us what we'd been missing for so long. But despite popular opinion, Terry Fenwick isn't a complete dimwit and he wanted Bradders back.

Another star to leave during the season was Martin 'Buster Buster Boing Boing' Phillips sold to Alan Ball's Manchester City for £500,000. Now I'm not going to complain at half a million quid for the pint-sized young winger, but I still can't quite help feeling that we've been conned somewhere along the line. After all, when Ballie was our manager, I remember him saying Buster was going to be the first £10m footballer. Now unless we get a huge crowd and record gate receipts when Man City come to play us in a friendly next year as the second part of the deal, it looks to me as though we're some way short of that figure. The other bad thing about the deal is that we now have a relationship (ooh err) with the Mancs whereby they loan us some of their reserves until they're good enough for Ballie's first team. So far it hasn't worked too well. They gave us John Sharpe, brother of Man United's Lee - and it's obvious who got the footballing genes in that family! Still it does worry opposing fans for a couple of minutes at least when we shout "Come on Lee Sharpe's brother!"

But the sale of Buster did put some much needed cash back into the club, and that, together with the considerable help of the City Council seems to have averted the threat of closure. The Council (don't switch off folks this isn't a party political broadcast) came to our rescue by applying for a compulsory purchase order on the ground, which we sold to a property developer the year before, and bought it back for us. They now lease St James Park to us. If they hadn't come in we would have been homeless when Beazer Homes started building houses on the pitch. The club has also come out of administration which means it is allowed to handle its own affairs again. Previously, the administrators had decided what we could and couldn't spend. This exercise was imposed by the Football League, and while it did stop a lot of wastage it also cost us £250,000 paying their wages - almost three times more than we've ever spent buying a player. But at least now the club can go forward for the first time in years. Although there's still not much cash around, the League have lifted their transfer ban on us and we're allowed to buy players again - although so far all we've done is pick up free transfers.

Foxy says it's difficult to attract players down to Devon and maybe he's right. Don't think I'm paranoid or anything but teams don't seem to like us. Take Colchester for example. We've got nothing against them but they seem to think we are their biggest rivals. At half time during the match at Layer Road a group of their fans got onto the pitch and stormed the away end for a 70's, scarves around your wrist era, punch-up. The police and stewards just left them to it. What *is it* with them? The year before when they came to us they attacked our supporters' club and hurled a beer barrel through the window. If we were a bit richer I would send Colchester a map and explain to them that we're *not* their local rivals. Colchester/Exeter is *not* a derby. We couldn't give a toss about them; it's Plymouth we hate.

But Colchester aren't the only team who don't like us. We laid out the red carpet for Preston by giving their large support our home end and they responded by locking us out of the final match of the season at Deepdale! Some 400 City fans made the 500 mile round trip up North and those that went straight to the ground got in. But those of us who enjoy a pre-match pint rolled up at quarter to three to be told it was sold out! What happened was that 18,000 Preston fans turned up to see their team crowned Champions. Prestonites who were locked out of the home sections quickly ran round to fill the away end, leaving 200 City fans pissed-off and banished to the nearest pub.

Not everyone has it in for us though. Scarborough made us very welcome and even introduced us to a quaint after-match custom of theirs - a game called Pile

On. One chap lies spread-eagled on the floor of their social club and everyone else takes a run up and jumps on top, building a human mountain. We couldn't work out why they do it. The best explanation was that it has something to do with the fact that their team is always near the bottom and their supporters want to know what it feels like. In that case, I suggest Smallcock's lot down the road start playing Pile On - because they'll be back at the bottom next year.

Fanzine Facts

There's A Good Time Coming (Be It Ever So Far Away) is a new Exeter City fanzine started last season after the merger of The Exe Directory and In Exile mags. The new 'zine takes its name from the song that City ran out to on the greatest day in the club's history, an FA Cup quarter final replay against Sunderland in front of a record 20,984 fans at St James Park in the '30-31 season. Editor Dave Peters muses that they had thought about calling it 'Parklife', which would not have been a bad name for a fanzine about life at the Park, "but the next line 'All the people, so many people' forced us to admit that Blur probably had something other than St James Park in mind."

THERE'S ONLY ONE F IN FULHAM

Fulham

So it's farewell, and bloody good riddance, to yet another record breaking season down by the Thames. For the third successive term (and the fifth time in seven seasons) Fulham recorded their worst ever final League placing. And en route they slumped to their worst ever position - one off the foot of the basement Division. No wonder it's said that 'There's only one F in Fulham'. Come to that there's only one F in Frustration, and we know that sensation only too well!!

A grotesque sequence of 27 League game produced just one measly win and meant that the unthinkable drop into the Vauxhall Conference became a real possibility, only 21 years on from an FA Cup Final appearance. Following years of despair and decay the rot had well and truly set in; this was surely the nadir (it couldn't possibly get any worse, could it?). No-one knew where the next win was coming from. Fortunately Torquay had been having an even worse time of it than us and were adrift at the foot of the table. Plus, there was the added bonus that Conference leaders Stevenage Borough's ground was deemed not up to League status.

Nevertheless after losing to Torquay, and with the club languishing just above the trap-door, the vultures came out in force for the visit of Hartlepool in February. Fulham received ample doom 'n' gloom exposure leading up to and immediately after what was to prove Ian Branfoot's last game in charge. Officially, that is.

Branfoot had persevered with a long ball 'style' to very little effect. The huff 'n' puff tactics were simply not conducive to the squad. Mike Conroy, a £75,000 buy from Preston, and the latest in a long line of would-be 20 goal-a-season strikers, never looked like reaching that target. Clearly at his best looking for the vital lost touch in and around the six yard box, Conroy was instead asked to chase and harry. His lack of pace showed up alarmingly and you have to ask why was he bought to play in a manner so alien to his strengths.

The squad members were fitter and, largely, more determined than under previous regimes. But that ain't a lot of good if you don't have the ball! Or when schoolboy errors were ensuring a steady increase in the 'goals against' column.

Yet it was all so different back in August. On the back of a camaraderie-engendering Scottish tour, on which they were unbeaten, Fulham stormed into the new season, seemingly making light of losing midfield general and concerted collector of yellow cards Terry Hurlock with a career-ending double fracture in a behind-closed-doors pre-season encounter with Brentford. The buzz after the 4-2 win over Mansfield on the opening day was almost tangible. So many chances had been created that the 'goals for' tally, which for a couple of weeks was actually the best in the country, could have been more than doubled. It really was a much needed breath of fresh air.

By November however, things reeked of old boots. Injuries contributed, not least that to Micky Adams. 'But the persistence in sticking to a playing 'style' so unsuitable to the squad was surely the telling factor. No sooner was the ball pumped up-field than it was back and the defence was again on the rack.

Several 'performances' plumbed new depths, including both encounters with Northampton and a cowardly show against Lincoln at an ice-bound Sincil Bank (we lost 0-4!). The absence of guile or pace was pitifully highlighted when nine man Hereford held out with considerable ease for a draw at Craven Cottage.

Curiously, in amongst these showings came another record: the 7-0 destruction of Swansea was the best ever FA Cup result by a team against another from a higher division. Swansea were pretty poor, it's true, but Fulham played it on the deck and made chance after chance. The much maligned Conroy grabbed a hat-trick. To Ian Branfoot's credit he promptly offered young winger Paul Brooker, the star of that show, a longer contract.

After the aforementioned Hartlepool game, which Fulham only drew after being 2-0 up going into the closing stages, Ian Branfoot marched into the press room and showed the larger than usual throng a clutch of 'we hope you die soon' leaflets. He quite wrongly went on to blame a voluble, mischievous yet hugely supportive group of Fulham fans who were accordingly slated in the national press.

The fanzine was quick to criticise such over-the-top sentiments - no-one deserves such treatment - but also damned Branfoot's wild allegations. Yet this was clearly a watershed. (The leaflets were later blamed on Southampton fans by the powers that be at Fulham).

However, things were certainly getting to the manager. He was mysteriously 'sick' for the midweek game at Cambridge (0-0 and Conroy missed a late sitter) and was strangely 'scouting for a striker in the north east' the following Saturday while the team gained a 1-1 draw at Rochdale. Player/coach Micky Adams, who followed Branfoot from The Dell, took over the reins in his absence and was subsequently appointed to the hot seat the following week.

Adams turned things around somewhat. His insistence that the team play the ball to feet obviously pleased the Fulham cognoscenti. Hot on the heels of a bright win over Exeter, Fulham recorded their first away success of the season, at Doncaster. Some decent results followed, particularly the 4-0 trouncing of Plymouth who eventually went up via the play-offs. Hopefully the appalling effort against Cambridge - as bad as anything served up this season - was but a blip.

Much will now depend on the new manager's close season activity. He's been at pains to express that he wants to be judged on a squad of his own choosing - a squad which will do things his way. A summer clear-out is on the cards but with very little money to play with it's unlikely that we'll get in any star names - although I've heard Asprilla's grandmother is on the wanted list. But then we couldn't afford the air fare, let alone her signing-on fee!

All Fulham supporters are hoping and praying that Micky Adams will be the one to get the club moving upwards at long, long last. And I'm prepared to stick out my neck and suggest that with a fair rub of the green Fulham could be among the front-runners this season. It won't be for the lack of trying on Adam's part, that's for sure.

The other good news will hopefully concern the ground. This particular saga has dragged on interminably, the latest chapter being a public enquiry into Fulham's proposed redevelopment of the Craven Cottage site which they claim would raise the capital to buy back the freehold of the ground - currently held by the Royal Bank of Scotland after property developers Cabra Estates went into liquidation.

The inquiry was called after a small band of local residents, keen to see the club go under and thereby increase the values of their properties, made enough noise to influence Matthew Carrington, MP for Fulham. Previously the green light had been given by the local Labour-led council who have given steadfast support to Fulham (and Chelsea and QPR, the other clubs of the borough) throughout the struggle. Carrington, a Tory, begged to differ.

The current viewpoint is that the purchase price of the freehold is much nearer half the £7.5m previously demanded by the Royal Bank. It hasn't helped that the fund-raising efforts of 'Fulham 2000' have been balked by all manner of in house wranglings. The fans, meanwhile, have had to make do with occasional strands of information from the club rather than regular meaty bulletins.

Certainly no Fulham fan relishes the prospect of flats on two sides of the picturesque Craven Cottage site, but we're prepared to accept them as a necessary evil if it's the only way of ensuring that Fulham stay at the Cottage. October '96 marks Fulham's 100th year at the site: a successful outcome to this drawn-out saga would be the ultimate centenary present. Promotion would, as they say, be the icing on the cake.

Fanzine Facts

There's Only One F In Fulham first appeared at Aldershot in February 1988, with the aim, claims editor David Lloyd, of "having some fun; initially to be a sort of footballing Private Eye, with the emphasis on stupid haircuts, ugly players, best/worst players, dreams, nostalgia, and one or two serious bits." David explains that *TOOFIF* got its name from a combination of "dead-of-night inspiration and a hark back to the raucous chant by Fulham fans at Anfield when 10-0 down to Liverpool in the League Cup." Prize for cheek goes to the Fulham programme editor, who for the second leg gave details of extra time "should the contest be level after 90 minutes!"

THE THIN BLUE LINE

Cardiff City

When we left our heroes at the end of the '94-95 season, the Bluebirds were still reeling after a season packed with incidents - none of them good. We'd had a failed take-over, two changes of manager, early exits from Cup competitions at the hands of lesser clubs, the sale of most of our best players, and then to cap it all, we'd been relegated. So was the '95-96 season to be any better? Well, unfortunately, the simple answer is 'No'. If anything, after a promising start, things got worse, and then worse again. But let's start at the beginning...

With just weeks to go before the end of the 94-95 season, manager Eddie May had returned from Barry Town to replace Terry Yorath, who'd quit following the failure of the Cadman consortium's take-over bid. Once the season was over, and we were relegated, Eddie's final task (before returning to Barry) was to decide which of the squad were staying, and which were to be released. As is normally the case with managers, his idea of who was any good didn't entirely agree with the majority of the fans', and all too predictably, certain players left who perhaps should have been kept on. It didn't help matters when two of the players released by 'Rock Steady' Eddie later signed for him when he returned to Barry Town. A coincidence? Who knows! But the end of the season saw us left with just a handful of experienced players, the remainder of the squad being youngsters placed on long-term (and very lucrative) contracts by chairman Rick Wright.

But then something happened that was to change everything, and raise all our hopes, for a while at least. The club had been officially up for sale for at least the last two years, but no-one seemed interested enough to pay the asking price. Then just before the start of the new campaign, the club was sold (Yippee!) to Samesh Kumar, who'd previously been involved at Birmingham City. It appeared that our saviour had arrived at last. A new manager was appointed, in the shape of Kenny Hibbitt, who strangely enough would also have been the Cadman group's first choice, if they'd ever managed the impossible and got the money together. Hibbitt immediately started the well-known procedure that managers adopt when they can't afford new players i.e. playing every man in the squad a few times, blooding youngsters, and drafting in loan players or triallists where he could. Players who didn't fit into Hibbitt's great scheme were off-loaded, ostensibly to enable

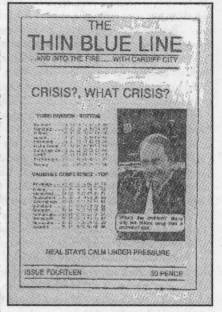

others to come in, but their replacements weren't always up to the same (already poor) standard, and as a result, the side began to struggle almost immediately. This isn't exactly what we'd been expecting from our new owners, and the poor football on show was even more of a shock. Attendances plummeted.

But the management was made of sterner stuff, and promised that the club would have to be set on the straight and narrow path to profitability, before any major spending could take place. To be fair, the previous regimes' 'boom and bust' policies had seen us go up and down like a yo-yo over the last 20 years, so it was good to see that our new guardians had more long-term plans. The majority of fans were prepared to accept this scheme, although we all knew it meant no new faces, and almost certainly nine months of struggle. Of course we didn't realise just how much of a struggle it would turn out to be.

Anyway, Kumar's backroom team was comprised of Bill Coldwell (who'd also been at Birmingham), and Joan Hill, who'd had commercial experience at a few League clubs, and who was coincidentally Kumar's fiancee. Hill started to build her commercial department (which she named the 'A Team'), comprising Mike Lewis and Howard King, both of whom were to resign later following King's revelations of attempts to bribe him with call-girls when he was an international referee (now that brightened our season up a bit, we can tell you). The plan was that this trio would raise the money to launch the club's expansion.

Although Kumar's policy of financial stability before funding player spending was, as stated before, eminently sensible, Cardiff's recent successes had shown that a good side would pull in decent crowds - excellent ones, in fact. So we were in a Catch 22. Without new blood we would flounder, crowds would suffer and revenue would drop: "You have to speculate to accumulate" came to mind. But that was a strategy the club's management wouldn't, or couldn't, consider. And sure enough, within a matter of a few short months, clues began to appear in the programme notes, and in quotes in the local press, that made it quite clear no money was available, and nothing was going to happen this season.

And sure enough, nothing did. A brief blaze of glory facing Southampton in the Coca Cola Cup was all we got, except for another splash in the nation's press when we managed to defeat non-league upstarts Rushden and Diamonds in the FA Cup. The truth is that the press all turned up expecting us to get a hiding, but when the anticipated 'giant'-killing didn't happen, they were forced to report rather reluctantly that Cardiff had won. Still, how often do we make the pages of the national press? But apart from those two admittedly hardly wondrous events, the season was beginning to fall into a recognisable pattern - i.e. Cardiff losing. Even the arrival of a proven goal-getter, in the shape of Tony Philliskirk, failed to help matters. Philliskirk seemed to have left his scoring boots back at Burnley, and despite a few goals late on in the campaign, has been a massive disappointment. By now it was February, and it was becoming more and more clear to most fans that we were on a crash course for relegation to the Conference, unless something drastic occurred. And something did - but even then, it didn't help much.

The club's owner and chairman, Samesh Kumar, had obviously taken City's attendance figures into account when calculating his finances, but the regular defeats and poor football being served up at Ninian Park meant that even the weary regulars were going elsewhere for their Saturday afternoon entertainment. The untimely death of director of football Bill Coldwell meant that Hibbitt was effectively doing two jobs, and the strain was beginning to show. So Kumar moved Hibbitt to Coldwell's old job, and brought in ex-Liverpool and England star Phil Neal as manager.

Whether this was a good move, or just an expensive knee-jerk reaction, is still not certain. But Neal waded in, and repeated Hibbitt's player-swapping moves almost exactly. This just seemed to upset an already troubled side, and they slid down the table, finding their true level (last but two), and stayed there.

The football was dreadful, and the local press was full of letters calling Neal's side "the worst ever seen at Ninian Park." Was it any wonder the fans (and fanzines) were disgruntled? The club's reaction to criticism from fanzines and Supporters Club alike was simply to haul in the editors, give them a real tongue-lashing, and threaten to ban their respective publications from the ground unless they toed the party line. All very democratic, and a classic case of putting your head in the sand. "You need to portray a more positive attitude", they said. Hard to do when your club is staring relegation to non-league obscurity in the face.

There were one or two little flickers of light in the gloom, in the shape of top scorer Carl Dale, who hit 30 goals (more than the rest of the side put together), and more or less kept us up by himself. He deservedly scooped the Player of the Year award, and was named in the Division's representative side - not bad going, considering we finished last but two. Lee Jarman and Scott Young also look like outstanding prospects at the back, with most Premier sides sending scouts to watch them over the last six months. But Kumar has already hinted that one or more of these three may have to go "to help the club progress." It's still the same old story...

So, 90th out of 92, our lowest ever League position. It must be said though that if the players showed the same enthusiasm as some of the management team, then we'd have finished up there with Preston and Plymouth, not down in the depths with Torquay and Scarborough. Still, on the bright side, no-one in the entire playing staff appears to be safe from Neal's restructuring.

And that's probably just the motivation they need to get off their arses and put some pride back into this club.

Fanzine Facts

The Thin Blue Line has just completed its second full season. The 'zine is still basically the work of Editor Andrew Turton, along with 'guest' writers, some regular, others not. Andrew's stance on not pulling any punches regarding the problems at the club, has landed TTBL in trouble with the owners more than once, but recently things seem to have settled down, and he reports that current relations are much more cordial.

THIS CHARMING FAN

Manchester City

Most clubs spent the summer unveiling new players. Manchester City spent it trying to sign a new manager. The board announced they were looking at a top six manager with proven European experience who the fans would warm to. Favourites for the job included George Graham (if he wasn't banned), Brian Kidd, Bruce Rioch, Bobby Robson and Franz Beckenbaur. Also in the frame were Mick McCarthy, Martin O'Neill and more disturbingly Trevor Francis and Dave 'Harry' Bassett. At one time, it was reported that chairman Francis Lee would take training if necessary. It wasn't necessary, as out of the blue and with permission from the Southampton board (perhaps they knew something we didn't?), Alan Ball was approached and appointed team manager on the eve of the pre-season tour. City fans questioned the appointment, referring to the board's promises about the manager's CV. The response was that Ballie was their first choice all along! Asa Hartford was recruited as assistant manager, a choice that seemed to quiet the discontent.

UNOFFICIAL SPONSOR OF EURO 94

This Charming Fan

Another Bloody Manchester City Fanzine

GOD SAVE THE QUINN

6th and Retiring Issue　　50p

Nationally, most of the top players seeking a transfer had already moved clubs, so City were left to look abroad for new recruits. The chairman had been tracking the Georgian International George Kinkladze for some time, and showed Ballie a 30 minute video, which prompted a £2m signing. Red tape held up the transfer so Gio was unable to appear in any of the disastrous pre-season friendlies, climaxed by a 5-0 defeat at the hands of the crack Scottish Premier League side, er, Hearts.

Forty eight hours before the season began, two more players were bought in: Kit Symons (Portsmouth's Welsh International) and goalkeeper Eike Immel from Stuttgart; described in some papers as 'the new Bert Trautman' whilst the Manchester (United) Evening News investigated further and informed us "he is the first German goalkeeper City have signed since Bert Trautman." Really! Although City had three experienced keepers on their books, all were injured, and with John Burridge presumably having signed for someone else for that week, Ikie was bought on a one year contract, as cover, we thought; yet strangely enough, both Ikie and Kit were the only two ever-presents all season.

Our three new boys appeared in an encouraging 1-1 home draw with Spurs that gave little indication of what was to follow. Eight games later our record read:

played 9, Won 0, Drew 1, Lost 8, For 3, Against 15, Points 1.

We needed new blood, and fast, but some of the dead wood had to be cleared first. And this was a problem. Take Michel Vonk for instance; he refused three approaches from Oldham and Portsmouth, preferring the Pontin's League Division Two, because neither could match his current wages. Eventually he did join Old-ham - on loan - before signing to Sheffield United. Other players were also off-loaded, notably Paul Walsh, Fitzroy Simpson and Carl Griffiths, all to Portsmouth, and Adie Mike and David Brightwell (son of Robbie Brightwell and Ann Packer, Olympic medal winners, Tokyo 1964, and brother to City's Ian). In came Gerry Creaney from, er, Portsmouth, who came with a reputation for hitting the back of the net and hitting the bar too, which probably explained his Jan Molby-esque frame and failure to last the Premier League pace. By March, he had joined Old-ham on loan, saving them from relegation with a couple of goals.

October 21st. At long last, our next point arrived (0-0 home to Leeds) and the joke changed from 'What's the difference between City and a cocktail stick' to '...City and a triangle'. If you don't know the answer - tough shit!

During the previous few weeks, The Manchester (United) Evening News, as sympathetic and supportive of the Blue cause as ever, started the first of its frequent articles attempting to undermine the running of the club. It followed up with one of those ridiculous phone-in-polls, asking "Should Francis Lee resign?"; a vote open to anyone bothered to do so regardless of team supported The result was predicta-ble, and rightly dismissed by chairman Lee.

Back on the pitch, and the week beginning October 23rd. City slumped to the lowest of lows. We faced Liverpool twice in four days and built an aggregate score of 0-10 which started the Blue's fans mock chant of "Alan Ball is a football genius!." Surely November couldn't get any worse. It didn't. By the end of the month Alan Ball, much to the amusement of the tabloids, was Manager of the Month, and City's souvenir shop released 'Alan Ball - a football genius' T-shirts! One nil wins over Bolton, Villa and Leeds, plus a draw at Sheffield Wednesday, had moved City up to 15th in the League. It was no coincidence that this turn-around was given the highest accolade that could be bestowed on a player - front cover status on the last issue of TCF.

During December, City made history becoming the first club to (legally) play more than three foreigners, when on loan Ronnie Ekelund (Barcelona) joined Im-mel, Rösler and Kinkladze against Chelsea only days after the European Court ruled in favour of Jean Marc Bosman. Before the season would finish, four more foreigners joined the club - Michael Frontzeck (German), Mikhail Kavelashvili (Geor-gian), Guiseppe Mazzareli (Swiss) and Edward Abajaz (Albanian), though Ekelund returned to Spain after four weeks.

It wasn't a good Christmas, with a Boxing Day defeat at Blackburn, but New Year was celebrated in spectacular style. Niall Quinn's two goals against West Ham not only boosted after-match sales of TCF, but it was the first occasion that City had scored two goals all season (with due respect to the League Cup second round, second leg 4-0 victory against Wycombe!). The reason for the lack of goals was obvious. Peter Beagrie (?) who had only appeared in four games (four too many as he was clearly unfit), aggravated his ankle again and was out for the remainder of the season. The other winger, Summerbee, dropped to full back to cover for the losses of Rae Ingram, Richard Edgehill, John Foster, Ian Brightwell and Scott Hiley.

Of these five full backs, only Brightwell (son of Robbie and Ann Packer etc. etc.) finished the season fit. Talking of injuries, it was sad to hear the announcement that City favourite Paul Lake's career was finally over. His five year battle against a knee injury deserved a better ending, and I hope that the club arranges a testimonial in his honour.

To compensate for the lack of wingers, Ball bought Martin 'Buster' Phillips from his old club Exeter for £500,000. At Exeter, Ball had said Phillips would become the first £10m player! Despite the signing, Ball seemed reluctant to play the teenager, "one for the future" it was stated. January and February saw more comings and goings. Frontzeck and Nigel Clough joined the fold, and more controversially, Tony Coton, fit again but unable to win his place back from Immel, left for City's 'cross town rivals. (Sunderland were to sign him, but couldn't supply the readies). As with the sale of Terry Phelan to Chelsea in November, it is alleged that City received very little from the sale, because, although both players had said they were not happy about playing reserve team football (putting themselves in the shop window?) neither had asked for a transfer; therefore each players' contract had to be bought out by the club. City only benefited by saving wages on two of the high earners.

After home replay wins against Leicester and Coventry, the fifth round Littlewoods sponsored FA Cup paired the two Manchester clubs together. The watching nation was as shocked as everyone else at Old Trafford to discover a United player, oops sorry!, referee Alan Wilkie, had awarded a penalty for judging Frontzeck to have fouled the 'New Saint'. Yes, there was an infringement, but a penalty? After that incident there was only to be one winner. Ask any Southampton fan (same fate in the sixth round); they'll know what I mean.

More rumours in the papers again. This time that Kinkladze was to sign a new contract (£13,000 a week) to fend off the Italian and Spanish giants. Lee claimed this info was being fed to the media by a Premier League manager, keen to unsettle Gio and sign him for his own club.

The week after the Cup defeat, the players responded by producing their best scoring rate for a League game, putting three past runaway leaders Newcastle, Quinn again scoring twice. Oh, Newcastle scored three too, but it was a thrilling game.

City were out of the bottom three but just couldn't pull clear with a decent run. Too many games were drawn at home and not enough points won away. One win against Southampton in March produced the goal of the season; Kinkladze's spellbinding run through the defence had Beasant on his arse before the chip was made. The standing ovation continued as the Saints kicked off. However, a dreadful Easter witnessed the Blues crash 3-0 at Wimbledon, and then plunge back into the relegation zone after a derby day defeat at Maine Road. Soon there were three games left. Each one in turn became 'the most important game of the season!' City were level on points with Coventry and Southampton, but with an inferior goal difference. City won their first two games, but each victory was counteracted by wins from both the other two clubs fighting not to join Bolton and QPR.

Prior to the final game, the M(U)EN again disgraced itself by reporting that some directors were unhappy about the manager and a meeting was to be held to discuss the issue. Again, this was dismissed by our chairman. At such a time, one would expect the local media, whose 'alleged' journalist is both a former player and fan, would give the club its support, but this was obviously too much to expect.

Three days before the final game the news broke that former chairman Peter Swales had died after suffering two heart attacks. Despite the bitterness felt towards Swales, the very fans who had hounded him out stood impeccably to observe the tribute of a minute's silence; acknowledgement perhaps that he *was* a City fan first and foremost.

The club also announced that they were to lift the ban on taking flags into the ground to create a carnival atmosphere. Strangely, Jack Richards, the safety officer, then asked fans not to bring huge sticks - because these could be used as a jousting weapon (?) and even more bizzarely, the huge Italian style flag (probably the largest in England) that was provided by the now defunct City fanzine *Blue Print* was also not welcome as (and I quote) "an obvious fire risk!" Obviously. In the end, the only flags that appeared to be in the ground were the ones that you could only buy from, er, the club souvenir shop or official sellers!

In the end, City, Coventry and Southampton all drew, and a very quiet, yet full stadium waited for confirmation: that was it. <u>DOWN</u>

All we were left with were IFs. What if Middlesbrough's 'well offside' goal at Maine Road had been rightfully disallowed? What if Dion 'Donkey' Dublin hadn't scored late goals, both home and away? What if that Bolton player hadn't stupidly played the ball across the area, for Matt Le Tiss to score a vital winner? What if...

THERE IS A LIGHT - THAT HAS JUST GONE OUT

Fanzine Facts

When City's first fanzine, Blue Print, ceased to function, Phill Gatenby, a regular contributor went solo and produced *This Charming Fan*; the title inspired by The Smiths. Notoriously irregular from the start (Jan '93) the sixth and final issue appeared in December '95, and like all previous issues, quickly sold out. After eight years of fanzinedom the pen has been hung up, mainly due to promotion at work, "I've got to some work now, rather than skiving off to produce *TCF*! Also, with two City supporting daughters (aged 4 and 2), arriving early and flogging copies at the back of the Kippax is, according to Phill "just is not practical." However, don't rule out special (no deadline required) one-off's. This final output by *TCF* is dedicated to the three unsung heroes of the 'zine: Kirsty Raybould (typist) Andy (printer) and the photocopying machine!

TIGER RAG

Hull City

If you're looking for a humorous chapter full of laughs and good times, celebrations and trophies, please turn over now. This is about Hull City AFC, and we've had a season so depressing that even Leonard Cohen would rip up his season ticket.

In terms of reasons to celebrate, '95-96 was akin to a launch party at the European Space Agency. Relegated a full month before the season's end, with many depressing records set on the way, support for the team dropped to an all-time low. And no surprise, either. Never before have we been the subject of such ridicule by others in East Yorkshire. Attendances have not only dipped below the local rugby league club, but at one point looked like falling below that of the local ice hockey team. Even Torquay fans would have a pop at us for our woeful choice of football team.

After just failing to reach the play-offs in the previous two seasons, optimism was high that this could be third time lucky. Manager Terry Dolan reminded fans of his "Five Year Plan", the time period he said it would take to turn the club around and generate upward momentum. This was to be his fifth season in charge, and with one relegation under his belt this club was ready for turning.

However, among the waves of optimism came a certain amount of caution; the club were forced to call off pre-season friendlies as they couldn't actually raise a team, a quarter of their small squad seemingly picking up injuries whilst on holiday. Worrying stuff, especially a couple of weeks before the official start. Defender Simon Dakin hit the headlines - and the floor - whilst on holiday in Tenerife, amazingly managing to fall 50ft down a lift shaft. And you thought *your* team has bad luck when your star striker twists his ankle on a dance floor in Magaluf.

Swindon rolled into a sweltering Kingston-upon-Hull to get the campaign underway, and everything went well for a tantalising hour. City were well on top as the woodwork was rattled three times before the interval. The Tigers tired, however, and after the hour the visitors showed their class by scoring, then sitting on the lead. We looked an eager but inexperienced team.

The following Saturday, City travelled to exotic Millmoor and at the time we joked that two incidents could end our season - and our words proved prophetic. Mike Quigley - hugely impressive in pre-season since his transfer from Man City -

broke his leg early in the game, putting him out for over six months. In the second half defender Rob Dewhurst made a brilliant tackle which was rewarded with a red card and a penalty from the git in black. We drew, lost two important players, and it was downhill from there.

If this was a video of the season we'd advise you fast-forward now, as it's not worth listing all the clubs we lost to, but probably a lot easier to embarrass the ones we actually beat: Blackpool, York (our only away win), Burnley (3-0!), Walsall and Wycombe. Feeling suitably sheepish? You should be!

During the season, our God Dean Windass was sold to Aberdeen for £600k, coincidentally (?) the same amount as the club's current debt. Several months later Northern Ireland International goalkeeper (and goalscorer) Alan Fettis also went for an amount equal to that which the club reportedly owed the bank (£250k). Both transfers smacked of a desperate club clearing the debt at all costs. With our best players sold, there was no escape. Terry Dolan stood firm, however, confidently predicting we'd finish above clubs like Brentford. He'd have been right as well, had the Football League deducted 27 points from them for fielding a fat goalkeeper.

Windass' wonder goal at Wycombe (receives ball with back to opposing goal from Fettis' punt upfield, flicks ball over head and over closely-marking defender, volleys home from 40 yards in one movement) would surely have been Goal of the Season if Deano had been Ghanian and wearing a Leeds Utd shirt. Deano drinking the bars and clubs in Europe dry with the Dons this season is a frightening thought.

Hero of the season was a supporter called Phil Pinder, who launched his own one-man pitch invasion during the home match with Rotherham. As the Merry Millers gleefully slammed home their fourth goal he charged onto the pitch, and in the centre circle proceeded to animatedly tear up his season ticket in front of the director's box. Sad as it may seem, this got the biggest cheer of the season at Boothferry Park. A heartfelt plea from a true fan.

However, bizarrely, the real talking point came on the final day - Bradford at home. The Bantams needed the win to confirm their play-off place; we needed a win to finish *nine* points behind everyone else. "Under police instruction", Hull City's chairman, the under-fire Martin Fish, booted Tigers fans out of their regular home end at Boothferry Park, generously giving it to the visitors, shoving us all in our poxy away end. It was a final insult to the fans who had dutifully turned up week-in, week-out to watch the rubbish on offer. Unsurprisingly, there were several pitch invasions - the first at precisely the minute the terrace rumours suggested it would be - with the game itself having to be stopped several times as sporadic fighting broke out. Bradford won 3-2, their second coming via a cross deflected off a pile of police horse shit on the pitch and into the path of a Bantams player; the winner from the perennially nasty Carl Shutt. The police were weak and disorganised, and this public disorder (their words) continued into the streets after the game as Hull City's small yob element thrust us into the national headlines once more.

That insult to all supporters was compounded by the news that we were forced to wait two months for, and which proved the proverbially damp haddock when it finally came. "It's really big news that will really please all Hull City fans" oozed Martin Fish, and which basically boiled down to: if you all raise half a million quid between you we'll build you a small new stand down one side of the ground. Oh yes, and Terry Dolan and his assistant Jeff Lee were handed extensions to their contracts, which will keep them at Boothferry Park until 1999, even after guiding the Tigers to a famous Double (relegations in five years, that is). This was an amazing announcement, coming as it did in the same week that Man Utd were publicly mulling over whether to extend Alex Ferguson's contract by a year, even after his Double (Championship and FA Cup, that is). One wonders what Dolan and Lee would've been offered had we done the impossible and stayed up (something to do with the chairman's first born springs to mind).

This decision angered the City so much that a pressure group - TIGERS 2000 - has been formed with the aim of ousting the Fishy one. Several (very wealthy) local businessmen have come forward with the express wish of buying the club out, but none will touch Hull City until the old boardroom power structure has disappeared. Of the three directors that were there at the start of the season, two have since 'resigned', leaving Martin Fish in charge of all the shares, so at the moment it's stalemate. During the close season Hull City have released three of their most experienced players (club captain Greg Abbott, the impressive and in-form Andy Williams and cult hero Jimmy Graham), who have approaching 1,000 appearances between them, to make way for... err... "experienced players." Work that one out! Cheaper players more like. The Player of the Season award went to our 19-year-old goalkeeper who played his first game in January, which says a lot about the rest of the team. Dolan released ten players a week before the season's end, informing them all - *together* - in an amazingly quick ten-second speech in his office. Man-management obviously isn't his strong point.

We wonder what is.

Hull City finished the season bottom, and were the first team to succumb to the drop in the whole country. They scored the lowest number of goals ever in their history, and let in the second highest ever at the other end. They were rock bottom of the League from September '95, and they boasted the worst player disciplinary record in the club's history. Roll on '96-97. Torquay - you have been warned.

Fanzine Facts

Tiger Rag, produced by Andy Medcalf and Geoff Bradley, is now 11 issues old. Andy explains: "Our attitude to the club changed as last season fizzled out. From our relatively strong support of the management duo at the beginning, their increasingly negative tactics, combined with poor man-management and absurd public claims, means our respect for them has diminished. Our glorious chairman also appears to have lost the plot completely. This season is going to prove very interesting, both on and off the field. If Hull City don't get off to a good start, expect fireworks!"

TILL THE WORLD STOPS

Leeds United

If football, with all its drama, intrigue and hyperbole, is the world's biggest soap opera, then Leeds United's '95-96 season was an episode of Eldorado. You know - the show where over-rated, has-been performers frequently lost the plot in front of extremely expensive sets and a disillusioned audience. It sounds strangely familiar. Wearers of rose-tinted glasses will no doubt be describing Eldorado as a cult show very soon; for Leeds fans, who have seen better, expected more and received nothing, the past season was nothing short of a farce.

The opening scenes of our little show were sensational. Three straight wins, top of the League for ten minutes and the goal of the season thrown in for good measure - a truly stunning, absolutely unforgettable winner by Tony Yeboah against the boys from Anfield. Leeds then pressed the pause button, one point from six, but then our Ghanaian leading man stunned Europe with a hat-trick in Monaco. Suddenly you couldn't open the back pages of the tabloids without reading of the magical properties of Yorkshire pudding. United supporters at last had the hero that they had yearned so desperately for since that French actor departed for Coronation Street

Mediocre performances followed, but no matter; up stepped 'The Predator' Yeboah, a manufactured nickname, which like the copyrighted 'Stan the Man', thankfully never caught on, to claim the third prize in the BBC's Goal of the Season competition too. Then, a twist in the plot, as the words 'fortress' and 'Elland Road' went spinning off in opposite directions, as within four days Leeds conceded not only eight goals in two home games, but their chance of glory in both the Premiership and the UEFA Cup. First Arsenal scored three without reply, then Dutch masters, PSV Eindhoven, taught us a lesson, and early season optimism disappeared quicker than the hike in season ticket prices following promotion. Eindhoven with their poise, flair and finishing ran out 5-3 winners at Elland Road (or ER, if you will, judging by the subsequent scenes of carnage and dismembered defenders witnessed at the ground).

The cardiogram of Leeds' season continued to record mighty peaks and desperate troughs. Within the space of 80 days we suffered a humiliating 6-2 defeat at Hillsborough and celebrated a Christmas present, the 3-1 win against Manchester

United. The team were so consistently bloody inconsistent, that somehow I just *knew* one would follow the other. Call it a football fan's sixth sense, or being wise after the event, but like sunshine on the first day of the season, some things just seem pre-destined.

The scriptwriters then decided to introduce a couple of new characters; a blue-eyed, blond heart-breaker from Sweden, one Tomas Brolin - a member of the 'scored a goal to end England's hopes' club, who for four and a half million quid looked like taking centre-stage, but ended the season as nothing more than a bit player. No doubt the mists of time will clear to reveal why our director (of football) Howard Wilkinson was a doubting Tomas - maybe not. Perhaps Messrs. Rocastle, Hodge and Cantona have the answer. And lo! Who is that stepping out of the shower? Surely not! He was killed off in an earlier episode wasn't he? Or have the past few seasons all been a very bad dream? Yes, Leeds fans reached for the Prozac at the sight of Lee Chapman once again donning the famous white shirt. Unfortunately for him he was sent off early in his return match for playing just like Lee Chapman.

Mr Wilkinson in his questionable wisdom, decided that the time was right to allow young strikers Jamie Forrester and Noel Whelan to be sold. To Leeds fans, that seemed as appropriate as a beef sandwich at an EU buffet, particularly bearing in mind that Yeboah and Phil Masinga had received their New Year call-up papers for the African Nations Cup. Come on Wilko, if Sun readers could work out that they needed to replace Yeboah in the fantasy League mid-season transfer window, why couldn't you anticipate that we were going to be short on goal scorers?

Dismal performances in the League however were deflected from intense criticism by stuttering Cup runs, and after defeating Barry Fry, snooker balls and Birmingham City, Leeds reached their first Wembley final for over a century, or so the media would've had everyone believe. The Coca Cola Cup Final was played on March 24th, and what a great day it was - up until five o'clock of course, when they kicked off. No-one would have been surprised if Leeds supporters had gone into self-imposed hibernation after this non-performance. The team played without spirit, cohesion and almost without interest, and that is inexcusable. This was the day that Leeds United, for all their pretensions, were finally 'found out' and Wilkinson, his players et al, were booed off at Wembley after handing Villa the Cup.

So why had the team who made flattering to deceive into an art-form suddenly stopped performing at all? Was it a deliberate policy by the players to undermine the manager as suggested by Alex Ferguson after they raised their game at Old Trafford? If so, they managed to prove a point in the final seven games of the season - because that is just what they earned - one point. Leeds players: cunning or crap? That's a tough one.

Anyway, this little sub-plot failed to kill off the principal character. Leeds fans chanted "Wilko, it's time to go!", but it wasn't to be Wilko and out. A £20m take-over from asset-stripper (allegedly) and former QPR chairman (allegedly) Richard Thompson and new old signing Ian Rush's insistence that he would only stay if Wilkinson did, look to be providing the strands for an exciting cliff-hanging final scene of Dallas proportions.

Tune in for next-season's exciting episode...

Fanzine Facts

Till the World Stops was born at the beginning of the '91-92 season as a direct result of the editor, Pete Vale, choosing the mundane security of the civil service over a temporary summer position at 'When Saturday Comes'. The title of the magazine was taken from a terrace chant, "we're gonna stay with you forever, at least till the world stops spinning round" and although the world does appear to have stopped at times (March 24th, 1996), Leeds fans will be relieved to know that the 'zine's still going!

PHIL BABB'S PASSING MANUAL
(WHAT IT SAYS, AND WHAT IT MEANS)

1. KEEP YOUR EYE ON THE BALL
   "SHIT, IT'S COMING TOWARDS ME"

2. USE THE SIDE OF THE FOOT TO STOP THE BALL
   "COME HERE, YOU LITTLE ROUND BASTARD"

3. LOOK UP AND TRY TO FIND A TEAM MATE
   "HEEEEEELP!!!"

@. STROKE THE BALL CALMLY TO A COLLEAGUE
   "OOPS! DIDN'T SEE HIM"

THE TOMMY COOK REPORT

Brighton & Hove Albion

Bellotti is a w****r

It is difficult to look back on '95-96 and pick out any memorable footballing moments that stood out from the inevitable lethargy that gripped the on-pitch activity. No money, no ambition, no future - and that was at the *start* of the season. As far as Brighton & Hove Albion was concerned, football wasn't the issue. It was about money, politics, arrogance, frustration, lies, more lies, possible extinction, nonsensical ground-sharing schemes, public mud-slinging, accusations, writs - oh, and of course *the* riot (more of that later).

So, football played a fairly insignificant part in the lives of Seagull supporters throughout the whole of the campaign. The team had their usual moments of Cup glory: knocked out of the Coca Cola Cup in the first round by Fulham 5-0 on aggregate and humbled in the first round of the FA Cup by Canvey Island, after which Liam Brady finally let the lack of boardroom support get the better of him and walked away from the false promises he had been made by the Chairman. Guilt rather than skill saw us ease (!) past Canvey in the replay at the Goldstone and marked a winning start for Jimmy Case. There was hardly a whimper of protest from supporters at the demise of Brady, and the crowning of Jimmy proved to be the only politically astute move the board made throughout the season. The ghost of Brady may, however, live to haunt his boardroom detractors.

Despite Liam's demise we had put together an FA Cup run - well, jog would be more appropriate. Who should we meet round the corner? The mighty Fulham. A 0-0 draw in London was quickly followed by an equally awe-inspiring 0-0 draw in Brighton (Hove actually). Humiliation was heaped upon us; our exclusion from future rounds being sealed by a 4-1 defeat on penalties. The omens were not good. At least we had the play-offs to aim for and of course the Windscreen Wipers Shield - that was *bound* to be a crowd pleaser. 1,191 watched our attempts to secure this illustrious trophy at the Goldstone Ground in October. And 1,191 saw us lose to a Bristol Rovers reserve team. One co-editor of *The Tommy Cook Report* received a phone call from his Bristol-born grandfather to make sure the result had been duly noted. Despite this set-back we made it through to the next round, only for our dreams to be shattered by Shrewsbury.

Between our exit from the Coca Cola Cup and our humiliation at Canvey, the Seagulls visited our friends down at Bournemouth. The match was broadcast live on

Meridian TV (pretty heady stuff eh!). The banners asking for the removal of the board were prominent, but unfortunately their impact was overshadowed by a pitch invasion and eager TV directors focusing on the futile violence that followed. The name of Brighton & Hove Albion was on the lips of the tabloid press once more. Some say football would have been a more appropriate way of reaching the back pages of the news sheets, but as the board kept telling us, there was no money available to strengthen the squad. Football was therefore not an option.

1996 arrived - a winning run did not. The play-offs were no longer viable and relegation was becoming a distinct possibility. Gates fell game after game, reaching their lowest point against Oxford in mid March (3,953). New players did eventually arrive - Paul McDonald, Craig Maskell and Derek Allan (all from Southampton), Gary Hobson (Hull City) and Zeke Rowe (Chelsea). It was too little too late. Relegation was inevitable and it was clear that Case had one and a half eyes on the future - a team to get us straight back up from the Third Division. Evidence indeed that forward planning was not dead at the Albion!

Relegation of course did follow, not that anyone really noticed - activity off the pitch drew attention away from poor performances on it. The final irony was dealt in footballing terms before the kick-off of the York game. Player of the Year was awarded to defender Ian Chapman - one of the few players who had shown determination throughout the season. Brighton-born and with Brighton running through his veins he must have allowed himself a rueful smile as he collected his prize, knowing that his future lay elsewhere. Ian was not included in Jimmy's plans and had been advised of the fact two weeks earlier. His final game for the Albion ended prematurely at 3.16pm on the 27th April 1996.

So what caused the frustration that spilled so publicly onto the pitch during the game with York? Why should a proposal to share playing facilities with another South Coast team cause such an outburst of emotion? The truth is that the ground-sharing scheme with Pompey was not initially the issue, despite what was written in the press. The Goldstone Ground had been sold before the start of the '95-96 campaign without a site for a new ground being secured for future seasons. The board insisted that the move to Portsmouth would only be temporary while a new ground was built to provide a home for the club, together with a commercial and retail development. This (according to them) was the dawning of a new era for the Albion. Unfortunately for the board, the 'perfect' site they had identified had already been rejected by the council some two weeks before the announcement by the club had been made! The FA put a further spanner in the works - they had not endorsed the move to Pompey and were insistent that they would only allow such a move if plans and permission were in place for a new stadium within the Brighton & Hove area. This was still the position of the FA (and League) right up to the final home game of the season. No plans, no planning permission, no ground-share. Many at the York game felt that without an extension to the Goldstone lease this could only mean one thing - no future.

Combined with this was the fact that the club's Articles Of Association that prevented any member of the board from benefiting financially from the sale of the ground had been changed during the summer of '95. Understandably supporters grew suspicious. Discussions between FA officials and the club resulted in the Articles being returned to their original status, but by now it was too late. Any trust the supporters still felt for the board evaporated. Further attempts to pacify the FA and fans came to nothing (a proposed ground-share with Crawley Town was a non-starter

- according to the local paper, discussions were held with the Crawley chairman as he was mowing the pitch!). Hove Council seemed to want to help, but they were not prepared to allow a commercial development alongside a football stadium, something the club said was essential to secure future finances. Council and club fell out, resulting in a writ being issued against council leader and Albion fan Ivor Caplin at the same time that a planning application was being prepared for a new location. It was against this background that the game with York took place.

Of course it was the 'riot' that hit the front pages of the tabloids on the following Sunday. The word 'riot' was used endlessly during debates about the incident and by people who should have known better. Don't believe everything that you read (something Brighton fans have reminded themselves every time they opened a match program and read the words of chief executive David Bellotti). Yes, it was an example of the fact that wherever a protest (of whatever nature - sporting, political or other) takes place the presence of mindless idiots intent on causing maximum damage will be felt. Yes, it was a genuine outpouring of emotions from a large number of Brighton supporters desperate to make their feelings known to the board of directors. It was not a riot. York City supporters were in no danger throughout the scenes that engulfed the Goldstone Ground. The breaking of the goals and damage to the ground cannot be condoned, but then again the reporting by the press which blamed the chaos on the actions of the many, when in reality the responsibility lay with the few, was also wrong. It was nevertheless an acutely embarrassing day for many Albion supporters who felt shame as the name of the club was dragged across the national news and Sunday papers.

The question remains however: how does the genuine supporter protest about the boardroom activities of directors, particularly when they have no desire to listen to the people for whom they are supposed to bring glory through the success (!) of the football club they share? This may well be the future dilemma of Seagull followers. The board does not appear to want to listen to our voices on the terraces. They presumably will not notice the decline in the number of season ticket sales that will be an inevitability of the season's debacle. None of this adds up. The reason the board gave for the sale of the Goldstone was to pay off debts. Fair enough, but if money is the issue, why alienate the supporters? Why jeopardise your very life blood in the name of securing the future? Why, oh why, oh why?

The questions are endless but the truth is harder to accept. At the end of the day, when money is involved (and the commercial development of a football ground involves vast potential amounts of cash) the fans simply don't matter. The board was happy to move to Portsmouth as a 'temporary' arrangement, despite the fact that gate receipts were likely to tumble as supporters refused to watch away games week after week. Support for the team simply did not come into the equation, therefore the conclusion must be that if the performance of the team did not matter then as far as the board was concerned, Brighton & Hove Albion Football Club did not matter.

Of course, few of the broadsheets or tabloids mentioned this in their reporting of April 27th. They could have picked up on the issues behind the headline-grabbing events at the Goldstone; then the fans may have felt that they had someone on their side. *Gulls Eye* (Britain's most prolific fanzine) pursued the indefensible remorselessly. The *Evening Argus* highlighted any about-turn and nonsensical statement that was issued from the boardroom and were banned from the Goldstone on several occasions for their trouble. The Brighton Independent Supporters Association organised meetings to highlight the ever-spiralling situation. The second of these gatherings resulted in hundreds being locked out (including the editors of *TTCR!*). We listened through open windows in miserable conditions to the empty words of our once-revered president, Greg Stanley, promising this and promising that. As previously mentioned, the local council offered to help and had a writ slapped on them by the club - very forward-thinking, especially when the board kept citing Huddersfield Town as an example of a football outfit working successfully with their local authority.

The national press and TV merely scratched the surface. The local council, local press, fanzines, FA, League, Toads Hole Valley Residents Association (potential site of a new ground/office/retail development?), Liam Brady and most importantly the supporters have all been alienated by the actions of the board. An impressive list and a potential entry for the Guinness Book Of Records. There are rumours that 'Sussex By The Sea' will be replaced by 'No One Likes Us' as the club song. Others suggest 'Pretty Vacant' - but there's no point in asking, you'll get no reply.

Footnote: Ex-Crystal Phallus strikers have never been high on our Christmas card list, but dear old Steve Claridge has changed all that. His devastating, God-like, last second of extra time strike for Leicester against our eternal Surrey pals in the First Division play-off final is, we believe, the turning-point for the Albion. That day when 5,000 Seagull fans, as an experiment for New Scientist Magazine, smashed mirrors in unison is now but a distant memory - it is in fact just over seven years ago. The tide has turned dear friends, our march back up the divisions begins right now, as they say in all the best establishments: *"Brighton are back! Brighton are back!"* Ahem.

Fanzine Facts

The Tommy Cook Report was founded in the summer of 1995 by Matthew Griffin and David Jarvis, two Tunbridge Wells based supporters, although the idea for producing a fanzine had been in their minds for some time. The monumental events of *that* summer finally pushed them in to initiating it. Another reason for starting 'Tommy' was due to the lack of Albion fanzines mentioned in the back pages of *When Saturday Comes* - even *Gulls Eye*, one of the longest running fanzine in the country was not mentioned. With supreme timing a third Brighton fanzine *On The Up* appeared at the same time - the club were now in danger of having more fanzines than they did points.

TTCR is (surprisingly) named after a gentleman called Tommy Cook, a veritable legend at the Albion in that he was the first Brighton player to win an England cap, and he also played cricket for Sussex - albeit not at the same time!

THE TRICKY TREE

Nottingham Forest

A Tale Of Two Strikers

Finishing ninth in the Premiership and reaching the quarter-finals of two major Cup competitions may, at first glance, appear to signal a relatively successful season.

The truth, however, is a wholly different story.

OK, so there may be 80-odd sets of supporters up and down the country who would gladly have swapped positions with us at the end of it all. Understandable on the face of it, but the undeniable truth is that we Nottingham Forest supporters expected more from our team. That's not arrogance; it's just that after two seasons of almost total nirvana, to end up with nothing but half baked-plaudits for being the last British club left in Europe was simply not good

Who needs lots of hair when you've got an England Cap!

Bald is Best for the Geordie Genius

enough. Worst of all, however - and whisper this - the popular notion of Forest being an entertaining side to watch, no matter what, looked at times as fanciful as the idea of a Kevin Campbell hat-trick.

Mention of the C-word brings me neatly onto the indisputable reason for our demise - the failure to replace Stan Collymore. As soon as Stan decided to pack up his Pedigree Play Centre and suck his dummy elsewhere, we were quids in. Eight and a half million of them to be exact, and Forest fans sat back awaiting the arrival of the world class talent which would have us asking "Stan who?" as we stormed to the top of the Premiership. Swedish international Martin Dahlin was for a long time the man rumoured most likely to be taking over the number ten shirt, and expectation reached fever pitch when the local paper screamed out the near legendary headline of 'It's Baggio', as the pony-tailed wonder was reported to have expressed in interest in setting up his monasterial home on the banks of the Trent.

We rubbed our hands, licked our lips and laughed at the sheep-shagging nobodies from down the A52 who had nothing but another season of Endsleigh League obscurity to look forward to. Little were we to know, however, that Frank Clark's exemplary record in the transfer market was about to crash and burn in spectacular fashion. Frank retained the fanciful notion that Campbell would miraculously rediscover the form that he had shown as a sprightly 17 year-old, when, on loan to a Leyton Orient side then managed by the moustachioed one, he scored goals for fun to almost single-handedly get his temporary team-mates promoted.

Seven years and two and a half million pounds of our money later, the two were re-united, but the goals were nowhere to be seen. We wept. And the tears weren't of joy for the happy couple, but at the thought that we'd paid Arsenal £500,000 more for their fifth choice centre-forward than Newcastle had passed on to Paris St Germain for the mercurial talents of David Ginola. As though realising that Campbell was not exactly the replacement supporters had in mind (heck, he only had to ask), Clark brought in the additional talents of Italian international striker... Andrea Silenzi. No, we hadn't heard of him either, but general opinion was that if his ability half matched the size of his nose, we had great things to look forward to.

Unfortunately, Silenzi disappointed, and we were left to be grateful for the 100% effort but 10% ability of our very own dreadlocked destroyer, Jason Lee. Messrs Baddiel and Skinner may think themselves oh so funny for their weekly jibes at Jason's expense, but the sad truth is that Aston Villa fans beat them to the pineapple jokes by a good season, and anyway, there are worse strikers around in the Premiership - and Forest fans should know, we've been watching two of them for the past 12 months!

Still, at least we enjoyed the opening fixture of the season before doubts began to creep in regarding Frank's summer spending spree. An attacking display bordering on the kamikaze saw us edge out Southampton in a seven goal thriller on the sun-soaked south coast as Bryan Roy grabbed a brace - one of very few meaningful contributions to a season of largely infuriatingly inept performances from the Dutch would-be master. Four games in, and Campbell returned to Highbury and rode the torrent of time honoured "what a waste of money" chants before hitting a late equaliser. Tucked away in the corner of the old Clock End we mockingly returned the chant, little knowing that six months later we would be singing the same with an altogether more meaningful edge to the prose.

September brought the long-awaited return to European action, but a pitiful display in Malmo saw us go down 2-1, although those of us who'd made the gruelling 30 hour journey by coach returned relieved - it should have been far worse. Seven days later and the cracks grew even wider as we were comprehensively outfought by Bradford City in the League Cup; only a freak injury-time header from Lars Bohinen keeping the scoreline within the realms of respectability.

We got past Malmo but Bradford proved too much as Ian Haemorrhoids piled on the agony with a last minute equaliser to provide the Yorkshiremen with a well deserved aggregate victory. The press labelled it a 'Cup shock' but anyone who had witnessed both legs knew differently, and one in particular wasn't slow in doing something about it. Could it have been the straw which broke Bohinen's back? Well it was either that or the 'double your money' offer from Jack Walker that did the trick. Forest fans were certainly in no doubt as to which of the two evils was to blame, and Lars was given a rather (ahem) 'hostile' reception as he lined up for his new team at Ewood Park on November 18th.

Q: Which team holds the record for going most games undefeated in the FA Premiership since its conception in 1991?

A: Nottingham Forest, with 24 games between February 21st 1995 and... November 18th 1995.

Blackburn Rovers 7 (seven) Nottingham Forest 0 (nil). Man of the Match? Lars Bohinen. Mother told me there'd be days like these.

Three days later and it was back to the magic of the Cup, the UEFA Cup. A backs-to-the-wall performance against one French team, Auxerre, had earned us a tie against another, the supposedly less formidable Lyon. As appears to be his want in important fixtures against continental opposition, the skipper missed a penalty, but thankfully on this occasion rebounds were allowed, and the hitherto largely unknown Paul McGregor netted it. The first 'Britpop Footballer' (a title of which he is apparently very proud) suddenly found himself splashed all over the back pages, and sales of The Verve's somewhat underrated album, 'A Northern Soul', soared dramatically. However, unable to handle the pressures of such instant acclaim, the band were to split just a few weeks later.

Meanwhile, League form continued to peak and trough in equal measures, outplaying Manchester United one week, sneaking a point at Bolton thanks to a last minute equaliser the next. Still, it was in Europe where we were king.

Everyone in the nation's media, even Alan Hansen, climbed into bed with us as we carried the flag for the sorry idea of sporting supremacy that is English football. "One team in Europe - there's only one team in Europe" was the chant resurrected from our Euro heydays of the late 70's and early 80's. A nil-nil draw on a preposterously cold night in Lyon ensured its continuation for at least another three months.

Unfortunately, the smugness of that chant alone was nowhere near enough at Anfield on New Year's Day when the obligatory hangover was treated to an immensely unwelcome hair of the dog from, of all people, Mr S Collymore. Two-nil ahead after 20 minutes and we were in heaven. 4-2 down 60 minutes later thanks to a Stan-inspired fight-back - including the biggest indignation of them all, a goal directly in front of us - and the wait for a win against Liverpool at Anfield clocked on yet another season. Twenty-seven years and counting...

It was around this time that Campbell found his goalscoring boots, starting with a cracker against Stoke in the FA Cup. He then proceeded to hit a further three goals in his next six games, before it all proved too much for 'Super Kev' (sic) and, despite it being only the middle of February, those goalscoring boots were carefully cleaned of the barely visible scuff-marks and packed away.

A freak blizzard and the necessity of a replay delayed the inevitable, but come the drama of a penalty shoot-out at White Hart Lane there was only ever going to be one winner. If Psycho's spot kick was sublime, then the unerring pace and accuracy of Steve Chettle's effort was ridiculous, compounded in fine style by Big Norm (that's Mark Crossley to you lot) belly-flopping his way to save after save, and Des Lyttle doing his best to revive the art of break-dancing as celebrations both on and off the pitch went into overdrive.

Oh, and I nearly forgot to mention, all this came just four days after the first leg of the UEFA Cup quarter-final against Bayern Munich in the Olympic Stadium. Steve Chettle scored then, too. Mother told me there'd be weeks like these.

But, no rest for the wicked, eh? Another four days on, we were playing host to Aston Villa in the quarter-finals of the FA Cup, which, they tell us, is the World's Most Famous Domestic Cup Competition. It's where David meets Goliath, where the BBC get to show that Ronnie Radford goal time after time, year after year, and where, try as he might, Frank Clark never *does* close down Radford quickly enough. It's also where the Forest board get their wake-up call to the fact that supporters only have so much money to spend and - big game or not - if they ain't got it they can't spend it. The attendance for our first home game at this stage of the WMFDCC since 1981 was just 21,067, and a good 4,000 of them were from the West Midlands. Franz Carr's annual shot on target gave Villa victory in a poor game, but the abiding memory is of a disgraceful display from Campbell, whose disinterest in such an important fixture was startlingly apparent from the first whistle to the last. Lack of ability is one thing, but such an obvious lack of effort is another entirely, and Campbell all but dug his own grave that evening.

Klinsmann and co then visited the City Ground a week later and issued the last rites, promptly burying Forest's season as a whole with a highly fortunate 5-1 victory. Well, OK, not that fortunate, but if we'd got the goal that our football in the first half hour undoubtedly deserved... the sort of goal, in fact, that Stan Collymore often produced during his two year tenure on Trentside.

Unfortunately for us he wasn't there on March 19th 1996. Unfortunately for him, he was four days later. Not that he did anything, mind; he didn't need to. I don't think there is any way that Collymore could have expected the atmosphere of pure hatred that overwhelmed the City Ground that afternoon. The media had a field day, of course, calling us a disgrace and even having the temerity to register words of sympathy for Collymore. Sadly for them, it showed up their blissful ignorance of what it means to be a TRUE football fan. The fact of the matter is that a player we had worshipped like few before him had walked out on OUR club midway through his contract. Yet from their post-match pontifications they seemingly expected us to welcome him back a with a wink and a smile and a "thanks for the memories, duck." No, sorry, but wake up and smell the coffee. Believe it or not, we took exception to the way Stan Collymore used his last six months at OUR football club as an extended PR opportunity to appeal to any club with ambitions as big as his own to come in and entice him away from 'smalltown' Nottingham Forest. Except he couldn't find anyone with ideals that big, so he settled for Liverpool instead, though still claimed the half a million pounds he was entitled to as his part of the deal because he hadn't 'technically' asked for a move. No, and the Pope isn't catholic either, Stan.

So we registered our disapproval in the only way we could. We booed him. And booed him. And booed him. And Stoney put us one-nil up. And we booed him. And he changed his red boots at half time because he hadn't had a kick. And we booed him. And he got into a scuffle with the Geordie Genius which should have resulted in a red card. And we booed him. And he got substituted because he hadn't had a kick. And we laughed at him.

I'd still have him back tomorrow though.

And there the season ends - well, almost. Blackburn stuffed us again and we still had some small part to play in the destination of the Premiership title. Fifty five thousand tricolor flag-waving Mancs bayed for our blood and duly got it, five times over, before a stunning equaliser from Woany against Newcastle all but packed the trophy back off to Old Trafford. But don't take it out on us. We weren't fooled into feeling sorry for Newcastle by countless images of Geordies crying into their replica shirts as it all went so horribly wrong. They may not have landed the ultimate prize this time around, but they will do eventually - Sir John Hall's millions will see to that.

If you have to feel sorry for anyone, how about us? We haven't got any money to spend on new players, which means we've little to look forward to next season except Kevin bloody Campbell again. Oh, and six points off those sheep-shagging nobodies from down the A52 of course.

Fanzine Facts

The Tricky Tree hit the streets in 1989, and was started by Andy Lowe and Neil Shaw, who continue to run the fanzine today. The fanzine's name derives from an alternative nickname given to Forest by the inhabitants of the old Trent End, who were often heard to shout "Come on you tricky trees!.".

A mis-caption surely - How about something like 'A fat headed arse and a streaker'?!
Thanks to *Nigel Burrough* for the picture

TRUMPTON TIMES

Bristol Rovers

Those of you who read last season's *Survival of the Fattest* probably thought the same as me - with the exception of the Champions of the respective divisions, and those lucky enough to be promoted automatically: why is it that everyone else had a crap season that failed to live up to supporters expectations? And why did nearly everyone label events or happenings 'things could only happen to us'? I expect there were quite a few readers who were thinking 'you think that's unique? You ought to hear what *I* heard about our centre forward, the club chairman, the club mascot and a plate of porridge!'. I suppose it's one of the great imponderables of our times like 'why does my belly button still collect fluff even when I haven't got a shirt on?', or 'why does Old Country cider taste so good?'

So as the *Trumpton Times* makes its one and only appearance (to find out why see the fanzine facts), are we going to be any different? Well, no not really. We had a crap season, and the Dallas scriptwriters would have difficulty topping what happened to us. Well almost. At least space aliens didn't kidnap our leading scorer Marcus Stewart, although Barry Fry had a bloody good go.

But back to the beginning. The run up to the start of the season should have warned us all what to expect: first, our assistant manager Dennis Booth galloped off to Huddersfield to join Brian Horton; second, with three days to go, new kit manufacturers Le Coq Sportif (better known to all Rover's fans as Le Coq Up) still had not delivered a kit for the team to wear; and finally, from the other end of the spectrum completely, came the news that we'd waited nine years to hear: ICI had given 60 acres of land to Rovers to build a new home. A 20,000 all-seat stadium IN BRISTOL was planned, and the artist's impressions looked terrific.

Shrugging off the disappointment of failing to win promotion by the width of a Wembley crossbar, hopes were high that the 'Gas' (as Bristol Rovers are affectionately known) would go one better this time, and an unbeaten August with third spot in the table gave us all false hope that everything was going to plan. This was coupled with a dreadful start made by the 'Shitheads' (as Bristol City 1982 Ltd are affectionately known). But of course it didn't last.

September arrived, along with Ron Noades and Steve Coppell bearing gifts from Palace. They paid an extraordinary amount of money for a very average striker while ignoring the diamond, Marcus Stewart. After the board had practically snatched Ron's hand off and banked the cheque double quick before he could change his mind, the guy lined up to replace Gareth Taylor promptly got injured, which meant we were effectively playing with just one striker. Now that wouldn't be quite so bad if you were 6ft 3in and 13 stone of evil muscle, but at 5ft 9in and ten stone, Marcus Stewart was always going to struggle. Sure enough, the defeats started and the Endsleigh slide began. We were hoofed out of the Fizzy Pop Cup by a very poor-looking West Ham side (who perked up dramatically after beating us though) and the only consolation during this period was watching the Shitheads drift down into a relegation position.

Our season was going nowhere and we were getting dumped on both home and away by mediocre teams. Not content with that, Brian Parkin, who had been a model of goalkeeping consistency for five years, suddenly took it into his head to buy a pair of Teflon coated goalkeeping gloves. Then the other teams in the Division twigged that our left back was totally unable to tackle or kick the ball with his left foot, and our midfield players, seeing that our strike force had gone on strike, came out in sympathy and seven October games yielded a paltry two goals.

November arrived along with the FA Cup. Drawn away to Hitchin, who were effectively eight divisions below us and without a home league win all season, we reckoned that even we couldn't bugger this one up. Pah. Ten minutes into the game and 2-0 down we knew the answer to that one. We pulled a goal back after half an hour, but couldn't even force a replay: the worst defeat in the history of the club. For the first time, dissenting voices were heard questioning the performance of manager John Ward, who promptly panicked and spent the princely sum of £50,000 on a striker. Why didn't he do this two months ago?

The player's name was Beadle. Oh no, - here it comes: "YOU'VE BEEN FRAMED." But wait, he wasn't a funny looking bearded bloke clad in a Gas shirt, he was a big bugger, and though a bit slow and cumbersome at first, when he got match fit he started to look the business. Defeats dried up as the goals started to flow, and Peter Beadle achieved cult hero status on Tuesday January 16th 1996, when in the first Bristol derby for three years he scored both goals in a 2-0 win at Trashton Gate. A never-to-be-forgotten night by those Gasheads who got in, for not only did we win, but it also showed up the total ineptitude of Bristol City 1982 Ltd both on and off the field.

Deep in the financial mire, City '82 didn't bother to make the game all-ticket (Bristol football fans are notoriously bad at buying tickets), determined as they were to grab as much cash as they could. Well, there were people standing in the aisles, blocking the exits, perching anywhere to get a view - who knows what would've happened if there'd been an emergency. But best of all, season ticket holders (those that got in - many couldn't!) arrived to find that *their* club had sold *their* seat. Oh, how we laughed. Then when they went down 2-0, several of their 'supporters' reverted to type and started to smash their own ground up, breaking down gates and ripping up advertising hoardings.

So, things were looking up in '96 and we started to creep up the table again, but hold your horses, little at Bristol Rovers ever runs smoothly. February breezed in with headline news from ICI: "new stadium now unlikely to go ahead." Apparently the land deal hinged on a junction off the new Severn Bridge motorway being sited in the correct place, but some berk from the Dept of Transport decided the junction should be one and a half miles away from the proposed stadium instead of next to it, which buggered up all the plans. So it was back to square one on the ground front - still at Bath for the foreseeable future.

Idiots in the media with NO understanding of how a true football fan feels kept calling for us to share Trashton with City '82. That was like asking Tottenham to move into Highbury, or suggesting that Celtic cuddled up to Rangers at Ibrox. Fortunately, our directors weren't that daft. And to their credit they're still trying to salvage something from ICI.

After February's body blow, March arrived with us on the fringe of the play-offs, and 90 minutes from another Wembley trip in the Auto Windscreens Nodding Dog Trophy. After drawing 1-1 away in the first leg of the area final, all we had to was keep a clean sheet and we were there. The ref tried to help; he gave us a penalty which we missed and then, a few minutes later, we conceded a goal and promptly gave up. Oh well, there was always next Saturday. Beat the Shitheads and all would be forgotten. Gulp, horror of horrors, our one and only home League defeat against City '82 in ten years at Trumpton. Our season was over in a week, and although we flirted on the fringe of the play-offs till the end, we ultimately missed out by three points.

End of the season on the pitch, but all action off it. A debut on TV for the *Trumpton Times* in a local football debate was followed by news that Rovers were leaving Bath after ten years to return to Bristol and play at the Memorial Ground, home of the Bristol Rugby Club. Next, manager John Ward was told that his contract wasn't being renewed. Some were sorry to see him go but here are three reasons why *we* weren't: (1) most embarrassing ever defeat (Hitchin), (2) the Shithead's Twerton first, and (3) for the first time since being elected to the League in 1920, an entire home campaign without being able to score three goals

Now the news has filtered through that prodigal son Ian Holloway (a hero from our last Championship season and self-confessed Gashead) has returned from QPR to take over as player-manager, and his assistant is to be Geoff Twentyman, who was captain in our Championship season.

The club is moving its headquarters from portakabins in the grounds of a chocolate factory to a salubrious mansion on the outskirts of Bristol with its own training facilities. Things are happening so quickly, everything will probably be out of date by the time you read this. ROLL ON NEXT SEASON!

Thought for the day: Can anyone explain why a club with the official title of Bristol City 1982 Ltd is planning to celebrate a centenary next year? I may not be very good at sums but I do know that 1997 minus 1982 is not 100. With maths like that no wonder they've got into financial difficulties!!

Fanzine Facts

Trumpton Times first dished the dirt in 1992. The fanzine takes its name from the nickname given to Twerton Park - Trumpton, so with Rovers leaving Twerton to return to Bristol, it looks as if the fanzine will have to be renamed, hence its one and only appearance in this publication. Main editors The Eternal Optimist and Mr Angry are given considerable help by Dr John Dee, Old Country Cider and Carling Black Label. They are also grateful to their regular contributors, who can be relied on to churn out good quality copy at extremely short notice.

TWO TOGETHER

Barnet

The season got under way in August with a slight setback at Hereford: a narrow 4-1 defeat which included a goal scored by their 'keeper from a long punt up-field! Never mind, everyone thought, weÕll soon start winning. Six games later we were wondering where the first win would come from. Lincoln had the courtesy to give us an easy win and Dougie Freedman's last goals wearing a Barnet shirt. Crystal Palace signed him for a down payment of £300,000 (which was swallowed up by the overdraft at the bank), rising to £900,000 if he played for Scotland on a wet Tuesday afternoon. So there we were, our best player sold, one win from the first seven games, none of the money raised available for new players. It was going to be a long season!

After beating Lincoln we then had to wait another six games for our next result, a run which included our fall to (and brief stay at) the bottom of the table after losing at home to Plymouth.

Then came what turned out to be the turning point of the season - Sean Devine, a Millwall and Fisher Athletic cast-off who had tried his luck in Cyprus. Thanks to chairman Tony Kleanthous' connections (think about it), Devine signed for the Bees. With his first touch against Exeter he scored, and carried on doing just that for the rest of the season.

It took a little while longer for the results to start turning our way. A 4-0 home defeat by Rochdale ended with the fans calling for the head of Ray Clemence. Rumour had it that he was for the old heave-ho if things didn't improve in the next two games. The team duly responded with a draw at Hartlepool and a win at Northampton to save the manager's bacon, for a few more weeks at least. Then came the dreaded FA Cup home draw against a top non-league team. Woking - again! They went 2-0 up in the first 20 minutes and the chairman was seen to leave his seat and dash to the social club. We assumed that this was for one of three reasons: (1) to type out Clemence's P45, (2) to have a few stiff drinks, or (3) to kill himself. When asked later what he'd actually been doing, he explained that as club chairman there were some things that he couldn't do in public. He needed to get a bit of pent-up frustration out of his system, apparently. Barnet pulled back the two goals and so off we went to Woking for the second year running. Surely this year we would beat them? Nope. Even after going one up in the first minute and been gifted a penalty through a perfectly fair and justified refereeing decision, we lost it in extra time.

That was it, the fans wanted Clemence out, and quick! The chairman and manager traded blows via the local and national press; it was fairly obvious that they weren't getting on too well. However there was no chance of Clemence getting the push since the club couldn't afford to pay off his contract, worth between £70,000 and £200,000 a year, depending on which rumour you wanted to believe. As things turned out in the end, it was just as well.

The team contrived to lose only six of the last 29 League fixtures, compared to the opening record of six reverses in the first 15 matches. After going out of the Cup to Woking they embarked on a unbeaten run of seven matches including wins over Chester and Preston. Come February, after a 5-0 thrashing of Wigan, things were looking up. We were on the verge of a play-off place and Devine and Hodges were scoring freely. Then came the kiss of death. Clemence won the Manager of the Month award. We duly lost at Mansfield in our first game of March and then dropped two points at home to Chester the following week.

From a personal point of view, the highlight of the season came when *Two Together* won a raffle. The prize was a full match sponsorship package. Meal, football, booze; what a night! A home win against Cardiff, with Mr Devine getting the winner was followed by the consumption of vast qualities of alcohol after the game.

Glenn Hoddle, Frank Clark and Joe Kinnear were all at the game, but wouldn't discuss which Barnet star they were watching. In retrospect they would have been unlikely to understand us. The evening finished with a drunken discussion with Ray Clemence about Barnet, the players, life in general. From what we remember of the conversation, Ray came across as someone dedicated to the cause and not just 'here for the ride'. We have to grudgingly admit that our opinion of him changed for the better that night. It's amazing what 12 pints of lager, two bottles of wine and a cup of Bovril can do.

Things were getting a bit tight now. Easter weekend saw us beat Northampton yet again. Oh, we *do* enjoy winning against them. This was followed by a 4-0 revenge thumping of Rochdale with Lee Hodges getting all four goals. We won't mention that they had nine players out injured that day. The following Saturday came a 5-1 win over Hartlepool with Hodges only getting three this time. Tut, tut...

So with three game to go we had finally reached the holy grail that was seventh place. We duly bottled it and lost at Doncaster to a last minute goal. But even going into the last two games against Orient and Fulham we still had a good chance of making the play-offs.

At Orient we were 2-0 and 3-1 up but thanks to two huge errors form our normally reliable 'keeper Mark Taylor, we contrived to snatch a draw from the jaws of victory. The short journey home was made more stressful when we heard that all of our nearest rivals for the play-offs had also lost. Now we had to beat Fulham and hope that everyone would lose again on the final Saturday. Much to their fans' delight we didn't make it. Sean Devine obliged with two goals in our 3-0 win but the other results didn't go our way. When praising his fans after the game, Fulham manager Micky Adams obviously hadn't heard the racist and anti-Semitic chants from the Fulham 'supporters' directed at our players and fans. The abuse was the worst heard at Underhill for years and shattered the myth of Fulham as a friendly family club.

The season ended with Barnet two points shy of the play-offs but with a collection of players that we can at last call a team. Next season... who knows! Mind you, at least one player will be moving, especially with the club so strapped for cash. Barnet fans have become used to the sad fact that any time we find a half decent player, he won't be around for long. Given that we have already offered £95,000 for a Stevenage Borough striker, you can bet your life that either Sean Devine or Lee Hodges won't be marauding around Underhill next year.

Clemence appears to have turned things around and has built a stable platform for the club to build on. There are even plans afoot for a new stadium. Jeez - things must be getting better!

Fanzine Facts

Two Together was named after the activities of Barnet's famous ex-chairman Stan Flashman. If you had the dosh, Stan could always be guaranteed to get you 'Two Together' for a swish night out at Les Misérables. John Cosgrove and Hugh Godwin started the fanzine in November 1993 and were 'respectful' of Mr Flashman's business empire. So respectful in fact, that the fanzine initially operated from a PO Box with anonymous contributions. With a new regime in place at Underhill, they have come out into the open a little more, and along with regular contributor Doron Garfunkel, a stalwart of the original Barnet fanzine Buzztalk, produce *Two Together* as often as possible.

THE UGLY INSIDE

Southampton

It was the sort of feeling you get if you stand near the edge of a cliff. You look over the side and your legs go to jelly. There's a horrible sickly feeling in the pit of your stomach as you break out into a cold sweat. All the symptoms of being a Southampton fan during the last ten minutes of the season.

All our hopes hung on Man City not scoring a winner against Liverpool. There seemed no way we were going to beat Wimbledon in a most atrocious nerve-wracking game. City had pulled a two goal deficit back and there were still 11 minutes left for them to get the winner. The Dell, which had earlier been a sea of happy faces, turned into a stress-filled cauldron of noise. We shouted, we screamed, will-ing our team to score a winner and

put us out of our misery. Everyone with a radio was besieged as the latest news filtered through from Maine Road. It was totally unbearable as City piled on the pressure. Every minute seemed like an hour till finally, finally, the Dell erupted as Liverpool clung on. Still we needed to survive the last few seconds at the Dell but Wimbledon had long since settled for a draw. The final whistle was as good as winning the Cup. The team did a lap of honour and it really did feel like we'd won something. Saints fans, who had been outstanding with their vocal support in the final games, gave the team an emotional send-off then it was off to town to celebrate the great escape.

Anyone who has survived a last day escape from relegation will understand the elation and the enormous sense of relief. Southampton have only ever been relegated twice in their history, and it was an enormous irony that this year's escape was at the expense of Alan Ball and Man City. You see, Alan Ball departing was where our season started. To this day nobody knows the truth behind why Ballie went, but the majority of Saints fans believe it was only for the money. Personally, I'm not so sure and think the board could and should have done more to hang onto a man who had rescued us from the oblivion Branfoot was sending us to, and in some style too. Unfortunately, Alan Ball's statements when he joined Southamp-ton such as "walking over broken glass to get the job" seriously backfired on him. It's fair to say he is now a hated man down here and this was reflected in the mail we received throughout the season. "Judas! Judas!" they chanted on his return to the Dell, but he still has a minority of support that appreciates his past contribution to the club. Was he pushed or did he run for the money? We will never know.

Alan Ball gone, it was time to search for a replacement. Big Fat Ron, Bobby Robson, Jack Charlton even? You've got to be joking; we've got the tightest chairman in the Premier League. During the 'Branfoot Out' campaign we were invited into the boardroom for a meeting with him and were amazed when he offered us chocolate bourbons. Chocolate bourbons! That's about as much luxury as Southampton can afford! Guy Askham, the chairman, is actually a nice old boy with a pleasant nature, we call him 'the vicar of Bumble'. However in the cut-throat world of the Premiership our board, despite being good local businessmen with the club at heart (Lawrie McMenemy excepted), have been left behind and seem to lack the ambition, drive and most importantly, financial clout needed to survive at the top level. Southampton, apart from signing Kevin Keegan, has always been a club that eventually follows trends, never seeming to be bold or dynamic enough to set them. It was no surprise then when Dave Merrington was appointed à la Liverpool boot room style from reserve team coach to first team manager.

Dave Merrington after all had guided the likes of Alan Shearer, Rod Wallace, Jason Dodd and Matt Le Tissier from youth players to highly successful professionals. The fans were certainly happy about the appointment but it was one hell of a step up for Dave to make. He is a straight talking Geordie who bleeds red and white stripes, totally committed to the cause as he is to his Christian beliefs. After finishing tenth the previous season hopes were high and the clouds that loomed when Ballie left seemed to be blowing away.

The *Ugly Inside* made a venture into the record business on the back of a campaign to get Matt Le Tissier in the England team. Local group "The Valley Slags" brought out 'Legend of the Saint' written by Rich Charley and Perry Flatt. It is not your typical 'we're going to Wembley' anthem, but has more of a 'Clash' sound to it. Locally it sold very well, and had Venables given Matt the chance he richly deserved it would have been a major hit. As it is we are left with a couple of thousand unsold copies, waiting for Le Hod to pick Le God and poised to change our name from The Ugly Inside to the Ugly Bank Balance! Yes it wasn't just the team that struggled, the fanzine nearly got relegated as well. We are eternally grateful to everybody who had contributed to our survival and happily things seem to be moving in the right direction.

Back on the pitch the season got off to a poor start with a home defeat against Forest. Matty scored a hat-trick but the defence were awful. An unexpected home win against Newcastle lifted spirits but to be honest our League form wasn't up to much. Many times the reality dawned on me that this really could be it, "we're definitely going down" I thought. There just didn't seem any backbone in the side. Team selection was a complete mystery, there was no consistency, the players lost confidence and so did the supporters. When Sheffield Wednesday turned us over at home in March, doom and gloom reached epidemic proportions. The only cure would come if all the teams around us were equally bad. Then came the amazing yo-yo run-in, starting with a deserved 1-0 win against Coventry when Big Ron spat at the dummy on Sky TV.

A massive turnout trekked up to Loftus Road to witness our very worst performance, a 3-0 defeat actually flattering Saints. All hope of salvation seemed lost and I remember people walking out of QPR resigned to the Endsleigh League. A week later and Saints reserves (Blackburn) were the visitors. For some reason Bruce

Grobbelaar was back in goal in place of Player of the Season Dave Beasant. Again the fans were mystified, but a workmanlike performance was rewarded when a late penalty gave us all three points. Easter Monday and a fruitless visit to Villa Park - stitched up by the ref - treated like crap by their stewards - and another 3-0 defeat made it a very bad day.

Then Man Utd came to the Dell where we hadn't beaten them for seven years. In the words of their own fans "they came out and posed about for 45 minutes." Never mind all that grey kit bollocks, we murdered them with good passing football. Matt was back to his best and the Saints were staying up! For the first time in ages we actually believed it, but next up was the massive hurdle of Bolton away.

Burnden Park was one of those brilliant unforgettable away days. Everyone got totally pissed, Saints won and the vocal support never stopped. Even hearing that Man City and Coventry had both won didn't spoil things because surely we wouldn't muck it up at home to Wimbledon, would we?

Finally, I can't leave without mentioning the FA Cup run and the thrashing of our south coast rivals Portsmouth. They call us scummers and we call them skates. Why skates you ask? Well, it's something to do with their ancient seafaring history, and a sexual preference for fish. And don't they realise that the scum always floats to the top?

Fanzine Facts

Started in 1987 by Nick Illingsworth and Clive Foley, *The Ugly Inside* was named after The Ugly Men And Inside Crew's of the mid 80's. It has been influential in forming of Southampton Independent Supporters Association - SISA, and is heavily involved in fighting for a new stadium. Clive thanks Neil Gange and Darren Wheeler for the quality of cartoons and reckons that regular contributors Kevin Filth, Perry on Left Wing, Dave Juson, Chris Newman and Rich Chorley also deserve a glowing tribute. Despite a circulation approaching 3,000, *TUI* nearly went bankrupt this year, so as Clive says "any donations would be gratefully accepted, including milk tokens."

UNITED WE STAND

Manchester United

June '95. In the space of four weeks, we'd seen our team lose the League to Blackburn on the final day of the season, and in the Cup Final a week later, United had lost a drab game to a single Everton goal. These defeats hurt, but part of being a football fan means accepting defeat. Besides, they make the successes, when they come, all the more enjoyable. But Manchester United fans were confused.

Why? Because three star players, Paul Ince, Mark Hughes and Andrei Kanchelskis, had been allowed to leave the club. Bewildered, I went away.

July '95, Kuala Lumpur. The arrival of Manchester United to play two friendly games caused a stir, and two thousand Malaysian Reds descended on the airport to see their heroes in the flesh for the first time.

UNITED WE STAND

Just like a team...

The Independent Voice of Manchester United Fans

ISSUE 53a • £1.00

United's first XI were used to crowds (if not quite such large ones) meeting them at the airport. Indeed, Galatasaray fans had questioned the parentage of Giggs *et al* on placards at Istanbul airport, but this was different. United were being received as heroes; their arrival made National news headlines.

Watching the scenes on television in Malaysia gave me an enormous sense of pride, but also a feeling of unease. The subjects of the adulation on the screen in front of me looked so young, so inexperienced. Could they really challenge for the title when Liverpool were paying £8m for players, and United weren't even interested in adding to the squad? Match-going United fans hadn't, as some elements of the media suggested, voted for Fergie to leave. You'd have to be a very shallow and uneducated person to demand a new manager when the one you've got has brought more trophies than you could ever have dreamt of.

That said, even the most optimistic United fan doubted the team's credentials as challengers of genuine pedigree, and the first half performance at Villa Park on the opening day compounded Reds' worst fears. Villa 3, United 0. If we were to have a sticky patch, it would only last 45 minutes, for in the second half they performed much better. Two weeks later, the young Reds side destroyed Champions Blackburn in their own back-yard. Fergie had taken a massive gamble, but his instincts were already starting to pay off. United didn't need to bring in replacements, because the manager had seen the nucleus of a fine young side four years earlier, when Butt, Beckham, Scholes and Gary and Phil Neville were all FA Youth Cup winners. Given the chance of first team football, they didn't take long to find their feet, and grew in stature on the pitch as quickly as the giant North Stand did alongside it.

Local rivals Bolton were swept aside 3-0 in September by one of the youngest ever sides to be fielded by Manchester United. That stunning performance offered an insight into what to expect later in the season. But there was still something (or someone) missing.

September saw the team travel to Volgograd, scene of one of the bloodiest battles in World War Two. On the pitch, United rode the Russian assault, and the 150 travelling fans, for once staying in a better hotel than the players, relaxed safe in the knowledge that United would win back in Manchester. If only life could be so predictable!

At Old Trafford, the Russians were two up, and although the Reds pulled both goals back, they went out in the most painful manner (after penalties): away goals.

So, United were dumped out of Europe once again, to another unknown but technically superior side. In the League Cup, another equally superior side had come to Old Trafford and gone home with a deserved 3-0 victory. No, not Liverpool or Newcastle, but Second Division York City.

October 1st '95. A key player returned from a nine month suspension, and although his name eludes me, I was sure he'd do well...

Newcastle were playing fine football, and to some extent taking all the pressure. In our first meeting, the Geordies were brought down to earth by a 2-0 Christmas defeat at Old Trafford. Either side of that morale-boosting victory, United had been beaten away at Liverpool and Leeds, not to mention a 4-1 drubbing at White Hart Lane on New Year's Day. All three of these defeats were televised, much to the delight of the watching nation.United may be the most popular team in the land, but they are also the most despised. Week in, week out, we'd hear "If you hate Man United clap your hands", and the now ubiquitous "Do you come from Manchester?." I do, actually, and so do plenty of others. But that's not the point. Blackburn fans may live in each others' back yards, but do all Chelsea fans come from SW6? Or Villa fans from Birmingham? And do all Leeds fans come inside sheep?

Why alienate the supporter who travels miles to watch your team play at home, and who has done so for years? Fair-weather fans have been picked up by the thousand, but they're not true fans, and shouldn't be classed as such. Crystal Palace won the small-time supporter of the year award last season. This time, it had to be Reading. With their Umbro manager's coats and Hi-Tec trainers, they insisted upon doing their best to make Elm Park a hostile venue. They failed, but then a ground named after a tree hardly puts the fear of God in you! If the mouthy Reading fans spent more of their time actually attending games and not just making their presence felt at big matches, they might have something to genuinely shout about.

The Christmas slips had cost us dear. Newcastle's defeat at Old Trafford had merely dented their sky-high morale, and by late January they had opened up a 12 point lead at the top. When prior to the game at Upton Park, Alex Ferguson stated that his side was still capable of winning the Double, I was surprised. I couldn't work out whether he genuinely believed this, or was just trying to boost the team's confidence. It was both, and that statement was to turn out to be no blunder. If only United fans were as careful with their words. A self-assured section of K Stand bellowed "Have you ever won the Double?" to Villa fans in mid-January. Actually, they had, albeit 100 years ago. Oops!

In this game, United just couldn't break down Villa's formidable defence, and the strain of Cole's misses was starting to show. He made up for it two days later though, scoring a last-minute winner in the FA Cup third round replay at Roker Park. That victory brought about a change in our fortunes, as United marked the start of a ten game winning streak. Things were starting to click at Old Trafford. The young players were becoming as solid and efficient as a BMW; the Frenchman was the fuel injection, and the catalyst off whom the youngsters fired. But United needed to do more than get their own house in order. They needed Newcastle to crack. And sure enough, by March, those cracks were starting to appear.

March 4th '96. The clash of the top two sides had loomed ominously for a month, and the change in both clubs' fortunes had made it a classic six-pointer. The victorious team would gain a huge psychological advantage, and create the momentum needed to see them through the final two months of the season towards the Championship.

Black and white shirts pounded Schmeichel's goal for the first 45 minutes. But the Reds absorbed the pressure, and struck back with a clinical goal from Cantona after the break. I stayed up in Newcastle that night to witness the devastation Cantona's goal had caused first-hand. To a man, they were totally desolate. Their expressions said it all - they looked worse than I felt in the aftermath of Anfield in '92 and Upton Park in '95, when we had lost the League. But there were no excuses because their team had no answers to Manchester United.

The Championship was now thrown wide open, and the momentum was firmly with the United team from Manchester. Progress was being made in the Cup too. Manc rivals City had been defeated in the fifth round. It was a dubious penalty which afforded us our first goal, but there were no doubts about Lee Sharpe's second, which would confine City to their 20th trophy-less year.

Aside from a blip at the Dell where United scored one goal, sported two kits, and conceded three goals, things were working out remarkably well. Chelsea, despite inspired performances from Gullit and their fans, were defeated in the FA Cup semi-final, setting up a classic Wembley tie against Liverpool. Amazingly, the prospect of that Double which Fergie had bravely talked about in January was now on.

It all happened so quickly, but by May 4th, the 3,000 United fans lucky enough to have tickets were travelling to the Riverside stadium in Middlesbrough to celebrate our third Championship in four years. A week later, a single goal in the 85th minute of the Cup Final ensured that United became the first English team to win the domestic Double twice.

He didn't have a bad season, our kung fu-kicking, garlic-smelling, nuclear bomb-testing, arrogant, dirty Frenchman. I forget his name again, but I know that's what the tabloid press had called him. And they're always right, aren't they? Just like when they said he should leave English football for the good of the game.

Fanzine Facts

United We Stand, one of British football's biggest selling fanzines, first appeared around Old Trafford in October '89. Editor Andy Mitten and co-editor Steve Black are assisted by a large team of contributors, not to mention the 11 or so ground sellers, and the mag is now on issue 53a (cock-up on the numbering front!).

VOICE OF THE BEEHIVE

Brentford

Brentford-inary

Being a football fan entitles me to be fickle; we all are. So, I'll conveniently gloss over the fact that in the '94-95 season Brentford finished second in Division Two and just lost out in the play-offs on penalties. In fact the previous season's near-miss made last year's shambles even worse. On paper we should have walked our way to promotion; sadly on the pitch we almost limped into Division Three to join our close pals, Fulham, in the bottom flight. Should Brentford manager Dave Webb ever decide to hang up his sheepskin coat and quit the world of football - a move which some Bees supporters would like to see sooner rather than later - he could do worse than apply for a job in the customer services department at British Rail.

His excuses for Brentford's failures this year were certainly up to the standard required, and although he never actually blamed the wrong type of ball or grass on the pitch he certainly hinted at it. But for whatever the reasons, the team failed to get going, and no matter how many changes of players, formation or style were made during the course of the season things just didn't gel. The defence forgot how to defend, strikers forgot how to strike and the midfield spent the majority of their time picking daises and looking at the pretty clouds. Our pint-size 'keeper, Kevin 'Bloody' Dearden, even lost the ability to catch the ball. Whatever they had been doing in pre-season training, it clearly had very little to do with football.

Much of our previous success had been down to the influence of three key players: the potent strike force of Robert Taylor and Nicky Forster and the powerhouse defender Martin 'the new Steve Stone' Grainger. And had they all lived up to the potential they'd already shown, things may have been very different. Unfortunately only Robert Taylor carried on from where he had left off and I can confidently say that without his 16 goals and all-round effort we would have suffered the drop. As for the two other heroes of '94-95, they had nightmare seasons. Forster, who had drawn much attention from the Premiership, had obviously signed a new sponsorship deal with Dunlop. At least that's the only explanation I can think of for his switch to wearing rubber boots. A simple pass? *BOING!* Into the stands. A shot on goal? *BOING!* Into another time-zone. It was all very disappointing. This sponsorship deal could only have been struck by his agent, the ever popular Eric Hall (with that cigar always in his mouth don't you think he looks like a Hollywood film star? Lassie taking a crap). As for Grainger, he totally lost the plot. In his 'golden season' he had the tackling ability of Bobby Moore (RIP), the pace of Linford Christie and the shot of Stuart Pearce. Last season, alas, he had the pace of Stuart Pearce, the shot of Bobby Moore and the tackle of Linford Christie (maybe I should re-phrase that). Anyway, I suppose you're reading this chapter of the book to learn about Brentford's '95-96 campaign, not to read my cheap willy jokes, so I'd better take you on some sort of guide through the season...

On the whole, things started off pretty well with two wins and two draws in our first four games; what's more, the partnership of Taylor and Forster had carried on where they had left off, netting four goals between them. But once again Brentford fans had fallen for the 'false sense of security' trick. It gets us every time. Over the next 14 matches the Bees only managed to scrape together three wins, and one of those was in the Auto Windscreens Shield against Bournemouth. Burnley, Swindon, Rotherham, Bristol Rovers, Chesterfield and Blackpool all took three easy points at Brentford's expense and left us sitting at the bottom of the League. The club was metaphorically wearing a big sign on its back saying 'KICK ME', and they all lined up for a good boot. In the Coca Cola Cup Bolton beat us 1-0 at their place and 3-2 in an admittedly exciting encounter (I woke up several times) at Griffin Park. In the middle of this poor run Dave Webb decided the time had come to take action. What the team needed was an experienced midfield player, someone who could slow the play down a bit and create chances for others. A player with class, skill and flair. Instead, we signed Paul Davis on a free from Arsenal. Paul had an immediate effect on the Griffin Park crowd - it was hate at first sight. He played eight games in total for the Bees before being dropped to the reserves, where he played out time until Webb put him on the free transfer list. According to Davis himself, his lack of success in the lower branches of this great tree we call football (in case you are wondering, yes, I am trying to pad things out) was that he couldn't get used to the pace. Whether it was too fast for him or too slow he never revealed, but the fact that he complained that a snail was stalking him might give some clue. Former 'Eastenders' actor, Tom 'Lofty' Watt, in an article for my fanzine (I know all the stars me), said Arsenal were "foolish" to let Davis go - they certainly were from Brentford's point of view. But then again, he married pizza-face Michelle Fowler, so what does he know?

In late October Brentford were obviously worried that supporters may have rumbled the fact they were crap and so decided to have a decent win to regain our confidence. Peterborough were beaten 3-0 and the team actually turned in a good performance. Star of the show was new signing, or should that be singing, Dean Martin. He was brought in to replace a sulky girl's blouse of a player called Paul Stephenson, a winger, who had been sold to York for a packet of frozen peas and a hat. Martin had been eking out a living in the Icelandic League after being released by West Ham and had in fact just won the Icelandic Player of the Year award (the trophy was a large plastic fish I believe.) He was a troublesome winger blessed with an armoury of tricks and flicks, a bit of pace and, unusual in a winger, a slice of aggression. For one brief afternoon we thought the team had got its act together and a star had been born. Alas, we'd been fooled again. Beating the Posh had been a mere blip, and Martin's sparkling wing play had been but a fluke. The following four League matches saw a return to the club's true form - Crewe, Notts County, Shrewsbury and Bournemouth all saying "Thank you very much" for maximum points. The only success came when we managed to scrape a 1-1 draw with Farnborough Town in the FA Cup. Oh yes, the streets of Brentford were awash with champagne that night I can tell you. (You may be interested to know that the phrase "born under a bad sign" refers to a sign on the Great West Road which says 'You are now in Brentford.') The Bees did manage to redeem themselves in the replay, beating Farnborough 4-0, the ever reliable Taylor netting two of them (the match was shown live on Sky TV which is another good reason not to have one of those ugly dishes outside your house). This resounding victory spurred the Bees onto a 2-1 win over Bradford, but the fun was not to last. Our next match was against well respected, much loved neighbours Fulham in the AWS. Games against Fulham were usually the highlight of the season - the one 'must win' game. With Fulham being in Division Three we hadn't met them in the League for a while, so the Shield provided us with the chance for a spot of morale-boosting. Naturally, we lost 1-0. There was even a punch-up on the terraces. It was awful. Getting beaten by Fulham, especially at home, was just about as low as things could get.

An away win at Bournemouth (again) in the second Round of the Cup the following Saturday did little to cheer up the faithful, and the next four games saw three draws and one defeat to compound the gloom around Griffin Park. Just to put the icing on the cake, one of Brentford's promising youngsters, Marcus Bent, managed to drop a mirror on himself (I don't know how he managed it, he just did) severely cutting his neck and putting himself out of action for a few games. Still, we did have the thrill of the FA Cup and an away trip to Norwich to look forward to. And strangely enough we *were* looking forward to it. Having given up any hope of League success, the Cup gave us the chance of a taste of much-needed glory. This led Brentford fans to snap up all the tickets for the trip to East Anglia. Norwich is a strange town, the sort of place where they still look upon the motor car as being a modern fad and think producing vast amounts of mustard is something to brag about. All things were in place for a giant-killing, as the Norwich team were down in the dumps, and the crowd (what there was of them) were calling for the resignation, nay lynching, of the chairman. Sure enough, the Bees put up a fighting, gritty performance and came away 2-1 winners. We sang our team to victory for the full 90 minutes, and for that one short afternoon we all felt proud of being Brentford supporters. Seven days later we lost 1-0 at Oxford and supporting Brentford didn't seem so much fun after all!

Once more the glamour of the Cup helped ease the disappointment as we made the short journey across London to the New Valley to take on Charlton. Again the Bees showed the sort of commitment and fight they'd been lacking in the Endsleigh and were unlucky to lose 3-2; once again though, it did give Bees fans a glimpse of how things could be if the players pulled their fingers out a bit more often. Now, our season was as good as over, and it was only early February.

A short run of wins and draws in March even deprived us of the excitement of the battle against relegation (though we certainly helped other teams near the drop zone by giving points to all the strugglers below us). As the season began to fizzle out (good news for me as I'm nearing my allotted number of words) supporters started to lose interest. This reached its nadir on a dull Tuesday in March when the club recorded its lowest ever attendance for a League game when only 3,104 people turned up to watch an equally dull 1-1 draw with Carlisle. When the final whistle of the final game blew (a 2-0 win against perennial victims Bournemouth), Bees fans left Griffin Park without many happy memories from a fairly aimless, anonymous and above all average season.

Dave Webb made the usual utterances about "new faces" for next season, but with Brentford's meagre finances that probably means he's going to sign a gurner. Still, that would be better than signing another Gunner. It was no surprise when Robert Taylor swept the board at the Player of the Year poll - there really were no other choices. On the brighter side, some of Brentford's younger players did start to shine, although in many cases it was their inexperience that proved to be our undoing. Hopefully, next season, youngsters like Marcus Bent (accidents with mirrors permitting), Joe Omigie, Carl Asaba, Carl Hutchings, Gus Hurdle (Hello! Gus Hurdle!) and Ijah Anderson will all live up to their early promise, and we'll see some of the "on the floor" and "exciting" football Dave Webb has been talking about, but not delivering, since his arrival at Griffin Park. Brentford chairman Martin Lange has promised to move the club to a purpose built all-seater stadium by the year 2000. Another season like the last one and he can forget the seats. We'll need beds instead.

Fanzine Facts

You may think that *Voice of the Beehive* got its name simply because Brentford are the 'Bees'. Actually, editor Rob Bartram tells a different story. In fact he knew the members of the band 'Voice of the Beehive' before they had achieved any fame. This was at the time, 1988-ish, that Rob was considering starting Brentford's first fanzine. This, along with the fact that Griffin Park had a pub called the Beehive on one of its corners, and the fact that Brentford were the Bees, produced its name. *Voice of the Beehive* is pretty much a one man band and Rob has become 'The Godfather of Brentford fanzines'. Produced three times a season *Voice of the Beehive* tries to avoid any sort of relationship with the club, just in case the unpalatable truth needs to be told.

VOICE OF THE VALLEY

Charlton Athletic

Charlton's '95-96 campaign was brimful of pleasant surprises, but somehow we always expected it to end in tears. Those of us with a sense of history strongly suspected Crystal Palace would be involved as well.

And so it proved. But no one could quite have anticipated the local surge in demand for Kleenex when Leicester's Steve Claridge shot down the Eagles with his last-minute extra-time winner in the play-off final at Wembley. Funny or what? And we'd only just got over Millwall's kamikaze climax.

What would we do without the neighbours to entertain us?

The answer, actually, is plenty. If the end of the season was all about the folk down the road, the rest of it had been brilliantly illuminated by the

Voice of The Valley
THE INDEPENDENT ADDICKS MAG

No. 17   May 1996   £1

Inside — why Tranmere spell disaster to me

OAPs outwit Valley price rises

Paul Weller — another closet Addick owns up

Charlton kit — in your high street at last

Addicks' own youngsters. For the first time in a decade, all the talk among Charlton fans was about the team and not the ground. Some of us have attended as many meetings as matches in the last ten years, so it made a pleasant change.

Going solo for the first time, manager Alan Curbishley started the campaign with plenty to prove to the fans and their fanzine, neither of whom were entirely convinced his divorce from four-year partner Steve Gritt would be enough to see the Addicks improve on their previous faltering form. There had been no cash signings in the summer and the season opened, as indeed it was to close, amid rumours the club would sell outstanding central defender Richard Rufus, voted 1995 Player of the Year after less than 30 senior games.

After a scrappy opening day defeat at The Hawthorns, Curbishley was jeered by a section of the travelling support following a goalless Coca Cola draw at Barnet. And when the team fell behind at home to Birmingham four days later, bets were already being taken on the manager's chances of surviving until Christmas. But events were to prove us wrong. *Very* wrong.

It took a goal from Garry Nelson - better known as the author of *Left Foot Forward* than for his contribution on the field last season - to turn things sharply around. A minute later young midfielder Lee Bowyer stepped up for his first in senior football and the show was on the road. The 18-year-old scored again in midweek as Charlton saw off Barnet and then panicked Palace with a deliciously arrogant chip at Selhurst Park on the Saturday. Not only could he pass and shoot, but he ran and ran. Rumour had it he was first out of the ground at the final whistle and ran straight home.

Three days after the draw with Palace, Bowyer equalised against Watford at The Valley. And if a penalty miss against Huddersfield blotted his copybook, he soon came storming back with an extraordinary hat-trick against Wimbledon at Selhurst Park. The double-header with the Dons was a Coca Cola draw few had relished, but the sceptics again proved to be badly mistaken as the goals flew in at either end. In a see-saw first leg, Charlton trailed 1-0, led 2-1, trailed 3-2, led 5-3 and finally won 5-4. Only 3,717 had bothered to share the experience, meaning there was even less atmosphere than usual at Selhurst Park. But it was no surprise that the attendance climbed to almost 10,000 for the return. And for once, the second game lived up to expectations created by the first, with John Robinson eventually making it 3-3 in extra time to seal an 8-7 aggregate win.

In between had come another goal glut, this time at Ipswich Town where cult hero Carl Leaburn secured an historic hat-trick from the penalty spot in extra-time. Incredibly, all three of the towering target man's goals were scored with his feet. Charlton won 5-1, their biggest away victory for more than 30 years, although Ipswich did have the considerable excuse of losing their goalkeeper Craig Forrest following a second-half collision with Kim Grant.

Even though October failed to produce a League win until the trip to Luton on the final weekend, the Addicks' ambitions were now looking up. As well as Bowyer and Rufus, 20-year-old utility man Shaun Newton had recovered his best form after struggling the previous term. His right-side displays were good enough to keep Mark Robson on the sidelines for most of the season. On the left flank, meanwhile, intermittently at left or right back and ultimately central midfield, was the real revelation. So versatile was John Robinson that rumour had it he drove the team bus to away games and spent his days off in the box office selling tickets.

The one thing he definitely couldn't have done though is worked on the turnstiles. After all, he'd spent the best part of three years burdened by the reputation of predecessor Robert Lee, who'd provided endless programme editors with material by doing just that. Robinson started the season on the transfer list, but now the former Brighton winger was the first name on Curbishley's teamsheet. This transformation, in particular, was ascribed to the one-to-one approach of new first-team coach Les Reed, recruited from the FA and a key behind-the-scenes figure in the Addicks' transformation. Now his always consistent work-rate was allied to confidence in his own ability, Robinson exceeded everyone's expectations, to the extent that he eventually romped home with a massive majority in the Player of the Year poll.

It remained Charlton's weakness, however, that too many of their goals were being scored from midfield. After the glut came nine consecutive autumn games in which the Addicks failed to score more than once.

Previously prolific scorer David Whyte had made an indifferent start and then got injured, but hopes were high that his return would spark a real promotion challenge. Instead, he came back looking overweight and under-motivated. Despite scoring a crucial penalty at Grimsby, he failed even to hold on to his place in the side.

More significant, as it transpired, was the return of midfielder Paul Mortimer, who had missed the early season after snapping an Achilles tendon in the spring.

This painful injury deprived the Addicks of a key inspiration, but his importance was underlined in only his second substitute appearance. Just two minutes remained against Reading at The Valley, but it was enough for him to reach the byline and pull the ball back for Robinson to steer home the winner.

Significantly, it represented Charlton's first home win in eight attempts, a sequence which had seen them slide into mid-table. In the midst of that came a disappointing Coca Cola Cup exit in a Valley replay against Wolves. The other fly in the ointment was the fact that neighbours Millwall, popularly renamed the Spanners after said piece of hardware somehow found its way on to the Reading pitch during one of their games, were top of the First Division.

It has long been an unfathomable fact of SE London life that Charlton cannot beat Millwall, regardless of circumstances. A rare victory for the Addicks at Upton Park in '92 had been the first win for 14 years. So there was little cause for optimism on a snowy December night at the New Den, even once we were safely in the ground.

Hope flared briefly when Kim Grant put Charlton ahead, but within minutes Bowyer had responded to a carefully timed off-the-ball assault from Alex Rae with a pair of reckless challenges that saw him collect a pair of yellow cards. Then central defender Phil Chapple was carried off with a serious leg injury. Millwall briefly rallied. But the Lions still looked clueless on an increasingly treacherous-looking surface. And after Keith Stevens sportingly elbowed Jamie Stuart in the face to allow the referee to even the numbers up, an historic victory began to look very likely. Then the diving Kasey Keller decided to stop Robinson's long-range shot with his head and Grant tucked in the rebound to add a measure of security to the scoreline. The occasion was really sealed, however, by Mortimer, who danced delightedly round the leaden-footed home defence, even stumbling over and then recovering to beat his man again. By five minutes from time, the New Den was even emptier than usual.

Boxing Day saw Charlton go second with a late Nelson winner against Portsmouth. It was a position they would hold for two months and signalled the start of the most impressive phase of the season. FA Cup visitors Sheffield Wednesday were not just beaten but outclassed, while Barry Fry's Birmingham were routed again at St Andrews, even though they pulled back from 4-1 down to 4-3 in the closing stages. Home fans sought moronic retribution by stoning the Charlton coaches while the police were conveniently detained elsewhere. Or perhaps the locals were just upset about Greenwich getting the Millennium Exhibition instead of the NEC.

What worried us was the extent to which the season was shaping up as a repeat run of two years earlier, when a promising position had been squandered with a late season collapse after the diversion of an FA Cup run ending in sixth round defeat at Old Trafford. The parallels were uncanny. And although Mike Salmon tried to ruin the plot by dropping the ball into his own net in the fourth round against Brentford, substitute David Whyte appeared on cue with a perfectly placed free-kick winner to send us to Anfield.

Once Liverpool had finally been allowed to put Shrewsbury out of their misery we headed north in numbers, but the sense of occasion had been undermined by the delay and the fact that it was now a midweek game. Although always on top, the home side were strangely careless finishers and when Grant pulled a spectacular goal back in the closing minutes hope briefly flared. But the moment turned out to have significance only for the scorer. Five years after his first team debut, it proved to be the Ghanaian-born striker's last goal in Charlton colours because he was surprisingly sold to Luton in transfer deadline week.

In 1994 the fans' major criticism had been that no money was spent on the run-in to consolidate the team's promotion chances. This time Charlton moved for Millwall's Chris Malkin just days before the clubs were due to clash at The Valley. Malkin got as far as signing, but the deal then collapsed over doubts about an old knee problem. "Conspiracy!" cried the Spanners - or expletives to that effect - as Malkin sat out the SE London derby and Charlton completed their first double in the fixture since 1935. The last time it happened the teams didn't meet again for 30 years. Here's hoping!

Birmingham's Chris Whyte did make his debut that day after signing on a free transfer, and he was followed by Everton's Matt Jackson, who provided some much needed loan cover at right back. Finally, Curbishley signed Bradley Allen from QPR for £400,000. And when Allen scored on his debut to earn a 1-0 win at Norwich and leave Charlton still handily placed in third, things looked very hopeful. The manager himself predicted that only suspensions and injuries could deny the Addicks promotion. And did fate work overtime to prove him right!

In the event, Charlton won just once in their last nine games, failing even to score in the next six, but the miracle was that they managed to field a team all. Bowyer, in particular, appeared to be playing entirely from memory as tired young legs staggered towards the finishing line. Agonisingly, the Addicks slipped from third to fourth and fourth to fifth. Then it was down to sixth on the final day of the normal season, their lowest placing since December. But over the hill came the cavalry, in the unlikely shape of the Spanners, whose noble sacrifice prevented Ipswich pushing Charlton into seventh.

Our own play-off place secure, the Valley faithful showed proper respect by hanging on as one to hear the Lions' last rites from Huddersfield, where Portsmouth's victory sent them down.

And so to the play-offs. But Charlton were a spent force by now and Palace's victory in both legs was little surprise. After all, who were we to deny Claridge his date with destiny?

Fanzine Facts

Voice of The Valley first appeared in January '88, taking its name from legendary SE7 tannoy man Dick Neve, who was also a prominent local politician and Mayor of Greenwich. Although launched to spearhead the successful campaign for the club's return to its spiritual home, it has continued to flourish since this goal was finally achieved four years ago, and editor Rick Everitt shows little sign of shutting up.

WE ARE LEEDS

Leeds United

Miserable '95 to bloody awful '96. The year Eric Cantona rubbed Wilkinson's nose in it for the 100th (and hopefully last) time. No, it's not sour grapes; he is the best player in the country, but it was really no surprise that in a season in which he should never have played, the scum bum-licking press finally voted him Player of the Year. What do you expect from the same body of men who nominated Howard Wilkinson for England manager, then stood around bemused when the only ones in agreement were Wilkinson's own supporters?

So Manchester United won the Championship again, and commiserations are due all round. Apparently in a brilliant campaign they closed a twelve point gap, to win the League,

losing only six games along the way. We at Leeds know how that feels; after all we won the League four years ago, losing only four games along the way. Then again we didn't win it did we? Manchester United gave it to us, or so we're still being told. It's strange, but I still haven't heard anyone say Manchester United never won the League, Newcastle lost it... Anyway, enough of this petty moaning - on with the whinging.

Before the season started, curiously just as season tickets went on sale, we were apparently going to sign 'Tino Asprilla. Every source inside the club claimed he was coming over in a couple of days and was desperate to sign for Leeds. Three long months later, curiously just as the season tickets had all been sold, it all fell through, despite Bill Fotherby jetting all over the world to finalise the deal. Some months later when it was discovered what Newcastle were paying him, our now happily ex-chairman admitted that Leeds never even got as far as discussing terms with him. Never mind; instead we signed Paul Beesley, one of Sheffield United's lesser known, ageing reserves. Then came the mandatory declaration that "This is the strongest squad we've had here for many years."

Despite all this, the season couldn't have started better. Three straight wins, at West Ham (2-1), home to Liverpool (1-0) and Villa (2-0), AND Leeds were top of the League. When asked to comment on our fine start, the ever-enthusiastic Mr Wilkinson growled that three games wasn't a start, and to ask him again after ten. As you can imagine, with that kind of motivation, as if to prove a point, the season went rapidly downhill from then on.

The last ounces of optimism were drying up faster than a Yorkshire reservoir when we went to Monaco. Ah yes, that glorious night amongst the jet-set in Monte Carlo, when we frightened Europe with a 3-0 win over one of the UEFA Cup favourites. My God, we fooled them didn't we? Next round we depended on our ever-reliable defence and PSV put five past us at home. In five weeks we went from Britain's best performers to Britain's biggest embarrassment.

Then again there was always Tony Yeboah, the wonderful Tony Yeboah. The world thought he'd scored the best ever goal against Liverpool, but Tony knew better. He equalled it in Monaco, then a couple of games later he beat it in front of the cameras on Match of the Day against Wimbledon. He'd said better would come, and he was right...

November brought a dearly beloved old friend to Elland Road with his new team. Changing his club certainly hadn't altered his playing style. Anyway even though we didn't play particularly well, we beat Chelsea one nil.

Soon it was back to normal - beaten at home by struggling Manchester City. Then a lucky home draw against struggling Wimbledon. After that a trip to Wilko's Alma-Mater and a very poor, struggling Sheffield Wednesday put six past us. By now we had Tomas Brolin. You know - the one, the little Swedish genius who'd just completed five very good years in Italy. Little did we know he was doomed to suffer the same fate as a certain French genius a few years back.

At this point, I would like to declare that, for the first time since I was five, I believed in Father Christmas. Out of the blue, on Christmas Eve, we murdered THEM. Cantona and all. They were squabbling amongst themselves as we played them off the park. Little did we realise that a measly four months later we would consider losing only 1-0 at Old Trafford a high point. A further good measure of how we felt about the season's performances was that Richard Jobson, who only played in 12 games, would come third in the supporters club Player of the Year.

Just as the winter of our discontent was turning into the spring of our outrage, it became clear that we were blundering our way to Wembley in the Coca Cola Cup. We were also doing very well in the FA Cup. Don't let a Wembley appearance and a quarter final fool you; the first decent teams we played in both competitions wiped the floor with us. When people wondered why we were calling for Wilkinson's head at Wembley, they didn't realise that we'd struggled in every round to beat the likes of: Notts County, Derby, Port Vale, Reading, Birmingham and Blackburn by the odd goal. "What about Derby and Blackburn?" you may ask. Well, at the time Derby were in the Endsleigh relegation zone and Blackburn hadn't won away all season. Notts County and Port Vale both held us at Elland Road and after going a goal behind, it took very late winners against the run of play to beat them both. For most of us, losing at Wembley was not the beginning of our disillusionment; it was the last straw. I can't believe a manager has ever had to take so much stick at a Cup Final. Then again, I can't remember such a passionless, boring, unambitious performance either.

But if anything, our League form was even worse. All three relegated teams, QPR, Bolton and Manchester City got their first away wins at Elland Road. Here's an example of the 'ambition' which was now overwhelming our board and manager: everybody knew that come January, Tony Yeboah and Phil Masinga would be away for a month in South Africa. David White had already been sold, Jamie Forrester had been given away and Brian Deane was hovering on the brink of suspension. At this most opportune of moments (mid-December actually), it was deemed appropriate to sell the best covering striker at the club. Noel Whelan went on to save Coventry's season and maybe even Ron Atkinson's job. The folly of the sale was matched only by the timing.

Then something really bizarre happened. If I wasn't used to the transfer dealings of Howard Wilkinson I would never have believed it . Three years earlier we'd sold a striker who was well past his sell-by date. Since then he'd been rejected by Portsmouth, West Ham and most recently Ipswich. Now, after appearing just twice all season for the Suffolk outfit, Lee Chapman was brought back on loan and put straight into the side. At this point I should remind you that Tomas Brolin could hardly get a game. OK, so he'd only started five times for Parma, plus a couple of internationals. Yeah, he was a touch short of match practice. So what did Wilkinson do to get a world-class player back to his England-beating best? Kept him on the bench, of course!

Funnily enough, Lee Chapman was sent off in his first game, and with only ten men we beat West Ham 2-0. Both goals came from Brolin, before Wilkinson decided he was getting far too popular and, to the anger and amazement of the crowd, took him off with 15 minutes to go. That day Brolin was the best man on the pitch, and far from tiring, he was improving as the game progressed. Tomas Brolin was hardly seen again until his confidence and interest in Leeds United were crushed. Much later the downtrodden and disheartened Swede was played a couple of times, but out of position. It looked like some of the other Leeds 'professionals' were deliberately avoiding giving him the ball. Clearly, somebody had taken a lot of stick over Brolin and somebody wanted to say "told you so."

At Anfield the sprightly Lee Chapman was played alone against Liverpool's powerful defence, with only his zimmer frame for support. Gary Kelly was sent off and even though we hadn't played badly up to then, we defended abysmally and lost 5-0.

Anyone who saw us last year could see we couldn't defend, yet we stuck to a 'sit back and defend' policy all season. As attendances fell and the shouts for the manager's head grew, still nothing changed. The bare fact remains that we lost ten of our last 13 games. This should have been the title/European run-in that we'd been promised. Instead, it was form which would have shamed the relegated teams. Thank God for those three wins at the beginning, and more to the point for Tony Yeboah's early season form, otherwise relegation would surely have been here by Easter.

Fanzine Facts

We Are Leeds began life in 1992 as a fanzine/newsletter exclusive to members of the Knaresborough branch of the LUSC. Due to outside commitments, the original editor Graham Spink was forced to resign. Main contributor Steve Abbot took over and turned *We Are Leeds* into a regular fanzine for the start of the '95-96 season. Now on issue nine, Steve, assisted by Chrissie Colman, still does most of the writing, organising and selling, though one or two casual contributors are now surfacing. "Having to compete with three well established fanzines, *We Are Leeds* is gradually making headway" comments Steve, adding that the fanzine takes its name "from the only song Leeds fans seem to chant these days."

WHAT A LOAD OF COBBLERS

Northampton Town

If you had asked any Cobblers fan at the start of the season for their hopes and aspirations for the coming campaign, the vast majority would have settled for a mid-table position. And so it came to pass. However after years of financial instability and basement football, any glimmer of hope was instantly seized upon, and come the season's end a number of fans were disgruntled that a play-off chance had been spurned. They must have known in their heart of hearts that we weren't good enough to go up, even via the play-offs, and a season of consolidation under Ian Atkins can only (hopefully) lay the foundations for next year.

But back to the beginning. For the first time in living memory, we

What A Load Of Cobblers !!
An Alternative View Of Northampton Town FC

£1

Stewards Introduce New Method of Persuasion to get North Standers To Sit Down

looked forward to true home games; farewell County Ground and Northants CCC, hello a full season at Sixfields. But the fixture list computer must have had it in for the Cobblers. Our opening match was against Bury. The Shakers had beaten us 5-0 - twice - in the later months of the previous season. Cobblers were unable to field new £35,000 signing Jason White (from Scarboro) due to suspension, and in front of a decidedly average crowd of 4,500 we gained a modicum of revenge by thrashing Bury 4-1. A visit to the much improved Hawthorns followed in the Fizzy Pop Cup, and a thoroughly justified draw with over 1,000 Cobblers travelling to see it. Four days later and we were TOP (well second on goals scored, but it felt good anyway) thanks to a Dean Peer goal at Cardiff. Manager Ian Atkins had faith in the midfielder, suggesting he would score quite a few goals; indeed, 'Wigan' (Wigan Pier - gedditt? Oh well, suit yourselves) added to his tally in the second leg against West Brom. Trouble was, we were 4-1 down at the time. It was to be his last goal of the season, the 'Wigan' tag was dropped and he became known as 'Dissa' instead. But he just wouldn't (disappear, that is), as Atkins saw something in him that no-one else could.

An exciting 3-3 draw at Sixfields with Mansfield (from 3-1 down) followed, and nose bleed was definitely setting in; we just weren't used to being so high up. Hartlepool ended our best League start for years; the only consolation was that for once the weather was actually quite mild (anything above freezing is T-shirt weather up there). A taste of things to come, however, materialised in that game, i.e. our manager's desire to bore the pants off everyone by getting 11 men behind the ball, relying on the quick break. It was to prove a problem as the season wore on; the defence could only take so much pressure, and consequently we conceded several late goals, including one on that balmy night on the North East Riviera.

A boring draw with Exeter followed. What should have been a good day was spoiled by some West Country morons who clearly hadn't been at the affable previous meeting between the clubs, when it seemed likely to be Exeter's swansong. Leyton Orient were next at Sixfields. No problem; they hadn't won away from home for 42 games and were below us in the table. We'd only lost once in the League, and a win would see us back into second place. No problem. We lost. I think everyone knew we'd lose; we always do against teams with that sort of record. What I couldn't fathom out was how Orient failed to win again away all season. They were, on the night, the best footballing side we've seen at Northampton. That left us in seventh position, never to climb back to those dizzy heights again. Two weeks later we were even more despondent, when Torquay beat us 3-0. OK, they did have Mr Clive Wilkes on their side, but, I mean, *Torquay*, and *3-0...*

Next came a great 3-0 victory over local rivals Cambridge (although I can't get worked up about it as a 'derby', the only local rivals for both us and them are Peterborough; still, it's fun to hear both sets of fans singing "We hate Peterborough"). Unfortunately the game was marred by more violence, as a group of Cambridge dickheads decided to try and rearrange the decor in the local watering hole. It was to be our last League win for two months as we slumped to 18th in the table; once more we were looking at the points gap between us and those below us, especially as Lincoln had started to win. However, during this spell we had progressed to the knock-out stage of the AWS, and actually reached the second round of the FA Cup, courtesy of non-league Hayes. They also brought trouble with them, but it was easy to spot the real Hayes fans from the 'hangers-on'. The real fans carried a flask in a plastic bag and wore bobble hats, not to mention a bemused look as some neanderthal looking types with Union Jack tattoos and extremely short hair chanted "We are A's." They too re-arranged the decor in another local hostelry.

We were drawn away to Oxford in the next round, and a totally spineless performance saw hopes of a money-spinning trip in the next draw disappear. Mind you, the reward would have been a home tie with Millwall. Perhaps losing at Oxford was not so bad after all.

A good day out in London with a 3-1 win at Fulham showed what the team was capable of if the manager had the bottle to let the players attack, instead of sitting back on a 0-0 and inviting the opposition to come at us. This negative attitude was reflected in the falling crowds, with gates hovering around the 4,000 mark, 1,000 less than last year. We even managed an all-time Sixfields low of 3,090 for the visit of Rochdale; this on the back of a run of only one defeat in eight League games. Mind you that was a defeat at Orient, where we became the first team they had done the double over since the first war, or something like that. The run also included our own double over Bury, albeit by a solitary Jason White goal, nevertheless it was so sweet after last year's 5-0 drubbings.

Four days later saw one of the most exciting games at our newish and still magnificent stadium. Doncaster were the visitors, and at half past two the match was in severe doubt; the heavens had opened and the pitch was awash. Fortunately the rain stopped and for once a sensible referee (Mr J. Brandwood) checked the weather forecast, allowed the pitch to be forked to help the drainage, and delayed kick-off until 3.25. The only drawback was the bars had already closed 40 minutes earlier! But what a great game followed amongst the puddles - Cobblers went 2-0 up early on and were coasting. Then Doncaster got a penalty - Woodman saved it. Five minutes later they got another - and scored. Two-one at half time. A few minutes after the restart, it was 2-2, and mid-way through the half Doncaster's comeback was complete as they took the lead. The rest of the game saw Cobblers camped in Donny's penalty area, but couldn't find a way through until, in the last minute, the ref spotted a handball in the box. Leading scorer Jason White hammered home the penalty to end a brilliant game which had seen 28 shots, 17 corners and three penalties (for the Stattos out there).

By now we were comfortably in mid-table, but hopes of a play-off place still dangled tantalisingly thanks to wins over Exeter, Scarborough and Chester. However, defeats to fast-improving Hereford and Plymouth more or less put paid to those hopes, the Plymouth game encapsulating Atkins' tactics: ten men behind the ball (including Garry Thompson), hoping Jason White would snatch something on the break, which he nearly did, hitting the post mid-way through the second half. Plymouth's pressure told in the end though, and a scrappy 83rd minute goal won it for the Division's big spenders. (Another Statto note: we conceded 44 League goals all season, 12 of those - over a quarter - coming in the last ten minutes).

With play-off hopes realistically ended following our home defeat to Scunthorpe, the season still had some life in it. At Champions-elect Preston, where we had never won in 11 attempts, we thrashed them. Neil 'Larry' Grayson grabbed his second hat-trick of the season as 11,000 Lancastrians in party mood were well and truly silenced (including the bloody drummers). That elusive play-off place was still mathematically possible, but we all *knew*; well most of us did anyway. It was finally confirmed at Chester, as the home side beat us 1-0, with, yes you've guessed, a last-minute winner.

The season had one final twist though. Over 1,000 of us travelled to Wigan for the last game. They needed a win to be certain of the fourth play off place and were soon in the driving seat with an early goal. But Cobblers were destined to spoil another party as Ian Sampson equalised, and with a few minutes left in the game, Jason White rose from the bench to grab the winner. So it's back to Springfield Park again next season and Holts at £1 a pint!

All in all, then, a satisfactory season, given our aspirations at the outset. We won almost as many away games as we had done in our Championship-winning season of '86-87, but results at home let us down. Despite an upturn in our League position gates decreased (perhaps Groundhoppers had 'done Sixfields' now), but at times the football was just so dull. We showed we could play in our wins over Bury, Cambridge, Fulham and Wigan on that last Saturday, but there were many dire performances, notably home and away against Barnet. We still have no money, so new signings will rely on 'frees', but hopefully the long nightmare is over and a new dawn is approaching. Watch this space...

Fanzine Facts

WALOC's first appearance was at Northampton's opening game of the '88-89 season. It now bulges with 48 pages, and this year will see its 50th issue. Editor Rob Marshall now has 15-16 regular contributors, the longest standing of whom are Quentin Jones and 'Abraham Anstruther'.

WHEN SKIES ARE GREY

Everton

Upwards and Onwards

Summer '95 saw most blues basking in the ridiculously hot weather and the glory of the club's fairytale Wembley triumph on that never-to-be-forgotten tear-strewn, balmy May afternoon. Indeed, the fans responded with an unparalleled level of season ticket madness, albeit aided by a canny direct debit scheme initiated by the club's new lean and mean commercial department.

Excitement reached fever pitch (oh shite, I promised I wouldn't namecheck that loathsome, middle class, angst ridden fuckin' nonsense) with the signing of the mercurial Andrei Kanchelskis from United; season ticket sales topped the 25,000 mark.

With Andrei and his carbon copy Anders providing the ammunition for the rampaging Duncan 'animal' Ferguson, only blue skies were forecast. Unfortunately, the weather was soon to turn very nasty.

The pre-season games got underway with Neville Southall's richly deserved testimonial against Celtic, and the bizarre spectacle of 8,000 comedy drunken Scotsmen in self-parody. Kanchelskis was introduced to the crowd in a jacket that even Barry Venison might have thought twice about, and we all sat back and waited for his work permit to come through. The following Sunday, news broke of a hitch surrounding the Kanchelskis deal. The cynics amongst us immediately rounded on our blustering board who had made a drama of previous transfer deals involving the likes of Ferguson, Barrett and Short. However the truth soon became apparent as Man U's incompetent and despicable conduct was revealed. For three weeks the transfer hung in the balance as United tried to worm more money out of the Goodison coffers and Kanchelskis' hard-up Russian club. Everton stood firm. Meanwhile, the FA did their best Iscariot impression. Eventually when the Mancs realised they were getting nowhere, they played ball, but not before Andrei missed the deadline for the first two Euro rounds.

Back on the pitch, the team started slowly, with only the newly shorn Anders Limpar displaying any form. Indeed, as soon as Anders ditched his Scandinavian Ah Ha head for a Paddock suede, he showed possibly the best form of his Everton career. Unfortunately all was not well elsewhere. Duncan Ferguson was patently unfit, and after three games departed for a groin operation. The rest played like the near-relegation duffers of 12 months previous. Off the pitch, fans arriving at the ground for the early games were greeted by some seven foot foam-filled fucker in an Everton kit, purporting to be the club mascot. Outrageously this embarrassment was named Dixie after our 1920's legend. Not only was the supposition an insult to a true legend, but it was given a nickname that Bill Dean himself despised. Ultimately, and after a long campaign (not least within the pages of WSAG), 'Dixie' was sacrificed at the end of the season.

Other causes for concern were the launch of Everton chocolate and the fact that many long-standing season ticket holders found their seats transformed into executive lounges. All of these issues were the subject of lively debate. Some fans argued that they were needed to help generate the cash to keep the club up there with the Liverpools and Man Utds, whilst others thought that the heart and soul was being ripped out of the place. What everyone agreed on was that the commercial department had needed its revamp, and the powers that be had definitely got it right with the opening of the unique and impressive souvenir shop, the building design being based on the famous Everton tower (off the badge) which still stands today in Everton Park.

Back to playing matters, and the first embarrassing Cup defeat of the season. Millwall, then riding high in the first, turned a 2-0 deficit with half an hour to go into an amazing 4-2 extra time victory. Although being pegged back by a more than dubious penalty, the Everton players that night showed a distinct lack of character.

By the end of October, Europe had been and gone and Duncan Ferguson was slopping out. Obviously the case should've never got to court when compared to other on-field misdemeanours, but once it did, old Fergie was only going one way. Down.

The turning point probably came with a narrow 1-0 Sky victory over the fallen Champions Blackburn in early November. With Graham Stuart buzzing up front and Kanchelskis back after his injury (sustained inevitably against Man United), prospects looked a little better.

However, even the bluest noses were not over-confident for the Anfield derby. With the catwalk ponces banging in the goals left right and centre and Liverpool desperate to put poor recent derby results behind them, things looked ominous. November 18th was the day Andrei Kanchelskis became a Goodison hero. Aided by the sexy Limpar, the speedy soviet (he'll always be a soviet to me) tore the arse out of the red defence. Two-one was the final score, but Liverpool were extremely flattered by this. We obviously needed this result, an unbeaten run ensued and within a couple of weeks DF was back to a hero's reception. Everton and Evertonians were hammered in the media for the way in which they welcomed the big man back, but what were we supposed to do, have him publicly flogged in the centre circle?

Christmas was celebrated with a 4-0 eclipse of the then high-flying 'Boro, plus a hard fought victory over Leeds, whilst Ferguson welcomed in the new year with two first half goals to sink the Dons at Selhurst. Next it was back to the Cups and more humiliation. Stockport County, compete with that knob with the Gazza head, were unlucky to leave Goodison needing a replay, and in the return they took us all the way before John Ebbrell scored an improbable 25 yarder to edge us through. In the League, Arsenal was the latest in an impressive list of away scalps, before we had to face a lower League outfit again in the Cup. Port Vale was a mirror image of the Stockport game, when with seconds left Dunc looked to have got us out of jail (boom-boom). However, a looping, deflected Ian Bogie effort seconds later took us to another replay. Why is it that lower League clubs still think it's 1985 whenever they play one of the big boys? The Potteries cavemen were no exception, and there were numerous altercations between weary blues and badly dressed midlanders, before and after both games.

Valentine's Day brought possibly the worst Everton performance for many a year when Vale in the replay triumphed with a scandalous 2-1 scoreline; four or five would have been a more realistic reflection, the majority of the Everton team playing like their tea had been laced with Tomazepam. The 7,000 blues contingent were rightly outraged. A furious Joe Royle promised changes, and in the next few games gave youth its chance. Jon O'Connor and 17 year old reserve striking sensation Michael Rush were given debuts, whilst the mercurial Tony Grant got an extended run. Like a young Le Tissier, Grantona (crap nickname alert) exudes class and is going to be massive; he's a blue as well, a true hero in the making.

However, the true star of the run-in was undoubtedly Kanchelskis, with an unbelievable run of form from March onwards. Two particular performances at Blackburn and Wednesday will live long in the memory. Sixteen goals made him the top scorer and outlined why he got so much shit off the Man U fans when they realised that he didn't want to play for them anymore. Andrei is a true world star, and whatever happens in the future it's been a pleasure to see him in blue. That late season surge put us within five minutes of Europe. Unfortunately, Arsenal pissed on our strawberries.

Still, sixth place after three or four relegation struggles marked significant progress, and with one or two summer additions, Everton will once again be a major force. Joe Royle continues to mix witty and thought-provoking after-match comments with managerial genius. His apparent Indian sign over the red heathens has further endeared him to blues fans. It's just a shame that the Cup form was so iffy; speaking of which, the season's final act gave everyone in the blue half of this city the chance to be a Manc for the day, with the pure humour of Eric Cantona's late Wembley strike. Most blues fans are mystified by the national hatred of United. Why hate them when Liverpool are around? We've never really had any problems with the Mancs and besides, we've got a good record of stuffing them when it matters, something we've been doing to Liverpool over the past couple of years. What a lovely thought.

Fanzine Facts

Phil Redmond and Graham Ennis have been producing **WSAG** since 1991, although the 'zine was first introduced to the Goodison faithful by Chris Collins as early as 1988. This year, **WSAG** continues to go from strength to strength, with more readers, more contributors and now better software to boot, according to Phil. But he adds; "There's no truth in the rumour that Peter Johnson's been bankrolling us!"

WHEN YOU'RE SMILING

Leicester City

Plans are well under way for a fantastic new theme park to be built in the East Midlands. It will have the biggest rollercoaster ride in the world, giving the highest peaks and the lowest troughs; it will make you feel sick with exhilaration, and then nauseated with horror; it'll turn you inside out, take every penny you own and leave you screaming for more. There'll be plenty of Mickey Mouse comic characters wandering about for your amusement and entertainment as well. The only draw-back will be that you'll have to cram it all into one visit. The venue? Filbert Street. Its name? 'LeicesterCityLand' was one suggestion. But it's far more likely to be called 'WhatTheFuck'sGoing-OnLand'!

It's hard not to sound dramatic when you're a Leicester City fan, but it's true to say that most seasons send your emotions spinning as we lurch along the tight-rope separating 'glory' (used relatively!) and disaster. This season more than any other on record has left us completely breathless and exhausted by its sheer extremes. And as for that annual day-trip to Wembley? It left us not so much 'high' as friggin' 'heavenly'!

But that all seemed a long way distant when we kicked off in August. Our first game was our usual victory away at Sunderland, notable for two factors: (1) it was our first on our travels since last January (at Maine Road), and (2) our last-minute Aussie signing, Steve Corica, burst on the scene with a blistering debut goal. The curtain-raiser at Filbert Street was to set a home pattern which would be duplicated with alarming frequency. In our own half we passed the ball around like Champions. We looked calm. We looked collected. And we were 3-0 down in under 32 minutes! So what had happened to our defence? Precisely nothing. It was virtually the same shower who'd helped our speedy exit from the Premiership the previous season. The second half saw a mini-revival, but it was shockingly late. A Gary Parker penalty for a more than dubious foul on Steve Walsh sparked off frenzy in the Kop. Walsh's second contribution followed shortly afterwards - chipping into an empty net when Stoke weren't watching. We were baying for an equaliser - hammering on fixtures and fittings... everything. But it wouldn't come, and a 3-2 scoreline stood. And not for the last time that season.

A pathetic draw against Luton left us with no hint of the delights to come, but a run of four straight wins powered City to the top of the League. Portsmouth found themselves 4-1 down at half-time through a Iwan Roberts hat-trick, Corica also impressing greatly. This, as it happens, was to be our most convincing home performance for eight months. Then it was Wolves. There was a supposed 'revolution' going on at Molineux; favourites for easy promotion under Graham Taylor, the crowds were pouring in to see the 'delights' of De Wolf and Steve Bull. Yet, true to form, they were struggling. But even though we were managing to outclass everyone in the Division for 45 minutes, we still weren't convinced that Whitlow's blazing strike would be enough. Wolves, though, had been battered out of midfield and chose route one (to Bull and Goodman) to no effect at all. It was a sweet victory against the cocky West Midlanders. But if we hated them then, it was *nothing* compared to the venom reserved for Wolves now!

Derby away was a joy to behold. In front of Central's TV cameras, Kevin Poole saved a second minute penalty, Iwan got himself sent-off, Julian Joachim scored his final League goal (as it turned out) for City and we went home happy. Derby had looked totally inept, and were well rooted in the bottom half of the table (where they belong), and oh, how we taunted the sheep-shaggers with rousing (and very wet) choruses of "Derby are going nowhere!", which, by and large, they seemed to agree with. The day's events had really annoyed the nazi skinheads above us, and even more infuriated the dickheads who'd been gesturing to the effect that we were about to get our throats cut... NOT! Walking away from the Baseball Ground, the pitiful shaggers were looking even more 'sheepish' than usual. "Did you cry at WEMB-ERR-LEY! AAHHHHHHHHH!!"

After four wins on the trot, we were top of the table. But the engine was beginning to stutter as the Gary Parker-inspired team began to crack - most noticeably at home. Humiliated by Southend 3-1, and several bore-draws later, it was obvious all was not well. Without Aussie ace Corica (now sidelined with a broken leg), if Parker wasn't on top form, then we were nothing.

Scrambled away draws and some magnificent away wins, such as Emile's late winner at Norwich and the glorious second half against Sheffield Utd, kept us on course. But our home form became more and more suspect, until eventually we surrendered the top spot. To whom? Millwall!

Looking back at those 'glorious' early days objectively, it doesn't seem so marvellous. But when the football was going well, it was fantastic. It was just that a majority of City fans probably only saw a glimpse of it due to our appalling home form. We were sliding steadily downhill, although November 5th, which marked the debut of our magnificent Swedish international defender Pontus Kamaark, saw fireworks of a different type at West Brom. In the best single 45 minute display of football from a City side I have ever seen, Pontus strode around like a God - a playmaker, attacker, and a supreme defender in one package. Gary Parker also rose to the occasion and we opened up West Brom almost at will. Iwan Roberts blasted a goal from distance following some beautiful build-up play. And then Scott Taylor took over, scoring two peaches whilst we basked in the glory of a world-beating side. Well, for half a game anyway! The Baggies wouldn't roll over and die though; after all, they could have gone top themselves. They scrambled two goals and made us sweat (even in the freezing Brummie gale!), but not even our lanky Aussie debutante goalie could conspire to lose this one for us. Also nice to hear some serious humble pie being eaten by Jimmy 'tosser' Greaves!

However things took a sharp turn for the worse against Bolton in the home replay of the Coca Cola Cup third round. Some more stunning passing football, but this time Zeljko Kalac was determined to stamp his mark on the game. In a goalkeeping display about as secure as a Group Four detainee on a pub crawl, he committed three whacking great HUMUNGOUS mistakes which ensured our usual early exit from the competition. But more importantly, our star right back was stretchered off with a serious knee injury. One hundred and fifty minutes of joyous football, and that was it for the season... oh, apart from 15 seconds of a reserve game at Grimsby (his 'comeback') when he collapsed under the weight of his own body!

By late November, our first away defeat had crushed any myths of invincibility, and wild rumours were flying about linking Mark McGhee with the vacancy created at Wolves. Surely not. Within the week, he and his entire backroom staff had buggered off! *Déjà vu*, City?!

We were unanimous in our disgust with McGhee's treachery, but how come LCFC can never sack their managers; they all walk out first! Fingers pointed in all directions. It was a city in mourning, and mostly 'cos McJudas had persuaded us that we WOULD achieve success under him - even though at the time we quite clearly weren't going to. Even mild, moderate Cityites began to doubt our board's man-management! Our season looked to be over before Xmas: a promising beginning, a slight slip in form, and the manager buggers off and leaves us in the sh*t!

Norwich at home on December 17th was of great significance. First, Martin O'Neill had quit Norwich that morning. Second, the game itself - a staggering fight-back from two down - "Are you watching Mark McGhee?" Glorious. Third, it was our first victory in over a month... and was to be our last for another two!

Martin O'Neill was swiftly appointed, and at least we seemed to have 'got our man' (at the third attempt!). The board can't keep 'em - but they certainly pick 'em!

His first match saw Iwan and Walshy force a draw at Grimsby. The Xmas programme was decimated by freezing weather (shame no one told me and my mate as we'd travelled 45 miles down the M1 early on Boxing Day morning to find out it'd been frozen off! Gits!). Disappointing results, including a disastrous five goal drubbing in the away replay of the F**k All Cup at Maine Road, showed us that we were not yet at a dawning of a new era.

So, all did not bode well for our big game of the season: away at McJudas' W**ky Wanderers. Martin O'Neill hadn't seen us win a game, and we'd forgotten what it felt like! But aaghh! Revenge was sweet! The beast of McJudas was slain.

It should also be noted that McGhee had bought our Aussie starlet, Steve Corica, for a paltry £1.1m. At the time, we had stood aghast - blasphemy! "I'm gonna sign someone much better" said O'Neill. He was on about Neil Lennon from Crewe, and we all scoffed. It wasn't long before we realised O'Neill was right. Lennon was immediately impressive, especially in the often extremely violent clash (both on and off the pitch) against Derby - fighting, battling, tackling-back, ball-winning and skilfully distributing.

And we were soon to be introduced to another battler, Steve Claridge. What an impact he was to have! (More of that later). Meanwhile, an Emile double strike staved off a riot, as we clinched a 2-1 home win over Grimsby - our first for nearly three months. Claridge and Lennon both looked superb, but Grimsby were the worst side I'd seen at Filbo this season, apart from us!

Our inconsistency and comparative lack of activity in the transfer market had got the Blue Army riled. Years of under-investment were taking their toll, on top of which a row between O'Neill and City's play-making hero Gary Parker had led to a thrown cup of tea, after which Gary was dropped and stripped of the captaincy (although he was now injured too). Rowdy protests followed a crap performance in a 2-0 defeat against a lacklustre Sheffield United. Chairman Martin George was in Barbados at the time, so O'Neill caught a lot of the flak.

Following a couple of unlikely victories, there were also some hard-fought draws and unlucky reverses. All seemed lost. But then 'Super Stevey Claridge' destroyed Oldham, joined with Steve Walsh and Emile to kill-off Huddersfield, combined with Heskey and Lennon to murder Birmingham... and suddenly we were within spitting distance of the play-offs. Ipswich cocked-up, new boy Muzzy Izzet scored a much-deserved winner and we were there!

Stoke were hard to break down in the home play-off leg, and we barely created a chance. They had two within five seconds and Kevin Poole saved 'em both! Nil-nil. The Stoke fans and almost every bugger in the land thought they'd got it in the bag. Gary Parker was welcomed back to the fold for that away second leg, and not only did he murder them in midfield, but pulverised the back of the net with a superb half-volley! Yet again, it should have been more. But after the season we've had, that'd do!

Our big day. And even with an early kick-off, several hours pre-match drinking ensured my memory of the final is sketchy. Just total midfield domination, a soft Palace goal, more domination but few chances. More of the same in the second half, then two Palace chances (way off in the distance) followed by more City dominance, a couple of our own chances, a crippling Walshy challenge that put Hopkins out of the game, and more domination. Then Muzzy through... brought down... PENALTY!... Gary 'F***ing Hero' Parker... SCORES!! Walshy header... off the line! Full-time. Extra time consisted of Lennon's superb tackling back, more domination, a couple of half-chances either way, more domination, Muzzy Izzet's excellent late challenge on new sub Simon Rodger, which left him as walking wounded for the rest of the game, more domination, Walsh off, Hill on, penalties looming... Kalac on, Poole OFF!, Parker - long free kick... Watts knock-down... Claridge half-volley... IT'S THERE!! BLLLLOOOOOOO ARRRMMEEEEEE!!

After the game consisted of dodgy chips on Wembley Way, a skinful on the M1, more domination... of the bar back in Leicester. "Martin O'Neill's Blue Army!" indeed. But for how long this time, eh? "Super, Super Steve...!"

PS We're only in the Premiership to piss Derby off! Oh, and for three months of basking in summer glory! "Are you watching, are you watching, ARE YOU WATCHING MARK McGHEE...?!!" And bloody hell! Things are even beginning to shift in City's boardroom! Who knows - they might even be thinking of keeping the City up!

Fanzine Facts

When You're Smiling (previously Filbo Fever!) was originally kicked off by the organisers of Leicester City's anti-racist group, Foxes against Racism, during the summer of '93. Written after closing time by the FAR crew, the current editorial staff are Geoff, Tom and recent returnee Jock Lobster. WYS was re-named after the golden oldie which has found its way into the Filbert Street hymn-book .

WHERE WERE YOU AT THE SHAY?

Bury

"When we win promotion, this is what we'll sing."

Let us take you on a musical ride through a topsy turvey Bury season. A season which was constantly on the edge, a season which threatened disappointment even beyond the final whistle on the last day. Before this though, cast your mind back to those balmy days of August.

"Go now."

The optimistic convoy, still wearing its Wembley colours and smiles, rolled into Sixfields confident of starting the campaign with a stuffing of the Cobblers (who had been beaten 5-0 home and away last year). The tone of the early season was set though, as the Shakers were trounced 4-1 and declared 'tactically inept' by one local sports reporter. Trouble immediately began to rack up and it took a half time rollicking (followed by the remainder of half time back on the pitch) to gee them up to a first win at Hereford two weeks later. Not even this could lift the side, still suffering from post-Wembley blues and a shocking 5-0 home reverse by 'big nose' Warnock's Plymouth (who had barely got a point before then). This resulted in Mike Walsh being handed the club revolver and pointed into the woods. Walsh was announced as 'having left by mutual consent' but the rumours of a Machiavellian plot surfaced instantly. The hideous Sam Ellis had been sacked by Lincoln only an hour later. Stan Ternent (Walsh's assistant) took over as caretaker, but Ellis, who had endeared himself to the faithful by walking out in November '90 with the club on the edge of extinction, was suddenly in the running...

WHERE WERE YOU AT THE SHAY?

Rochdale revival has the whole town buzzing.

"Sammy Mac, when are you coming back?"

Ternent was immediately installed as favourite, despite former hero Sammy McIlroy being the fans' choice. On the pitch he was helped by revenge being completed over Wembley victors Chesterfield in the Coke Cup (which just made the play-off defeat harder to take, we are *surely* better than the Spireites) and then another away win at Wigan. But still we couldn't win at home.

That was until Sheffield United came to Gigg defending a 2-1 lead, and by far the best performance of the early season saw the Blades leave well beaten 4-2, out of the Cup and Dave Bassett mumbling about "Lack of application." At last a home League win followed but our form still wasn't consistent.

"When the rain comes, they run and hide their heads. They might as well be dead."

The reward (?) for beating United was a trip to Royal Berkshire and Reading, easily the worst ground in the top three Divisions. A downpour before the game didn't dampen our spirits, since on current form the Royals were probably as bad as we were. The Shakers went 2-0 up; fine goals and still the rain came down. Just before half time, as the Reading players bleated to the referee about the pitch getting waterlogged, he took them off to allow the pitch to be forked. A single geriatric with a rusty Spear & Jackson gave the pitch a token prod before the ref (from Sheffield, no doubt a Blade) abandoned the game. Of course we lost the rematch to a last minute goal. Hey-Ho.

"Hello Hello, I'm back again."

Former Stags hero Phil Stant's return was eagerly awaited in Mansfield (it's that kind of town). For the Shakers fans it was a chance to get the Reading robbery out of our systems, if the lads would oblige. At 1-0 down it wasn't looking promising, then Sergeant Stant began his amazing day. Equaliser before half time , then goals three, four and five left player and supporters in a state of delirium. Even the Stag's fans gave him a standing ovation (the only thing that they had to cheer all season).

"You're an embarrassment."

Blyth Spartans in the Cup. A non-league team at home is usually a no-win situation, and it certainly was for us. The Shakers had the sort of day that you always have when the telly cameras are in town, and once usually dependable goalie Gary Kelly had gifted them the first goal the upset was always on. A second goal (so far offside that linesman and defenders all missed him) gave them the game, and gave weeks worth of ammunition to people who don't go to watch Man U but claim to be fans. Oh and by the way, Sam Ellis was back as Ternent's assistant. Discontent rumbled on.

"Welcome to the cheap seats."

Following the disaster of Blyth, and the public relations nightmare of the Ellis appointment, the club decided on a sweetener of cheap prices for a few games around Christmas. The experiment worked with larger than usual crowds for the Exeter and Colchester games, and the team saying that the extra backing was noticeable. This is surely a way forward for the lower divisions: cheaper prices means bigger and better support. It was around the time of the improved relations between club and fans that the season really kicked into gear.

"I'm a loser baby, so why don't you kill me."

John Beck, king of the kick and rush and tactics of unsettlement and intimidation, had applied for the Shakers job in September; well he finally made it to Gigg in February, but as Lincoln manager. Things by now were greatly improved, the lads were playing some good stuff and were moving into the play-off area. For once this season almost everything went right and Beck and his boys were beaten out of sight. The 7-1 goal-fest was the biggest win for 15 years and could have possibly have been bigger but for the woodwork a couple of times late on.

"Aint no stoppin' us now."

At 2-0 down at Cambridge, with the influential Tony Rigby carried off, you wouldn't have given us a hope. But the belief and team spirit that was bonding started to show its worth. So many times in the second half of the season the lads responded to adversity with a terrific performance and (for me) this was the best. After the referee (Gene Hackman) had ignored a foul on Rigby that led to the second goal (he has a track record for this, having ignored a foul on Gary Kelly that put him out of football for a year a couple of seasons ago), the lads were on a different footballing planet to Cambridge and ended up worthy 4-2 winners. Suddenly we were going up.

"Are you going to Scarborough Fair."

By Easter, Bury were up to third place, and a massive, vocal following journeyed to Scarborough. Our new signing Gary Brabin probably doesn't rank the Yorkshire Riviera in his top 100 places to visit; he was sent off for the third time in three visits (including the second time this season). Again this adversity spurred the team on, along with the new, big blue and white checked flag that was passed up and down the away end, and two goals in five minutes killed off the 11 man opposition.

"Don't let me down."

With the right results, promotion was now within touching distance. People who hadn't seen the inside of an away ground since Wembley were back on the road, destination Darlington for the big third v fourth place game. The atmosphere within the Bury camp was verging on the celebratory but of course with such a large following it had to go wrong, and it did. Four-nil style wrong. Despite this though, we were still third and with two games to go, two wins would see us up. Away at Exeter a week later we were leading 1-0 and looking good before 'keeper Bracey had the kind of aberration saved for Alan Rough or Dave Felgate, and we only managed a draw. Worse still, Darlington won their game and we were down to fourth place.

"You just keep me hanging on."

We had to win and just hope that the Feetham's crew wouldn't at Scunthorpe (and Darlington with the best away record in the League, aagh). Five thousand plus filed to the shrine to watch us play Cardiff. It seemed that just about everyone was listening to the radio for news of Darlo. The 'headset set' were soon on cloud nine as word of an early goal for the Iron came through. By the time that we scored, the news was even better - 2-0 at Glanford park. A second Bury goal killed our game and by the time we were 3-0 up, news of a Darlington come-back was reaching the ground. With their game at 2-2 Manchester local radio went for live commentary. On 86 minutes Scunthorpe scored, on 87 Darlington equalised. Our game ended and we spilled on the pitch waiting for news, and waited, and waited. For five agonising minutes they played on at 3-3 and we waited in silence at Gigg Lane. Then it was over, we were up and the party could begin.

After 11 years of disappointments, four failed play-off bids and a relegation year, we had something to celebrate. Souvenir newspapers, promotion mugs and a civic reception. Could this really be the Bury we all love? I suppose it must be, but I won't really believe it until we are running out at Millwall, Luton, Watford and the many other new grounds we will be visiting. To misquote once again;

> "Farewell to Spotland and Scunthorpe,
> McCain stadium, fare thee well."

Fanzine Facts

WWYATS? is now in its sixth season and continues to grow. This year editor Craig Clarkson and his team launched a fortnightly information service called 'shaking all over' for the use of Bury exiles who in his words "can't get access to those titbits of information from local newspapers, TV and Radio and are embarrassed to arrive at a game and have to ask who the new guy in the no. 4 shirt is."

WHERE'S THE MONEY GONE?

Leicester City

The Shin Of God

The Ramones used to cram five minutes of post-punk anthem into two and a half. Elvis could scoff down the entire agricultural output of a small African nation at one sitting, as long as it was deep fried and smothered in peanut butter. I once saw a woman in Kwiksave on the Saffron Lane stuff five tins of "Ye Old Oake" ham down the elasticated waistband of her trousers. And since 1974 Frank Worthington has shagged more women than the combined male population of Hinckley, Loughborough and Market Harborough. Yet all of this pint-pots-into-gallons sort of malarkey pales into insignificance when you put it up against Leicester City Football Club's '95-96 Endsleigh promotion campaign.

Forget tabloid hype about 'rollercoaster rides', 'fantasy football' and 'Roy of the Rovers'. The fact is that Leicester's '95-96 season went so far beyond all cliché, that the highlights video is being released in 23 episodes, just like 'Murder One'. Only, our villain got off and got fatter and is still at large (very large) in the West Midlands contemplating his third successive crime.

The pre-season build-up set the tone. Mark "loyalty is for fans and players only - I have to be professional" McGhee attempted to turn Filbert Street into Ramsey Street. Quicker than you could light a beach barbie on Christmas Day, Sydney United's Lurch look-alike 'keeper, 'Spider' Kalac, so named because of his uncanny ability to pop up through bath-time plug holes in the dead of night, plus the pocket-sized Soccer Roo Steve Corica, joined David 'Queen of the Desert' Old-field at what was becoming the East Midlands' answer to Summer Bay.

And so, like a demented kangaroo ("What's that Skippy? You've snagged your bollocks on the wire fence?"), Leicester hopped to the top of the Endsleigh pile as early as the first week of September to the tune of "Who ate all the pies, sport?." For a while it was looking good Ma, top of the world, fair dinkum.

The team was piling up points like Tommy on whizz, not acid...

From Roker down to Derby we went and beat them all.

That money-grabbing fat bloke, sure played some neat football!

Even so, there was a sneaking sense of emptiness at the heart of it all, on the pitch as much as in the manager. So it was not a great shock when the house of cards, increasingly held up single-handedly by Gary Parker, began to tumble down around our ears. Not surprisingly, Fat Bloke decided it was high time he pissed off, converting the points he'd already won into pounds, with the cash safe he then went for the star prize on Jack Hayward's 'Going For Gold'. Fat Bloke told the world that his new giant in the West Midlands was only sleeping. By the end of the season, however, after an expensive dose of McGhee's quack remedies, the giant was to be seen on a Black Country mortuary slab, laid out in its best bib and tucker with 1970 Derek Dougan ESSO coins over its eyes.

But we couldn't laugh. While Fattie McGhee's master plan was taking effect at Molineux (24 weeks and £3m to propel Wolves from 19th place to the dizzy heights of 20th), back at Filbert Street in the meantime, Leicester, holding hands with the other early pace-setters Millwall, had jumped off the First Division summit. Only unlike Butch and Sundance, there was no mountain lake to cushion their fall, just Griffin Park and a cold thankless slog up to Deepdale.

'Shite' wasn't the word for it, as crap performance piled on crap performance. New boy O'Neill seemed to be taking forever to find his feet; the board, as always in times of trouble, suddenly became invisible, and almost every Leicester fan seemed to launch their own blueprint for dragging City out of the mire. And come match days, the club car park was awash with unfunny slogans plastered onto bedsheets.

Even the ball-boys were being booed onto the pitch; something had to give, and it wasn't long before it all boiled over. After a legendarily dismal performance at home to Sheffield United, when even The Fast Show's small boys, enduring image, would have picked up their jumpers-for-goal posts and pissed off early, had they been half as shite as Leicester were that day.

The scenes that followed the final whistle led the Independent to label Leicester fans as "the most petulant in England", which in retrospect seems a bit unfair on Spurs. But just how do you get loyal fans - and they certainly are that - to go on the rampage against the club they love?

Its a simple formula really, as boards from Hull to Brighton have most recently demonstrated. First, you take a club that contested FIVE major Cup Finals in the 1960s then tell the fans, "That's your lot mate, fini, full stop. No Mas." Not even a quarter-final since 1982. Then you go from breaking the British transfer record by luring 'Sniffer' Clarke from Fulham, to draining the club of money quicker than a Yorkshire reservoir on a hot day. Money disappeared to the point where, twenty five years after Clarke signed for Leicester, the club couldn't even scrape together one tenth of the then British transfer record.

But don't stop there. Oh no, you have to chip away at the credibility of the club, from the 1970s when the cream of English football, entertainers like Worthington, Weller and Birchenall, genuinely wanted to come and play at Filbert Street, to the point where even journeymen footballers from the lower Divisions would think twice (or thrice) about a move to Leicester. And just to rub salt into the wound, if by chance the club did unwittingly unearth a peach, like Lineker or Alan Smith or McAllister or Newell or Joachim, you have to flog it off quick with the proceeds mysteriously disappearing into thin air with a puff of cigar smoke. But in case all this isn't enough to provoke madness among the fans, you also have to lure in promising young managers under false pretences, thereby raising fresh hope, only to crush it underfoot when the promised transfer cash fails to materialise, so the gaffer walks out, preferably in mid-season.

Finally, and most important of all, you need fans who'll stick with you doggedly throughout all this Chinese torture, through the decades when rare wins over Bournemouth and Hull were to be savoured, still buying twice as many season tickets as, say, Chelsea fans, and spending as much on club merchandise as the top 12 in the Premiership. But getting nothing but lies and evasion in return. The bittersweet Euro 96 song could have been written for Leicester fans and sums it all up - "Thirty years of hurt, never stopped me dreaming."

That was the mess that Martin O'Neill was unfortunate enough to have just taken over when the dam finally burst. And surely it won't be lost on him that, even after only 13 weeks in charge, the board looked to him to be the lightning conductor for the fans' fury, when it was them, not the manager who were the real target.

Somehow, in an aftermath that seemed to have settled nothing, the improbable began to happen. Leicester won in London, something we'd achieved about as often as Adolf Hitler. Then we did it again, at Palace a few days later. Like Dumbo in mid- nose-dive off the big trapeze, the club was suddenly flying again, and we said tarra to the circus, with Millwall sawdust-bound.

The team began to play like one, they had spirit, they had a system, they had ideas! The fans at last realised what O'Neill was about, that he wouldn't lie down and give up like the directors had. He generated his own much-needed cash by selling Joachim and Corica. Brave decisions; this manager had got bottle and was not about to hide or let the fans down like his governors seemed prepared to. Even though he'd copped the fans board-induced frustration, he was about to prove that he had a heart every bit as big as the barn door that Mark Robins was still regularly practising against (without success).

And as we began to win again, in a comeback that made Lazarus look like he was pissing about, the Ipswiches and Huddersfields suddenly faltered. Leicester City, cheered on by a massive blue fez-wearing hoard at Watford, swept into the play-offs on the last day of the season.

And so to Wembley, and the day when Basset's boys were out of (all-) sorts. Are You Watching Mark McGhee, now officially added to the Wembley songsheet, squeezed in between Abide With Me and the National Anthem, rang around the tunnel end. And Wolves, if you fancy a play-off final next season, get rid of the fat twat, he'll walk out on you eventually anyway. It certainly worked for us and Reading. Leicester fans outdid the Palace in number, voice and imagination (point of note, Palace fans: a few red and blue wigs and one fancy dressed Tango man is simply not good enough, now is it?).

Our celebrities like Gary Lineker, with his young son proudly wearing a City shirt and waving a blue flag, mingled as one with the mighty Blue Army. Theirs, like Neil Morrissey, seemed afraid of men behaving badly, surrounding himself with minders while shouting twatitudes like "it's going to be 4-1 to the Palace." Ha Ha.

The game itself showed how far O'Neill and his team had come. One down early, they made you proud with their passing, their vision, their cool. Imperious was the word. And eventually victory was theirs. In 1966 Geoff Hurst hammered home an unstoppable shot in the last second of extra time. In 1996, it was Stevie Claridge, the man swearing at a screen at a Ladbrokes near you, the man who misspent his Hampshire youth not in arcades or cider drinking, but selling strawberries by the side of the road, the man who looks (and is) knackered by the end of the pre-match warm up, who 'shinned' it in.

And so Leicester are back where they rightly belong, whatever William Hill might say. History is against O'Neill; history and the skinflint ownership of the club. But if he can break the mould and find out "Where's The Money Gone?" this big-hearted Ulsterman might yet keep us up. And if he continues to pick winners - like Lennon, Claridge, Izzett and Watts - then who knows, Stevie Claridge might end up in the black, and we might get a crack at Europe, like O'Neill wants, like *we* want. At the very least he's helped us to carry on dreaming, for just a little longer...

Fanzine Facts

Where's the Money Gone? saw the light of day in March 1994. This piece was written by 'Little Jimmy Osmond' who claims that there is no 'real' editor; just a lot of arguing until the owner of their Apple Mac decides what goes in. The fanzine was launched "to show our frustration at the conspiracy of silence and lies perpetrated on Leicester fans by the club through an unchallenging and unquestioning local media", explains Little Jimmy. As if to prove his point, rather than the expected congratualtory piece some fans expected to see in the Leicester Mercury following the play-off final victory, the paper published a centre spread proclaiming "I'LL NEVER EVER FORGET IT" - WEMBLEY WON'T WIPE OUT O'NEILL'S MEMORY OF FILBERT STREET HATE MOB.

Where's the Money Gone has been voted Fanzine of the Year by 'Football Monthly' magazine, and is characterised by 'Wortho the dog', whose defecatory exploits prove the point that "if you mess with the City, it's gonna get shitty."

WHITE LOVE

Bolton Wanderers

Two words haunted Bolton Wanderers all season; perhaps you can guess what they were. One began with an M, the other with an I. Give up? (Like the Wanderers did right from the start of the season.) Oh all right I'll tell you, perhaps you've guessed already. "Mathematically Impossible." Easy wasn't it! The season created a lot of cynics amongst the Burnden faithful, players and supporters alike; it saw our loyalty tested to the limit and beyond in many cases.

It all started with our messiah of a manager Bruce Rioch leaving us for the Arsenal and being replaced by a joint management duo of Colin Todd and Roy McFarland. Some wag suggested we would have had more chance with Robson and Jerome at the helm, or Fred and Rose West for that matter,

maybe even Richard and Judy. McFarland was way out in front as first management casualty of the Premier League at Ladbrokes. We would have put some serious money on it, here at *White Love*, but the odds were way too short. To add to our pessimism, the only new additions to the side were Chris Fairclough, and the overweight and over-rated Barnsley captain Gerry Taggart, who like our beloved 'Supa' John McGinlay, had a fondness for the lager. Before a ball had even been kicked Bolton Wanderers already had the 'feel-crap factor'.

August 19th and the Wanderers lost 3-2 to the mighty Wimbledon away at Selhurst Park on perhaps the hottest day of the year, then followed it up with a midweek home defeat at the hands of the Toon Army. 'Welcome to the Premier League' sang the away end at Burnden in mocking irony. August 26th witnessed the Wanderers first win against Blackburn Rovers, with a 2-1 scoreline courtesy of Fabian 'Disabled' and an Alan Stubbs header. The victory was soured by Stubbs' consistent moaning on Match of the Day, and our first month finished with a 1-0 defeat at Villa Park; a scoreline that flattered a dismal and inept Wanderers.

Last year, in what we dubbed "The Dream Season", two of our more promising players, McAteer and Stubbs, were threatening huge baby-like tantrums if they didn't get their way and a move to a 'big' club; the pre-season papers, desperate for a story, had linked them with every club west of the Rhine, and their prices had inflated faster than those at a Belgrade petrol station. Worse for the both of them, they believed the hype. So now, Stubbs and McAteer went into what can only be described as tantrum overdrive. The rumour machine had Stubbs and Macca going to Blackburn for a small fortune, but McAteer went to Liverpool, while Stubbs went into a sulk and into hiding as the Salman Rushdie of Burnden Park. September came and Bolton snatched another point with a 1-1 draw against newly promoted Boro through a spectacular John McGinlay goal, but the week after it was business as usual as we narrowly lost 3-0 to that 'nearby' club. Meanwhile Roy McFarland signed his Bolton death warrant by declaring how good that 'nearby' club was on Match of the Day. Another couple of hammerings were handed out by Liverpool and QPR before the month ended unexpectedly with Bolton snatching a victory in the Capital at the expense of... wait for it, wait for it... Brentford in the Coca Cola Cup.

The inevitable slide continued towards bottom spot, interrupted fleetingly by a 'thumping' of Rioch's Arsenal, live on Sky. Our Serbian messiah with the unpronounceable name, Sasa Curcic, made his debut against the goons but it was to be the only bright spot this side of Christmas. Sasa for his part turned out to be perhaps the best buy in the Premier League, and his performances in a Wanderers shirt were nothing short of electrifying. It was a pity that no-one else in the team knew the Serbo-Croat for "pass the ball you bastard!"

On a cold and bitter November day Bolton reached their nadir with a 3-0 home defeat to West Ham. A near riot by the home fans after the match resulted in a rash of abusive graffiti appearing around the ground, mostly involving McFarland whose days were numbered at Burnden Park (the writing was *literally* on the wall). It led ironically to **White Love's** 'sack McFarland front cover issue' becoming a best-seller.

December, and even the arrival of Scott Sellars from Newcastle failed to halt the teams' plummeting performances. His Burnden debut couldn't stop Liverpool snatching a one goal victory during their very lean spell, and it soon became apparent that any Premier outfit experiencing a tough time should take a visit to Bolton to perk themselves up. Sellars tried to revive us with a goal at Loftus Road, but the Whites again succumbed to a late winner.

Then the form book was turned inside out and upside down with a 2-2 draw at White Hart Lane to give the Wanderers faithful a little spot of festive cheer. At 2-0 down and dead and buried, Gudni Bergsson, Icelandic international and one time Spurs player, equalised with just minutes to go to silence the White Hart Lane regulars. For those Wanderers fans at the game, it was the first time we saw a Bolton team capable of taking the opposition to the cleaners, and the first time a point had been gained on foreign soil. It was also the debut of Bolton's latest signing, Nathan 'Jah Wobble' Blake. How Howard Kendall must have laughed when he off-loaded this duffer on us.

Yet again though, inconsistency ruled the roost in the Bolton team. A 2-1 home defeat at the hands of Coventry sparked another near riot situation at Burnden, with more calls for McFarland's head to roll (Roy was held in the same reverence by the Bolton supporters as an American flag would be at a Muslim wedding). The Wanderers were drinking in the Last Chance Saloon, and for the rest of the season they steadfastly refused to leave, despite kicking on the door a number of times. However, on January 23rd the saloon doors did swing open for McFarland and he rode out into the sunset. Colin Todd was now head honcho, and not before time.

The team sharpened up their act on the pitch, yet couldn't keep the ball out of the net when it mattered. After defeat at Newcastle, Keegan went on record to praise the team and the fans in particular, saying we were the best bunch to visit St James' Park. Bloody right too; we out-sang and out-danced the Geordie home crowd and bellowed our new chant... "The Premier League is upside down, we're staying up with the City, and the Scum are going down." Considering how it all ended the chant was somewhat prophetic.

On February 17th Bolton travelled to the Riverside Stadium, and once again failed to deliver the goods, but the goods in this case being three points to the opposition, as Bolton came back with their first away win of the season courtesy of 'Jah Wobble', 'Disabled', David Lee and the newly returned and much missed Simon Coleman. Talk was rife of Bolton's 'Great Escape', and the March issue of *White Love* saw us honour that with Steve McQueen in his best Virgil Hilts pose on our front cover. The Sunday after, just as the tunnel was taking shape, we narrowly lost again to another local team. So the escape committee at Burnden opted for plan B instead, with two away victories at Leeds and Coventry getting us to the perimeter fence ahead of fellow escapees QPR.

Then it all came together: the thrashing of Spurs, Sheffield Wednesday, fellow strugglers Man City, Everton, Chelsea, and West Ham meant Bolton had made it across the border and would live to fight another day, after one of the biggest comebacks since Lazarus. There was dancing in the streets for days on end, and many a sore head the morning after as we kept our place in the Premier League. Everything would be alright forever... Oh alright then, we got carried away with deeds of derring-do. Mind you, watching Bolton's final run-in was like being at Custer's last stand. Despite narrowly losing to Spurs, beating Sheffield Wednesday and then Chelsea, we were still stranded in no-man's land when Southampton arrived to finally put out of our misery; and who'd have believed that our own Jimmy Phillips would have collaborated with Le Tissier and so allow the Channel Islander to virtually guarantee the Saints' liberation. The dream was over, and losing to Arsenal a week later mattered not one jot.

The mistakes had been made long before we even kicked a ball in the Premier League. We all know that it's money that counts these days, and the fossils in the Wanderers boardroom had sent us on a mission impossible, under-funded and without the tools to do the job properly. Like Steve McQueen in the Great Escape, Bolton tried against overwhelming odds to jump the fence, but in the end got entangled in the barbed wire with safety just out of reach. Maybe in the end it would be for the best.

Fanzine Facts

White Love, Bolton's Premier Fanzine, is the bastard re-incarnation of Come On Feel The Wanderers, and has presented a critical perspective of events at Burnden Park for the last four seasons. It has won the Bolton Evening News Fanzine of the Year for the last three years in succession, a feat unparalleled anywhere in Britain. *White Love* is the work of co-editors Dick Smiley and Ray Burke, along with regular contributor Paul Hanley. All three are committed Marxist-Leninists being in favour of the destruction of the capitalist oligarchy through a popular uprisng of the working classes. All are committed Wanderers fans and share an irrational hatred of all things to do with Man Utd.

THE WITTON WAG

Aston Villa

Asked if sex was dirty, Woody Allen replied, "Only if it's done right", in as much the same way that if Brian Little were to be asked if football was beautiful, he would surely answer "Only if it's played properly." In a manner that was about to confound his sternest critics and appease the most demanding Villan, Brian Little was quietly masterminding a Claret and Blue revival that was about to be unleashed on an unsuspecting and complacent football world. So, as we gathered with fragile optimism barely intact for season '95-96, the doom and gloom vultures were already out in force circling around Villa Park, expecting rich pickings come Yuletide, not knowing that they would starve to death come May.

There were still many Villa fans who mourned the demise of Fatkinson and remained publicly opposed to the appointment of our chosen saviour. Under this spotlight, Brian Little had only the miserly few weeks of the close season to transform our team from the relegation haunted cannon fodder of Fat Ron's making into something that didn't contravene the Trade Descriptions Act and resembled a combative football force. Despite the short summer involving the usual ludicrous transfer speculation, August saw Villa lining up with several new faces: the desperately needed Draper, Crystal Palace's ex-captain Southgate (at that stage what else was there to say?), and the potential video nasty Savo Milosevic. As summer's blistering heatwave shimmered over Birmingham 6, Deadly Doug reminded Little that now that hefty wads of the benevolent one's (whose?) cash had been spent, the team had better deliver or else. Another League season kicked off. Gulp!

To the cynics and doubters - and there were many - Villa's opening set of fixtures had all the hallmarks of a recipe for propping up the table come mid-September. Despite the brazen optimistic bluster emanating from *TWW's* prestigious garret, even we were taken aback by the style in which the new Villa mean machine set about the task of re-establishing the club back amongst the elite. From the opening day onwards, when happy Alex Ferguson must have spent the whole journey back to Manchester changing the nappies of his youngsters after Villa had frightened the shit out of them, we never looked back. So even before the first swallows had reached Keetmanshoop (look it up), the season was becoming one splendid surprise after another.

That was unless your name was Savo Milosevic. Obviously, if you cost £3.5m, then more than a little might be expected of you, especially if you toss idle boasts about of bagging 25 goals or more in your first season. Savo struggled to look the part. Hardly surprising, taking into account the change of country and the anxiety of leaving your closest family in a war zone. By the close of the season, Savo was to show enough to suggest that by growing up a bit, and learning from the harsh reality of his first English season, then he may well become something special. Savo did OK - just.

What Savo didn't deserve was the xenophobically spiteful vitriol in the press, particularly Birmingham's own local media, who thought that it was good copy to ridicule and undermine Savo at every opportunity. Savo, and more importantly Brian Little, persevered, and with each game Milosevic started to find his feet and the back of the net (Coventry's in particular, to my eternal gratitude), culminating in him joyously stunning Wembley with his left footed ground-to-net-seeking exocet of a shot that crushed a shambolic Leeds side and catapulted Villa into Europe. All in all, £3.5m very well spent methinks. Ironically, when Les Ferdinand turned us down in the summer because he wanted a club that would win something, it's Savo, the so-called misfit, who clutches a winner's medal when all Les has are broken dreams. Funny old game, football...

Exciting and determined League form apart, Villa donned a cloak of near invincibility in the knock-out competitions. The League Cup became a procession which more than deservedly saw us win, disembowelling what was ultimately the most demoralised team ever to play in a major Wembley final, Leeds United (we say *major* because Birmingham City have also played at Wembley recently). Staggeringly, Villa reached an FA Cup semi-final despite the best efforts of the Football Association to perpetually exclude them from the latter stages of this competition. In what was to be a fated semi-final, where Villa's loyal support who had waited so long for this game were inexcusably priced out of the club's hour of need through the gross stupidity and greed of Graham Kelly and his minions, only referee Paul Durkin's inexplicable inability to make match-changing decisions in favour of the team not playing in red unfairly handed Liverpool an undeserved FA Cup final against The Despised.

Can't moan and be bitter through; the season was a revelation: Dwight Yorke's mesmerising ability and toothpastey smile lighting the way; Andy Townsend leading by fine example; the potential of Southgate, Ugo and Allen Wright; the eccentricity of Bosnich; the true Brummy Taylor; Johnson discovering he was a footballer; the phenomenon that is Paul McGrath; the arrival of some pretty young things from the youth ranks. All this left Villa for the first time in many a long winter really looking and acting the part. You know you are doing well when teams who usually see you as their home banker don't beat you and go off in a huff. Top prize here again goes to laugh-a-minute Ferguson for his verbal buffoonery following our solid performance at the Theatre of Wet Dreams, where happy Alex got silly and upset because we didn't let his little boys win. We took four points off everyone's second favourite team, and in my book that makes us better than them. So nah nah nee nah nah!!!

What else happened? Well, Deadly Doug couldn't find anything to moan about, so basically he regularly congratulated himself for sacking Big Fat Ron and appointing *The One that walks on Water*. Didn't you just know that he would find some way of taking all the credit? Though grudgingly, in this instance his decision has turned out to be beyond reproach. (I can't believe I said that.) Our near neighbours and rivals (ha ha ha ha, sorry) kept up their tradition of abysmal mediocrity and stayed down another season. So very well done to the now-departed Barry Fry. Let's all hope Clever Trevor keeps up the good work.

We would also like to discover what secret attraction Teesside holds. Whatever it is, it must be pretty irresistable because half of the crowd at The Riverside Stadium left with 20 minutes of their game with us to go. It was also nice to see the Champions bringing all their supporters to Villa Park. Hey, Blackburn fans, did you tip your taxi driver when he got you home?! Can you believe that Stockport, Peterborough and Gravesend brought more fans to Villa park than the so-called reigning Champions? Pathetic. I'm sure though, for most Villans, their abiding memory will be Wembley Stadium in the half hour after the Cup was won, when 36,000 Brummies had one of the biggest Claret and Blue parties ever! The tears of joy said it all.

We've been here before, of course; on the brink of something very good, only to let golden opportunities slip through our fingers. So is this another false dawn? We don't think so; the management and team are young and too good. As season '95-96 closed, this team have only fulfilled their initial burst of potential. As the team matures and learns together, and with the careful introduction of new faces, it will only go from strength to strength. In one of the first editions of *TWW*, we suggested that Brian Little offered Doug Ellis his last best chance of leaving some positive mark as chairman of Aston Villa. It looks like that chance may finally be realised.

With the League Cup nailed down at Villa Park and a European jaunt booked in the calendar, it's been questioned whether Villa fans have been left with a twinge of disappointment. Seeing the FA Cup so close, and wondering but for the shortfall of 15 or 20 goals, whether the Championship couldn't have been secured. To even think of Villa in these circumstances little more than a season after it could have all ended in disaster is remarkable. Within the cosmic scheme of things, Villa were within an ace of scooping the lot, and for an emerging side that can only get better, what we have been given will do for now. Plus it tantalisingly whets the football appetite for more.

In drawing together the threads of our season in true Villa fashion, our fortunes took everyone by surprise. The danger in all of this is that we start taking ourselves too seriously, expecting and demanding success, behaving like the contemptuous glory hunters in their red/blue/green/yellow/grey Umbro shirts. This season has given us priceless success, some reward for the thin times, and yes, it leaves you expectant for more. But we won't demand it just in case, though when it does come along, we shall be ready. In football, success breeds respect. '95-96 was a vintage Villa year. At its start we were a laughing stock, but at the season's close we had achieved some of our dreams - to be successful, to be feared, but above all to be respected. You can ask no more. In August '95 I would have settled for the building blocks of a bright future. Finishing fourth, winning a cup and qualifying for Europe are skyscrapers of building blocks. Only in football can 12 months offer such a turnaround.

Fanzine Facts

Having written for other fanzines for a number of years, editor David Rogers reckoned that it was time to put idle boasts to the test, and see whether he could launch one himself. With the tolerant support and production expertise of Clare Billingham, *The Witton Wag* saw the light of day in August 1995. As with the renaissance of the Villa, the signs are goods, with *TWW* well received by Villa park regulars. The fanzine takes its name from the suburb adjacent to the Villa ground.

CONFUSED & BEWILDERED

YIDAHO!

Wimbledon

Crime and Punishment

For those of you unfamiliar with Dostoyevskey's *oeuvre*, it basically tells the story of a student called Raskolnikov who comes to the conclusion that a terrible action is justifiable if it results in a greater good. To this end he murders an old woman pawnbroker in the belief that the poor people will no longer owe her money and will be better off, and therefore the action is justifiable. Unfortunately for him though, the guilt of the murder drives him slowly mad before he finally confesses to the crime and gets carted off to Siberia for 20 years' hard labour.

So, I hear you ask, what the hell has all this got to do with Wimbledon Football Club and the '95-96 season? Well, for Raskolnikov read Dons boss Joe Kinnear whose actions and

rambling became more and more irrational as the season wore on. The whole situation basically arose from the club's plans to move to Dublin after indulging in their annual moan about there not being enough support to survive. Of course, we could all understand that, although this season the average home gate was nearly 13,500 - a huge increase compared to the Plough Lane days. They also complained of a lack of atmosphere; "it's like playing in a morgue." Well, there's a surprise, Selhurst lacks buzz when Palace play at home! And hey, the fans knew this when we left SW19. You can't compare the two, especially when Plough Lane was something of a tiny fortress, where a crowd of 8,000 often sounded four times that number.

The plan for Dublin, involving the building of a brand new 70,000 capacity arena, was backed by several leading Irish businessmen, including U2's manager Paul McGuiness. The logistics involved in moving the club lock, stock and barrel to Dublin thankfully appeared to be insurmountable. Not only were the Irish FA and our own FA opposed to it but UEFA had also expressed their concerns.

It was about this time that Joe Kinnear committed his 'crime'. He turned on Wimbledon fans for having the audacity to complain about the possibility of our club being taken away from us. We were spoken of as brainless idiots. Kinnear had recently turned down an opportunity to become the Republic of Ireland manager out of "loyalty" to Wimbledon, because he "hadn't finished his job" here. It soon became obvious that his 'job' at Wimbledon was to take them back to Dublin with him. During the last few months of the season it was impossible to open the sports pages without reading of a possible relocation, be it to Dublin, Cardiff or even

Wigan! Our match reports were littered with quotes, week after week, and Kinnear's post-match comments became more and more vindictive - "As far as I can see, only die-hards, an idiot in Cowdenbeath or an 86 year old on a committee somewhere can stop us moving to Dublin. Manchester United say 'fantastic', Liverpool and Everton are supporting us - 60 percent of people involved in the decision are for it. Who are we going to upset? Four thousand punters here? We can give 4,000 season tickets away free." It's rather sad for a club's manager to consider the views of Man Utd, Liverpool and Everton to be far more important than those of his own fans, and it caused deep resentment towards him. Don't get me wrong, I think Kinnear is a fine manager, but how can a club employ someone with such an insensitive lack of respect for his team's own followers? He's always been very popular; in the four years he's been manager I've never once heard anyone call for his head, something so commonplace at other clubs. Kinnear seemed genuinely indignant though when the supporters finally snapped and started giving him abuse. Couldn't he figure out why? Surely he's not that stupid. After a 3-0 win over Manchester City virtually ensured our Premiership survival for another season, Kinnear applauded the fans for the level of support in the game, although most of us found this to be a rather hollow gesture and an attempt to squirm out of what he'd done. In any other business can you imagine how a manager would be dealt with after repeatedly insulting him customers? At Wimbledon, you are rewarded with a new four year contract.

Surprisingly, despite all the off-field trauma, some football was played. For once, Wimbledon were quick out of the blocks and were third in the League after five games. These involved the usual (at least for us) two sent off (one of which was reduced to a booking after an appeal), and another one accidentally sent off before coming back from the dressing room to rejoin the game. Then however, the club was hit with a massive injury crisis. We seem to have one of these every season, but even this one was a bit special. For three months we had anything up to 20 players out, and unsurprisingly we dropped like a stone, going 15 without a win. The press, as usual, wrote us off, some with obvious glee. It's always been a particular annoyance to me that whenever a Man Utd or a Liverpool have about three crocked players it's called an injury crisis, and excuses are made for them if they lose or fail to perform. But true to form, the media painted a different picture for Wimbledon; our genuine injury crisis was reported as a lame excuse, as the scribes secretly relished the demise of their most irritating club.

The 'hospital run' produced some nightmares, including: a 6-1 defeat at Newcastle after 'keeper Paul Heald was sent off and Vinny Jones had to play in goal; a 2-1 home defeat to Southampton despite a wonder goal from 18 year old debut boy Jason Euell - a lad already dubbed the 'new Pele' by our over-enthusiastic owner Sam Hamman, and a 4-1 defeat at Forest with Vinny sent off yet again, although this time, incredibly harshly. Sky viewers voted Vinny Man of the Match, so clearly felt the referee's decision was ridiculous too. In the same game, the ref pulled up one of our players for dissent. Not so surprising, apart from the fact that the dissent was not aimed at the ref, but at an *opponent* (yes, really!), and Forest scored their second goal from the resulting free-kick. Unbelievable!

Our season finally began to turn around with a thrilling 3-3 draw with leaders Newcastle, and a few games later we were celebrating that first League win in three and a half months after a 2-1 victory at Chelsea (Vinny getting his third red card of the season). Four days later we were at it again, outclassing Arsenal for a 3-1 win and becoming one of only two teams to beat them at Highbury all season.

A return to League form also brought its rewards as we reached the sixth round of the FA Cup - and we certainly did it the hard way. After being drawn away to Watford, Middlesbrough and Huddersfield, we managed to despatch them all in replays at Selhurst. This pattern seemed set to continue as we gained a draw at Stamford Bridge after a late Dean Holdsworth equaliser. Sadly though, things didn't go for us in the replay as we went down 1-3.

Although the threat of relegation was there for us throughout the campaign, a run of five games without defeat meant that we avoided the spectre of a last game relegation decider at Southampton. We were safely in the Premiership for an 11th season.

Highlights included excellent victories over Liverpool, Arsenal, Man City and a big away win at Everton. Another plus was our goalscoring - we always looked likely to put the ball in the net, and were the seventh highest scorers in the League despite finishing 14th. Holdsworth, as ever, was top scorer with 16, and Earle after missing much of the previous season with injury scored an excellent 14 goals from midfield. Ekoku and Goodman also chipped in well and there were excellent performances from young Chris Perry in defence and Leonhardsen in midfield too. Indeed, Leonhardsen was voted the supporters' Player of the Year.

On the minus side, there was of course the Dublin fiasco (something which is still being fought against now by the recently formed Wimbledon Independent Supporters Association) and our abysmal defence. Only bottom club Bolton conceded more.

Still, in the best backs-to-the-wall Wimbledon tradition, hopes are high for next season, despite everything. If we can avoid another major injury crisis, there is plenty of belief that the squad can take us back to our usual top ten finish. And won't that just piss off the hacks!

Fanzine Facts

Back in December 1988 when fanzines were at their peak of chic, Wimbledon were suffering their very own 'winter of discontent'. Several of that year's FA Cup winning side had been sold off and the present side were hovering around the relegation zone. Editors Colin Leonard and Peter Jones decided that the club needed an independent voice. "It was something we had to do" says Colin, "and if as a result we became the object of the amorous advances of female Dons (or 'Cholets' as we prefer to call them), well, that was a sacrifice we were prepared to make."

In the early years *Yidaho!* had a good relationship with the club. Sam Hammam would regularly buy 20 copies of *Yidaho!* at a time. But the move to Selhurst changed the atmosphere. Colin explains "No Wimbledon fan wanted to go there. But more importantly, where were Dons fans supposed to drink before and after games?." Jamie, an outspoken critic of the move, was physically attacked in the club car park by Sam Hammam and accused of making him a target. Given that *Yidaho!* carried a target on the back page with Sam's head as the bullseye, he may have had a point. A few years on, relations with the management seem to have been restored and *Yidaho!* is read widely within the club.